Adobe
Design
Collection
REVEALED

CHRIS BOTELLO

Acknowledgments

Grateful acknowledgment is given to the authors, artists, photographers, museums, publishers, and agents for permission to reprint copyrighted material. Every effort has been made to secure the appropriate permission. If any omissions have been made or if corrections are required, please contact the Publisher.

Cover Image Credit:

Anton Vierietin/Getty Images

Adobe® Photoshop®, Adobe® InDesign®, Adobe® Illustrator®, Adobe® Flash®, Adobe® Dreamweaver®, Adobe® Edge Animate®, Adobe® Creative Suite®, and Adobe® Creative Cloud® are trademarks or registered trademarks of Adobe Systems, Inc. in the United States and/or other countries. Third party products, services, company names, logos, design, titles, words, or phrases within these materials may be trademarks of their respective owners.

Adobe product screenshot(s) reprinted with permission from Adobe Systems Incorporated.

For product information and technology assistance, contact us at Customer & Sales Support, 888-915-3276

For permission to use material from this text or product, submit all requests online at **www.cengage.com/permissions**

Further permissions questions can be emailed to **permissionrequest@cengage.com**

National Geographic Learning | Cengage
20 Channel Center Street
Boston, MA 02210

National Geographic Learning, a Cengage company, is a provider of quality core and supplemental educational materials for the PreK–12, adult education, and ELT markets. Cengage is a leading provider of customized learning solutions with employees residing in nearly 40 different countries and sales in more than 125 countries around the world. Find your local representative at **NGL.Cengage.com/RepFinder**

Visit National Geographic Learning online at **NGL.Cengage.com**

ISBN: 978-0-357-92577-5

Printed in the United States of America.

Print Number: 01
Print Year: 2023

In this contemporary collage, Anton Vierietin merges elements of modern design and geometric form with color and black and white photography.

CONTENTS

UNIT 1 PROJECT

| **NATIONAL GEOGRAPHIC STORYTELLER**
ANAND VARMA:

CONTENTS

UNIT 2 PROJECT

NATIONAL GEOGRAPHIC STORYTELLER
NIRUPA RAO: CAPTURING COMPLEXITY

UNIT 3 INDESIGN

CHAPTER 12 GET STARTED WITH INDESIGN

CHAPTER 13 WORK WITH TEXT

CHAPTER 14 SET UP A DOCUMENT

UNIT 4 SKILLS INTEGRATION

CHAPTER 18 DESIGN A PROJECT THAT INCORPORATES ILLUSTRATOR, PHOTOSHOP, AND INDESIGN

REVIEWERS

Dahlia Acosta
Socorro High School
El Paso, Texas

Andrea Batts-Latson
Frederick Community
College
Frederick, Maryland

Andrea Bays
Charles Page High School
Sand Springs, Oklahoma

Jessica Campbell
Buchholz High School
Gainesville, Florida

Eric Cornish
Miami Dade College
Miami, Florida

Linda Dickeson
Adobe Certified Instructor
Lincoln, Nebraska

Rachele Hall
Yerington High School
Yerington, Nevada

Beverly Houwing
Adobe Certified Instructor,
Squid Gallery
Los Angeles, California

Diana Johnston
Northside Health
Careers High School
San Antonio, Texas

Emmalee Pearson
Madison Area Technical
College
Madison, Wisconsin

Dr. Marilyn Proctor-Givens
Lincoln High School
Tallahassee, Florida

Linda Robinson
Winter Haven High School
Winter Haven, Florida

Jessica Salas
George Jenkins High
School
Lakeland, Florida

Natasha Smith
Union High School
Tulsa, Oklahoma

Alison Spangler
John Paul Stevens High
School and Northwest
Vista College
San Antonio, Texas

Odemaris Valdivia
Santa Monica College
Santa Monica, California

CREATIVE STORYTELLING | *THE REVEALED SERIES VISION*

The *Revealed* series extends step-by-step software instruction to creative problem solving for real-world impact with more projects than any other Adobe® curriculum. Through our exclusive partnership with National Geographic, students create unique and meaningful projects inspired by National Geographic Creatives with a focus on how design principles create meaningful compositions, layouts, and infographics.

This book includes professional, visually impactful examples from *National Geographic®* magazine. Students will connect concepts with real-world projects through featured interviews with National Geographic Creatives for an authentic, professional perspective.

These comprehensive books teach the skills behind the application, showing you how to apply smart design principles to multimedia products such as dynamic graphics, animation, and websites.

A team of design professionals including multimedia instructors, students, authors, and editors worked together to create this series. We recognized the unique learning environment of the multimedia classroom and produced a series that:

- Gives you comprehensive step-by-step instructions.
- Offers in-depth explanation of the "Why" behind a skill.
- Includes creative projects for additional practice.
- Explains concepts clearly using full-color visuals.
- Keeps you up-to-date with the latest software upgrades so you can always work with cutting-edge technology.
- Integrates Photoshop, Illustrator, and InDesign for a comprehensive approach to the Adobe suite.

The *Revealed* series speaks directly to the digital media and design community and gives students the tools to pick up the conversation and make an impact with their work.

ABOUT THE AUTHOR

Chris Botello began his career as a print production manager for *Premiere* magazine. He designed and produced movie and TV campaigns for Miramax Films and NBC Television and was the art director for Microsoft's launch of sidewalk.com/boston. Chris is the author of the *Revealed* series of books on Photoshop, Illustrator, InDesign and the Design Collection, and the co-author of *YouTube for Dummies*. He lives in Los Angeles, where he teaches graphic design at a private high school and uses his own Revealed books as the text for his classes.

AUTHOR'S VISION

It has been a joy to prepare *Adobe Design Collection—Revealed*. It has been wonderful to share my favorite tips, tricks, strategies, and inspirations for working with Photoshop, Illustrator, and InDesign, and to integrate skills across the Adobe suite.

A book like this is always a team effort. I have been honored by all the hard work, joy, and creativity the many people involved in this project have delivered. Thank you to Ann Fisher for your intelligence, dedication, and friendship in developing the books in this series. Thank you to Karen Caldwell and Mary Ann Lidrbauch for always keeping us informed and up to speed in all aspects of this series. Thank you to the reviewers for their invaluable real-world feedback. Thank you to Chris Jaeggi for your clarity and consistent leadership. Thank you to Raj Desai for your vision and commitment to imagine what is possible. Thank you to Alex von Dallwitz and Brian Nehlsen for the readable and sophisticated layouts. Thank you to Allison Katen Lim for keeping this book on track and to you and Jessica Livingston for developing the National Geographic features that compliment this book so well.

To the teachers, the students, and the readers: These are my favorite tricks and my best-kept secrets. Now they're yours. I hope something of what I've shared with you here launches you on an unforgettable journey.

—Chris Botello

INTRODUCTION TO ADOBE® DESIGN COLLECTION

Welcome to *Adobe Design Collection—Revealed*. This book offers creative projects, concise instructions, and coverage of basic to advanced skills across Photoshop, Illustrator, and InDesign, helping you to create polished, professional-looking artwork. Use this book both in the classroom and as your own reference guide.

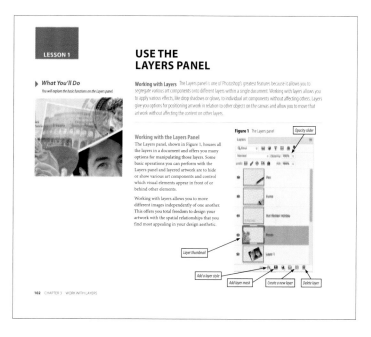

Chapter Opener

To set the stage for learning, each chapter opens with an impactful, full-page image to engage students visually. If a students chooses to pursue an Adobe certification, the lesson topics and the Adobe Certified Professional Exam Objectives covered in the chapter are clearly laid out so students and instructors can easily track their progress in acquiring skills for preparing for the exam.

What You'll Do

A What You'll Do figure begins every lesson. This figure gives you an at-a-glance look at what you'll do in the chapter, either by showing you a reference figure from the project or a feature of the software.

Comprehensive Conceptual Lessons

Before jumping into the instruction, in-depth conceptual information tells you "why" skills are applied. This book provides the "how" and "why" through the use of professional examples. Also included in the text are tips and sidebars to help you work more efficiently and creatively or to teach you a bit about the history or design philosophy behind the skill you are learning.

PREVIEW

Step-by-Step Instructions

This book combines in-depth conceptual information with concise hands-on steps to help you learn Photoshop, Illustrator, and InDesign. Each set of steps guides you through a lesson where you will create, modify, or enhance a file. Steps reference large colorful images and quick step summaries round out the lessons.

Skills Review

A Skills Review at the end of the chapter contains hands-on practice exercises that mirror the progressive nature of the lesson material.

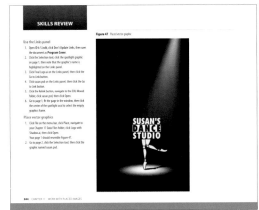

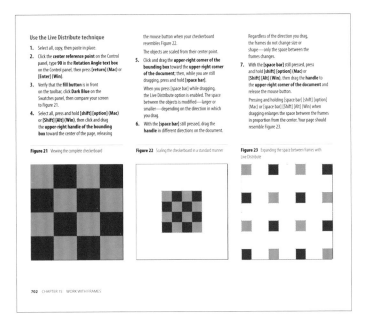

Chapter Projects

This book contains a variety of end-of-chapter materials for additional practice and reinforcement. Most chapters conclude with two to three Project Builders and one Design Project. Together, these projects provide a valuable opportunity for students to practice and explore the concepts and techniques learned in the chapter. For the instructor, they are an opportunity to evaluate students' abilities as they work independently.

You are an illustrator for a small-town quarterly magazine. You're designing an illustration to accompany an article titled "A Walk Down Main Street." You decide to distort the artwork in perspective to make a more interesting illustration.

1. Open AI 4-25.ai, then save it as **Main Street Perspective**.
2. Select all the buildings on the left, then click the Free Transform tool.
3. Click and begin dragging the upper-right handle straight down.
4. While still dragging, press and hold [shift] [Ctrl] [Alt] (Win) or [shift] [command] [option] (Mac) and continue dragging until you like the appearance of the artwork.
5. Release the mouse button.
6. Click and drag the middle-left handle to the right to reduce the depth of the distortion. Figure 86 shows one possible result.
7. Using the same methodology, distort the buildings on the right in perspective. Figure 87 shows one possible solution.
8. Save your work, then close the Main Street Perspective document.

Figure 86 Distorting the left of the illustration

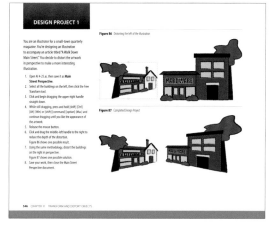

Figure 87 Completed Design Project

To create this fun and highly effective zombie image, you'll have to rely on many different skills you've learned so far in this book; those include making accurate selections and masks, crafting smart layer strategies, clipping layers, and using blending modes to achieve a desired visual effect. You will be given two flattened images: the cityscape and the zombie. Study the final image, then ask yourself if you can figure out on your own how to achieve it. Try it on your own to see how far you can get. If you can't complete it, follow the steps to the end. Have fun!

AUTHOR'S NOTE   In the steps, you'll be instructed to select the zombie with the Magic Wand tool. If this were a professional project, you'd be expected to mask it with the Brush tool and a layer mask. When you're done with the project, you should take 30–40 minutes to mask the zombie anyway, which will give you more valuable experience masking images—one of the most important skills for any advanced Photoshop user to master.

1. Open PS 6-15.psd, then save it as **Hancock Tower**.
2. Click the Magic Wand tool, set the Tolerance to 32, then verify that the Contiguous option is activated.
3. Select the entire sky, and only the sky, in as few clicks as possible.
4. Click Select on the menu bar, click Inverse, copy, then paste.
5. Name the new layer **Skyline Only**.

6. Open PS 6-16.psd, use the Magic Wand tool to select the background, click Select on the menu bar, then select Inverse to select the zombie.
7. Click Select on the menu bar, click Select and Mask, type **4** in the Smooth text box, then click OK.

8. Copy the zombie.
9. Return to the Hancock Tower document, target the Background layer, paste, then name the new layer **Zombie**.
10. Using the Options panel, scale the layer 55%, then position it as shown in the Figure 26.

Figure 26   Positioning the zombie

This project will show you how to create a "tinted black and white" effect in which parts of the image appear in color and other parts appear as a faintly colored black and white image. After you have progressed through the exercise, find your own images and experiment with different techniques for creating this effect.

1. Open PS 5-21.psd, then save it as **Tinted Black and White**.
2. Add a Hue/Saturation layer mask, then drag the Saturation slider all the way to the left.
3. Mask the adjustment so the apples are in full color and the remainder of the image is black and white.
4. Reduce the Opacity on the adjustment layer to 80% so your work resembles Figure 60.
5. Save your work, then close Tinted Black and White.

Figure 60 Vibrant apples and a tinted background

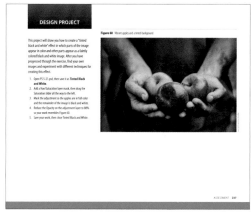

NATIONAL GEOGRAPHIC | STORYTELLERS

Adobe Design Collection—Revealed provides multiple opportunities for students to discover the work of National Geographic Creatives and be inspired to pursue their own creative careers.

Mid-unit features are based on in-depth interviews and images designed by the Creatives. These features give students a window into their career development, creative process, and passion for their work. Students learn firsthand how accomplished creative professionals use their skill and talent to capture impactful, meaningful works that bring their projects to life.

The projects encourage students to create their own work based on the feature they have just studied. Students are guided to create pieces that relate to their lives; to research local and community issues; and to incorporate photographs, data, or copy that tie directly to their school, community, and interests.

Three end-of-unit features incorporate longer creative projects that allow students to explore designing for impact, with an emphasis on visual storytelling, inspired by the featured National Geographic examples. These features incorporate either a "Skills Challenge" or a "Soft Skills Challenge" to allow students to further explore skills learned and to collaborate and engage with peers about the projects.

NATIONAL GEOGRAPHIC STORYTELLER **NIRUPA RAO**

DEVELOPING AN APPRECIATION

Growing up in Bengaluru, India, Nirupa Rao spent much of her childhood exploring the nearby jungle with her family. Their walks through the wild, tropical forest cultivated Nirupa's fondness for and appreciation of nature. Her granduncle, a field botanist, collected plant specimens from the jungle surrounding her grandfather's farm. Her mother's stories of this research inspired an air of adventure and excitement. A storyteller at heart, Nirupa enjoyed putting on plays for her family and also took an interest in creating handcrafted items, such as toys and books. Nirupa has carried her artistic talent and passion for nature into her career as a botanical illustrator. Her detailed works depict impactful stories about the unique behaviors of plants in India.

EDUCATION AND EARLY CAREER

With the exception of one online course, Nirupa is mostly a self-taught artist. While studying in Singapore, Nirupa had the opportunity to learn from other creatives and experiment with different mediums. Her interest grew when her cousin, a botanical researcher, shared photographs of plants and flowers with her. This inspired Nirupa to begin painting. She then took an internship in the children's division of a publishing house in the United Kingdom. While there, she learned about media research and further developed her creative skills using software programs such as Adobe Creative Suite. This helped Nirupa visualize her next step—providing children in India with similar content, so they, too, could learn about plants native to India.

CREATIVE PROJECTS AND PUBLICATIONS

In 2016, National Geographic awarded Nirupa a Young Explorers Grant to create an illustrated book of plant life in the Western Ghats of India. Published in 2019, *Hidden Kingdom—Fantastical Plants of the Western Ghats* sets Nirupa's colorful and intricately detailed illustrations to rhyme and helps open children's minds to the magical plants that exist in their own backyard. In addition to publishing other pieces, Nirupa's work has been displayed in the museum at Harvard's Dumbarton Oaks Museums. She collaborates with botanists and naturalists to ensure scientific accuracy in every illustration.

In Nirupa's book, *Hidden Kingdom*, she shares this watercolor painting titled *Strangler Fig*. The painting shows a tropical wild fig tree, which is part of the Ficus genus. This particular fig is often referred to as a strangler fig because of its unique behavior. This keystone species produces fruit throughout the year, providing food for birds, bats, and small mammals. In turn, birds drop strangler fig seeds on the branches of grown trees. The seeds germinate upon existing trees as a means to access sunlight more quickly. Over time, the roots of the strangler fig engulf the host tree, cutting off its access to sunlight and eventually strangling it to death with its roots.

Looking to capture this unique plant behavior, Nirupa created a watercolor painting of the strangler fig. Sitting low on the ground, she sketched the fig from below to capture the shapes of the branches, which she has described as "a hand grasping for sunlight." Nirupa often uses notes, photographs, and detailed sketches of the plants, which she then brings back to her studio to paint, scan, and manipulate using different software. Nirupa's process is very detail-oriented and thorough. She believes if you take the time to comprehend the complexity of an ecosystem, you can begin to understand how individual plants evolve, and what that communicates about the ecology of a place as a whole.

UNIT 2 PROJECT **549**

UNIT 2 PROJECT

CAPTURING COMPLEXITY

Strangler Fig, a watercolor painting by Nirupa Rao, highlights the plant's unique role in its ecosystem.

Images courtesy of Nirupa Rao

Writing Project gives graphic arts students a chance to become master storytellers by analyzing the intentional key elements of photographs, layouts, and compositions created by a National Geographic professional. Students explore multiple design concepts as they practice creative analysis. They prepare for future careers as they develop an eye to pick up on the design elements in each example, learn and employ professional terminology, use critical thinking skills, and give feedback before starting their own composition.

Design Projects give students hands-on practice creating their own artifacts, inspired by the featured theme or topic. Using their own research, students build their own composition, illustration, or layout. Design Projects include examples of pre work to encourage student planning and preparation.

Portfolio Projects allow students to build a more complex piece, and incorporate more advanced skills from the current unit. Students have the freedom to be creative and choose from a list of recommended skills and tools to use in their project. These projects encourage students to provide information about a given topic, incorporating both visual and textual elements.

RESOURCES

A FULL SUITE OF SUPPORTING RESOURCES

Instructor Companion Site

Everything you need for your course in one place! This collection of product-specific lecture and class tools is available online via the instructor resource center. You'll be able to access and download materials such as PowerPoint® presentations, data and solution files, Instructor's Manual, Industry-Aligned Credential correlations, and more.

- Download your resources at **companion-sites.cengage.com**.

Instructor's Manual

The Instructor's Manual includes chapter overviews and detailed lecture topics for each chapter, with teaching tips.

Syllabus

A sample Syllabus includes a suggested outline for any course that uses this book.

PowerPoint® Presentations

Each chapter has a corresponding PowerPoint® presentation to use in lectures, distribute to your students, or customize to suit your course.

Solutions to Exercises

Solution Files are provided to show samples of final artwork. Use these files to evaluate your students' work, or distribute them electronically so students can verify their work.

Test Bank and Test Engine

Cognero®, Customizable Test Bank Generator is a flexible, online system that allows you to import, edit, and manipulate content from the text's test bank or elsewhere, including your own favorite test questions; create multiple test versions in an instant; and deliver tests from your LMS, your classroom, or wherever you want.

- K12 Teachers, log on at **nglsync.cengage.com**, or **companion-sites.cengage.com**.

- Higher Education Teachers, log on at **www.cengage.com**.

 CENGAGE | MINDTAP

 SYNC

THE ONLINE SOLUTION FOR CAREER AND TECHNICAL EDUCATION COURSES

MindTap for *Adobe Design Collection—Revealed* is the online learning solution for career and technical education courses that helps teachers engage and transform today's students into critical thinkers. Through paths of dynamic assignments and applications that you can personalize, real-time course analytics, and an interactive eBook, MindTap helps teachers organize and engage students. Whether you teach this course in the classroom or in hybrid/e-learning models, MindTap enhances the course experience with data analytics, engagement tracking, and student tools such as flashcards and practice quizzes. MindTap also includes the following:

- Bonus modules for using the Adobe suite on the iPad

- A Career Readiness Module for the Arts, A/V Tech & Communications Career Cluster

K-12 teachers and students who have adopted MindTap can access their courses at **nglsync.cengage.com**.

Don't have an account? Request access from your Sales Consultant at **ngl.cengage.com/repfinder**.

Higher education teachers and students can access their courses at **login.cengage.com**.

ACCESS RESOURCES ONLINE, ANYTIME

Accessing digital content from National Geographic Learning, a part of Cengage, has never been easier. Through our new login portal, NGLSync, you can now easily gain access to all Career & Technical Education digital courses and resources purchased by your district, including: MindTap, Cognero Test Bank Generator, and Instructor/Student Companion Sites.

Log on at **nglsync.cengage.com**, or **www.cengage.com**

SUBJECT MATTER EXPERT CONTRIBUTORS

Adobe on the iPad
Chana Messer
Artist, Designer, Educator
Adobe Education Leader
University of Southern California (USC), FIDM
Los Angeles, California

GETTING STARTED

INTENDED AUDIENCE

This text is designed for beginners who want to learn how to use the most readily used tools in Photoshop, Illustrator, and InDesign, and integrate skills learned in these programs. The book provides in-depth material that not only educates, but also inspires you to explore the nuances of these exciting programs.

APPROACH

The text allows you to work at your own pace through step-by-step tutorials. A concept is presented, the process is explained, followed by the actual steps. To learn the most from the use of the text, you should adopt the following habits:

- Proceed slowly: Accuracy and comprehension are more important than speed.

- Understand what is happening with each step before you continue to the next step.

- After finishing a skill, ask yourself if you could do it on your own, without referring to the steps. If the answer is no, review the steps.

The first three units in this book have been designed as an introduction to the program at hand. Each make up a perfect one-semester introductory course. If you're new to the Adobe suite, this book will provide you with a solid foundation. Do not rush through the material. Build your skills steadily and solidly.

GENERAL

Throughout the book, students are given precise instructions regarding saving their work. Students should feel they can save their work at any time, not just when instructed to do so.

Students are also given precise instructions regarding magnifying/reducing their work area. Once students feel more comfortable, they should feel free to use the Zoom tool to make their work area more comfortable.

ICONS, BUTTONS, AND POINTERS

Symbols for icons, buttons, and pointers are shown in the step each time they are used. Once an icon, button, or pointer has been used on a page, the symbol will be shown for subsequent uses on that page without showing its name.

FONTS

The data files contain a variety of commonly used fonts, but there is no guarantee these fonts will be available on your computer. If any of the fonts in use are not available on your computer, you can make a substitution, realizing that the results may vary from those in the book.

WINDOWS AND MAC OS

The Adobe programs work virtually the same on Windows and Mac OS operating systems. In those cases where there is a significant difference, the abbreviations (Win) and (Mac) are used.

SYSTEM REQUIREMENTS

For a Windows operating system:

- Processor: Intel® or AMD processor with 64-bit support; 2 GHz or faster processor with SSE 4.2 or later

- Operating System: Windows® 10 (64-bit) version 20H2 or later; LTSC versions are not supported

- RAM: 8 GB minimum; 16 GB or more recommended

- Graphics card: GPU with DirectX 12 support; 1.5 GB of GPU memory minimum or 4 GB of GPU memory for 4K displays and greater recommended; GPUs less than 7 years old

- Storage space: 4 GB of available hard-disk space minimum; 16 GB of available hard-disk space recommended; additional space is required for installation

- Monitor resolution: 1280 × 800 display at 100% UI scaling minimum; 1920 × 1080 display or greater at 100% UI scaling recommended

- Internet connection and registration are necessary for required activation, validation of subscriptions, and access to online services

For a Mac OS operating system:

- Processor: Intel® processor with 64-bit support; 2 GHz or faster processor with SSE 4.2 or later

- Operating System: macOS Big Sur v11 or later

- RAM: 8 GB minimum; 16 GB or more recommended

- Graphics card: GPU with Metal support; 1.5 GB of GPU memory minimum or 4 GB GPU memory for 4K displays and greater recommended

- Storage space: 4 GB of available hard-disk space minimum; 16 GB of available hard-disk space recommended; additional space is required for installation

- Monitor resolution: 1280 × 800 display at 100% UI scaling minimum; 1920 × 1080 display or greater at 100% UI scaling recommended

- Internet connection and registration are necessary for required activation, validation of subscriptions, and access to online services

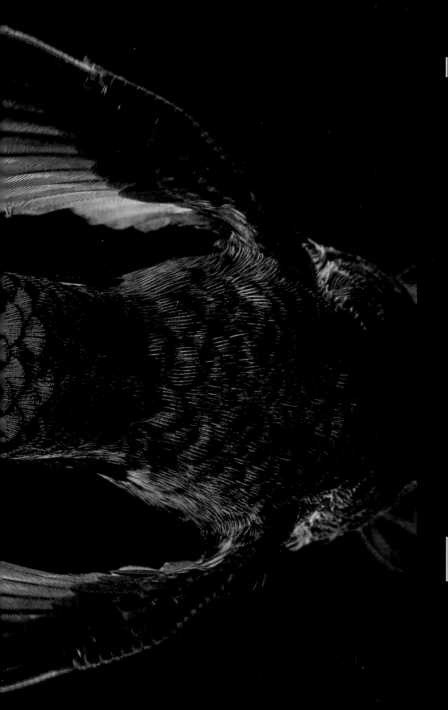

| UNIT 1 |

PHOTOSHOP

Anand Varma, Hummingbird using its forked
tongue to drink

CHAPTER 1

GET STARTED WITH PHOTOSHOP

1. Learn About Photoshop and Digital Images
2. Set Important Photoshop Preferences for Using This Book
3. Create, Open, and Save Documents
4. Explore the Toolbar and the Options Panel
5. Create a Customized Workspace for Using This Book
6. Work with Grids, Guides, and Rulers

Adobe Certified Professional in Visual Design Using Photoshop CC Framework

2. Project Setup and Interface

This objective covers the interface setup and program settings that assist in an efficient and effective workflow, as well as knowledge about ingesting digital assets for a project.

2.1 Create a document with the appropriate settings for web, print, and video.
  A Set appropriate document settings for printed and onscreen images.
  B Create a new document preset to reuse for specific project needs.

2.2 Navigate, organize, and customize the application workspace.
  A Identify and manipulate elements of the Photoshop interface.
  B Organize and customize the workspace.
  C Configure application preferences.

2.3 Use non-printing design tools in the interface to aid in design or workflow.
  A Navigate a document.
  B Use rulers.
  C Use guides and grids.

2.4 Import assets into a project.
  A Open or import images from various devices.

5. Publishing Digital Media

This objective covers saving and exporting documents or assets within individual layers or selections

5.2 Export or save digital images to various file formats.
  A Save in the native file format for Photoshop (.psd).

LEARN ABOUT PHOTOSHOP AND DIGITAL IMAGES

▶ *What You'll Do*

In this lesson, you'll read about Photoshop, the history of its original launch, and learn about digital images.

About Adobe Photoshop

Adobe Photoshop is the famous and revolutionary image-editing program created by Thomas and John Knoll in 1988. The Knoll brothers sold the license for distribution to Adobe Systems, based in San Jose, California. Adobe released Photoshop 1.0 in February 1990 exclusively for the Macintosh platform.

Photoshop immediately captured the imaginations of not just graphic designers but the world. The idea that image editing—the ability to manipulate an image in any and all kinds of ways—was now available to the general public for $895 was revolutionary. The launch of Photoshop, along with the launch of Adobe Illustrator in 1988, reinvented graphic design as it is now known in the modern, computer-based world. Adobe Systems, along with other pioneering software companies, created a new platform that revolutionized the entire printing industry.

In 1993, Adobe chief architect Seetharaman Narayanan "ported" Photoshop to Microsoft® Windows®. The Windows port led to Photoshop reaching a wider mass market audience as Microsoft's global reach exploded over the next few years.

Over the next 10 extraordinary years starting with the launch of Photoshop in 1990, the entire offset printing process, which had evolved over centuries strictly as a table-based operation, changed to an entirely computer-based operation. Whole industries and new technologies were created, while other traditional systems were suddenly out of date. Jobs were lost, but thousands of new and unprecedented jobs were invented. Service bureaus were created to help people learn to print "camera-ready" type on "repro paper" from their desktop computers and to output the digital layouts they sent in on "floppy" disks. Then, suddenly, service bureaus were outputting not to paper but to film—film that could be used to burn plates to be used on a conventional offset printing press.

Film was the bridge. Once desktop computers could print to film, the connection between the desktop computer and the traditional offset printing press was established. And there was no turning back.

Today, even film has disappeared and people can print "direct to press," meaning they hit the Print button on their computers and are able to download directly—and wirelessly! — to multimillion-dollar "digital printers," often thousands of miles away, that produce professional-grade reproductions. That this has occurred over the course of just 30 years is astounding.

All of this happened because of the release of one program: Adobe Photoshop. Yes, Adobe Illustrator came first, but Illustrator wasn't unique. There was a competing software package called Aldus Freehand. But to date, Adobe Photoshop is a one and only. Think of it—there has never been another mass-market, image-editing software package. Never. No other software company has ever released "another Photoshop." There is no alternative to Photoshop. Photoshop is a monolith.

It's not overstating to say that Photoshop has freed the human spirit. With Photoshop, people could suddenly live the life of the artist. "Art" up to that point, be it "fine" art or "commercial" art, was accessible as a career only to a rarefied segment of society. Before Photoshop, the idea that you could make money as an artist or have a career as an artist was a daunting ambition. Going to art school was a must and something of a luxury, for betting all one's chips on a career in art was a genuine risk. "Help wanted" ads for artists were few and far between, and career jobs for artists existed almost exclusively in the big cities. There were, as always, the successful and celebrated artists, but for every David Hockney, Peter Max, and Roy Lichtenstein, there were thousands of innately gifted would-be artists working in obscurity, working as a hobby, or not working at all.

Photoshop changed all that too. It's not going too far to say that, like Prometheus giving fire to the mortals, Photoshop made a career in art possible for the everyman and everywoman. Suddenly, from their homes, on their computers, people were able to make art using Photoshop. They were able to *sell* art they made in Photoshop—and feed themselves, pay the rent, and get hired—because of Photoshop. Photoshop provided the tools and the venue for people who might never have even thought of themselves as artists to be able to express themselves as such.

So much has been written about the Photoshop software story. What has not been written about Photoshop is the human story.

About Adobe Creative Cloud

In the early days, you purchased Photoshop at a store, in a box. In the box, you found a couple of floppy disks that contained the software and a user's manual. As time went by, the floppy disk turned into a CD, and then into a DVD. Then the printed user's manual vanished and was relocated to the DVD as a digital document.

The question for Adobe, of course, was how to continue to make money on Photoshop. They didn't want Photoshop to be a one-time-only purchase, so versioning became the method for repeat sales. Every two years or so, Adobe would release an updated version of Photoshop with new features so people would pay to upgrade.

The advent of the Internet made purchasing software on physical disks obsolete, and Internet downloads became the delivery method of choice for Adobe. Around 2015, Adobe transitioned out of versioning Photoshop and its other products and switched to a monthly subscription-based model (and its stock skyrocketed).

That's where Adobe Creative Cloud comes in. Creative Cloud is the Adobe website that houses all Adobe programs. You subscribe to Creative Cloud for a monthly fee; then you can download and install the Creative Cloud software. Once you have the Creative Cloud software on your computer, you have access to all of Adobe's software packages to download, install, and use. Now, when there's an update to Photoshop or any of the other Adobe products, you simply click the Update button to access those new features.

Defining Image-Editing Software

Photoshop is an image-editing program. An **image-editing program** offers you a wide variety of tools and settings that allow you to manipulate electronic images. You can use those images for on-screen presentations, whether on the Internet or on a single laptop computer, and you can also print those images, either on your home printer or professionally with a high-quality printer. Because Photoshop is so versatile, you can open images from many different sources, including from your phone, your digital camera, and images you download from the Web.

The following are just some of the tasks you can use Photoshop to accomplish:

■ **Acquire images from a variety of devices**
Transfer images from CDs, DVDs, digital cameras, and scanners into Photoshop. Download images from the Web and open them in Photoshop. With some digital cameras, you can use Photoshop to preview images from your camera before you open them in Photoshop.

■ **Apply basic processing procedures**
Crop an image to get rid of unwanted elements or to focus more dramatically on your subject. Rotate an image if it is upside down, on its side, or crooked. Resize an image so it prints to fit the frame you just bought. All of these are essential and practical procedures that Photoshop can do quickly and efficiently.

■ **Improve the color and quality of images**
Photoshop has many sophisticated color tools that allow you to enhance the appearance of photographs. You can brighten images that are too dark or darken images that are overexposed. Turn an otherwise plain image into something striking with a quick increase in contrast. Make the color more vivid or remove it entirely to create a dramatic black-and-white image.

■ **Fix image flaws**
Photoshop's retouching tools and production filters offer you many options for fixing flaws in an image, such as dust and scratches, graininess, and red eye. You can also retouch photos of your family and friends. Best of all, retouch and restore old family photos, and give them as gifts to be treasured.

- **Add special effects**

  If you can think of it, you can probably do it in Photoshop. Turn a brand-new photo into an old-looking photo, or take a typical black-and-white photo and make it look hand-tinted. Add grain effects or blur effects to give an ordinary photo a custom look. Distort photos by giving your friends big heads on little bodies or making your sister appear to be a giant 40-foot woman crashing her way down Fifth Avenue. Photoshop makes your imagination a reality.

- **Batch-process image files**

  Photoshop is also a production workhorse. For example, Photoshop can automatically process a batch of files for one type of output, such as professional printing, and then reprocess the same batch of files by reducing their physical size and file size and changing their format for use on the Web. And that's literally with the click of one button.

- **Output to various devices**

  You can use Photoshop to create graphics for slide shows, video presentations, and electronic billboards. Photoshop is used every day to create elements for on-screen animation projects. Photoshop comes complete with software you can use to save images for your cell phone or your iPad. Photoshop can even process many different-sized images into one contact sheet.

Understanding an Electronic Image

A **digital image** is a picture in electronic form, and it may be referred to as a file, document, graphic, picture, or image. You can create original artwork in Photoshop, or you can manipulate images that you bring into Photoshop from your camera or online sources.

Every electronic or "digital" image is made up of very small squares, which are called **pixels**, and each pixel represents a single color or shade. The word "pixel" is a combination of the words *picture* and *element*. Pixels are always square, and they are the smallest component of an electronic image.

Digital cameras, like the one in your phone, create the digital image the moment you snap a photo. The light from the live image that you capture is recreated digitally; it is converted into pixels inside your camera. The number of pixels per inch that your camera can access to recreate the image is the **camera resolution**.

Modern-day phones, like your iPhone or Android, are amazing machines with amazing cameras able to store hundreds upon hundreds of high-resolution and large-file-size images. For example, an iPhone 10, by default, creates an image that is 3,024 × 4,032 pixels and 34 megabytes. That's more than 12 million pixels in each photo on your phone. You could print one photo as is, at high resolution, at 13 inches tall. That's the size of a coffee table book.

When Photoshop was introduced in 1989, these high resolution levels and storage capabilities were as fantastic as space travel would have been to the Wright brothers at Kitty Hawk. And think about it, that's just one of the hundreds and hundreds of photos you have on your phone!

SET IMPORTANT PHOTOSHOP PREFERENCES FOR USING THIS BOOK

▶ *What You'll Do*

In this lesson, you'll set important preferences for working in this book.

Understanding Preferences

Think of the millions of people who use Photoshop every day and have used it for years and even decades. Just as with any traditional work area, Photoshop users like to set up their workspace to use the software in a particular way that they find logical and comfortable. For example, some users might prefer to work with tools that are arranged in two columns rather than one, and they might prefer dark panels with white type rather than light panels with black type. They might have created an arrangement of panels that are docked and positioned exactly as they want them to be, and they want that arrangement to be consistent every time they launch the software. For these reasons, Photoshop offers an array of options, which are referred to as **preferences**.

The Preferences dialog boxes are where users choose from a variety of preferences for using Photoshop, a list far too long to present here. Once chosen, these preferences become part of the software package itself. Whenever you launch Photoshop, even if you're opening a file that's not your own, the software will launch with *your* preferences intact.

Understanding Platform User Interfaces

Photoshop is available for both Windows and Mac OS platforms. Regardless of which platform you use, the features and menu commands are the same. Some Windows and Mac OS keyboard commands use different keys. For example, [command] and [option] keys are used on Macs and [ctrl] and [alt] keys, respectively, on the Windows platform. There are also cosmetic differences between the Windows and Mac OS versions of Photoshop due to the user interface differences found in each platform.

One glaring difference is the location of the Preferences command. On a Mac, to access the Preferences dialog box, click the Photoshop command on the menu bar, point to Preferences, and then choose the dialog box you want to open. On a Windows PC, the Preferences command is located at the bottom of the Edit menu.

Set important preferences for using this book

1. Launch Photoshop.

TIP You don't need to have any files open to set preferences.

2. If you are working on a Mac, click **Photoshop** on the menu bar, point to **Preferences**, then click **General**.

3. If you are working on a Windows PC, click **Edit** on the menu bar, point to **Preferences**, then click **General**.

4. Match your settings to Figure 1.

5. Click the word **Interface** in the left column to show the Interface preferences dialog box, then match those settings to Figure 2.

Continued on next page

Figure 1 General Preferences

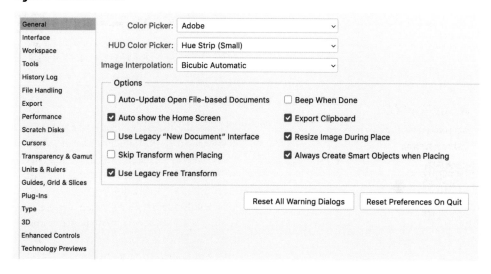

Figure 2 Interface Preferences

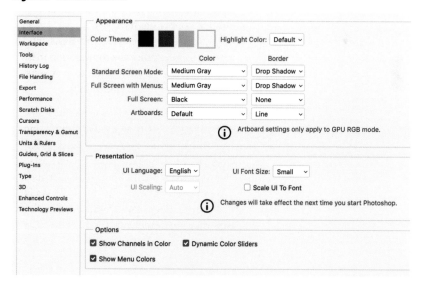

6. Click the word **Workspace** in the left column to show the Workspace preferences dialog box, then match those settings to Figure 3.

7. Click the word **Tools** in the left column to show the Tools preferences dialog box, then match those settings to Figure 4.

Figure 3 Workspace Preferences

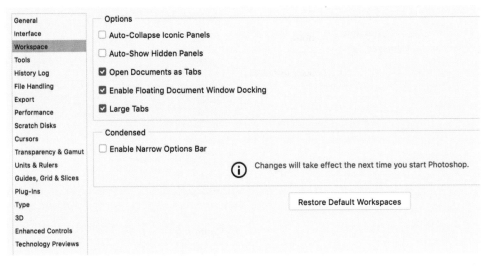

Figure 4 Tools Preferences

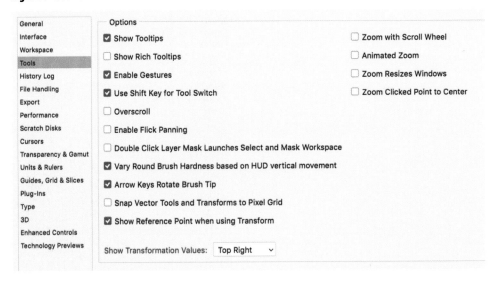

8. Click the word **Cursors** in the left column to show the Cursors preferences dialog box, then match those settings to Figure 5.

9. Click the words **Transparency & Gamut**, then match those settings to Figure 6.

Continued on next page

Figure 5 Cursors Preferences

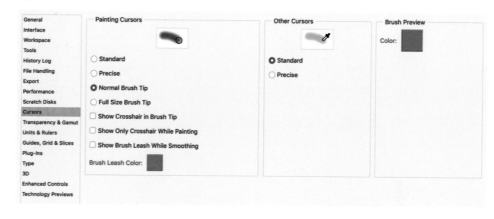

Figure 6 Transparency & Gamut Preferences

10. Click the words **Units & Rulers**, then match those settings to Figure 7.

11. Click the words **Guides, Grid & Slices**, then match those settings to Figure 8.

Figure 7 Units & Rulers Preferences

Figure 8 Guides, Grid & Slices Preferences

12. Click the word **Type**, match those settings to Figure 9, then click **OK**.

13. Exit Photoshop, then relaunch Photoshop.

You must exit and restart Photoshop for some of the changes you made to take effect.

You set preferences in nine different dialog boxes so your software behavior will mirror that which you see in the figures in this book.

Figure 9 Type Preferences

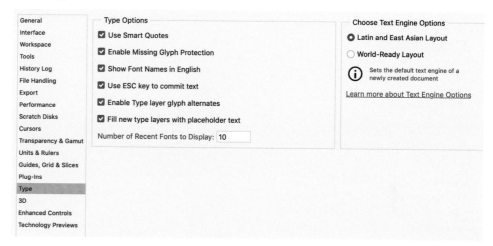

Remove the Siri keyboard shortcut on a Mac computer

1. On your Mac, click the **Apple menu**, then click **System Preferences**.

    If you are working on a Windows PC, skip this set of steps.

2. Click the **Siri icon**.

    The Siri dialog box opens.

3. Click the **Keyboard Shortcut list arrow**, then click **Off**.

    Your dialog box should resemble Figure 10. The keyboard shortcut for Siri is the same as an important Photoshop keyboard shortcut, so you need to disable this option or customize it to a sequence that doesn't involve the [shift] [control] [option] [command] or [spacebar] keys. A good key to use would be one of the [function] keys, which aren't used in any common Photoshop keyboard shortcuts.

4. Close the Siri dialog box.

Turn off the Spotlight keyboard shortcut on a Mac computer

1. On your Mac, click the **Apple menu**, then click **System Preferences**.

2. In the top row, click the **Spotlight button**.

    The Spotlight dialog box opens.

3. In the lower-left corner, click **Keyboard Shortcuts**.

    The Keyboard dialog box opens.

4. Uncheck both options so your Keyboard dialog box resembles Figure 11.

    The Mac keyboard commands for accessing the Spotlight search feature are the same keyboard commands Photoshop uses to access the Zoom tool, so they have been disabled.

5. Close the Keyboard dialog box.

You disabled a Mac system keyboard shortcut that conflicts with an important keyboard shortcut in Photoshop.

Figure 10 Turning the Siri keyboard shortcut off

Figure 11 Disabling the keyboard command for accessing the Spotlight search feature

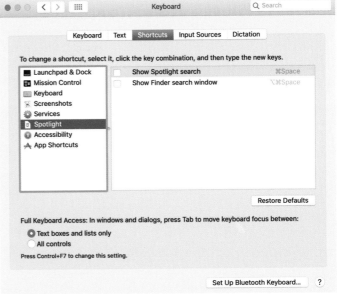

CREATE, OPEN, AND SAVE DOCUMENTS

▶ **What You'll Do**

In this lesson, you'll create a new Photoshop document, open an existing document, and save both.

✓ Photoshop
Large Document Format
BMP
Dicom
Photoshop EPS
GIF
IFF Format
JPEG

Creating a New Document

After you start Photoshop, you can create a file from scratch using the New Document dialog box. In the New Document dialog box, you determine the dimensions of the file you want to create by typing values into the Width and Height text boxes. You also set the number of pixels you want, per inch, in the file. The number of pixels per inch in a Photoshop file is called the **image resolution**.

Opening an Existing Document

Much of the work you do in Photoshop will be working on image files you open from another source—in other words, image files you didn't create from scratch in Photoshop. Photoshop can open image files from a wide variety of sources, such as files from your phone camera, your digital camera, or files you download from the Internet. Once opened in Photoshop, those images are editable using all of Photoshop's features.

Saving Files

Photoshop provides several options for saving a file. Often the project you're working on determines the techniques you'll use for saving files. For example, you might want to preserve the original version of a file while you modify a copy. You can open a file and then immediately save it with a different filename as well as save files in many different file formats. When working with graphic images, you can open a Photoshop file that has been saved as a bitmap (.bmp) file and then save it as a JPEG (.jpg) file to use on a web page.

Understanding File Formats

When you save a Photoshop file, you must choose a file format in which to save it. You can think of file formats as different types of coding that an image can be saved with or, if you like, different languages. Photoshop can open images saved in many different file formats, and it can save those images in different file formats as well.

Perhaps the most important file format for you to understand is PSD. Saving a file as a PSD is saving it as a Photoshop file. The PSD format is called a **proprietary format**. That means it's the property of someone; in this case, it's Adobe's format for Photoshop files. Because the PSD format is itself the Photoshop format, it saves all Photoshop elements and features with the file with no compression and thus no loss of image quality. As a rule of thumb, you should always save your files as PSD files for your own work. If you need to deliver PSD files to others, ask them which file format they prefer. Make a note: Because the PSD format is proprietary, PSD files can only be opened and edited in Photoshop, and they can be placed only in other Adobe software packages, such as InDesign, Illustrator, or Dreamweaver.

Other file formats are **nonproprietary formats** and choosing them can have a big effect on how the image is saved. The following is a list of the most commonly used nonproprietary formats.

- **JPEG** (Joint Photographic Experts Group) Named for the group that created it, the JPEG file format is widely used, especially for web graphics. Because it is so common, many programs other than Photoshop are compatible with JPEGs. For example, Microsoft Word, PowerPoint, and Excel can all place and display JPEG files. On the contrary, these programs cannot place or display a PSD file, because that format is proprietary to Adobe.

Despite the fact that the JPEG format is so common, beware of choosing JPEG as a format for your work. The JPEG format cannot save layered artwork from Photoshop. If you save a file as a JPEG, the layered artwork will be "flattened" into one layer, and the layer structure lost.

Another reason to avoid the JPEG format is that it is "lossy," meaning that it degrades Photoshop image data to compress the image down to a smaller file size. Thus, you must think of JPEG as *only* an output file, as opposed to a file you'll use while you're working on a Photoshop document. You must always think of JPEG as a format you use for a *copy* of your artwork. The only real reason to use the JPEG format is to create a flattened copy of your artwork that you want to share for use online or in other programs where the quality of the image isn't a priority.

- **TIFF** Another common format is the TIFF (Tagged Image File Format). TIFF files are a good choice for saving a Photoshop file if you need it to be in a nonproprietary format. TIFF files save Photoshop files in their existing state; for example, TIFFs will save the Photoshop files with their layers intact. You must always be aware of compression when choosing a file format other than PSD. The TIFF format is "non-lossy compression," meaning that the compression algorithm will make the file size smaller without degrading the image data in any way.

- **GIF** (Graphics Interchange Format) The GIF format, pronounced with a hard or soft G, is a lossy compression format created in the late 1980s. You can think of GIF as only for output and sharing an image; it's not a format you'd ever use while working on a Photoshop document, because it doesn't save layers and it heavily compresses an image. GIFs have become very popular for creating low-resolution and small-file-size animations shared on the Internet because they are able to contain multiple images simultaneously.

- **PNG** (Portable Graphics Format) PNG is a relatively new format created to replace GIF files. One of the big benefits of the PNG file format is that it is "lossless"; it doesn't degrade the quality of the image like JPEG and GIF. PNG files, like GIFs, support transparent backgrounds, and they too can be animated. However, like GIF and JPEG, PNG files do not support layered artwork, so they are not an option for saving in-progress Photoshop documents.

To summarize, PSD is the format you want to always use when saving Photoshop documents because it saves everything with no loss in quality. Use the other formats only for copies of the artwork you want to use online or deliver to someone else who can't open or doesn't need layered Photoshop artwork.

TIP Photoshop files that are larger than 2 GB cannot be saved in the PSD format. Instead, they must be saved in the Large Document Format (PSB), which is also a proprietary Adobe format. PSB supports documents up to 300,000 pixels, keeping all Photoshop features such as layers, effects, and filters intact.

Using Save As Versus Save

Sometimes it's more efficient to create a new image by modifying an existing one, especially if it contains elements and special effects you want to use again. The Save As command on the File menu creates a copy of the file. It prompts you to give the duplicate file a new name, so it doesn't overwrite the original file.

Throughout this book, you will be instructed to open your data files and use the Save As command. Saving your data files with new names keeps the original data files intact in case you have to start the lesson over or you want to repeat an exercise.

TIP You can also create a copy of the active file by clicking Image on the menu bar and then clicking Duplicate. Click OK to confirm the name of the duplicate file.

Create a new Photoshop document

1. Start Photoshop.
2. Click **File** on the menu bar, then click **New** to open the New Document dialog box.
3. Click the **Print tab** at the top of the dialog box.
4. Click the preset template named **Letter** in the first row.
5. In the **Preset Details pane** on the right side of the dialog box, note the words **Untitled-1** at the top.

   Photoshop automatically names new documents with the word "Untitled" followed by a sequential number.

TIP Depending on how many Photoshop files you have open on your computer, your default name might be different.

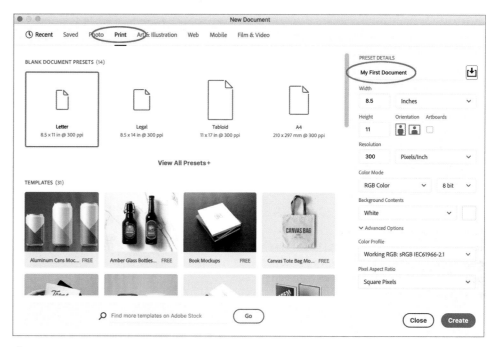

Figure 12 New Document dialog box

6. Change Untitled-1 to **My First Document**.

   Your New Document dialog box should resemble Figure 12.

   Entering a name for the document does just that—it gives the document a name. Understand that naming the document is *not* saving the document. This new document won't be saved on your computer until you actually save it.

7. Note the value in the **Resolution text box**.

   This file will have 300 pixels per inch, which is the default resolution when you choose Letter as your document type.

   Continued on next page

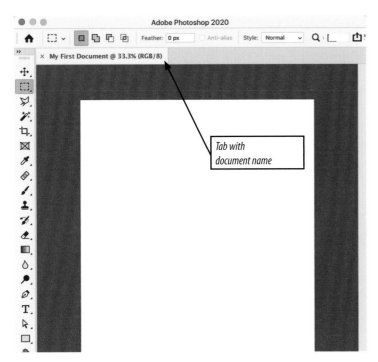

Figure 13 The new document opened in the Photoshop window

Tab with document name

Figure 14 PS 1-1.psd file open in the Photoshop window

8. Click **Create**.

 A document opens. As shown in Figure 13, the new document appears as a white rectangle, which is called the **canvas**, but it is actually a bed of millions of pixels, all of which can be colorized to render any image you can think of. Be sure to note that a tab appears at the top of the window with the name My First Document.

9. Press the **letter [D]** on your keypad to set the foreground color to black and the background color to white.

10. Click **Filter** on the menu bar, point to **Render**, then click **Clouds**.

 The pixels on the canvas change to a pattern of clouds, which were rendered using the foreground and background colors on the toolbar.

11. Keep this document open as you move to the next set of steps.

You used the New command to open the New Document dialog box. You then loaded the Letter document type and noted its default dimensions and resolution. You created the document and then noted it appears as a white canvas. You then used the Render filter to see the pixels rendered as clouds.

Open an existing Photoshop document

1. Click **File** on the menu bar, then click **Open**.

2. Navigate to the folder where your data files are stored, then open **PS 1-1.psd**.

 As shown in Figure 14, the file opens in a new tab with the name PS 1-1.psd.

3. Keep this document open as you move to the next set of steps.

You opened a second Photoshop document and noted that a second tab appeared in the window for this document.

Explore options for viewing multiple open documents

1. At the top of the Photoshop window, click the **My First Document tab**.

   Photoshop switches to the My First Document file, and it becomes the active file.

2. Click the **PS1-1.psd tab**.

   PS1-1.psd becomes the active file.

3. Click **Window** on the menu bar, point to **Arrange**, then click **Tile All Vertically**.

   As shown in Figure 15, the two documents now appear side by side.

AUTHOR'S **NOTE** As you work in Photoshop, you will often have many documents open simultaneously. Sometimes you'll even want to drag elements from one file into another. Use these commands on the Arrange menu when you need to see multiple documents at the same time.

4. Click **Window** on the menu bar, point to **Arrange**, then click **Consolidate All to Tabs**.

   The two documents revert to tabbed documents at the top of the Photoshop window.

5. Click **Window** on the menu bar, point to **Arrange**, then click **Float All in Windows**.

   Each document is no longer tabbed; each is now a "floating" window.

6. Click and drag **each document** by its name to move it to a different position in the window.

   Figure 16 shows one arrangement.

7. Click **Window** on the menu bar, point to **Arrange**, then click **Consolidate All to Tabs**.

8. Keep both documents open as you move to the next set of steps.

You used the Arrange commands to show the two open documents side by side and to return them to tabbed documents at the top of the Photoshop window.

Figure 15 Two documents arranged side by side in the Photoshop window

Figure 16 Two documents "floating" in the Photoshop window

Save and Save As

1. Click the **My First Document tab** to activate that document.

This file has not been saved since you created it. It has been named in the New Document dialog box, but it hasn't been saved.

2. Click **File** on the menu bar, then click **Save**.

TIP The first time you save a new file, you will be asked if you wish to save it on your computer or to cloud documents. If you do not wish to make this choice every time you save a Photoshop document, simply click the Don't show again check box in the lower-left corner.

3. Click **Save on your computer**, if necessary.

The Save As dialog box opens. Note that the name you gave the file, My First Document, has automatically been loaded into the Save As dialog box.

4. Navigate to where you save your working files for this chapter.

5. Click the **Format list arrow**.

As shown in Figure 17, the Format menu offers many file formats you can use to save your document.

6. Click **Photoshop** on the list.

7. Click **Save**.

8. Click the **PS 1-1.psd tab** to switch to that image.

9. Click **Image** on the menu bar, point to **Adjustments**, then click **Hue/Saturation**.

10. Drag the **Hue slider** left to **−77**, then click **OK**.

All the colors in the image shift, and the bird's beak changes to red. If the file were saved now, it would over-write the original image with this altered image. This is undesirable because the original image may be needed at some other time.

11. Click **File** on the menu bar, then click **Save As**.

12. Type **Red Beak Eagle** in the Save As text box.

13. Verify that **Photoshop** is selected as the **Format**, then click **Save**.

A new file is created; the original PS1-1.psd document has not been altered and is no longer open.

Figure 17 File formats available in the Save As dialog box

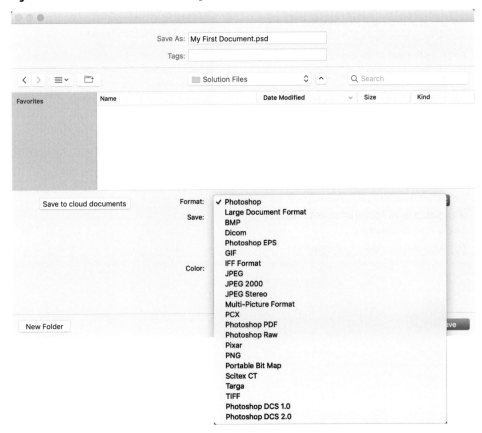

14. Close My First Document, and then close Red Beak Eagle.

Note that even though no documents are open, Photoshop is still open.

You saved the My First Document file. You used the Hue/Saturation dialog box to alter the PS 1-1.psd image, then you used Save As to save the altered image as a new file.

Save a custom document preset

1. Click **File** on the menu bar, then click **New**.

The New Document dialog box opens. Listed across the top of the dialog box are different types of output destinations for the new file.

2. Click **Photo**, then click **View All Presets**.

The window offers preset document sizes in both portrait and landscape orientations that you might use for a photo. For example, the preset Portrait, 5×7 would fit a standard-sized frame.

3. Click **Mobile**, then click **View All Presets**.

The window offers many presets for Apple devices, such as for the iPhone X or an Apple Watch. It also offers presets for an Android phone and a Microsoft Surface Pro 4, among others.

4. Click **Print**, then click **View All Presets**.

5. In the **Preset Details pane**, change the settings to those shown in Figure 18.

The standard size for a billboard, like what you'd see along a highway, is 14-feet by 48-feet. To design a billboard in Photoshop, you would build a high-resolution image file at a scale of 1-foot=1-inch. Therefore, the Photoshop file would be 14-inches by 48-inches.

6. Click the **Save Document Preset button** ⬇, identified in the figure.

7. Type **14 x 48 BILLBOARD** at the top of the window, then click **Save Preset**.

The new 14 x 48 BILLBOARD preset is now listed in the Saved window. You can use this preset as a template each time you want to create a file for a 14" × 48" billboard.

8. Click **Close** at the bottom of the New Document dialog box.

You explored different file output categories in the New Document dialog box to view different preset documents. You entered settings for a 14" × 48" billboard document and then saved those settings as a custom preset on the Saved tab.

Figure 18 Settings for a custom preset for a billboard document

EXPLORE THE TOOLBAR AND THE OPTIONS PANEL

Explore the Toolbar

The **toolbar** presents a tool with an icon representing its function. For example, the Zoom tool shows a magnifying glass. You can place the pointer over each tool to display a tool tip, which tells you the name or function of that tool. Some tools have additional hidden tools, indicated by a small black triangle in the lower-right corner of the tool. Press and hold the tools with the small black triangle to reveal the hidden tools.

You can view the toolbar in a one-column or two-column format by clicking the expand arrow in its upper-left corner.

Each tool has a corresponding one-letter shortcut key. For example, the shortcut key to access the Type tool is T. If a tool has hidden tools, you can cycle through them by pressing and holding [shift] and then pressing the tool's shortcut key until the desired tool appears.

TIP The Edit toolbar button on the toolbar (represented by a three-dot icon) opens the Customize Toolbar dialog box. Here you can customize the toolbar by placing tools into groupings based on your work style. Tools that are not used often can be dragged into the Extra Tools pane. You can choose whether to hide or show these tools.

Explore the Options Panel

The **Options panel**, located directly under the menu bar, displays the current settings for the selected tool. For example, when you select the Type tool, the default font and font size appear on the Options panel, which can be changed if desired. If you choose the Lasso tool (a selection tool), the Options panel switches to show options for the Lasso tool. As you work, whenever you select a tool, the first place your eye should go is to the Options panel to check the settings for the tool you're about to use.

Quick-Accessing the Move Tool and Zoom Tool

As you progress with Photoshop, you will often find yourself switching between the Move tool and the Zoom tool. This is because, no matter what other operation you're doing, the need to move artwork and zoom in or out to view artwork comes up regularly.

Moving your mouse pointer to click back and forth between the Move tool and the Zoom tool takes too much time and is too much of a distraction. Instead, you can use simple keyboard shortcuts that allow you to temporarily switch to those tools without clicking on them on the toolbar.

For example, let's say you are using the Brush tool to paint artwork. At any time, you can temporarily switch to the Move tool by pressing and holding the [command] (Mac) or [ctrl] (Win) key on your keypad. Your mouse pointer will switch to the Move tool for you to move artwork. Then, when you're done, simply release the key, and you're back to the Brush tool.

In the same scenario, let's say you need to access the Zoom tool. Press and hold [spacebar][command] (Mac) or [spacebar] [ctrl] (Win) and your Brush tool will change to the Zoom Plus tool, which you can use to enlarge the view of the canvas. Add [option] (Mac) or [alt] (Win) to switch to the Zoom Minus tool, which reduces the view of the canvas.

Explore the Toolbar and the Options panel

1. Open PS 1-1.psd.

2. Click **Window** on the menu bar, point to **Workspace**, then click **Reset Essentials**.

   Essentials is a default workspace, which refers to how the Photoshop window is arranged. Clicking Reset Essentials restores the window and its panels to the default arrangement.

3. Note the toolbar on the left side of the window, then note the Options panel at the top, under the menu bar.

4. At the very top of the toolbar, click the **two tiny arrows** pointing to the right.

   As shown in Figure 19, the toolbar switches from a single column to a double column. Clicking the arrows toggles between a single- and double-column toolbar.

   AUTHOR'S **NOTE**   It is suggested you work with a double column of tools when using this book to match the figures in the book.

5. At the top of the toolbar, note the series of **tiny vertical lines**.

6. Click and drag those **vertical lines** to move the toolbar away from the left edge and "float" it anywhere in the Photoshop window.

   Some Photoshop users like their toolbar locked against the window's edge, and others like to float it in different locations.

7. Position your mouse pointer over the **top-left tool** and keep it there.

   A tool tip appears, telling you the name of the tool. This is the Move tool. Note the letter V in parenthesis. That is the shortcut for the Move tool.

8. Press the **letter [V]** on your keypad (lowercase works too) and the **Move tool** will be selected on the toolbar.

Continued on next page

Figure 19 Toolbar set to a double column of tools

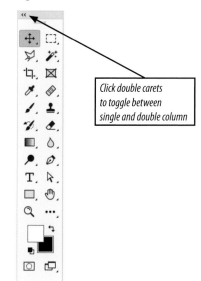

Click double carets to toggle between single and double column

Figure 20 Showing hidden Marquee tools

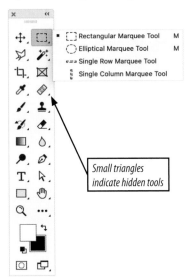

Rectangular Marquee Tool   M
Elliptical Marquee Tool   M
Single Row Marquee Tool
Single Column Marquee Tool

Small triangles indicate hidden tools

9. Press the **letter [M]** on your keypad.

    The Rectangular Marquee tool ⬚ is selected. Note the small black triangle at the lower-right corner of the tool. The triangle indicates that there are hidden tools behind the tool that is showing.

10. Press and hold the **Rectangular Marquee tool** ⬚.

    As shown in Figure 20, all four marquee tools become visible.

11. Press and hold **[shift]**, then press the **letter [M]** on your keypad repeatedly.

    Each time you press the letter [M], the toolbar toggles between the Rectangular and Elliptical Marquee tools. The combination of the [shift] key and a tool's keyboard shortcut will toggle through all hidden tools for that tool.

12. Press the **letter [V]** on your keypad to access the **Move tool** ⊕.

    Note how the Options panel changes from the Marquee tool settings to show the Move tool settings.

13. On the Options panel, verify that **Auto Select:** and **Show Transform Controls check boxes** are not checked.

14. Press the **letter [Z]** on your keypad to access the **Zoom tool** 🔍.

15. On the Options panel, verify that none of the check boxes are checked.

    Your Options panel should resemble Figure 21.

16. Note the two colors at the bottom of the toolbar.

    The top color is the foreground color, and the color beneath the foreground color is the background color.

17. Click **Window** on the menu board, then click **Swatches**.

    The Swatches panel opens. The Swatches panel contains numerous default colors for you to work with.

18. Click the **red swatch** at the top of the Swatches panel.

    The foreground color changes to the red swatch you clicked. Clicking a swatch in the Swatches panel always changes the foreground color.

19. Press the **letter [X]** on your keypad repeatedly.

    The foreground and background colors switch.

20. Press the **letter [D]** on your keypad.

    Pressing [D] restores the foreground and background colors to their defaults, which are black over white.

You changed the toolbar to a double column, you viewed hidden tools, you selected tools using keypad shortcuts, and you selected tools and verified their settings on the Options panel.

Figure 21 Zoom tool settings on the Options panel

🏠   🔍 ⌄   ⊕ 🔍   ☐ Resize Windows to Fit   ☐ Zoom All Windows   ☐ Scrubby Zoom   100%   Fit Screen   Fill Screen

Use keyboard keys to quick-access the Zoom tool and Hand tool

1. Press the **letter [Z]** on your keypad to access the **Zoom tool** 🔍.

2. On the Options panel, *remove* the **check marks** next to **Resize Windows to Fit**, **Zoom All Windows**, and **Scrubby Zoom**.

3. Press the **letter [L]** on your keypad to access the **Lasso tool** ⬭.

   The Lasso tool is a selection tool that allows you to select a randomly shaped area of pixels. Let's practice working with the Lasso tool to quickly change the view of the canvas.

4. Use your index finger and your ring finger to press and hold **[spacebar] [command] (Mac)** or **[spacebar] [ctrl] (Win)** on your keypad.

   The Lasso tool ⬭ changes to the Zoom Plus tool 🔍.

5. Click the **Zoom Plus tool** 🔍 three times between the eagle's eyes.

   The image of the eagle is so large now that it exceeds the window. You would have to use the scroll arrows or scroll bars at the side of the window to see other parts of the image, but there's a faster way.

6. Press and hold only **[spacebar]** with your index finger.

   The tool changes to the Hand tool 🖐, which is a panning tool.

7. Click and drag the **Hand tool** 🖐 to pan to see different parts of the enlarged image.

8. With your index finger still on **[spacebar]**, bring down your middle and ring fingers so that you are pressing and holding three keys: **[spacebar] [command] [option] (Mac)** or **[spacebar] [ctrl] [alt] (Win)**.

   The tool changes to the Zoom Minus tool 🔍.

9. Click the **Zoom Minus tool** 🔍 five times between the eagle's eyes.

   AUTHOR'S **NOTE**   You *must* learn these keyboard shortcuts to access the Zoom tools quickly. You can easily remember these commands by the number of fingers needed to execute them: one finger = scroll, two fingers = zoom in, three fingers = zoom out. For the remainder of this book, you will never be asked to "click the Zoom tool." Instead, you will be asked to "access the Zoom tool" or "zoom in on the image."

10. Click **View** on the menu bar, then click **Fit on Screen**.

11. Use the keyboard shortcut to access the **Zoom Plus tool** 🔍.

    Using Figure 22 as a guide, click and drag a box around both of the eagle's eyes, then release the mouse pointer.

    The area you drew the box around is enlarged in the window. This method is called a "marquee zoom," and it is a very effective way to zoom in on the area of the canvas that you want to see.

TIP   If you are unable to create a marquee with the Zoom tool, it is because you have options activated for the Zoom tool that need to be turned off. Click the Zoom tool 🔍, then uncheck Resize Windows to Fit, Zoom All Windows, and Scrubby Zoom.

12. Press and hold **[command] [0] (Mac)** or **[ctrl] [0] (Win)** to fit the artwork on the screen.

    These are the keyboard shortcuts for the Fit on Screen command on the View menu. You will do this thousands of times. Use the keyboard shortcut to do it quickly.

TIP   The keyboard shortcuts are zeros, not the letter O.

13. Keep this file open for the next exercise.

You used keyboard shortcuts to access the Zoom Plus and Zoom Minus tools.

Figure 22   Executing a marquee-zoom

CREATE A CUSTOMIZED WORKSPACE FOR USING THIS BOOK

▶ *What You'll Do*

In this lesson, you'll explore the toolbar and the Options panel, set preferences for different tools, and learn important quick keys for accessing tools.

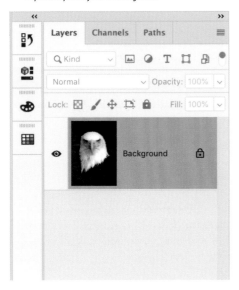

Working with Panels

Imagine you were a designer on the Photoshop interface. In the early days, you could use the menu commands on the menu bar to contain all the commands and launch all the dialog boxes necessary for users to use Photoshop. But that was a long time ago. Photoshop now has so many features that Adobe needed to create individual panels to house them.

Panels are small control windows that house settings you use to modify images. By default, panels appear in stacked groups at the right side of the window. A collection of panels is called a **panel group**.

The **panel dock** is a gray vertical bar that contains a collection of panels, panel groups, or panel icons. The arrows in the dock are used to expand and collapse the panels.

You can display a panel by simply clicking the panel tab, making it the active panel by clicking its name from the Window menu, or by clicking its icon in the icon dock (if it's displayed).

Panels can be separated and moved anywhere in the workspace by dragging their tabs to new locations. To manage screen space, you can package panels into groups, or you can dock them so that they move together as a unit.

Each panel has its own menu that you can access by clicking the Panel menu button in its upper-right corner.

Working with Rulers

Rulers in Photoshop are positioned along the top and down the left edge of the Photoshop window. Rulers can help you precisely measure and position an object in the workspace. Rulers do not appear the first time you use Photoshop, you display them by clicking Rulers on the View menu.

Photoshop offers a variety of units to choose from for your rulers. You can display rulers as pixels, inches, centimeters, millimeters, points, picas, or percentages.

Learning Shortcut Keys

Keyboard shortcuts can make your work with Photoshop faster and easier. For example, rather than clicking the Edit menu, then pointing to the word Transform, and then clicking the word Scale to scale an image, you can simply enter [command][T] (Mac) or [ctrl][T] (Win) to do the exact same thing. Commands on the menu bar list their keyboard shortcut to the right of the command.

As you become more familiar with Photoshop, you'll gradually pick up shortcuts for commands and tools you use most often, such as saving a file, opening a document, copying, pasting, duplicating a layer, or transforming artwork. You'll notice that as you learn to use shortcut keys, your speed while working with Photoshop will increase, and you'll complete tasks with fewer mouse clicks.

You can find existing keyboard shortcuts by clicking Edit on the menu bar and then clicking Keyboard Shortcuts. The Keyboard Shortcuts and Menus dialog box allows you to add shortcuts or edit those that already exist. You can also display the list of shortcuts by exporting it to an HTML file and then printing it or viewing it in a browser.

Customizing Your Workspace

The term **workspace** refers to how you set up your Photoshop window—specifically, which panels you keep open, how you group them, and where you position them. Once you establish the workspace the way you like it, you can name it and save it as a customized workspace, and it will be available to every document you create. Even if you modify your own customized workspace, you can always restore it to its default by hitting the Reset command under the Window/ Workspace command.

Many designers name and create different customized workspaces based on the work they might be doing. For example, if a project calls for a lot of work with type, you might want to create a workspace that has the type-formatting panels available, such as the Character, Paragraph, and Paragraph Styles panels. For a different project that involves a lot of color correction, you might create a workspace heavy with color adjustment panels, like Curves, Levels, Hue/Saturation, and Color Balance panels.

You can easily switch between different workspaces using the Workspace submenu command on the Window menu or the Workspace Switcher icon at the top right of the Photoshop window.

You can also change the color of your workspace by clicking Edit on the menu bar, pointing to Preferences, and then clicking Interface (Win) or by clicking Photoshop on the menu bar, pointing to Preferences, and then clicking Interface (Mac). Here you can choose one of four gray themes, from light gray to the darker charcoal gray.

Specify the keyboard shortcut for hiding extras

1. Verify that the file **PS 1-1.psd** is still open.

2. Click the **Rectangular Marquee tool** 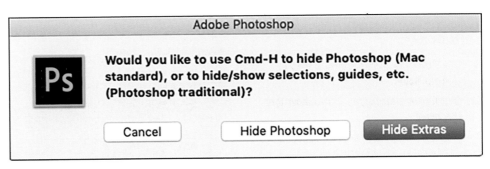 on the toolbar, then click and drag to make a rectangular marquee anywhere on the image.

   Occasionally, you may want to hide things Photoshop refers to as "extras" on the canvas. For example, you might want to work with this selection you just made, but you might want it to be invisible, or hidden, while you work. You can use a keyboard shortcut to do that, which you will do in the next step.

3. Press **[command] [H] (Mac)** or **[ctrl] [H] (Win)**.

   A dialog box may appear, as shown in Figure 23. (If the dialog box does not appear, skip to Step 5.) The shortcut you entered can be used to hide extras, which is what you want to do, or it can be used to hide Photoshop entirely, which you most definitely do not want to do.

Figure 23 Specifying the result of entering the Hide Extras keyboard shortcut

4. Click the **Hide Extras button**.

   The selection still exists, but the selection marquee is hidden.

5. Press **[command] [H] (Mac)** or **[ctrl] [H] (Win)** again.

   The selection marquee becomes visible. The keyboard shortcut toggles between hiding and showing extras.

6. Press **[command] [D] (Mac)** or **[ctrl] [D] (Win)** to deselect the pixels.

   You made a simple selection and then tried to hide it using the keyboard shortcut for Hide Extras. If this was the first time you used that shortcut on a Mac, Photoshop wanted to know if you meant it to Hide Extras or to Hide Photoshop. You specified that you wanted to Hide Extras. You will not be asked to specify this again.

Customize the View menu and the Move tool

1. Click **View** on the menu bar, point to **Snap To**, then click **None**.

2. Click **View** on the menu bar, point to **Show**, then click **None**.

3. Click **View** on the menu bar, point to **Show**, then click **Selection Edges** to activate it.

   Always keep Selection Edges checked. Selection edges can be hidden or shown when you choose [command] [H] (Mac) or [ctrl] [H] (Win).

4. Click the **Move tool** ✛ on the toolbar.

5. On the Options panel, verify the **Auto-Select** and **Show Transform Controls** options are not checked.

You customized options on the View menu and for the Move tool.

Customize the Photoshop workspace

1. Click **Window** on the menu bar, point to **Workspace**, then click **Reset Essentials**.

   The panel arrangement throughout the Photoshop window resets to a default workspace named Essentials.

2. At the very top of the toolbar, click the **two arrows** pointing to the right to make the toolbar a double column.

3. From the right side of the screen, click and drag the **Learn panel** by its name tab to the center of the window, so that your screen matches Figure 24.

Figure 24 "Floating" the Learn panel on its own at the center of the window

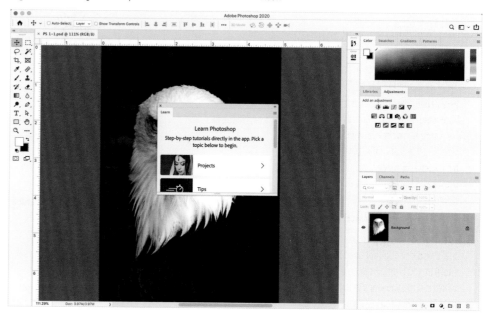

By clicking and dragging the Learn panel by its name tab, it is removed from the panel dock on the right edge of the window.

TIP The Learn panel is on the Window menu.

4. Click the **small x** at the upper-right corner of the Learn panel to close it.

5. Using the same method, close the following panels: **Adjustments**, **Libraries**, **Patterns**, and **Gradients**.

If you do not see the same panels mentioned in the steps, substitute them for panels that you do see to practice working with panels.

TIP Drag each panel to the center of the canvas and then click the x on the panel to close it.

Continued on next page

6. Drag the **Color panel** by its name toward the left side of the image, then drag the **Swatches panel** by its name toward the center.

Your figure should match Figure 25. Note that the Layers panel now takes up the full height of the window. You will be working with many layers (often dozens, sometimes hundreds!), so having this much vertical space for the Layers panel is a good thing.

TIP Note that the Color panel and the Swatches panel are now "floating" panels; you can move them to any area of the window that you like.

7. Note the tall, narrow panel dock outlined in red in Figure 25. Note also that two icons are stored at the top.

This tall, narrow panel dock is spring loaded. It contains full panels, but it displays them as small icons.

8. Click the **top icon** on the panel dock.

The top icon is a thumbnail for the History panel. When you click it, the History panel pops open to the left of the vertical bar.

9. Click the **top icon** again.

The History panel collapses.

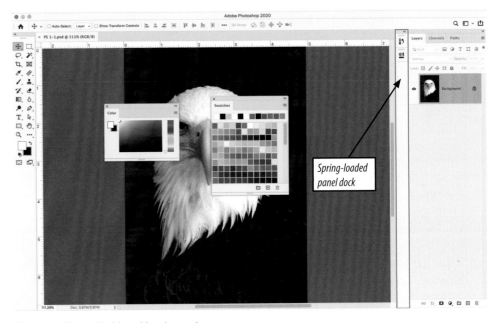

Figure 25 "Floating" the Color and Swatches panels

10. Click the **second icon** on the panel dock.

The second icon is a thumbnail for the Properties panel, one of the most important and most used panels in Photoshop.

11. Click the **second icon** again to collapse the Properties panel.

12. Note the **gray bar** across the top of the Color panel.

13. Click and drag the **Color panel** by the gray bar, position the **gray bar** over the bottom of the Swatches panel until you see a horizontal blue bar appear, then release the mouse pointer.

As shown in Figure 26, the two panels are now docked.

14. Click and drag the **Swatches panel** by its gray bar.

Both panels move together because they are docked.

15. Click and drag the **Color panel** by its name tab out of the dock.

The Color panel is released from the dock and is now a floating panel on its own.

16. Click and drag the **Color panel** by its name tab into the Swatches panel to the space at the right of the Swatches name tab.

As shown in Figure 27, the panels are grouped. You can click on each tab to view each panel.

17. Click and drag the **Color panel** by its name tab out of the group so that the two panels are separated again.

Continued on next page

Figure 26 The Color and Swatches panels docked

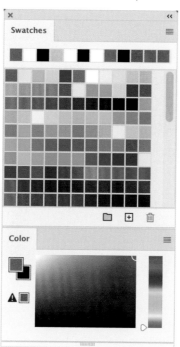

Figure 27 The Color and Swatches panels grouped

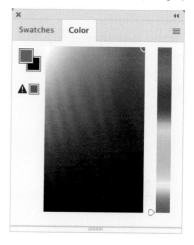

18. Click and drag the **Color panel** by its name tab beneath the second icon in the tall, narrow spring-loaded dock.

The Color panel is added to the dock and now appears as the third icon in the spring-loaded dock.

19. Click and drag the **Swatches panel** into the spring-loaded dock.

Your window should resemble Figure 28.

You closed panels that you didn't want open in your workspace. You docked two panels, you grouped two panels, and then you separated two panels. Finally, you dragged two panels into the spring-loaded dock.

Save a customized workspace

1. Click **Window** on the menu bar, point to **Workspace**, then click **New Workspace**.

The New Workspace dialog box opens.

2. Type **REVEALED WORKSPACE** in all caps.

Your dialog box should resemble Figure 29.

3. Click **Save**.

4. Click **Window** on the menu bar, then point to **Workspace**.

REVEALED WORKSPACE is now listed as a workspace and is checked because it is the active workspace.

5. Close PS 1-1.psd, and don't save it if prompted.

You named and saved the workspace you customized in the previous set of steps. You will use this workspace as the basis for the remainder of this book.

Figure 28 The Color and Swatches panels displayed as icons in the spring-loaded dock

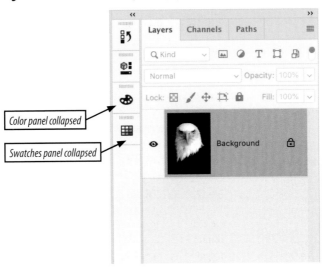

Color panel collapsed

Swatches panel collapsed

Figure 29 Naming the new workspace

WORK WITH GRIDS, GUIDES, AND RULERS

▶ *What You'll Do*

In this lesson, you'll rotate and flip the canvas, and then you'll show rulers, create guides, modify guide colors, and view the document grid.

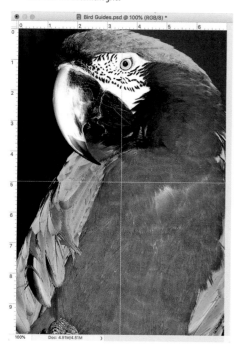

Using Guides

Guides are nonprinting horizontal and vertical lines that you can display on top of an image to help you position a selection. You can create an unlimited number of horizontal and vertical guides. You create a guide by displaying the rulers, positioning the pointer on either ruler, and then clicking and dragging the guide into position. You delete a guide by selecting the Move tool on the toolbar, positioning the pointer over the guide, and then clicking and dragging it back to its ruler. If the Snap feature is enabled, as you drag an object toward a guide, the object will be pulled toward the guide. To turn on the Snap feature, click View on the menu bar, and then click Snap. A check mark appears to the left of the command if the feature is enabled.

To delete a guide, first select the Move tool, and then click and drag the guide off of the canvas. You can also clear all guides from the document by clicking the Clear Guides command on the View menu.

You can lock guides on the canvas so they are not accidently moved. Click View on the menu bar, and then click Lock Guides. This menu also contains the Extras command, which you learned about in Lesson 5 of this chapter. The Extras command hides and shows guides along with other "extras" on the canvas, which are listed on the Show menu.

Using the Document Grid

In the pre-digital days, graphic designers and production artists designed and produced their layouts on grid paper—paper with intersecting lines that formed a grid. This was useful for aligning images and blocks of text. Photoshop documents have a document grid that you can hide or show using the Show/Grid commands on the View menu.

Changing the Color and Style of Guides and the Document Grid

The color and style of guides in a document are preferences that you set in the Preferences dialog box for Guides, Grid, and Slices. You use this same dialog box to change the space increments of the document grid. To access that dialog box quickly, double-click any guide. Change the color of guides or the document grid by clicking the appropriate Color list arrow, selecting a color, and then clicking OK.

Rotating and Flipping the Canvas

Another positioning element is the canvas itself. Sometimes an image will open on its side or even upside down and will need to be rotated. This happens most often when you download from a phone camera or other digital camera when the photographer has taken the photo with the camera in a side orientation.

In other circumstances, you might want to rotate the image just for artistic considerations. You might want to also flip the canvas so that you achieve a mirror image of the original.

To rotate or flip the canvas, click Image on the menu bar, point to Image Rotation, and then select the operation you want to execute.

Viewing the Canvas at 100%

Photoshop allows you to zoom in to enlarge an image or to zoom out to reduce an image on your screen. You can use the Fit on Screen command to view the entire canvas at the largest size it can fit on your screen.

When you click the 100% command on the View menu, you view the image at 100%. That sounds simple enough, but it actually requires some additional information to understand what that means. It's important to keep in mind that the monitor on your computer has its own screen resolution, which is by default 72 pixels per inch. At that setting, if you have a document that is 720 pixels × 720 pixels, that document at 100% would take up 10 inches × 10 inches on your screen.

Why does this matter? Because viewing a document at 100% is the minimum most accurate view of the document. As you progress with Photoshop, you will be adding very fine details to an image, such as noise or film grain or edge sharpening. In order to view those details with minimum accuracy, you must be viewing the document at a minimum of 100%. You may zoom in to enlarge the details but a view of less than 100% will not show a fully rendered view of the image.

Rotate and flip the canvas

1. Open **PS 1-2.psd**, then save it as **Bird Guides**.

2. Click **Image** on the menu bar, point to **Image Rotation**, then click **90° Clockwise**.

3. Click **Image** on the menu bar, point to **Image Rotation**, then click **Flip Canvas Horizontal**.

   The image is "flipped" to become its mirror image. Your canvas should resemble Figure 30.

4. Save the file.

You rotated the canvas 90° clockwise, and you flipped the canvas horizontally.

Figure 30 The image rotated and flipped

Work with guides and the document grid

1. Click **Image** on the menu bar, then click **Canvas Size**.

   The Canvas Size dialog box opens showing that the document is 7" × 10".

2. Click **Cancel**.

3. If you do not see rulers along the canvas, enter **[command] [R] (Mac)** or **[ctrl] [R] (Win)** so that the rulers are showing along the top edge and left edge of the canvas.

4. Double-click the **top-edge ruler**.

   The Preferences for Units & Rulers dialog box opens.

5. In the Units section, click the **Rulers list arrow** to see the list of measurements available.

   You can set your rulers to pixels, inches, centimeters, millimeters, picas, points, or percent.

   TIP Right-click the ruler to see a pop-up menu of the available measurements.

6. Verify that **Inches** is selected as the measurement, then click **OK**.

7. Click **View** on the menu bar, then click **100%**.

   The view of the canvas changes to 100%.

   TIP Memorize the keyboard shortcuts **[command][1]** or **[ctrl][1]** to view the canvas at 100%.

8. Click anywhere in the **top ruler**, then begin **dragging down** to create a horizontal guide across the image.

   As you drag, an info window appears, telling you, in inches, the position of the guide from the top edge of the canvas.

9. Position the guide so that it is **5"** from the top edge of the canvas.

10. Click anywhere in the **left ruler**, then begin **dragging right** to create a vertical guide.

11. Position the guide so that it is **3.5"** from the left edge of the canvas.

    As shown in Figure 31, the guides divide the image into four equal quadrants, and the intersection of the guides identifies the center of the document.

12. Press and hold **[command] (Mac)** or **[ctrl] (Win)**, then press the **semicolon key (;)** on your keypad to hide and show guides.

    TIP The semicolon key is one key to the right of the [L] key.

13. Press and hold **[command] (Mac)** or **[ctrl] (Win)**, then press the **apostrophe key (')** on your keypad to hide and show the document grid.

    TIP The apostrophe key is two keys to the right of the [L] key.

14. Click **View** on the menu bar, then click **Lock Guides**.

15. Save your work, then close Bird Guides.

You positioned a horizontal and a vertical guide at specific locations. You used keyboard commands to hide and show the guides and to hide and show the document grid. You used a View menu command to lock guides.

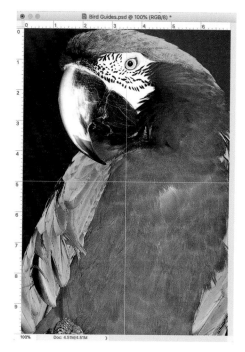

Figure 31 Two guides intersecting at the center point of the image

PAINT, SELECT, AND MOVE PIXELS

CERTIFIED PROFESSIONAL

Adobe Certified Professional in Visual Design Using Photoshop CC Framework

2. Project Setup and Interface

This objective covers the interface setup and program settings that assist in an efficient and effective workflow, as well as knowledge about ingesting digital assets for a project.

2.1 Create a document with the appropriate settings for web, print, and video.
  A Set appropriate document settings for printed and onscreen images.

2.5 Manage colors, swatches, and gradients.
  A Set the active foreground and background color.
  C Create, edit, and organize swatches.

3. Organizing Documents

This objective covers document structure such as layers and managing document structure for efficient workflows.

3.3 Differentiate between and perform destructive or nondestructive editing to meet design requirements.
  B Destructive editing: painting, adjustments, erasing, and rasterizing.

4. Creating and Modifying Visual Elements

This objective covers core tools and functionality of the application, as well as tools that affect the visual outcome of the document.

4.3 Make, manage, and manipulate selections.
  A Make selections using a variety of tools.
  B Modify and refine selections using various methods.
  C Save and load selections as channels.

FILL THE CANVAS AND MAKE SIMPLE SELECTIONS

▶ *What You'll Do*

In this lesson, you'll use keyboard commands to fill the entire canvas and simple selections with color.

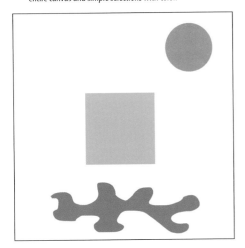

Photoshop is so popular and such a best seller that it's likely this is not your first time using it. You have probably done some exploring of the program and figured out how a lot of it works on your own. You might even be a self-taught user who has gone pretty far with the program. That's great! However, do not skip this chapter because you think it's too basic and you already know this content. Chapter 2 contains the ABC skills of Photoshop, and even the most accomplished self-taught user will find a valuable refresher course here. The chapter is designed to reinforce fundamental skills and behaviors. There are tips and tricks included and the selection tools are explored in depth. Don't pass this chapter over. You'll walk away a stronger user for the time you put in here.

Of course, if you are brand new to Photoshop, then this chapter is exactly what you are looking for. Welcome! And no matter what, don't rush! These are the skills that will strengthen your Photoshop muscles, and the time you put in here will build your entire foundation for working like a superhero with the program.

Filling with Color

"Filling" is one of the first commands most people learn in Photoshop. To fill in Photoshop means to choose a color and "fill" an area of the canvas—or the entire canvas—with that color. Even though filling is one of the most basic of Photoshop's operations, it's one you'll use over and over again, even in complex situations.

The Fill command on the Edit menu takes you to the Fill dialog box, which you use to fill a selection or the entire canvas with the foreground or background colors or other colors available in the dialog box. In most cases, however, you should use simple keyboard shortcuts to fill quickly. Press and hold [option] (Mac) or [Alt] (Win), then click the [delete] key to fill with your foreground color.

Understanding Pixels

All digital images are made up of small squares of color called **pixels**. The word pixel is a combination of two words—picture and element. The pixel is the smallest component, or element, of a digital image. There's no such thing as a half-pixel; the pixel is as small as it gets. Pixels are also only one color. A pixel is either black or white or red or pink or peach or brown. There are no "shades" in a pixel, and there are no "blends" of color. A pixel is one color and one color only.

Figure 1 shows an image, and it also shows an area of the image magnified so you can see the component pixels. When we see a digital image, we see the image and not the pixels because the pixels are so small. The number of pixels per inch is called the **resolution** of the image and is measured in pixels per inch (ppi). In an on-screen presentation such as a slideshow, on-screen images are saved with a resolution of 72 ppi. For high-quality printing, images are saved with a resolution of 300 ppi. Think of that—each pixel is so small that 300 of them can fit in one inch.

Filling Selections

To modify just some of the pixels on the canvas, you need to first select those pixels. Photoshop offers several selection tools that do just that—select pixels. These include the **Marquee tools**, which are the **Rectangular Marquee tool** and the **Elliptical Marquee tool**. As their names suggest, they create rectangular and square selections and elliptical and circular selections, respectively. The **Lasso tool** allows you to make freehand selections of any shape or size.

Once you make a selection, only those pixels on the canvas can be modified. For example, if you apply a fill color, only the selected pixels will be filled with the new color.

Figure 1 Image showing enlarged pixels

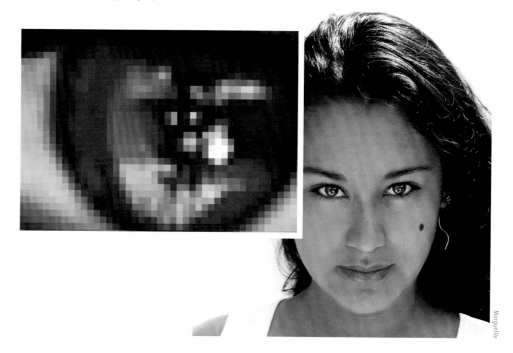

Morguefile

Fill the canvas

1. Open PS 2-1.psd, then save it as **Basic Fills**.

2. Click **Window** on the menu bar, point to **Workspace**, then click **Reset REVEALED WORKSPACE**.

   REVEALED WORKSPACE is the workspace you created in Chapter 1. Resetting a workspace restores it to the exact setup you saved and resets any modifications you might have made since.

3. Click **Window** on the menu bar, then click **Swatches**.

   The Swatches panel opens. This workspace has been saved with the Swatches panel as a thumbnail on the narrow spring-loaded panel dock. From this point on, rather than using the Window menu, you can access the Swatches panel by clicking the thumbnail.

   TIP All of Photoshop's panels are listed on the Window menu. This is a big help because whenever you are looking for a specific panel, you know it's located on the Window menu.

4. Click a **bright red swatch** on the Swatches panel.

   The foreground color on the toolbar changes to the red color you clicked.

5. Press the **letter [X]** on your keypad.

   The foreground and background colors switch. Red is now the background color.

6. Click a **blue swatch** on the Swatches panel.

   The foreground color changes to blue.

7. Click **Edit** on the menu bar, then click **Fill**.

   The Fill dialog box opens.

8. Match your settings to Figure 2, then click **OK**.

Figure 2 Fill dialog box

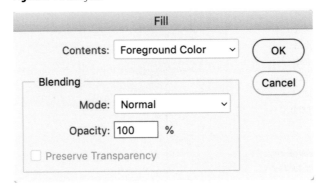

9. Compare your screen to Figure 3.

The entire canvas fills with the foreground color.

10. Press the **letter [X]** on your keypad so that the foreground color changes to red.

TIP To switch the foreground and background colors, you can also click the Switch Foreground and Background Colors icon ⇄ on the toolbar.

11. Press and hold **[option] (Mac)** or **[Alt] (Win)**, then press the **[delete] key** on your keypad.

The canvas fills with the red foreground color. It is important that you memorize this keyboard shortcut for filling with the foreground color. This is an operation you will do countless times in your Photoshop work, so you need to know how to do it quickly, without having to use the Edit menu.

12. Save your work.

You reset the workspace. You selected a red foreground color and then switched the foreground and background colors. You then selected a blue foreground color. You used the Fill dialog box to fill the canvas with the blue foreground color. You switched the colors again and then used a keyboard command to fill the canvas with red.

Figure 3 Filling the entire canvas with the foreground color

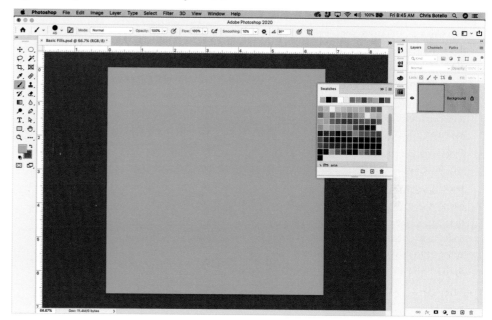

Fill simple selections

1. Press the **letter [D]** on your keypad.

   The foreground and background colors change to their default colors, which are black over white.

2. Press and hold **[command] (Mac)** or **[Ctrl] (Win)**, then press the **[delete] key** on your keypad.

   The canvas fills with the white background color. Memorize this keyboard shortcut for filling with the background color.

3. Select the **Rectangular Marquee tool** 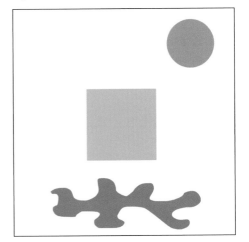 on the toolbar, then make roughly a 2″ square near the center of the canvas.

TIP Press the letter [M] on your keypad to access the Marquee tool. Hold [shift] and press the letter [M] repeatedly to toggle between the Rectangular and the Elliptical Marquee tools.

4. Click a **green swatch** on the Swatches panel.

5. Use the keyboard shortcut to **fill** the selection with the green foreground color.

   For the remainder of this chapter (and the whole book), use the keyboard shortcut to fill.

TIP The keyboard shortcut to fill a selection is **[command] (Mac)** or **[Ctrl] (Win)**, then **[delete]**.

6. Click **Select** on the menu bar, then click **Deselect**.

7. Select the **Elliptical Marquee tool** on the toolbar, then make roughly a 1.5″ circle in the upper-right corner of the canvas.

8. Fill the circle with **pink**.

9. Press and hold **[command] (Mac)** or **[Ctrl] (Win)**, then press the **letter [D]** on your keypad.

   The circle is deselected. It's important that you memorize this keyboard shortcut to deselect; using the Select menu takes too long.

10. Select the **Lasso tool** on the toolbar.

    The Lasso tool makes freeform selections.

TIP Press the letter [L] on your keypad to access the Lasso tool. Hold [shift] and press the letter [L] repeatedly to toggle between all the Lasso tools.

11. Click and drag the **Lasso tool** to make any shape you like at the bottom of the canvas.

12. Fill the selection with **orange**.

13. **Deselect**, then compare your canvas to Figure 4.

14. Save your work.

You made three simple selections with the Rectangular Marquee tool, the Elliptical Marquee tool, and the Lasso tool and then filled them with green, pink, and orange.

Figure 4 Three selected areas with three different fill colors

---

GROUPING, IMPORTING, AND EXPORTING NEW SWATCHES

The Swatches panel comes with default groups of swatches to make your design work easier. For example, you can choose colors from the Pastel group or the Dark group, depending on your needs. While these swatch groups are helpful, you may want to create your own group of colors to work with. To create a new swatch group, click the Swatches panel menu button, click New Swatch Group, name your group with a descriptive name, then click OK. Drag swatches from other groups into your new group or create new colors using the Color panel or the Color Picker. Clicking the Add to Swatches button in the Color Picker will place your new color in whichever swatch group is selected on the Swatches panel. To use your colors in another program or to send to someone else to use, you can export color swatches by first selecting all the swatches you want to export, click the Swatches panel menu button, then click Export Selected Swatches. Your swatches will be saved with the (*.ACO) filename extension. You can also import swatches by clicking the Swatches panel menu button, selecting Import Swatches, and then navigating to the (*.ACO) file on your computer.

PAINT WITH THE BRUSH TOOL

▶ *What You'll Do*

In this lesson, you'll use the Brush tool with three different modes to paint on the canvas.

Painting with the Brush Tool

The Brush tool is Photoshop's version of a paintbrush. You click and drag it to paint, and it always paints with the foreground color. In addition to clicking and dragging to paint, you can single-click the brush and then [shift]-click the brush on a different area of the canvas. When you do that, a straight brush stroke will automatically connect the two points.

When you click the Brush tool on the toolbar, the Options panel at the top of the window changes to show settings for the Brush tool, and the **Brush Preset picker**, shown in Figure 5, becomes available. The Brush tool's size is measured in pixels. When the Brush tool is selected, the Options panel shows the current brush size and a rendering of the brush edge.

Clicking the Brush Preset picker list arrow reveals settings for the brush's **Size** and **Hardness**. The Hardness setting is measured in percentages. While 100% Hardness produces a brush that has a well-defined, smooth edge, 0% Hardness produces a brush with a very soft edge that fades or blends. These soft brushes

are often referred to as having a "feathered" edge. Even with a 0% Hardness setting, however, the center of the Brush tool will paint 100% of the foreground color.

While you can always use the Size slider on the Options panel to change the size of the Brush tool, you'll want to use the left and right bracket keys on the keypad to do so far more quickly. These keys are immediately to the right of the letter P on the keypad. The right bracket key ( ]) increases the brush size, and the left bracket key ([ ) decreases it.

The Options panel also displays the Opacity setting for the Brush tool. The word "opaque" means "not see-through," so the term **opacity** in Photoshop describes how opaque the Brush will paint. At 100% opacity, the brush paints 100% opaque; you can't see through the paint. At 50% opacity, the paint will be 50% see-through. Whenever the Brush tool is selected, you can quickly change the Opacity setting by pressing numbers on your keypad. Press [5] for 50% opacity, press [4] for 40% opacity, and so forth. For 100% opacity, press [0].

Figure 5 Brush settings on the Options panel

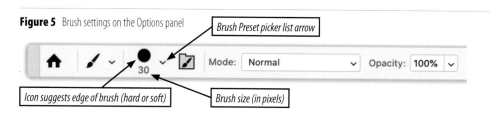

Brush Preset picker list arrow

Icon suggests edge of brush (hard or soft)

Brush size (in pixels)

Introducing Blending Modes

Blending modes are some of the most complex user algorithms in Photoshop, and they're available to you both for painting and for superimposing images and colors on the Layers panel. The basic definition of a blending mode is a computer **algorithm** (an ordered set of instructions to process data in a certain way) that controls how overlapping colors interact with one another. You will study and explore blending modes in great depth starting in Chapter 6. In this chapter, you will be introduced to blending modes as a concept when you use two of them to paint with the Brush tool.

When the Brush tool is selected, the Options panel displays a **Mode** setting with a list arrow, also identified in Figure 5. Click the list arrow to reveal all the blending modes available for you to paint with.

The default blending mode for the Brush tool is **Normal**, which you can think of as using no blending mode at all. In Normal mode, whatever color you paint changes the pixel to that color. For example, let's say your canvas is filled with bright yellow pixels, and you decide to paint with cyan. Wherever you paint, those yellow pixels will become cyan.

When the **Multiply** blending mode is activated, painting the same yellow canvas with the same cyan brush will yield green wherever you paint. This is because the Multiply blending mode causes the Brush tool to paint with transparent paint. One of the most useful features of the Multiply algorithm is that black pixels cannot

MULTIPLY BLENDING MODE

CYAN STROKE MULTIPLIED OVER A YELLOW STROKE PRODUCES GREEN

SAME COLORS MULTIPLIED OVER THEMSELVES PRODUCE DARKER COLOR

ANY COLOR MULTIPLIED WITH BLACK BECOMES BLACK

SAME PRIMARY COLORS MULTIPLIED DO NOT PRODUCED A RESULT

DARKER COLOR BLENDING MODE

CYAN STROKE DOMINATED BECAUSE IT IS THE DARKER COLOR

SAME COLORS PRODUCE NO CHANGE BECAUSE NEITHER IS DARKER

BLACK STROKE ALWAYS DOMINATES BECAUSE NO COLOR IS DARKER THAN BLACK

Figure 6 Multiply and Darker Color blending modes detailed

be altered by any other colors. Thus, Multiply mode is a great choice for painting white areas of an image without affecting any of the black areas, like in a coloring book.

You can think of using the Brush tool in Multiply mode like coloring with overlapping magic markers. If you overlap paint strokes of the same color, a darker color will appear where they intersect, as shown in the top section in Figure 6. This can be a cool effect. However, if it's an effect you don't want, you'll need to paint in a way that strokes don't overlap, or you can use a different blending mode.

In Multiply mode, the only colors that don't create a darker shade where they overlap themselves are the six primary colors—red, green, blue, cyan, magenta, and yellow. This is because the first three are the additive primary colors and the last three are the subtractive primary colors.

The **Darker Color** blending mode, detailed in the lower section of Figure 6, is a straightforward algorithm. Wherever two colors overlap, the darker color will dominate and replace the lighter color. Painting with the Darker Color blending mode, as with the Multiply blending mode, leaves black pixels unaffected by any color. This is because no other color is darker than black.

The Fill dialog box on the Edit menu offers you the ability to fill a selection or the entire canvas with a color using a blending mode. Figure 7 shows a line art illustration composed of black lines after half the canvas is filled with a green color using the Multiply blending mode. The white areas become green, but the black areas are not affected.

Figure 7 Line art illustration half filled with the Multiply blending mode

Alka5051/Shutterstock.com

Paint with the Brush tool

1. Open PS 2-2.psd, then save it as **Paint Palette**.
2. Select the **Brush tool** on the toolbar.

   When you select the Brush tool, the Options panel at the top of the window changes to show options for the Brush tool.
3. Click the **Brush Preset picker list arrow** to show Size and Hardness settings, as shown in Figure 8.
4. Drag the **Size slider** to **100 px**, then drag the **Hardness slider** to **100%**.
5. On the Options panel, verify that **Mode** is set to **Normal**, **Opacity** is set to **100%**, **Flow** is set to **100%**, and **Smoothing** is set to **10%**.
6. Open the Swatches panel, then click **any blue swatch**.
7. On your keypad, note the **left bracket ([ )** and **right bracket ( ])** keys, which are immediately to the right of the letter [P].
8. Press the **right bracket ( ])** key repeatedly until the **Size** on the Options panel reads **500 px**.

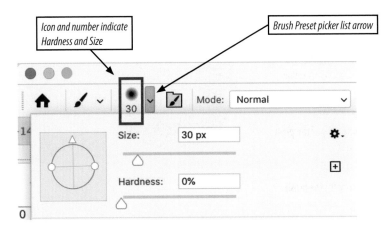

Icon and number indicate Hardness and Size

Brush Preset picker list arrow

Figure 8 Brush Preset picker list arrow on the Options panel

Pressing the right bracket ( ]) key enlarges the brush size. Pressing the left bracket ([ ) key reduces the brush size.

9. Click the **brush** one time on the upper-left quadrant of the canvas.

   A circle with a hard, smooth edge is painted.

10. Change the **Hardness** setting to **0%**, then click the **brush** one time on the upper-right quadrant of the canvas.

    A circle with a soft, feathered edge is painted.

11. Reduce the brush size to **250 px**, then click one time on the bottom-left quadrant.

12. Press and hold **[shift]**, then click one time on the bottom-right quadrant.

A straight stroke is painted connecting the two places you clicked. Your canvas should resemble Figure 9.

13. Change the **Hardness** setting to **100%**.

14. Change the **foreground color** to any of the **pink** swatches on the Swatches panel.

15. Press the **number [3]** on your keypad.

On the Options panel, the Opacity for the brush now reads 30%.

16. Increase the brush size to **600 px**, then click and drag the **brush** over different areas of the canvas.

Wherever you paint, a transparent pink color appears. It is only 30% opaque, so the blue lines you created are still visible.

17. Paint with the brush a second time, overlapping one of your pink brush strokes.

Wherever you overlap the pink, the opacity doubles.

18. Press the **letter [D]** on your keypad, then press the **letter [X]** to change the foreground color to white.

19. Press and hold **[option] (Mac)** or **[Alt] (Win)**, then press the **[delete] key** on your keypad.

The canvas is filled with white.

20. Save your work.

You examined a brush with a Hardness setting of 100% and a brush with a Hardness setting of 0%. You created an automatic brush stroke using the [shift] key, and you painted with opacity. Finally, you filled the canvas with white to erase your work.

Figure 9 Hard brush, soft brush, and an automatic brush stroke

Examine brush edges and opacity

1. Verify that the **Brush tool** is selected, then press **[0]** on your keypad to set the Opacity to 100%.

2. Set the brush size to **250 px**.

3. On the Swatches panel, click **any blue swatch**.

4. Click and drag to paint a curved arc approximately two inches long anywhere on the canvas.

5. Click a **red swatch** on the Swatches panel, then paint another **curved ark** anywhere on the canvas.

Continued on next page

Figure 10 Painting the wide, hard-edged strokes

Figure 11 Painting the narrow, soft-edged strokes

6. Using Figure 10 as an example of the look you are trying to achieve, paint the whole canvas with different colors.

As you paint, observe that whenever you overlap colors, there's no "mixing" of colors. When the Mode is set to Normal for the Brush tool, the current color replaces whatever color was previously there.

7. Press and hold **[option] (Mac)** or **[Alt] (Win)**.

The Brush tool 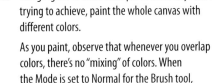 changes to the Eyedropper tool.

8. Click the **Eyedropper tool** on any **yellow color** on the canvas.

The foreground color changes to the yellow color you sampled with the Eyedropper tool.

9. Release **[option] (Mac)** or **[Alt] (Win)** to return to the **Brush tool**.

10. Click the **Brush Preset picker list arrow**, then set the **Hardness** to **0%**.

11. Click the **left bracket key ([ )** on your keypad until the brush size on the Options panel reads **60 px**.

12. Toggling between the **Brush tool** and the **Eyedropper tool**, paint thin, soft-edged strokes in different colors all over the canvas.

Figure 11 represents an example of the look you are trying to achieve.

13. Save your work without making any other changes, and continue *directly* to the next set of steps.

You painted the canvas with wide, hard-edged, multicolored brush strokes. You toggled between the Brush tool and the Eyedropper tool to sample colors off the canvas, then you painted narrow, soft-edged strokes on top of the existing colors.

Use Keyboard Shortcuts to Undo and Redo

1. Press and hold **[command] (Mac)** or **[Ctrl] (Win)**, then press the **letter [Z]** on your keypad 12 times.

   This keyboard shortcut executes the Undo command, which is on the Edit menu. Every time you press [Z], you undo a previous move that you made. By default, Photoshop saves 50 "history states," so you can step backward 50 times.

2. Press and hold **[shift] [command] (Mac)** or **[Shift] [Ctrl] (Win)**, then press the **letter [Z]** on your keypad 12 times.

   This keyboard shortcut executes the Redo command, which is also on the Edit menu. Every time you press [Z], you step forward through the moves you made until you are back to the current state of the document.

3. Using the keyboard shortcut, undo 20 times.

4. Using the **Brush tool** ✐ , paint a stroke of color anywhere on the canvas.

   Because you made a new move after using the Undo command, you can no longer redo your way forward to the state of the artwork when you started this series of steps. The new stroke you painted is now the current state of the artwork. All you can do is undo from here.

5. Click **File** on the menu bar, then click **Revert**.

   The Revert command restores the file to the state it was in when you last saved, which, in this case, was Step 13 of the previous set of steps.

AUTHOR'S **NOTE**   You can think of the Revert command as a "Super Undo" you can use to go way back if you really mess up, even if you've made hundreds of moves. This is an example of why you must make it a habit to save your work as you go.

You used keyboard shortcuts to undo and redo steps you made while working. After undoing a second time, you made a new move, which made it impossible to redo to the state of the art-work when you started this series of steps. You used the Revert command to restore the file to when it was last saved.

Use filters with painted artwork

1. Click **Filter** on the menu bar, point to **Blur**, then click **Gaussian Blur**.

2. Type **23** in the **Radius text box**, then click **OK**.

3. Click **Filter** on the menu bar, point to **Pixelate**, then click **Crystallize**.

4. Drag the **Cell Size slider** to **40**, then click **OK**.

5. Click **Filter** on the menu bar, point to **Stylize**, then click **Oil Paint**.

6. Set **Stylization** to **10.0**, **Cleanliness** to **2.0**, **Scale** to **6.0**, and **Bristle Detail** to **10.0**.

7. Verify that the **Lighting option** is checked, then click **OK**.

Continued on next page

8. Click **View** on menu bar, click **100%**, then compare your artwork to Figure 12.

   The result of the Oil Paint filter is a perfect example of why you must view the canvas at 100% to see fine details. You would not get an accurate rendering of the filters you applied if you viewed the canvas at anything less than 100%.

9. Press the **letter [F]** on your keypad two times to view the canvas in full screen mode against a black background.

   AUTHOR'S **NOTE**   Considering the simple steps we took to paint the canvas, now that the filters have been applied, it's quite remarkable that this has become a reasonably interesting piece of artwork.

10. Press the **[esc] key** on your keypad to exit full screen mode.

11. Save your work, then close Paint Palette.

You applied three filters to the painted artwork to create the effect of an oil painting. You viewed the artwork at 100% in full screen mode against a black background.

Figure 12   Viewing the artwork with three filters applied

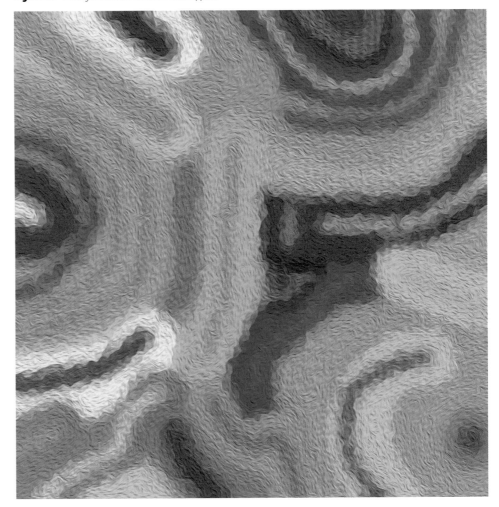

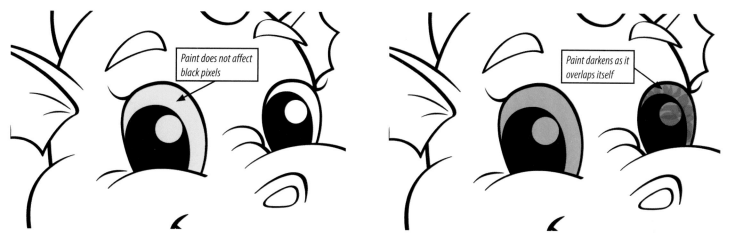

Figure 13 Painting the left eye yellow

Figure 14 Overlapping transparent paint strokes in the right eye

Paint with transparent paint in Multiply mode

1. Open PS 2-3.psd, then save it as **Coloring Book**.

2. Assess the image as a painting project, like a child's coloring book image.

   The challenge of trying to "color" the artwork with the same methods we've used so far in this lesson wouldn't be possible. That's because we'd have to paint right up to every black line without painting over the black lines. Fortunately, the Brush tool offers other options.

3. Select the **Brush tool** ✐ on the toolbar; set the **Size** to **20 px** and the **Hardness** to **100%**.

4. On the Options panel, change the **Mode** to **Multiply**.

5. Click the **yellow swatch** at the top row of the Swatches panel.

6. Paint the **left eye yellow** so your artwork resembles Figure 13.

   When you paint over black areas in the eye, they aren't affected by the Brush tool and don't change color. In Multiply mode, black pixels don't change color; they will remain black, regardless of what color is being painted by the Brush tool.

7. Click the **cyan swatch** at the top row of the Swatches panel.

8. Paint over the **yellow area** of the same left eye.

   Even though you are painting with cyan, the color of the eye changes to green. This is because you are painting with transparent paint, and transparent cyan over yellow produces green.

9. Click a **peach-colored swatch** on the Swatches panel.

10. Using at least 10–12 short strokes, paint the **right eye** with overlapping strokes.

    As shown in Figure 14, because the paint is transparent, it darkens when it overlaps itself. The effect is just like overlapping magic markers. A challenge when painting with Multiply mode is that every area must be painted in one move. If not, the colors will darken when overlapped. We will use a different blending mode to avoid this problem.

    TIP The following colors will not darken when they overlap themselves in Multiply mode: red, green, blue, cyan, magenta, and yellow.

11. Click **File** on the menu bar, then click **Revert**.

You set the Brush tool to Multiply mode, noting black pixels remain unaffected by any paint color. You painted cyan over yellow, noting these areas become green because they are transparent. You painted multiple strokes with a peach color, noting where they overlap themselves, they create a darker color. You reverted the file.

Paint in the Darker Color mode

1. On the Options panel, change the **Mode** to **Darker Color**.

2. Click an **orange swatch** on the Swatches panel. Then paint the **left eye** orange, except the circle; leave it white.

   When you paint over the black areas in the eye, they aren't affected by the Brush tool and don't change color. In Darker Color mode, when two colors overlap, the darker of the two dominates and remains. Because no color is darker than black, black cannot be replaced by any other color. Also, in Darker Color mode, colors do not darken when they overlap themselves, so you can feel free to paint with multiple strokes.

3. Using different colors and adjusting the brush size as necessary, paint the remaining areas of the head.

   Figure 15 shows one result. Take the time to finish the whole head to practice resizing the brush with the bracket keys.

4. Save your work.

You set the Brush tool to Darker Color mode, noting black pixels remain unaffected by any paint and the same color does not darken when it overlaps itself. Using different colors, you painted the remainder of the dragon's head.

Figure 15 An example of the painted dragon's head

Alka5051/Shutterstock.com

Fill selections with a blending mode

1. Use the **Eyedropper tool**  to sample a **pink color** from the artwork, or select a **pink swatch** from the Swatches panel.

2. Select the **Magic Wand tool** on the toolbar.

   When you select the Magic Wand tool , the Options panel at the top of the window changes to show options for the Magic Wand tool .

3. On the Options panel, type **4** in the **Tolerance text box**, then verify that the **Anti-alias** and **Contiguous** options are both checked.

   For this lesson, you are going to use the Magic Wand tool to select large areas to fill.

4. Note the **circles** on the dragon's arms.

   There are 19 circles in the artwork.

5. Click the **Magic Wand tool** in the **center** of any of the circles.

   The entire white center of the circle is selected. The Magic Wand tool selects pixels based on their similarity in color, so it selected all the white pixels at the center of the circle. It didn't select the gray or black pixels that draw the circle because they are too dissimilar from the white center that you clicked.

6. Press and hold **[shift]**, then click the **Magic Wand tool** in the **centers** of the 18 other circles.

   Because you are pressing and holding [shift], you add to the selection.

7. Press and hold **[option] (Mac)** or **[Alt] (Win)**, press the **[delete] key** on your keypad, then deselect.

Figure 16 Fill dialog box with the Darker Color blending mode activated

The selection fills with the pink foreground color. Where the pink pixels meet the lines that draw the circles, there is potential for some white or light gray pixels to remain. We will use a different method in the next steps to address that.

8. Choose a **green foreground color** to paint the dragon's leg.

9. Click the **Magic Wand tool** on the dragon's tail.

   The white pixels in the tail and the dragon's front leg are all selected.

10. Click **Select** on the menu bar, point to **Modify**, then click **Expand**.

11. Type **1** in the Expand By text box, then click **OK**.

    The entire perimeter of the selection is expanded by one pixel. The selection now overlaps the black lines that draw the dragon.

12. Click **Edit** on the menu bar, then click **Fill**.

13. Enter the settings shown in Figure 16, click **OK**, then deselect.

    The leg and tail are filled with the foreground color, but the black lines you overlapped weren't affected because you used the Darker Color blending mode for the fill.

14. Using any of the methods you learned in this lesson, finish coloring the drawing.

    Figure 17, shown on the following page, is one result.

15. Save your work, then close Coloring Book.

You made selections with the Magic Wand tool, then you expanded the selections by one pixel to overlap the black line art. You then used the Fill dialog box to fill with the Darker Color blending mode activated, noting the black line art was not affected. This allowed you to be sure that no white or light gray pixels were left after applying the fill.

Figure 17 The colorized artwork

MAKE SELECTIONS WITH THE MARQUEE AND LASSO TOOLS

▶ *What You'll Do*

In this lesson, you'll use the Marquee and Lasso tools to select objects on the canvas.

Understanding the Goals of this Lesson

While working your way through Lesson 3, imagine a collection of kids' toys that need to be stored neatly on three shelves. You will work with images of toys and put them all together into a final image. This type of work is called *compositing*. A **composite image** is one in which many different images are brought together—in a *composition*—to create one single image or effect.

The main goal of this lesson is for you to learn to make basic selections with the Marquee and the Lasso tools. The challenge of selecting and moving the objects onto the shelves will allow you to explore many options for working with these essential selection tools.

Along the way, you will be asked to notice aspects of the composite image that *don't work well* and to consider some of the challenges you would face if you were working at a more advanced or professional level. Therefore, while you're making basic selections and moving the artwork, you will also learn to think like a more advanced user about such topics as size, spatial relationships, perspective, and shadows, along with more advanced Photoshop features like layers. This will be a great opportunity for you to explore the considerations that professional designers must keep in mind when they work.

Selecting Pixels

Making selections is one of the most fundamental procedures you'll do in Photoshop. The toolbar houses three types of selection tools—the Marquee tools, the Lasso tools, and the Tolerance-based tools—the Magic Wand, the Quick Selection, and the Object Selection tools. Making selections is just one component of working with selections. In this lesson, you'll also learn how to define a selection edge—with a feather, for example— how to transform and save a selection, and how to refine a selection's edge. You'll also gain an understanding of issues involved with moving pixels to a new location on the canvas.

Using the Marquee Selection Tools

The Marquee tools are the most basic tools available for making selections in Photoshop. The Rectangular Marquee tool is used for making rectangular or square selections, and the Elliptical Marquee tool is used for making oval or circular selections. Press and hold [shift] while you drag to constrain the tools to make perfect squares and circles, respectively.

When you make any kind of a selection, what you see on your screen is called a **selection marquee**. Some users call the marquee "marching ants" because it appears as tiny creatures moving in a clockwise direction.

Actually, the term "marquee" refers to a real-world entity. Think of the great old movie palaces you find in the theater districts in big cities. The sign out front that announces the movie's title is called a marquee, and marquees are known for the blinking lights that attract attention, often blinking in patterns that create the illusion of movement. Thus, in Photoshop, the blinking result of making a selection is called a selection marquee.

You can add to an existing selection and remove pixels from an existing selection using simple quick keys. Press and hold the [shift] key to add pixels to an existing selection, and use the [option] (Mac) or [Alt] (Win) keys to remove pixels from a selection.

Doing Double Duty with the Shift Key

The [shift] key plays two important roles when making selections. It allows you to add to an existing selection, and it constrains the Marquee tools so that they create a perfect square or circle when dragging. But what if you want to do both? What if you select a square and you want to select an additional square? You'll need to use the [shift] key to select the second square, *and* you'll need the [shift] key to constrain the new selection to a perfect square. How can you use the same key to do both? First, press and hold [shift] to make a square marquee. Next, to make the second square, press [shift] to add to the first selection. Then, while dragging the second marquee, release the [shift] key and then press it again

to constrain the second marquee to a square shape. This method also works for making multiple perfect-circle selections.

Using the Lasso Selection Tools

The Lasso tool is a freeform selection tool. Unlike the Marquee tools, which limit you to rectangular and elliptical selections, you can use the Lasso tool to make selections of any shape. When selecting a complex shape with the Lasso tool, you will usually find it easier to make small selections and then add to them with the [shift] key.

The Polygonal Lasso tool functions like the Lasso tool, but it does so with straight lines. This makes the tool extremely effective for making quick selections or selecting areas of the canvas that are geometric in shape, as the tool's name implies.

The Magnetic Lasso tool will amaze you the first time you use it. Like the Lasso tool, it makes freeform selections. Its specialty, however, is that it "snaps" to the shape of the object you are trying to select, as if it knows what you are trying to do. For example, let's say you have an image of a black cat on a white background, and you want to select the cat. Drag the Magnetic Lasso tool near the cat, and it will align itself with the edge of the cat image automatically. The Magnetic Lasso tool achieves this ability because Photoshop recognizes contrasting pixels that abut. In this example, Photoshop is able to calculate that

the black pixels of the cat are abutting the white pixels of the background. The Magnetic Lasso tool "understands" that you are trying to make a selection around the black object (the cat) only. This makes the Magnetic Lasso tool valuable for selecting objects photographed against solid backgrounds of contrasting color.

Transforming a Selection Marquee

The word **transformation** means change. After you make a selection, you can enlarge, reduce, rotate, or distort the selection marquee using the Transform Selection command on the Select menu. A bounding box appears around the marquee you are transforming. A **bounding box** is a rectangle that contains eight handles you click and drag to change the dimensions of the marquee.

Press and hold [shift] while dragging a handle on the bounding box to maintain the proportion of the marquee when you are scaling it to be larger or smaller. Press and hold [option] (Mac) or [Alt] (Win) to scale it from its center; this can be very useful when scaling selection marquees. You can use transform commands individually or in a chain. In other words, you can first scale a marquee, and before committing the transformation, you can rotate it too. Once you are done, press [return] (Mac) or [Enter] (Win) to execute the transformation. Press [esc] to abandon the transformation.

Make selections with the Rectangular Marquee tool

1. Open PS 2-4.psd, then save it as **Marquee and Lasso Selections**.

2. Press the **letter [D]** on your keypad to change the foreground and background colors to the default black over white, then press the **letter [X]** to switch them.

3. Click the **Rectangular Marquee tool** on the toolbar, then verify that **Feather** is set to **0 px** and **Style** is set to **Normal** on the Options panel.

4. Use the keyboard shortcut to access the **Zoom tool**.

   If you need a review of accessing the Zoom tool via the keyboard, see Chapter 1, Lesson 4, Exercise 2.

5. Use the **Zoom tool** to drag a box around **both comic books** at the top-right corner of the white section.

   The view of the two comic books is enlarged in the Photoshop window. If you don't see a selection marquee while dragging the Zoom tool, deselect the Scrubby Zoom option for the Zoom tool on the Options panel.

   TIP To make selections accurately, it is *essential* that you zoom in enough to see what you are doing. If you need to squint or move closer to your computer screen, you're not zoomed in enough.

6. With the **Rectangular Marquee tool**, position the **center of the crosshair** on the upper-left corner of the blue comic book, drag downward until the center of the crosshair is on the lower-right corner, then release the mouse pointer.

7. Press and hold **[shift]**, position the **crosshair** over the upper-left corner of the red comic book, then drag a **second marquee** to add the red comic book to the selection.

   Both comic books are selected. Pressing and holding [shift] when making a selection adds to the existing selection.

8. Press the **letter [V]** on your keypad to access the **Move tool**.

   For the remainder of this chapter and the whole book, use this method to access the Move tool.

9. Drag the **two comic books** to the top shelf in the position shown in Figure 18, but don't deselect.

   When you move a selection, the current background color is used to fill the original location of the selection. In this example, the area is filled with black, which is the current background color on the toolbar.

Continued on next page

Figure 18 Positioning the two comic books

10. Deselect.

Once you deselect, the pixels are embedded into the canvas. If you wanted to move the comic books to another location, you'd have to select them again to do so. However, if you move the comic books a second time, you would leave behind the black background color. The blue back wall of the shelves "behind" the comic books is no longer there. This situation is a great example of why working with layered artwork is so important. If the comic books were on their own layer, you could move them without affecting any other pixels on the canvas. You will learn all about layers in Chapter 3.

11. Press the **letter [M]** on your keypad to access the **Rectangular Marquee tool** , use the keyboard shortcut to access the **Zoom tool** , then zoom in on the **pink frame** beneath the "WOW" poster.

You are going to select just the frame and then move it on top of the poster above it to frame the poster.

12. Select the **pink frame**.

We need just the frame, not the white interior, so we need to remove the white pixels from the selection.

13. Press and hold **[Alt] (Win)** or **[option] (Mac)**, then select the **white inner rectangle** inside the pink frame.

Pressing and holding [Alt] (Win) or [option] (Mac) when making a selection removes pixels from the existing selection. As shown in Figure 19, the white inner rectangle is removed from the selection, and just the frame is selected.

Figure 19 Deselecting the interior section of the pink frame

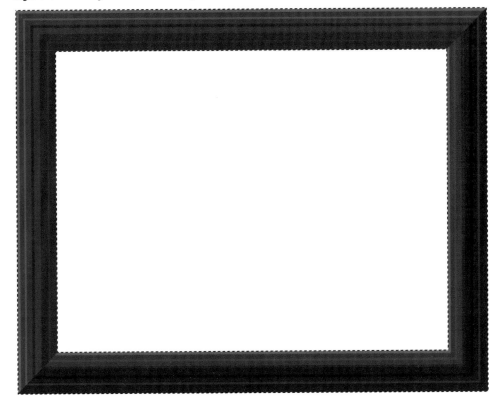

14. Access the **Move tool** ⊕ , press and hold **[shift]**, drag the **frame** straight up, position it over the poster so that the poster completely fills the frame, then deselect.

Now we want to move the framed poster over to the shelves, so we need to *reselect* the frame.

15. Select the **pink frame**.

This time, the interior is not a problem; we *want* the image inside the frame.

16. Move the **framed artwork** to the second shelf in the position shown in Figure 20.

17. Save your work.

You used the [shift] key to select the two comic books. You used the [option] or [Alt] key to deselect the interior of the pink frame, positioned the frame over the poster artwork, and then positioned the framed artwork on the second shelf.

Figure 20 Positioning the framed artwork

Use the Elliptical Marquee tool and transform a selection marquee

1. Click the **Elliptical Marquee tool** ⬭ on the toolbar, then verify that **Feather** is set to **0 px** and **Style** is set to **Normal** on the Options panel.

2. Zoom in on the **dartboard** so that it fills the screen but remains fully visible.

3. Click and drag the **Elliptical Marquee tool** ⬭, and try to select the **dartboard**.

   Chances are you won't be able to select it accurately. For selecting circular objects, starting at the center is the best method.

4. Press and hold **[shift] [option] (Mac)** or **[Shift][Alt] (Win)**, position the **crosshair** over the **center** of the dartboard, then drag out a **circle** that is approximately 75% the size of the dartboard.

   The [option] and [Alt] keys draw the ellipse from its center, and the [shift] key constrains the result to a perfect circle. The circle is not as large as the dartboard, but it can be enlarged.

5. Click **Select** on the menu bar, then click **Transform Selection**.

   A bounding box appears around the selection marquee.

6. Press and hold **[shift] [option] (Mac)** or **[Shift] [Alt] (Win)**, then drag the **top-right corner handle** to enlarge the marquee until it selects the entire **dartboard**.

   Don't try to be perfect. Go just up to the edge of the dartboard, but leave a little room for error. The last thing you want is to have a white halo around the dartboard that will show against the blue background of the shelves.

Figure 21 Positioning the dartboard

7. When the selection is where you want it, press **[return] (Mac)** or **[Enter] (Win)** to execute the transformation.

8. Zoom out, move the **dartboard** to the position shown in Figure 21, then deselect.

9. Fit the whole canvas on the screen, then assess the "shelves" section of the artwork.

   AUTHOR'S **NOTE**   The more you work with Photoshop, the more you will "learn to see." To the untrained eye, the three shelves are identical, but if you look closer, you will see that each is entirely different from the other two. We are looking straight on at the middle shelf; we see neither its top nor its bottom surface. We are looking up at the top shelf, so we see its bottom surface. We are looking down at the bottom shelf, so we see its top surface.

   Our perspective of the shelves affects how we view the objects on the shelves. The framed poster is believably standing at the front edge of the middle shelf because we are looking at it and the shelf straight on. It could also be believably back against the wall, except in that case, the shelf above would cast a shadow on it, so it must be at the front of the shelf.

The dartboard and the comic books on the top shelf don't pass the reality test. They appear to be standing at the very front edge of the shelf, but that makes no visual sense, because they couldn't stand on their own. Either they would have to lean back against the wall or they would be positioned deeper into the shelf and up against the wall. In that case, because we are looking at them from below, we would not see the bottoms of the dartboard or the comic books.

Figure 22 shows an example of an edit that looks more realistic. This was achieved by slicing off the bottom of the books and the dartboard. Because we see the bottom surface of the top shelf, it makes sense that we wouldn't see the bottom of the books or the dartboard. Now they appear as though they are up against the wall, deeper into the shelf. Note also a shadow was added to the top of the framed poster, which makes it appear to be positioned at the back of the shelf and under the top shelf. It's another touch that adds more reality points to the composite.

These are the kinds of complex perspective considerations you'll have to keep in mind when compositing multiple images on a more advanced level, which is exactly what you'll be doing in Chapter 3.

10. Save your work.

You used the Elliptical Marquee tool to select most of the round dartboard artwork. Rather than trying to get the selection dead on in just one move, you made just a 75% selection and then used the Transform Selection command to scale the marquee. This allowed you as many tries as you needed to get the best selection of the artwork. You then analyzed the top shelf of the artwork, noting the round dartboard could not be positioned on the shelf in a way that looks realistic.

Figure 22 A more realistic crop of top-shelf images

Use the Lasso tool and the Magnetic Lasso tool

1. Be sure your work is saved at this point.

2. Click the **Lasso tool**  on the toolbar, then verify that **Feather** is set to **0 px** and **Anti-alias** is checked.

3. Zoom in on the **teddy bear**.

4. Using Figure 23 as a guide, click and drag the **Lasso tool** to make a rough selection of the interior of the artwork.

5. Using the **[shift] key**, click and drag to add to the selection to select the **whole teddy bear**. Use the **[option] (Mac)** or **[Alt] (Win)** key to remove from the selection if you accidentally select the white background.

   You will quickly realize that this is not the right tool for the job. The Lasso tool is good for making quick, inaccurate selections of areas of the canvas, but it's not a precision selection tool.

6. Deselect whatever selection you have made.

Figure 23 Rough selection of the interior of the artwork

7. Select the **Magnetic Lasso tool** 🧲 on the toolbar, then enter the settings shown in Figure 24 on the Options panel.

   The Width setting determines the number of pixels Photoshop samples to identify an edge. The Contrast setting is the minimum amount of contrast, measured in pixel brightness, for Photoshop to identify an edge. The Frequency is a measurement of how often the Magnetic Lasso tool will position an anchor point on the line. These are the default settings for the Magnetic Lasso tool. The Magnetic Lasso tool works by placing a selection line on the "edge" of artwork. Photoshop can't really "see" what the edge of any piece of artwork is in relation to other artwork. All Photoshop "sees" is pixels with different color and brightness values. In this case, Photoshop recognizes that a lot of brown-colored pixels are adjacent to white pixels and that the contrast between those pixels, in terms of their brightness values, is very different. Based on that information, Photoshop will position the Magnetic Lasso tool on the edge of the teddy bear artwork.

8. Zoom in so that you can see the **whole head** of the teddy bear.

9. Position the **Magnetic Lasso tool** 🧲 on the **left edge** of the head at the eye level, click just once, then drag along the edge until you have gone around both ears and are on the right edge of the head at the eye level.

TIP You don't need to hold down the mouse pointer while you drag; just drag. However, when you come to a corner or a sharp turn, you can click the mouse on that point. This will help you switch directions sharply.

10. When you reach the right side of the head, at the eye level, double-click.

    When you double-click, the Magnetic Lasso tool automatically closes the selection with a line. Your selection should be similar to Figure 25.

Continued on next page

Figure 24 Settings for the Magnetic Lasso tool

Feather: 0 px   ☑ Anti-alias   Width: 10 px   Contrast: 10%   Frequency: 57

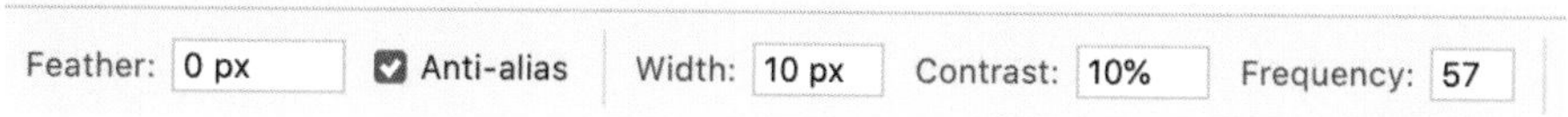

Figure 25 Selecting just the top half of the head

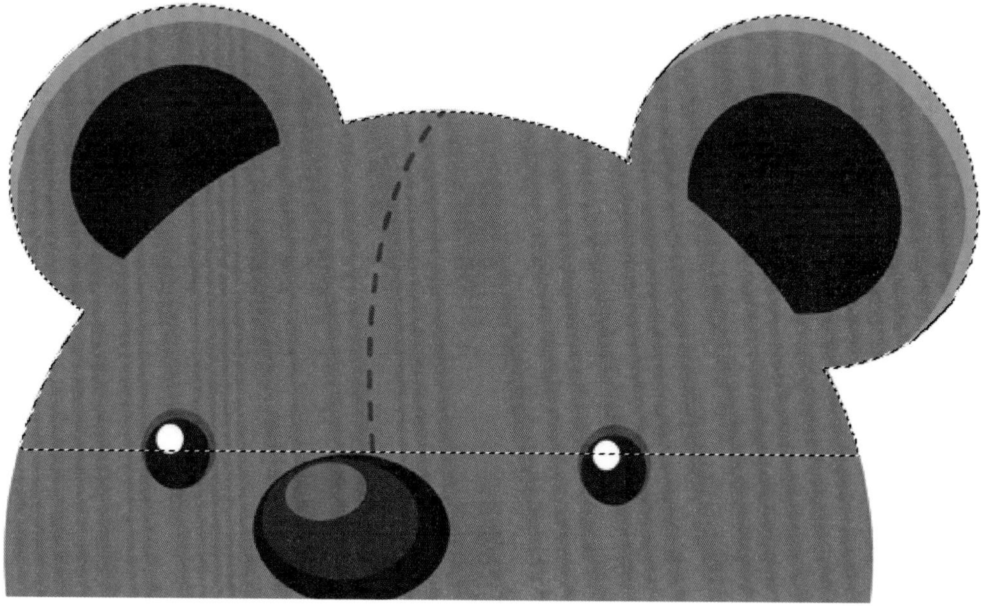

11. Starting in the *interior* of the current selection, press and hold **[shift]**, then add more to the current selection.

It's tempting to try to go around the whole of the artwork in one move, but you'll do a better job if you stay zoomed in and make multiple selections, adding along the way. You should be able to finish selecting the entire teddy bear with five or six selections.

12. When you have finished selecting the perimeter of the teddy bear, press and hold **[option] (Mac)** or **[Alt] (Win)**, then *remove* the white triangle under the arm from the selection.

13. Zoom in on an **edge** of the teddy bear, press and hold **[spacebar]**, then pan around the artwork to assess the selection.

You can use the "add to" or "remove from" technique to improve the selection if you need to.

14. Access the **Move tool** , then move the **teddy bear** to the position shown in Figure 26.

While the Magnetic Lasso tool is not perfect, it does a remarkably good job.

15. Zoom in on the **dart** so that it fills the entire screen.

16. Use the **Magnetic Lasso tool** to select the **dart**, then move it to the position shown in Figure 27.

17. Save your work.

Figure 26 Positioning the teddy bear on the shelf

Figure 27 Positioning the dart

The teddy bear sits on the shelf in a way that looks very realistic; the angles all make sense. However, an issue you'd have to consider on the advanced level is that the bear would cast a shadow on the shelf. Figure 28 shows painted shadows for the bear. Note the shadow from the bear is complex, especially where its leg hangs off the shelf. Shadows, your ability to understand how they would be cast, and your ability to paint them, are all major challenges when making composite images.

You tried to use the Lasso tool to select the teddy bear but quickly realized that it's not accurate enough to do the job. You switched to the Magnetic Lasso tool, which was much more effective. Rather than trying to select the entire artwork in one move, you used [shift] to combine multiple selections as you worked.

Figure 28 Shadows on the bear artwork

Use the Polygonal Lasso tool

1. Zoom in on the **blue O block** so that it fills your screen.

2. Select the **Polygonal Lasso tool**  on the toolbar. Then, on the Options panel, verify that **Feather** is set to **0 px** and **Anti-alias** is checked.

3. Press the **[caps lock] key** on your keypad.

   With the [caps lock] key activated, the cursor switches to a crosshair, which is more precise.

4. Click the **crosshair** one time on the **top-left corner** of the O block.

5. Move the mouse pointer down, and click the crosshair on the **bottom-left corner** of the O block.

6. Click the **next two corners** of the O block.

7. Moving counterclockwise, work your way all the way around the blocks.

   As you move the mouse pointer, the screen will scroll automatically.

8. When you near the end, float over the **original point** you clicked so the Polygonal Lasso tool icon appears with a small "o" beside it, then click to close the selection.

TIP You can also double-click the mouse pointer to close the path. When you double-click the mouse pointer, the path will automatically close by drawing a straight line from your current location to the starting point.

9. Zoom out, then move the **blocks** to the second shelf, as shown in Figure 29.

   The blocks cannot realistically be positioned on the second shelf. We are looking straight on at the shelf, so the surface of the shelf is not at all visible. Therefore, as shown in the figure, the O block is floating in thin air. Even though the R block and the M block are touching the front edge of the shelf, they make no logical sense. They too are floating away.

10. Move the **blocks** down to the bottom shelf, then compare your work to Figure 30.

    The placement of the blocks on the bottom shelf makes visual sense. Both the blocks and the shelf are photographed from the same angle. Note how we see the tops of the O, R, and M blocks exactly as we see the top of the shelf itself. We see the surface of the bottom shelf, and we see the blocks resting on the shelf.

11. Save your work, then close Marquee and Lasso Selections.

You used the Polygonal Lasso tool to select the straight edges of the blocks. You positioned the blocks on the second shelf, noting the perspective was too far off to look real. You then positioned the blocks on the bottom shelf, which worked much better.

Figure 29 Positioning the blocks on the second shelf doesn't work

Figure 30 Assessing the final artwork

EXPLORE A GRAYSCALE IMAGE WITH THE MAGIC WAND TOOL

▶ **What You'll Do**

In this lesson, you'll gain an understanding of a grayscale image while learning to use the Magic Wand tool.

Moving a Selection Marquee vs. Moving Pixels

When you make a selection, as long as a selection tool is active on the toolbar, you can move the selection marquee to another location on the canvas without moving any pixels. When the Move tool is active, moving a selection marquee moves the selected pixels.

The arrow keys on your keypad are very useful when moving a selection marquee or moving pixels. Press an arrow key and the selection will move one pixel in that direction. Press and hold [shift] plus an arrow key, and the selection will move 10 pixels in that direction. Using arrows helps you to be very specific when moving pixels or a selection marquee.

Using the Magic Wand Tool

The Magic Wand tool is a powerful selection tool. Click any pixel on the canvas, and the Magic Wand tool selects other pixels based on the similarity of their color. The **Tolerance** setting on the Options panel will determine the number of pixels the Magic Wand tool either includes or doesn't include in the selection. The greater the Tolerance value, the greater the number of pixels the Magic Wand tool will select.

By clicking the **Contiguous check box** on the Options panel, you are specifying that the Magic Wand tool selects only pixels that are contiguous to (touching) the pixel where you click the image. Otherwise, it will select pixels throughout the image that are within the current Tolerance value.

Understanding the Grayscale Image and the Tolerance Setting on the Magic Wand Tool

The Magic Wand tool and other tools and dialog boxes in Photoshop do their work based on the function of tolerance. The key to understanding tolerance is to understand that every pixel in the image has a number between 0 and 255.

A **grayscale image** is a single-color image, one that you would normally refer to as black and white. The single color is black, and the image is produced as a range of grays, from black to white. You are already familiar with this concept if you've ever printed an image on a black-and-white printer. The printer has only black ink, but it can use that one color to reproduce an image by creating the *illusion* of a range of grays. The word "illusion" is appropriate because there are no actual gray inks coming out of your black and white printer; the printer just uses fewer dots of black ink in lighter areas to create the illusion that those areas are gray.

In a grayscale image, Photoshop produces an image using a range of 256 gray pixels, from black to white. Each pixel can be one—and only one—of 256 shades of gray. Keep the following important points clear in your understanding:

- Black pixels have a grayscale value of 0.
- White pixels have a grayscale value of 255.
- Values 1–254 are shades of gray.
- "Middle gray" has a grayscale value of 128.
- The range in a grayscale image is 0–255, for a total of 256 shades of gray available per pixel.

Tolerance settings for the Magic Wand tool are directly related to a pixel's **grayscale value**. When you click the Magic Wand tool on an "area" of an image, you are *only* clicking on one pixel, and that pixel has a grayscale value. Because pixels are so small, you won't know the specific pixel you are clicking or its grayscale value, but nevertheless, you are clicking on one pixel. The Magic Wand tool selects other pixels based on the grayscale value of the pixel you clicked and the Tolerance value that you set on the Options panel.

For example, let's say you set the Tolerance value for the Magic Wand tool to 10, and you click the Contiguous check box. Next, you click the Magic Wand tool on a pixel whose grayscale value is 75. The Magic Wand tool would select all contiguous pixels whose grayscale value falls within the range of 65–85, 10 grayscale values higher and 10 grayscale values lower than the pixel that you clicked. If the Contiguous option is *not* checked, the Magic Wand tool would select all the pixels whose grayscale values were 65–85 *throughout the image*.

When working with the Magic Wand tool, you don't need to know the number of the pixel you are clicking, that would be impractical. Your goal is simply to select pixels of similar color. Experiment with different tolerance settings until you get the selection you want.

This discussion of tolerance is a great example of how working effectively with Photoshop requires a broad understanding of the program itself. Sure, you can click around mindlessly with the Magic Wand tool and figure out, "Hey, it selects the same colors." That's great, but it's in no way an in-depth understanding of the program that will take you where you want to go. To understand how the Magic Wand tool *really* works requires that you understand what the grayscale image *really* is—a grid of tiny gray pixels, each of them having one grayscale value.

Understanding Selection Edges

The outline of a selection is called the **edge** of a selection; the type of edge that you choose will have a big impact on how your work appears. The edge of a selection is always either aliased or anti-aliased. An **aliased** edge is a hard edge—the hard "stair-stepped" pixels are very obvious. The edge is noticeably blunt and seldomly used. An **anti-aliased** edge is a crisp but smoother edge. With an anti-aliased edge, Photoshop creates a smooth transition between the edge and its background using many shades of the edge pixel color.

Think about it this way. The Photoshop canvas is made of square pixels. How could you possibly reproduce a round image, like an orange, if all you are using is square pixels? The answer is a combination of resolution and an anti-aliased edge. The resolution of the image, the number of pixels per inch, must be high enough that the pixels are too small to be seen individually. The anti-aliased edge uses edge pixels to create a visual color transition at the edge between the object and the background, so the viewer sees the *illusion* of a smooth, curved edge. That's what all curved objects are in Photoshop—an illusion created with an anti-aliased edge.

Most selection tools have an anti-alias option. Whenever you see it, 99.9% of the time you should activate it.

Working with a Feathered Edge

A **feathered edge** is a blended edge. Photoshop creates a blend at the edge of a selection between the selected pixels and the background image. Photoshop offers settings for controlling the length of the blend at the edge. The feather value is equal to the length of the feathered edge. When you apply a feathered edge to a selection, the edge is equally distributed inside and outside the selection edge. In Photoshop, vignettes are created with feathered edges. A **vignette** is a visual effect in which the edge of an image, usually an oval, gradually fades away.

Figure 31 shows three circles—one with an aliased edge, one with an anti-aliased edge, and one with a feathered edge.

Understanding the Relationship Between Computer Monitors and Viewing Selection Edges

Your computer monitor acts as the middleman between you and the Photoshop image. Everything you are seeing is through your monitor. Monitors have resolution as well; most have a resolution of 72 pixels per inch. This fact has a big impact on how you view your Photoshop image because your monitor's resolution is constantly trying to display the image's resolution. When you're viewing your image at less than 100%, your monitor is not giving you an accurate visual representation of the pixels in your image. When you're analyzing subtle components of your image—like selection edges!—be sure that you're viewing your image at least at 100%.

Sampling Pixels and Saving Swatches

The term **sampling** refers to either taking information from a pixel or accessing its color.

The Info panel offers readouts that tell you a pixel's color information. When you position your mouse pointer over a pixel, the Info panel gives you a readout on that pixel, and that readout can be in terms of RGB, CMYK, Grayscale, or HSB, among other settings you can choose. Most designers set the Info panel's readouts to RGB, which provides grayscale information on each pixel.

Click the Eyedropper tool on any pixel to sample its color. When you do, the color of the pixel you click becomes the foreground color on the toolbar. Press [option] (Mac) or [Alt] (Win) when you click a swatch or use the Eyedropper tool to change the background color.

When using the Brush tool, pressing [option] (Mac) or [Alt] (Win) changes the Brush tool to the Eyedropper tool.

If you click a swatch on the Swatches panel, the foreground changes to that color.

The Color panel is an interactive panel. You create a color on the Color panel by dragging the available color sliders, based on the current color mode. Any new color you make on the Color panel becomes the foreground color on the toolbar.

Figure 31 Examples of three selection edges

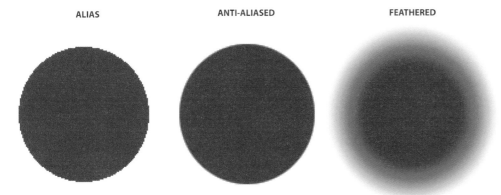

ALIAS   ANTI-ALIASED   FEATHERED

The Swatches panel houses lots of preset colors for you to work with. In addition to the default set of colors, the Swatches panel offers you different collections of swatches, such as Pastel, Dark, Light, and Pale.

When you create a new color by either using the Color panel or sampling a color with the Eyedropper tool, you can save it to the Swatches panel. The Swatches panel allows you to name and save your color using the Create new swatch button on the panel. The new color will appear at the bottom of the panel, under the default swatch categories.

You can also add a new color to the Swatches panel from the Color Picker dialog box. Click the Add to Swatches button in the dialog box. You will be prompted to name your new color and choose which library to add it to. To delete a swatch, click to select it, then click the Delete swatch button.

Move a selection marquee and move pixels

1. Open PS 2-5.psd, then save it as **Balloon Puzzle**.

2. Select the **Magic Wand tool** 🪄 on the toolbar.

3. On the Options panel, set the **Tolerance** to **8**, then verify that the **Contiguous** and **Anti-alias options** are both checked.

4. Use the **Fit on Screen** keyboard shortcut.

TIP The keyboard shortcut is [command] [0] (Mac) or [Ctrl] [0] (Win).

5. Click the **Magic Wand tool** 🪄 on the **center of the white circle** on the right side of the canvas that corresponds with the Number 4 puzzle piece on the left side of the canvas.

   The white circle, and only the white circle, is selected. The other white areas of the image are not selected because the Magic Wand tool is set to select *only* contiguous pixels.

6. Position your mouse pointer over the selection.

   Your mouse pointer changes to a move selection marquee cursor ▸.

7. Click and drag the **selection marquee**, and align it with the **Number 4 puzzle piece**.

8. Press and hold **[spacebar] [command] (Mac)** or **[spacebar] [Ctrl] (Win)** to access the **Zoom tool** 🔍.

9. With the **Zoom tool** 🔍, zoom in around the **Number 4 puzzle piece**, then release **[spacebar] [command] (Mac)** or **[spacebar] [Ctrl] (Win)**.

   The puzzle piece fills the window.

10. Use the arrow keys on your keypad to align the selection marquee exactly to the puzzle piece.

    The marquee moves one pixel every time you press an arrow key.

11. Click **View** on the menu bar, then click **Fit on Screen**.

12. Press and hold the **letter [V]** to switch to the **Move tool** ✛.

13. Click and drag the **Number 4 puzzle piece** until it is close to aligning with the corresponding white circle on the right side of the canvas.

Continued on next page

14. Use the keyboard to access the **Zoom tool** 🔍, then zoom in on the selected circle.

15. Use the **arrow keys** to move the pixels to the best alignment, as shown in Figure 32.

Because the Move tool ✛ is the active tool on the toolbar, pressing the arrow keys moves the pixels along with the selection marquee.

16. Deselect.

17. Using the same methods, including zooming in and out of the image, finish the puzzle. Your result should resemble Figure 33.

There is no "perfect" in this exercise. The pieces will align, but there will be a white halo around all the pieces in the final image.

18. Save your work, then close Balloon Puzzle.

You used the Magic Wand tool to select white areas of the image. You moved the marquee selection to align it with pixels of the same shape. You used arrow keys to get the best alignment possible. You used the Move tool to move the image pieces into the puzzle. You used the arrow keys again, this time to move and align pixels. Throughout the exercise, you used keyboard commands to access the Zoom tool, to zoom in on the image, and to fit the image on the screen.

Figure 32 Positioning the Number 4 puzzle piece

Figure 33 Finishing the puzzle

Morguefile

Experiment with Tolerance settings

1. Open PS 2-6.psd.

   This file has a gradient that gradates horizontally from black to white. This is a grayscale image. In a grayscale image, each pixel can be one of 256 shades of gray. Black pixels have a grayscale value of 0, and white pixels have a value of 255. Thus, the range of black to white pixels is 0–255, for a total of 256 shades of gray per pixel. Each pixel is one of those shades.

2. Click **Window** on the menu bar, then click **Info**.

   The Info panel opens. You use the Info panel to sample the grayscale values of pixels. Since this might be the first time you are using the Info panel, we must first verify that your Info panel displays the same settings as this book.

3. On the left side of the Info panel, click the **Eyedropper icon** , then click **RGB Color**.

Your Info panel should resemble Figure 34. It doesn't matter what the setting is on the right side of the Info panel. The RGB Color readout displays grayscale information for each pixel. If this were a color image, each pixel would have a different number for red, for green, and for blue. For example, a yellowish pixel would have high numbers for red and green and a low number for blue, because red and green produce yellow. In a grayscale image, no color dominates. Each is the same, and that produces a "gray" pixel. A black pixel is RGB 0/0/0. A white pixel is RGB 255/255/255. A middle gray pixel is RGB 128/128/128. And so forth.

4. Press the **letter [I]** on your keypad to access the **Eyedropper tool** , position it on the far-left edge of the image, then note the readout on the left side of Info panel.

   Because you are positioned over a black pixel, the RGB values on the Info panel are 0/0/0.

Continued on next page

Figure 34 The Info panel showing the left side set to RGB Color

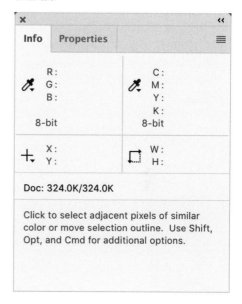

5. Slowly move the **Eyedropper tool**  from left to right while noting the changes on the Info panel.

    As you move from left to right, the grayscale values on the Info panel move up incrementally. The gradient on the canvas goes from 0 (black) to (255) white, with every value in between. The lighter the pixel, the higher the grayscale value will be.

6. Click the **Magic Wand tool** on the toolbar.

7. On the Options panel, set the **Tolerance** to **10**, then verify that the **Contiguous** and **Anti-alias options** are not checked.

8. Click the **left edge** of the canvas.

    As shown in Figure 35, a small slice of the artwork is selected from top to bottom. You clicked a black pixel on the left edge, and black pixels have a grayscale value of 0. With the Tolerance set to 10, the Magic Wand tool selected pixels with a grayscale value of 0–10.

    AUTHOR'S **NOTE** This explanation of how the Tolerance setting works on the Magic Wand tool is correct, but it's also simplified. Photoshop's computing algorithms are sophisticated and complex, and the Magic Wand tool will produce selections that won't always correspond exactly with the Tolerance setting that has been input. Don't worry about that; just keep in mind the essential understanding of how the tool works with the Tolerance setting.

Figure 35 Selection with a Tolerance setting of 10

9. Deselect, change the **Tolerance** to **64**, then click the **left edge**.

   Roughly the left quarter of the canvas is selected because 64 is one-quarter of 256.

10. Deselect, change the **Tolerance** to **128**, then click the **left edge**.

    Roughly half of the canvas is selected because 128 is half of 256.

11. Deselect, change the **Tolerance** to **20**, then click roughly the **center** of the canvas.

    Roughly 40 pixels are selected. Let's agree that when you clicked, you clicked on a pixel whose grayscale value is 128. With tolerance set at 20, pixels in the range of 108–148 were selected. In the case of this specific graphic, that means 20 pixels to the right and 20 pixels to the left of where you clicked were selected.

12. Close the file.

You used a black-to-white gradient to better understand the concept of a tolerance-based tool like the Magic Wand tool and to better understand the concept of a grayscale image as a whole. You set the Info panel to display in RGB color, which shows pixel information as grayscale values. By increasing the tolerance, you saw that the selection was expanded. You also clicked the center of the gradient to better understand that a tolerance setting selects pixels that are higher and lower than the pixel that is clicked.

Experiment with the Contiguous setting

1. Open PS 2-7.psd, then save it as **Contiguous Concentration.**

2. Select the **Magic Wand tool** 🪄. Then, on the Options panel, set the **Tolerance** to **0**, verify the **Contiguous option** is checked, then verify that **Anti-alias** is *not* checked.

   With a tolerance value of 0, the Magic Wand tool 🪄 selects just the grayscale value of the pixel you click and *zero* others.

3. Click the **topmost pink square**.

   Because the Contiguous option is activated, the other pink square is not selected. Only the pixels that are touching the pixel you clicked are selected (if they are within tolerance).

4. Click a **yellow swatch** on the Swatches panel, then click **[option] [delete] (Mac)** or **[Alt] [delete] (Win)** to fill with the foreground color.

5. Uncheck the **Contiguous option** on the Options panel.

6. Click **either** of the **blue squares**.

7. Fill the **blue squares** with **purple**.

8. Check the **Contiguous option** to activate it.

9. Click the **top-left black square**, press and hold **[shift]**, then add the three other **black corner squares** to the selection.

10. Fill the **corner squares** with **red**.

11. Uncheck the **Contiguous option**.

Continued on next page

12. Click any of the **green squares**.

    All four green squares are selected.

13. Check to activate the **Contiguous option**.

14. Press and hold **[option] (Mac)** or **[Alt] (Win)**, then click the **top-right green square**.

    The top-right green square is deselected. This was a *very tricky* move. Holding the [option] or [Alt] key removes from a selection. However, if the Contiguous option had remained off, all four of the green squares would have been deselected when you clicked the top-right green square. With the Contiguous option activated, only that square was deselected.

15. Fill the **three selected squares** with **orange**.

16. Select all the **black squares**.

17. Click **Select** on the menu bar, point to **Modify**, then click **Contract**.

18. Type **8** in the Contract By text box, then click **OK**.

    The Contract and Expand dialog boxes do exactly that. They contract or expand a selection marquee by a specific number of pixels. In this case, the selection was contracted by eight pixels.

19. Fill the selection with **blue**, then deselect.

    Your canvas should resemble Figure 36.

20. Save your work.

You alternated activating and deactivating the Contiguous option for the Magic Wand tool to fill different squares on the checkerboard.

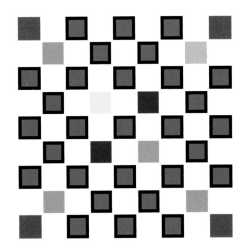

Figure 36 The multicolored checkerboard

Explore Select Inverse vs. Invert

1. Ask yourself how you could use the **Magic Wand tool** with one click to select all the different colored squares on the canvas.

2. Click the **Magic Wand tool** on any white area.

3. Click **Select** on the menu bar, then click **Inverse**.

    OK, so we cheated a little bit. You had to use the menu command as well. The Inverse command deselects the pixels that are selected and selects the pixels that aren't.

4. Fill the selection with **white**.

Figure 37 The black and white checkerboard

5. Click **Select** on the menu bar, click **Inverse**, fill the selection with **black**, then deselect.

    Your canvas should resemble Figure 37.

6. Verify that nothing is selected on the canvas, enter **[command] [I] (Mac)** or **[Ctrl] [I] (Win)** repeatedly to execute the Invert command.

    The Invert command inverts pixels' grayscale values. Black pixels (0) become white pixels (255) and vice versa.

7. Use the **Magic Wand tool** to fill the squares with **blue**.

8. Fill the background with **green**.

9. Deselect, then invert the canvas repeatedly.

   Colored pixels also invert their grayscale values and become their "opposite" colors.

10. Save your work, then close Contiguous Concentration.

You selected the background color of the checkerboard and then used the Inverse command to select the multicolored squares. You then used the Invert command to invert the canvas with nothing selected, noting that the black squares became white and vice versa.

Use the Magic Wand tool to select an image

1. Open PS 2-8.psd, then save it as **Orange Balloon**.

2. Click the **Magic Wand tool** 🪄 , then on the Options panel, set the **Tolerance** to **64**, verify that **Contiguous** is not activated, then verify that **Anti-alias** is checked.

3. Click the **bright yellow area** of the balloon above the green diamond at the upper-left corner of the balloon.

4. Press and hold **[shift]**, then click **two other areas of darker yellow** so that your selection resembles Figure 38.

   Three clicks should be enough to get a clean selection of all yellow areas, as shown in the figure. Note the basket under the balloon was also selected. We will remove that from the selection.

   Continued on next page

Figure 38 Selecting the yellow areas of the balloon

The basket is also selected

5. Click the **Rectangular Marquee tool** , press and hold **[option] (Mac)** or **[Alt] (Win)**, then drag a **box around the basket** below the balloon.

   The basket is deselected, so just the yellow areas of the balloon are selected.

6. Press **[command] [H] (Mac)** or **[Ctrl] [H] (Win)** to hide the selection marquee.

   If a dialog box appears asking what you want to hide, click Hide Extras.

7. Click **Image** on the menu bar, point to **Adjustments**, then click **Hue/Saturation**.

   The Hue/Saturation dialog box opens.

8. Drag the **Hue slider** left to **−99**, then click **OK**.

   The yellow pixels change to bright purple.

9. Click the **Magic Wand tool** , increase the **Tolerance** to **100**, then activate **Contiguous**.

10. Click the **blue sky** at the top-left corner of the image.

    The entire sky, or background, is selected.

11. Click **Select** on the menu bar, then click **Inverse**.

    The sky is deselected, and the balloon is selected. Unfortunately, the basket is also selected, which you must now deselect.

12. Click the **Lasso tool** , press and hold **[option] (Mac)** or **[Alt] (Win)**, then deselect the basket.

13. Click **[command] [U] (Mac)** or **[Ctrl] [U] (Win)** to open the Hue/Saturation dialog box.

14. Drag the **Hue slider** to **+87**, click **OK**, then compare your artwork to Figure 39.

15. Save your work, then close Orange Balloon.

You used the Magic Wand tool to select only the yellow areas of the balloon, which you changed to purple. You then selected the sky and inversed the selection to select the balloon. You then removed the basket from the selection and changed the color of the whole balloon.

Figure 39 Changing the color of the whole balloon

Explore selection edges

1. Open PS 2-9.psd, then save it as **Selection Edges**.

2. Click the **Magic Wand tool** 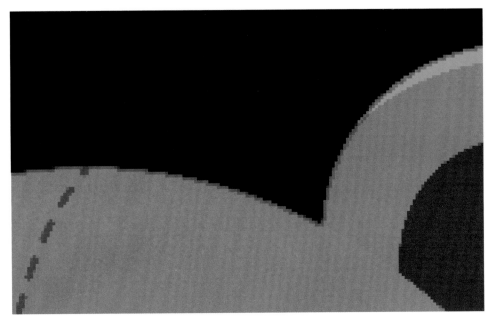, set the **Tolerance** to **8**, then verify that **Contiguous** is checked.

3. Uncheck **Anti-alias**.

4. Click the **white background**, press and hold **[shift]**, then click the **black background** to add it to the selection.

5. Click **Select** on the menu bar, then click **Inverse**.

6. Click the **Move tool** on the toolbar, press and hold **[option] (Mac)** or **[Alt] (Win)**, then drag the **bear** completely into the black area.

   Pressing and holding [option] (Mac) or [Alt] (Win) when dragging a selection makes a copy of the selection.

7. Zoom in to examine the aliased edge.

   The edge is hard and uneven. It is unacceptable.

8. Click **File** on the menu bar, then click **Revert**.

9. Click to activate **Anti-alias** on the Options panel.

10. Using the same method as before, select the **bear**, then move it into the black area.

Figure 40 Examining the anti-aliased edge

11. Zoom in to examine the anti-aliased edge.

    The edge is smooth. As shown in Figure 40, the Anti-alias option uses the edge pixels of the selection to create a color transition between the edge of the bear and the black background.

12. Revert the file, then using the same method, select the **bear**.

13. Click **Select** on the menu bar, point to **Modify**, then click **Feather**.

14. Type **24** in the Feather Radius text box, then click **OK**.

15. Move a **copy of the bear** into the black area.

The artwork appears with a white glow. The bear gradates out to the illusion of a soft white "feathered" edge, which is really a range of white pixels blending with the black background.

16. Save your work, then close Selection Edges.

You used the Magic Wand tool to select the bear first with an aliased edge and then with an anti-aliased edge and examined both edges. Lastly, you applied a feather to the selection and then examined that effect against the black background.

Smooth selection edges

1. Open PS 2-10.psd, then save it as **Robot on White**.

The robot was photographed against a black background for contrast. However, we want to position it over a white background. Removing a black background can often be challenging.

2. Click the **Magic Wand tool** , verify that the **Tolerance** is set to **8**, then verify that **Contiguous** and **Anti-alias** are both checked.

3. Click the **black background**, press and hold **[shift]**, then click the **white background** to add it to the selection.

4. Click **Select** on the menu bar, then click **Inverse**.

5. Click the **Move tool** on the toolbar, press and hold **[option] (Mac)** or **[Alt] (Win)**, drag a **copy** completely into the white area, then hide the selection marquee.

A black edge surrounds the "silhouette" of the image, like a dark halo. Also, even though Anti-alias is activated, the pixels along the edge aren't smooth. Because the white robot abuts a black background in the original photograph, the Magic Wand tool cannot make a selection that visually appears smooth, not even with an anti-aliased edge. Adding a feathered edge will soften and fade the edge, which is not an option for a plastic and hard-edged toy.

TIP Press **[command] [H] (Mac)** or **[Ctrl] [H] (Win)** to hide the selection marquee.

6. Revert the file.

7. Using the same method, select the **robot**.

8. Zoom in so that you are viewing the artwork at **400%**.

9. Click **Select** on the menu bar, point to **Modify**, then click **Contract**.

10. Enter **2** in the Contract By text box, then click **OK**.

Viewing the artwork at this magnification, we can see the selection edge shift. Contracting the selection will remove the black edge pixels from the selection. However, just contracting the selection won't make its edge any smoother.

11. Zoom out, click **Select** on the menu bar, then click **Select and Mask**.

The Select and Mask workspace opens, with the Properties panel on the right and its own set of tools on the left. This workspace offers many options for altering selections. For our purposes in this lesson, we will use it for viewing the artwork and for simply smoothing a selection.

12. On the Properties panel, in the View Mode section, verify that **High Quality Preview** is the only one of the three check boxes that is checked.

13. Click the **View list arrow**, then click **Overlay**.

The View menu offers options that will change the background of the artwork to help you better see the edges of the selection and the overall appearance of the silhouette.

14. Drag the **Opacity slider** to **100%**.

15. Click the **Color box** to open the **Color Picker**.

Continued on next page

16. Drag the **Hue sliders** (along the rainbow graphic) to a blue area. Then, in the large color square, click a **bright blue area** in the upper-right corner.

17. Click **OK**.

The selection of the robot appears against the blue background. With the Overlay view, you can preview your selection against any color. This can be very useful. For example, this preview would give you a good sense of how the robot would look against an image of a blue sky. In this case, however, we want to position the robot against a white background.

18. Click the **View list arrow**, then choose **On White**.

19. Press and hold **[command] [spacebar] (Mac)** or **[Ctrl] [spacebar] (Win)** to access the **Zoom tool** ⊕., then zoom in on the **inside of the robot's arm** on the left side of the image.

You should be viewing the inside of the arm at 500%. At this magnification, you can see clearly that the edge is not smooth.

20. On the Properties panel, drag the **Smooth slider** to **2**.

As shown in Figure 41, the edge pixels are made smoother without a feathering or fading effect taking place.

21. Click **OK**.

22. Zoom out, click the **Move tool** ⊕. on the toolbar, press and hold **[option] (Mac)** or **[Alt] (Win)**, then drag a **copy of the robot** completely into the white area.

Figure 41 Examining the smoother edge

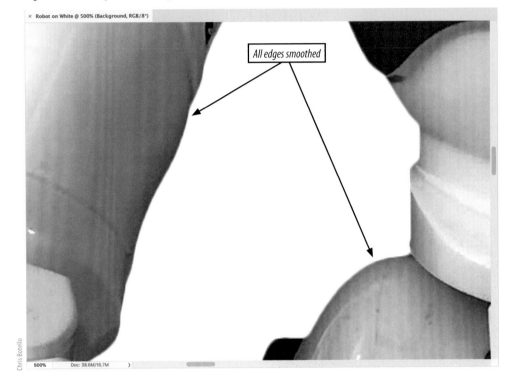

All edges smoothed

23. Deselect, then examine the edge.

The edge is smooth, exactly as it was previewed in the Select and Mask workspace.

24. Save your work, then close Robot on White.

You used the Magic Wand tool to select the robot, then you contracted the selection trying to remove the black halo from the edge. You opened the selection in the Select and Mask workspace and viewed it against a custom blue background. You then used the Smooth option to smoothen the rough edge.

POSTERIZE AN IMAGE AND SAVE SELECTIONS

▶ *What You'll Do*

In this lesson, you'll gain a deeper understanding of a grayscale image while creating a posterized effect.

Saving Selections

After you've made a selection, especially a complex selection, you can save it for future use. The Select menu offers you the Save Selection command, which gives you the ability to name and save multiple selections with a file. Use the Load Selection command, also on the Select menu, to load any of the selections you've saved.

When you save a selection, Photoshop creates a new channel, called an alpha channel, on the Channel menu. An **alpha channel** is a grayscale image that Photoshop creates and uses to render the selection. Photoshop uses white pixels to represent pixels that are selected and black pixels to represent pixels that aren't selected. For example, let's say you selected an image of an airplane against a blue sky. When you save the selection, Photoshop will create a new channel with the shape of the airplane filled with white, meaning that those pixels are part of the selection. All the other parts of the image, the sky in this example, will be black, meaning they're not part of the selection. When you load a selection, Photoshop uses the channel information, the white pixels specifically, to know what will be selected.

Converting from RGB to Grayscale and Vice Versa

RGB is the color mode that Photoshop uses to render color images. In an RGB image, each pixel can be one of 256 shades of red, 256 shades of green, and 256 shades of blue. The pixel is just one color—"orange," for example—but that color is represented by its RGB components. One specific hue of orange can be rendered as 255R/128G/0B. In an RGB image, each pixel has three times the amount of color information than in a grayscale image, so the file size is three times larger. Given a combination of 255 potential reds, 255 potential greens, and 255 potential blues per pixel, the RGB mode can produce more than 16.5 million colors ($256 \times 256 \times 256$).

Sometimes, you will want to use an RGB image as a black and white image. To do so, use the Grayscale mode on the Image menu. The color data per pixel will be discarded, and the image will be rendered as a single-color black and white image.

You can also convert an image from Grayscale mode to RGB mode. For example, you might want to paint colors over a black and white image. You wouldn't be able to do that in

Grayscale mode because there are no colors available in Grayscale mode, only shades of gray. But if you convert to RGB mode, each pixel's *potential* to be one of 16.5 million colors is restored. However, the image will continue to appear as a black and white image.

Posterizing a Grayscale Image

Figure 42 shows a grayscale image and the same image posterized. Posterizing is an effect created by reducing the range of colors in an image. In the figure, the top image is rendered with 256 shades of gray available per pixel. It has a smooth range of color from black to white, also known as "continuous tone." The posterized image is rendered with just four shades of gray—black, dark gray, light gray, and white. The image is still recognizable, but the result is colors that "jump" drastically from black to white.

In the top image, each pixel can be one of 256 shades of gray. In the posterized version, each can be just one of four shades of gray. Photoshop runs this simple equation: 256/4 = 64. Photoshop then identifies all the pixels whose grayscale values are 0–64 and makes them all black. Pixels that were 65–128 become dark gray. Pixels that were 129–192 become light gray, and those that were 193–255 become white. So what appears to be a complex effect, from the computing perspective, is quite simple. Now that you know each pixel in a digital image has a number, you can understand that Photoshop is producing those effects by playing with the numbers.

Figure 42 A grayscale image posterized

Morguefile

Investigate an RGB image

1. Open PS 2-11.psd, then save it as **Posterized Eagle**.

2. Click the **Eyedropper tool** , then open the **Info panel**.

3. Zoom in on the image until you can see the individual pixels.

4. Move the **Eyedropper tool**, over the pixels, and note the readout on the Info panel.

   This is an RGB image, and each pixel has a red, green, and blue component. Each pixel is one of 256 reds, one of 256 greens, and one of 256 blues. Thus, a yellow pixel in the bird's beak might read, in terms of RGB, 250/243/12.

5. Fit the image on the screen.

6. Click **Window** on the menu bar, then click **Channels**.

   The Channels panel opens.

7. Click the word **Red** on the Channels panel.

   Figure 43 shows the Red channel. In the Red channel, each pixel can be one of 256 shades of red. The color range in the channel is from black to red. Black pixels have a value of 0; red pixels have a value of 255. Everything in between is a range between black and red.

Figure 43 Viewing the Red channel in an RGB image

Morguefile

8. Click **Green** to see the Green channel.

9. Click **Blue** to see the Blue channel.

10. Click **RGB** to see the composite channel.

    As you learned in the beginning of this chapter, the word composite refers to one thing that is created by bringing other things together. The RGB channel is called the composite channel because it is rendered by combining the three color channels.

    AUTHOR'S **NOTE** The pixels in an RGB image are one color composed of a red, a green, and a blue component, each with 256 available shades per pixel per channel.

11. Click **Image** on the menu bar, point to **Mode**, then click **Grayscale**.

12. Click **Discard** to discard other channels, if a warning box appears.

    All of the color data per pixel is discarded, and the image changes to a black and white image.

13. Note the Channels panel.

    The Channels panel now contains only one channel named Gray. Grayscale mode is a single-channel mode.

    Continued on next page

14. Float the **Eyedropper tool**  over the pixels, and note the readout on the Info panel.

The RGB readout shows the same number in R, G, and B. The Info panel has a Grayscale readout, but that readout is in percentages; it doesn't give you information from 0 to 256. Therefore, when sampling a grayscale image, you use the RGB readout and infer that when you're looking at three identical numbers on the Info panel, they represent just one number in this single-channel image. Don't let this confuse you. This is a single-channel image, and the single channel is Gray. Each pixel has just **one** grayscale value, and that one grayscale value can be 0–255.

15. Save your work, then continue to the next set of steps.

You sampled pixels in RGB mode, noting each is one color with an RGB component. You looked at each of the three color channels that make up the image in the Channels panel. You then converted the image to Grayscale, noting it becomes a single-channel image named Black in the Channels panel.

Posterize an image and save selections

1. Click **Image** on the menu bar, point to **Adjustments**, then click **Posterize**.

2. Highlight the **number in the Levels text box**, then use the up and down arrows on your keypad to increase and decrease the number of levels.

3. Set the number of levels to **8**.

The Posterize dialog box is a valuable key for understanding the concept of rendering an image in Grayscale mode. For example, if you enter eight levels, that's what a black and white image would look like if only eight shades of gray were available per pixel—clearly not enough to create the

illusion of an invisible transition, or "continuous tone," from black to white.

4. Set the number of levels to **16**.

At 16 shades of gray available per pixel, the image is still clearly posterized, and there's no illusion of continuous tone.

5. Set the number of levels to **32**.

At 32 shades of gray available per pixel, the illusion of continuous tone starts to take hold. Even in the eagle's beak, which is a smooth range of grays, the tone appears continuous. Consider that, if the image looks this good at just 32 shades of gray per pixel, imagine how invisible the transition from black to white is with 256 shades.

6. Set the number of levels to **4**, click **OK**, then sample the pixels with the **Eyedropper tool** .

Your canvas should resemble Figure 44. The pixels in this image are black, dark gray, light gray, or white. In grayscale values, they are 0, 107, 187, or 255.

7. Click the **Magic Wand tool** , set the **Tolerance** to **0**, then verify that **Contiguous** and **Anti-alias** are not checked.

8. Click **any white area** of the image to select all the white pixels in the image.

9. Click **Select** on the menu bar, then click **Save Selection**.

The Save Selection dialog box opens.

10. Type **White Pixels** in the Name text box, then click **OK**.

Note that on the Channels panel, a new alpha channel has appeared named **White Pixels**.

Figure 44 Viewing the image posterized at 4 levels

11. Deselect, then click the words **White Pixels** on the Channels panel.

As shown in Figure 45, the alpha channel uses white pixels to represent the area of the canvas that you selected, and it uses black pixels to represent the pixels that weren't selected.

TIP When you view channels, click the channel's name or the thumbnail image on the panel; don't click the eye icons on the left.

12. Click the **Gray channel** on the Channels panel to return to the posterized artwork.

Figure 45 Alpha channel representing the selection of the white areas of the posterized image

13. Click the **Magic Wand tool** on a **light gray area** of the image, then save the selection with the name **Light Gray Pixels**.

14. Select the **dark gray pixels**, then save the selection with the name **Dark Gray Pixels**.

15. Select the **black pixels**, then save the selection with the name **Black Pixels**.

Your Channels panel should resemble Figure 46.

16. Save your work, then continue to the next set of steps.

You used the Posterize dialog box to explore the concept of "number of shades of gray per pixel." You increased the number of shades available until the illusion of a smooth transition from black to white, or "continuous tone" was achieved. You then posterized the image to four levels. You used the Magic Wand tool to select each of the four colors and saved a selection for each as an alpha channel on the Channels panel.

Add color to a posterized image

1. Click **Image** on the menu bar, point to **Mode**, then click **RGB Color**.

Nothing appears to change. The image still looks like a black and white image. However, this is now an RGB image.

2. Click **Select** on the menu bar, then click **Load Selection**.

The Load Selection dialog box opens.

3. Click the **Channel list arrow**, click **Black Pixels**, then click **OK**.

The Black Pixels selection is loaded on the canvas.

4. On the Swatches panel, click a **dark blue swatch**, then fill the selection with that color.

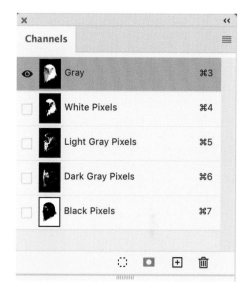

Figure 46 Channels panel showing four alpha channels for saved selections

---

5. Using the same methodology, load the **Dark Gray Pixels selection**, then fill it with a **medium green color**.

6. Load the **Light Gray Pixels selection**, then fill it with an **orange color**.

7. Load the **White Pixels selection**, then fill it with a **pale yellow color**.

8. Deselect, then compare your canvas to Figure 47, shown on the following page.

9. Save your work, then close Posterized Eagle.

You converted the grayscale image to an RGB image, noting that pixels in an RGB image are gray when none of the three colors dominates. You then loaded saved selections and filled them with a color, creating a dramatic color posterized effect.

Figure 47 The saved selections filled with color

Paint with the Brush tool

1. Open PS 2-12.psd, save it as **Connect the Dots**, then click the Brush tool.
2. Set the foreground color on the toolbar to black.
3. On the Options panel, set the Size to 32, set the Hardness to 100%, then set the Opacity to 100%.
4. Leave the Options panel, then press the right bracket ( ]) on your keypad until the brush size increases to 80 px.
5. Target the Hard brush layer on the Layers panel, then click point #1 on the canvas.
6. Press and hold [shift], then click point #2.
7. Using the same method, continue to point #6.
8. Target the Soft Brush layer on the Layers panel, then change the foreground color to white.
9. Click the left bracket ([ ) on your keypad until the brush size is 30 px.
10. Change the Hardness to 0%.
11. Click where point #1 would be if it were visible, press and hold [shift], then click point #2.
12. Using the same method, continue to point #6.
13. Save your work, then move directly into the next set of steps.

Use keyboard shortcuts to undo and redo

1. Press and hold [command] (Mac) or [Ctrl] (Win), then press the letter [Z] on your keypad 12 times.
2. Press and hold [shift] [command] (Mac) or [Shift] [Ctrl] (Win), then press the letter [Z] on your keypad 12 times.
3. Save your work, then close Connect the Dots.

Paint and fill with Darker Color mode

1. Open PS 2-13.psd, then save it as **Skills Coloring Book**.
2. Select the Brush tool on the toolbar; set the Size to 20 px and the Hardness to 100%.
3. On the Options panel, change the Mode to Darker Color.
4. Click a blue swatch on the Swatches panel to paint water.
5. Use the brush to paint the water drops coming from the elephant's trunk at the top of the illustration. Change the brush size as needed. Because you are painting in Darker Color mode, you can paint over the black lines of the image without affecting them.
6. Select the Magic Wand tool on the toolbar.
7. On the Options panel, type **4** in the Tolerance text box, then verify that the Anti-alias and Contiguous options are both checked.
8. Click the Magic Wand tool in the puddle of water at the bottom of the illustration.
9. Click Select on the menu bar, point to Modify, then click Expand.
10. Type **1** in the Expand By text box, then click OK.
11. Click the Edit menu, then click Fill.
12. Set the Contents to Foreground Color, set the Mode to Darker Color, set the Opacity to 100%, then click OK.
13. Using any of the methods you learned in this chapter, finish coloring the drawing.
    Figure 48, shown on the following page, shows one result.
14. Save your work, then close Skills Coloring Book.

Use the Marquee and Lasso tools to make selections

1. Open PS 2-14.psd, then save it as **Skills Puzzle**.
   You used this same file in Lesson 4 to move marquees you made with the Magic Wand tool. In this exercise, you'll build the puzzle to review using the Marquee and Lasso selection tools.
2. Zoom in on the #1 piece, then click the Rectangular Marquee tool.
3. Position the center of the crosshair on the upper-left corner of the puzzle piece, drag downward until the center of the crosshair is on the lower-right corner, then release the mouse pointer.

4. Click View on the menu bar, click Fit on Screen, click the Move tool, drag the piece to the correct position on the hot air balloon image, then deselect.

5. Click the Rectangular Marquee tool, select the top square in the #2 piece, press and hold [shift], position the crosshair over the lower-right corner, drag a second marquee around the bottom square that overlaps the first square, then release the mouse pointer.

   Pressing and holding [shift] when making a selection adds pixels to the existing selection.

6. Move the selected pixels into place in the puzzle.

7. Select the outer square in the #3 piece, press and hold [option] (Mac) or [Alt] (Win), then select the white inner rectangle.

   The white inner rectangle is removed from the selection. Pressing and holding [option] (Mac) or [Alt] (Win) or when making a selection removes pixels from the existing selection.

8. Move the selected pixels into place in the puzzle.

9. Select the Elliptical Marquee tool, then position the crosshair icon over the green pixel at the center of the #4 piece.

Figure 48 Viewing the painted artwork

10. Press and hold [option] (Mac) or [Alt] (Win), begin dragging, add the [shift] key, then drag to the edge of the circle to complete the selection.
Pressing and holding [option] (Mac) or [Alt] (Win) when no pixels are selected creates a marquee selection that starts in the center and grows outward. Pressing and holding [shift] while dragging a Marquee tool constrains the marquee selection to a perfect circle or square.

11. Move the selected pixels into position in the puzzle.

12. Zoom in on the #5 piece, then click the Lasso tool.

13. Click and drag to select just an interior section of the piece.

14. Press [shift], then use the Lasso tool to keep adding to the selection until the entire shape is selected.
If necessary, press [option] (Mac) or [Alt] (Win) while using the Lasso tool to remove unwanted selected areas you might create outside of the shape. Your result will not be ideal. This selection calls for more precision than the Lasso tool can provide.

15. Move the selected pixels into place in the puzzle.

16. Zoom in on the #6 piece, click the Polygonal Lasso tool, then press [caps lock] so that the Lasso tool is a precise crosshair.

17. Position the crosshair at the tip of the upper-right point of the shape, click, and release the mouse button. Then move the mouse pointer to the next corner on the shape, and click.

18. Using the same method, move the mouse pointer around the shape, clicking on the next 12 corners of the shape.

19. Float over the original point you clicked so the Polygonal Lasso tool icon appears with a small "o" beside it, then click to close the selection.

20. Move the selected pixels into place in the puzzle.

21. Click the Magnetic Lasso tool.

22. Click and drag the Magnetic Lasso tool to select the #7 piece.

23. Move the selected pixels into place to complete the puzzle.

24. Save your work, then close Skills Puzzle.

Experiment with the Contiguous setting

1. Open PS 2-15.psd, then save it as **Contiguous Skills Test**.

2. Using Figure 49 as a reference, use the Magic Wand tool change the squares to match the figure using as few moves as possible. If you're working in a group, count the number of steps it takes you to finish, then compare with the group to see who used the fewest steps.
If you have problems, refer to the third exercise in Lesson 4.

3. When you are finished, Invert the canvas.

4. Save your work, then close Contiguous Skills Test.

Figure 49 The multicolored checkerboard

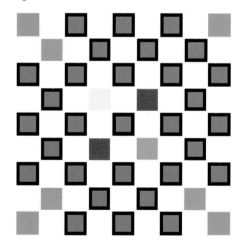

Use the Magic Wand tool to select an image

1. Open PS 2-16.psd, then save it as **Blue Stop**.
2. On the Options panel, set the Tolerance to 32, then verify that Anti-alias and Contiguous are both checked.
3. Click the red area of the stop sign directly above the letter O.
   The Contiguous option is activated to avoid any of the pixels in the red bricks of the building being accidentally selected.
4. Press and hold [shift], then click the center of the red areas inside the letter O and inside the letter P.
5. Click Select on the menu bar, point to Modify, then click Expand.
6. Type **2** in the Expand By text box, then click OK.
7. Click Select on the menu bar, then click Select and Mask.
8. At the top of the Properties panel, in the View Mode section, verify that High Quality Preview is the only one of the three check boxes that is checked.
9. Click the View list arrow to see the viewing options available to you.
10. Click Black and White (K), then zoom in on the image to better see the edge pixels.
    Viewing the selection in black and white makes it easy to see that the selection edge is very uneven—not the straight and smooth edge one would expect when looking at color on a stop sign.
11. On the Properties panel, drag the Smooth slider to 3.
    The edge pixels are smoothed without a feathering or fading effect taking place.

Figure 50 The blue stop sign

12. Click OK.
13. Press [command] [H] (Mac) or [Ctrl] [H] (Win) to hide the selection marquee.
14. Click Image on the menu bar, point to Adjustments, then click Hue/Saturation.
    The Hue/Saturation dialog box opens.

15. Drag the Hue slider left to −128, then click OK.
    As shown in Figure 50, the stop sign is blue, but the white letters and border are not affected.
16. Save your work, then close Blue Stop.

Posterize an image and save selections

1. Open PS 2-17.psd, then save it as **Posterize Skills**.
2. Click Image on the menu bar, point to Mode, then click Grayscale.
3. Click Image on the menu bar, point to Adjustments, then click Posterize.
4. Set the number of shades to 4, then click OK.
5. Click the Magic Wand tool, set the Tolerance to 0, then verify that Contiguous and Anti-alias are not checked.
6. Select all the white pixels in the image.
7. Click Select on the menu bar, then click Save Selection.
8. Type **White Pixels** in the Name text box, then click OK.
   Note that in the Channels panel, a new alpha channel has appeared named White Pixels.
9. Deselect, then click the words White Pixels in the Channels panel.
   The alpha channel uses white pixels to represent the area of the canvas that you selected, and it uses black pixels to represent the pixels that weren't selected.
10. Click the Gray channel in the Channels panel to return to the posterized artwork.
11. Select all the light gray pixels in the image, then save the Selection with the name **Light Gray Pixels**.
12. Select the dark gray pixels, then save the Selection with the name **Dark Gray Pixels**.
13. Select the black pixels, then save the selection with the name **Black Pixels**.
14. Click the Gray channel to return to the posterized image.
15. Save your work.

Add color to a posterized image

1. Click Image on the menu bar, point to Mode, then click RGB color.
2. Click Select on the menu bar, then click Load Selection.
3. Click the Channel list arrow, click Black Pixels, then click OK.
4. On the Swatches panel, click a dark maroon or dark purple swatch, then fill the selection with that color.
5. Using the same methodology, load the Dark Gray Pixels selection, then fill it with a medium purple color.
6. Load the Light Gray Pixels selection, then fill it with a light purple color.
7. Load the White Pixels selection, then fill it with a pale purple color.
   You can use the Color panel to create a pale purple color.
8. Deselect, then compare your canvas to Figure 51.
9. Save your work, then close Posterize Skills.

Figure 51 The posterized, colorized image

1. Open PS 2-18 .psd, then save it as **Painting Skills**.
2. Click the Magic Wand tool, set the Tolerance to 8, then verify that Contiguous and Anti-alias are not checked.
3. Click one of the black eyes so all the black pixels in the image are selected.
4. Click Select on the menu bar, point to Modify, then click Expand.
5. Type **1** in the Expand By text box, then click OK.
6. Save the selection with the name **All Black Pixels**.
7. Deselect.
8. Zoom in on both eyes so they fill your screen.
9. Click the Magic Wand tool, set the Tolerance to 8, then verify that Contiguous is checked and Anti-alias is not checked.
10. Select both orange sections of the eyes, then hide the selection marquee.
11. Click the Eyedropper tool, then sample the orange color from the eyes so it becomes the foreground color.
12. Click the Brush tool, set the Size to 60 px, then set the Hardness to 0%.

13. Set the Opacity to 80%.
14. Set the Mode to Multiply.
    In Multiply mode, the orange foreground color will darken the orange eye color if painted.
15. Paint darker orange on the insides of both eyes so your artwork resembles Figure 52.
16. Change the foreground color to white.
17. Change the Opacity of the brush to 40%, then change the Size to 25 px.
18. Change the Mode of the brush to Screen.
    Screen blending mode functions as the opposite of Multiply. In Screen mode, lighter colors lighten a painted area. Note the selection is still active, so you cannot paint outside and affect the black lines that draw the eye.
19. Paint lighter orange on the outside of the eyes so your artwork resembles Figure 53.
20. Click Filter on the menu bar, point to Blur, then click Gaussian Blur.
21. Type **3** in the Radius text box, then click OK.
    The Gaussian Blur filter smooths the lines made by the brush. Instead of being one color, the eyes now have a range of tone from shadows to highlights in orange. Even though no black pixels are selected,

some of the black from the black lines blur into the orange.

22. Using the skills covered in steps 1–15, select different parts of the image, then paint shadows and highlights to create dimension.
    Use Figure 54 as a guide. You will need to alter the size and the opacity of the brush as well as the amount of the Gaussian Blur, depending on your preferences.
23. When you are done painting, load the All Black Pixels selection, then fill it with black.
    The fill replaces some of the blurring that occurs with the original black lines.
24. Save your work, then close Painting Skills.

Figure 54 Painted shadows and highlights create dimension

Figure 52 Darkening the eye with Multiply mode

Figure 53 Lightening the eye with Screen mode

1. Open PS 2-19.psd, then save it as **Pink Flip Flops**.
2. Click the Magnetic Lasso tool.
3. On the Options panel, verify that the Feather is set to 0, Anti-alias is checked, the Width is set to 10, the Contrast is set to 10, and the Frequency is set to 57.
4. Select both flip flops with the Magnetic Lasso tool. Use [shift] to add to the selection. Use [option] (Mac) or [Alt] (Win) to remove from the selection.
5. When you finish making the selection, use the Lasso tool to improve the selection by adding to or removing from it.
6. Click Select on the menu bar, then click Select and Mask.
7. Click the View list arrow, then click Black & White (K).
8. Type **3** in the Smooth text box, then click OK.
9. Press and hold [command] (Mac) or [Ctrl] (Win), then press the letter [U] on your keypad to open the Hue/Saturation dialog box.
10. Type **-100** in the Hue text box, click OK, then compare your results to Figure 55.
    These results were achieved using exactly these steps and no additional "extras" to help the process. The results are a testament to the ability and power of the Magnetic Lasso tool.
11. Save your work, then close Pink Flip Flops.

Figure 55 Viewing the altered flip flops

Morguefile

1. Open PS 2-20.psd, then save it as **Contiguous Colors**.
2. Convert to the file to Grayscale.
3. Posterize the image to six levels.
4. Convert the file to RGB Color.
5. Set the Magic Wand tool to a Tolerance of 4, verify that Contiguous is checked, then verify that Anti-alias is not checked.
6. Make contiguous selections and fill them with color. Use Figure 56 as a guide. Filling contiguous selections with color will create a different effect than the other two posterize exercises from this chapter, both of which were done with the Contiguous option turned off. You should use all the selection techniques you learned in this chapter to create the final image.

Figure 56 Design Project completed

Courtesy of Alison Wright

Alison Wright travels around the world to meet people and uses photography to tell their stories. Many of her photos focus on people who have suffered from disaster, war, or infringement of their basic human rights. Her goal is to create images that help people and their communities by increasing awareness of their situations and reminding viewers of the connection we all share as human beings.

Alison is passionate about the people of Tibet and has traveled there many times. In 2005, while working on a story about Tibet's nomads for *National Geographic*, she met a group of people returning from a horse festival. In this group, Alison saw a young girl dressed in traditional clothing and beautiful jewelry and asked for the opportunity to take her photo.

Because it was pouring rain, Alison took the girl indoors and used natural light from a side window to illuminate the photograph. Not knowing each other's languages, Alison said she and the girl connected through communication of the heart. The girl's expression was not coached. Instead, the moment unfolded naturally to produce an image that Alison feels captures not only the sadness of this girl's community and culture, but also its resilience and tenacity.

© Alison Wright

Alison Wright, Tibet girl, near Manigango, Kham, Tibet

PROJECT DESCRIPTION

In this project, you will analyze and respond to Alison's image. You'll have the opportunity to investigate the different elements of the image and interpret the story for yourself. After looking at the photo closely, you will write a brief analysis consisting of your observations, your interpretation of the story, any questions you may have, and the messages you take away.

QUESTIONS TO CONSIDER

What stands out to you?

What surprised you?

What questions would you ask?

What do you think the story is about?

GETTING STARTED

Research the Tibetan culture and people. Look into where they live and how they work. Understand how the culture has changed over time and what that means for Tibetan people today. Understanding the topic of the photo you're analyzing will help you better interpret and comprehend the story.

Analyze the photo. Take note of anything that catches your attention. Look closely at the girl and how she is posed. Pay attention to her facial expression and what she is wearing. Make observations about how the different visual elements are interacting with each other in the photo. If you can, talk to your classmates and discuss your ideas. Decide which elements of the photo are impactful to you and write a brief analysis of your findings.

Our Roman Holiday

WORK WITH LAYERS

1. Use the Layers Panel
2. Transform Layered Artwork
3. Incorporate Layer Styles
4. Employ a Layer Mask
5. Mask Out the Background of an Image and Modify the Canvas Size

 CERTIFIED PROFESSIONAL

Adobe Certified Professional in Visual Design Using Photoshop CC Framework

3. Organizing Documents

This objective covers document structure such as layers and managing document structure for efficient workflows.

3.1 Use layers to manage design elements.
- **A** Use the Layers panel to manage visual content.
- **C** Recognize the different types of layers in the Layers panel.

3.2 Modify layer visibility using opacity, blending modes, and masks.
- **B** Create and edit masks.

4. Creating and Modifying Visual Elements

This objective covers core tools and functionality of the application, as well as tools that affect the visual outcome of the document.

4.4 Transform digital graphics and media.
- **A** Modify the canvas or artboards.
- **B** Rotate, flip, and modify individual layers, objects, selections, groups, or graphical elements.

USE THE LAYERS PANEL

Working with Layers The Layers panel is one of Photoshop's greatest features because it allows you to segregate various art components onto different layers within a single document. Working with layers allows you to apply various effects, like drop shadows or glows, to individual art components without affecting others. Layers give you options for positioning artwork in relation to other objects on the canvas and allow you to move that artwork without affecting the content on other layers.

Working with the Layers Panel

The Layers panel, shown in Figure 1, houses all the layers in a document and offers you many options for manipulating those layers. Some basic operations you can perform with the Layers panel and layered artwork are to hide or show various art components and control which visual elements appear in front of or behind other elements.

Working with layers allows you to move different images independently of one another. This offers you total freedom to design your artwork with the spatial relationships that you find most appealing in your design aesthetic.

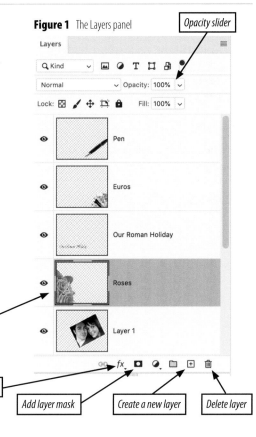

Figure 1 The Layers panel

Opacity slider

Layer thumbnail

Add a layer style

Add layer mask

Create a new layer

Delete layer

Working with Layer Opacity

The Layers panel offers you controls to modify the opacity of artwork on the Layers panel. In Photoshop, the term **opacity** refers to how *opaque* artwork is. For example, if artwork has 100% opacity, it is completely opaque—no part of it is transparent. Conversely, artwork with 0% opacity is completely transparent and thus invisible. In between the two extremes is a whole range of transparency, from 99% down to 1%. For example, artwork with 50% opacity would be visible, but any artwork on a layer or layers beneath it would be visible *through* it.

Layer opacity can be a very effective design tool, especially when you want to merge multiple images by having them "blend" into one another.

Merging Layers

At any point during your design process, you can merge some or all of the layered artwork in a file onto one layer. The more layers in a file, the larger the file size, so merging layers reduces file size. Remember, though, that merging layers is a commitment: once artwork is merged onto a single layer, it can't be unmerged later on in the project (other than by using the Undo or Revert commands, which are very limited). For example, if you merge two layers and then exit Photoshop, there will be no way to unmerge that artwork.

Even though you'll learn how to merge layers in this lesson, it's almost always best to not merge. Generally speaking, it's best to keep artwork segregated on different layers simply to keep your options open for any modifications you might need to make as your project evolves.

Duplicating, Deleting, and Pasting New Layers

Layers are created in Photoshop in a variety of ways. For example, you can click Layer on the menu bar, point to New, then click Layer. The fastest and easiest way is to click the Create a new layer button on the Layers panel. This creates a new "empty" layer on the Layers panel.

Another common way that layers are created is when you duplicate an existing layer in the panel. Perhaps the most common way that new layers are created occurs when you copy and paste an image from another file into your current file. Whenever you copy artwork and then paste, the copied artwork is pasted onto a new layer, directly above the active layer on the Layers panel. This is a great feature in Photoshop because you can be confident that when you paste artwork, the new artwork will always be isolated on its own layer and will not directly affect any existing artwork in the file.

To delete a layer, simply drag it to the Delete layer button on the Layers panel.

Loading a Selection from a Layer

Any artwork on a layer is, by definition, selectable as a selection. Press and hold [command] (Mac) or [Ctrl] (Win), then click the layer's thumbnail to load a selection of the artwork on the canvas. You can then use that selection for different operations, such as adding a shadow behind the selected object.

Set preferences for working with layers

1. Open PS 3-1.psd, then save it as **Roman Holiday**.

   Be sure you don't save the file again until you are instructed to.

2. Click the **Photoshop menu** (Mac) or the **Edit menu** (Win) on the menu bar, point to **Preferences**, then click **General**.

3. Verify that **Use Legacy Free Transform** is checked, as shown in Figure 2, then click **OK**.

   "Legacy" is an option Photoshop Creative Cloud offers you for some tools, features, and dialog boxes. It allows you to work with older versions of features that have since been updated. Use Legacy Free Transform is the only legacy feature we use in this book. We do so because it allows you to transform layers in a way that is most consistent with making marquees and shapes in Photoshop and making shapes in Illustrator and in InDesign.

4. On the Layers panel, note the size of the "thumbnail" for each layer.

   The thumbnail icons present a visual of the artwork that is on each layer. These icons are currently very small and would be more helpful if they were larger.

5. Click the **Layers panel menu button** 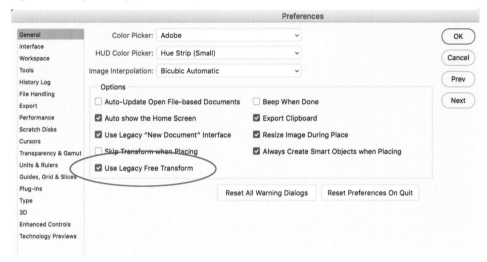, then click **Panel Options**.

6. Click the **largest thumbnail option**, then click **OK**.

You set a preference to use the legacy version when transforming, and you changed the size of the thumbnails on the Layers panel.

Figure 2 Activating the Use Legacy Free Transform preference

Perform basic operations on the Layers panel

1. Note that all layers have been given an identifying name except the one named "Layer 1."

   By default, whenever you create a new layer, it is assigned a layer number.

2. Double-click the name **Layer 1**, then rename it **Couple**.

3. Save the file.

   Be sure you save the file in this step, and don't save again until you are instructed to.

4. Click the **eye button** 👁 on the **Pen layer** repeatedly.

   The layer toggles between visible and invisible. Verify that the pen artwork is visible when you're done with this step.

5. Click and drag vertically over **multiple eye buttons** 👁 on the Layers panel.

   Clicking and dragging over multiple eye buttons hides those layers.

6. Repeat Step 5 to make **all layers** visible again.

7. Press and hold **[option] (Mac)** or **[Alt] (Win)**, then click the **eye button** 👁 on the **Couple layer**.

   Only the artwork on the Couple layer is visible. Pressing and holding [option] (Mac) or [Alt] (Win) while clicking an eye button shows only that layer and hides all other layers.

8. Still holding **[option] (Mac)** or **[Alt] (Win)**, click the **eye button** 👁 on the **Couple layer**.

   All the layers become visible again.

9. Target the **Colosseum layer**.

10. Click the **Opacity slider** at the top of the Layers panel, then drag the **slider** to **50%**.

    As shown in Figure 3, the Colosseum artwork is now 50% transparent. You might have noticed that dragging a slider to an exact number can be difficult. There's a better way to change opacity.

11. Click the **Move tool** ⊕ on the toolbar, then press the **number [2]** on your keypad.

    The Colosseum artwork opacity changes to 20%. With the Move tool activated, pressing numbers on the keypad changes the opacity and the Opacity setting is updated on the Layers panel. 5 = 50%, 2 = 20%, 1 = 10%, and 0 = 100%.

12. Click anywhere on the **Coin layer** to target it.

    In Photoshop, you don't "select" a layer; you *target* it. Designers use this distinction to avoid confusion with making "selections" with the selection tools.

    Continued on next page

Figure 3 The Colosseum artwork at 50%

13. Press the **letter [V]** on your keypad to verify that the Move tool  is still selected, float over the **coin artwork**, then click and drag it to another position on the canvas.

The Move tool moves artwork only on the targeted layer. You will use the Move tool all the time when working with layers. Get used to using the [V] shortcut key to access the Move tool.

14. Target the **Couple layer**, press and hold **[command] (Mac)** or **[Ctrl] (Win),** then click the **Pen layer** so that both layers are targeted.

Pressing and holding [command] (Mac) or [Ctrl] (Win) allows you to target multiple and nonadjacent layers on the Layers panel.

15. Drag the **Couple** and **Pen artwork** to another location on the canvas.

Because both layers are targeted on the Layers panel, the artwork on both layers moves as you drag.

16. Click **File** on the menu bar, then click **Revert.**

The artwork returns to the state when you last saved it. Note, however, that the thumbnails on the Layers panel are still large. Preferences are saved separately from individual files, so when you reverted this file, it did not revert the preference you changed.

17. Target the **Coin layer**, then click and drag it up to the top of the Layers panel.

As you drag, a blue horizontal line appears, indicating where the layer will be repositioned when you release the mouse pointer. Changing the *stacking order* of layers changes which artwork is in front of or behind other artwork.

TIP Photoshop has hundreds (if not thousands) of features for you to keep track of. Knowing the names of different features helps you keep track of all your options. So, when

Figure 4 Moving the coin with the arrow key

you learn a term like *stacking order*, it's worth your time to incorporate it into your understanding of the program.

18. Verify that the **Coin layer** is still targeted, then press **[command] [J] (Mac)** or **[Ctrl] [J] (Win).**

The coin layer is duplicated. A new layer named Coin copy automatically appears on the Layers panel above the original Coin layer.

19. Enter **[command] [J] (Mac)** or **[Ctrl] [J] (Win)** again.

A third Coin layer is created.

20. Click and drag the **Coin copy 2 layer** to the **Delete layer button** 🗑 on the Layers panel.

The layer is deleted.

21. Target the **Coin copy layer**, press and hold **[shift]**, then press the **right arrow** on your keypad six times.

Your coins should resemble Figure 4.

TIP Pressing an arrow key on the keypad moves artwork on the targeted layer **one** increment in that direction. Holding [shift] and pressing an arrow key moves artwork on the targeted layer **10** increments in that direction.

22. Target both the **Coin** and the **Coin copy layers**, click the **Layers panel menu button** ▤ , then click **Merge Layers**.

The artwork is merged onto one layer. Even though you are being taught that you *can* do this, you seldom should merge layers. Think of Photoshop as a "Hansel & Gretel" application—you always want to have a trail of breadcrumbs so that you can backtrack if you need to. Once you merge artwork, you're stuck with it, other than using the Undo command.

23. Click **File** on the menu bar, then click **Revert.**

You named a layer, made layers hidden and visible, changed the opacity of layers, then moved artwork on layers and duplicated layers.

Load a selection from artwork on a layer

1. Target the **Couple layer**.

2. Press and hold **[command] (Mac)** or **[Ctrl] (Win)**, then click the **Create a new layer button** ⊞ on the Layers panel.

   A new blank layer is created below the Couple layer. Pressing and holding [command] (Mac) or [Ctrl] (Win) when you click the Create a new layer button ⊞ adds a new layer below the currently targeted layer.

3. Rename the new layer **Couple Shadow**, then verify that the Couple Shadow layer remains targeted.

4. Press and hold **[command] (Mac)** or **[Ctrl] (Win)**, then click the **thumbnail image on the Couple layer**.

   A selection of the couple artwork is loaded.

5. Click **Select** on the menu bar, point to **Modify**, then click **Feather**.

6. Enter **4** in the Feather Radius text box, then click **OK**.

7. Press the **letter [D]** on your keypad to set the default colors on the toolbar to black (foreground) and white (background).

8. Press and hold **[option] (Mac)** or **[Alt] (Win)**, then press **[delete]** on your keypad.

   The selection is filled with the foreground color on the Couple Shadow layer and remains selected.

9. **Deselect**, then click the **Move tool** ⊕ on the toolbar.

10. Press and hold **[shift]** on your keypad, then press the **down arrow** on your keypad three times.

11. Set the **Opacity** on the Couple Shadow layer to **50%**, then compare your canvas to Figure 5.

12. Save your work, then close Roman Holiday.

You created a new layer beneath a targeted layer, you loaded a selection from artwork on a layer and feathered it, then you filled it with black to create a drop shadow effect.

Figure 5 Viewing the drop shadow

TRANSFORM LAYERED ARTWORK

▶ What You'll Do

In this lesson, you'll scale and rotate artwork on layers.

Using the Transform Commands

Any kind of transformation is a change. In Photoshop, transforming artwork means doing any of the following:

- moving
- scaling
- rotating
- skewing
- distorting

You can **transform** (change the shape, size, perspective, or rotation of) an object or objects on a layer using one or more of the Transform commands on the Edit menu. You can transform a single layer or transform multiple layers simultaneously.

When you use some of the transform commands, a bounding box appears around the object you are transforming. A **bounding box** is a rectangle that surrounds an image and contains eight handles that you click and drag to change the dimensions of the artwork.

After you transform an object, you can apply or execute the changes by pressing [return] (Mac) or [Enter] (Win). Alternatively, clicking the Move tool on the toolbar will also execute the transformation.

You can use transform commands individually or in a chain. After you choose your initial transform command, you can try out as many others as you like before you apply the changes by pressing [return] (Mac) or [Enter] (Win). In other words, you can first scale artwork, and before committing the transformation, you can rotate it too.

You don't have to keep going back to the Edit menu every time you want to transform. A faster method is to simply enter [command] [T] (Mac) or [Ctrl] [T] (Win). This causes the bounding box to appear around the artwork on the targeted layer so you can begin transforming. Drag any handle with your mouse pointer to scale the artwork. Float your pointer outside of the bounding box, and it turns into the rotate icon. Click and drag the rotate icon to rotate the artwork.

Transforming artwork is one of the preeminent features of Photoshop. Transforming is a key skill in Photoshop, especially when creating a montage, because montages involve specific positioning and size relationships between elements.

Flipping and Rotating Artwork

Flipping and rotating are two transformations that can be especially useful when creating a montage of various images. **Flipping** artwork creates a mirror image of the artwork. You can flip images horizontally or vertically. **Rotating** an object moves it clockwise or counterclockwise around its center point, just like a windmill spins. You can rotate an image by hand or by entering a specific rotation value on the Options panel.

Rotating and flipping are very different transformations that produce different results. You can compare rotating artwork with your tire rotating as you drive. By default, artwork in Photoshop is rotated around its center point unless you move the crosshair icon from the center point to a new location.

Figure 6 shows an image flipped horizontally and vertically.

Flipping an image can produce odd results, especially when the image shows peoples' faces. Flipping the image of a person's face may yield unexpected results because nobody's face is perfectly symmetrical. Also remember, if there's text anywhere in an image when flipped, that text is going to read backwards or upside down, which is a dead giveaway that the image has been flipped!

Figure 6 The same image, flipped horizontally and vertically

ORIGINAL

FLIP HORIZONTAL

FLIP VERTICAL

Chris Botello

Understanding the Point of Origin in a Transformation

The **point of origin** defines the point from which a transformation occurs. In Photoshop, the point of origin is represented by the crosshair icon, as shown in Figure 7.

When you click and drag *outside* the bounding box to rotate, by default, the artwork will be rotated at the location of the crosshair icon. By default, the crosshair is at the center of the artwork when you first apply a transform command. However, you can move the crosshair icon. Figure 8 shows the crosshair

icon moved to the upper-left corner of the image. Clicking and dragging outside the bounding box will rotate the image around that point.

Scaling artwork functions differently than rotating. To scale artwork, you drag a handle on the bounding box. The transformation occurs at the location of the handle you drag. Press and hold [option] (Mac) or [Alt] (Win) while dragging a handle and the crosshair will become the point of origin for the scale. For example, if you create a 2" × 2" square and then reduce it by 50% using its center point as the point of origin, all four sides of the square

will move equally toward the center until the new size of the square is 1" × 1". This is a very powerful technique for managing your artwork when doing scale transformations.

Remember, before you make any kind of transformation, you can move the crosshair icon to any point that you want to remain fixed, then transform the artwork using that point as the point of origin.

Rather than click and drag to scale or rotate, you can enter values on the Options panel. When you do, the crosshair icon determines the point of origin automatically.

Figure 7 The crosshair icon, representing the point of origin for the transformation

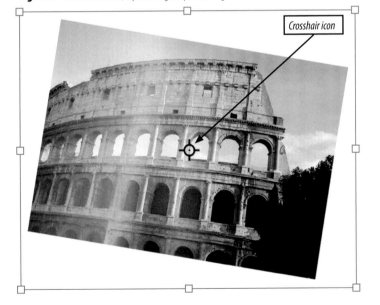

Crosshair icon

Figure 8 The crosshair icon, relocated

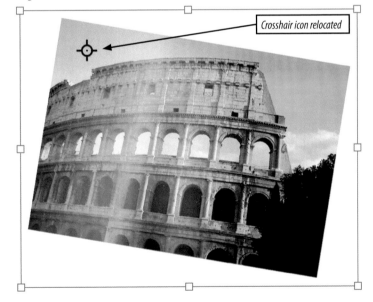

Crosshair icon relocated

Scale artwork

1. Open PS 3-2.psd, then save it as **Roman Holiday 2.**

2. Target the **Colosseum layer**, click **Edit** on the menu bar, point to **Transform**, then click **Scale.**

   As shown in Figure 9, the bounding box appears around the artwork. The bounding box has a square handle at each corner that you click and drag to transform the artwork. The handles are sometimes referred to as resizing handles.

TIP If you do not see the crosshair pointer in the center of the bounding box, click **Edit (Win)** or **Photoshop (Mac)** on the menu bar, point to **Preferences**, click **Tools**, and then click the **Show Reference Point when using Transform check box**.

3. Position the mouse pointer on the **lower-right corner handle** until a double-headed arrow appears, click and drag in different directions to modify the image, then release the mouse pointer.

   Clicking and dragging the corner handle allows you to enlarge, reduce, and/or distort the image.

4. **Undo** your last step.

5. Position the mouse pointer on the **lower-right corner handle**, press and hold **[shift]**, click and drag in different directions, then release the mouse pointer.

   The [shift] key constrains the scale proportionately. Using the [shift] key, you can enlarge or reduce the artwork, but you can't modify the proportional relationship between the width and height.

6. **Undo** your last step.

Continued on next page

Figure 9 The bounding box and crosshair icon

7. Note the crosshair icon in the middle of the bounding box.

   The crosshair icon is automatically positioned at the center of the bounding box and therefore at the center of the artwork.

8. On the Options panel, double-click the **W text box**, type **80**, press **[tab]**, type **80** in the **H text box**, press **[tab]**, then compare your screen to Figure 10.

   The artwork is scaled 80% at the crosshair, which is at the artwork's center point. By default, when you enter a scale value in the W and/or H text boxes on the Options panel, the artwork is scaled using the crosshair icon as the point of origin for the scale.

9. Press the **[Esc]** key on your keypad to cancel the last transformation.

   Note that throughout these steps, we have been experimenting with different transformations. All of them were previewed, but none of them were executed. The bounding box allows you to experiment endlessly without necessarily committing.

10. Click and drag the **Coin layer** to the top of the Layers panel so that the coin artwork is the topmost artwork.

11. Click the **Coin layer**, then enter **[command] [J] (Mac)** or **[Ctrl] [J] (Win) two times** to create two duplicate coin layers.

12. Rename the layers **Bottom Coin**, **Middle Coin**, and **Top Coin**.

Figure 10 Scaling the artwork 80% at its center

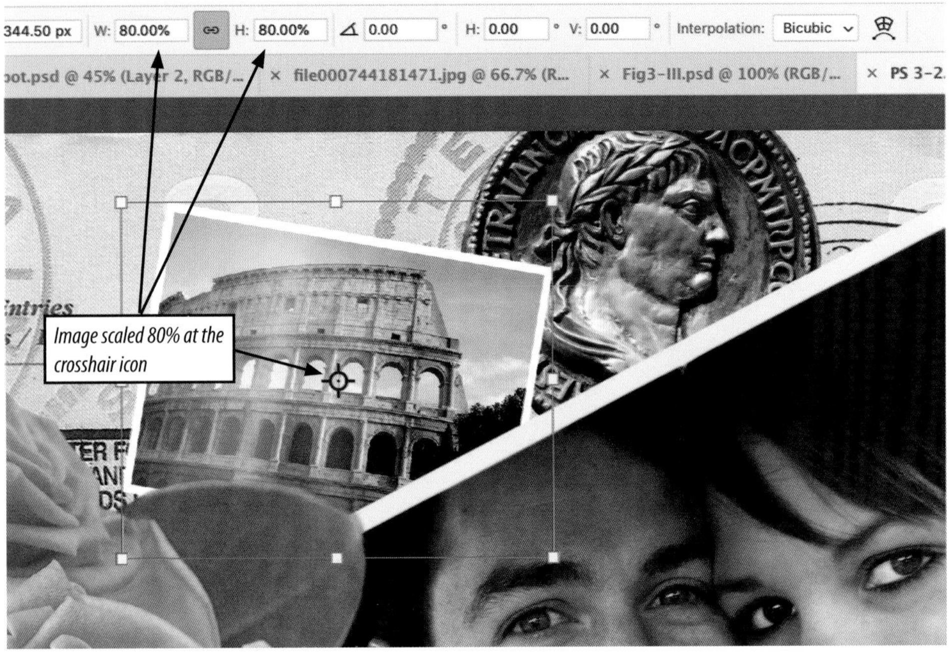

Image scaled 80% at the crosshair icon

13. Drag the **Bottom Coin layer** down below the Couple layer, then position the artwork as shown in Figure 11.

14. Target the **Bottom Coin layer**, press **[command] [T] (Mac)** or **[Ctrl] [T] (Win)**, then drag the **crosshair icon** to the position shown in Figure 12.

Entering [command] [T] (Mac) or [Ctrl] [T] (Win) is a fast way to access the bounding box.

15. Press and hold **[shift][option] (Mac)** or **[Shift][Alt] (Win)**, position the mouse pointer over the **lower-left handle**, drag to experiment with resizing the coin artwork, then release the mouse pointer.

Pressing and holding the [option] (Mac) or [Alt] (Win) key ensures that any transformation will be executed using the location of the crosshair as the point of origin. The [shift] key is used in this step to constrain the width and height ratio of the artwork while scaling.

16. **Undo** the last step.

Rather than resizing by dragging, we are going to enter a specific value for the scale.

17. Double-click the **W text box** on the Options panel, type **67**, press **[tab]**, type **67** in the **H text box**, then press **[tab]**.

By default, when you transform by entering values on the Options panel, the transformation uses the crosshair icon as its point of origin.

TIP If you activate the link icon 🔗 between the W and H text boxes on the Options panel, the value you enter in one box automatically appears in the other. This forces a scale transformation to be in proportion. The link icon's official name is Maintain aspect ratio.

18. Click **[return] (Mac)** or **[Enter] (Win)** to execute the transformation.

19. Save your work.

You scaled artwork using the bounding box and by entering width and height percentage values on the Options panel.

Figure 11 Repositioning the bottom coin artwork

Figure 12 Repositioning the crosshair icon

Crosshair icon

Rotate and Flip artwork

1. Target the **Couple layer**, click **Edit** on the menu bar, point to **Transform**, then click **Flip Horizontal.**

   The artwork is flipped horizontally.

2. Position the **couple artwork** as shown in Figure 13.

3. Click the **Bottom Coin layer,** then press **[command] [T] (Mac)** or **[Ctrl] [T] (Win)**.

   The bounding box appears.

4. Press and hold **[shift]**, then position your mouse pointer *outside* of the bounding box so that it changes to the rotate icon ↱ .

5. Click and drag counterclockwise outside the bounding box to rotate the bottom coin **−45°**, then click the **Move tool** ⊕ on the toolbar.

   Clicking the Move tool executes the transformation. The bottom coin is rotated and no longer appears as an obvious duplicate of the larger coin. Holding [shift] while you rotate constrains the rotation to 15° increments as you drag. Rotating counterclockwise produces a negative rotation. In terms of spatial relationships, the coin is now a bit too far from the couple, so we're going to move the coin.

TIP Note that the rotation uses the crosshair as the point of origin for the rotation—even though you weren't pressing [option] (Mac) or [Alt] (Win); those keys are only required when you are scaling artwork from the point of origin.

6. Position the coin as shown in Figure 14.

7. Using the same techniques, scale and rotate the top coin to resemble Figure 15.

   Save your work, then close Roman Holiday 2.

You flipped artwork horizontally and rotated artwork.

Figure 13 Flipping and repositioning the couple artwork

Figure 14 Repositioning the rotated coin

Figure 15 Scaling and rotating the top coin

INCORPORATE LAYER STYLES

▶ *What You'll Do*

In this lesson, you'll add Drop Shadow and Outer Glow layer styles to artwork. You'll also copy layer styles between layers.

Adding Layer Styles to Artwork

Layer styles are built-in effects that you can apply to layers; they include glows, shadows, bevels, embosses, and chiseled edges, among many others. When you apply layer styles to artwork on a layer, they will be listed on the Layers panel beneath the layer they've been applied to. Click the small black caret icon to the right of the layer to expand or collapse the list of layer effects for that layer. Click the eye button to hide or show the effect. Once a layer style has been applied, all the artwork on that layer takes on the effect.

Using the Layer Style Dialog Box

The Layer Style dialog box houses all the styles available to add effects to your work. You have several options to add a layer style to a targeted layer. You can click Layer on the menu bar, then click Layer Style, or you can click the Add a layer style button on the Layers panel. Either of these actions will open the Layer Style dialog box. The fastest and easiest way to open the Layer Style dialog box is to simply double-click a layer on the Layers panel.

The Layer Style dialog box is "sticky," meaning any styles you apply will remain in the dialog box even if you close and open the dialog box repeatedly.

All styles you've applied will be checked in the dialog box. Note that you must target the *name* of a style on the left column to display the settings associated with it.

Working with Layer Styles Settings

The Layer Style dialog box contains 10 styles, and each of these styles offers many options for modifying and customizing the style you are applying. When working with layer styles, you will run into many different terms for these options. In this chapter, you will encounter terms such as *distance*, *size*, and *spread* for applying a drop shadow and an outer glow. While those terms might seem self-explanatory, they can get confusing because they overlap. For example, the "spread" option for a drop shadow appears to alter the size of a drop shadow more than the "size" option does. These three options are covered in context in the steps in this lesson.

Generally speaking, most designers don't overthink the options available for a given layer style. Instead, they experiment with the options while watching the visual changes to the artwork. In this sense, applying styles is more about the visual result rather than a calculation of every option.

Copying Layer Styles Between Layers

The *fx.* icon on the Layers panel indicates that one or more layer styles have been applied to that layer. If you drag the *fx.* icon to a different layer, the layer styles will move to that layer and the styles will be applied to the artwork on that layer. Press [option] (Mac) or [Alt] (Win) and drag the *fx.* icon to copy styles between layers.

Copying styles between layers is a good solution for applying styles quickly; however, don't fall into the trap of just assuming that the settings for one style work for all the artwork you copy them to. Take the time to adjust the settings to customize the effect for all the artwork to which you apply styles. The differences might be subtle, but you'll find with experience that subtle customization is what makes all the difference.

Apply a Drop Shadow layer style

1. Open PS 3-3.psd, then save it as **Roman Holiday 3**.

   This file picks up where the previous lesson left off.

2. Target the **Couple layer**.

3. Click **Layer** on the menu bar, point to **Layer Style**, then click **Drop Shadow**.

   The Layer Style dialog box, shown in Figure 16, opens. Because you clicked Drop Shadow when you opened the dialog box, Drop Shadow is checked and activated in the left column, and the settings shown are those of the Drop Shadow layer style (your specific settings will be different).

Figure 16 Layer Style dialog box

4. Position the Layer Style dialog box so that you can see as much of the artwork on the canvas as possible.

   As you work with the Layer Style dialog box, the selections you make are updated dynamically on the artwork on the canvas. Even though the Layer Style dialog box is quite large, you want to be able to see as much of the artwork as possible.

5. Experiment with the **Opacity slider**, then set it to **50%**.

   The Opacity setting determines how opaque the shadow is. A 100% opacity shadow is totally opaque—you can't see through it no matter what color it is. A 0% opacity shadow is not

visible. Since you want to see a shadow and see through it, a midrange Opacity setting is usually the best choice.

6. Experiment with the **Distance slider**, then set it to **35**.

   The Distance slider determines how far away from the object the shadow will appear. The greater the distance, the more the object will appear to "float" above the background.

7. Experiment with the **Spread slider**, then set it to **10**.

   The Spread slider expands the size of the shadow itself before it is blurred by the Size slider.

8. Experiment with the **Size slider**, then set it to **20**.

   The Size slider determines the size of the feathered edge of the shadow. A value of 0 would create a hard-edged shadow.

9. Experiment with dragging the **Angle wheel** and notice the effect it has on the shadow in the collage.

   The Angle setting determines the position of the shadow in terms of the artwork casting the shadow. The angle of a shadow and the distance of a shadow in relationship to the object casting the shadow is often referred to as the "offset" of the shadow.

10. Set the **Angle** to **19°**.

    AUTHOR'S **NOTE**   In a collage like the one you're creating here, generally speaking, you'll want all shadows to move in the same direction. Your choice of angle for a drop shadow will be based on the shadows in the photos in the collage. For example, when choosing an angle for the shadow on the picture of the couple, you should match the angle of the shadow that's in the photo of the euros. That shadow is not a layer style; it's in the photograph itself.

11. Click **OK**, then compare your artwork to Figure 17.

12. Save your work, then continue to the next set of steps.

You added a Drop Shadow layer style to artwork and specified settings for the style.

Figure 17   Viewing the Drop Shadow layer style on the couple artwork

Copy layer styles between layers

1. Note the layer styles listed on the Layers panel.

   As shown in Figure 18, the Drop Shadow layer is now listed on the Layers panel as a subset of the Couple layer. The *fx* icon indicates that layer styles have been applied to this layer.

2. Press and hold **[option] (Mac)** or **[Alt] (Win)**, then drag the *fx* icon to the Colosseum layer.

   The shadow is copied to the Colosseum layer. You must hold [option] (Mac) or [Alt] (Win) to copy the layer style. Simply dragging the *fx* icon only moves the style from one layer to another.

   TIP Even if you can't see the Colosseum layer on the Layers panel when you begin dragging, you can still do this step. The layers on the Layers panel will scroll as you drag, so you can get to the layer you want.

3. Using the same method, copy the **layer style** from the **Colosseum layer** to the **Top Coin layer**.

Figure 18 Layer style listed on the Layers panel

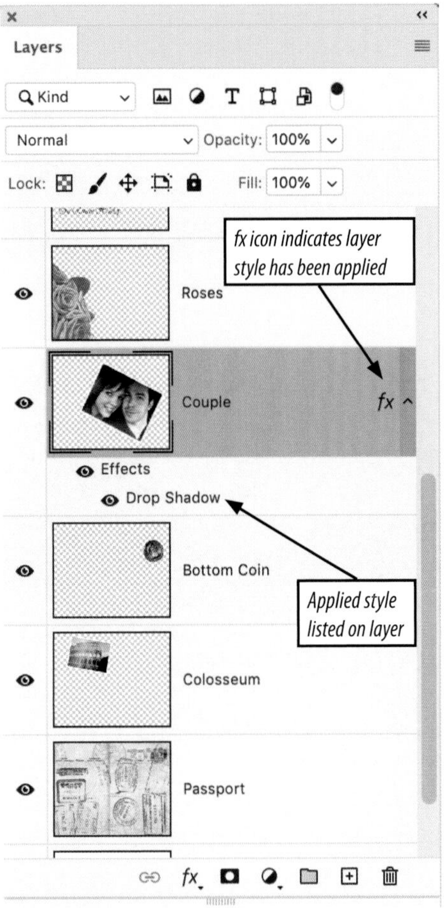

fx icon indicates layer style has been applied

Applied style listed on layer

Copying styles with this method is often referred to as "drag and drop." Dragging and dropping styles between layers is a good, quick way to get the job done, but don't think one size fits all. Different objects cast shadows with different qualities. For example, both the Colosseum and top coin objects would cast a shorter shadow than the one copied from the couple, and the Top Coin layer would cast a shadow with a harder edge. The shadows in this collage now need to be adjusted to work better visually with the individual artwork.

4. On the Layers panel, double-click **Drop Shadow** under the Colosseum layer to open the Layer Style dialog box.

5. Change the **Distance value** to **18**, then click **OK**.

6. Double-click **Drop Shadow** under the Top Coin layer, change the **Distance value** to **14**, change the **Size value** to **5**, then click **OK**.

7. Drag and drop the **Drop Shadow layer style** from the **Top Coin layer** to the **Middle Coin** and the **Bottom Coin layers**.

8. Compare your artwork to Figure 19.

9. Save your work, then continue to the next set of steps.

You copied a Drop Shadow layer style from one layer to another, then modified the settings for the drop shadow to better fit the new artwork.

Apply an Outer Glow layer style

1. Hide and show the **Our Roman Holiday layer**.

In a collage design like this one, type plays an important role. In this collage, it explains the collage. When you read the type, you understand immediately that this is a couple who took a trip to Rome together. They saw the Colosseum. The coins indicate that they experienced the old-world charm of this ancient city, and the euros remind

us that it's also a modern city. The passport in the background conveys travel, and the flowers tell us it was romantic. All of this information comes to us through the type. Perhaps they wrote home with the pen, or perhaps they wrote the headline itself with the pen. When you hide the type, you can still understand the image, but not quite so specifically.

2. Verify that the **Our Roman Holiday layer** is visible.

As a design element, the type is well positioned in its own space in the lower-left quadrant. It has plenty of "air" around it—it's not crammed in there. However, the type overlaps both the image of the roses and the image of the couple, and it is slightly difficult to read. The typeface itself is elegant and charming, but it's also thin, and this too makes it difficult to read.

3. Double-click the **Our Roman Holiday layer**.

The Layer Style dialog box opens. This is the fastest and easiest way to access the Layer Style dialog box. Note that no specific layer style is targeted in the left column when you open the dialog box using this method.

4. Click the words **Outer Glow** in the left column.

The settings for the Outer Glow layer style appear. It is tempting to just click the check box and be done. Clicking the check box activates the style, but if you want to see the settings for the style, you must click on the words themselves.

Continued on next page

Figure 19 Shadows copied and customized to multiple layers

5. In the **Structure** section, set the **Blending Mode** to **Screen**, then set the **Opacity** to **75**.

The Screen blending mode makes bright colors visible and darker colors invisible. We cover this extensively in later chapters. For the time being, just know that you want the Screen blending mode for any bright glows like hot whites, pinks, yellows, blues, etc.

6. Position your pointer over the unlabeled **black square** in the lower-left corner of the Structure section until **Set color of glow** appears.

This is the official name of the black square.

7. Click the **square**.

The Color Picker dialog box opens, offering you 16.5 million choices for the color of the outer glow. For the remainder of this chapter and this book, we will refer to the square you clicked as the "Color Picker square."

8. Choose **white** for the color, then click **OK**.

9. In the **Elements** section, set the **Spread** to **20** and the **Size** to **60**.

10. Click **OK**, then compare your artwork to Figure 20.

Not only does the Outer Glow layer style add an interesting (and charming) visual element to the collage, look what it does for legibility. The glow makes the type stand out—it's effortless to read the type. Because the glow hides so much of the background elements (the image of the roses and the image of the couple), those elements no longer compete with the type for your attention.

11. Save your work for the next set of steps in Lesson 4.

You added an Outer Glow layer style to type outlines so they would be more legible. You specified settings for the glow in the Layer Style dialog box.

Figure 20   The Outer Glow layer style applied to the type

EMPLOY A LAYER MASK

What You'll Do

In this lesson, you'll use a layer mask to hide aspects of layered artwork.

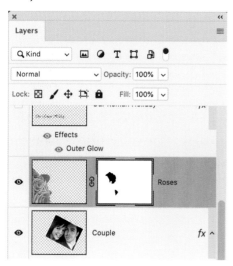

About Layer Masks

You use layer masks to hide or reveal specific artwork on a layer. A layer mask can affect an entire layer or specific areas within a layer. When a layer has a mask, the layer mask thumbnail appears on the Layers panel between the layer thumbnail and the layer name.

The basic concept of a layer mask is that you use black to hide specific areas of the artwork on that layer, or you use white to show specific areas. You add black or white by painting in the layer mask or making selections and filling them with black or white. **Note**: You may also use shades of gray in a layer mask, which is covered in Chapter 4. For this chapter, we are sticking with black or white to get the basic concept down.

As you hide or reveal portions of a layer, the layer mask thumbnail mirrors the changes you are making, and the artwork hides or shows dynamically. One of the many great features about layer masks is that they are endlessly editable. Simply repaint or refill areas you altered previously, and those areas will be updated. Furthermore, nothing you do in a layer mask is permanently altering the actual artwork. You can disable the layer mask or delete it if you want. Because you alter the mask and not the image, no actual pixels are modified in the artwork.

> **TIP** You can think of a layer mask as a type of temporary eraser. When you add black to the mask, you erase pixels from the image—they disappear. If you go back and add white to the mask, those pixels from the image reappear.

Creating a Layer Mask

To add a layer mask to a layer, first target the layer, then click the Add layer mask button on the Layers panel.

By default, Photoshop adds an all-white mask, meaning no artwork is hidden and essentially nothing changes. Note the frame around the layer mask thumbnail. The frame indicates that the mask is activated, so when you paint on the canvas, for example, you are painting in the mask, not on the actual artwork. Because you can switch between activating the artwork or the mask on a given layer, it's important to be aware of which is activated. If you lose track, it is easy to accidentally paint the artwork when you think you're painting in the layer mask.

Figure 21 conveys the entire concept of a mask. The designer made a rectangular marquee selection in the mask and filled it with black. Therefore, the corresponding artwork (the image of the man on the Couple layer) is no longer visible. The frame around the mask indicates that the mask is active. If the designer were to paint black anywhere *on the artwork*, more of the Couple layer artwork would disappear because the mask is activated.

Viewing, Editing, Disabling, and Deleting a Mask

Once you've painted a mask, you can actually view the mask rather than the artwork. Press and hold [option] (Mac) or [Alt] (Win), then click the mask to view it. When you do, you'll see the black and white sections of the mask. Note that you can paint directly in the mask! You might see a spot you missed—for example, a small white area in a field that is supposed to be all black. You can paint that small white area you missed black directly in the mask. This is a great method for ensuring that all the areas of the mask that you intend to be black are indeed black.

At any time, you can disable or "turn off" a mask simply by shift-clicking the mask. A red X will appear over the layer mask thumbnail. To delete a layer mask, simply drag the layer mask thumbnail to the Delete layer button on the Layers panel.

TIP The term "mask" has its origin in printing. Traditionally, a mask was opaque material or tape used to block off an area of the artwork that you did not want to print.

Figure 21 The activated layer mask with a black rectangle and its effect on the corresponding artwork

Masked area in the layer mask and on the artwork

Add and employ a layer mask

1. Open Roman Holiday 3.psd from Lesson 3, then hide the **Our Roman Holiday layer**.

2. Target the **Roses layer**.

   You are going to "mask out" the two green leaves to see if the roses look better without them.

3. Click the **Add layer mask button** 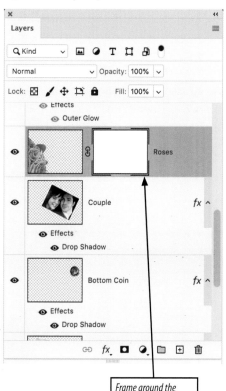 on the Layers panel.

   As shown in Figure 22, an all-white mask is added to the layer, and by default, a frame appears around the mask thumbnail, indicating that the mask is activated. Because the mask is all white, nothing is hidden on the layer, so adding a mask has no immediate effect on the artwork.

4. Note the foreground and background colors on the toolbar.

   No matter what colors you currently have displayed on the toolbar, when you activate a layer mask, the foreground and background colors change to black, white, or a shade of gray because you can only paint black, white, or a shade of gray in a layer mask.

5. Press the **letter [D]** on your keypad to access the default colors, which are foreground (white) and background (black) when a mask is activated.

6. Press the **letter [X]** on your keypad to reverse the foreground and background colors.

   When you paint, you will now be painting with the foreground color, which is black. In other words, anything you paint will disappear.

   TIP Get in the habit of using the [D] and [X] keys when you're working in a layer mask to be sure you're painting with pure black and pure white.

Figure 22 Adding the layer mask

Frame around the layer mask thumbnail indicates it is activated

7. Type the **letter [B]** on your keypad to access the Brush tool, click the **brush settings** on the Options panel, then set the **Brush Size** to **30** and the **Hardness** to **75**.

   If you need a refresher on brush settings, refer back to Chapter 2, Lesson 2. To mask effectively, it is critical that you use the best brush size and brush hardness (which is essentially the brush "edge") to get the job done. This cannot be overstated. Your willingness to take the time to experiment with the best brush size and especially the best hardness setting will have a huge impact on the success of any mask you ever create.

8. **Zoom in** on the **top green leaf** to enlarge it.

   Taking the time to enlarge the view of the area that you intend to mask is another critical choice for success in masking. Condition yourself to make zooming in a default step when you work with masks.

9. **Paint on the green leaf** so the entire leaf disappears.

   Use the left and right bracket keys (to the right of the letter [P] on your keypad) to adjust the size of the brush, as necessary. Taking the time to adjust your brush size as you work is key to success in masking.

10. Using the same method, mask out the **small lower leaf**.

Continued on next page

11. Compare your artwork and your Layers panel to Figure 23.

12. Press **[command] [0] (Mac)** or **[Ctrl] [0] (Win)** (Fit on Screen), press and hold **[option] (Mac)** or **[Alt] (Win)**, then click the **layer mask thumbnail**.

As shown in Figure 24, the entire mask becomes visible. You can see where you painted black in the mask. Evaluate the mask. Note, if you missed a spot—if there's a bit of white in a field of black that you intended to be all black—you could paint that spot black directly in the mask.

13. Click the **Roses layer thumbnail** (the artwork thumbnail) on the Layers panel.

The view switches back to the artwork. Note that the double border around the artwork thumbnail indicates that the artwork is activated, not the layer mask.

14. Press and hold **[shift]**, then click the **layer mask thumbnail**.

The layer mask is disabled, and a red X appears over the layer mask thumbnail. Because the mask is disabled, the two green leaves are visible again.

15. Evaluate the image.

Let's agree that you decide you like the artwork better with the green leaves visible. You decide the leaves add some unique color, and you like the way the big green leaf overlaps the couple image. Should you delete the layer mask? No. You've already put in the work, and you never know if you might change your mind later in the process, so don't discard the mask. Simply keep it disabled.

16. Save your work, then close Roman Holiday 3.

You used a layer mask along with the Brush tool to mask out parts of artwork and make them invisible.

Figure 23 Viewing the roses without the green leaves and the corresponding layer mask thumbnail on the Layers panel

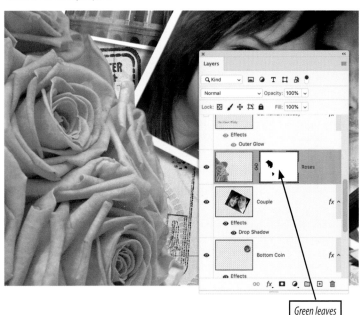

Green leaves masked

Figure 24 Viewing (and evaluating) the mask itself

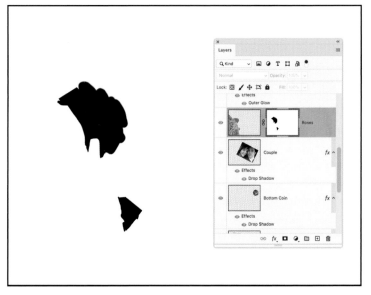

MASK OUT THE BACKGROUND OF AN IMAGE AND MODIFY THE CANVAS SIZE

▶ *What You'll Do*

In this lesson, you'll use a layer mask to remove the background from an image. You'll also enlarge the canvas size to make room for a frame.

Masking Out the Background of an Image

In Lesson 4, you used a layer mask to make two leaves on the roses artwork disappear. That type of work—removing unwanted details from artwork—is a common task layer masks are used to achieve.

Layer masks are most often used to remove the background of an image so that the main subject of the image can be used in a collage or positioned in a different environment. For example, when you see a movie poster that shows the movie's star floating in space or hanging from the edge of a cliff or standing in the middle of Manhattan with no cars or people to be seen, that movie star was not photographed in those locations. He or she was photographed in a studio, most likely against a white screen. Designers then use layer masks to remove the white background. Once the subject is "isolated" or "silhouetted" and the background is removed, the subject can be positioned against any other background—like in space, or hanging from a cliff, or standing in an empty New York street.

Masking out a background is a fundamental skill in Photoshop, a skill that must be practiced and honed. Professional designers are expected to be able to quickly "drop out" a background so that they can begin building their designs, and when a design is chosen, advertising agencies and other types of art departments hire highly skilled (and highly paid) "finishers" to do exactly that—finish the artwork. Finishing the artwork includes painting a flawless mask. You might ask, is that really so hard to do? What if the actor has curly hair? How do you mask out the background but keep the curls? What if the actress's hair is blowing in the wind? How do you mask around that? What if the actress is wearing a cape that is somewhat transparent and the white background is partially showing through? How do you keep the see-through cape and lose the white background? As you can see, masking out a background can be very challenging, so much so that it requires professional-level skills.

When you mask out a background, you can do so in the original image file, then drag the masked layer from the original file into the collage file you are building. Alternatively, you can copy and paste the original file into the collage file and mask it in the collage file.

Pasting an Image

When you paste an image into a Photoshop file, Photoshop automatically creates a new layer for the pasted artwork and assigns it a number. It's always a good idea to rename the layer with a descriptive term.

Here's a great tip: use the Fit on Screen command on the View menu so the entire canvas is visible before you paste. Now when you paste, the pasted artwork will be centered on the canvas. This simple move can be very useful in the right time and place for alignment considerations.

About the Canvas Size

The canvas size is the size of the artwork on your screen. If you fit the artwork in the window so that you can see all of it, you are seeing all the canvas. If you create a new document in Photoshop that is 8" × 8", the canvas size for that document is 8" × 8". If you open an image from the camera on your phone, the canvas size for that image is whatever size your phone is set to. Imagine for a moment that you have an image from a recent vacation, and you want space below the image to type the location and the date you were there. Let's be clear: you don't want to type over the image—you want *more* space to type the info. You can add that space by increasing the canvas size in the Canvas Size dialog box.

The Canvas Size dialog box allows you to add more pixels to the canvas at the bottom, top, left, right, or all around the image. Figure 25 shows an image with added space at the bottom to accommodate type.

Figure 25 An image with pixels added to the bottom to create space for type

Bleeding an Image off the Canvas

Once you've pasted an image, you can use the Move tool to position the pasted artwork anywhere you want on the canvas, including partially off the canvas. When you position artwork off the canvas, it does not show—only that which is on the canvas is visible.

Figure 26 shows the same image with a robot pasted in the foreground. The robot has been positioned so that it *bleeds* off the canvas. "Bleed" is a term from the days of conventional printing that has survived into modern lingo.

Any artwork that extends all the way to the edge of the canvas is said to bleed. In this image, the parts of the robot image that are not on the canvas are not visible, but at any time, you could move the robot artwork back on to the canvas to show more of the artwork that's not currently visible. It's still there; it's just not visible.

When you position artwork off the canvas, Photoshop creates space to accommodate that artwork. It does NOT change the canvas size—the new space is virtual. However, you should consider that the file size of the image—how

Figure 26 The same image with a robot bleeding left and bottom

The risk of cropping a file is that all the off-canvas data will be lost with the crop. In the preceding example, if you cropped the image, you would lose all options for showing more of the robot artwork in the future. On the other hand, if you manage your files properly, you will have saved another copy of the entire robot artwork for future access, so cropping here would be a good choice to manage the file size.

Instead of using the Crop tool, you can quickly crop the entire image by choosing All on the Select menu, then clicking the Crop command on the Image menu.

Figure 27 The Reveal All command exposes all the artwork

much memory it takes up—increases based on how much virtual space needs to be added to accommodate the bleed image.

Using the Reveal All Command

The Reveal All command on the Image menu expands the canvas size to show you the totality of all artwork that bleeds off the canvas. This is not a much-used command, but it can be useful to remind yourself of the artwork that's not visible and how much content is placed off of the canvas.

Figure 27 shows the canvas after the Reveal All command has been applied. Like an iceberg, there was a lot more to this file than could be seen. The file size, in terms of memory, was also a lot bigger than one might have guessed looking at the original file.

Cropping an Image with the Crop Command

Sometimes designers choose to crop an image to delete content that's off the canvas and reduce the file size. When you crop an image, anything that's outside of the crop is deleted.

Paste an image

1. Open PS 3-4.psd, then save it as **Roman Holiday Final**.

   This collage is in the same state as it was at the end of Lesson 4.

2. Target the **Top Coin layer** at the top of the Layers panel.

3. Open PS 3-5.psd, click **Select** on the menu bar, then click **All**.

4. Copy the artwork, then close the file.

5. In the Roman Holiday Final document, click **View** on the menu bar, then click **Fit on Screen**.

6. Paste the artwork.

   The ring artwork is pasted into the document and a new layer is created above the Top Coin layer. Pasted artwork is always placed in a new layer above the targeted layer on the Layers panel.

   TIP When you choose Fit on Screen, any artwork you paste will be pasted at the center of the canvas. This can be a strategic choice in the right situation.

7. Rename the new layer **Ring**.

8. Save your work.

   You pasted artwork into a working document.

Use a layer mask to remove a background

1. Target the **Top Coin layer**, then click the **Create a new layer button** ⊞ on the Layers panel.

   A new layer is created above the Top Coin layer and below the Ring layer. Since the new layer has no content, it doesn't change the image in any way.

2. Click the **Foreground color** on the toolbar to open the Color Picker.

3. Choose a **bright lime green color**, then click **OK**.

4. Press and hold **[option] (Mac)** or **[Alt] (Win)**, then press **[delete]** on your keypad to fill the layer.

   Your canvas should resemble Figure 28.

5. Name the layer **Temp Green Bkg**.

   You will use this green background as a visual aid when masking the ring artwork. Rather than mask the ring against the busy collage artwork, you will mask it against this simple green background, which will make it easier for you to see the outline you are creating.

6. Click the **Ring layer**, then click the **Add layer mask button** ▣ on the Layers panel.

7. Press the **letter [B]** on your keypad to access the Brush tool 🖌, then **zoom in** on the ring so you can analyze its edge.

   The edge is fairly hard.

8. Click the **Brush Preset picker arrow** ● ∨ on the Options panel, choose an appropriate brush size, then set the **Hardness** to **75**.

9. Press the **letter [D]** on your keypad, then press the **letter [X]** to verify that your foreground color is black.

10. **Mask** the **ring** so your artwork resembles Figure 29.

    Don't go past the point shown in Figure 29.

    The best method for masking this ring would be to use the click + [shift]-click. If you need a refresher on this, go back to Chapter 2, Lesson 3.

Figure 28 Filling the entire layer with green

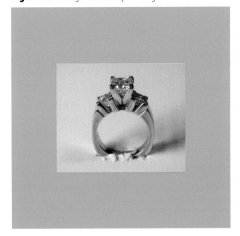

Figure 29 Masking around the ring

TIP Remember, there are no "mistakes" in masking. If you want to undo a move you made at any time, you can always paint white to show the image.

11. Press and hold **[option] (Mac)** or **[Alt] (Win)**, then click the **layer mask** to see the mask.

We want to find a fast way to get rid of all the white in the mask that's outside the mask you've painted so far.

12. Click the **Magic Wand tool** ![magic wand icon], set the **Tolerance** to **16**, then verify that the **Contiguous option** is checked.

13. Click the **Magic Wand tool** ![magic wand icon] anywhere in the white background.

The entire white background is selected, up to the edge of the mask you painted.

14. Click **Select** on the menu bar, point to **Modify**, then click **Expand**.

15. Enter **3**, then click **OK**.

The selection is expanded by three pixels to overlap the mask you painted. This is like painting a wall in your house with a roller—you overlap the previous roll a little bit to be sure you don't miss a spot. In this case, we want to be sure we don't leave a white line around the painted mask.

16. Fill the selection with the **black foreground color**, then **deselect**.

Your mask should resemble Figure 30.

17. Click the **Ring artwork thumbnail** to show the artwork.

18. Hide the **Temp Green Bkg layer**.

19. Enter **[command] [T] (Mac)** or **[Ctrl] [T] (Win)**, scale the artwork **75%**, rotate the artwork **28°**, then click the **Move tool** ![move tool icon] on the toolbar to apply the transformation.

20. Position the ring as shown in Figure 31.

21. Save your work.

You created a new layer with a bright green background so you could mask artwork against a simple background. You masked around the ring artwork, viewed the mask, then masked the entire background of the ring image.

Figure 30 Filling the layer mask background with black

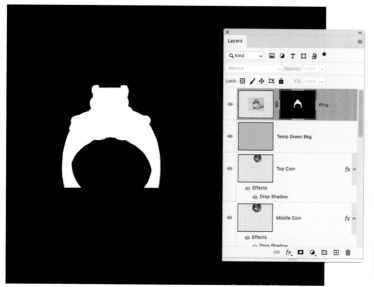

Figure 31 Positioning the scaled and rotated ring artwork

Ring artwork in position

Our Roman Holiday

Change the canvas size to create a frame

1. Click **Image** on the menu bar, then click **Reveal All**.

   All the artwork that bleeds off the canvas is now revealed, including the ring artwork you positioned.

2. **Undo** the last step.

3. Click **Select** on the menu bar, then click **All**.

4. Click **Image** on the menu bar, then click **Crop**.

   The image is cropped at the edge of the canvas. All the images end at the canvas edge. You wouldn't be able to use the Reveal All command now because there's nothing to reveal.

5. Click **Image** on the menu bar, then click **Canvas Size**.

   The Canvas Size dialog box opens, revealing that the canvas is 6.573" wide and 4.987" tall. You are going to add a thin black frame around the canvas.

6. Click once in the **Width dialog box** to the immediate right of 6.573, then type **+.25**.

7. Press **[tab]** on your keypad.

   Note that Photoshop automatically does the calculation for you. The new width will be 6.823".

8. Click once in the **Height dialog box** to the immediate right of 4.987, then type **+.25**.

   Your dialog box should resemble Figure 32.

9. Press **[tab]** to execute the calculation.

   The new height will be 5.237".

10. Click the **Color Picker square** at the bottom of the dialog box.

11. Set the color to **black**, click **OK**, then click **OK** to close the dialog box.

12. Compare your canvas to Figure 33.

    A black frame appears around the image. The frame is .125" on all four sides, because you expanded the canvas by .25" on the width and .25" on the height.

13. Save your work, then close Roman Holiday Final.

You enlarged the canvas size to create a black frame around the image.

Figure 32 Adding .25" to the height

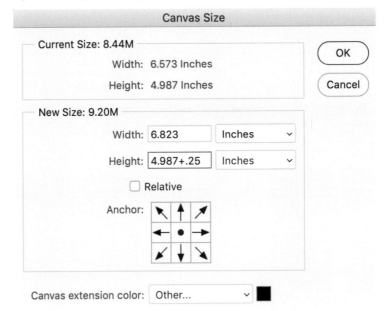

Figure 33 Viewing the final artwork with the frame

Set preferences for working with layers

1. Open PS 3-6.psd, then save it as **Chapter 3 Skills Review 01.**
   Be sure you don't save the file again until you are instructed to.
2. Click Photoshop (Mac) or Edit (Win) on the menu bar, point to Preferences, then click General.
3. Verify that Use Legacy Free Transform is checked, then click OK.
4. Click the Layers panel menu button, then click Panel Options.
5. Verify that the largest thumbnail option is selected, then click OK.

Perform basic operations on the Layers panel

1. Note that all layers have been given an identifying name except the one named Layer 1.
2. Double-click the name Layer 1, rename it **Pink Globe**, then save your work.
3. Click the eye button on the Pink Globe layer repeatedly to hide and show the artwork, then verify that the Pink Globe layer is visible.
4. Click and drag vertically over all the eye buttons on the Layers panel to hide all layers.
5. Repeat Step 4 to make all layers visible again.
6. Press and hold [option] (Mac) or [Alt] (Win), then click the eye button on the Pink Globe layer to hide all other layers.
7. Still holding [option] (Mac) or [Alt] (Win), click the same spot on the Pink Globe layer to show all other layers.
8. Target the Blue Globe layer.
9. Click the Opacity slider at the top of the Layers panel, then drag the slider to 50%.

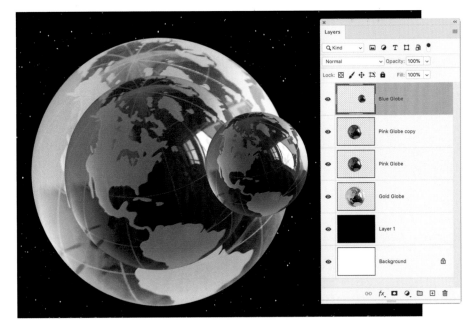

Figure 34 Repositioning the Blue Globe artwork

10. Click the Move tool on the toolbar, then press the number [2] on your keypad to set the opacity to 20%.
11. Press the number [7] on your keypad to set the opacity to 70%.
12. Press the number [0] on your keypad to set the opacity to 100%.
13. Click anywhere on the Gold Globe layer to target it.
14. Press the letter [V] on your keypad to verify that the Move tool is still selected, then click and drag the Gold Globe artwork to another position on the canvas.
15. Target the Blue Globe layer, press and hold [command] (Mac) or [Ctrl] (Win), then click the Pink Globe layer so that both are targeted.
16. Drag the blue globe and pink globe artwork to another location on the canvas.

17. Click File on the menu bar, then click Revert.
18. Target the Pink Globe layer, then click and drag it up to the top of the Layers panel.
19. Press [command] [J] (Mac) or [Ctrl] [J] (Win) to duplicate the layer.
20. Drag the Blue Globe layer to the top of the Layers panel, then position the blue globe artwork as shown in Figure 34.
21. Target both the Blue Globe and the Pink Globe copy layers, click the Layers panel menu button, then click Merge Layers.
22. Move the merged layer artwork to any other location on the canvas.
23. Save your work, then close Chapter 3 Skills Review 01.

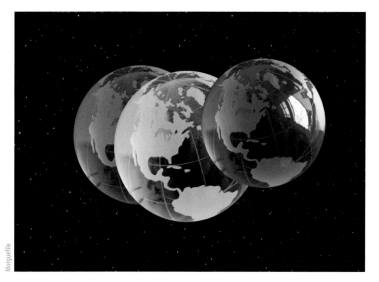

Morguefile

Figure 35 Reordering and repositioning the globes

Figure 36 Repositioning the scaled globes

Scale artwork

1. Open PS 3-7.psd, then save it as **Chapter 3 Skills Review 02.**
2. Reorder and reposition the globes as shown in Figure 35.
3. Target the Pink Globe layer, click Edit on the menu bar, point to Transform, then click Scale.
4. Position the mouse pointer on the lower-right corner handle until a double-headed arrow appears, click and drag in different directions to modify the image, then release the mouse pointer.
5. Undo your last step.
6. Position the mouse pointer on the lower-right corner handle, press and hold [shift], click and drag in different directions, then release the mouse pointer.
7. Undo the move.
8. Note the crosshair icon in the middle of the bounding box.
9. On the Options panel, double-click the W text box, type **80**, press [tab], type **80** in the H text box, press [tab], then click the Move tool on the toolbar to execute the transformation.
10. Target the Blue Globe layer, then press [command] [T] (Mac) or [Ctrl] [T] (Win).
11. Press and hold [shift] [option] (Mac) or [Shift] [Alt] (Win), position the mouse pointer over the lower-left handle, drag to experiment with resizing the globe artwork, then release the mouse pointer.
12. Undo the last step so you can enter specific values.
13. Double-click the W text box on the Options panel, type **60**, press [tab], type **60** in the H text box, press [tab], then click [return] (Mac) or [Enter] (Win) to execute the transformation.
14. Position the globes as shown in Figure 36.
15. Save your work.

Rotate and flip artwork

1. Target the Gold Globe layer, click Edit on the menu bar, point to Transform, then click Flip Vertical.
2. Click the Blue Globe layer so it is the only targeted layer, then press [command] [T] (Mac) or [Ctrl] [T] (Win).
3. Press and hold [shift], then position your mouse pointer *outside* of the bounding box so it changes to the rotate icon.
4. Click and drag outside the bounding box to rotate the blue globe −60 degrees, then click the Move tool to execute the transformation.
5. Save your work, then close Chapter 3 Skills Review 02.

Apply an Outer Glow layer style

1. Open PS 3-8.psd, then save it as **Chapter 3 Skills Review 03**.
2. Double-click the thumbnail on the Gold Globe layer.
3. Click the words Outer Glow in the left column of the Layer Style dialog box.
4. In the Structure section, set the Blend Mode to Screen, then set the Opacity to 75.
5. Position your mouse pointer over the Color Picker square in the lower-left corner of the Structure section, then click it. Choose a similar shade of yellow/gold to the golden globe artwork, then click OK.
6. In the Elements section, set the Spread to 14 and the Size to 200, then click OK.
7. Save your work.

Figure 37 Viewing the scaled green globe

Copy layer styles between layers

1. Note that the Outer Glow layer style is now listed on the Layers panel as a subset of the Gold Globe layer. The *fx* icon indicates that layer styles have been applied to this layer.
2. Press and hold [option] (Mac) or [Alt] (Win), and drag the *fx* icon to the Blue Globe layer.
3. Using the same method, copy the layer style from the Gold Globe layer to the Pink Globe layer.
4. On the Layers panel, double-click Outer Glow under the Pink Globe layer to open the Layer Style dialog box.
5. Change the color of the glow to the same hot pink as the globe.
6. Drag the Size slider to 120, then click OK.
7. On the Layers panel, double-click Outer Glow under the Blue Globe layer to open the Layer Style dialog box.

8. Change the color of the glow to the same blue as the globe.
9. Drag the Size slider to 100, then click OK.
10. Save your work.

Add and employ a layer mask

1. Duplicate the Blue globe layer, then rename it **Green Globe**.
2. Move the green globe artwork to the lower-right quadrant of the canvas.
3. Enter [command] [U] (Mac) or [Ctrl] [U] (Win) to open the Hue/Saturation dialog box.
4. Drag the Hue slider to -57, then click OK.
5. Scale the Green Globe layer 75% proportionally.
6. On the Layers panel, click the eye button to hide the Outer Glow layer style on the Green Globe layer. Your artwork should resemble Figure 37.

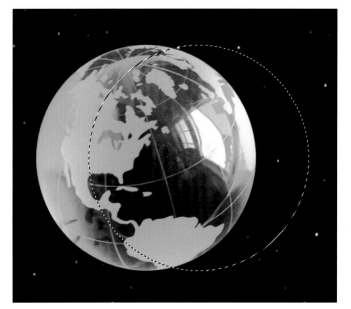

Figure 38 Moving the selection marquee with the arrow key

![Figure 39]

Figure 39 Four glows

7. Verify that the Green Globe layer is still targeted, then click the Add layer mask button on the Layers panel.
8. Press and hold [command] (Mac) or [Ctrl] (Win), then click the thumbnail image on the *artwork* thumbnail on the Green Globe layer.
9. Press the letter [M] on your keypad to access a marquee tool on the toolbar.
10. Press and hold [shift], then press the right arrow on your keypad eight times.
    Your Green Globe artwork should resemble Figure 38.
11. Set the foreground color on the toolbar to black.
12. Press and hold [option] (Mac) or [Alt] (Win), then press [delete] on your keypad.

13. Deselect.
14. Show the Outer Glow layer style on the Green Globe layer on the Layers panel.
15. Change the outer glow color to the same green as the green globe artwork.
16. Compare your canvas to Figure 39.
17. Save your work.

Paste an image

1. Target the Green Globe layer at the top of the Layers panel.
2. Open PS 3-9.psd, click Select on the menu bar, then click All.

3. Copy the artwork, then close the file.
4. In the globes document, click View on the menu bar, then click Fit on Screen.
5. Paste the artwork.
6. Rename the new layer **Rocket**.
7. Save your work.

Use a layer mask to remove the background

1. Verify that the Rocket layer is targeted.
2. Press and hold [command] (Mac) or [Ctrl] (Win), then click the Create a new layer button on the Layers panel.

(continued)

3. Click the foreground color on the toolbar to open the Color Picker.
4. Choose a bright lime green color, then click OK.
5. Press and hold [option] (Mac) or [Alt] (Win), then press [delete] on your keypad to fill the layer.
6. Name the layer **Temp Green Bkg**.
7. Click the Rocket layer, then click the Add layer mask button on the Layers panel.
8. Press the letter [B] on your keypad to access the Brush tool, then zoom in on the rocket artwork so you can analyze its edge.
   The edge is fairly hard.
9. Click the Brush Settings panel button on the Options panel, choose an appropriate brush size, then set the Hardness for the brush to 75.
10. Press the letter [D] on your keypad, then press the letter [X] to verify that your foreground color is black.
11. Mask the rocket so your artwork resembles Figure 40. Don't go past the point shown in Figure 40.
    The best method for masking the rocket would be to use the click + [shift]-click method. If you need a refresher on this, go back to Chapter 2, Lesson 3.

12. Press and hold [option] (Mac) or [Alt] (Win), then click the layer mask to see the mask.
13. Click the Magic Wand tool, set the Tolerance to 16, then verify that the Contiguous option is checked.
14. Click the wand anywhere in the white background.
15. Click Select on the menu bar, point to Modify, then click Expand.
16. Enter **3**, then click OK.
17. Fill the selection with the black foreground color, then deselect.
18. Click the Rocket artwork thumbnail to show the artwork.
19. Hide the Temp Green Bkg layer.
20. Enter [command] [T] (Mac) or [Ctrl] [T] (Win), scale the artwork 63%, rotate the artwork 45°, then click the Move tool on the toolbar to execute the transformation.
21. Copy the Outer Glow layer style from the Blue Globe layer to the Rocket layer.
22. Position the rocket as shown in Figure 41.
23. Save your work, then close Chapter 3 Skills Review 01.

Figure 40 Masking the rocket

Morguefile

Figure 41 Positioning the rocket

Using a layer mask to remove an object from a background is one of the most important skills in Photoshop, and one you'll have to master if you want to achieve larger goals with the program. This project builder uses an image of flip flops, an item you are likely very familiar with. The goal is to use a mask to remove the background, but it's also for you to use the right brush size and the right hardness setting to get the best edge for the mask. These sandals would have a relatively hard edge, even though the rubber material is flexible. Think about that when you choose the hardness for your brush and when you're painting the mask.

1. Open PS 3-10.psd, then save it as **Flip Flop Mask.**
2. Duplicate the Background layer, then rename the new layer **Flip Flops**.
3. Target the Background layer, then fill it with red.
4. Target the Flip Flops layer, then add a layer mask.
5. Zoom in on the image until you are viewing the image at minimum 500%.
6. Select the Brush tool, set the Size to 10 pixels, then set the Hardness to 80%.
7. Mask both flip flops so your mask resembles Figure 42.
   The best method for masking the flip flops would be to use the click + [shift]-click. If you need a refresher on this, go back to Chapter 2, Lesson 3.

TIP Remember, there are no "mistakes" in masking. If you want to undo any move you made at any time, you can always paint white to show the image.

Figure 42 Masking the flip flops

8. Press and hold [option] (Mac) or [Alt] (Win), then click the layer mask to see the mask.
9. Click the Magic Wand tool, set the Tolerance to 16, then verify that the Contiguous option is checked.
10. Use the Magic Wand tool to select all the white areas that need to be filled with black.
11. Click Select on the menu bar, point to Modify, then click Expand.
12. Enter 3, then click OK.
13. Fill the selection with the black foreground color.
14. Click the flip flop artwork thumbnail to show the artwork.
15. Compare your artwork to Figure 43.

Figure 43 The flip flops fully masked

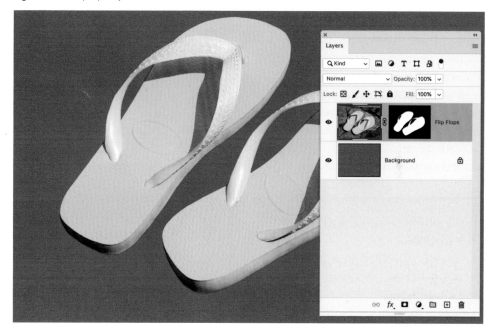

PROJECT BUILDER 2

(continued)

Working with layers in Photoshop is a game of strategy. This project builder is designed to teach you a fundamental strategy for layering one image "inside" another. Starting with an image of an empty basket, you'll be asked to arrange fruit "inside" the basket. You'll use the front of the basket strategically with a layer mask to create the illusion. This technique is fundamental and can be applied to other projects with similar objectives.

1. Open PS 3-11.psd, then save it as **Still Life**.
2. Click Select on the menu bar, click Load Selection, verify that your Load Selection dialog box matches Figure 44, then click OK.
3. Click the Rectangular Marquee tool on the toolbar, press and hold [shift] to add to the selection, then select the top-half of the canvas.
   Your selection should resemble Figure 45.
4. Click Select on the menu bar, then click Inverse.
5. Target the Background layer, copy the selection, then paste.
   A new layer is created.
6. Name the new layer **Basket Front**, then drag it to the top of the Layers panel.

Figure 44 The Load Selection dialog box

Figure 45 Adding to the elliptical marquee

Figure 46 The final effect

7. Make the Purple Grapes layer visible, then move the artwork around the canvas to see the effect you've created.

   The grapes appear to be "inside" the basket because they are behind the Basket Front artwork.

8. Undo your last move so the grapes are in the same location as when you made the layer visible.

9. Duplicate the Purple Grapes layer, rename it **Purple Grapes in Front**, then drag it to the top of the Layers panel.

10. Add a layer mask, then fill the layer mask with black so that the Purple Grapes in Front artwork is not visible.

11. Painting with white, "unmasks" some of the purple grapes so that the artwork appears to be "hanging over" the front of the basket. Use Figure 46 as a guide. The illusion is very effective because some of the grapes appear to be "inside" the basket while others are hanging "outside" the basket.

12. Save your work, then close Still Life.

Fine art school students are usually required to create still life artwork. The same can be done with digital art. You are given images of various fruits and asked to arrange them into a beautiful and balanced still life. This is a great challenge for working with layers, transforming images, and bringing images into a working file from other files.

1. Open PS 3-12.psd, then save it as **Still Life Composition**.
2. Target the Background layer.
3. Click File on the menu bar, click Open, then navigate to the Fruit folder in the Chapter 3 Data Files folder.
4. Open the file named Green Grapes.
   The file has been masked for you.
5. Drag the Green Grapes file by its name down from the Photoshop window so that it is a floating window. Your screen should resemble Figure 47.
6. Click the Move tool, then drag the Green Grapes layer into the Still Life Composition file.
   The artwork, along with the mask, is moved into the Still Life Composition file.
7. Close Green Grapes.
8. Open the file named Orange Navel.
9. Mask out the background.
10. Drag the Orange Navel artwork into the Still Life Composition file, then close Orange Navel.

Figure 47 Dragging the masked Green Grapes layer into the Still Life Composition file

11. Using the same method, open other fruit image files you want to work with, mask out their backgrounds, then add them to the Still Life Composition file until you have enough fruit images to build a still life.

12. In the Still Life Composition file, transform artwork as needed and reposition artwork to build a still life collage.
    Figure 48 shows one outcome that you can use as a guide.
13. Save your work, then close Still Life Composition.

Figure 48 One example of the completed still life

Morguefile

CHAPTER 4

WORK WITH TYPE AND
GRADIENTS

1. Set and Format Type
2. Create Bevel & Emboss Effects on Type
3. Create and Apply Gradients
4. Clip a Gradient and an Image into Type
5. Fade Type with a Gradient and a Layer Mask
6. Clip Multiple Images into Type

Adobe Certified Professional in Visual Design Using Photoshop CC Framework

2. Project Setup and Interface
This objective covers the interface setup and program settings that assist in an efficient and effective workflow, as well as knowledge about ingesting digital assets for a project.

2.5 Manage colors, swatches, and gradients.
    B Create, customize, and organize gradients.

4. Creating and Modifying Visual Elements
This objective covers core tools and functionality of the application, as well as tools that affect the visual outcome of the document.

4.1 Use core tools and features to create visual elements.
    A Create and edit raster images.

4.2 Add and manipulate text using appropriate typographic settings.
    A Use type tools to add typography to a design.
    B Organize and customize the workspace.
    C Convert text to graphics.

SET AND FORMAT TYPE

▶ *What You'll Do*

In this lesson, you'll use the Type and the Character panels to set and format type. You'll rasterize type and learn to lock transparent pixels so that you can paint type outlines.

Working with Type and Gradients

When people think of Photoshop, their first thought usually is of images, photographs, and special effects. But another great Photoshop feature is the ability to create sophisticated typographical effects. Photoshop makes it easy to create classic effects like beveled and embossed text, chiseled text, and text that shines as though it were made of chrome. Even better, you can combine type with photographic images to produce truly unique typographical designs.

When you start working extensively with type, you often find yourself working with gradients as well. **Gradients** are blends between two or more colors, and they are visually striking when applied to type and typography. A white-to-black gradient can add weight to a title, or a green-to-yellow gradient can make for a vibrant headline that appears to glow. Gradients offer many more options than a simple solid color for filling type.

Setting Type

Adobe has outfitted Photoshop with all the text-editing capabilities you'd expect from any top-notch word processing or page layout package. When you create type in Photoshop, it is "live type" just like in any other application; you can select it, copy it, paste it, and so on. The toolbar offers you a tool to set type horizontally and a tool to set type vertically.

When you set type, a new type layer is shown on the Layers panel. A type layer is a "live type" layer: the type can be edited at any time. Simply by targeting the layer on the Layers panel, you can change the type size, typeface, and color of the type. You can do this without clicking and dragging to highlight and select the type as you would in a word processing program.

Type layers can be transformed like any other artwork. In fact, rather than change the font size on type, most designers simply scale the type to the size they think looks good. In addition to scaling, type can be rotated, skewed, warped, and flipped horizontally and vertically.

Working with the Character Panel

The Character panel is command central for formatting type in Photoshop. You can do all formatting you need to do—setting the typeface, the size, the tracking, the kerning, and so forth—on the Character panel.

Figure 1 shows the Character panel and identifies the many options available to you when working with type. The Tracking and Kerning options are used to perfect the appearance of typography in terms of spacing. Tracking controls the overall spacing between letters in a given word or paragraph. Kerning controls the spacing between any two specific letters. The Horizontal and Vertical scale options resize selected text, making it wider or taller, respectively. Be sure to experiment with the style buttons at the bottom of the panel, which are useful for making all caps, small caps, superscripts, and other classic examples of typographical formatting.

Figure 1 The Character panel

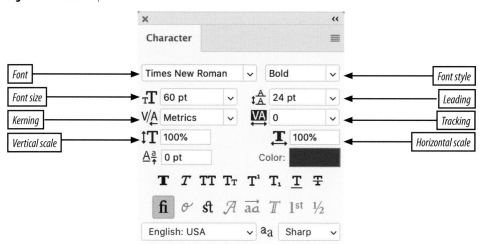

Working with the Paragraph Panel

Most designs in Photoshop that call for type usually call for what is referred to as display type. Headlines and other large, free-standing typographical elements in a design are examples of display type. Some designs, however, call for type to be laid out in paragraph format. In those cases, you will rely on the Paragraph panel. The Paragraph panel offers standard paragraph formatting tools, including margin indents, first line indents, space after and space before paragraph measures, and text alignment.

Tracking and Kerning Type

When setting type in Photoshop, don't just assume that the way the type lays out when you type it is visually satisfying. Many fonts, when they are typed, leave you with awkward or inconsistent spacing between letters. Neglecting to address these issues is neglecting the typographical considerations that are critical for producing elegant and sophisticated type. Unfortunately, many inexperienced designers either overlook or don't bother correcting this. You'd be amazed at how many posters, flyers, and advertisements—even billboards!—are printed and released to the public with obviously neglected typographical considerations.

Tracking and **kerning** are options on the Character panel that control the space between letters. Tracking is the more global of the two. When tracking type, you select the whole word (or words) then reduce the space or increase the space between letters evenly. Kerning is more specific. With kerning, you click the cursor between two letters and affect the spacing only of that pair of letters. With both tracking and kerning, a negative value brings letters closer together, and a positive value moves letters further apart.

Rasterizing Type

Sometimes a designer will want to create an effect or a look that can't be done with live type. For example, live type cannot be painted, you can't apply filters to live type, and you can't apply the Distort command with the transform bounding box. If you want to do these or other operations to type, the only option is to first rasterize the type using the Rasterize command on the Type menu.

To **rasterize** type means to convert type to pixels. Adobe users refer to this as changing the live type to "outlines." Once rasterized, the type outlines don't appear to change, but they can be manipulated like all other Photoshop artwork.

That's because, once rasterized, type outlines are just that, outlines. They're not type. They're simply pixels.

Rasterizing type is a commitment. Once you do so, other than using the Undo command or reverting the file, you can never go back and convert the rasterized text back into live type.

Another reason designers rasterize type is to avoid font issues. When you share a Photoshop file that includes font information, the person who opens your file will need the same font installed on their computer to render the type. When type is rasterized, you no longer need the font installed because the type has been converted to pixels.

Understanding Transparency on a Layer

When you create a new layer in Photoshop, you'll see no changes to the artwork on your canvas. This is because each new layer is automatically a transparent layer. It's empty because it has no artwork on it. Until you fill the layer or paint in the layer, you can think of the pixels on the layer as being transparent, or "empty."

Transparency on a layer is rendered visually as a gray and white checkerboard.

The idea that a layer or part of a layer is transparent is an important concept to understand, especially when working with type. On a type layer, the pixels on the layer that *aren't* used to render the type are transparent by default. Similarly, if you have masked artwork on a layer, like a coin or a pen, the pixels on the layer that aren't used to render the artwork are transparent by default.

Filling and Painting Live Type and Rasterized Type

Live type can be filled with any solid color, but it can't be filled with a gradient. Live type also cannot be painted with multiple colors.

Once rasterized, type outlines can be painted like any other artwork. When painting or filling rasterized type with colors, you'll want to preserve the shapes of the type outlines. To do so, click the **Lock Transparent Pixels button** on the Layers panel, or activate the Preserve Transparency option when it appears in dialog boxes, like the Fill dialog box.

When you lock transparent pixels or preserve transparency, the transparent pixels on the layer won't be affected by any fills or painting that you do on the layer.

Set type

1. Open PS 4-1.psd, then save it as **Typography**.

2. Press the **letter [D]** on your keypad to set the foreground and background colors on the toolbar to the default black over white.

3. Click the **Horizontal Type tool**  on the toolbar, set your type size to 24 points on the Options panel, then set your foreground color to black.

4. Float over the canvas, then click the cursor on the left side of the canvas.

   A blinking type cursor appears, prompting you to begin typing.

TIP When you click the Type tool, default "Greek" text appears that reads "Lorem ipsum." This is intended to give you a preview of the typeface and the type size you have preset before you started typing. The Greek text disappears the moment you type a character.

5. Type the word **Typography**.

   A type layer appears on the Layers panel. The word or words you type will be set in whatever typeface, type size, and foreground color you have active when you click the Type tool. Make a note of this, because you want to be set up to succeed before you start typing. For example, if your foreground color were set to white, you wouldn't see the type against the white background. Or, if your type size were set to 150 points, it would be too large to fit on the canvas.

6. Click the **Move tool** on the toolbar.

   Once you click the Move tool, the name of the new layer becomes the same as the word or words you typed.

TIP Clicking the Move tool is a good way to escape from type mode when you're done typing.

7. On the Character panel, click the **Font family list arrow**, then choose **Times New Roman** (or a similar typeface).

   Even though the Move tool is selected, the typeface changes. In Photoshop, when a type layer is targeted on the Layers panel, changing the typeface on the Character panel changes the typeface of the type on the canvas. Also note that when the Move tool is selected, type formatting options are no longer available on the Options panel.

TIP If you don't see the Character panel, click Window on the menu bar, and then click Character.

8. Move the type so that it's centered on the canvas.

9. Click the **Font style list arrow**, click **Bold**, click the **Set the font size list arrow**, then click **60 pt**.

10. Show the Swatches panel, then click **any blue swatch**.

    Your Character panel should resemble Figure 2.

    You used the Type tool and the Character panel to set and format type.

Figure 2 Formatting the type

Typography

Track and kern type

1. Click the **Horizontal Type tool** T. on the toolbar, then double-click the word **Typography** on the canvas to select the whole word. On the Character panel, enter **−75** in the **Tracking text box**, then compare your results to Figure 3.

2. Change the **Tracking value** to **−25**.

3. Click the **cursor** between the letters **p** and **h**.

4. On the Character panel, enter **−25** in the **Kerning text box**.

5. Click the **cursor** between the letters **h** and **y**, then enter **−25** in the **Kerning text box**.

   The two letters move closer together.

6. Save your work.

You used the Character panel to track and kern type.

Rasterize and paint type

1. Verify that the **Typography layer** is targeted, click **Layer** on the menu bar, point to **Rasterize**, then click **Type**.

   When you rasterize a type layer, all layer content is converted from type to pixels. The type icon disappears from the layer on the Layers panel, and the layer is no longer editable as type.

2. Hide the Background layer.

   The many transparent pixels on the Typography layer are rendered as a gray and white checkerboard.

3. Press the **letter [D]** on your keypad to access the default foreground and background colors.

4. Press **[option] [delete] (Mac)** or **[Alt] [Delete] (Win)** to fill the layer with the black foreground color.

   All the pixels on the layer—transparent and nontransparent—are filled with black.

   AUTHOR'S **NOTE**   For the remainder of this chapter, use [option] [delete] **(Mac)** or [Alt] [Delete] (Win) when you are instructed to "fill."

Figure 3 Tracking type

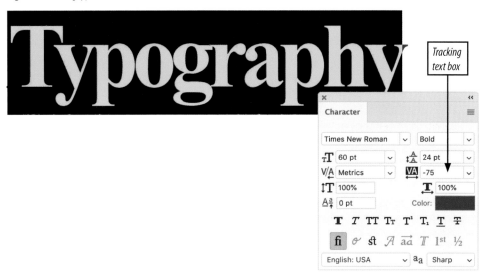

5. Undo the fill, then click the **Lock transparent pixels button** 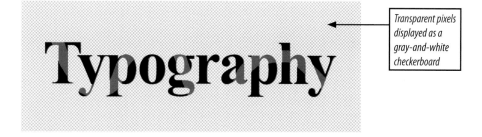 on the Layers panel, as shown in Figure 4.

A padlock icon appears at the right of the layer on the Layers panel. Locking the transparent pixels on the layer ensures that they will remain transparent when other pixels are being modified.

6. Fill the layer with the black foreground color.

The type outlines are filled with black, but the transparent pixels on the layer are not filled.

7. Click a **bright red swatch** on the Swatches panel, press **the letter [B]** on your keypad to access the Brush tool , set the **brush size** to **50 px**, set the **Hardness** to **100%**, then set the **Opacity** to **100%** on the Options panel.

8. Paint different areas of the type red, then compare your result to Figure 5.

Because transparent pixels are locked, only the black pixels are affected by the Brush tool.

9. Show the Background layer, save your work, then close Typography.

You rasterized type, converting it to pixels on a transparent layer. In order to fill only the rasterized type with the foreground color (and not the whole layer), you first had to click the Lock transparent pixels button for that layer on the Layers panel. You were then able to paint only in the type outlines with the Brush tool.

Figure 4 Locking transparent pixels on the Typography layer

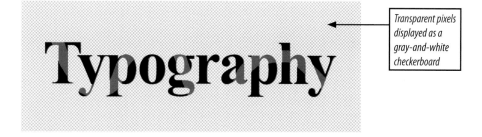

Lock transparent pixels button

Figure 5 Painting parts of rasterized type with transparent pixels locked

Transparent pixels displayed as a gray-and-white checkerboard

Typography

CREATE BEVEL & EMBOSS EFFECTS ON TYPE

▶ *What You'll Do*

In this lesson, you'll apply the Bevel & Emboss layer style to type.

Creating Bevel & Emboss Effects on Type

Prepare to fall in love with Bevel & Emboss, especially when you use it to design type. Bevel & Emboss is a layer style—a built-in effect that you can apply to layers—just like the Drop Shadow and Outer Glow layer styles you learned in Chapter 3. Bevel & Emboss is especially effective for type because you can use it to create classic effects like raised text and chiseled text. Rather than offering only a single option, the Bevel & Emboss dialog box features a number of different styles and techniques that you can use to create a variety of bevel and emboss effects. It's a great opportunity to experiment to see the different looks you can achieve.

Figure 6 shows an illustration of type that has been carved with a chisel into stone, type you'd expect to see carved into ancient Greek buildings or, in modern times, carved into everything from banks to gravestones. Note that, because of the carving, each letter has an angle with a highlight and a shadow. The effect that results is a letterform with a bright edge and a contrasting dark edge.

The Bevel & Emboss layer style in Photoshop mimics this real-world look. The Bevel & Emboss layer style dialog box offers you myriad options to create different bevel and emboss effects, including inner bevels, outer bevels, chisel effects, and emboss effects. These are

Figure 6 Type chiseled in stone

some of the most popular effects designers use when working with type. The results can be both sophisticated and eye-popping.

Using a Stroke Layer Style

A **stroke** is a basic artistic element that places an outline on an object or on type. For example, you can apply a black fill to type and then apply a colored stroke as an outline. In Photoshop, the best method for applying a stroke is to apply it as a layer style. This method allows you to apply the stroke and choose its color and its size. As with all layer styles, you can modify it or remove it at any time. Figure 7 shows a Stroke layer style applied to type with a Bevel & Emboss layer style.

Once you've applied the Stroke layer style, you can then apply a Bevel & Emboss layer style to the stroke. To do this, click the Style list arrow in the Layer Style dialog box and then choose Stroke Emboss. As a result, only the stroke will be beveled and embossed.

Applying Gloss Contours to Layer Styles

Gloss contours are a set of 12 preset adjustments that affect the brightness and contrast of a layer style to create dramatic lighting effects. They are available for many different kinds of layer styles, not just Bevel & Emboss. Gloss contours fall into the "click and choose" category of Photoshop features—you simply click through them to see what they do and how they affect the current artwork you're working with, then choose the one you like best. After a while, you'll get a sense of what to expect from each of them. However, the gloss contours will produce different results for different types of artwork.

Understanding the Use Global Light Option with Layer Styles

Many layer styles produce their effects by adjusting the brightness and contrast of the artwork they're applied to. The effect is often created with a "light source," meaning that the artwork appears to be brightened from a certain direction. For example, if you apply a Bevel & Emboss layer style to text and set the light source to light the artwork from the right, you will create interesting shadows on the left side of the artwork.

You will apply multiple layer styles to multiple pieces of artwork when working in Photoshop, especially when creating collages. The **Use Global Light** option exists as a simple solution to help you maintain a consistent light source for multiple layer styles. With the Use Global Light option checked, all your layer styles will create their individual effects using "light" from the same direction.

Sometimes consistency is desired, and if you want a consistent light source, the Use Global Light feature is a great option. But don't think that you *must* have a consistent light source. Sometimes different layer styles applied to the same artwork look even more interesting when they strike the artwork from different angles or light sources. You can turn off the Use Global Light option and manually set the angle and the altitude of the light source by dragging the Direction of light source icon in the Shading section of the Layer Style dialog box.

Be open to experiment when working with any feature associated with layer styles. Experimenting will lead to surprising yourself with a new look or a new effect, and that's always a great moment.

Figure 7 Stroke layer style

Creating a Double Emboss Effect

Layer styles are a lot of fun, and they produce interesting and useful effects. But at some point, you're bound to feel that you're not really *creating* artwork with a layer style, because the result is something anyone could achieve by dragging the sliders to the same settings you did. That is the truth about layer styles—they are canned effects, manufactured by Adobe Systems and packaged with the program. As a designer, it's your job to see past this built-in limitation of layer styles and figure out how to create *unique* artwork with these effects. The key to doing so is to work with *many* layer styles, combining them in inspired and insightful ways to produce artwork that is unexpected and brand-new.

One way you can achieve this is by duplicating artwork and applying different layer styles that work together to create one visual effect. A double emboss effect is achieved by creating two copies of the text. One copy has an outer bevel, and the other has an inner bevel. The result appears to be one block of type with a complex bevel and emboss effect.

Apply a Bevel & Emboss layer style to type

1. Open PS 4-2.psd, then save it as **Bevel & Emboss**.

2. Click the **HEADLINE layer** on the Layers panel, click **Layer** on the menu bar, point to **Layer Style**, then click **Bevel & Emboss**.

   The Layer Style dialog box opens with the default Bevel & Emboss settings selected.

3. Set the **Style** to **Emboss**, set the **Technique** to **Smooth**, then set the **Depth** to **100%**.

Figure 8 Bevel & Emboss effect

Figure 9 Different settings produce a different bevel and emboss effect

4. Set the **Size** to **24 px**, set the **Soften value** to **0 px**, then click **OK**.

   Your canvas should resemble Figure 8.

5. Double-click the **Bevel & Emboss layer style** on the Layers panel to open the Layer Style dialog box.

6. Set the **Style** to **Inner Bevel**, set the **Technique** to **Chisel Hard**, then set the **Depth** to **120%**.

7. Set the **Size** to **44**, set the **Soften value** to **0**, then click **OK**.

   As shown in Figure 9, the modified settings produce an entirely different bevel and emboss effect.

8. Save your work.

You applied a Bevel & Emboss layer style to type outlines.

Apply a gloss contour to a layer style

1. Double-click the **Bevel & Emboss layer style** on the Layers panel to open the Layer Style dialog box.

2. Move the **Layer Style dialog box** out of the way so you can see at least one of the letters on your canvas.

3. Click the **Gloss Contour list arrow**, then position the mouse pointer over the **third square in the second row**.

   The gloss contour is identified in Figure 10. If you position the mouse pointer over this gloss contour, a tool tip appears, revealing the name of the gloss contour, which is Ring - Double.

4. Click **Ring - Double**, then move the dialog box out of the way to see the effect on the artwork.

5. Click **each of the remaining 11 gloss contours** to see its effect on the type artwork.

6. Click the **second gloss contour**, named **Cone**, on the top row.

7. Click the **Anti-aliased check box** beside the Gloss Contour list arrow, then click **OK**.

   Your artwork should resemble Figure 11. You can use the Undo/Redo commands to see a before and after view of the change.

8. Save your work.

You applied a Gloss Contour preset in the Layer Style dialog box.

Figure 10   The Ring - Double gloss contour

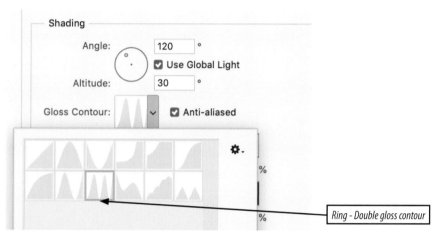

Ring - Double gloss contour

Figure 11   The Cone gloss contour applied to the type outlines

Apply an Outer Bevel layer style to create a double emboss effect

1. Verify that the **Headline layer** is targeted, then press **[command] [J] (Mac)** or **[Ctrl] [J] (Win)** to duplicate the layer.

2. Rename the new layer **Inner Bevel**, then **hide** it.

   In this exercise, we are hiding the Inner Bevel layer style so you can see the Outer Bevel layer style being built. However, if you were designing this type in a real-world project, you would probably want to show the Inner Bevel layer style to see the final effect of both layer styles together as you are designing.

3. Target the **Headline layer**, then rename it **Outer Bevel**.

4. Drag the **Layer effects button** *fx* on the Outer Bevel layer to the **Delete layer button** 🗑 on the Layers panel.

   Your Layers panel should resemble Figure 12.

5. Double-click the **Outer Bevel layer** to open the Layer Style dialog box, then click the words **Bevel & Emboss** in the left column.

6. Set the **Style** to **Outer Bevel**, set the **Technique** to **Chisel Hard**, then set the **Depth** to **100%**.

7. Set the **Size** to **13**, then set the **Soften value** to **0**.

8. Uncheck the **Use Global Light option**.

   We want to change the lighting on this layer style. However, we do not want to change the lighting on the Inner Bevel layer style, so we must uncheck Use Global Light.

9. Set the **Angle** to **139**, then set the **Altitude** to **32**.

10. Click the **Cove - Deep gloss contour**.

    Your Layer Style dialog box should resemble Figure 13.

Figure 12 Two layers, one hidden

Figure 13 Layer Style settings

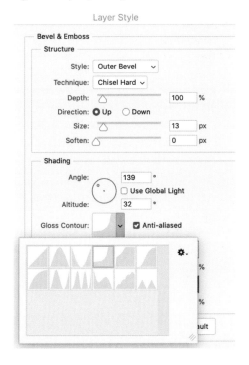

11. Click **OK**, then compare your artwork to Figure 14.

12. Show the **Inner Bevel layer**, then compare your artwork to Figure 15.

The two layer styles work together to create one single visual effect. If you hide and show the Outer Bevel layer, you can see the top layer with and without the effect.

13. Save your work, then close Bevel & Emboss.

You duplicated the type layer, then applied an Outer Bevel layer style to the copy. The result was two layer styles working together to produce a more complex and dimensional effect.

Figure 14 The Outer Bevel effect on its own

Figure 15 The Outer Bevel and Inner Bevel effects combined

CREATE AND APPLY GRADIENTS

What You'll Do

In this lesson, you'll use the Gradient tool and the Gradient Editor dialog box to create and apply gradients to the canvas and to type.

Applying a Gradient

A **gradient** is a blend of two or more colors. Often, a gradient between two colors creates a third distinct color. For example, any gradient between red and yellow will produce orange somewhere in between.

The Gradient tool is the tool that you use to apply gradients. It determines the placement and the length of the gradient. The tool works by clicking, dragging, and releasing. Where you click determines where the gradient begins, where you drag determines the length of the gradient, and where you release determines where the gradient ends.

When you click the Gradient tool on the toolbar, the Options panel changes to show the Gradient Picker box and list arrow, identified in Figure 16. Click the list arrow beside the box, which shows you a menu that contains dozens upon dozens of preset gradients that come with the program. These presets are housed in different folders. Click the caret beside the folder to see the preset gradients. This menu is also the location that automatically stores gradients you create on your own in the Gradient Editor dialog box.

In addition, when you click the Gradient tool, the Options panel shows options that allow you to determine the *type* of gradient you are applying. A **linear** gradient blends from one color to another in a straight, linear fashion. A **radial** gradient blend radiates outward from one color to another, like a series of concentric circles.

Creating a New Gradient

In addition to the preset gradients that come with Photoshop, you can create your own customized gradients in the Gradient Editor dialog box, shown in Figure 17. The colors that make up a gradient are called **color stops**. In the Gradient Editor dialog box, you create a customized gradient on the **gradient ramp**. You can create gradients between two color stops or between multiple color stops. You add color stops simply by clicking the gradient ramp, and you remove them by dragging them down and off the gradient ramp. You determine the length of the gradient between color stops by moving color stops closer to or farther away from each other. The diamond-shaped **color midpoint slider** between color stops determines where the gradient is a 50–50 mix between color stops. The **Location** text box below the gradient ramp identifies a selected color stop's location, from left to right, on the gradient ramp.

Figure 16 Gradient picker box and list arrow

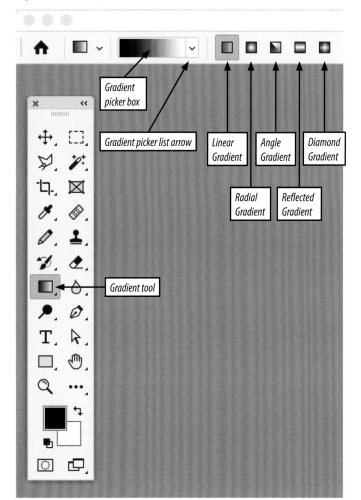

Gradient picker box

Gradient picker list arrow

Linear Gradient

Angle Gradient

Diamond Gradient

Radial Gradient

Reflected Gradient

Gradient tool

Figure 17 Gradient Editor dialog box

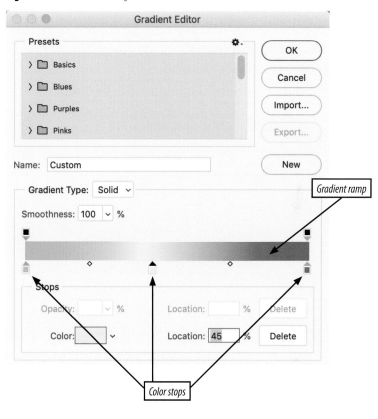

Gradient ramp

Color stops

Apply a gradient

1. Open PS 4-3.psd, then save it as **Making the Gradient**.
2. Click the **Gradient tool** 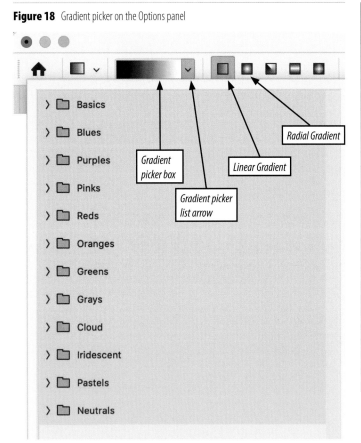 on the toolbar.
3. Click the **Gradient picker list arrow**, identified in Figure 18.

As shown in the figure, clicking the list arrow shows a list of folders, all of which contain preset gradients that come with Photoshop.

4. Expand the **Reds folder**, then click the **first gradient** in that folder.

The Options panel updates to show the gradient you clicked.

5. Click the **Linear Gradient button** on the Options panel.

TIP See Table 4-1, which describes the five types of gradients available on the Options panel.

Figure 18 Gradient picker on the Options panel

Gradient picker box
Gradient picker list arrow
Linear Gradient
Radial Gradient

> Basics
> Blues
> Purples
> Pinks
> Reds
> Oranges
> Greens
> Grays
> Cloud
> Iridescent
> Pastels
> Neutrals

TABLE 4-1: FIVE TYPES OF GRADIENTS		
Type of Gradient	**Button Icon**	**Description**
Linear		Blends from the start color to the end color in a straight line.
Radial		Blends from the start color to the end color in a circular pattern, with the start color in the center.
Angle		Blends in clockwise sweep from the start color to the end color. Think of an angle gradient as the big hand and the little hand being in the same place on a clock, like at midnight. The gradient is created from the foreground color to the background color from the big hand to the little hand in a clockwise direction.
Reflected		Blends using symmetric linear gradients on either side of the starting point. Think of a reflected gradient as a mirror. Click and drag from your foreground to background color, and it creates a linear gradient *plus* a mirror image of that gradient at the point where you first clicked. Practically speaking, this type of gradient would be useful for making something that looks like a lead pipe or some other kind of metal tube.
Diamond		Blends from the start color outward in a diamond pattern. The end color defines one corner of the diamond. The result appears three-dimensional and could be especially useful for creating flares or web graphics.

6. Position the mouse pointer at the **left edge** of the canvas, click and drag to the **right edge** of the canvas, then release the mouse button.

A linear gradient is created from the left edge of the canvas to the right edge of the canvas. The gradient blends from gray to rose to dark purple.

7. Click and drag from the **top** of the canvas to the **bottom** of the canvas.

The gradient is re-created from top to bottom.

8. Click and drag from the **upper-left** to the **lower-right corner** of the canvas.

The gradient is re-created diagonally from the upper-left to the lower-right corner of the canvas.

9. Click near the **center** of the canvas and drag from **left to right** for approximately one inch, then compare your result to Figure 19.

The length of the entire gradient is approximately one inch long. Any pixels outside of the one inch range are filled with solid start and end colors, which in this case are gray and dark purple.

10. Click the **Radial Gradient button**  on the Options panel.

11. Position your pointer at the **center** of the canvas, click and drag approximately one inch to the right, then compare your result to Figure 20.

The gradient starts where you click and ends where you release. With a radial gradient, however, the gradient "radiates" out from a center point, like concentric circles, with the start color as the center color.

12. Save your work.

You used the Gradient tool and a preset gradient to create a gradient on the canvas.

Figure 19 Short linear gradient

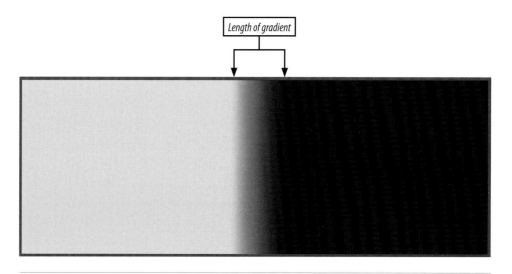

Figure 20 Radial gradient with the start color at the center by default

Create a new gradient

1. Click the **Gradient picker box** 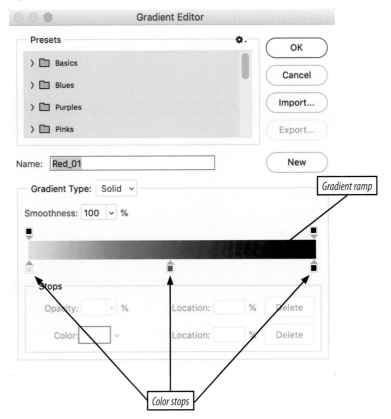 on the Options panel.

   The Gradient Editor dialog box opens, shown in Figure 21. The Gray/Rose/Dark Purple gradient appears in the gradient ramp in the dialog box. The color stops on the gradient ramp from left to right represent gray, rose, and dark blue. Note that the name given to the preset gradient is Red_01.

2. Click the **first (leftmost) color stop**.

   The name of the gradient in the Name text box changes to "Custom" once you click the color stop.

3. Click the **Color box** below the gradient ramp to open the Color Picker.

4. Type **29** in the **R text box**, type **5** in the **G text box**, type **170** in the **B text box**, then click **OK**.

   The color stop on the gradient ramp changes to a royal blue.

5. Click the **last color stop**, then change its color to the same royal blue, 29R/5G/170B.

6. Click **right below the gradient ramp** between the first and second color stops.

   A new color stop is added to the gradient ramp where you clicked.

Figure 21 Gradient Editor dialog box

7. Drag the **new color stop** until the Location text box reads **25%**.

The Location text box indicates where a color stop is positioned on the gradient ramp, from left to right. For example, at 25%, the new color stop is exactly between the first stop at 0% and the middle stop at 50%.

8. Change the color of the new color stop to **246R/142G/86B**.

9. Drag the **Color Midpoint diamond slider** between the first and second color stop to 75%, as shown in Figure 22.

The blue and orange color stops are blended equally three-quarters of the way between the two stops.

10. Type **Blue, Orange, Rose, Blue** in the Name text box, then click the **New button.**

The new gradient is added to the group of presets in the Gradient Editor.

11. Click **OK**.

TIP The new gradient is also added to the bottom of the list of gradient preset folders on the Options panel.

12. Save your work, then close Making the Gradient.

You used the Gradient Editor dialog box to modify and save a new gradient.

Figure 22 Changing the midpoint between two color stops

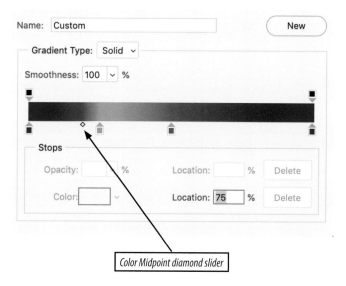

Color Midpoint diamond slider

CLIP A GRADIENT AND AN IMAGE INTO TYPE

Clipping a Layer with a Gradient Fill into Type

Clipping refers to using artwork on one layer to mask the artwork on a layer (or multiple layers) above it. The simplest example of clipping and a clipping mask would be of a type layer with a layer above it filled with a gradient. If you target the gradient layer and then create a clipping mask, the gradient will be clipped into the type layer beneath it and will be visible only within the type. The transparent areas of

the type layer will mask the gradient artwork. Figure 23 shows a radial gradient clipped into type and visible only in the type.

The layer functioning as the clipping mask—the type layer in the preceding example—is referred to as the **base layer**. For artwork to be clipped, it must be immediately above the base layer. Base layers can have multiple layers clipped into them, but all those layers must be immediately above the base layer on the Layers panel.

Figure 23 Radial gradient clipped into type

Clipping Layers on the Layers Panel

Let's say you have two layers on the Layers panel—Layer A and Layer B—and you want to clip Layer B into Layer A. Select Layer B, then click the Create Clipping Mask command on the Layers panel menu.

A faster way to clip a layer is to use a quick and easy keyboard technique. Using the previous example, press and hold [option] (Mac) or [Alt] (Win), then float your cursor over the line between the two layers on the Layers panel. A square icon with a small black arrow will appear. Click the small black arrow on the line that separates the two layers, and the top layer will be clipped into the layer beneath it.

Clipping Imagery into Type

Clipping imagery into type works the same way as clipping a gradient into type, except that you are clipping a picture instead of a gradient fill. Figure 24 shows a landscape image clipped into type.

Another good example of clipping a picture into type would be an old-fashioned postcard with the word *FLORIDA* and different scenes of Floridian attractions inside the letters. Clipping an image into type is a classic type of design that is visually interesting and communicates an idea with strength and clarity. Remember, when you clip an image into text that has layer styles applied to it, the image takes on the effects of the layer style.

Applying a Gradient Directly to Live Type

You're already familiar with "filling" type with color. You can also apply a gradient to live type using the Gradients panel. The Gradients panel houses all the gradients that come preset with Photoshop and all the custom gradients you create in the Gradient Editor dialog box. When you target a live type layer and click a gradient on the Gradients panel, the gradient is applied directly to the live type as a Gradient Overlay layer style. When you apply a gradient with this method, you can't use the Gradient tool to control how the gradient fills the live type. Instead, use the Gradient Overlay layer style dialog box to control how the gradient is applied.

Clip a layer with a gradient fill into type

1. Open PS 4-4.psd, then save it as **Clipped Gradient**.

2. On the **TYPE layer**, click the **eye button** beside the word Effects to hide the layer styles that have been applied.

3. Create a new layer above the TYPE layer, then name the new layer **Gradient**.

4. Click the **Gradient tool** , then click the **Gradient picker box** on the Options panel.

Continued on next page

Figure 24 Landscape image clipped into type

5. Click the **Blue, Orange, Rose, Blue gradient** at the bottom of the list of presets in the Gradient Editor dialog box, then click **OK**.

This is the gradient you created in the previous set of steps.

6. Click the **Radial Gradient button** ⬛ on the Options panel.

7. Verify that the **Gradient layer** is targeted on the Layers panel, position the mouse pointer at the top edge of the canvas, then click and drag the **Gradient tool** from the top edge to the bottom edge of the canvas.

Your canvas should resemble Figure 25.

8. Click the **Layers panel menu button** ≡ , then click **Create Clipping Mask**.

As shown in Figure 26, the Gradient layer is clipped into the TYPE layer, indicated by the bent arrow on the Gradient layer. The gradient artwork is visible only where there is artwork on the TYPE layer. The gradient artwork is not visible—it is masked—where there are transparent pixels on the TYPE layer.

9. Click the **Move tool** ⊕ , then drag the **gradient artwork** around the canvas to show different areas of the clipped artwork.

The gradient artwork moves but continues to be masked by the TYPE layer.

Figure 25 Radial gradient

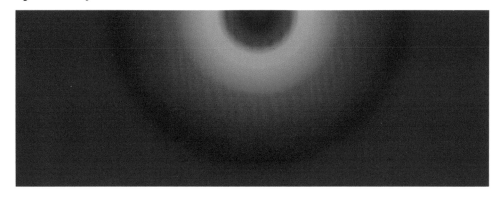

Figure 26 Clipping the gradient

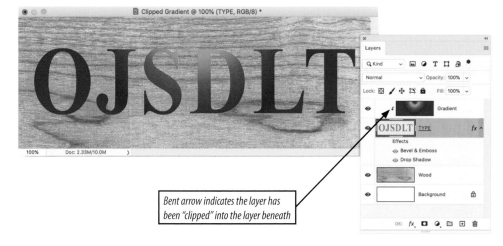

Bent arrow indicates the layer has been "clipped" into the layer beneath

10. Undo your last step.

11. Make the **Effects layer** visible on the Inner Bevel layer, then compare your canvas to Figure 27.

The gradient artwork is beveled and embossed. When a layer style is applied to a layer, any artwork that is clipped into the layer will take on the appearance of the layer style. The colors of the gradient have lightened because they are taking on the highlight and shadow colors specified in the Bevel & Emboss layer style.

12. Save your work.

You used a radial gradient on a layer then used the Create Clipping Mask command to clip the gradient layer into the type layer beneath it, noting that the gradient took on the layer effects from the type layer when clipped.

Clip an image into type

1. Hide the effects on the **TYPE layer**.

2. Drag the **Wood layer** to the top of the Layers panel.

3. On the Layers panel, press and hold **[option] (Mac)** or **[Alt] (Win)**, then float your mouse pointer over the line between the **Gradient layer** and the **Wood layer**.

The clip icon ⬚ will appear. The clip icon is a small white square with a bent black arrow ⬚ .

Figure 27 Making the styles on the base layer visible

Figure 28 Layer styles on the base layer affect the clipped image

4. Click the **line between the layers** with the clip icon ⬚ .

The wood artwork is clipped into the TYPE artwork. It's important to understand that the Wood layer is being clipped into the TYPE layer, not into the Gradient layer. The gradient artwork has no visual impact on the final artwork because the gradient artwork is beneath the wood artwork.

5. Show the effects on the **TYPE layer**, then compare your canvas to Figure 28.

6. Save your work, then close Clipped Gradient.

You used a keyboard command to clip an image layer into the type layer beneath it, noting that the image took on the layer effects from the type layer when clipped.

Apply a gradient directly to live type

1. Open PS 4-5.psd, then save it as **Overlay Gradient**.

2. On the Layers panel, click the **Typography layer** to target it.

3. Open the **Gradients panel**.

   The Gradients panel houses all the gradients that come preset with Photoshop and all the customized gradients you create in the Gradient Editor dialog box. A thumbnail for the Blue, Orange, Rose, Blue gradient you created is at the bottom of the Gradients panel.

4. Click the **Blue, Orange, Rose, Blue gradient thumbnail** on the Gradients panel.

   The gradient is applied to the type and a layer style named Gradient Overlay appears beneath the layer. When you target a live type layer and click a gradient swatch on the Gradient panel, the gradient is applied with this method. The gradient cannot be manipulated with the Gradient tool. Instead, you manipulate the gradient as you would any other layer style.

5. Double-click the **Gradient Overlay layer style** to open it.

   The Layer Style dialog box opens with the Gradient Overlay settings, as shown in Figure 29.

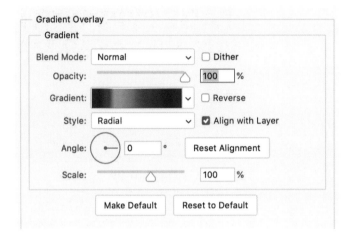

Figure 29 Gradient Overlay layer style settings

6. In the Layer Style dialog box, set the **Angle** to **0**.

   The gradient now fills the type from left to right.

7. Change the **Style** to **Radial**, then click **OK**.

8. Click the **Gradient tool** , position your pointer over the **type** on the canvas, then note that the tool won't work.

   You cannot use the Gradient tool on a gradient applied as a Gradient Overlay layer style. Because using the Gradient tool is a faster and more direct method for manipulating a gradient, many designers prefer to clip a layer with a gradient fill into type, as you did in the first exercise in this lesson. With that method, you can use the Gradient tool to modify the gradient rather than using slider controls.

9. Save your work, then close Overlay Gradient.

You applied a gradient directly to type and used the Gradient Overlay layer style to modify the gradient settings.

FADE TYPE WITH A GRADIENT AND A LAYER MASK

Using a Gradient in a Layer Mask to Fade Artwork

Gradients play an important visual and artistic role when they function as a color element in artwork. Gradients play an important *practical* role when used in layer masks. The fundamental rule of a layer mask is that white areas of the mask reveal 100% of the artwork on the layer, and black areas of the mask hide or mask 100% of the related artwork on the layer. Therefore, it follows logically that gradients in a layer mask that blend from white to black affect the artwork as a blend from "revealed" to "masked." Thus, a gradient in a layer mask becomes a powerful tool for gradually fading artwork on the layer.

Use a layer mask to fade type

1. Open PS 4-6.psd, then save it as **Fade Type**.

2. Target the **FADE OUT layer**, then click the **Add layer mask button** on the Layers panel.

   An all-white layer mask is added to the layer.

3. Press the **letter [D]** on your keypad to set default colors to a white foreground color and a black background color.

4. Click the **Gradient tool** on the toolbar, then click the **Linear Gradient button** on the Options panel.

5. Click the **Gradient picker list arrow** on the Options panel, expand the Basics folder, then click the **Foreground to Background thumbnail**.

   We want to make a white-to-black gradient in the mask, so a white-to-black gradient must be active.

   Continued on next page

6. Click and drag from the **top edge** of the type down to the **bottom edge** of the type, then compare your result to Figure 30.

   Because the layer mask was targeted, you applied the gradient to the layer mask. The layer mask graduates from white to black from the top to the bottom of the type. Thus, the type is fully visible at its top edge, completely invisible at its bottom edge, and gradually fades from top to bottom.

7. Click and drag from the **top edge** of the type down to the **bottom edge** of the canvas, then compare your result to Figure 31.

   The bottom edge of the text is no longer invisible.

8. Press and hold **[option] (Mac)** or **[Alt] (Win)**, then click the **layer mask** to view the layer mask.

   The area of the mask that corresponds to the bottom of the type is dark gray, not black. Thus, the type does not fully disappear at its bottom edge because the gradient in the mask becomes fully black only at the bottom of the canvas.

9. Press and hold **[option] (Mac)** or **[Alt] (Win)**, then click the **layer thumbnail** to view the layer artwork.

10. Save your work, then close Fade Type.

You used a linear gradient in a layer mask to fade type artwork from visible to transparent.

Figure 30 Fading the type with a gradient in a layer mask

Figure 31 Changing the way the type fades

CLIP MULTIPLE IMAGES INTO TYPE

▶ *What You'll Do*

In this lesson, you'll clip multiple images into one type layer, using transformations and layer masks to achieve the final look.

Clipping Multiple Images into Type

Clipping images into typography has a long and much-beloved history in graphic arts. Figure 32 shows an old postcard with images of Paris clipped into the word. The appeal of the effect never gets old, never gets dated, and never gets tired. Clipping multiple images into type inevitably involves transforming the images to achieve the best fit between the images and the type itself. It also involves using layer masks to isolate the images in the targeted letter outlines. Clipping multiple images into type will challenge you on many levels and offers the potential for producing charming and eye-popping results.

Figure 32 Old postcard with images clipped into type

Clip images into type

1. Open PS 4-7.psd, then save it as **Japan Postcard**.

2. Show the **Mt. Fuji layer**, then show the **Blue push-back layer**.

3. Target the **Blue push-back layer**, then reduce its **Opacity** to **40%**.

4. Click **File** on the menu bar, click **Open**, navigate to where you store your data files, open the folder named **Japan Images**, then open the file named **Waterfall.psd**.

5. Select all, copy, then close Waterfall.psd.

6. In the **Japan Postcard file**, target the **JAPAN layer**, then paste the **waterfall artwork**.

7. Name the new layer **Waterfall**, then hide it.

8. Using the same method, open, copy, and paste the following four files: **Pagoda.psd**, **Arch.psd**, **Blossom.psd**, and **Bamboo.psd**.

9. When you're done pasting and naming the new layers, hide them all.

   Your Layers panel should resemble Figure 33, with the layers named the same and in the same order.

Figure 33 All five images pasted into the document

Figure 34 Positioning the clipped waterfall image

10. Show the **Waterfall layer**, then clip it into the **JAPAN layer**.

TIP Float your mouse pointer over the line between the Waterfall layer and the JAPAN layer, then click when you see the clip icon ⌐□ . Use the **Move tool** ⊕, to position the waterfall into the J of Japan.

11. **Scale** the **waterfall artwork** so that it's positioned in the J in a way you find appealing.

    Figure 34 shows one possibility.

TIP If you need a refresher on scaling and transforming, see Chapter 3.

Figure 35 Positioning the clipped pagoda image

Figure 36 Masking unwanted parts of the pagoda image

12. Show the **Pagoda layer**, clip it, then scale it and position it as shown in Figure 35.

    The pagoda artwork is extending into the letter J and covering the waterfall artwork.

13. Add a **layer mask** to the **Pagoda layer**.

14. Click the **Brush tool** [icon], then use a hard-edged brush to mask out the pagoda artwork where it overlaps the waterfall artwork.

    Your canvas and your Layers panel should resemble Figure 36.

Continued on next page

Figure 37 Clipping and positioning all five images

TIP You have a faster alternative than using the brush. You can use the Rectangular Marquee tool ⬚ to drag a rectangular selection around the J and then fill the selection with black. The black fill will fill the selection in the mask because the mask is targeted. The objective is to get black into the layer mask, you can use whatever means you like to achieve that objective.

15. Using the same methods and skills, clip, transform, and mask the remaining images so that your canvas and Layers panel resemble Figure 37.

16. Show all the layer styles on the JAPAN layer, then compare your artwork to Figure 38.

17. Hide and show the Blue push-back layer to see the role it plays in the finished artwork.

When you hide the layer, the colors in the background image are so deep and vivid that they *compete* with the images inside the letters. As a designer, you must resolve this competition so there is one clear focal point. In this image, the first thing the viewer should see is the word JAPAN in vivid color. Therefore, we use the Blue push-back layer to dull the background and make it more uniform in color.

18. Save your work, then close Japan Postcard.

You pasted five images into the working file, clipped them, transformed them, and positioned them in a type layer.

Shutterstock photo credits: Mt. Fuji: Guitar photographer; Waterfall: PixHound; Pagoda & Bamboo: Sean Pavone; Cherry blossoms: picture cells

Figure 38 The final artwork

DESIGN NOTE

Don't overlook the critical role the layer styles play in this artwork. Without them, the word JAPAN is hardly legible against the background image. The layer styles, especially the black stroke and the bright orange outer glow, define the letter outlines from the background and make the word readable. The drop shadow behind the layers plays a subtle role, but also contributes to making the letters stand out from the background.

AUTHOR'S NOTE I am pleased to share this stunning piece of artwork created by my student, Kishan Shah, in our Digital Design class at Sierra Canyon High School in Chatsworth, CA. At the time, Kishan was a freshman who signed up for the course and likely never thought he'd be published. We were working on clipping images into type as I was writing this chapter, and when he showed me this artwork, I knew it had to be part of this book. This story says a lot about how rapidly young people can learn and how far they can go when empowered by learning a great program like Photoshop. Thank you, Kishan.

Set type

1. Open PS 4-8.psd, then save it as **Skills Type**.
2. Click the Horizontal Type tool, then click on the left side of the canvas.
3. Type the words **Type It**.
4. Click the Move tool.
5. On the Character panel, click the Fonts list arrow, then choose Impact (or a similar typeface).
6. Set the font size to 96 pt by typing **96** in the Set the font size text box.
7. Center the type on the page, then click a red swatch on the Swatches panel.
8. Save your work.

Lock transparent pixels

1. Verify that the Type It layer is targeted, click Layer on the menu bar, point to Rasterize, then click Type.
2. Hide the Background layer.
3. Press the letter [D] on your keypad to access the default foreground and background colors.
4. Press [option] [delete] (Mac) or [Alt] [Delete] (Win) to fill with the black foreground color.
   The entire layer fills with black.
5. Undo the fill, then click the Lock transparent pixels button on the Layers panel.
6. Fill the layer with the black foreground color.
   Only the type outlines are filled with black.
7. Click a bright red swatch on the Swatches panel, click the Brush tool, set the Size to 50 px, then set the Hardness to 100%.

8. Paint different areas of the type.
9. Show the Background layer, save your work, then close Skills Type.

Create bevel and emboss effects on type

1. Open PS 4-9.psd, save it as **Bevel Skills Type**, then target the HEADLINE layer on the Layers panel.
2. Double-click the HEADLINE layer to open the Layer Style dialog box, then click the words Bevel & Emboss in the left column.
3. Set the Style to Emboss, set the Technique to Smooth, then set the Depth to 100%.
4. Set the Size to 24, set the Soften value to 0, then click OK.
5. Double-click the Bevel & Emboss layer style on the Layers panel to reopen the dialog box.
6. Set the Style to Inner Bevel, set the Technique to Chisel Hard, then set the Depth to 100%.
7. Set the Size to 48, set the Soften value to 0, then click OK.
8. Save your work.

Apply gloss contours to layer styles

1. Double-click the Bevel & Emboss layer style on the Layers panel to open the dialog box.
2. Click the gloss contour named Cone.
3. Click the Anti-aliased check box, then click OK.
4. Save your work.

Create a double emboss effect

1. Duplicate the HEADLINE layer, rename the new layer **Inner Bevel**, then hide it.
2. Target the HEADLINE layer, then rename it **Outer Bevel**.
3. Drag the Layer effects icon fx on the Outer Bevel layer to the Delete layer button on the Layers panel.

4. Click Layer on the menu bar, point to Layer Style, then click Bevel & Emboss.
5. Set the Style to Outer Bevel, set the Technique to Chisel Hard, then set the Depth to 100%.
6. Set the Size to 12, then set the Soften value to 0.
7. Apply the Ring - Double gloss contour, then activate the Anti-aliased check box.
8. Click OK, then show the Inner Bevel layer.
9. Save your work, then close Bevel Skills Type.

Apply a gradient

1. Open PS 4-10.psd, then save it as **Gradient Skills**.
2. Click the Gradient tool on the toolbar.
3. Click the Gradient picker list arrow.
4. Expand the Oranges folder, then click the 12th gradient in that folder, named Orange_12.
5. Click the Linear Gradient button on the Options panel.
6. Position the mouse pointer at the left edge of the canvas, click and drag to the right edge of the canvas, then release the mouse button.
7. Click and drag from the top of the canvas to the bottom of the canvas.
   The gradient is recreated from top to bottom.
8. Click and drag from the upper-left to the lower-right corner of the canvas.
   The gradient is recreated diagonally from the upper-left to the lower-right corner of the canvas.
9. Click near the center of the canvas and drag from left to right for approximately one inch.
   The length of the entire gradient is approximately one inch long. Any pixels outside of the one inch range are filled with solid start and end colors, which in this case are yellow and purple.
10. Click the Radial Gradient button on the Options panel.

11. Position your pointer at the center of the canvas, then click and drag approximately two inches to the right. The gradient starts where you click and ends where you release. With a radial gradient, however, the gradient "radiates" out from a center point with the start color as the center color.
12. Save your work.

Create a new gradient

1. Click the Gradient picker box on the Options panel to open the Gradient Editor dialog box.
2. Click the first (leftmost) color stop, then click the Color box below the gradient ramp to open the Color Picker.
3. Type **255** in the R text box, type **208** in the G text box, type **0** in the B text box, then click OK.
4. Click the last color stop, then change its color to 29R/5G/170B.
5. Click just below the gradient ramp roughly in the middle of the two color stops.
   A new color stop is added to the gradient ramp where you clicked.
6. Drag the new color stop until the Location text box reads 65%.
7. Change the color of the new color stop to 0R/211G/194B.
8. Drag the Color Midpoint diamond slider between the second and third color stop to 20%.
9. Type **Yellow, Cyan, Blue** in the Name text box, then click the New button.
10. Click OK.
    The new gradient is added to the bottom of the Gradient Editor dialog box.
11. Save your work, then close Gradient Skills.

Figure 39 Clipping the granite image into type

Clip a layer with a gradient fill into type

1. Open PS 4-11.psd, then save it as **Clipping Skills**.
2. Hide the effects on the TYPE OUTLINES layer.
3. Create a new layer above the TYPE OUTLINES layer, then name the new layer **Gradient**.
4. Click the Gradient tool.
5. Click Gradient picker list arrow, then click the Yellow, Cyan, Blue gradient thumbnail at the bottom of the menu.
6. Click the Linear Gradient button on the Options panel.
7. Verify that the Gradient layer is targeted on the Layers panel.
8. Position the mouse pointer at the top edge of the letters, then create a gradient from the top to the bottom of the letters.
9. Click the Layers panel menu button, then click Create Clipping Mask.
10. Make the effects visible on the TYPE OUTLINES layer, then save your work.

Clip imagery into type

1. Hide the effects on the TYPE OUTLINES layer.
2. Move the Granite layer to the top of the Layers panel.
3. Press and hold [option] (Mac) or [Alt] (Win), then click the line between the Granite layer and the TYPE OUTLINES layer to clip the Granite layer. Show the

effects on the TYPE OUTLINES layer, then compare your result to Figure 39.
4. Save your work, then close Clipping Skills.

Fade type

1. Open PS 4-12.psd, then save it as **Fade Skills**.
2. Target the FADE AWAY layer, then click the Add layer mask button on the Layers panel.
3. Set the foreground color to white and the background color to black.
4. Click the Gradient tool on the toolbar, then click the Linear Gradient button on the Options panel.
5. Click the Gradient picker list arrow on the Options panel, expand the Basics folder, then click the Foreground to Background thumbnail.
   We want to make a white-to-black gradient in the mask, so a white-to-black gradient must be active.
6. Click and drag the Gradient tool from the left edge of the letter F to the right edge of the letter Y.
7. Click and drag the Gradient tool from the middle of the letter D to the right edge of the canvas.
8. Press and hold [option] (Mac) or [Alt] (Win), then click the layer mask to view the layer mask.
9. Press and hold [option] (Mac) or [Alt] (Win), then click the layer thumbnail to view the layer artwork.
10. Save your work, then close Fade Skills.

This exercise focuses on creating a simple type-based post card for an event. It's a terrific example of how a gradient can so effectively make a basic layout visually interesting.

1. Open PS 4-13.psd, then save it as **Sunset Gradient**.
2. Fill the Background layer with black, then lock transparent pixels on both type layers.
3. Fill the type on the two type layers with white.
4. Click the Gradient picker box on the Options panel to open the Gradient Editor dialog box.
5. In the Presets section, expand the Basics folder, then click the first Gradient thumbnail, which is named "Foreground to Background."

TIP Position the mouse pointer over a gradient and wait for a moment for its name to appear.

6. Change the color of the left color stop to 255R/228G/0B.
7. Verify that the color of the right color stop is 0R/0G/0B.
8. Add a third color stop between the first and second color stops.
9. Change the color of the new color stop to 255R/0G/0B, then change its location to 75%.
10. Add a new color stop between the first color stop and the new color stop.
11. Change the color of the new color stop to 255R/132G/0B, and change its location to 50%.

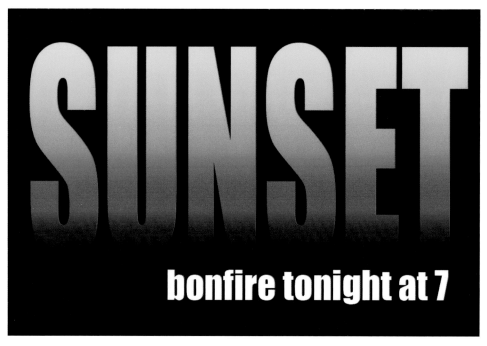

Figure 40 Gradient clipped into type

12. Name the new gradient **Sunset Gradient**, click New, then click OK.
13. Create a new layer above the SUNSET layer, then name the new layer **Sunset Gradient**.
14. Click the Gradient tool on the toolbar, then verify that the Linear Gradient button is selected on the Options panel.
15. Position your cursor at the top edge of the SUNSET type, then create a linear gradient from the top of the SUNSET type to the bottom of the SUNSET type.
16. Click the Layers panel menu button, then click Create Clipping Mask.
17. Compare your canvas to Figure 40.
18. Save your work, then close Sunset Gradient.

Project Builder 2 is designed specifically to get you to remember the Stroke Emboss effect. So many designers aren't even aware of it, so that's even more reason to get it into your skill set. Once you've completed the steps, take a moment to appreciate the sophisticated and stunning impact it has on the artwork.

1. Open PS 4-14.psd, then save it as **Sunset Stroke Emboss**.
2. Target the SUNSET layer on the Layers panel.
3. Click Layer on the menu bar, point to Layer Style, then click Stroke.
4. Click the Color box, type **128** in the R, G, and B text boxes, then click OK.
5. Set the Size to 10, then set the Position to Center.
6. In the Styles column at the left of the dialog box, click the words Bevel & Emboss.
7. Set the Style to Stroke Emboss, set the Technique to Chisel Hard, then set the Depth to 110%.
8. Set the Size to 2, then set the Soften value to 0.
9. Click the Gloss Contour list arrow, click the Ring - Double gloss contour, then verify that the Anti-aliased check box is checked.
10. Click OK, then compare your artwork to Figure 41.
11. Save your work, then close Sunset Stroke Emboss.

Figure 41 Bevel & Emboss layer style applied to the stroke

The entire focus of this Project Builder is on clipping. Clipping is where many of the "magic tricks" in Photoshop happen. In this case, your result will have what appears to be the same image used twice, but look closer and you'll see a neat visual trick being played.

1. Open PS 4-15.psd, then save it as **Sunset Image Clipping**.
2. Verify that only the Background and Original Image layers are showing on the Layers panel.
3. Show, then hide the Sunset layer, comparing the artwork to the Original Image artwork.
   The Sunset artwork is a duplicate of the Original Image artwork. It has been colorized orange, and sunset artwork has been added at the center.
4. Show all layers, then drag the Sunset layer above the HEADLINE layer.
5. Clip the Sunset layer into the HEADLINE layer.
6. Add a layer mask to the Sunset layer.
7. Set the foreground and background colors to white and black, respectively.
8. Click the Gradient tool, then position it at the horizon line in the image.
9. Make a white-to-black gradient in the layer mask from the horizon line to bottom edge of the artwork.

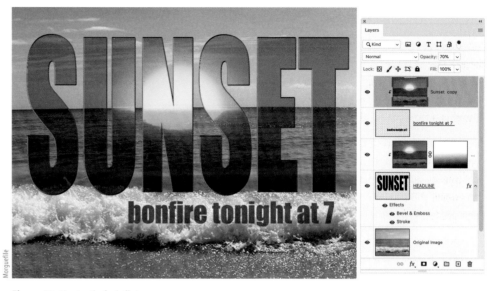

Figure 42 Viewing the final effect

Morguefile

10. Press [command] [J] (Mac) or [Ctrl] [J] (Win) to duplicate the Sunset layer, then move the Sunset copy layer to the top of the Layers panel.
11. Drag the layer mask on the Sunset copy to the Delete layer button on the Layers panel, then click Delete when prompted.
12. Clip the Sunset copy layer into the type layer beneath it.
13. With the Sunset copy layer still targeted, drag the Opacity slider on the Layers panel to 70%.
14. Compare your Layers panel and your artwork to Figure 42.

The eye recognizes immediately that it's the same image inside the letters as outside the letters but, on second glance, realizes that the sunset is only inside the letters. The stroke emboss delineates the word "SUNSET" from the background but is thin enough that it doesn't interrupt the continuity between the two images. You can create a lot of tricky effects like this by duplicating and modifying an image and clipping it strategically into type.

15. Save your work, then close Sunset Image Clipping.

DESIGN PROJECT

This project gives you the opportunity to incorporate the layer skills you have learned in Chapters 3 and 4. You are going to type the name of a city, then place images into the letters, as you did with the "JAPAN" artwork in Lesson 6 of this chapter.

The way to do this project is to work methodically, don't rush. Think about color and about finding the right typeface and images. Think about which layer styles would work best for you about how a gradient might add to the effect.

1. Open PS 4-16.psd, then save it as **City Images**. This file is blank, a clean slate to get you started.
2. Decide what city you want to work on.
   Keep in mind that the shorter the name, the larger the letters will be on the canvas, and the more of the images you'll be able to see inside those letters.
3. Type the name of the city on the canvas.
4. Choose the best typeface for the city.
   You have many considerations when choosing a typeface. Your most important consideration though, is finding a typeface that's very bold and thick so that when you put images into the type, they will show substantially.
5. Track and kern the type as necessary.

Figure 43 Final artwork

6. Go online and find a background image that you think will work and paste it in.
7. Research and choose the best images for the collage and clip them into the type.
8. Apply the layer styles you think will best make the type and images stand out from the background.
9. Incorporate a gradient over the background to perhaps darken it or lighten it. Figure 43 shows one result.

Shutterstock photo credits: Christ the Redeemer: Dmitri Kalvan; Night view of Rio de Janeiro & Mosaic sidewalk: Catarina Belova; Brazilian woman: Gold Stock Images

CHAPTER 5

EMPLOY ADJUSTMENT LAYERS

1. Explore Fundamental Adjustments
2. Adjust Levels
3. Investigate the RGB Color Model
4. Investigate the HSB Color Model

Adobe Certified Professional in Visual Design Using Photoshop CC Framework

3. Organizing Documents

This objective covers document structure such as layers and managing document structure for efficient workflows.

3.1 Use layers to manage design elements.

    C Recognize the different types of layers in the Layers panel.

3.2 Modify layer visibility using opacity, blending modes, and masks.

    A Adjust a layer's opacity, blending mode, and fill opacity.

    B Create and edit masks.

3.3 Differentiate between and perform destructive or nondestructive editing to meet design requirements.

    A Nondestructive editing: adjustment layers.

    B Destructive editing: painting, adjustments, and erasing.

4. Creating and Modifying Visual Elements

This objective covers core tools and functionality of the application, as well as tools that affect the visual outcome of document elements.

4.5 Use basic reconstructing and retouching techniques to manipulate digital graphics and media.

    A Apply basic auto-correction methods and tools.

    C Evaluate or adjust the appearance of objects, selections, or layers using various tools.

    D Apply photographic changes to images using tools and adjustments.

EXPLORE FUNDAMENTAL ADJUSTMENTS

▶ *What You'll Do*

In this lesson, you'll apply four different adjustments to an image.

Improving Images with Adjustments

Our digital world offers unprecedented access to professional-level, high-quality photography, images that are flawless and require no improvements or corrections. On the contrary, our digital world has put phone cameras in the hands of almost everyone, and while these cameras are also high quality, the photos an amateur photographer captures are often just average.

Photoshop offers many practical adjustment operations to improve the quality of images—their color, contrast, and overall effect. Brightness/Contrast, Levels, and Color Balance are three common, powerful, and highly useful adjustments for improving the overall appearance of an image.

Once you understand the concepts of the Grayscale, RGB, and HSB color modes, you'll be ready and able to dramatically alter or improve your images with a variety of adjustments.

Understanding Nondestructive Editing

In the course of a project, you will execute hundreds and even thousands of moves that affect the original image or images you are working with. Regardless of all changes you make, you never want to permanently change your original artwork, which is also referred to as the **base artwork** or the **base image**. You want all your changes to be editable or removable, if necessary. You can achieve this by working effectively with the Layers panel, which gives you the ability to execute all operations on *layers* rather than on the base image itself.

Nondestructive editing is the term used to describe this working behavior. With nondestructive editing, your original artwork is protected from permanent changes.

One of the big misconceptions new designers have regarding more experienced designers is that they know where they're going and what their goal is at all times, and the finished product is exactly what they planned from the start. That is very seldom (if ever) the case. Design is a process, one that often involves experimentation, trial and error, and redirection. Nondestructive editing allows you endless flexibility to experiment, to try something out. If it works, great, and if it doesn't, edit and move in a new direction. Once you are close to finishing the piece, the fact that all your steps are editable allows you to tweak everything to perfect the final look.

Working with Adjustments

Photoshop offers 22 types of operations, called **adjustments**, that affect the appearance of an image. These include fundamental adjustments such as Levels, Curves, Hue/Saturation, and Brightness/Contrast. Adjustments can be applied using commands on the Image menu, but you should always make adjustments using the Layers panel. If you make adjustments using the commands on the Image menu, those fall under the category of **destructive editing** because they are applied directly to the image.

Adjustments made using the Layers panel are referred to as **adjustment layers**. When an adjustment is applied as a layer, it is always editable. You can hide or show the adjustment, you can delete it if you no longer want it, and you can change its settings whenever you like. For example, if you create a new adjustment layer to brighten an image with the Brightness/Contrast adjustment, the base image will be affected only as long as the Brightness/Contrast adjustment layer is showing. In addition, you can return to this Brightness/Contrast adjustment at any time to change its settings.

Adjustment layers are created on the Layers panel by clicking the Create new fill or adjustment layer button on the panel and then choosing the type of adjustment you want. Once created, the Properties panel opens showing the adjustment's default settings. Settings on the Properties panel allow you to change the appearance of the adjustment. For example, Figure 1 shows a Brightness/Contrast adjustment layer and the settings for it on the Properties panel.

You can use the Opacity setting on the Layers panel to decrease or increase the effect an adjustment has on the base artwork. By default, all new adjustment layers are created at 100% opacity. All adjustment layers are also created with a layer mask, which you can use to hide or show the adjustment in different areas. The ability to "brush in" adjustments this way, in specific areas and with specific strengths, is a powerful option for working with adjustments.

Figure 1 Brightness/Contrast adjustment layer and settings on the Properties panel

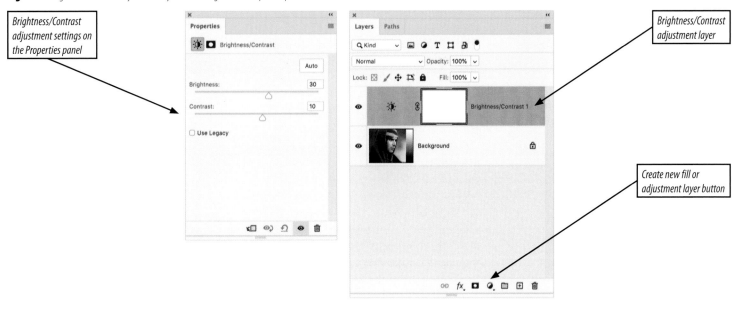

Understanding Grayscale

A grayscale image is a digital image in which each pixel can be one—and only one—of 256 shades of gray. With 256 shades of gray available per pixel, the illusion of a continuous tone image can be created. The grayscale range is 0–255. Pixels with a grayscale value of 0 are black. Pixels with a grayscale value of 255 are white. Any number in between 0 and 255 is gray—light gray or dark gray—with 128 being the middle point in the grayscale range.

The first step in analyzing the appearance of any image is to identify the highlights, midtones, and shadows. **Highlights** are the lightest areas of the image and are represented by pixels whose value falls in the upper third of the grayscale range. **Shadows** are the darkest areas represented by pixels in the lower third of the grayscale range. **Midtones**, as the name suggests, fall into the middle of the grayscale range.

When you look at a digital image, you don't see individual pixels; you see the illusion of continuous tone, a smooth transition from shadows to midtones to highlights. To create this illusion, there must be enough grays available per pixel so that the eye perceives smooth transitions between tones.

Applying an Invert Adjustment

The **Invert adjustment** achieves its effect by flipping the grayscale range. Black pixels change to 255 and become white, and white pixels change to 0 and become black. In a black and white image, applying the Invert adjustment creates an x-ray effect.

Applying a Threshold Adjustment

Like the Posterize effect you explored in Chapter 2, the **Threshold adjustment** creates its effect by manipulating the number of colors available per pixel. The Threshold adjustment forces each pixel to be either black or white, thus creating the ultimate high-contrast effect. By default, the adjustment splits the image right down the middle: pixels with a grayscale value of 128 or higher all become white; pixels with a grayscale value of 127 or lower all become black. You can adjust where that split occurs by dragging the Threshold Level slider left or right. The number you stop on specifies the grayscale value at which pixels become white.

Applying a Gradient Map Adjustment

The **Gradient Map adjustment** applies a gradient to the transition from shadows to highlights. For example, if you created a gradient from dark blue to yellow and used it as a Gradient Map adjustment, the image would transition from dark blue shadows to yellow highlights. You can use any gradient you create in a gradient map, including multicolor gradients. Thus, with the Gradient Map adjustment, you can create dynamic images that transition through multiple hues from shadow to highlight.

Applying a Brightness/Contrast Adjustment

The Brightness/Contrast adjustment, as the name suggests, affects the brightness and contrast in an image. **Brightness** is defined by a pixel's grayscale value. The higher the number, the brighter the pixel, because the closer it is to white.

Contrast is represented by the relationship between the shadows and highlights of the image. Good contrast is created when shadows and highlights are distinctly different in tonal range—that is, when shadow areas are richly dark and highlights are gleaming white and there's a "dynamic range" between shadows and highlights. On the other hand, when the highlights aren't bright enough and the shadows aren't dark enough, the image will lack contrast and appear drab and "flat" in its tonal range.

Bad contrast can also occur "in camera" when the available lighting is poor or the camera settings are not correct for the given lighting conditions. In these cases, the highlights can "blow out and "bleach" the image, or the shadows can "plug up" to the point that there's no range of gray in the dark areas. When this occurs in the camera, there is very little that can be done to fix it. On the other hand, be sure you don't overdo the Brightness/Contrast adjustment in Photoshop and create these problems yourself!

Figure 2 shows an example of good contrast and three examples of bad contrast.

Understanding Legacy Settings

Photoshop is more than 30 years old, and some users have been using it for that long. Many users find their groove with Photoshop and are resistant to changes or evolutions Adobe might make to long-standing features. For some of these features, Adobe offers the *Use Legacy* option, which restores the functionality of a given feature to its *classic* state. The Brightness/Contrast adjustment is one of many Photoshop features that offers the "Use Legacy" option.

Figure 2 Four examples of contrast

Poor contrast: "weak" shadows and "closed" highlights

Good contrast: "strong" shadows and "open" highlights

Poor contrast: shadows are "plugged" and have no range

Poor contrast: highlights are "blown out" and have no detail

Morguefile

Sample shadows, midtones, and highlights in an image

1. Open PS 5-1.psd, then save it as **Basic Adjustments**.

2. Click **Image** on the menu bar, point to **Mode**, then note that **Grayscale** is checked.

   This image has been saved in Grayscale mode, meaning that one of 256 shades of gray is available per pixel.

3. Open the **Info panel**, then verify that the left-side readout is set to **RGB**.

4. Click the **Eyedropper tool** 🖊 on the toolbar, then position it over different areas of the image, noting the readouts on the Info panel.

5. Position the **Eyedropper tool** 🖊 at the very bottom of the gradient on the right, then move it slowly to the top of the gradient.

   The pixels in the gradient range from 0 at the bottom to 255 at the top. Try to see the image of the young man as a similar gradient from black to white.

6. Make the **Chart layer** visible on the Layers panel.

   The chart shows the general ranges for shadows, midtones, and highlights on the gradient. Try to see these ranges in the image of the young man.

7. Assess the image for its **shadows**. Which areas do you identify as the shadow areas of the image?

   The dark area under the young man's chin and the dark jacket on his shoulder are the shadow areas. Note that a *range* of dark gray pixels exists at his shoulder. They are not all black, and there is detail in the jacket; therefore, you can see the folds in the cloth and the scrunching of the material along the

collar. Note too that even though the area under the chin is very dark, you can still see the detail of the *inside* of the hood. These are great examples and reminders that shadow areas *must* have a range of dark grays to show detail. Otherwise, all you'd be looking at is a field of black.

8. Assess the image for its **highlights**. Which areas would you guess contain the brightest pixels in the image?

   The pixels with the highest grayscale value can be found in the highlight along the man's nose. His face and the lighter stripes of the knit cap are the highlights in the image.

9. Assess the image for its **midtones**. Which areas would you guess contain pixels closest to 128?

   If you're thinking it's the man's hood, you'd be wrong. Those pixels are darker than you might first guess, somewhere in the range of 64. The midtones in the image are the blurry background to the right of the man's nose.

In terms of contrast, the hood is an interesting component of the image. The fabric is not shiny, so there's no bright highlight, and the fabric is not overly dark in color, so there's no deep shadow. Nevertheless, try to see that there is a *range of tone* that renders the hood. The vertical, diagonal shadow has grayscale values from 20 to 40, and the soft highlight at the back of the hood is rendered with grayscale values from 90 to 105. Consider, therefore, that even though the hood is not rendered with deep shadows or bright highlights, there is a limited range of contrast in the hood.

10. Hide the **Chart layer** on the Layers panel.

11. Assess the whole image in terms of **shadows**, **midtones**, and **highlights**.

As shown in Figure 3, this image has great contrast. The shadows are deep and dark, yet they never go black or lose detail. The face is bright, the highlight along the nose delivers, and there's detail in all areas of the face. Note how this good contrast serves the whole image. The pupils in the young man's eyes are dark and intense. There's a highlight on his bottom lip and a very sharp and bright highlight on the edge of his hood where it meets the knit cap. The image is a study in textures. The outer jacket reads as a smooth nylon, like a windbreaker; the softness of the hood is visible, and the texture of the knit cap is rendered with bright pixels abutting very dark pixels at the holes in the knitting. When you view the image in terms of shadow, midtones, and highlights, there's much to appreciate.

Figure 3 Identifying shadows, midtones, and highlights

MorgueFile

12. Continue to the next set of steps.

You used the Eyedropper tool in conjunction with the Info panel to explore the shadows, midtones, and highlights in the image.

Create an Invert adjustment layer

1. Drag the **Chart layer** to the **Delete layer button** 🗑 on the Layers panel.

The Chart layer is deleted.

2. Click **Image** on the menu bar, point to **Adjustments**, then click **Invert**.

This image is inverted. By using the menu command, the change is applied directly to the image on the Background layer. This is an example of destructive editing.

TIP For every adjustment layer on the Layers panel, there is a corresponding adjustment menu item on the Image/Adjustments menu. Remember that adjustment layers are nondestructive, making them a far superior method for applying adjustments than using the commands on the Image/Adjustments menu, which permanently alter the base image.

3. Undo the last step.

Next, you will apply the same adjustment using an adjustment layer.

4. Click the **Create new fill or adjustment layer button** ⬤ on the Layers panel, then click **Invert**.

As shown in Figure 4, an Invert adjustment layer appears on the Layers panel with a default layer mask. As indicated on the gradient to the right, the entire range from black to white has been inverted: black pixels have changed from 0 to 255, and white pixels have changed from 255 to 0.

5. Hide and show the **Invert adjustment layer**.

Because the adjustment has been applied as an adjustment layer, it can be made visible or invisible like any other layer. The original artwork is affected only when the adjustment layer is visible. This is an example of nondestructive editing.

Continued on next page

Figure 4 Invert adjustment layer and the inverted artwork

6. Save your work and continue to the next set of steps.

You applied the Invert menu command, noting that it affected the image directly. After undoing that move, you applied the Invert adjustment as an adjustment layer, noting that you could hide and show the adjustment and the original image was not permanently affected.

Create a Threshold adjustment layer

1. Verify that the **Invert adjustment layer** is hidden and the **Background layer** is targeted.

2. Click the **Create new fill or adjustment layer button** 🔘 on the Layers panel, then click **Threshold**.

   All the pixels in the image become either black or white.

3. Verify that the **Properties panel** is visible.

   The Properties panel shows the settings for the current selected adjustment layer. For a Threshold adjustment, the default setting is 128, the midpoint of the grayscale range. Thus, in the image, the pixels whose grayscale values were 128 or above have all changed to white, and the pixels that were 127 or below have all changed to black. Note that the gradient on the right is now split vertically at the halfway point, its top half is white, and its bottom half is black.

4. Assess the effect on the image.

   It's a pretty cool effect. The man is recognizable, but his eyes and eyebrows are almost completely black and lack detail.

5. On the Properties panel, drag the **Threshold Level slider** to **108**.

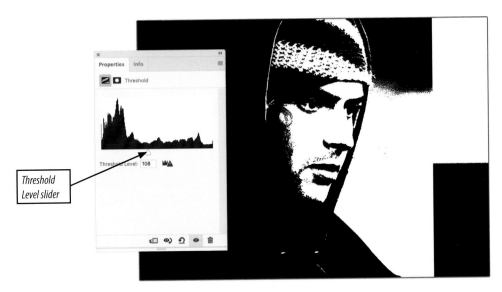

Threshold Level slider

Figure 5 The image threshold set to 108

As shown in Figure 5, all pixels with a grayscale value of 108 or above are white. Note that the gradient on the right is no longer split 50-50 white over black; there's now more white than black. More pixels in the image of the man are now white, and his eyes are now rendered with more detail.

6. Show the **Invert adjustment layer**.

   The Threshold effect is inverted. Multiple adjustment layers affect other adjustments.

7. Hide the **Invert adjustment layer**, save the file, then continue to the next set of steps.

You created a Threshold adjustment layer then adjusted it to render the effect with more white pixels.

Create a Gradient Map adjustment layer

1. Hide both **adjustment layers**, then target the **Background layer**.

2. Click **Image** on the menu bar, point to **Mode**, then click **RGB Color**.

   If a warning box opens asking whether or not you want to flatten the image, click **Don't Flatten**.

3. Press the **letter [D]** on your keypad to set the foreground color to black and the background color to white.

4. Click the **Create new fill or adjustment layer button** 🔘 on the Layers panel, then click **Gradient Map**.

5. On the Properties panel, click the **black-to-white gradient** directly above the **Dither option**.

The Gradient Editor dialog box opens.

6. In the **Gradient Editor dialog box**, click the **left color stop** , click the **Color box** ▭, choose a **dark blue**, then click **OK**.

The image changes from a black-to-white color range to dark blue to white.

7. Change the **right color stop** to a pale yellow color.

8. Add a **color stop** in the middle of the gradient, change its color to **orange**, then set its location to **45%**.

Your gradient settings should resemble Figure 6.

TIP Click the base of the gradient bar to add a new color stop.

9. Click **OK**, then compare your artwork to Figure 7.

10. Save your work, then close Basic Adjustments.

You added a Gradient Map adjustment layer, and then you specified the colors of the gradient applied to the image.

Adjust Brightness/Contrast

1. Open PS 5-2.psd, then save it as **Adjust Brightness and Contrast**.

2. Click **Select** on the menu bar, click **Load Selection**, click the **Channel list arrow**, click **Gradient at Bottom**, then click **OK**.

The gradient is darker on the left side than it is on the right, but the tonal range is short, from 108 to 212.

Continued on next page

Figure 6 Customizing the colors of the gradient

Figure 7 Viewing the Gradient Map adjustment

3. Click **Image** on the menu bar, point to **Adjustments**, then click **Brightness/Contrast**.

   The Brightness/Contrast dialog box opens.

4. Click the **Use Legacy check box**, then drag the **Contrast slider** to **60**.

   The darker pixels in the gradient are darkened to black, and the lighter pixels are lightened to white. Adding contrast moves pixels toward the extremes of the grayscale range

5. Drag the **Contrast slider** to **–60**.

   The ends of the gradient move toward the middle of the grayscale range. These two steps are illustrated in Figure 8.

6. Click **Cancel**, click **Select** on the menu bar, then click **Inverse**.

7. Click **Image** on the menu bar, then click **Crop** to remove the gradient from the image.

8. Take a moment to assess the image and its tonal range.

   As was the case with the gradient at the bottom, the shadows in the image are weak, and there are no highlights.

9. Using the Info panel, sample the highlight areas of the face, including the whites of the eyes, to get a general range of the values of the highlights in the image.

   The values are generally 140–170, far too low for highlights, which should be greater than 200. This image is not bright enough.

10. Sample the hair and the image background area to the left of the face to get an idea of the general range of the shadows in the image.

The values are generally 40–70, which puts them at the high end of the shadow range.

11. Click the **Create new fill or adjustment layer button**  on the Layers panel, then click **Brightness/Contrast**.

12. On the Properties panel, click the **Use Legacy check box**, then drag the **Brightness slider** to **50**.

    Increasing brightness increases the grayscale values of all the pixels in the image.

13. Drag the **Contrast slider** to **78**.

    The shadows darken, and the highlights brighten. The shadows are improved dramatically, especially in the hair and the dark details of the face, like the pupils and the eyelashes.

14. Hide and show the **Brightness/Contrast adjustment layer** to see its effect.

    Figure 9 shows the before and after views of the image. The improvement in the image is stunning.

Figure 8 Illustration of the relationship between contrast and grayscale

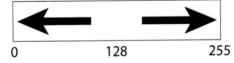

Figure 8 appears with the illustration below.

Compared to the improved image, the original image looks like you're seeing it through a dusty and dirty window.

15. Save your work, then close Adjust Brightness and Contrast.

You added a Brightness/Contrast adjustment layer, then adjusted both the brightness and the contrast to dramatically improve the image.

Figure 9 Before and after views of the Brightness/Contrast adjustment

ADJUST LEVELS

▶ *What You'll Do*

In this lesson, you'll improve the tonal range of an image using the Levels adjustment.

Understanding the Levels Adjustment

Levels is an adjustment in Photoshop that allows you to manipulate the range of tone in an image, from shadow to highlight. The word "levels" refers to the concept that a grayscale image has 256 "levels" of gray and that an RGB image has 256 "levels" of in each channel. You can use the Levels adjustment to define the darkest and brightest point in an image, and you can define the middle tone between the two extremes. Making these adjustments with levels redistributes the image data along the grayscale range. Generally speaking, you use the Levels adjustment to improve the contrast in an image.

Adjusting Black and White Points with Levels

In addition to the shadow, midtone, and highlight ranges, every image has a **black point**, the very darkest pixel in the image, and a **white point**, the very lightest pixel in the image. The black and white points are critical to the appearance of the image because they represent the start and the end of the tonal range.

Today's digital cameras, including the camera in your phone, are so sophisticated that most images need little or no correction for contrast or color balance. However, when an image is captured in poor lighting conditions, the image quality will also be poor, regardless of how sophisticated the camera is. That's where Photoshop adjustments can help.

In some cases, professional photographers will define their camera settings so the darkest pixel will be no darker than 15, and the brightest pixel will be no lighter than 240. This forces the camera not to make shadows too dark or highlights too white. It results in an image that has a smooth tonal range from shadow to highlight, and it allows for the black and white points to be improved in Photoshop.

When adjusting images with levels, the first standard move is to verify that the black and white points are at their optimal grayscale value—that is, that the black point is at or close to zero and that the white point is at or close to 255.

Figure 10 shows the Levels adjustment settings on the Properties panel. Notice the three eyedropper tools on the left. These are sampling tools for setting the black (shadow) point, gray (midpoint) point, and white (highlight) point. You use these tools by clicking in the image. For example, where you click the white point eyedropper determines the whitest point in the image, and where you click the black point eyedropper determines the darkest point. Use these tools to get a sense of what the image might look like with different white and black points. The moves are not permanent, and you can always readjust. Not everyone uses the eyedroppers to set black and white points, but it's a great way to identify the 255 and 0 pixels before you make any adjustments.

These tools offer another great feature. If you click the white point eyedropper, then press [option] (Mac) or [Alt] (Win), the entire image turns black, except for the pixels with a grayscale value of 255, which remain white. This is a great way to know where you can find white pixels in the image. (If the entire canvas displays black, that's because the image contains no white pixels.)

Conversely, when you click the black point eyedropper, then press [option] (Mac) or [Alt] (Win), the entire image turns white, except for the pixels with a grayscale value of 0, which remain black.

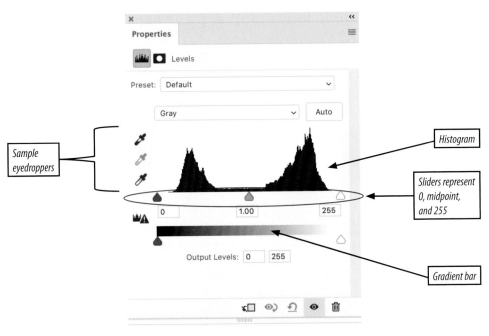

Figure 10 Levels adjustment on the Properties panel

Understanding the Histogram

The most striking component of the Levels adjustment is the histogram. The **histogram** is a graph of the image data and where that data is positioned on the grayscale range.

Using Figure 10 as a reference, imagine that the Levels adjustment has 256 slots between the black triangle on the left and the white triangle on the right, one slot for each of the 256 available colors in the grayscale image. The slot for the 0-value pixels is on the left, and the slot for the 255-value pixels is on the right. Imagine that the image is composed of 100,000 pixels and 1,000 of them have a grayscale value of 64. Using a black marble to represent each pixel, imagine that you drop 1,000 marbles into the 64-value slot on the slider. Next, imagine that the image contains 2,000 pixels with a grayscale value of 72, and you drop 2,000 black marbles into the 72-value slot. The marbles in that slot will go twice as high as in the 64-value slot.

Imagine that you do this for each of the 256 slots on the slider. Your result would be the histogram—exactly what you see on the Properties panel. From left to right, the histogram shows the distribution of the pixels in the image, from 0 to 255. The varying heights of the histogram show the concentration of pixels at any given point on the grayscale range.

Understanding How the Levels Adjustment Works

With the Levels adjustment, you modify the tonal range of the image by manipulating the sliders directly below the histogram. The black triangle represents 0 on the grayscale range. The white triangle represents 255. The gray triangle represents the midpoint between the two.

When you move any of the triangles, you readjust how the histogram relates to the full *potential* grayscale range, from shadow to highlight. For example, wherever you place the white triangle, the grayscale values of the pixels at that spot on the histogram change to 255. Wherever you place the black triangle, those pixels change to 0. All the data between those two points will now be redistributed.

The gray triangle, or midpoint slider, separates the light half of the image from the dark half. Wherever you place the gray triangle sets those pixels at 128; therefore, any part of the histogram to the right of the gray triangle must have grayscale values higher than 128, and any pixels to the left must have grayscale values 127 or lower. To put it another way, the more you move the gray triangle to the left, the brighter the image will become, because more of the histogram will be to the right of the gray midpoint triangle.

Adjusting the tonal range of an image is a lot like knowing which fork to use in fine dining—you start at the outside and work your way in. First, set your black and white points—the extremes. If that one move delivers satisfactory contrast throughout the image, you are ready to (if you want) adjust the midpoint. Essentially, the midpoint darkens or lightens the image. Interestingly, a midpoint adjustment is often only subjective, depending on your preference for a lighter or a darker image overall.

TIP Because of the complexity of Photoshop's algorithms, where you place the gray channel will define those pixels as the middle value of the histogram, but not necessarily as 128. We used the number 128 in the preceding explanation because 128 is the middle number between 0 and 255. Photoshop's calculation of the midpoint won't be quite so simple. Nevertheless, you should think of the gray midpoint slider as the "middle gray" of the image.

Understanding the Relationship Between Contrast and Color

When improving a black and white image, a dynamic range of shadow to highlight produces a dynamic black and white image. When it comes to color images, the relationship between contrast and color isn't quite as intuitive. This is because, when considering the improvement of color in a color image, most people think that means shifting the color balance of the image, for example, making the photo less red or less yellow or more neutral.

In fact, good contrast and good color are inextricably linked. For an image to have vibrant color, it's necessary to have a dynamic tonal range with deep shadows and bright highlights. Just like a black and white image with poor contrast, you can't get bright yellows and deep blues in a color image with poor contrast.

Today's digital cameras are of such high quality and so finely calibrated—even those in most smart phones—that color balance problems and contrast problems have become somewhat rare. Even in poor lighting conditions, most cameras will produce an image with neutral, balanced color. For those images, you will find that correcting the highlight and shadow points and improving the overall contrast will be enough to bring out vibrant and balanced color in the image.

Using Layer Masks with Adjustments

When you create an adjustment layer, it is created with a layer mask by default. The layer mask is often an essential component of working with adjustment layers. Sometimes, you will make an adjustment that you can apply completely to the artwork, but more often, you will want to use the layer mask to apply the adjustment selectively in different strengths to different areas.

Some designers make it an automatic part of their process to mask the adjustment completely and then use a low-opacity brush to paint white in the mask, thus "brushing in" the adjustment gradually in specific areas. Working with this method allows you to apply an adjustment in a way that is more customized and unique to the given artwork.

Because masking is so essential, you need to choose the right brush for the job. This means using the best brush size and edge hardness for a given goal. The decisions you make—especially for the edge hardness—will have a direct effect on the success of the mask.

Brush settings allow you to specify the edge of a brush in terms of hardness: 100% is the hardest-edged brush, and 0% is the softest-edged brush. You can think of a hard brush as having a smooth, crisp, anti-aliased edge, and you can think of a brush with 0% hardness as having a feathered edge. The size of the feathered edge increases and decreases proportionately with the size of the brush.

In other words, if you're using a soft brush with a brush size of 100 pixels, the feathered edge on that brush will be much wider than the feathered edge on a brush with a brush size of 10 pixels.

Investigate the histogram

1. Open PS 5-3.psd, then save it as **Adjusting Levels**.

2. Enter **[command] [L] (Mac)** or **[Ctrl] [L] (Win)**.

    The Levels dialog box opens. The histogram shows the distribution of the pixels in the image, from the darkest pixels to the lightest pixels. For this exercise, you are going to make selections and note where those pixels appear on the histogram.

To keep things simple, you're going to use the Levels dialog box on the Image menu, not a Levels adjustment on the Layers panel.

3. Click **Cancel**.

4. Click the **Rectangular Marquee tool** ⬚, then make a small selection of the **interior of one of the petals**.

5. Enter **[command] [L] (Mac)** or **[Ctrl] [L] (Win)**.

    As shown in Figure 11, the histogram now shows only the selected pixels. The petal is a lighter area of the image, and those pixels are located at the upper half of the histogram.

6. Click **Cancel**, then make a selection of the **top-left corner of the background**.

Figure 11 A selection of lighter pixels represented on the histogram

7. Enter **[command] [L] (Mac)** or **[Ctrl] [L] (Win)**.

As shown in Figure 12, the selected pixels appear on the lower half of the histogram, closer to the black triangle.

8. Click **Cancel**.

9. Deselect, click **Image** on the menu bar, point to **Adjustments**, click **Posterize**, enter **3** in the Levels text box, then click **OK**.

The pixels in the image are now black, gray, or white. There are far fewer white pixels compared to gray and black.

10. Enter **[command] [L] (Mac)** or **[Ctrl] [L] (Win)**.

As shown in Figure 13, the histogram is just three vertical lines: one at the 0 representing the black pixels; a taller line at the center, representing the majority gray pixels; and a short line at 255, representing the few white pixels.

11. Click **OK**, click **File** on the menu bar, then click **Revert**.

The file is returned to its original state to be used in the next set of steps.

You explored how the histogram represents the image by selecting light and dark areas of the image and noting where they appear on the histogram. You posterized the image to three levels and then noted that the histogram showed just three lines.

Figure 12 A selection of darker pixels represented on the histogram

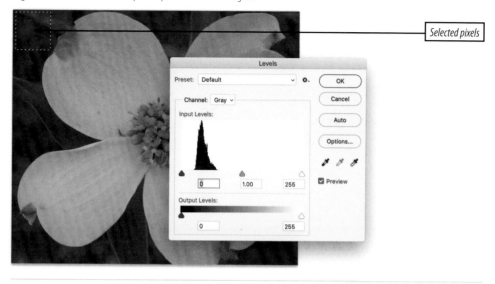

Selected pixels

Figure 13 The posterized image represented by three lines on the histogram

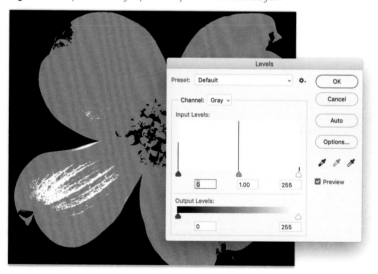

Employ the Levels adjustment

1. Click the **Create new fill or adjustment layer button** 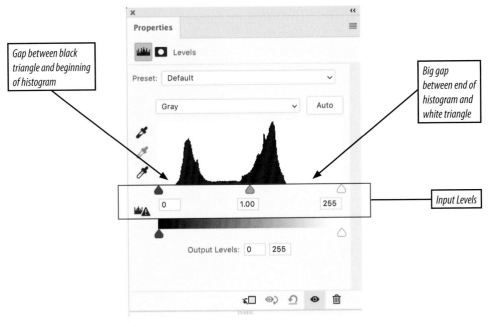 on the Layers panel, then click **Levels**.

   Note that merely creating a new adjustment layer does nothing to affect the image. Only when you manipulate the settings in an adjustment layer do you affect the image.

2. Assess the image for contrast and assess the histogram on the Properties panel.

   The image has poor contrast. The shadows are weak, and the highlights are gray and dull. As shown in Figure 14, the histogram reflects this assessment of the image. Left to right, the histogram has a short range. On the left side, it does not extend into the darker areas of the grayscale range, and on the right side, there's a big gap between the end of the histogram and the white triangle. That gap represents a range of high-numbered bright pixels on the grayscale range not being used to render the highlights in the image. The same is true for the darker pixels on the left side of the histogram.

3. Drag the **black triangle**, directly below the histogram, to the right to line it up with the beginning of the histogram.

   The shadow input level should be 22. Before you moved the black triangle, the darkest pixels in the image had a grayscale value of 22. Now those pixels have a grayscale value of 0 (black).

   TIP In this lesson, you will only drag the triangles in the Input Levels section—those immediately below the histogram, not those in the Output Levels section.

Figure 14 Assessing the histogram

4. Click the **set black point eyedropper tool** on the Properties panel float over the image, then press **[option] (Mac)** or **[Alt] (Win)**.

   The entire canvas turns white except for any pixels that have a grayscale value of 0, which remain black. In the case of this image, those pixels are very few and at the center of the canvas.

5. Drag the **white triangle** to the left to line up with the end of the histogram.

   The highlight input level should be 183. Before you moved the white triangle, the brightest pixels in the image data had a grayscale value of 183. Now, those pixels have a value of 255 (white).

6. Click the **set white point eyedropper tool**, float over the image, then press **[option] (Mac)** or **[Alt] (Win)**.

   The entire canvas turns black except for any remaining white pixels. There are very few of those pixels on the bottom-left petal, where it folds over itself. The fact that so few pixels are 0 and 255 tells you that the image is using the full range of the grayscale, but not overly so.

7. Drag the **gray triangle**, directly below the histogram, to the left so that the **midtone input level** is **1.04**.

   The image is slightly brighter.

8. Assess the improvements to the image.

The petals in the image are now white, not light gray. They are dramatically brighter, but the fine detail in the petals has all been retained. The shadows are darker, but there is still detail throughout.

9. Select the **Eyedropper tool** on the toolbar, then float it over the shadow and highlight areas of the image.

The Info panel shows before and after readouts that reflect darker shadows and brighter highlight areas. These changes are particularly dramatic on the petals, where you can find before and after readouts with a difference of more than 50 grayscale levels.

10. Add a **second Levels adjustment layer**, then compare its histogram to Figure 15.

The image data in the histogram is now distributed across the length of the grayscale, from 0 to 255. Thus, the shadows are deep and dark, and the highlights are bright. Compare this histogram in Figure 15 to the histogram in Figure 14, and you can see that the work you did in Steps 3–5 affected the *entire* image. All the data has been *redistributed*; the tonal range has been *extended* to take full advantage of the available range of tones.

11. Drag the **white triangle** left to change the **highlight input level** to **218**, drag the **black triangle** to the right to change the **shadow**

input level to **17**, then compare your results to Figure 16.

These changes are not acceptable for the flower because the highlights on the petal are blown out. Note that the petals are now just "flat" white; there's no longer any detail. This is represented on the histogram. All the data to the right of the white triangle—all those pixels—are now all 255. At the left side of the histogram, all the pixels to the left of the black triangle, which used to be a range of shadow values, are now black.

TIP Read the *Explore Extreme Adjustments* sidebar.

Continued on next page

Figure 15 Assessing the adjusted histogram

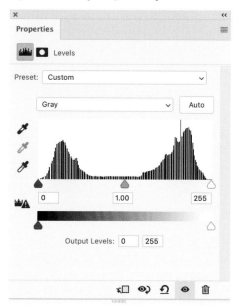

Figure 16 Blown-out highlights on the image reflected in the histogram

12. Focus on the **buds** at the center of the flower, then hide and show the **second Levels adjustment layer**.

The second Levels adjustment layer is an improvement to the buds, despite being bad for the petals. The buds' highlights are brighter without blowing out, and the shadows are deeper.

13. Enter **[command] [I] (Mac)** or **[Ctrl] [I] (Win)** to invert the second Levels adjustment layer.

The entire Levels adjustment is masked.

14. Click the **Brush tool** 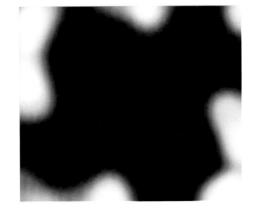 on the toolbar, set the **Size** to **100 px**, set the **Hardness** to **0%**, set the **Mode** to **Normal**, then set the **Opacity** to **30%**.

15. Set the **foreground color** to **white**, then paint over the buds to "brush in" the Levels adjustment in that location only.

16. Look past the flower petals and focus only the background of the image.

The leaves in the background have brighter edges, but those brighter edges are a dull gray. We will use a third adjustment layer to improve the dullness of the leaf edges.

17. Add a **third Levels adjustment**, then assess the histogram.

By now, you've noted that the histogram for this image has the appearance of two mountains. If you look at the image itself, it only makes sense

that the larger mountain on the right represents all the brighter pixels that render the petals, and the smaller mountain on the left represents the darker pixels that make up the background.

18. Drag the **white triangle** left past the right "mountain" until the **highlight input level** is **158**, then drag the **black triangle** to the right until the **shadow input level** is **8**.

The entire flower is blown out to white, and the background lightens dramatically. The shadows in the background are darker. The tonal range of the background is now using the full range of the grayscale, as you can see on the highlights of the edges of the leaves, which are now brighter.

19. Invert the mask.

The entire adjustment is masked.

20. Change the brush **Size** to **200 px**, then change the **Opacity** to **40%**.

21. Working from the outside in, gradually "brush in" the adjustment on the background only without affecting the petals.

AUTHOR'S **NOTE**   If you're a new user, you might have the instinct to brush this adjustment in at 100% opacity with a hard line along the flower so as to not affect the petals. That's not the way you want to go. Think of this adjustment as a subtle adjustment. You want to gradually "bump up" the areas you can get

to with the big soft brush. Consider avoiding small, "surgical" moves in narrow areas such as those between the petals. If you do go into those areas with a small brush, it will be challenging to show the adjustment while keeping your presence invisible. Smaller brushes have a smaller feather at their edges and leave behind harder lines.

22. Press and hold **[option] (Mac)** or **[Alt] (Win)**, then click the **mask** to view the mask.

Figure 17 shows the **mask** the author painted.

23. Click the **histogram thumbnail** on the Levels 3 layer on the Layers panel to view the image instead of the mask.

Figure 17 Viewing the mask

24. Shift-click to select all **three adjustment layers** on the Layers panel, then enter **[command] [G] (Mac)** or **[Ctrl] [G] (Win)** to place them into a group.

The three Levels adjustment layers are grouped into a new group layer (named Group 1 by default).

25. Hide and show the **Group 1 layer**.

Figure 18 shows the image before and after the adjustments.

26. Save your work, then continue to the next set of steps.

AUTHOR'S **NOTE** This exercise is a great example of how gratifying adjusting images can be. One enjoyable element of this work is the designer's invisible role. If you executed this assignment well, there should be no trace of you anywhere in the image. You shouldn't see any kind of a white halo at the center where you brushed in the brighter buds, and you shouldn't see any "hot spots" on the edges of the petals where you brushed in the background. None of your Levels adjustments should have been so extreme that they catch the eye. It should not appear manipulated or doctored in any way. Instead, the image should be simply beautiful on its own. The greatest compliment you, as the designer, can get is the viewer's total lack of awareness that you were ever there at all.

You made a Levels adjustment to correct the shadow and highlight points for the flower image, thereby improving the contrast throughout the entire image. You then used two more Levels adjustments in conjunction with layer masks to adjust specific areas of the image. Finally, you grouped the three adjustment layers so you could hide and show all three simultaneously to see a before and after view of the image.

EXPLORE EXTREME ADJUSTMENTS

Sometimes, the best method for making effective adjustments is to walk the fine line between going far enough to make the adjustment the best it can be and then going too far. As a designer, you can do exactly that—push the adjustment to the extreme to see what it looks like when it's too much. When you find that line, pull back a bit, and you'll know you've gone far enough but not too far. When you work this way, seeing what you don't want can make it easier to find what you do want. You're training your eye to recognize when an image looks its best, and recognizing when an image looks *bad* is a big part of that training.

Figure 18 Before and after views of the Levels adjustments

Adjust levels on a color image

1. Verify that the **Group 1 layer** is showing.

2. Click **Image** on the menu bar, point to **Mode**, click **RGB Color**, then click **Don't Flatten** if a dialog box appears.

   When the flower image and the three Levels adjustments are converted from Grayscale to RGB Color, the adjustments affect the flower image differently. The lower petals are now blown out. The Levels 1 adjustment needs to be readjusted.

3. Expand the **Group 1 layer**, then target the **Levels 1 adjustment**.

4. On the Properties panel, drag the **white triangle** to **203**, drag the **black triangle** to **29**, then collapse the **Group 1 layer**.

   With minor tweaks, the image once again has excellent contrast and is visually dynamic.

5. Save your work and keep this file open.

6. Open PS 5-4.psd.

   This is the same image in color that you've been working on in black and white.

7. Select all, copy, close the file, then return to the Adjusting Levels file.

8. Verify that the **Group 1 layer** is collapsed and targeted, then paste.

   Because the Group 1 layer was collapsed and targeted, the pasted image was placed in a new layer above the Group 1 layer and not inside it.

9. Target the **Group 1 layer**, click **Layer** on the menu bar, then click **Duplicate Group**.

   The Duplicate Group dialog box opens.

10. Type **Color Adjustments** in the As text box, then click **OK**.

11. Drag the new **Color Adjustments group layer** above Layer 1 on the Layers panel.

    As shown in Figure 19, the impact that the three Levels adjustments have on the color flower is dramatic. The highlights are bright without being blown out, the shadows have substance, the colors are rich, and the whole image is vibrant. The same adjustments that were applied to improve the black and white image did the exact same thing for the color image. The color is much more vibrant in the corrected image because the highlight and shadow points are on target and the contrast is excellent. You could not achieve this level of vibrant color without excellent contrast.

    AUTHOR'S NOTE Converting modes with adjustments, as we did in Step 2, is something you'll likely never do in your own work. As you saw, it adversely affected the adjustments. We did this only as part of a teaching exercise.

12. Save your work, then close Adjusting Levels.

You converted the grayscale file to RGB Color. You noted that the shift to a different color mode negatively affected how one of the Levels adjustments was affecting the image, so you tweaked that adjustment. You duplicated the adjustments and applied them to a color version of the same image, noting that the same adjustments improved the color in the image and making the connection that excellent contrast is the key to excellent color.

Figure 19 Before and after views of the same Levels adjustments on a color image

INVESTIGATE THE RGB COLOR MODEL

▶ *What You'll Do*

In this lesson, you'll learn about the RGB Color model in depth.

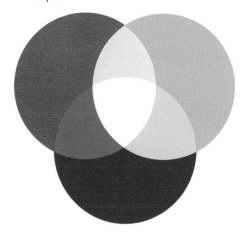

Investigating RGB in Photoshop

A **color model** is a mathematical model that describes how colors can be represented as numbers, usually as a way for computers to process color. Photoshop incorporates many different color models, including RGB, HSL, CMYK, Lab color, and Hexadecimal color.

RGB (Red, Green, Blue) is the primary color model that Photoshop uses to render color images. In an RGB image, each pixel can be one of 256 shades of red, 256 shades of green, and 256 shades of blue.

On the Channels panel, you will find a Red, a Green, and a Blue channel. Each is a grayscale image displaying pixels from 0 to 255 for that channel. In the Red channel, for example, the range is from black, at 0, to red, at 255.

Whenever red, green, and blue values are equal, the pixel's color will be black, white, or a range of gray in between. Black pixels have an RGB value of 0R/0G/0B. White pixels are 255R/255G/255B. Middle gray pixels have an RGB value of 128R/128G/128B.

Whenever red, green, and blue values are not equal, they produce colors. For example, orange colors are created with a high percentage of red and a lower percentage of green and little or no blue. One specific hue of orange can be rendered as 255R/128G/0B.

Investigating RGB on Your Computer Screen

Think of a white screen on your computer. Imagine, for example, that you're looking at a blank document in Microsoft Word or a white canvas in Photoshop. That white screen is actually composed of three colors—red, blue, and green, mixed together in equal measure. Now imagine a rainbow across your screen, perhaps a gradient in Photoshop with a spectrum of pink, purple, orange, yellow, cyan, and magenta. Those colors, too, are all produced on your monitor with the same three colors: red, green, and blue. In fact, in the actual hardware of your computer screen, the light emitting components are red lights, green lights, and blue lights. Figure 20 shows an illustration of this concept. With those three colored lights, your computer can render all the color you see every day on your screen.

If you flick a few drops of water onto a computer monitor, the water droplets will magnify and refract the light on the computer screen, enabling you to see the tiny red, green, and blue lights that are the light source for the computer screen. The white that you see on the screen is actually red, green, and blue monitor pixels combining equally to produce white light.

Investigating RGB in the Natural World

Red, green, and blue lights making all the colors on your computer screen, including white, mimics color in the natural world. Use Figure 21 as an illustration for this discussion. The great light source in our world is, of course, the sun. The sum total of light radiation from the sun is called the **electromagnetic spectrum**. The spectrum is measured in waves and includes such familiar components as radio waves, microwaves, x-rays, and ultraviolet rays.

Figure 20 Illustration of red, green, and blue light on a computer monitor

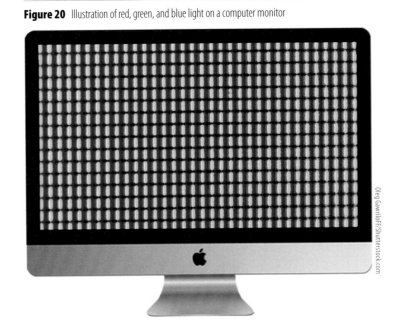

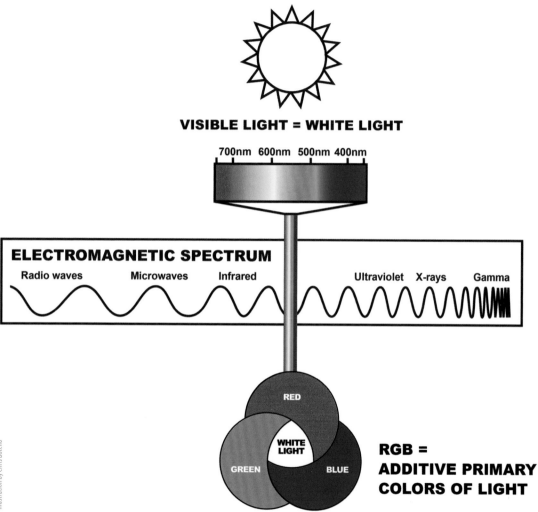

VISIBLE LIGHT = WHITE LIGHT

700nm 600nm 500nm 400nm

ELECTROMAGNETIC SPECTRUM

Radio waves   Microwaves   Infrared   Ultraviolet   X-rays   Gamma

Illustration by Chris Botello

RED

WHITE LIGHT

GREEN   BLUE

RGB =
ADDITIVE PRIMARY
COLORS OF LIGHT

Only a small subset of the electromagnetic spectrum is visible to the human eye. The typical human eye can see wavelengths between 380 and 750 nanometers. This subset is called **visible light**. As humans, we perceive all visible light as colorless; therefore, the visible spectrum is also called **white light**.

Through the process of **refraction**, white light can be broken down to make its component wavelengths visible. Figure 22 shows a prism refracting white light, making the visible spectrum visible. The **visible spectrum** is red, orange, yellow, green, blue, indigo, and violet, which has the nickname *roygbiv*.

Red light, green light, and blue light (RGB) are the **additive primary colors** of white light. The term "additive" refers to the fact that RGB light can combine in infinite measures to produce all the colors of the visible spectrum; the term "primary" refers to the fact the red light, green light, and blue light cannot themselves be refracted or broken down. For example, yellow light is a component of the visible spectrum, but it is not primary, because yellow light is created when red light and green light combine. Therefore, yellow light can be broken down to red light and green light. Those two primary colors, however, cannot be broken down.

This phenomenon occurs in nature, as you know, when you see a rainbow. For a rainbow to occur, there must be rain and bright sunlight. The droplets of water function as tiny prisms that refract the sunlight and make the visible spectrum visible in the sky. It's quite profound to consider that something so beautiful and magical to our human eyes exists as a scientific fact of nature.

When RGB combine in equal measure, they produce white light. Therefore, what we perceive as white is the combination of all colors. Black, on the other hand, is the absence of light, and therefore the absence of all colors.

Investigating How Our Eyes Interpret RGB

It is fascinating to think of our tiny human eyeball as the receptor for the immense ball of light that we call the sun, but the identification is correct. Light makes human vision possible, and the only true light in the world is sunlight. Consider the millions of years of evolution that have fashioned the human eye not only to perceive our world but also to perceive the infinite range of beautiful color in our world. It is a consideration both astounding and humbling.

Figure 22 Illustration of a prism refracting white light into the visible spectrum

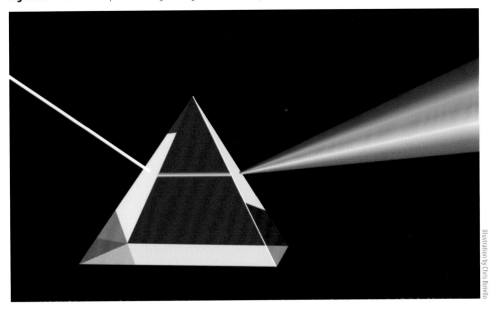

Illustration by Chris Botello

Figure 23 shows an illustration of the human eye. Our eyes contain receptor cells called **rods** and **cones**.

Rod cells process and perceive light as a range from highlight to shadow. Therefore, our perception of shape and size and distance and perspective relies on the rod receptors in the physiology of our eyes. It has likely never occurred to you how bizarre it is that we watch old black and white movies and fully accept them as reality, when in fact not one of us has ever lived in a black and white world. The rod receptors in our eyes make sense of those images, and that suggests we don't rely on color as much as we think we do to understand our world.

Cone cells perceive color. Some cone cells are sensitive to red light, some to green light, and some to blue light. Therefore, our eyes essentially break down white light into reds, greens, and blues.

One can only imagine the delicate balance and calibration our eyes rely upon to process and perceive color. People who are color blind have a deficiency in the cone cells in their eyes for a specific color. Red-green colorblindness is the most common, and those people have difficulty distinguishing between some red and green hues.

Humans have discovered all kinds of ways to manipulate (and have fun with) these physiological realities of color perception. You are probably familiar with old-fashioned 3-D glasses with a red plastic lens on one side

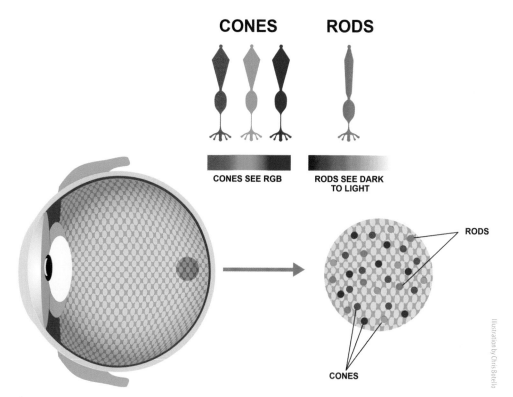

Figure 23 Illustration of rods and cones in the human eye

and a blue plastic lens on the other. Those glasses created a three-dimensional effect by separating the perception of red and blue light in each eye and using that separation to create an artificial perception of different depths. In the late 1960s, people would create outdoor "red rooms," which were small rooms lit with only red light. Standing in that room for a short amount of time would overstimulate the red cone receptors in their

eyes and simultaneously starve the green and blue receptors. Then, when they stepped out into the bright white light of day, their minds would "see" the intense greens of nature's flora and the profound blues of an immense sky. What was really happening was that those starved green and blue receptor cells were drinking in all the sudden green and blue light while the overstimulated red receptors had had their fill.

Another interesting optical color phenomenon is called a green flash. You can see a green flash shortly after sunset or just before sunrise. When the sun is almost entirely behind the horizon, with only the barest edge still visible, the eye might perceive a sky full of green for just a few seconds.

All of this is a great reminder that color is perception and entirely dependent on the lighting conditions in our world.

Investigating Subtractive Primary Colors

Cyan, magenta, and yellow (CMY) are the **subtractive primary colors**. Each is created by *subtracting* one of the additive primary colors. To put it a different way, each is created by combining two additive primaries. Figure 24 shows the subtractive primary colors.

Cyan is created by removing red light and combining green and blue light equally. Thus, cyan is also referred to as "minus red."

Magenta is created by removing green light and combining red and blue light equally. Thus, magenta is also referred to as "minus green."

Yellow is created by removing blue light and combining red and green light equally. Thus, yellow is also referred to as "minus blue."

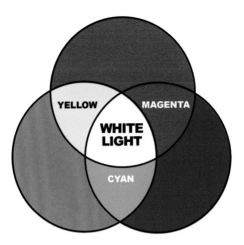

Figure 24 Subtractive primary colors

This relationship between CMY and RGB is reflected in the Color Balance adjustment, shown in Figure 25. The Color Balance settings show that Cyan is opposite Red, Magenta is opposite Green, and Yellow is opposite Blue. Therefore, any adjustment you make is either a move toward or away from an additive primary.

The world of subtractive primary colors is a world unto itself. For the purposes of this discussion, think of cyan, magenta, and yellow as "primary" *not for light* but only for human-made colors, such as pigments, inks, paints, and the like. For example, you might know that cyan, magenta, and yellow are the three

Figure 25 Color Balance adjustment settings

ink colors used to produce all other colors in conventional offset printing. When it comes to working with Photoshop (and using this book), all you should focus on is that CMY are each created by subtracting red, green, and blue light, respectively. Only RGB are the primary colors of light because they can't be refracted and broken down to other colors. Based on that definition, cyan, magenta, and yellow are *not* primary colors of light because each is composed of two additive primary colors.

View RGB on your computer monitor

1. Open PS 5-5.psd, then verify that only the **Background layer** is showing.

2. Make the **Freak Flag layer** visible.

3. Move the **Layers panel** out of the way so you can see the entire flag.

4. Position the mouse pointer over the **eye button** 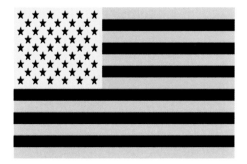 on the **Freak Flag layer** so you will be ready to hide the layer in the next step without looking away from the flag.

5. Stare at the **lower-right black star** for a full 30 seconds then, without looking away, click the **eye button** to hide the flag and stare at the white canvas for 45 seconds longer.

   Instantly you see the red, white, and blue American flag on the white canvas. If you continue to stare, it will fade in and out. As you stare at the flag, shown in Figure 26, your eyes are starved for red light in the stripes, blue light in the square, and all light in the black areas. When the white screen is restored, all colors are present in equal measure. However, the color receptors in your eyes that were deprived of certain colors are now overly sensitive to them. They are "drinking them in," so to speak. Therefore,

Figure 26 Minus red, minus white, and minus blue flag

your eyes are literally pulling red light out of the white light for the stripes and pulling blue light out of the white light in the rectangle. Even the white stripes on the flag are brighter white.

6. Show the **RGB layer**.

7. Stare for 30 seconds at the center blue and red stripes, then hide the layer.

   You instantly see cyan, magenta, and yellow stripes. When you stare at the red stripes, your eyes are starved for green light and blue light. When the red stripes are removed, your eyes pull green light and blue light from the white light in those

areas. Those areas appear as cyan, because cyan is created from combining green and blue light. The same principle explains why you see magenta and yellow stripes in place of the other two additive primary colors.

8. Close the file without saving changes.

You used two illustrations to perceive the color receptors in your own eyes.

Mix colors with RGB

1. Open PS 5-6.psd, then verify that your computer screen is turned up to full brightness.

2. Move the **Green circle** left so it overlaps the **Red circle**.

   The overlap is yellow because red light and green light combine to make yellow light.

3. Move the **Green circle** down so it overlaps the **Blue circle**.

   The overlap is cyan because green light and blue light combine to make cyan light.

4. Overlap the **Blue circle** with the **Red circle**.

   The overlap is magenta because red light and blue light combine to make magenta light.

Continued on next page

5. Overlap all three circles, as shown in Figure 27.

Where the three circles overlap, the area is white, with an RGB value of 255R/255G/255B. Overlapping RGB in equal measure produces white when the RGB components are each 255. White is the combination of all three additive primaries.

6. Reduce the **Opacity** on all three layers to **50%**.

The overlap area is gray, with an RGB value of 128R/128G/128B. At lower values, the overlap produces gray.

7. Increase the **Opacity** on the **Red layer** to **100%**.

As shown in Figure 28, the red/green overlap creates orange, the green/blue overlap creates a dark cyan, and the blue/red overlap creates a dark magenta. The area where all three colors overlap is a muted pink color. The RGB value of that pink is 255R/128G/128B.

8. Set the **Opacity** on the **Red layer** to **50%**, the **Green layer** to **20%**, and the **Blue layer** to **100%**.

As shown in Figure 29, purple hues are created when blue dominates and green is highly reduced. Note that where the red and green overlap produces a dark orange, bordering on a brown.

9. Close the file without saving changes.

You experimented with RGB in different combinations to produce white, gray, and different colors.

Figure 27 Mixing RGB to produce white

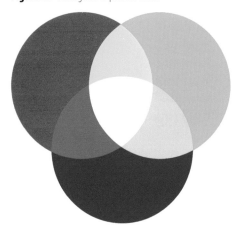

Figure 28 Mixing RGB with red dominating

Figure 29 Mixing RGB with blue dominating

Manipulate RGB in a Photoshop image

1. Open PS 5-7.psd, then save it as **RGB Color Balance**.

   This image has a yellow tone overall, which makes for a beautiful image. However, the color balance can be manipulated to create other tones that are equally interesting.

2. Verify that the **Sunset layer** is targeted, click the **Create new fill or adjustment layer button** on the Layers panel, then click **Color Balance**.

   Color Balance adjustment settings appear on the Properties panel. Each of the subtractive primaries is opposite its additive primary—Cyan is opposite Red, Magenta is opposite Green, and Yellow is opposite Blue.

3. On the Properties panel, note that **Tone** is set to **Midtones**. Drag the **top slider** to **+43**, then drag the **middle slider** to **−36**.

4. Click the **Tone list arrow**, then choose **Highlights**.

5. Drag the **top slider** to **+26**, then drag the **middle slider** to **−21**.

   Your screen should resemble Figure 30. Moving the midtones and highlights toward red and away from green has produced an overall red color balance to the image.

6. Click the **Reset to adjustment defaults button** on the Properties panel.

   The adjustments you made are removed.

7. Drag the **top slider** to **−28**, then drag the **bottom slider** to **+44** to adjust the midtones.

Continued on next page

Figure 30 Shifting the overall color balance to red

Morguefile

USE THE ERASER TOOL

The Eraser tool is a quick way to erase pixels from an image. When a layer is targeted, the Eraser tool will erase pixels leaving transparent areas. In a flattened image (all layers are flattened to one background layer), the Eraser tool paints with the current background color.

8. Click the **Tone list arrow**, choose **Shadows**, drag the **top slider** to **–27**, then drag the **bottom slider** to **+37**.

9. Click the **Tone list arrow**, choose **Highlights**, drag the **top slider** to **–20**, then drag the **bottom slider** to **+15**.

   Your screen should resemble Figure 31. Moving the midtones and highlights away from red and toward blue has produced an overall blue color balance to the image. If you compare the two figures from this exercise, you can see the dramatic difference in color that can be achieved by adjusting the color balance.

10. Save your work, then close RGB Color Balance.

You used the Color Balance adjustment to shift the color dramatically from its original overall yellow effect to an overall red then an overall blue effect.

Explore shape vs. color

1. Open PS 5-8.psd, then save it as **Rods and Cones**.

2. Click **Select** on the menu bar, click **Load Selection**, load the selection named **Circle**, then click **OK**.

3. Click **Edit** on the menu bar, click **Fill**, click the **Contents list arrow**, click **50% Gray**, then click **OK** to fill the circle with **50% Gray**.

4. Hide the **selection marquee**, click the **Brush tool** , then set the **foreground color** on the toolbar to **white**.

TIP To hide the selection marquee, press [command] [H] (Mac) or [Ctrl] [H] (Win).

5. Set the Brush tool **Size** to **400 px**, then set the **Hardness** to **0%**.

Figure 31 Shifting the overall color balance to blue

6. Set the **Opacity** to **20%**, then position the brush at the **center of the gray circle**.

7. Click the **brush** one time.

8. Move the brush **slightly to the right**, then click again to paint a highlight.

9. Repeat the preceding step 14 times (moving the brush slightly to the right each time) to complete the highlight.

   Your artwork should resemble Figure 32.

10. Change the **foreground color** to **black**.

11. Approaching the circle from the outside and overlapping slightly, paint a shadow counterclockwise from 9 o'clock to 5 o'clock.

12. Repeat Step 11 two or three times to create a deeper shadow without going all the way to black.

Your artwork should resemble Figure 33. With shadows and highlights, the flat gray circle has transformed into a sphere. As a circle, its shape was defined by its perimeter. As a sphere, its shape is defined by its dimensionality.

13. Click the **Create new fill or adjustment layer button** ◕ on the Layers panel, then click **Hue/Saturation**.

14. On the Properties panel, click the **Colorize check box**.

    The Colorize option applies a single hue, or color, to each pixel; however, it does not change the brightness of the pixel. The sphere now appears red.

15. Drag the **Saturation slider** to **50**.

    Increasing the saturation increases the intensity of the color.

16. Drag the **Hue slider** to **205**.

    Your artwork should resemble Figure 34. The sphere changes from red to blue.

17. Drag the **Hue slider** to different locations to see the sphere with different colors.

    Regardless of how you change the color, the sphere remains a sphere. This exercise is a great example of how we perceive shape through highlight to shadow, not through color.

18. Save your work, then close Rods and Cones.

You filled a circle with gray and then created the illusion of a sphere by first painting highlights using white and then painting shadows using black. You applied the Hue/Saturation adjustment to colorize the sphere, then changed it to different hues, noting that changing the hues did not change your perspective of the object as a sphere.

Figure 32 Painting a highlight

Figure 33 Painting a shadow

Figure 34 Shifting the hue to blue does not change the dimension of the sphere

As a teacher, one of the concepts I love to share with my students is the idea that they must "learn how to see." Each of them looks at me with a "does not compute" expression. One is born, and if one is fortunate, one sees. What is there to learn?

When we are children, we are amazed by what we see. Shapes and colors are endlessly fascinating. The color receptors in our eyes are brand new, so the colors we see are the most vivid of our lifetimes. Perspective, on the other hand, is mysterious (and seemingly impossible for us to render). Thus, with our crayons, we draw the stick-figure family and the red square house with the triangle roof and the round yellow sun and the blue rectangle sky, and it's all on one plane.

As we get older, our vision becomes for us, first and foremost, a *function*—our most essential *tool* for navigating the adult world of responsibility and goals. What we call "seeing" is how we parse and process the world around us—how we put a plate on a table, how we avoid an oncoming car, how we recognize the face of our loved ones in a crowd, how we find our own face in a group photo. Even our language recognizes this functionality. Consider that we use the same word, "sense," to describe our five mechanisms for perceiving the world *and* our concept of logic. We say, "It makes sense."

Somewhere in all this visual *function*, we "lose sight" of the miracle and the beauty in everything we are seeing. We say, "This coat is red," as though it were a fact, and we don't even consider that, in a room with no light, the coat is, in fact, *not red*. We say, "This coat

is red," as though it is one thing, and even as we look at it, we fail to see that it is a *range of reds*, with darker reds in the folds and more vibrant reds where the light strikes.

With all that is visible, so much becomes invisible. We fail to notice the blue hue on the shadowy side of the white building. We barely perceive the dart of white light glinting off the ripple in the brook as it babbles by. We aren't fascinated by the polygons of negative space created by the telephone wires crossing diagonal tree branches in the gray light of winter.

We look at ourselves in the mirror and tell ourselves, "This is what I look like," oblivious to the reality that we look completely different the moment we leave that spot, the moment we leave that light. We look different in every room we enter. On a rainy day, we look different than we do in the sunshine. We look different in the morning than we do in the afternoon and in the evening. When we bump into a long-lost friend, we are shocked at how much they've changed, yet we are blind to the fact that the face we see in the mirror would be a total stranger to our younger selves.

As the shadows move across our world from morning to night, week to week, year to year, all the shapes and all the colors in our visual space change constantly before our eyes, yet we seldom mark the difference.

Photoshop demands that we see again. Photoshop insists that we notice the difference in contrast between two images that we put together in a composite. It insists that we adjust them so that they share the same highlight and the same depth of shadow; otherwise,

what's the point? Photoshop expects us to see that the shadows on this layer are inconsistent with the shadows on that layer. Photoshop challenges the logic centers in our brain to "make sense" of the perspective of one image merged with another.

Photoshop asks that we debate between this red, or maybe that red, but not this yellow, because it's too green, and not this blue, because it's too red. In Photoshop, we find ourselves torn between one percentage point either way when resizing an image to fit in a collage. We negotiate the size and the space relationship between this shape and that, and we attempt to make peace with the negative space that is created between the two. Photoshop even, at times, asks us to harmonize that which is not visible with that which is.

Over time, Photoshop teaches us. Then, at some point, we transcend Photoshop. We find ourselves seeing the actuality of the world again, as Photoshop demands that we do. Ultimately, we can work truthfully in Photoshop only when we learn, once again, to bother, to

pause,

to stop,

to look,

and to see,

once again,

to see.

INVESTIGATE THE HSB COLOR MODEL

▶ What You'll Do

In this lesson, you'll learn about the HSB color model in depth.

Investigating HSB in Photoshop

HSB (Hue, saturation, and brightness) is a color model that is based on 360 colors or hues. In the HSB color model, 360 hues exist on an imaginary circle or color wheel, one hue for each of the 360 degrees on a circle. Figure 35 shows an illustration of a color wheel.

One could legitimately ask, "Does that mean there are only 360 hues in the HSB color model?" The answer would be yes … sort of. For each of the 360 hues, there is a Saturation component and a Brightness component, each of them measured in percentages from 0% to 100%.

Saturation is the intensity of the hue. At 0% saturation, there is no color; the hue is a neutral gray. The full intensity or vibrance of the hue is 100% saturation.

Hues in the HSB color model also have a brightness component: 0% brightness represents the absence of light and is black, and 100% brightness is the full illumination of the hue.

With a range of 0–100% saturation and 0–100% brightness available for each hue, each hue can be one of 10,000 colors (100 × 100 = 10,000). With 360 hues available, that creates a total of 3,600,000 color combinations available in the HSB color model.

Figure 35 Illustration of a color wheel

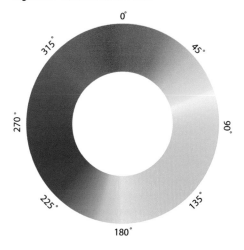

Figure 36 shows the Color Picker dialog box, which is one of the most essential dialog boxes in Photoshop. It allows you to choose any color as the foreground or background color. The Color Picker dialog box uses the HSB color model for its interface. In the figure, the color wheel is represented by the vertical rainbow rectangle. Move the sliders on the rectangle to choose a hue from 0° to 360°. In the figure, hue 225° has been chosen. Each hue number is followed by the degree symbol (°) to show its placement in the 360° color wheel.

The large rectangle that dominates the dialog box represents all the combinations of saturation and brightness available for hue 225°. Saturation increases horizontally from left to right. Brightness increases vertically from bottom to top. Therefore, the most vivid combinations are in the top-right corner, which all have higher saturation and brightness values. All the colors on the left edge are grays because they have 0% saturation. Those grays range from black on the bottom (0% brightness) to white at the top (100% brightness). All the pixels along the bottom edge are black, regardless of their saturation, because they have 0% brightness. The top-right corner of the rectangle represents the "pure hue" with 100% saturation and 100%

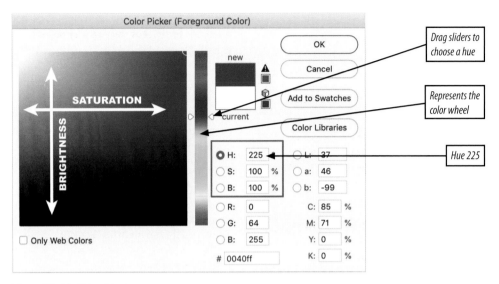

Figure 36 Color Picker dialog box

brightness. What's interesting is that the colors you see in the rectangle are all the same hue: 225°.

RGB and HSB Working in Tandem

In the Color Picker dialog box, you can specify color as RGB or HSB. They are independent of one another, but they don't conflict. It's like reading the same novel in English and in Italian—same story, just a different language.

The best way to approach the two color models is to keep them separate in your mind. When you are evaluating an image in terms of color balance, you're looking at the image in terms of RGB. Is it too red? Is the green too heavy in the highlights? At other times, you'll be evaluating images in terms of brightness/contrast, or you'll want to make the color of an image more intense. In that case, you're looking at the image in terms of HSB. Become comfortable with both because each offers a powerful and effective way to assess a color image.

Using the Hue/Saturation Adjustment

As much as you've gotten used to thinking of each pixel in a color image as having a red/green/blue component, you must also think of each as simultaneously having a hue/saturation/brightness component. That comes into play with the Hue/Saturation adjustment, which offers three controls (Hue, Saturation, and Lightness, along with a Colorize option) to manipulate HSB values in each pixel. The Hue/Saturation adjustment is one you will use often for both practical reasons and for special effects.

Hue is the name of a color. Red, blue, green, and yellow are all hues. The Hue slider shifts selected pixels' hues around the color wheel. In the Hue/Saturation adjustment, the Hue slider isn't listed as degrees. Instead, hues are listed as moving in two directions, toward +180 or –180. You can think of this as moving clockwise and counterclockwise around a 360° color wheel.

When you alter the hue of a given image, the brightness component is not affected by moving the Hue slider, so the tonal range from shadow to highlight is not affected. Therefore, the object simply appears to only change color. With this in mind, imagine that you have an online store selling sweaters, and you sell those sweaters in different colors. You could photograph a single red sweater; bring the image into Photoshop; and then use the Hue slider to quickly create new versions of the image for the orange, yellow, green, blue, and purple sweaters you also sell.

The Saturation slider either intensifies the color or removes color. When you desaturate an image, you set the saturation percentage for each pixel to 0%, thus creating what appears to be a "black and white" image. In that case, remember that the file is still a "color" file, because it's in RGB mode; it just appears black and white because the saturation is at 0%. In terms of your online sweater business, you could desaturate the image of the red sweater to create a gray sweater.

The third slider is the Lightness slider. (In the Color Picker dialog box, the third component is called "Brightness"; in the Hue/Saturation dialog box, it's called "Lightness." One must get used to this minor inconsistency.) The Lightness slider alters pixels' brightness values from black to white.

As a general rule, think of the Lightness slider as an option when using the Hue/Saturation adjustment for special effects; however, don't think of the Lightness slider as an alternative to brightening an image as you would with the Brightness/Contrast or the Levels adjustments. Those adjustments also offer controls for maintaining contrast; the Lightness slider does not. Therefore, looking back at your online sweater business, if you create a gray sweater image that is darker than the actual gray sweater you're selling, use the Brightness/Contrast or the Levels adjustment to brighten it, not the Lightness slider.

Colorizing an Image

When you click the Colorize option on the Hue/Saturation adjustment, it changes the hue of all selected pixels to 0°, which is a red hue.

You can change that hue by moving the hue slider; when you do, all the selected pixels will have that new hue. The result is that an image appears to be one color, like a black and white image that's been tinted with a single color. You can also modify the saturation and lightness when colorizing.

Loading Selections from Layer Masks

A layer mask is itself a selection. The act of painting in a layer mask is the act of making a selection. For example, let's say that you want to change a person's hair color from blond to blue. You would use a Hue/Saturation adjustment to colorize the image blue. You would then fill the layer mask with black and then paint white only in the areas that correspond with the person's hair. When you're done, the white area you painted in the mask represents a selection of the person's hair. At any time, you can load a layer mask as a selection by pressing [command] (Mac) or [Ctrl] (Win) and then clicking the layer mask.

Using the Replace Color Dialog Box

When you want to modify the color in areas of an image that are difficult to select with the selection tools, the Replace Color dialog box can be very useful. The Replace Color dialog box offers tools that allow you to target various areas of an image based strictly on similarity in color. When you target an area, the dialog box shows you a black and white mask, with the white areas representing the pixels that will be affected by any changes you make. Drag the Fuzziness slider to increase white in the mask and the pixels that will be affected. Use the Add to sample tool to click a specific area to add that area to the selection. Once you have targeted the areas of the image you want to affect, changing the Hue and Saturation values in the dialog box will modify the color only in those areas.

The Replace Color feature is another example of destructive editing—it directly affects the targeted artwork. Unless you use the Undo command (or the History panel), the change is permanent. Therefore, whenever you use the Replace Color feature, you should duplicate the layer you want to modify and apply the

Replace Color feature to the duplicate artwork. That way, you preserve the original artwork, and you can use a layer mask on the duplicate artwork layer to control how the Replace Color alteration affects the original.

USING TOOLS TO MAKE LOCAL ADJUSTMENTS TO BRIGHTNESS AND SATURATION

Most of the work you do to brighten and darken an image and adjust color saturation will be done with adjustment settings. However, the toolbar offers tools to make these moves by hand to specific (or *local*) areas of an image.

The Dodge tool 🔍 brightens areas that you paint. When the Dodge tool is selected, the Options panel offers an Exposure setting, which controls the strength of the tool and its effect. The Options panel also offers a Range menu, which allows you to choose to brighten shadows, midtones, or highlights with the tool.

The Burn tool 🖐 is the Dodge tool's partner and opposite. Use the Burn tool to darken local areas in an image. The Options panel offers the same settings for Burn tool as it does the Dodge tool.

Use the Sponge tool 🧽 to saturate or desaturate color in specific locations of an image. The Mode menu on the Options panel allows you to toggle between Saturate and Desaturate mode for the tool.

COLOR MODELS IN PHOTOSHOP	
Grayscale	Single-channel mode. Pixels can be one of 256 shades of gray, numbered 0–255. Grayscale mode is used to render black and white images.
RGB	Red, Green, Blue. This three-channel color mode offers 256 shades in the red channel, the green channel, and the blue channel, thus making more than 16 million colors available. RGB mode is the most-used color mode in Photoshop.
HSB	Hue, Saturation, Brightness. Each pixel can be one of 360 available hues. That hue is modified by saturation and brightness, each of which is measured in percentages. Saturation describes the vividness of the color and is measured from a neutral gray at 0% saturation to full intensity at 100%. Brightness is measured from 0% brightness, which is black, to 100% brightness, which is white. A pixel with a "pure hue" has 100% saturation and 100% brightness.
CMYK	Cyan, Magenta, Yellow, Black. This color mode is used for images that are to be printed using the conventional four-color printing process. Some modern-day digital printing presses work with RGB images, so talk to your printer about whether or not your color images should be saved in RGB or CMYK mode.
Indexed Color	The Indexed Color mode renders color images using a palette of 256 colors. When a color image is rendered with just 256 colors, it can appear as continuous tone, or it can appear to be posterized, depending on the image. Indexed color was used often in the early days of the Internet to render color images with small file sizes that could be downloaded quickly.
Lab Color	Lab Color is a color space in which color is described with a value for universal lightness (L) and four chromatic colors, the red/green axis (a) and the blue/yellow axis (b). The Lab color space is considered "device independent" meaning that it can be used to achieve the exact same color in different mediums. Lab Color is widely used in the plastics, automotive, and textile industries.

Explore hue, saturation, and brightness in the Color Picker

1. Open PS 5-9.psd, then save it as **Hue Sat Stripes**.

2. Press the **letter [D]** on your keypad to set the foreground and background colors to their defaults.

3. Click the **foreground color** on the toolbar.

   The Color Picker dialog box opens.

4. Verify that the **option button** 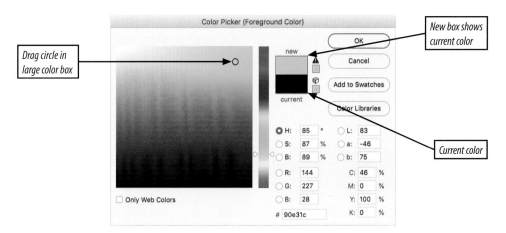 next to **H (Hue)** is activated, then drag the **Hue slider** up and down, noting the changes in the H text box.

   The H value refers to the hue number on a 360° color wheel.

5. Drag the **Hue slider** until the H value reads **85°**.

6. Click and drag **in the large color box** to the left of the Hue slider.

   As you click and drag in the large color box, the values in the S (Saturation) and B (Brightness) text boxes change depending on the direction you drag. Figure 37 illustrates this. The new box at the top of the dialog box shows the current color you are sampling, and the current foreground color is below it. Note, however, that wherever you sample, the H value remains at 85°. Any new colors you are sampling are all hue 85° with varying percentages of saturation and brightness.

7. Drag the **circle in the color box** all the way to the upper-right corner.

   In the upper-right corner, the S and B values are 100%. This color is the "pure" hue 85°—the brightest and most saturated.

Figure 37 Sampling a color with high saturation and brightness percentages

8. Drag the **circle in the color box** down along the right edge of the color box.

   As you drag down, the brightness is reduced, and the color is darkened. A color with 0% brightness is black, regardless of the hue and saturation values.

9. Click the **upper-left corner**, then drag the **circle** down along the left edge of the color box.

   Wherever you click along the left edge, you will see a shade of gray. At the left edge, there is 0% saturation, which means that only a shade of gray is possible. The left edge changes from white to black as the brightness decreases.

10. Click **near the center** of the color box, then drag the **circle** right and left, noting the changes in the S (Saturation) text box.

As you drag to the right, the saturation increases. As the saturation increases, the intensity of the color increases.

11. Click **near the center**, then drag slowly toward the upper-right corner.

    As shown in Figure 37, as you drag up and right, both the saturation and the brightness increase, and the color is brightened and intensified dramatically.

12. Click **OK** to close the Color Picker dialog box.

You sampled Hue 85° in the Color Picker dialog box and dragged the circle in the color box to better understand how to change the saturation and brightness of the hue.

Apply Hue/Saturation adjustment layers

1. Click the **Create new fill or adjustment layer button** 🔘 on the Layers panel, then click **Hue/Saturation**.

2. Drag the **Hue slider** to **–125**.

   The stripes on the shirt change to blue. White pixels are not affected by changes in hue because white pixels have HSB values of 0%/0%/100%. Since a white pixel has 0% saturation, it has no color, and a hue shift cannot affect it. Note in the image, however, wherever there are shadows in the white stripes, those are visibly affected by the adjustment.

3. Rename the adjustment layer **Blue**.

4. Verify that the **layer mask** is selected, then invert it by pressing **[command] [I] (Mac)** or **[Ctrl] [I] (Win)**.

   The layer mask on the adjustment layer is inverted to black.

   TIP Whenever you rename the layer, the layer mask becomes deselected, and the adjustment thumbnail becomes selected. You must select the mask to use it.

5. Choose a **brush size**, **hardness**, and **opacity**, then paint with a **white foreground color** to "brush in" the adjustment so your artwork matches Figure 38.

6. Add a second **Hue/Saturation adjustment layer**, drag the **Hue slider** to **+123**, then drag the **Saturation slider** to **–40**.

7. Rename the adjustment layer **Green**.

8. Invert the mask, then brush in the adjustment only on the **stripe immediately below the blue stripe** you just painted (including the sleeves).

9. Using the same steps for the blue and green stripes, add four more Hue/Saturation adjustment layers and paint each stripe a different color. Name each new adjustment layer by color.

   Your artwork should resemble Figure 39.

Figure 38 Changing the hue of a stripe to blue

Krakenimages.com/Shutterstock.com

Figure 39 Different Hue/Saturation adjustments applied to different stripes

10. Zoom in on the **sleeve** at the right side of the canvas.

   White is the most reflective color, and the white stripes above and below the green stripe are red in the shadows. They are reddish because they reflected the original red stripe, which is now green. Also, there are red reflections near the blue stripe.

11. Target the **Green layer**, then brush in the adjustment to change the pink reflections on the white stripes to green.

12. Target the **Blue layer**, then brush in the adjustment to change the pink reflections on the white stripes to blue.

   Your result should resemble Figure 40. When doing a project like this, reflections are always a challenge. For example, note the pink reflection on the skin on the inside of the man's arm. In this case, the reflection is not a problem because the stripe beside it is pink.

13. Zoom in and pan over the image, looking for other reflection color issues and correct them.

   TIP Look for another issue under the other sleeve.

14. Target **all the adjustment layers**, then click the **Create a new group button** 🗀 on the Layers panel.

15. Set the **Opacity** on the **Group 1 layer** to **50%**.

   As shown in Figure 41, reducing the opacity of all the adjustment layers reduces the opacity of the colored stripes.

16. Save your work, then continue to the next set of steps.

You used multiple Hue/Saturation adjustments and their layer masks to change colors throughout the image.

Figure 40 Adjusting red/pink reflections on the white stripes

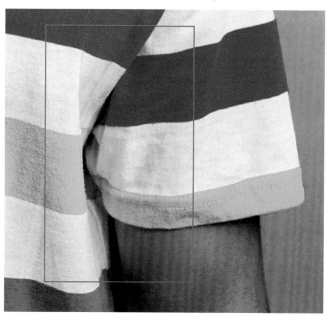

Figure 41 Reducing the opacity on all the adjustments

Desaturate an image and load selections from layer masks

1. Target the **Group 1 layer**, then add a new **Hue/Saturation adjustment layer**.

   The new adjustment layer appears above the Group 1 layer on the Layers panel.

2. Drag the **Saturation slider** all the way to the left to **−100%.**

   The entire image appears as a black and white image. White stripes on the shirt are not affected because they have 0% saturation to begin with.

3. Invert the layer mask.

   The adjustment no longer shows.

4. Expand the **Group 1 layer** to show the adjustments inside.

5. Press and hold **[command] (Mac)** or **[Ctrl] (Win)**, then click the **layer mask** on the **Blue layer**.

   The mask is loaded as a selection.

6. Add the **[shift] key** so that you're holding **[shift] [command] (Mac)** or **[Shift] [Ctrl] (Win)**, then click the **five other masks**.

   All six masks are loaded as selections.

7. Target the **layer mask** on the new Hue/Saturation layer at the top of the Layers panel.

8. Fill the selection with **white**.

9. Deselect, hide the **Group 1 layer**, then compare your results to Figure 42.

10. Save your work, then close Hue Sat Stripes.

You used a Hue/Saturation adjustment layer to desaturate the whole image. You then loaded selections from all the masks you painted on other adjustment layers to mask the desaturation adjustment to affect only the stripes on the shirt.

Figure 42 Desaturated stripes

Clip adjustment layers

1. Open PS 5-10.psd, then save it as **Clipped Adjustments**.

   This is the layers project you worked on in Chapter 3. The goal of this exercise is to desaturate the two coins.

2. Target the **Middle Coin layer**, then **add a Hue/Saturation adjustment layer**.

3. On the Properties panel, drag the **Saturation slider** all the way to the left.

   All the artwork on layers below the Middle Coin layer are affected.

4. Press and hold **[option] (Mac)** or **[Alt] (Win)**, then float over the horizontal line between the adjustment layer and the Middle Coin layer on the Layers panel.

   When you float over the line, your mouse pointer changes to a bent arrow icon ⤵□.

5. Click the **horizontal line**.

The adjustment is clipped into the Middle Coin layer and now affects only that artwork. As shown in Figure 43, the adjustment layer now shows the bent arrow icon, indicating that it is

Figure 43 Bent arrow icon indicates clipped layer

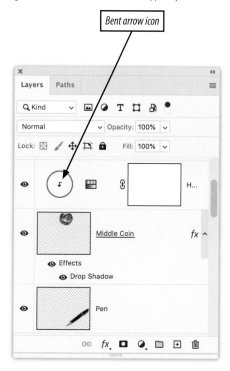

a clipped layer. The method you used to clip the layer is the manual method. Next, you will learn an alternative method.

6. Target the **Bottom Coin layer**.

7. Press and hold **[option] (Mac)**, then click the **Create new fill or adjustment layer button** ⊘ or press and hold **(Alt) (Win)** and **right-click** the **Create new fill or adjustment layer button** ⊘ on the Layers panel, then click **Hue/Saturation**.

The New Layer dialog box opens.

8. Click the **Use Previous Layer to Create Clipping Mask check box**, then click **OK**.

The new adjustment layer appears on the Layers panel as a clipped adjustment.

9. Desaturate the **Bottom Coin artwork** by dragging the **Saturation slider** all the way to the left.

10. Add a **Levels adjustment layer**, then clip it.

AUTHOR'S NOTE When working with multiple clipped adjustments, think of the adjustments as all being clipped into the base artwork. For example, in this case, don't think of the Levels adjustment being clipped into the Hue/Saturation adjustment. Instead, think of both adjustments as being clipped into the Bottom Coin artwork.

11. On the Properties panel, drag the **white triangle** to **215**.

12. Press and hold **[option] (Mac)** or **[Alt] (Win)**, then drag the **Levels adjustment** above the Hue/Saturation adjustment clipped into the Middle Coin layer.

A copy of the Levels adjustment is created. Pressing and holding [option] (Mac) or [Alt] (Win) when dragging a layer copies the layer. The new adjustment layer is unclipped and is affecting all artwork on layers beneath it.

13. Clip the Levels adjustment into the Hue/Saturation adjustment and thus the Middle Coin artwork.

14. Save your work, then close Clipped Adjustments.

You clipped two Hue/Saturation adjustment layers and two Levels adjustment layers into two different components of the collage.

Use the Replace Color dialog box

1. Open PS 5-11.psd, then save it as **Replace Color**.

2. Duplicate the **Background layer**, then rename the new layer **Replace Color**.

3. Click **Image** on the menu bar, point to **Adjustments**, then click **Replace Color**.

The Replace Color dialog box opens with the Eyedropper tool selected 🖉 in the upper-left corner.

4. Click the **Eyedropper tool** 🖉 on the **red stripe** at the center of the man's chest.

The mask turns white in areas representing what is selected.

Continued on next page

5. Drag the **Hue slider** to **–125**, then compare your screen to Figure 44.

   As shown in the figure, most but not all the red stripes have been affected by the hue shift. Some red patches remain.

6. Drag the **Fuzziness slider** to **94**.

   Fuzziness expands or contracts the selection based on where you sampled. The greater the Fuzziness value, the more white data will show in the mask and the more pixels will be affected by any changes you make.

7. Click the **Add to Sample tool** at the top of the dialog box.

8. Click the **Add to Sample tool** on a remaining red patch on the shirt, which is likely in shadow areas.

   Clicking the Add to Sample tool adds that area and similar areas of the image to the selection.

9. Click the **Add to Sample tool** until the stripes on the shirt are completely blue, as shown in Figure 45.

10. Click **OK**.

11. Add a **layer mask** to the Replace Color layer, then invert the mask.

12. Paint with white to brush in the blue stripes from the Replace Color layer.

Figure 44 Results of the first sample

Figure 45 Using the Add to Sample tool adds reddish areas to the selection

13. Save your work, then close Replace Color.

The Replace Color dialog box is okay for a quick change on a project that is not that important or one that you won't be making future changes to. The Replace Color feature is a dialog box utility, not an adjustment. When you're done with it, what you're left with cannot be edited effectively. In this project, for example, let's say you zoomed in and found some faint red pixels sprinkled throughout the blue stripes, pixels that the utility "failed" to modify. What could you do? Not much. On top of that, you still had to mask the change because it affected areas of the image you didn't want affected. Therefore, you would have been better off using a Hue/Saturation adjustment and masking in changes. For the same amount of work, you'd be left with an editable adjustment layer that cannot fail to affect the areas that you want affected.

You used the Replace Color dialog box to sample areas to change their hues.

Colorize an image

1. Open PS 5-12.psd, then save it as **Colorize**.

The sweater in this image is an excellent example of range of tone in shadows. Despite being overall a dark charcoal gray throughout, there is an abundance of detail in the sweater. You can see shadows in the fold under the sleeves and where the folded-over turtleneck meets the sweater. Furthermore, you can see the pattern of the knitting throughout.

2. Open the **Info panel**, click the **Eyedropper tool** on the *right half* of the panel, then click **HSB Color**.

3. Click the **Eyedropper tool** on the toolbar, then float over the **sweater**, noting the HSB information on the Info panel.

The pixels that make up the sweater have a range of hues from approximately 60° to 90° degrees, but their Brightness values are all less than 20 percent, so there's very little color in the sweater.

4. Add a **Hue/Saturation adjustment layer**, then drag the **Hue slider** slowly left and right.

No matter where you drag the Hue slider, the color of the sweater doesn't change.

5. Click **Colorize** on the Properties panel, then float the **Eyedropper tool** over the image to sample pixels' HSB values on the Info panel.

The Info panel shows before and after values. As shown in Figure 46 and on your Info panel, all the pixels in the image now have 0° as their hue, which is red.

6. Drag the **Hue slider** slowly to the right.

As you drag, the hue for all the pixels in the image changes. At all times, all the pixels in the image have the same hue.

Continued on next page

Figure 46 Viewing all pixels at Hue: 0°

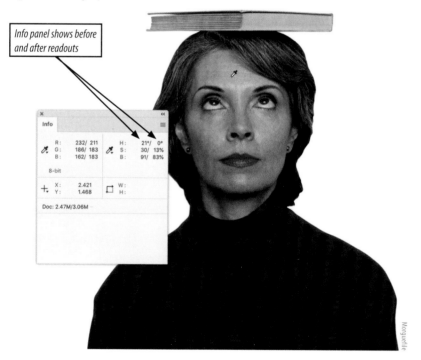

Info panel shows before and after readouts

7. Target the **layer mask** on the adjustment layer, click **Select** on the menu bar, click **Load Selection**, load the selection named **Sweater Mask**, then click **OK**.

8. Fill the selection with **black**, then **deselect**.

9. Invert the **mask**.

10. Select the **adjustment layer thumbnail**.

11. On the Properties panel, drag the **Hue slider** to **124**, then drag the **Saturation** slider to **50**.

    The sweater appears as a dark forest green.

12. Drag the **Lightness slider** to **13**.

    The color of the sweater lightens, and the sweater is now clearly green. However, the shadows were weakened with the Hue/Saturation adjustment, which you will now fix with a Levels adjustment.

13. Add a **Levels adjustment** above the Hue/Saturation adjustment.

14. On the Properties panel, drag the **black triangle** to **19** to darken the shadow point, drag the **white triangle** to **203**, then drag the **gray triangle** to **0.87**.

15. Select the **Hue/Saturation adjustment layer**, then reduce the **Saturation** to **45**.

    As shown in Figure 47, considering that was originally a dark charcoal gray sweater, the adjusted sweater is now very believably green.

16. Save your work, then close the Colorize file.

You colorized the image, masked the adjustment so that it affected the sweater only, then you brightened the sweater so the hue and saturation shifts became visible. You then used the Levels adjustment to restore contrast to the sweater without losing the new green hue.

Figure 47 Viewing the green sweater

Apply an Invert adjustment layer

1. Open PS 5-13.psd, then save it as **Skills Trio**.
2. Click the Create new fill or adjustment layer button on the Layers panel, then click Invert.
   The grayscale values of the pixels in the image are inverted: black pixels have changed from 0 to 255, and white pixels have changed from 255 to 0. As indicated on the gradient on the left, the entire range from black to white has been inverted.
3. Hide and show the Invert adjustment layer. Because the adjustment has been applied as an adjustment layer, it can be made visible or invisible like any other layer. The original artwork is affected only when the adjustment layer is visible.
4. Save your work, then continue to the next set of steps.

Apply a Threshold adjustment layer

1. Hide the Invert adjustment layer, then target the Background layer.
2. Click the Create new fill or adjustment layer button on the Layers panel, then click Threshold.
   All the pixels in the image become either black or white.
3. On the Properties panel, drag the Threshold Level slider to 74.
   All pixels with a grayscale value of 74 or greater are now white.
4. Save your work then continue to the next set of steps.

Apply a Gradient Map adjustment layer

1. Hide all the adjustment layers, then target the Background layer.
2. Click Image on the menu bar, point to Mode, then click RGB Color.
   If a warning box opens asking whether or not you want to flatten the image, click Don't Flatten.
3. Click the Create new fill or adjustment layer button on the Layers panel, then click Gradient Map.
4. On the Properties panel, click the gradient above the Dither option.
   The Gradient Editor dialog box opens.
5. Click the left color stop, click the Color box, choose a dark purple or maroon, then click OK.
6. Change the right color stop to a pale yellow color.
7. Add a color stop in the middle of the gradient, change its color to green, then set its location to 50%.
8. Click OK, then compare your artwork to Figure 48.
9. Save your work, then close Skills Trio.

Figure 48 Viewing the Gradient Map adjustment

(continued)

Adjust Brightness/Contrast

1. Open PS 5-14.psd, then save it as **Skills Brightness and Contrast**.
2. Sample the image, looking for the brightest pixels and darkest pixels.
   The brightest pixels are over the man's shoulder, but they are in the 120–124 range, which is below even a middle gray. The shadows overall are weak, with the darkest being around 30.
3. Click the Create new fill or adjustment layer button on the Layers panel, then click Brightness/Contrast.
4. On the Properties panel, click the Use Legacy check box, then drag the Brightness slider to 65.
5. Drag the Contrast slider to 65.
6. Sample the highlights over the man's shoulder, on his forehead, and in the white of his eye.
   The highlights are bright and white.
7. Sample the shadows in the man's hair.
   The shadows in the image are still too bright in the 28–32 range.
8. Reduce the Brightness to 55, then increase the Contrast to 69.
9. Hide and show the Brightness/Contrast adjustment layer to see its effect.
   Figure 49 shows the before and after views of the image.
10. Save your work, then close Skills Brightness and Contrast.

Employ the Levels adjustment

1. Open PS 5-15.psd, then save it as **Skills Adjusting Levels**.
2. Click the Create new fill or adjustment layer button on the Layers panel, then click Levels.

Figure 49 Before and after views of the Brightness/Contrast adjustment

3. Assess the histogram.
   On the right side of the histogram, it appears that some data goes all the way to the white triangle, but there's very little of that data. The bulk of the histogram ends halfway between the gray triangle and the white triangle. On the left side of the histogram, there's a gap between the black triangle and the data on the histogram, meaning there are no black pixels in the image.
4. Click the Set white point eyedropper tool on the Properties panel, float over the image, then press [option] (Mac) or [Alt] (Win).

   The entire canvas turns black except for any pixels that have a grayscale value of 255, which remain white. In the case of this image, those pixels are very few and in a line on the right side of the image.
5. Drag the black triangle right to 15 at the start of the histogram.
6. Click the Set black point eyedropper tool on the Properties panel, float over the image, then press [option] (Mac) or [Alt] (Win).

   The entire canvas turns white except pixels with a grayscale value of 0, which remain black.

7. Add a second Levels adjustment layer.
8. Drag the white triangle to 175—the end of the bulk of data on the histogram.

    The image is brightened, but many of the very bright areas have blown out to white and will need to be masked from this adjustment.
9. Click the Set white point eyedropper tool  on the Properties panel, float over the image, then press [option] (Mac) or [Alt] (Win).

    With this technique, you can see which highlights blew out to white.
10. Click the Brush tool, set the Opacity to 30%, then use a soft-edged brush to gradually mask out the second Levels adjustment where it blew out the highlights. When you are done, no highlight areas on the image should be overly blown out or glaring white.
11. Drag the gray triangle to the right to change the midtone input level to 0.92.
12. Shift-click to target both adjustment layers on the Layers panel, then enter **[command] [G] (Mac)** or **[Ctrl] [G] (Win)**.
13. Hide and show the Group 1 layer.

    Figure 50 shows the image before and after the adjustments.
14. Save your work, then continue to the next set of steps.

Figure 50 Before and after views of the adjustments

Morguefile

(continued)

Adjust levels on a color image

1. Verify that the Group 1 layer is showing.
2. Click Image on the menu bar, point to Mode, click RGB Color, then click Don't Flatten if a dialog box appears.
3. Open PS 5-16.psd.
4. Select all, copy, close the file, then return to the Skills Adjusting Levels file.
5. Verify that the Group 1 layer is collapsed and targeted, then paste.
   Because the layer is collapsed, the image was pasted above the layer, not inside the group.
6. Target the Group 1 layer, click Layer on the menu bar, then click Duplicate Group.
   The Duplicate Group dialog box opens.
7. Change the name of Group 1 to **Color Adjustments**, then click OK.
8. Drag the new Color Adjustments group layer above the Group 1 layer on the Layers panel.
   Figure 51 shows the image before and after the adjustments.
9. Save your work, then close Skills Adjusting Levels.

Figure 51 Before and after views of the same Levels adjustments on a color image

Apply Hue/Saturation adjustments

1. Open PS 5-17.psd, then save it as **Skills Stripes**.
2. Click the Create new fill or adjustment layer button on the Layers panel, then click Hue/Saturation.
3. Drag the Hue slider to +118.
4. Rename the adjustment layer **Green**.
5. Verify that the layer mask is selected, then invert it by pressing **[command] [I] (Mac)** or **[Ctrl] [I] (Win)**. The layer mask on the adjustment layer is inverted to black.

TIP Whenever you rename the layer, the layer mask becomes deselected, and the adjustment thumbnail becomes selected. You must select the mask to invert it.

6. Paint with a white foreground color to "brush in" the adjustment so that the longest stripe is green.
7. Add a second Hue/Saturation adjustment layer, drag the Hue slider to −63, then drag the Saturation to −26.
8. Rename the new adjustment layer **Purple**.
9. Select the mask, invert the mask, then brush in the adjustment on only the bottom-most stripe.
10. Using the same steps for the green and purple stripes, add three more Hue/Saturation adjustment layers to create three more colors, and paint the remainder of the shoe. Name each adjustment layer with its color.
    Figure 52 shows one example.
11. Target all the adjustment layers, then click the Create a new group button on the Layers panel.

12. Set the Opacity on the Group 1 layer to 50%.
13. Save your work, then continue to the next set of steps.

Desaturate an image and load selections from layer masks

1. Target the Group 1 layer, then add a new Hue/Saturation adjustment layer.
   The new adjustment layer appears above the Group 1 layer on the Layers panel.
2. Name the new adjustment layer **Desaturate**, then drag the Saturation slider all the way to the left.
   The entire image is affected and appears as a black and white image. White stripes on the shoe are not affected because they have 0% saturation to begin with.
3. Invert the layer mask.
   The adjustment no longer shows.

Figure 52 Different Hue/Saturation adjustments applied to different stripes

4. Expand the Group 1 layer to show all the adjustments inside.
5. Press and hold [command] (Mac) or [Ctrl] (Win), then click the layer mask on the Green layer.
   The mask is loaded as a selection.
6. Add the [shift] key so that you're holding [shift] [command] (Mac) or [shift] [Ctrl] (Win), then click all the other layer masks.
   All masks are loaded as selections.
7. Target the layer mask on the Desaturate group layer, then fill the selection with white.
8. Deselect, then hide the Group 1 layer.
9. Paint white in the Desaturate layer's layer mask to desaturate any areas of the image that are still in color, then compare your results to Figure 53.
10. Save your work, then continue to the next set of steps.

Figure 53 Desaturated stripes

(continued)

Use the Replace Color dialog box

1. Open PS 5-18.psd, then save it as **Replace Color Skills**.

2. Duplicate the Background layer, then rename the new layer **Replace Color**.

3. Click Image on the menu bar, point to Adjustments, then click Replace Color.
   The Replace Color dialog box opens with the Eyedropper tool selected in the upper-left corner.

4. Click the Eyedropper tool on the light purple sleeve on the woman's left arm.
   The goal is to change the purple elements of her costume to green.

5. Drag the Hue slider to −180 and the Saturation slider to +15.

6. Drag the Fuzziness slider to 40.

7. Click the Add to Sample tool  at the top of the dialog box.

8. Click the Add to Sample tool on a darker purple area of the costume.
   Clicking the Add to Sample tool adds that area and similar areas of the image to the selection.

9. Click the Add to Sample tool until the purple areas are completely green, as shown in Figure 54.

10. Click OK.

11. Add a layer mask to the Replace Color layer, then mask the face and hands to fix any areas that may have changed color.

AUTHOR'S NOTE You will repeat this exercise in this chapter using a layer mask instead of the Replace Color dialog box. As you will see, doing this with a mask will be a lot of work. This image is one for which Replace Color is a faster and more effective choice than using a mask.

12. Save your work, then close Replace Color Skills.

Colorize an image

1. Open PS 5-19.psd, then save it as **Colorize Skills**.

2. Add a Hue/Saturation adjustment layer, then drag the Hue slider slowly left and right.
   The color of the car changes very subtly—not a dramatic change or a vivid color.

3. Click the Colorize check box on the Properties panel.

4. Drag the Hue slider all the way to the left to 0.

5. Drag the Lightness slider to +10, then drag the Saturation slider to 60.

6. Mask the adjustment where it needs to be masked; you'll need to figure out what needs to be color and what should remain as is.

TIP Consider avoiding looking at the finished image on this page as you decide what stays and what gets masked. "Processing reality" is itself a challenge when masking.

7. When you're finished masking, change the Hue to 216, then compare your choices and your results to Figure 55.

8. Save your work, then close Colorize Skills.

Figure 54 Purple areas replaced with green

MorgueFile

Figure 55 Viewing the results of colorizing

This project is designed to give you more experience adjusting with levels. Creating the best contrast possible with levels is something you'll need to do often, and the only true way to get good at it is to practice on lots of images and develop an eye for tonal range, both in black and white and in color images.

For this project, you've been given seven images in black and white and the same images in color. All of them require adjustments for contrast. Feel free to use multiple Levels adjustments when necessary, and definitely feel free to use layer masks to brush in adjustments to specific areas. Don't use any other adjustments, such as Hue/Saturation or Color Balance.

Work on the black and white images first. When you move to the color images, don't go back and check the adjustments you made on the black and white versions. Instead, remember what you learned on the black and white versions to inform you how to approach the color versions.

The goal for both the black and white and color images is to produce the best contrast and tonal range while maintaining reality and leaving no evidence of your involvement in modifying the images.

1. Open the folder named Project Builder Images, then open the folder named Grayscale.
2. Open all seven images.

3. Working methodically, use the skills you learned in Lesson 2 of this chapter to use Levels adjustments to improve the contrast in each image.

TIP You might want to read through Lesson 2 again for a refresher on how we approached the work in those exercises.

4. When you are done with each image, save a separate PSD file for each.
5. Close each of the black and white images before moving on to the color images.

6. Open the seven color images in the Color Images folder.
7. Using what you learned when improving the black and white versions, adjust the color images for better contrast and, as a result, better color.
8. Save a separate PSD file for each.
   Figure 56 shows a before and after example of one set.

Figure 56 Before and after results of Levels adjustments

This project is designed to reinforce your skills using brush work for creating layer masks. You will first mask out the background of an image; then you will brush a Hue/Saturation adjustment into a complex costume. The image has only medium resolution, so fine details are missing, and you'll have to decide for yourself what to affect and what to leave alone as you work toward the goal. This exercise will also reinforce the need to clip adjustments when working with multiple images, as you learned to do in Chapter 3.

1. Open PS 5-20.psd, then save it as **Multiple Hues**.
2. Add a layer mask to the Purple layer.
3. Select the Brush tool, then set its Hardness to 75%.
4. Mask the image to remove the white background.
5. When you finish the mask, fill the Background layer with white.
6. Click Image on the menu bar, then click Canvas Size.
7. Click the Canvas extension color list arrow, then click White.
8. Click the arrow in the middle-left anchor box ←, change the Width to 8.25, then click OK.
9. Duplicate the Purple layer, then rename it **Green**.
10. Move the Green layer artwork directly to the right, as shown in Figure 57.
11. Press and hold [option] (Mac), then click the Create new fill or adjustment layer button or press and hold (Alt) (Win) and right-click the Create new fill or adjustment layer button on the Layers panel, then click Hue/Saturation.

Figure 57 Duplicating and moving the artwork

12. Click the Use Previous Layer to Create Clipping Mask check box, then click OK.
    The new Hue/Saturation adjustment layer is clipped into the Green layer and therefore will affect only the Green layer.
13. Drag the Hue slider to −180, then drag the Saturation slider to +27.
    The entire layer is affected.
14. Invert the layer mask on the Green layer.
15. Paint with white to brush in the adjustment in all the purple areas.
    Use Figure 58 as your guide. Expect to spend at least 30 minutes brushing in the adjustment.

Figure 58 Changing the purple hues to green

16. Target both the Green layer and its clipped adjustment layer on the Layers panel.
17. Press and hold [option] (Mac) or [Alt] (Win), then drag the artwork directly to the right as you did in Step 10. A copy of the artwork and the adjustment layer is created.
18. Shift the Hue and Saturation so the third costume is orange, not green.
19. Using the same steps as you did to create the green and orange costumes, create a yellow and blue version so your canvas resembles Figure 59 on the following page.
20. Save your work, then close Multiple Hues.

Figure 59 The finished project

This project will show you how to create a "tinted black and white" effect in which parts of the image appear in color and other parts appear as a faintly colored black and white image. After you have progressed through the exercise, find your own images and experiment with different techniques for creating this effect.

1. Open PS 5-21.psd, then save it as **Tinted Black and White**.
2. Add a Hue/Saturation layer mask, then drag the Saturation slider all the way to the left.
3. Mask the adjustment so the apples are in full color and the remainder of the image is black and white.
4. Reduce the Opacity on the adjustment layer to 80% so your work resembles Figure 60.
5. Save your work, then close Tinted Black and White.

Figure 60   Vibrant apples and a tinted background

mythja/Shutterstock.com

DESIGN WITH ESSENTIAL
BLENDING MODES
AND FILTERS

1. Use the Multiply Blending Mode
2. Explore the Screen Blending Mode
3. Apply the Overlay Blending Mode
4. Design with Blending Modes

Adobe Certified Professional in Visual Design Using Photoshop CC Framework

3. Organizing Documents
This objective covers document structure such as layers and managing document structure for efficient workflows.

3.2 Modify layer visibility using opacity, blending modes, and masks.

 A Adjust a layer's opacity, blending mode, and fill opacity.

4. Creating and Modifying Visual Elements
This objective covers core tools and functionality of the application, as well as tools that affect the visual outcome of the document.

4.6 Modify the appearance of design elements by using filters and styles.

 A Use filters to modify images destructively or non-destructively.

USE THE MULTIPLY BLENDING MODE

▶ *What You'll Do*

In this lesson, you'll use the Multiply blending mode for different effects.

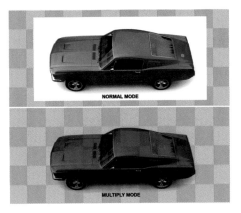

Working with Blending Modes

Because Photoshop offers the ability to work with layered artwork, it follows logically that pixels on one layer will directly overlap pixels in the same location on layers below it. **Blending modes** are mathematical algorithms that define how pixels affect pixels on layers beneath them. The Layers panel houses 27 blending modes (including Normal), many of which you'll use often and some you might never use. You'll use blending modes to create special effects, but the most essential blending modes have highly practical functions as well.

You specify the blending mode for a given layer on the blending mode menu, shown in Figure 1. Note that the list of blending modes is grouped into sections based on how they function. Four commonly used groups are as follows:

Darken blending modes (Darken, Multiply, Color Burn, Linear Burn, Darker Color): With these modes, white pixels become invisible, and black pixels are unaffected and remain opaque. These modes darken the areas of overlap.

Lighten blending modes (Lighten, Screen, Color Dodge, Linear Dodge, Lighter Color): With these modes, black pixels become invisible, and white pixels are unaffected and remain opaque. These modes lighten the areas of overlap.

Figure 1 Blending modes on the Layers panel

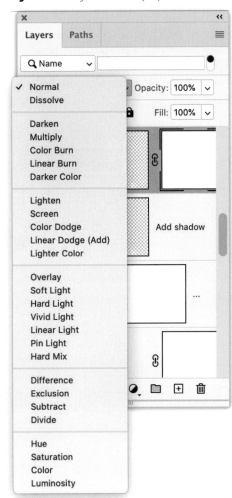

Overlay blending modes (Overlay, Soft Light, Hard Light, Vivid Light, Linear Light, Pin Light, Hard Mix): With these modes, gray pixels become invisible, and all pixels become transparent. These modes increase the contrast and saturation where pixels overlap.

Hue blending modes (Hue, Saturation, Color, Luminosity): These modes affect the color of pixels, specifically in terms of their hue, saturation, or brightness (luminosity).

The default blending mode for a layer is Normal, which is no blend at all. In Normal blending mode, the pixels on one layer completely hide pixels on layers below it. With other blending modes, pixels blend to create all kinds of color and special effects.

A good strategy for understanding blending modes is to think of three colors: the **base color** is the color of the pixel on the lower layer, the **blend color** is the color above it on the layer with the blending mode applied, and the **result color** is the color produced by blending the base and blend colors.

Figure 2 shows an example of the Multiply blending mode. The blue diamond is the base color, and the pink diamond is the blend color. In Normal mode, the pink color obscures the blue diamond below it where they overlap. When the Multiply blending mode is applied to the pink diamond, a third color is created where they overlap. This third color is the result color. If you were to apply a different blending mode to the pink diamond, the result color would be different; with some modes, there would be no change at all.

Figure 2 Example of the Multiply blending mode

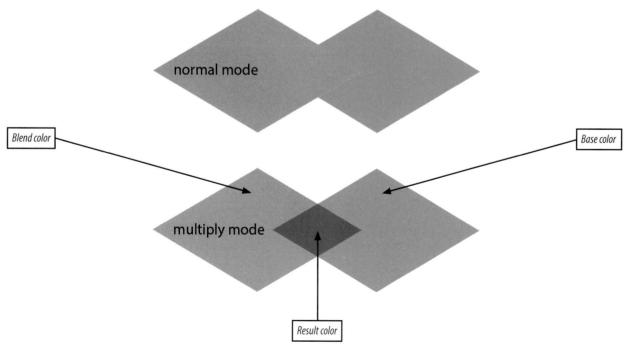

Examining the Multiply Blending Mode

The Multiply blending mode is one of the first blending modes most new Photoshop users encounter, primarily because it makes white pixels "invisible," and all colors appear "see-through" (except black). Figure 3 demonstrates this. In the top photo, an image of a blue car with a white background is positioned above an image of an orange and gray checkerboard. In the bottom photo, the Multiply blending mode has been applied to the layer with the car on it. The white background has disappeared completely. The car is now transparent: you can see the checkerboard through the car—except in the black areas like the tires, which are not affected by the blending mode.

What's fun about the Multiply blending mode is that its mathematical algorithm is basic enough for anybody to understand, so let's examine how it does what it does.

The calculation for the Multiply blending mode is the following:

(pixel 1 × pixel 2) / 255 = pixel 3

where pixel 1 is the base color, pixel 2 is the blend color, and pixel 3 is the result color. Figure 4 shows four examples of how pixels will blend with this calculation. In the top equation, a pixel with a grayscale value of 100 is multiplied with a pixel with a grayscale value

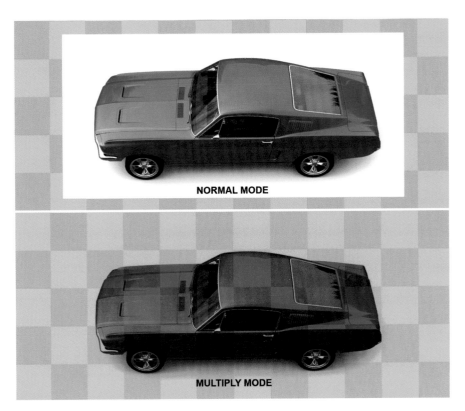

Figure 3 Multiplying the car image over the checkerboard

of 210, and then the result is divided by 255. The result is a pixel whose grayscale value is 82. It only makes sense that the resulting pixel (pixel 3) is darker than the base pixel (pixel 1) because you divided by a number (255) that

is higher than the number you multiplied by (210). Thus, the Multiply blending mode always darkens an image, as you can see in Figure 3. The blue of the car in Multiply mode is noticeably darker.

The second equation in Figure 4 shows what happens when you multiply with white. In the figure, a 100 pixel is multiplied by a 255 pixel and then divided by 255; thus, the resulting pixel (pixel 3) is 100. This explains why, in Figure 3, the white background behind the car disappears. The resulting pixel (pixel 3) is identical to the base pixel (pixel 1), so the blend color (the white pixel) has no role in the resulting image. Essentially, it "disappears."

The third equation in Figure 4 shows how colors blend in the Multiply mode. In this case, yellow and cyan are being multiplied to make green. You can see how each of the RGB components are run through the equation to produce the green result. (Note: this discussion of blending modes and their calculations has no relation to the additive primary and subtractive primary color model discussions from Chapter 5. They are two different and unrelated topics.)

The fourth equation in Figure 4 shows what happens when you multiply with black. A black pixel has a grayscale value of 0. Anything multiplied by zero is zero. Thus, anything multiplied with black results in black. This explains why the black tires and other black parts of the car do not change in Figure 3.

With all of this in mind, you can understand better what a *practical* tool the Multiply blending mode can be, offering you the ability to make images and colors transparent and make white disappear.

Figure 4 Examples of different calculations with the Multiply blending mode

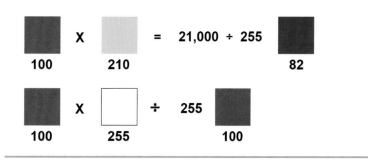

MULTIPLY MODE

(Pixel 1 x Pixel 2) / 255 = Pixel 3

Applying a Blending Mode to a Group

The Layers panel offers you the ability to use **groups**, which are like folders, to organize your layers. When you're working with multiple layers, especially when you're building collages that involve numerous pieces of artwork, a group becomes very useful for collecting related layers in one place, segregating different components of a project, and making the Layers panel more manageable.

By default, when you create a layer group, its blending mode will be Pass Through. **Pass Through mode** indicates that the group functions only as an organizational tool to house layers, nothing more complicated than that. Therefore, the act of grouping layers will cause no change to how layers with blending modes applied to them will affect one another or how they affect images outside the group.

Blending modes can be applied to groups themselves. When you apply a blending mode to a group, all the layers in the group take on that blending mode. For example, if you apply the Multiply blending mode to a group, all the layers inside the group will be multiplied. This offers you a powerful method for quickly applying blending modes to multiple layers.

Applying the Normal Blending Mode to a Group

Applying the Normal mode to a group prohibits blending modes on layers in the group from affecting images outside the group. For example, if you have two overlapping images set to Multiply inside a group that is set to Normal, they will only multiply over one another and over images *inside* the group. They will *not* multiply over any images on layers that are not inside the group.

You can think of a group set to Normal mode as being a collection of isolated layers—a world unto itself.

Using Adjustment Layers in Groups

An adjustment layer inside a group, such as Hue/Saturation or Levels, affects artwork outside the group only when the group is set to Pass Through. When a group is set to any other blending mode, an adjustment layer inside the group affects only the layers in that group.

Consider for a moment the time-saving opportunity this provides. Imagine that you have 10 layers of artwork, and you want to colorize all of them with a Hue/Saturation layer. Without creating a group, you'd need to create 10 Hue/Saturation layers, all with the same settings, and clip each into the 10 images. Instead, if you put all 10 images into a group and set it to Normal, you could create one Hue/Saturation adjustment layer to affect them all, and only them, with no clipping required.

Experiment with Multiply mode

1. Open PS 6-1.psd, then save it as **No Surrender**.

2. Show and target the **Magenta layer**, click the **blending mode list arrow** on the Layers panel, then click **Multiply**.

   The magenta fill becomes transparent. The effect is similar to looking at the brick wall through glass that is tinted magenta. All black areas, such as the shadow underneath the sofa, remain black.

3. Show the **Cyan layer**.

   Because the layer is set to Normal mode, the cyan rectangle obscures everything beneath it.

4. Set the **Cyan layer's** blending mode to **Multiply**.

   The cyan rectangle becomes transparent, and the overlapping area becomes blue. Figure 5 shows the Multiply blending mode calculation that creates this blue color.

5. Delete the **Magenta layer**.

6. Delete the **Cyan layer**.

7. Show and target the **Yellow-White Gradient layer**, then multiply it.

   The yellow-white gradient becomes transparent. The yellow-white gradient now transitions from transparent yellow to clear. The white area of the gradient at the bottom is no longer visible.

8. Delete the **Yellow-White Gradient layer**.

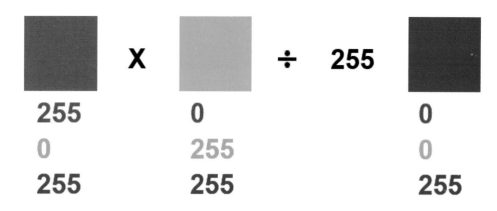

Figure 5 Calculation of magenta multiplied with cyan and producing blue

9. Show and target the **Black-White Gradient layer**, then multiply it.

   The black-white gradient transitions from black to clear. The black area at the top remains black. Black pixels have an RGB value of 0/0/0, and anything multiplied by zero becomes zero. Thus, the resulting pixel at the top of the image will be 0/0/0, regardless of what image is blended with it.

10. Delete the **Black-White Gradient layer**.

11. Save your work, then continue to the next set of steps.

You multiplied two solid fill colors to see their effect on the base image and on each other. You multiplied two gradients to demonstrate that multiplying white makes white disappear and multiplying anything with black results in black.

Applying blending modes to groups

1. Show and target the **Cyan Circle layer**, then multiply it.

2. Show and target the **Yellow Circle layer**, then multiply it.

   Where the yellow circle is multiplied over the cyan circle, a green area appears at the overlap. Both circles are multiplied over the background image.

3. Target **both layers**, then click the **Create a new group button** 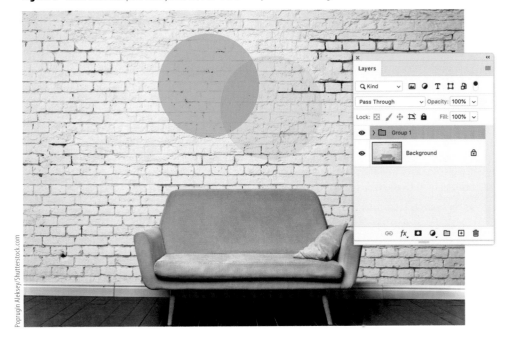 on the Layers panel to create a new group.

   The two circles are moved into a group named Group 1. The blending mode applied to the Group 1 is Pass Through, by default. Pass Through indicates that the group functions only as an organizational tool to house the two layers. As shown in Figure 6, the effect of the two multiplied circles "passes through," continuing to multiply over the brick wall.

TIP You can also press and hold [command] (Mac) [G] or [Ctrl] (Win) [G] to create a group.

Figure 6 Yellow circle multiplied over cyan circle; both circles multiplied over the background

Poprugin Aleksey/Shutterstock.com

4. Change the blending mode on the **Group 1 layer** to **Normal**.

As shown in Figure 7, the yellow circle continues to multiply over the cyan circle, but the two circles no longer multiply over the brick wall. When a group layer is set to Normal, you can think of it as a closed container. The elements inside the group only affect each other. Layers outside the group are not affected.

5. Target **Group 1**, then click the **Delete layer button** 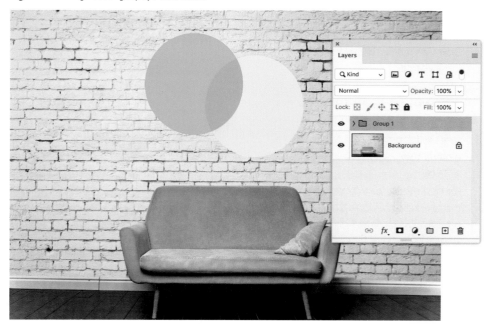 on the Layers panel.

When you delete a group, a dialog box opens, asking if you want to delete Group and Contents, Group Only, or Cancel. If you delete Group Only, the contents remain as individual layers.

6. Click **Group and Contents**.

7. Save your work, then continue to the next set of steps.

You moved two multiplied circles into a group, noting that, by default, the group was set to Pass Through, and the effect of the multiplied circles was not changed. You then changed the blending mode on the group to Normal, noting that the multiplied circles no longer affected the background image.

Figure 7 Blending mode on group layer set to Normal

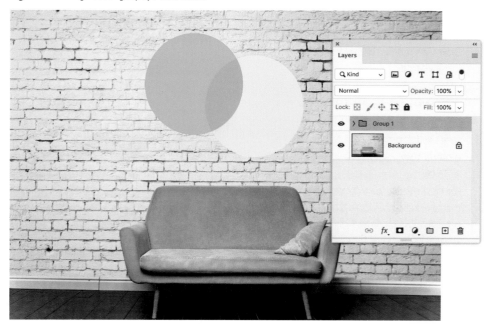

Remove a white background with the Multiply blending mode

1. Open PS 6-2.psd, then see Figure 8.

AUTHOR'S NOTE In Figure 8, the spray paint letters spell out NO RETREAT NO SURRENDER, which is a lyric from an old Bruce Springsteen song. In this exercise, you will layout the same phrase, because it has many repeating letters and will spur you to work more quickly by duplicating layers.

2. Select the **Rectangular Marquee tool** ⬚, drag a **box** around the **letter N**, copy it, then paste it into the No Surrender document.

3. Name the new layer "**N**" and then apply the **Multiply blending mode**.

   The white background disappears.

TIP Be sure to name every layer in this exercise.

4. Copy, paste, and multiply the following letters: **O**, **R**, **E**, and **T**.

5. Press and hold **[option] (Mac)** or **[Alt] (Win)**, then drag the **R layer** to the top of the Layers panel.

   A duplicate of the R layer is created.

   It is directly on top of the original R.

6. Move the **second R artwork** in place.

7. Duplicate the **E layer**, then move the **second E artwork** in place.

8. Using this method, finish the phrase so your artwork resembles Figure 8.

   This 20-letter phrase uses only eight different letters, so there are many opportunities for you to duplicate layers rather than copy and paste.

9. Target the **NO RETREAT letters**, then press and hold **[command] (Mac) [G]** or **[Ctrl] (Win) [G]**.

   The targeted layers are collected into a group called Group 1 with the Pass Through blending mode applied by default. Nothing changes in the artwork; the letters continue to multiply over the background image.

10. Rename the **Group 1 layer NO RETREAT**.

11. Create a new group for the **NO SURRENDER letters**, then rename the group **NO SURRENDER**.

12. Move the **NO RETREAT group** to the top of the Layers panel.

    It's always a good idea to organize your Layers panel logically.

13. Save your work, then continue to the next set of steps.

You copied and pasted letters into a document, and set their blending modes to Multiply to make their white backgrounds invisible. You created two groups to store each line of the phrase, noting that the Pass Through blending mode was applied to each group by default.

Figure 8 "Spray painted" phrase on the background image

Tomas Jasinskis/Shutterstock.com

Apply adjustment layers inside groups

1. Assess the No Retreat, No Surrender image.

   The type looks good, but because the letters are black, nothing of the brick shows through the "paint." It would be more effective if the details of the brick showed through the paint.

2. Expand the **NO RETREAT group**, target the **top layer** in the group, add a **Hue/Saturation adjustment layer**, then click the **Colorize check box** on the Properties panel.

   Because the blending mode of the NO RETREAT group is set to Pass Through, the adjustment affects the background image of the sofa.

3. Change the blending mode on the **NO RETREAT group** to **Normal**.

   Two things happen when the NO RETREAT group's blending mode changes to Normal. The Hue/Saturation adjustment continues to affect the letters because they are in the group, but it does not affect the background image because it is not in the group. In addition, the letters are no longer multiplied over the brick wall because the Normal blending mode prohibits blending modes on layers in the group from affecting images outside the group.

4. Change the blending mode on the **NO RETREAT group** to **Multiply**.

   The letters multiply over the brick wall. The Hue/Saturation adjustment layer affects all the letters, but it does not affect the background image.

TIP An adjustment layer in a group will only affect artwork on layers outside of the group when the blending mode is set to Pass Through.

5. Select the **Hue/Saturation layer**, set the **Hue** to **15**, set the **Saturation** to **40**, then set the Lightness to **+45**.

   The paint becomes rust colored, and the texture of the bricks is visible through the paint.

6. Change the blending mode on the **NO SURRENDER group** to **Multiply**, then expand it.

7. Duplicate the **Hue/Saturation adjustment layer**, then drag it into the **NO SURRENDER group** so that it's the top layer in the group.

8. Compare your artwork to Figure 9.

   Continued on next page

Figure 9 Viewing the brick texture through the spray paint

It's important to understand that the letters in each group are multiplying over the background image but the Hue/Saturation adjustments are not affecting the image even though they are in the same groups as the letters. The decision to make the spray paint lighter and give it a color is an example of the opportunities you look for as a designer. The black letters certainly had presence, but the ability to see the texture of the brick through the paint brings in additional detail and integrates the effect through the interaction between the paint and the wall. Also consider that if you didn't bother to use groups, you would have had to create 20 Hue/Saturation adjustment layers, one for each letter, and you would have had to clip each of those adjustment layers into its corresponding letter. This demonstrates how useful a group can be.

9. Save your work, close No Surrender, then close PS 6-2.psd.

You added an adjustment layer to a group, noting that it affected the background image outside of the group because the group's blending mode was set to Pass Through. You changed the group's blending mode to Normal, noting that the adjustment layer no longer affected the background image. You then set the group's blending mode to Multiply to multiply the letters, noting that the Hue/Saturation adjustment continued to only affect the letters and not the background image.

Multiply images

1. Open PS 6-3.psd, select all, copy, then close the file.

2. Open PS 6-4.psd, then save it as **The Man with the Dragon Tattoo**.

3. Paste the copied image into The Man with the Dragon Tattoo file, then name the new layer **Dragon**.

4. Add a **Hue/Saturation adjustment layer**, then clip it into the **Dragon layer**.

5. Click **Colorize**, drag the **Hue slider** to **100**, then drag the **Saturation slider** to **20**.

6. Target the **Dragon layer**, then multiply it.

7. Scale the **dragon artwork 50%**.

8. With the **Dragon layer** still targeted, add a **Levels adjustment layer**.

9. On the Properties panel, drag the **white triangle** to **219**, then drag the **middle gray triangle** to **1.05**.

10. Position the **dragon** so it is centered on the man's upper arm near his shoulder.

TIP If you have trouble moving the dragon, remove the check mark next to Auto-Select on the Options panel if it is checked.

11. Zoom in on the tattoo to **300%**.

The image of the dragon is a bit too sharp-edged and highly detailed to resemble an actual tattoo. You will use a filter to blur it slightly.

12. Click **Filter** on the menu bar, point to **Blur**, then click **Gaussian Blur**.

13. Drag the **Radius slider** to **0.5 Pixels**, then click **OK**.

The slight blur makes the illustration look more like an actual tattoo. Considering that the tattoo is supposed to be on the man's shoulder muscle, the artwork is too flat; it should be more rounded. You will use a different filter for that.

14. Press and hold [**command**] (**Mac**) or [**Ctrl**] (**Win**), then click the **Dragon layer thumbnail**.

A selection of the artwork on the layer is loaded. The selection is rectangular because, even though the artwork's white background is not visible in Multiply mode, it is still there and thus part of the selection.

TIP It is necessary to load this selection so the Distort filter you are going to use will use the center of this artwork as the center point for the effect.

15. Click **Filter** on the menu bar, point to **Distort**, then click **Pinch**.

    The Pinch filter makes images either convex or concave.

16. Drag the **Amount slider** to **−15**, then click **OK**.

    The filters' effects are subtle but necessary.

17. On the Layers panel, change the **Opacity** to **80%**, then compare your results to Figure 10.

18. Save your work, then close The Man with the Dragon Tattoo.

You colorized artwork green, then multiplied it over an image to create what appears as a tattoo. You used filters to blur and distort the artwork slightly.

Figure 10   Viewing the "tattoo"

EXPLORE THE SCREEN BLENDING MODE

▶ *What You'll Do*

In this lesson, you'll use the Screen blending mode for different effects.

Working with the Screen Blending Mode

The Screen blending mode functions as the exact opposite of the Multiply blending mode. With Screen, black pixels become invisible, and white pixels are unaffected and remain opaque. Regardless of what colors you use, Screen mode always lightens the overlapped area, and all colors except white become transparent.

Screen blending mode has many practical uses. In Photoshop, you can take a PDF file with black type on a white background, invert the page, and then screen it to position white type over an image. Screen mode is also commonly used and very effective for lighting effects such as flares, smoke, fog, steam, and lightning. All of these can be photographed against a black background, which can then be screened out, leaving only the light component. For example, professional photographers are known to photograph smoke against a black background because they know the background can be "dropped out" using the Screen blending mode.

Experiment with Screen blending mode

1. Open PS 6-5.psd, then save it as **Flares**.
2. Show and target the **Yellow-Purple Gradient layer**, then set its blending mode to **Screen**.

    The gradient becomes transparent, and the entire image is brightened. The brightening is most apparent in the deep shadow of the water ripple at the bottom, which is now bright yellow.
3. Delete the **Yellow-Purple Gradient layer**.
4. Show and target the **White-Black Gradient layer**, then screen it.

    The white-black gradient now transitions from white to clear. The white area at the bottom remains white.
5. Delete the **White-Black Gradient layer** and the **Water Droplet layer**.
6. Show the **Outer Bevel** and **Inner Bevel layers**, then target the **Inner Bevel layer**.
7. Create a new layer, name it **Lens Flare**, then fill it with black.

8. Click **Filter** on the menu bar, point to **Render**, then click **Lens Flare**.

Lens flare artwork is created by the Lens Flare filter. Note that the filter must have a pre-existing fill on the layer to render the artwork. Knowing that black will be dropped out with the Screen blending mode, it is the best color choice for the fill.

9. Set the **Brightness** to **100%**, then click **OK**.

10. Change the blending mode on the **Lens Flare layer** to **Screen**.

The black background becomes clear, and the underlying type artwork becomes visible.

11. Move the **center of the lens flare artwork** over the **letter S**, as shown in Figure 11.

When you move the lens flare artwork over the letter S, a hard line is revealed where the bottom of the lens flare artwork meets the black background. With the Screen blending mode, only black pixels with a grayscale value of 0 become 100% transparent. The Lens Flare filter lightened

Figure 11 Positioning the flare

most of the black fill; therefore, there's a faint line at the bottom because those pixels are a dark gray—not black—being screened. They must be made black.

12. Add a **Levels adjustment layer**, then clip it into the **Lens Flare layer**.

13. On the Properties panel, drag the **black triangle** right to **25**, then drag the **gray middle triangle** left to **1.32**.

The hard line at the bottom is darkened and is no longer visible. The midtones are brighter, so they remained vibrant with the adjustment.

Continued on next page

14. Add a **Hue/Saturation adjustment layer** above the Levels adjustment layer, then clip it.

15. On the Properties panel, click **Colorize**, drag the **Hue slider** to **223**, then drag the **Saturation slider** to **40**.

16. Target the **Lens Flare layer** and the **two adjustment layers**, then group them.

17. Verify that the **Group 1 layer** is targeted, click the **Layers panel menu button** ☰, then click **Duplicate Group**.

18. Click **OK** in the Duplicate Group dialog box to keep the name **Group 1 copy**.

TIP You can also right-click a group, then click Duplicate Group or drag the group to the Create a new layer button ⊞ on the Layers panel. If you drag the group to the Create a new group button ▢, the new group will be placed inside the original group.

19. Drag the **Group 1 copy layer** down below the Outer Bevel layer.

Figure 12 Duplicating, resizing, and repositioning lens flares

20. Expand the **Group 1 copy layer**, target the **Lens Flare layer**, scale the **lens flare artwork** to be larger, then position it **behind the letter O**.

21. Using Figure 12 as a guide, create two more duplicates of the original group, scale the lens flares to different sizes, then position them in different areas of the artwork.

22. Save your work, then close the Flares file.

You used the Lens Flare filter to create lens flare artwork on a black background. You screened the artwork to make the black background invisible and create the effect of a light shining on the type. You used a Levels adjustment to darken the background back to black after applying the filter. You then used a Hue/Saturation adjustment for a color effect.

APPLY THE OVERLAY BLENDING MODE

▶ *What You'll Do*

In this lesson, you'll use the Overlay blending mode for different effects.

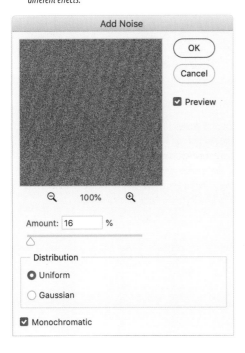

Understanding the Basics of the Overlay Blending Mode

Overlay is a blending mode that adds contrast where images or color fills overlap. Given that it adds contrast, it follows logically that Overlay lightens some parts of an image and darkens others.

The key component to remember about the Overlay blending mode is that gray pixels, exactly those at 128 at the middle of the grayscale, become invisible when overlayed. Pixels lighter than 128 lighten the image as they increase to 255. Pixels darker than 128 darken the image as they decrease to 0.

See Figure 13. The original image is at the top. The bottom image has been overlayed with black, gray, and white. The area overlayed with gray is not changed. The area overlayed with white is brightened significantly, and the area overlayed with black is darkened.

Figure 13 An image overlayed with black, gray, and white

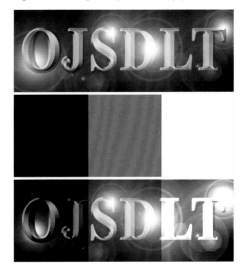

Sharpening with Overlay Mode

Sharpening is a technique for making an image appear less blurred and more in focus. Sharpening digital images is necessary because digital cameras have an anti-alias function in the lens that blurs the image slightly when it's captured to avoid creating artificial patterns (known as moire patterns).

Understanding sharpening with Overlay mode requires that you understand two concepts: edges and the results of overlaying an image on top of itself.

- The term **edges** in Photoshop refers to areas of the image where highly contrasting pixels meet. A black and white checkerboard would be an example of an image with extreme edges, because so many white pixels line up against so many black pixels.
- When you position a copy of an image on a layer on top of itself and then apply the Overlay blending mode, the result is a dramatic increase in contrast.

Sharpening with the Overlay blending mode utilizes these two concepts via the High Pass filter. As its most basic function, the High Pass filter fills a layer with gray. The High Pass filter allows you to manipulate the radius. The **radius** is a value that determines how many pixels to change on each side of the edge. When you increase the radius, the gray fill is gradually removed from the edge areas of the image; you could say those edge areas are exposed. Figure 14 shows the High Pass filter applied with a four-pixel radius. Notice the edge areas that have been exposed.

Figure 14 High Pass filter applied and exposing edge areas

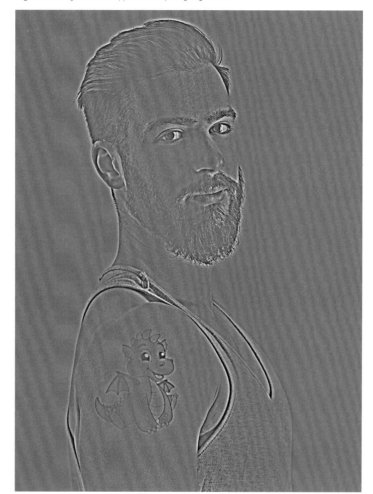

The sharpening effect is achieved when this filtered image is overlayed upon itself. With Overlay blending mode, all the gray areas of the image are rendered invisible. Thus, once the High Pass filter is applied and the image is overlayed, only the edge areas are overlayed, and the dramatic increase in contrast occurs only at the edge areas of the image. The result is the appearance of an increase of focus and detail in the image.

As you can see in Figure 14, a typical image contains many edge areas. Sharpening is very effective for bringing detail to hair, beards, clothing, and eyes. Sharpening with the Overlay blending mode is something you do at the end of a project because the high pass image must match the image underneath exactly. Otherwise, halo effects will appear as a result of overlayed edges that are not aligned.

Adding Noise with Overlay Mode

One of the last steps you'll take in any project is to add noise. **Noise**, created by the Add Noise filter, refers to tiny, random, pixel-sized squares of color or gray. When overlayed, they create a texture over the image, similar to grain you might see in conventional photography.

It might seem counterintuitive that you would want to make an image grainy, but noise is used pretty much in every commercial image you see, especially artistic and photographic images such as movie posters, album covers, and magazine covers. Look closely and you'll see the noise.

As previously stated, all digital cameras blur an image slightly when it is captured due to an anti-alias function in the lens. When you create noise, however, there's no anti-aliasing; those pixels are all hard squares. When they are overlayed over the image, those tiny, hard-edged, right-angle squares convey a subtle sense of sharpness, focus, and detail.

Adding noise is particularly useful for composite image projects where you're working with multiple images from different sources. Applying noise across the entire composite adds a consistent texture throughout. It may be subtle, but that consistency creates a familiar relationship between all images, making them appear that they all exist in the same universe.

One last major reason for adding noise is it does an incredible job of hiding subtle flaws left behind, such as softness from brush edges, aliasing from masks, and subtle color halos from Hue/Saturation adjustments. Professional designers will often comment, "Don't worry, you can hide that under the noise."

UNDERSTANDING THE IMPORTANCE OF VIEWING ARTWORK AT 100%

Sharpening images and adding noise are highly detailed functions, literally based at the pixel level. To view these results on your monitor requires that you view the image on your screen at 100%. Use the 100% command on the View menu. Even better, get used to using the keyboard shortcut, because you'll use this view thousands of times.

It's important to keep in mind that your monitor itself has pixels—tiny squares of electric light-transmitting hardware. When you view an image in Photoshop at 100%, the pixel grid of the image is aligned with the pixel grid of the monitor; one monitor pixel is used to render one pixel of the image. This provides you with an accurate view of the effect on the image.

To clarify this concept even more, imagine viewing the image at 50%. In that case, your monitor is showing you every other pixel in the image. At 25%, your monitor is showing you every fourth pixel. As bad as that is, at least the numbers are round. If you choose the Fit on Screen command and the image display is reduced to 53.7%, you can imagine the reduced accuracy of how the image is being rendered.

The rule of thumb whenever you're looking at your image to evaluate highly detailed or important areas is, view the image at a minimum of 100%.

Sharpen with the Overlay blending mode

1. Open PS 6-6.psd, then save it as **Sharpen and Noise**.

2. Target the **Ring layer** on the Layers panel, click **Select** on the menu bar, then click **All**.

3. Click **Edit** on the menu bar, then click **Copy Merged**.

   The Copy Merged command copies the composite of all visible layers, regardless of which layer in a layered document is targeted.

4. Click **Edit** on the menu bar, then click **Paste**.

   A flattened composite of the artwork is pasted.

5. Name the new layer **Merge Overlayed**, then set its blending mode to **Overlay**.

As shown in Figure 15, the effect of overlaying the image over itself results in a high-contrast version.

6. Duplicate the **Merge Overlayed layer**, then hide the **Merge Overlayed layer**.

7. Rename the **Merge Overlayed copy** layer **High Pass**, then set its blending mode to **Normal**.

8. Click **View** on the menu bar, then click **100%**.

   Whenever you are doing fine detail work like sharpening, you must view the image at 100% for the most accurate representation of the effect on the image.

9. Click **Filter** on the menu bar, point to **Other**, then click **High Pass**.

10. Drag the **Radius slider** all the way to the left until it reads **0.1**.

The image is filled with gray. Gray pixels set to the Overlay blending mode become invisible, so with this setting in the High Pass filter, all the artwork on the layer would be invisible.

11. Drag the **Radius slider** slowly to the right until it reads **3.0**.

As shown in Figure 16, the High Pass filter fills the artwork with gray, then, as you increase the Radius value, it finds edge areas of the image where highly contrasting pixels meet and makes them visible. Compare the roses with the coins. The coins are so much brighter because they contain so many more highly contrasting pixels that touch and are therefore exposed. The roses are more even in color, so the filter has less effect on them.

Continued on next page

Figure 15 Overlaying an image on top of itself creates a high-contrast version

Figure 16 The High Pass filter results

12. Click **OK**, set the layer's blending mode to **Overlay**, then hide and show the layer to see its effect.

The overall effect is that the image appears sharper and more in focus. The effect is stronger in high-contrast areas, such as the eyes, the coins, the diamond ring, and the details on the passport in the background. In some areas, it is not flattering. The man's skin tone is too detailed and ruddy. The rose petals and the coins are too sharp, and the line where the passport meets the black border is also too sharp.

AUTHOR'S **NOTE**   Consider this: the High Pass layer and the Merge Overlay layer produce the same result, with the one big difference being that the High Pass layer is filled with lots of gray. The High Pass layer produces its "sharpening" effect because the high-contrast overlay is happening only where high-contrast edge pixels meet. Therefore, those "edges" are more distinct and appear "sharper."

13. Add a **layer mask** to the **High Pass layer**, click **Edit** on the menu bar, then click **Fill**.

14. Set the **Contents** to **50% Gray**, set the Mode to **Normal**, set the **Opacity** to **100%**, then click **OK**.

The mask is filled with 50% Gray; therefore, the effect is reduced by half.

15. Paint **white** in the mask where you want to see more sharpening, and paint **black** in the layer mask where you want to see less sharpening. Consider increasing it in the eyes and the diamond and reducing it in the man's face, the passport, and the border.

16. Save your work.

You used the Copy Merged command to create a composite copy of all the visible artwork. You then overlayed that artwork to see the effect of overlaying an image on itself. You created a High Pass layer and overlayed it to sharpen the edges in the image. You used a layer mask to determine where in the image you wanted to increase and decrease the sharpening effect.

Add Noise with the Overlay blending mode

1. Target the **High Pass layer**, then add a new layer.

2. Name the new layer **Noise**, then fill it with **50% Gray**.

TIP   To fill the layer with 50% Gray, use the same method as you did in steps 13 and 14 in the previous exercise.

3. Click **Filter** on the menu bar, point to **Noise**, then click **Add Noise**.

4. Enter the settings shown in Figure 17, then click **OK**.

5. Set the **blending mode** of the **Noise layer** to **Overlay**.

6. Zoom in to **200%**, then hide and show the **Noise layer**.

The effect on the artwork is that of a texture of slightly darker or lighter pixels, similar to grain in a photograph.

AUTHOR'S **NOTE**   The appeal of adding a noise layer is that it creates a consistent texture across the composite image. That consistency helps to unite the images into a whole, making them appear more related to one another, as though they come from the same source. Typical noise values range from 8 to 12. In this exercise, 16 was used to make the effect very noticeable.

7. Save your work, then close Sharpen and Noise.

You filled a layer with 50% Gray, knowing that gray becomes invisible when multiplied. You then used the Add Noise filter to add noise to the gray layer. When you set the layer to Overlay mode, it became entirely transparent, and the noise added a grainy texture across the composite image.

Figure 17 Settings for the Add Noise filter

DESIGN WITH BLENDING MODES

Applying a Blending Mode to an Adjustment Layer

Let's say you have a single-layer image and you add an adjustment layer. If you don't modify the adjustment, it makes no change to the image. If you add a blending mode to the adjustment layer, the result is the same as if you copied the image, pasted the copy above it, and then applied the same blending mode to the copied image.

Even though the results are identical, applying the blending mode with the adjustment layer is the far better method, because you have all the controls available with the adjustment to modify the effect of the blending mode.

Blending modes can be applied to every type of adjustment layer. For example, you could create a Hue/Saturation adjustment layer, apply a blending mode, and then adjust the Hue, Saturation, and Lightness settings to modify the effect.

Using the Overlay and Soft Light Blending Modes to Enhance Images

The Overlay blending mode is known for making everyone and everything look better because of the dramatic increase in contrast it provides. Employing the Overlay blending mode brings with it more rich, vibrant, and intense color that results in images that take on a heightened reality and shine as though lit from within.

The Soft Light blending mode produces a similar effect to the Overlay blending mode, except that Soft Light is less intense. You can think of Soft Light as "baby Overlay."

Using Solid Color Adjustment Layers

In different situations, you'll want to fill a layer with a solid color. Often, you'll want to use the solid color with a blending mode, a technique that produces many dramatic and unexpected results. To fill a layer with a solid color, you can use the Fill command, but if you want to change the color of the fill again, you have to pick a new color and fill again. If you want to experiment with lots of different colors, it would become cumbersome.

A better method for working with fills is to add a Solid Color adjustment. When you do, the Color Picker opens for you to choose a color. You can then reopen the Color Picker, and as you sample different colors, the Solid Color adjustment updates dynamically. This can be particularly useful when you've applied a blending mode to the Solid Color adjustment because you can see the change of the effect dynamically as you sample different colors.

Using the Hue, Saturation, Color, and Luminosity Blending Modes

The Hue, Saturation, Color, and Luminosity blending modes are first cousins to the Hue/Saturation adjustment; they produce some of the same effects, and they produce different affects as well. These blending modes work well with solid color adjustments.

Let's say you choose a solid color with the HSB value of 10/80/70. Applying these four blending modes would result in the following:

Hue blending mode: All the pixels below the solid color will take on the hue of 10.

Saturation blending mode: All the pixels will take on the saturation of 80.

Color blending mode: All the pixels will take on both the hue of 10 and the saturation of 80.

Luminosity blending mode: All the pixels will take on the brightness of 70.

Knowing Which Blending Mode to Use

When introduced to blending modes, most new Photoshop users ask, "How do you know which one to use and when?" The best answer is probably, "Most of the time, you don't."

Once you understand the basic functions of the essential blending modes, situations arise in which you know for certain which mode to use. If you need to drop out a white background, you know to use Multiply. If you have an image of white smoke on a black background, you know to use Screen to just show the smoke. If you want to make artwork more vibrant and luminescent, you know to use Overlay, and if that effect is too dramatic, you know you can switch to Soft Light for a similar but diminished effect.

In addition to knowing the basic functions of the essential blending modes, you also know that they are grouped by similarity of effect. All the modes in the Darken section darken, all in the Lighten section lighten, and all in the Overlay section increase contrast. It also helps that Photoshop gives you a preview of a blending mode's effect just by floating your cursor over it.

Once you've worked a few hundred hours in Photoshop, you start to get a feel for specific blending modes, and you also start to create your own patterns and habits for working with them. Success, too, is a great instructor. For example, if you're going for a specific effect and you achieve it with a combination of blending modes, that naturally becomes a technique in your repertoire—one that you remember and one that you almost certainly will use again, perhaps with modifications. After a few thousand hours in Photoshop, you'll find that

you have discovered and built more techniques for your repertoire.

Ultimately, though, blending modes are about experimentation, and when it comes to design, you're seldom, if ever, certain which blending mode to use and at which setting. Instead, you try one out, combine it with another, bring in opacity as a factor, maybe add another adjustment, and before you know it, you've achieved a look you like.

Experiment with blending modes applied to adjustment layers

1. Open PS 6-7.psd, then save it as **Adjustments and Blending Modes**.

2. Target and show the **Merge Overlayed layer**.

    This is the same merged layer you created in the previous lesson. It is overlayed over the image, resulting in a dramatic increase in contrast across the image.

3. Hide the **Merge Overlayed layer**.

4. Create a new **Hue/Saturation adjustment layer**, then set its blending mode to **Overlay**.

    The result of overlaying the Hue/Saturation blending mode is identical to overlaying the merged copy of the artwork. Adding a blending mode to any adjustment layer has the same effect as duplicating the artwork and applying the same blending mode. The great difference is that, with the adjustment layer, you have all the controls available to you to adjust the effect of the blending mode.

5. Save your work.

You viewed the effect of the composite copy of the artwork overlayed upon itself. You then created a Hue/Saturation adjustment layer and set its blending mode to Overlay, noting that the effect is identical.

Enhance an image with the Overlay and Soft Light blending modes

1. Hide and show the **Hue/Saturation adjustment layer**.

   The bump in contrast makes the image more vibrant and saturated.

2. On the Properties panel, drag the **Saturation slider** all the way left to **–100**.

   As shown in Figure 18, this creates an entirely new effect. Even though the Saturation is set to –100, the image retains color because the Overlay blending mode is applied to the Hue/Saturation adjustment. The effect is a somewhat harsh, high-contrast image drained of color. The grittiness of the Noise layer adds to that effect.

TIP The term "desaturated" doesn't necessarily mean "black and white"; it refers to a reduction of color or vibrancy in an image.

TIP A good way to reference these two effects is as "pretty" and "gritty." The overlay with the saturation is pretty, and the desaturated overlay is "gritty." Associating your own words and phrases with effects you create is a great way to relate to them and remember them for future use.

Continued on next page

Figure 18 A gritty desaturated effect with the Overlay blending mode

3. Evaluate the "gritty overlay" effect for this image.

   Visually, it's a stunning image, but it's not at all right for this collage. This collage is about romance and a happy couple getting engaged on a trip to Rome. If perhaps they were spies working undercover or planning an art heist, then maybe this effect would work, but for a romantic story, it's all wrong.

4. Drag the **Saturation slider** back to **0**.

   The overlayed Hue/Saturation adjustment is "too hot," especially in the man's face, which appears bright red.

5. Change the blending mode on the Hue/Saturation layer to **Soft Light**.

   The effect is reduced in Soft Light mode and better for this image. The color isn't so harsh or glaring.

6. Hide and show the layer.

   Compared to the original, the blending mode effect creates a heightened reality in its vibrancy. However, the effect is making the man's face still too red.

7. Verify that the **Hue/Saturation adjustment** is showing, then paint **50% black** in the layer mask to reduce the adjustment by one-half.

8. Save your work, then close Adjustments and Blending Modes.

You modified the Hue/Saturation adjustment by dragging the Saturation slider all the way to the left. You noted that the image did not become desaturated because of the Overlay blending mode. Instead, the move created a dramatic desaturated effect that was not right for the tone and content of the artwork. You applied the Soft Light blending mode, which worked best for the artwork overall but required that you reduce the effect over the man's face.

Experiment with Darken blending modes

1. Open PS 6-8.psd, then save it as **Designing Modes**.

2. Target the **Background layer** on the Layers panel.

3. Add a **Hue/Saturation adjustment**, then name the layer **Sweater**.

4. On the Properties panel, click **Colorize**, then drag the **Hue slider** to **109**.

5. **Invert** the **layer mask**, then use a soft brush to brush the adjustment into the sweater only.

6. Press and hold **[option] (Mac)** or **[Alt] (Win)**, then click the **layer mask** to view it.

7. Verify that you did not miss any spots brushing in the adjustment on the sweater, paint white if you did, then click the **layer thumbnail** to return to the image.

8. Show the other **five adjustment layers**.

   These adjustments were created with the same method you used for the sweater layer. All are set to Colorize, and all are masked in with a soft brush. All six adjustment layers have the Normal blending mode applied.

9. Target the **Backdrop layer**, change the blending mode to **Linear Burn**, set the **Saturation** to **90**, then set the **Lightness** to **−27**.

   The background becomes a deep, rich gold. The goal in this exercise is to modify the other layers to mimic this look.

10. Set the **Sweater layer** to **Multiply**, set the **Saturation** to **77**, then set the **Lightness** to **−11**.

    The goal is not to use the same blending modes; the goal is to find the best blending modes to achieve the desired effect.

11. Set the **Face layer** to **Multiply**, then set the **Saturation** to **82**.

12. Set the **Mouth layer** to **Linear Burn**, then set the **Saturation** to **55**.

13. Set the **Eyes layer** to **Linear Burn**, set the **Saturation** to **47**, then set the **Lightness** to **+15**.

14. Set the **Hair layer** to **Multiply**, set the **Saturation** to **82**, then set the **Lightness** to **+37**.

    Your artwork should resemble Figure 19.

15. Save your work, then continue to the next set of steps.

You applied the Multiply and Linear Burn blending modes with different Hue, Saturation, and Lightness values to darken the image with bold colors.

Figure 19 A darkened image with bold colors

Experiment with Lighten blending modes

1. Target all **six adjustment layers**, then create a new group.

2. Name the new group **Darkening modes**.

3. Drag the **Darkening modes group** on top of the **Create a new layer button** to duplicate it.

   The duplicated adjustments create a dramatically different effect on the image.

4. Rename the new group **Lightening modes**, then hide the **Darkening modes group**.

5. Expand the **Lightening modes group**, then set the **Sweater layer** to **Color Dodge**.

6. Set the **Backdrop layer** to **Color Dodge**, set the **Saturation** to **70**, then set the **Lightness** to **–58**.

7. Set the **Face layer** to **Color Dodge**, set the **Saturation** to **50**, then set the **Lightness** to **–29**.

8. Set the **Mouth layer** to **Color Dodge**, set the **Saturation** to **73**, then set the **Lightness** to **–26**.

9. Set the **Eyes layer** to **Color Dodge**, set the **Saturation** to **55**, then set the **Lightness** to **–32**.

10. Set the **Hair layer** to **Color Dodge**, set the **Hue** to **44**, set the **Saturation** to **60**, then set the **Lightness** to **+5**.

11. On the **Backdrop layer**, change the **Hue** to **249**, then change the **Lightness** to **–39**.

    Your artwork should resemble Figure 20.

12. Save your work, then continue to the next set of steps.

You applied the Color Dodge blending mode with different Hue, Saturation, and Lightness values to create a bright, light, and glowing version of the artwork.

Experiment with Overlay blending modes

1. Collapse, then duplicate the **Lightening modes group**.

2. Rename the new group **Overlay modes**.

3. Hide the **Lightening modes group**.

4. Expand the **Overlay modes group**, set the **Sweater layer** to **Linear Light**, set the **Hue** to **190**, then set the **Lightness** to **–32**.

5. Set the **Backdrop layer** to **Vivid Light**.

6. Set the **Face layer** to **Vivid Light**, then set the **Lightness** to **–32**.

7. Set the **Mouth layer** to **Vivid Light**.

8. Set the **Eyes layer** to **Vivid Light**, then set the **Lightness** to **–42**.

9. Set the **Hair layer** to **Linear Light**, set the **Saturation** to **49**, then set the **Lightness** to **+24**.

   Your artwork should resemble Figure 21.

10. Save your work, then continue to the next set of steps.

You applied the Vivid Light and Linear Light blending modes to create a version of the artwork with deep, rich colors and good contrast from shadow to highlight.

Figure 20 A light and glowing version of the artwork

Figure 21 A version of the artwork with deep, rich colors

Use a Solid Color adjustment with blending modes that affect color

1. Hide the **Overlay modes group**, then show the **Darkening modes group**.

2. Create a new **Solid Color adjustment layer** at the top of the Layers panel above the **Overlay modes group**.

3. In the **Color Picker dialog box**, type **5** in the **H text box**, type **80** in the **S text box**, type **70** in the **B text box**, then click **OK**.

   The layer is filled with the color you specified.

4. Change the blending mode to **Hue**.

   All the pixels adopt the same hue (5) as the solid color.

5. Change the blending mode to **Color**, then compare your artwork to Figure 22.

   All the pixels adopt the same hue and saturation (5 and 80, respectively) as the solid color. The effect is similar, but if you click back and forth between the two, you will see there's a real difference.

6. Change the blending mode to **Saturation**.

   All the pixels adopt the 80% saturation of the solid color.

Figure 22   A version of the artwork with deep, rich colors

7. Change the blending mode to **Luminosity**.

   All the pixels adopt the 70% brightness of the solid color.

8. Change the blending mode to **Linear Dodge (Add)**.

9. Double-click the **solid color layer thumbnail** to open the Color Picker.

10. Drag the **Hue slider** to **150**.

11. Click and drag in the **color square** to sample different colors.

    As you sample different areas, the color updates dynamically on the canvas.

12. Choose a color that creates an effect you like.

13. Save your work, then close Designing Modes.

You created a Solid Color adjustment, then applied the Hue, Saturation, Color, and Luminosity modes. You then applied the Linear Dodge mode and sampled different colors in the Color Picker, noting that the artwork updated as you sampled.

Use the Multiply blending mode

1. Open PS 6-9.psd, then save it as **Multiply Skills**.
2. Hide the Original layer.
   The Masked layer is a duplicate of the Original layer with the sheet music behind the violin and carpet masked out.

TIP For an extra challenge and to practice critical masking skills, you should mask the violin yourself after completing this exercise.

3. Hide the Masked layer, then show the Sky and Clouds and Original layers.
4. Set the blending mode on the Original layer to Multiply.
   The entire image is multiplied, including the violin.
5. Add a Levels adjustment layer, clip it, drag the black triangle to 14, then drag the white triangle to 174.
   The adjustment makes the musical notes darker.
6. Show and target the Masked layer, add a Levels adjustment layer, then clip it.
7. Drag the black triangle to 13, drag the white triangle to 245, then drag the middle gray triangle left to 1.32.

8. Add a Hue/Saturation layer above the Levels adjustment layer, and don't clip it.
9. Set the blending mode to Hard Light, then drag the Lightness slider to +17.
10. Create a new layer above the Hue/Saturation layer, name it **Noise**, then fill it with 50% Gray.
11. Click Filter on the menu bar, point to Noise, then click Add Noise.
12. Set the Amount to 12, click Uniform, click to activate Monochromatic, then click OK.
13. Set the Noise layer blending mode to Overlay.
    Your artwork should resemble Figure 23.
14. Save your work, then close Multiply Skills.

Use the Screen blending mode

1. Open PS 6-10.psd, then save it as **Screen Skills**.
2. Open PS 6-11.psd, select all, copy, then close the file.
3. In the Screen Skills document, paste, then name the new layer **Coleridge**.
4. Press and hold [command] [I] (Mac) or [Ctrl] [I] (Win) to invert the layer.
5. Set the blending mode on the Coleridge layer to Screen.
6. Position the type where you like it.
7. Save your work, then close Screen Skills.

Figure 23 Sheet music multiplied over clouds image

Ingeborg Knol/image broker/Shutterstock.com

Enhance an image with the Overlay blending mode

1. Open PS 6-12.psd, then save it as **Gritty Overlay**.
2. Target the Hue/Saturation layer, then add a second Hue/Saturation adjustment layer.
3. Name the new layer **Gritty Overlay**, then set its blending mode to Overlay.
   The image becomes more vibrant and saturated with higher contrast.
4. Drag the Hue slider to −100.
   The image is desaturated. The shadow on the front apple has become too black.
5. Add a Levels adjustment layer, then drag the middle gray slider left to 1.55.
6. Invert the layer mask, then brush in the adjustment to lighten the shadow on the front apple.
7. Add a new layer, name it **Noise**, then fill it with 50% Gray.
8. Open the Add Noise dialog box, specify 24 for the Amount, then click OK.
9. Set the blending mode on the Noise layer to Overlay.
10. Save your work, then close Gritty Overlay.

Add a lens flare

1. Open PS 6-13.psd, then save it as **Skills Flare**.
2. Target the Color Balance 1 adjustment layer, add a new layer, fill it with black, then name it **Flare**.
3. Click Filter on the menu bar, point to Render, then click Lens Flare.
4. Set the Brightness to 100%, verify that the 50–300mm Zoom option is chosen in the Lens Type list, then click OK.
5. Remove the check mark next to Auto-Select on the Options panel if it is checked.
6. Set the Flare layer's blending mode to Screen, then drag it below the Color Balance adjustment layer.
7. Position the flare in the sky at the horizon as though it's a sunrise or a sunset between the two rightmost trees.
   As shown in Figure 24, the green and blue parts of the flare are especially visible against the darkness of the large tree at right. The overall effect is that the photographer's camera created a lens flare while photographing a sunrise.
8. Save your work, then close Skills Flare.

Figure 24 Positioning the lens flare

Design with blending modes

1. Open PS 6-14.psd, then save it as **Skills Blending Modes**.
2. Show each of the hidden Hue/Saturation adjustment layers one at a time.

   The Face, Shirt, and Backdrop layers have been colorized. The Eyes and Hair layers are not colorized, so those adjustment layers are not affecting the image in any way.
3. Set the blending mode on the Face layer to Overlay, set the Saturation to 58, then set the Lightness to +21.
4. Set the blending mode on the Shirt layer to Hard Light.
5. Set the Hue to 11, set the Saturation to 63, then set the Lightness to −2.
6. Set the blending mode on the Backdrop layer to Linear Light.
7. Set the Hue to 49, set the Saturation to 20, then set the Lightness to −13.

   The image is dramatically higher in contrast and more vivid in color. However, the hair and the eyes have not been altered from the original image. Even though the goal is not to add color to those areas, they still require the contrast bump from the blending modes to match the surrounding areas.
8. Set the Eyes layer to Overlay.
9. Set the Hair layer to Hard Light, then drag the Lightness slider to +23.
10. Press [command] [A] (Mac) or [Ctrl] [A] (Win) to select all, click Edit on the menu bar, then click Copy Merged.
11. Target the top layer, paste, then name the new layer **High Pass**.
12. Click Filter on the menu bar, point to Other, then click High Pass.
13. Enter **5** in the Radius text box, then click OK.

    Because the blending mode effects are so sharp and vivid, adding the High Pass filter at a high level makes sense.
14. Set the High Pass layer to Overlay.

    Your artwork should resemble Figure 25.
15. Save your work, then close Skills Blending Modes.

Figure 25 Blending modes making the artwork more vivid

To create this fun and highly effective zombie image, you'll have to rely on many different skills you've learned so far in this book; those include making accurate selections and masks, crafting smart layer strategies, clipping layers, and using blending modes to achieve a desired visual effect. You will be given two flattened images: the cityscape and the zombie. Study the final image, then ask yourself if you can figure out on your own how to achieve it. Try it on your own to see how far you can get. If you can't complete it, follow the steps to the end. Have fun!

AUTHOR'S **NOTE**   In the steps, you'll be instructed to select the zombie with the Magic Wand tool. If this were a professional project, you'd be expected to mask it with the Brush tool and a layer mask. When you're done with the project, you should take 30–40 minutes to mask the zombie anyway, which will give you more valuable experience masking images—one of the most important skills for any advanced Photoshop user to master.

1. Open PS 6-15.psd, then save it as **Hancock Tower**.
2. Click the Magic Wand tool, set the Tolerance to 32, then verify that the Contiguous option is activated.
3. Select the entire sky, and only the sky, in as few clicks as possible.
4. Click Select on the menu bar, click Inverse, copy, then paste.
5. Name the new layer **Skyline Only**.

6. Open PS 6-16.psd, use the Magic Wand tool to select the background, click Select on the menu bar, then select Inverse to select the zombie.
7. Click Select on the menu bar, click Select and Mask, type **4** in the Smooth text box, then click OK.

8. Copy the zombie.
9. Return to the Hancock Tower document, target the Background layer, paste, then name the new layer **Zombie**.
10. Using the Options panel, scale the layer 55%, then position it as shown in the Figure 26.

Figure 26 Positioning the zombie

tsuneomp/Shutterstock.com; Songquan Deng/Shutterstock.com

11. Duplicate the Zombie layer, then rename it **Zombie Reflection**.
12. Drag the Zombie Reflection layer to the top of the layer stack, click Edit on the menu bar, point to Transform, then click Flip Horizontal.
13. Clip the Zombie Reflection layer into the Skyline Only layer.
14. Change the Opacity to 50%, click Edit on the menu bar, point to Transform, then click Scale.
15. Using the Options panel, scale *only the width* 86%, position the artwork as shown in Figure 27, then execute the transformation.

    Skewing the artwork creates the effect that the reflection is on the same angle as the building.
16. Add a layer mask.
17. Click the Rectangular Marquee tool, select **only** the front face of the Hancock Tower, then fill it with black. The zombie couldn't possibly be reflected on this plane.
18. Set the Opacity back to 100%, deselect, then mask the Zombie Reflection where the legs are in front of the buildings.
19. Sample through the list of blending modes to see the different effects available.
20. Set the blending mode to Overlay, then set the Opacity to 50%.
21. Add a Noise layer with an Amount of 8.
22. Compare your artwork to Figure 28 on the following page.
23. Save your work, close Hancock Tower, then close PS 6-16.psd.

Figure 27 Skewing and positioning the reflection

Figure 28 The final image

Get your Brush tool ready for this exercise, which will ask you to do the most precise masking yet. The stunning aspect of the image is not only the smashed glass; it's also how we can see the tail inside the house as well as on either side of the windows. In many ways, it's seeing the tail *inside* the house that really makes the illusion work. This exercise provides great examples of blending modes (specifically the Screen mode), layer masks, transformations, and opacity choices all working together to produce an eye-popping effect. What you learn here can be applied to countless other situations.

1. Open PS 6-17.psd, then save it as **Komodo Attack**.
2. Show the Komodo layer, then show the House layer so you can see how the file has been built.
3. Open PS 6-18.psd, target the Tail layer, select all, copy, then close the file.
4. In the Komodo Attack document, target the House layer, paste the tail artwork, then name the layer **Tail**.
5. Remove the check mark next to Auto-Select on the Options panel if it is checked.

Figure 29 Positioning the tail

6. Position the tail exactly as shown in Figure 29, then hide the layer.
7. Save your work.
8. Open PS 6-19.psd, select all, copy, then close the file.
9. Target the House layer, paste, then name the new layer **Front Window**.
10. Set the blending mode to Screen.
11. Click Edit on the menu bar, point to Transform, then click Distort.

(continued)

12. Align the four corners of the bounding box to the position shown in Figure 30, then execute the transformation.

13. Add a layer mask, choose a soft brush, set the Opacity to 40%, then fade out the breaks in the glass where they near the edge of the window.
The center of the glass should remain bright white and not be masked.

14. Save your work.

15. Show the Side Window layer, then change its blending mode to Screen.

16. Press [shift], then click the layer mask to activate it.

17. Show the Tail layer, duplicate it, then name the new layer **Tail Left**.

18. Duplicate the Tail Left layer, name the new layer **Tail Inside**, then hide the two new layers so only the original Tail layer is showing.

19. On the Tail layer, add a layer mask, then invert the mask so that the tail is completely masked.

20. Brush in the tail so that it conforms to the line where it meets the broken glass in the front window. Use Figure 31 as a guide. You can use a big brush to bring back the tail, but when you get to the glass, use a small brush (around 9 pixels or smaller if necessary) at 70% Hardness and 100% Opacity. Be sure to zoom in.

Figure 30 Distorting the front window glass

Figure 31 Mask where the tail meets the glass

21. Show the Tail Left layer, add a layer mask, invert the mask, then brush in the tail as shown in Figure 32.
22. Fit in window, then set the Opacity on the Front Window layer to 70%.
    Because that window is in shadow, the smashed glass would not be so white.
23. Hide the Tail and Tail Left layers, then show the Tail Inside layer.
24. Show the Tail Inside layer, then drag it down below the Front Window layer.
25. Set the Tail Inside layer to Hard Light, then reduce its Opacity to 70%.
26. Show the Tail and Tail Left layers, then compare your results to Figure 33 on the following page.
27. Save your work, then close Komodo Attack.

Figure 32   Mask where the Tail Left meets the glass

Figure 33 The final image

Olivier Matthys/EPA/Shutterstock.com; Artoptimum/Shutterstock.com; Chris Botello

Producing this image of the rainbow-colored giraffe will put you squarely into advanced Photoshop territory. You're going to see the Threshold adjustment used for a different purpose here. It will be a great lesson for you of how Photoshop interrelates and interconnects strategically in ways you might not first notice. Starting at step 14, this exercise will also challenge you to work effectively with multiple adjustment layers and their masks. Finally, you'll see the power that one blending mode can have to turn a colorized image instantly into art.

1. Open PS 6-20.psd, then save it as **Chromatic Giraffe**.
2. Hide and show the Red adjustment layer.
   The goal is to colorize only the giraffe's spots, which would be a very painstaking challenge to attempt with the Brush tool. Instead, we will take a smart shortcut to create a usable mask.
3. Hide the Red layer, create a Threshold adjustment layer, then drag the Threshold Level slider on the Properties panel to 138.
4. Select all, click Edit on the menu bar, click Copy Merged, then paste.
5. Click Image on the menu bar, point to Adjustments, then click Invert.
   Based on what's white and what's black, this image can be used as a mask to affect just the spots on the giraffe.
6. Select all, copy the inverted image, then hide the layer.
   Do not deselect.
7. Delete the Threshold adjustment layer, then show the Red layer.
8. Press and hold [option] (Mac) or [Alt] (Win), then click the layer mask on the Red layer.
9. Click Edit on the menu bar, point to Paste Special, then click Paste Into.
   The canvas must be selected for the Paste Into command to be available.
10. Click the thumbnail on the Red layer to view the effect.
11. Deselect, duplicate the Red layer, name the new layer **Orange**.
12. Set the Hue to 25, Saturation to 66, and Lightness to +3.
13. Mask out the orange color in the head so the giraffe shifts from red to orange.
14. Using the same method, duplicate the Red layer four more times to create layers for the following colors: yellow, green, blue, and purple.
15. Use masks to make the giraffe's colors to shift through the six colors, from left to right.
16. Create a new Hue/Saturation adjustment layer at the top of the layer stack, then set its blending mode to Vivid Light.
    Your artwork should resemble Figure 34 on the following page.
17. Save your work, then close Chromatic Giraffe.

Figure 34 Vivid Light blending mode applied to the artwork

Omer Messinger/EPA-EFE/Shutterstock.com

NATIONAL GEOGRAPHIC **STORYTELLERS** | GABRIELE GALIMBERTI

© Gabriele Galimberti

When the Italian government issued lockdown orders on March 9, 2020, as a response to COVID-19, Gabriele Galimberti was staying in the city of Milano. Rather than return to his home in Tuscany, Gabriele decided to remain in the city and document the COVID-19 quarantine for *National Geographic*.

Gabriele's photography projects explore people's daily lives around the world. They include "In Her Kitchen," a cookbook featuring grandmothers and their best recipes, and "Toy Stories," portraits of children and their toys.

Gabriele wanted to use this approach to tell the story of COVID-19 in a meaningful way. Because public places were closed and people were not allowed to meet or socialize indoors, he spent a few days figuring out how to approach the project.

When Gabriele visited his friend Veronica Strazzari, he stood out on the sidewalk and talked through her window while she stayed inside. After taking a photo of her framed in the window, he realized photos like this could show the shared common experience of isolation during quarantine. He called the project "Inside Out."

Gabriele says that because his subjects helped him by placing sanitized lights inside their homes, they became his assistants. The result is that each portrait is also a conversation.

PROJECT DESCRIPTION

In this project, you will explore distance and connection by creating a composition that tells a personal story about COVID-19. Reflect on your own experiences during the pandemic, and communicate how the distance between you and the people around you affected your sense of connection.

Use what you have available to you — your own photos, found photos, pieces of writing, art, etc.,— and create an image that tells your personal story as it relates to being quarantined, socially distanced, and separated from the people you once interacted with regularly.

QUESTIONS TO CONSIDER

What stands out to you?

Can you relate to the subject?

What do you think the story is?

GETTING STARTED

Reflect on what your life was like before COVID-19. Make a list of the activities that made up your everyday routine. Think about tasks that were so regular they became a habit.

© Gabriele Galimberti

Gabriele Galimberti, Inside Out Project, Veronica Strazzari, Milano, Italy

Working from the list you made, note which of those activities and tasks changed the most. Describe how they changed and what was most challenging about the adjustment.

Reflect on the descriptive list you've made, and using what's available to you, create a group of illustrations that visually express your feelings and experiences. These illustrations will help guide the imagery, perspective, and overall tone of your story.

CHAPTER

7

INVESTIGATE PRODUCTION
TRICKS AND TECHNIQUES

1. Resize Images
2. Crop Images
3. Create Actions and Use the Image Processor
4. Use the History Panel and History Brush
5. Open an Image in Camera Raw

CERTIFIED PROFESSIONAL

Adobe Certified Professional in Visual Design Using Photoshop CC Framework

1. Working in the Design Industry
This objective covers critical concepts related to working with colleagues and clients as well as crucial legal, technical, and design-related knowledge.

1.4 Demonstrate knowledge of key terminology related to digital images.
   A Demonstrate knowledge of digital image terminology.

1.5 Demonstrate knowledge of basic design principles and best practices employed in the design industry.
   C Demonstrate knowledge of common photographic/cinematic composition terms and principles.

2. Project Setup and Interface
This objective covers the interface setup and program settings that assist in an efficient and effective workflow, as well as knowledge about ingesting digital assets for a project.

2.4 Import assets into a project.
   C Use the Adobe Camera Raw interface to import images.

4. Creating and Modifying Visual Elements
This objective covers core tools and functionality of the application, as well as tools that affect the visual outcome of the document.

4.1 Use core tools and features to create visual elements.
   A Create and edit raster images.

4.4 Transform digital graphics and media.
   A Modify the canvas or artboards.

RESIZE IMAGES

Understanding Image Resolution

All digital images are bitmap graphics. All bitmap graphics are composed of pixels. The word **pixel** is derived from the words picture and element—pixel. You can think of a **bitmap image** as being a grid of pixels—thousands of them.

Resolution is a term that refers to the number of pixels per inch (ppi) in a digital image. For example, if you had a 1" × 1" Photoshop file with a resolution of 100 pixels per inch, that file would contain a total of 10,000 pixels (100 pixels width × 100 pixels height = 10,000 pixels).

Often you will hear people refer to "high-resolution files" or "high-res files." High-resolution files are simply images that have more pixels. For any files that will be professionally printed, 300 ppi is considered a high resolution. For your home desktop printer, 150 ppi is generally enough resolution for a good-looking print. For web and other "on-screen" graphics, the standard resolution is low—just 72 ppi.

Image size refers to the dimensions of the Photoshop file. Image size is not dependent on

resolution; in other words, you could create two 3" × 5" files, one at 72 ppi and the other at 300 ppi. They would have the same image size, but different resolutions.

Image size however, is related to resolution, because anytime you modify a file's image size, that will have a direct effect on its resolution. And because resolution is so closely associated with image quality, resizing an image can affect quality.

Changing an Image's Size and/or Resolution

Many situations come up in which you will want to change an image's size or resolution. Here are some examples:

- You have a high-resolution image being used for a print project, but you also want to use the image on your website, so you must reduce its resolution from 300 ppi to 72 ppi.
- You have a 5" × 7" image that you want to use as an 8" × 10" image for a magazine cover.
- You've downloaded an image from a stock photography website. It is 11" × 17" at 300 ppi. The file size is 50 MB, and that's just too big for your needs.

All three of these cases require resizing, but only the second case is problematic, because it requires enlarging the image.

To best understand the ramifications of changing image size, the first thing you need to understand is the definition of captured data. **Captured data** is the digital image on your camera. The pixels in that image are the data your camera captured.

To keep the numbers easy, let's say your digital camera captures an image at 2,400 pixels wide and 1,800 pixels deep for a total of 4,320,000 pixels per image. Those numbers would be the resolution of the camera.

The image resolution is the number of pixels per inch, but that number is arbitrary and dependent on the output size of the document. For example, if you wanted to print your camera's image professionally, you would need 300 pixels per inch for the output file. Therefore, you could print an 8" × 6" image (300 pixels per inch times 8 inches equals 2,400 pixels).

Reducing the image resolution is not problematic, because all that you are doing is giving up captured data. Using your camera as an example, let's say you wanted to present the image at 8" × 6" on your website. The resolution for a web image is only 72 ppi, so you would reduce the resolution of your original image from 300 ppi to 72 ppi. If you run the numbers, that means your web image will be 248,832 pixels. So reducing the resolution from 300 ppi to 72 ppi means reducing the original image of 4,320,000 pixels to an image with just 248,832 pixels. Is this a problem? It is not, because the reduced image is still composed of original captured data.

Increasing image resolution is where the problems occur. Continuing with this example of your camera, let's say you wanted to use that original 8" × 6" image at twice the size, 16" × 12," for a poster. You are asking Photoshop to start with an image with 4,320,000 pixels and "res up" to an image of 17,280,000 pixels. You need all those extra pixels so that your 16" × 12" has the required 300 pixels per inch for professional printing. Photoshop can do that for you, but what is the

reality of what's happening? Where are those "extra" 12,960,000 new pixels coming from?

When you increase resolution as in the preceding example, Photoshop creates the new pixels based on a process called **interpolation**. Photoshop uses the captured data as its source and then creates new pixels based on that data. In the preceding example, the resulting image would be 75% interpolated data. The quality of the image would be degraded substantially, and the image would become blurry and lose fine detail. If you had no other choice but to use it, you could sharpen the image and add noise to add artificial sharpness and detail.

There's one saving grace regarding this example: at least when the image size was doubled, it had a high-resolution of 4,320,000 pixels! Trouble occurs when someone expects you to print a 5" × 7" image at 72 ppi as an 8" × 10" image at 300 ppi. This is called a "garbage-in/garbage-out" scenario. Starting with such a low-resolution image, there's nothing Photoshop can do to make it print at high quality. There's simply not enough captured data to work with.

Understanding "Effective Resolution" in an InDesign Document

Often, you will create images that will be used in a layout in Adobe InDesign. When the image is placed in InDesign, it's easy to enlarge it to your heart's content. However, once again, you must ask yourself exactly what it is you're doing.

Let's say you are building a layout in InDesign for a print document. That means all photos must be printed at 300 pixels per inch. Now let's say you have a Photoshop image that is 1" × 1" at 300 ppi that you place in the document, and you size it up to 2" × 2". InDesign does not do interpolation when you scale the image. It simply takes the data you give it and spreads it out over a larger area. Thus, at 2" × 2," the **effective resolution** of the image is 150 ppi, which is half of what's needed for professional printing. Figure 1 illustrates this concept.

Effective resolution in InDesign is the resolution of the image at its current size in the layout. The takeaway from this is example is that you should save your image in Photoshop at a high resolution and at the size you want to use it in your InDesign layout. In other words, if you need a 2" × 2" image in InDesign, start with a high-resolution image in Photoshop at that size.

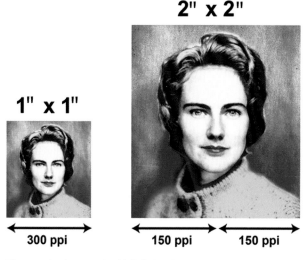

Figure 1   Resolution is reduced by half when the image size is doubled in InDesign

Reduce image size and resolution

1. Open PS 7-1.psd, then save it as **Resizing Images.**

2. Click **Image** on the menu bar, then click **Image Size**.

   The Image Size dialog box shows that this is a 2" × 2" file with a resolution of 300 ppi—thus making this a high-resolution file. The Dimensions section specifies that the full width of the file is 600 pixels (300 ppi × 2 inches), and the height is 600 pixels. Thus, this image is composed of exactly 360,000 pixels.

3. Click the **Resample check box** to remove the check mark.

   The Resample check box is the most important option in this dialog box. When Resample is **not** checked, the total number of pixels in the image must remain the same. In other words, no matter how you resize the image or change the resolution, no pixels can be added or discarded.

4. Type **100** in the **Resolution text box**, press **[tab]**, then note the changes in the Width and Height values.

   The width and height of the file changes to 6". Because the total number of pixels cannot change, when the number of pixels per inch is reduced to 100, the file must enlarge to 6" wide and high to accommodate all the pixels. In other words, no pixels were added or discarded with the change in resolution—they were simply redistributed.

5. Press and hold **[option] (Mac)** or **[Alt] (Win)** so that the Cancel button changes to the Reset button, then click the **Reset button**.

   The Image Size dialog box returns to its original values, and the Resample check box is once again checked.

6. Click the **Resample menu**, then choose **Bicubic Sharper (reduction)** from the menu, as shown in Figure 2.

   The Resample menu contains algorithms Photoshop uses to enlarge and reduce images with resampling. Bicubic Sharper is the best choice for the highest-quality result when reducing the image size or resolution.

7. Change the resolution to **150**, press **[tab]**, then note the changes to the Width and Height values and to the pixel dimensions.

As shown in the Image Size dialog box, the image size remains at 2" × 2". Note, however, that the pixel dimensions are now 300 pixels × 300 pixels. This means that when you click OK, the total number of pixels will be 90,000. In other words, 75% of the original 360,000 pixels will be discarded because of the reduction in resolution from 300 to 150 ppi. This reduction is reflected in the Image Size reading at the top, which has gone down to 263 KB from 1.03 MB.

8. Click **OK**.

Though the image doesn't look much different on your screen, 75% of its original data has been discarded.

9. Click **File** on the menu bar, then click **Revert**.

You removed the Resample check mark then changed the resolution of the image, noting that the pixels were merely redistributed. You then reset the Image Size dialog box, which activated the Resample check box, allowing pixels to be added or discarded. When you reduced the resolution by 50%, you noted that 75% of the pixels in the original image were discarded, and the file size also went down by 75%.

Figure 2 Decreasing resolution with resampling

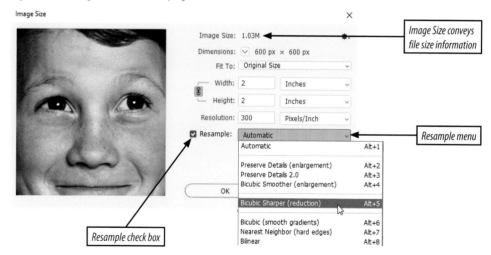

Increase Image Size and Resolution

1. Open the **Image Size dialog box**.

   Note that the Resample check box is checked by default. When the Resample check box is checked, pixels can be added or discarded when you resize an image. This file is 2" × 2", but it needs to be 4" × 4".

2. Type **4** in the Width text box.

   The Height value changes automatically because the Constrain Proportions feature is activated; this is represented by the link beside the width and height text boxes.

3. Note the **Resolution value**.

   The resolution remains at 300 ppi even though the image is being doubled in size. To maintain 300 ppi at the new, enlarged size, Photoshop must use interpolation to create the thousands more pixels necessary for this enlarged size. In fact, Photoshop will create three times the number of the original pixels.

4. Click the **Resample menu**, then click **Bicubic Smoother (enlargement)**, as shown in Figure 3.

Figure 3 Increasing image size and resampling pixels

This is Photoshop's best algorithm for enlarging images with resampling.

5. Click **OK**, then view the image at **100%** to evaluate the enlargement in terms of image quality.

   Photoshop has done a good job enlarging the image, and it still looks good overall. However, as a high-resolution image for quality print reproduction, this image would be considered problematic because it is composed of 75% interpolated data. In other words, only 25% percent of the pixels are actual pixels captured in a digital camera.

6. Revert the file.

7. Open the Image Size dialog box, and ensure that the **Resample check box** is checked.

   Next you will resize the file so it could be used on a website. Resolution for images to be used on-screen is 72 ppi.

8. Change the Width and Height values to **4**, change the Resolution to **72**.

9. Click the **Resample menu**, click **Bicubic Sharper (reduction)**, then compare your dialog box to Figure 4.

   All you need to do is look at the before and after Image Size values at the top of the dialog box to see that the new size requires fewer pixels than the original size. At the new specifications, the file size will be reduced from 1.03M (megabytes) to 243.0K (kilobytes). Even though the image doubled in size from 2" × 2" to 4" × 4", the reduction in resolution from 300 ppi to 72 ppi resulted in the need for fewer than 25% of the number of original pixels.

10. Click **OK**, then evaluate the enlargement in terms of image quality.

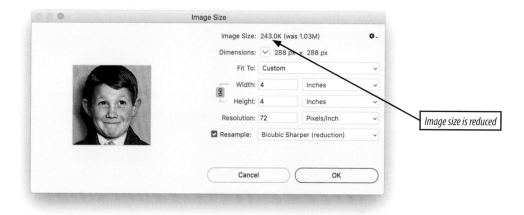

Figure 4 Decreasing image size and resampling pixels

Viewed at 100%, the image looks great on-screen, which is the goal, given that it will be used on a website. Even though Photoshop has discarded more than 75% of the original number of pixels, the reduced image contains only original data and no interpolated data.

11. Save your work, then close Resizing Images.

You increased the size and resolution of an image in the Image Size dialog box using the Bicubic Sharper (enlargement), noting that 75% of the data was interpolated. Because the quality of the image would not be acceptable, you reverted the file and then resized it using the Bicubic Sharper (reduction) option, noting that this method resulted in a better-quality image because it did not include interpolated data.

CROP IMAGES

▶ *What You'll Do*

In this lesson, you will use the Crop tool and the Straighten tool to crop images.

Cropping Images

Cropping might be the most underappreciated option and skill in all of Photoshop. Think of it this way: the iPhone 11 captures images at a width:height ratio of 4:3. Is 4:3 the best image size for every photo you take? Almost certainly not. But when was the last time you cropped any photo on your phone, or any of the images you post on Instagram or Snapchat?

Cropping can do wonders for an image. Figure 5 shows an uncropped image taken with an iPhone 10. It's a great photo of a great location in Utah, but the crop is not servicing the photo. There's too much unnecessary content in the foreground, and the left side also has redundant detail. In addition, the focal point of the image, where the two mountains meet, is off to the right side of the image.

Figure 5 Uncropped image from an iPhone 10

Chris Botello

Figure 6 shows the image cropped. Note the center of the image, and note also how the wideness of the crop conveys the expanse of the view.

The two images illustrate a central truth about graphic design: a designer's fundamental role is to put the viewer immediately at ease with the sense of "I know what I'm supposed to look at first." When a layout or a single image has too much information competing for attention, it creates unconscious stress for the viewer. When the message is focused and finessed, as with this crop, the viewer can fall into the image with no resistance.

Using the Crop Tool

The Crop tool crops images to any size or rectangular shape that you desire. In addition to cropping to change the shape of an image, the Crop tool has a rotate option, allowing you to crop and rotate the image so that the resulting image is rotated by the crop. This is a good method for resolving images that need straightening.

The Crop tool also offers the option to crop to a specific aspect ratio and to a specific

Figure 6 Cropped image

size. For example, you might have an 8" × 10" image at 300 ppi, but you can set the Crop tool to crop at 4" × 4" at 150 ppi. Regardless of what size you set the crop with the Crop tool, once executed, the image will be reduced to that size and resolution.

When the Crop tool is selected, the Options panel displays options for working with the tool and techniques for cropping. The default option is Rule of Thirds, in which the Crop tool preview is divided into three rows and three columns; the points where the vertical and

horizontal lines meet are where the focal points of your image should be.

Using the Straighten Tool

Another option for the Crop tool is the ability to crop an image by straightening it. The Straighten tool is a built-in tool option for the Crop tool on the Options panel. The Straighten tool draws a temporary line as you drag it across the photo. To straighten an image, drag the tool along an element in the image that should be horizontal or vertical.

Crop an image

1. Open PS 7-2.psd, then save it as **Mother's Love**.

2. Assess the image.

This is a charming image of a mother and child. What's particularly lovely about it is how much the mother and her daughter look alike, and how similar their haircuts are as well. The key to the image is the closeness between the two, with their faces pressed together, and the way their eyes and mouths meet. Uncropped, this closeness is not being expressed to its full potential, and their faces are off-center.

3. Press the **letter [C]** on your keypad to access the **Crop tool** 🛒 .

The eight-handled crop frame appears around the image.

4. On the Options panel, click the **Clear button** to clear any prior ratio values.

The Clear button only clears the existing values in the aspect ratio text boxes on the Options panel. It does not clear the crop grid from the image.

5. On the Options panel, click the **preset aspect ratio list arrow**, then click **Ratio**.

TIP The aspect ratio is also known as the crop size.

6. Click the **Overlay menu list arrow** ⊞ , then verify that **Rule of Thirds** and **Always Show Overlay** are both checked.

7. Drag the **center-left handle** of the crop frame to the right until the mother's and daughter's faces are centered.

8. Click and drag the **image** with the **Crop tool pointer** ▶ to position the crop as shown in Figure 7.

In the crop, the faces are centered, and the little girl's head is centered top to bottom.

9. Press **[return] (Mac)** or **[Enter] (Win)** to execute the crop.

The crop now emphasizes the closeness of the mother and daughter. All parts of the image that weren't part of the crop are discarded.

10. Save your work, then close Mother's Love.

You set the Overlay option for the Crop tool to Rule of Thirds. You then cropped the image.

Figure 7 Positioning for the crop

Morguefile

Rotate an image with the Crop tool

1. Open PS 7-3.psd, then save it as **Bird of Prey**.

2. Select the **Crop tool** 🔲, then position the crop frame as shown in Figure 8.

3. Position your mouse pointer at the **bottom-right corner** of the crop frame, about ¼ inch outside of the frame.

   The Crop tool pointer ▸ changes to a rotate icon ↵.

4. Click and drag counterclockwise until your screen resembles Figure 9.

   As you drag, the image is rotated behind the crop frame. Note that the eagle's eye is now at the intersection of the top-left squares.

5. Execute the crop, then compare your result to Figure 10.

   What was a very stagnant snapshot of a bird looking left is transformed into a dynamic and forceful square image. The eagle's beak pointing down diagonally toward the corner of the crop creates remarkable tension, and the diagonal white feathers in the top-right corner backed by the diagonal brown lines from the background now bring movement to the whole image. The original image was a photo of a bird. The cropped image is a bird of prey, swooping down for the kill. This is a stunning example of how much change a crop can bring to an image.

6. Save your work, then close Bird of Prey.

You rotated an image behind the crop frame, producing an entirely different effect with the resulting image.

Figure 8 Positioning for the crop

Figure 9 Rotating the image behind the crop frame

Figure 10 The dynamic cropped image

Crop to a specific size and resolution

1. Open PS 7-4.psd, then save it as **Bird Bookmark**.

   The goal of this exercise is to create a tall, thin bookmark from this image. The resulting image must be high resolution at 300 ppi.

2. Click **Image** on the menu bar, then click **Image Size**.

   This image has a resolution of 72 ppi.

3. Click **Cancel**.

4. Click the **Crop tool**, click the **preset aspect ratio list arrow** on the Options panel, then click **W × H × Resolution**.

5. On the Options panel, type **2** in the **set the width text box**, then press **[tab]** to set the height.

6. Type **6** in the **set the height text box**, then press **[tab]** to set the resolution.

7. Type **300** in the **px/in text box**.

   Your Options panel should resemble Figure 11.

TIP Be sure your ruler units are set to inches.

8. Position the crop as shown in Figure 12.

   As you drag the Crop tool, the image's width and height are constrained to the 2:6 proportion.

9. Execute the crop.

10. Open the **Image Size dialog box**.

    The image is 2" wide and 6" tall at a resolution of 300 ppi. In this case, there were enough pixels in the image that interpolation was not necessary to achieve this resolution at this size. However, had there not been enough original data, the crop would have interpolated the data to "res up" the image.

11. Save your work, then close Bird Bookmark.

You specified a width, height, and resolution for the crop. The resulting crop was produced at exactly those settings.

Figure 11 Options panel for the crop

W x H x Reso... ⌄	2 in	⇄	6 in	300	px/in ⌄	Clear

Figure 12 Positioning for the crop

Straighten an image with the Crop tool

1. Open PS 7-5.psd, then save it as **Straighten and Crop**.

2. Assess the image.

The image is the front entrance of a hotel named Cathedral. It is on a steep hill, so the doorway is on an angle from the horizontal bottom of the image.

3. Click the **Crop tool** 🔲, then click **Clear** on the Options panel.

4. Click the **Straighten button** on the Options panel, then float your mouse pointer over the image.

The cursor changes to the Straighten tool ⊹.

5. Click and drag the **Straighten tool** ⊹ down the **far-left edge of the door frame**, as indicated by the red line in Figure 13, then release the mouse pointer.

The image is rotated so the door frame is parallel to the left edge of the image.

6. Crop the image using Figure 14 as a guide.

7. Save your work, then close Straighten and Crop.

You used the Straighten tool to straighten the doorway of a building and then cropped the image. By doing so, the doorway and building were in alignment with the edge of the entire image.

Figure 13 Using the Straighten tool to straighten an image

Drag Straighten tool along door frame

Figure 14 The straightened and cropped image

Chris Botello

CREATE ACTIONS AND USE THE IMAGE PROCESSOR

▶ *What You'll Do*

In this lesson, you will use the Actions panel, the Image Processor, and the Batch feature to automate working with files.

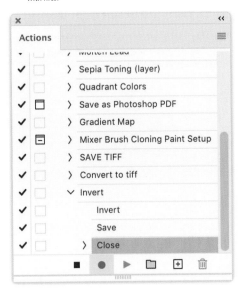

As designers, we like to focus on the big projects: the magazine covers, the posters, the billboards, the CD covers. But in the real world, it's not only the big projects that come across our desks; it's often the small stuff that you've got to handle as well. And the small stuff usually requires repetition. For example, you might receive 25 RGB files and be asked to convert them to CMYK and resize them so they are all seven inches wide. Or you might be given a folder full of PSD files and asked to convert them all to Grayscale mode and save them as 72 dpi JPEG files that can be used on a website. Sound like fun?

Fortunately, Adobe has made an enormous commitment to automation, especially since the advent of the Internet and the huge amount of image processing that creating and maintaining a website demands.

You might have played with the Actions panel before, but in this lesson, you're going to take a more rigorous and in-depth tour, and you're going to use more advanced features like batch processing and modal controls. You will also use Photoshop's Image Processor, which is a file conversion dream come true.

Using the Image Processor Dialog Box

In a professional ad agency or design firm, it's often the case that a client will send a folder full of images that need to be converted from one file format to another. This is where the Image Processor dialog box comes into play. The Image Processor can take a folder full of .psd files and quickly convert them into .tiff copies or .jpeg copies (or both) and put them into new folders. A situation in which literally hundreds or thousands of files need to be converted can be commonplace in some digital environments, and the Image Processor makes easy work of it.

Creating Actions on the Actions Panel

Once you've put 10,000 hours into Photoshop, you'll be amazed at how many repetitive sequences you do on a regular basis. For example, think of the sequence needed for creating a new noise layer: create a new layer, fill the layer with 50% Gray, open the Add Noise dialog box, enter the amount of Noise, click or don't click Monochromatic check box, click OK, set the layer's blending mode to Overlay. That's a lot of steps.

The Actions panel is designed to record a sequence just like this. Once recorded, you'll never have to step through it again. Instead, simply run the action on the Actions panel.

You might be thinking at this point, "But what about the amount of noise? What if I don't want the same amount of noise every time? What if I want to choose every time?" That's where modal controls come into play. A **modal control** stops the action at a specified step; a dialog box opens, allowing you to enter specific settings for that step. Continuing with the noise example, once you put a modal control on the Add Noise step, the action will stop when the Add Noise dialog box opens, allowing you to specify the amount of noise you want to use for the given project. Modal controls allow you to save an action sequence once and use it in different ways for different projects in perpetuity.

Using the Batch Dialog Box

The Batch dialog box gives you the power to apply an action sequence to a folder of files. Where the Image Processor is focused on changing file formats of a group of files, the Batch dialog box can apply more complex actions. For example, let's say you had a folder with 100 images downloaded from your camera. All of them are high resolution, and each of them is exactly the same size: 50 MB. You will give low-resolution images to your design team to produce ideas, because you don't want everybody working with 50 MB files. So you create an action that opens the Image Size dialog box and resizes the images to 6" × 8" at 150 ppi. That's when the Batch dialog box comes into play. Rather than you having to open each of the 100 files and apply the action, the Batch dialog box applies the action to all

the images in an instant. The Batch dialog box can save new, modified copies of the originals in the same folder and overwrite the originals, or you can create a new destination folder for the copies, leaving you with two sets.

Use the Image Processor

1. Open the seven files in the Automation folder located in the Chapter 7 Data Files folder.

   The files are all Photoshop (PSD) files. The goal of this lesson is to create one TIFF and one JPEG copy of each of the seven files.

2. Click **File** on the menu bar, point to **Scripts**, then click **Image Processor**.

3. In **Section 1 (Select the images to process)**, click the **Use Open Images button**.

   The Image Processor will only process the currently opened Photoshop files.

4. In **Section 2 (Select location to save processed images)**, click the **Save in Same Location button**.

5. In **Section 3 (File Types)**, click the **Save as JPEG check box**, then type **12** in the **Quality text box**.

6. In **Section 3**, click the **Save as TIFF check box**.

7. Verify that nothing is checked in **Section 4 (Preferences)**, then compare your Image Processor dialog box to Figure 15.

Continued on next page

Figure 15 Image Processor dialog box

8. Click **Run**.

The seven original PSD files remain open after the Image Processor is done.

9. Navigate to the **Automation folder**, then open it.

The Automation folder contains the seven original PSD files. It also contains a folder named JPEG and a folder named TIFF. These two folders contain the JPEG and TIFF copies generated by the Image Processor.

10. Return to Photoshop and keep all files open for the next set of steps.

You used the Image Processor dialog box to convert seven PSD files into seven new TIFF copies and seven new JPEG copies. You were able to specify where the files were saved to, and you were able specify the quality for the JPEG files.

Create and run an action on the Actions panel

1. Click **Window** on the menu bar, then click **Flowers.psd** at the bottom of the menu.

2. Click **Window** on the menu bar, then click **Actions**.

3. Click the **Actions panel menu button** ≡ , then verify that **Button Mode** is not checked.

4. Click the **Actions panel menu button** ≡ again, then click **New Action**.

5. Type **Invert** in the **Name text box**, then click **Record**.

A new action named Invert appears in the list on the Actions panel and is highlighted. The Begin recording button is activated. Any step you make at this point will be recorded as part of the action, so you need to be ready to go when you click the Begin recording button.

6. Click **Image** on the menu bar, point to **Adjustments**, then click **Invert**.

The Flowers.psd image is inverted.

7. Click **File** on the menu bar, then click **Save**.

8. Click **File** on the menu bar, then click **Close**.

9. Compare your Actions panel to Figure 16.

The three commands that you executed—Invert, Save, and Close—are listed as commands under the Invert action.

10. Click the **Stop playing/recording button** ▪ on the Actions panel.

11. Click **Window** on the menu bar, then click **Marble.psd**.

12. Click **Invert** on the Actions panel so that it is highlighted.

This is an easy step to miss—you must go back and target the action by its name before you can run it.

13. Click the **Play selection button** ▶ on the Actions panel.

You will only see the image closing. This is because "Close" is the final command of the action.

14. Repeat the **Invert action** for the remaining open images.

15. Open all **seven PSD files** in the **Automation folder**.

All seven images have been inverted.

16. Close all seven PSD files.

You used the Actions panel to create and specify a simple action of inverting an image, saving it, and then closing it. You applied that action to six other images.

Figure 16 Invert action with three commands

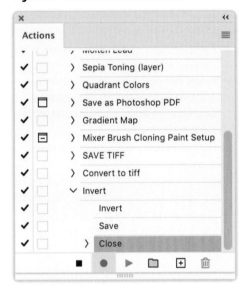

Batch process an action

1. Click **File** on the menu bar, point to **Automate**, then click **Batch**.

    No files need to be open.

2. In the Play section, click the **Action list arrow** to see all the actions available, then click **Invert**.

3. In the **Source section**, verify that **Folder** is chosen, then click **Choose**.

4. Navigate to and select the **Automation folder**, click **Select Folder**, then click **Choose (Mac)** or **OK (Win)**.

5. Verify that **none** of the **four check boxes** in the **Source section** are checked.

    Remember that the Automation folder now contains two subfolders—JPEG and TIFF—created from the first lesson of this chapter. This action should not be applied to the contents of those folders, so the *Include All Subfolders* option should not be checked.

6. In the **Destination section**, verify that **None** is chosen.

    No destination means that we want to affect the targeted images in the folder and for those images to be saved with the change. If you wanted to affect a *copy* of the images and save it in a new

location, you would need to specify a destination for the copies.

7. In the **Errors section**, verify that **Stop for Errors** is chosen, then compare your Batch dialog box to Figure 17.

8. Click **OK**.

    The seven images are all affected by the action and then closed.

9. Open all seven PSD files from the Automation folder.

    All seven files have been inverted again and therefore appear as they did originally.

10. Keep all seven files open and continue to the next set of steps.

You used the Batch dialog box to apply the Invert action to a folder of images.

Figure 17 Batch dialog box

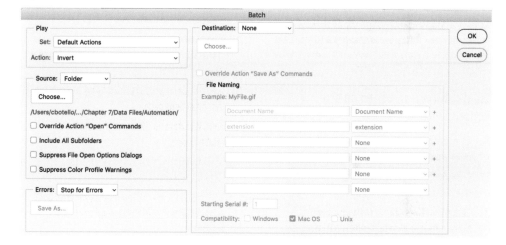

Create a complex action

1. Click **Window** on the menu bar, then click **Bricks.psd**.

2. Click the **Actions panel menu button** ≡, then click **New Action**.

3. Type **Processed Textures** in the **New Action dialog box**, then click **Record**.

4. Click **Image** on the menu bar, point to **Mode**, then click **CMYK Color**.

5. Click **Image** on the menu bar, then click **Image Size**.

6. Type **120** in the **Resolution text box**, then verify that your **Image Size dialog box** resembles Figure 18.

7. Click **OK**.

8. Click **Filter** on the menu bar, point to **Sharpen**, then click **Unsharp Mask**.

   Unsharp Mask is a sharpening filter. It produces similar results to the High Pass/Overlay technique you learned in Chapter 6.

9. Enter the settings shown in Figure 19, then click **OK**.

10. Click **File** on the menu bar, then click **Save As**.

11. Navigate to the **Automation folder**, open it, then create a new folder inside named **Processed Textures**.

12. Save **Bricks** as a PSD file in the **Processed Textures folder**.

13. Click the **Stop playing/recording button** ■ on the Actions panel.

14. Click 〉 to expand the **Unsharp Mask item** on the Actions panel.

    The settings for the Unsharp Mask are listed.

15. Click 〉 to expand the **Save action** on the Actions panel.

    The file format and the destination folder are recorded with the Save command.

16. Collapse the **Unsharp Mask** and **Save** items by clicking ∨.

17. Click **Window** on the menu bar, click **Wood.psd**, then click the **Processed Textures action** on the Actions panel.

Figure 18 Image Size dialog box

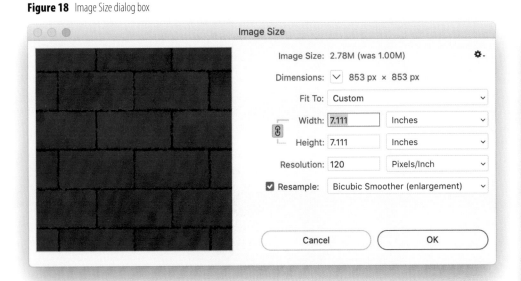

Figure 19 Unsharp Mask dialog box

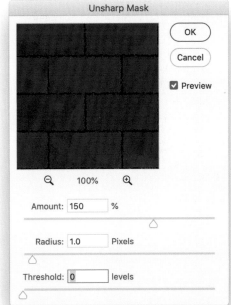

18. Click the **Play selection button** ▶ on the Actions panel.

The original file is left unchanged. The action is applied to a copy of the original whenever you choose a destination folder. The copy was saved as a PSD file with the same name in the Processed Textures folder. Both the original Wood.psd file and the new CMYK version remain open.

19. Continue to the next set of steps.

You used the Actions panel to create a complex action that involved converting an image's mode, resizing it, applying a filter, and saving a copy as a PSD file in a new folder.

Apply modal controls to an action

1. Click **Window** on the menu bar, then click **Water.psd**.

2. Click the **Toggle dialog on/off button** ☐ to the left of the **Unsharp Mask command** to activate it.

This button is known as a **modal control** ☐. With the modal control turned on, the action sequence will stop when it gets to the Unsharp Mask step and open the Unsharp Mask dialog box so you can adjust the settings if you so choose. Your Actions panel should resemble Figure 20.

3. Click the **Processed Textures action** on the Actions panel.

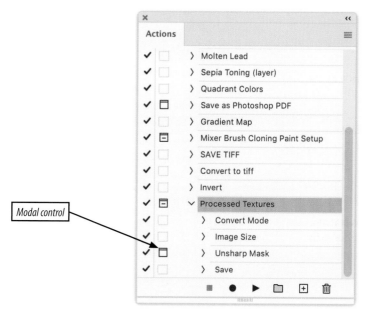

Figure 20 Modal control on the Actions panel

4. Click the **Play selection button** ▶.

The Processed Textures action pauses at the Unsharp Mask command, opens the dialog box, and awaits your input.

5. Change the **Amount value** to **75%**, then click **OK**.

The command is executed.

6. Apply the **Processed Textures action** to the remaining four PSD files, entering whatever settings you like for the Unsharp Mask filter.

7. Close all open files.

You added a modal control to the Unsharp Mask step, which pauses the action and gives you the option to enter new settings for that step.

USE THE HISTORY PANEL AND HISTORY BRUSH

▶ *What You'll Do*

In this lesson, you will learn how to return to a saved version of your work using the History panel, snapshots, and the History Brush tool.

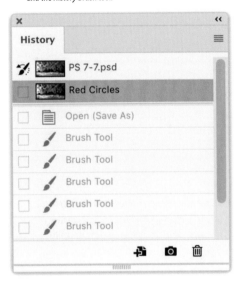

Working with the History Panel

The History panel is like a visual version of the Undo command on the Edit menu. As you work, the History panel records all moves you make and lists them as steps in a sequence. At any time, you can click on a previous step that you made, and your work on the canvas will return to that step in the process.

One of the keys to understanding the value of the History panel is to consider that you will work on Photoshop projects that can take days or even weeks to finish. When you see a project from this perspective, it becomes clearer how important it is that you save iterations of the project at different stages.

The History panel allows you to take a snapshot of your project at any given time. A **snapshot** is a record of the project as it is at that given moment. The snapshot is listed at the top of the History panel. Once you've created a snapshot, you can be assured that you can always return to that state of the artwork simply by clicking

the snapshot. Even if you've worked for days before realizing you've gone in the wrong direction and want to return to a previous state, you can simply click the snapshot on the History panel and instantly get back to the state. It's like a super Undo command.

Before the advent of the History panel, designers would save copies of the file at different stages to achieve this same ability to return to a state of the work. That method came at the cost of saving numerous large files and having to organize and manage them. With the History panel, saving a project at a certain iteration is as simple as clicking a button on the History panel.

Using the History Brush Tool

The History Brush tool is used for restoring part of the artwork back to what it was at an earlier stage of the project. You should think of the History Brush tool as a production tool *rather* than a creative tool.

The History Brush tool allows you to paint from any step that's been recorded in the History panel. Let's say you are working on an image that requires a lot of painting and masking. Now let's say you've made 100 moves with the Brush tool, and you realize that in one area, you liked it better the way it was when you saved a snapshot at step 40. You don't want to return the whole canvas to step 40 for just one object. In that case, you can use the History Brush tool to paint in just that object as it was recorded at step 40.

Using the Fill with History Option

The Fill command on the Edit menu offers the opportunity to fill a selection from a previous state. In the Fill dialog box, choose History from the Use menu. When you execute the fill, the selected pixels will be reverted to what they were when the image was last saved.

Use the Fill dialog box to fill using history

1. Open PS 7-6.psd, then save it as **Fill from History**.
2. Open the History panel.
3. Click **Image** on the menu bar, point to **Mode**, click **Grayscale**, then click **Discard**.

   On the History panel, the step is listed as Grayscale.
4. Click **Image** on the menu bar, point to **Mode**, then click **RGB Color**.

   RGB Color is listed as the next step on the History panel.
5. Click the **Rectangular Marquee tool** [::], then make a selection that encompasses the **eyes**, **nose**, and **mouth**.
6. Click **Edit** on the menu bar, then click **Fill**.
7. Enter the settings from Figure 21 in the Fill dialog box.
8. Click **OK**.

   The selection is filled with color because the pixels in this selection were in color when the file was opened.
9. Save your work, then close Fill from History.

You converted the file to Grayscale then back to RGB Color, producing a black and white image in RGB Color mode. You made a selection, then chose History from the Contents menu on the Fill dialog box. The fill restored the pixels in the selection to their status when the file was first opened.

Figure 21 Fill dialog box set to fill Contents using History

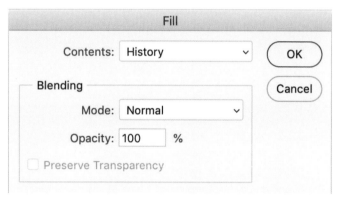

Revert to a snapshot on the History panel

1. Open PS 7-7.psd, then save it as **History Snapshot**.

2. Open the **History panel**.

3. Click the **Brush tool** 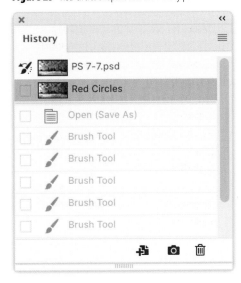, set the **Opacity** to **100%**, then set the **Hardness** to **100%**.

4. Set the **Size** to **500 px**, then set the **Mode** to **Soft Light**.

5. Choose a **red foreground color**, then click the brush **seven times** using different brush sizes so that your artwork resembles Figure 22.

6. Click the **Create new snapshot button** 📷 on the History panel.

   A new snapshot appears at the top of the History panel named Snapshot 1.

7. Double-click the name **Snapshot 1** to select it, then rename it **Red Circles**.

   Your History panel should resemble Figure 23.

8. Choose a **yellow foreground color**, then click the **Brush tool** to make **seven yellow circles** of different sizes that overlap the red circles.

   Note that the yellow circles *should* overlap the red circles.

Figure 22 Red circles painted on the canvas

Chris Botello

Figure 23 Red Circles snapshot on the History panel

9. Choose a **green foreground color** and a **smaller brush size**, then make **seven green circles** on the canvas that **overlap only red circles**.

Figure 24 shows one example of what your canvas might look like. The green circles should *not* overlap yellow circles.

10. Decide that you might have preferred the artwork with just red circles, then click the **Red Circles snapshot** at the top of the History panel.

The artwork is restored to its state when you created the snapshot.

11. Decide that you prefer the artwork with all the colors, scroll to the bottom of the History panel, then click the **bottommost Brush tool snapshot**.

The artwork returns to your last brush move.

12. Decide that there are too many yellow and green circles on the canvas, and you need to remove two of each.

13. Note the **Sets the source for the history brush icon**  beside the **top snapshot (PS 7-7.psd)** on the History panel.

14. Click the **empty box** ☐ beside the **Red Circles snapshot** so ✐ appears on the **Red Circles snapshot**.

15. Click the **History Brush tool** ✐, on the toolbar.

16. Paint over **any two yellow circles** and **any two green circles**.

The green and yellow circles are "removed." Wherever you paint, the canvas is restored

Figure 24 Yellow and green circles added to the artwork

to the state it was when you created the Red Circles snapshot.

AUTHOR'S NOTE Building the file this way would be silly because it's so destructive. You could just as easily have put the red circles on one layer, the yellow circles on another, and the green circles on another and set the blending modes for all three to Soft Light. That would have allowed you to mask out any circle you wanted to. However, this exercise was meant to demonstrate how the History Brush tool can save you from a tricky situation. Those situations often occur when you make a destructive move that you cannot undo or revert. In those cases, sometimes it's

the History Brush tool that can bail you out. One of the key takeaways from this lesson is to save often and to save snapshots often in the History panel, especially when you're working on long and involved projects. All it takes is losing three hours' work to learn the lesson the hard way.

17. Save your work, then close History Snapshot.

You painted red circles over an image and then saved a snapshot of that state in the History panel. You then painted yellow and green circles. You explored the option of restoring the artwork to the Red Circles state in the History panel. You then used the History Brush tool to restore just parts of the image to the Red Circles' state.

OPEN AN IMAGE IN CAMERA RAW

▶ *What You'll Do*

In this lesson, you'll open and edit an image in the Camera Raw utility window.

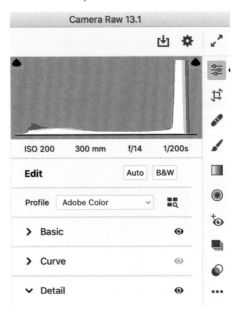

Investigating Camera Raw

A **Camera Raw** image is a digital image that hasn't been compressed or otherwise processed. When you set your digital camera to capture data in Camera Raw, the digital file that you download from your camera is as close to the actual image that was captured as possible. A Camera Raw file is not reduced by any compression algorithms, nor is the image manipulated by other algorithms that "ride" with the compression algorithms; therefore, the file size of a Camera Raw image is larger than compressed images.

The main alternative to shooting in Camera Raw is shooting in JPEG (or JPG) mode. JPEG is a compression algorithm that reduces the file size of images as they are captured. JPEG has become a standard format for digital cameras because it allows you to store more images on a photo card, and it allows the camera to capture frames more rapidly. Camera Raw images have file sizes that are much larger, so fewer of them fit on a card, and it's possible that your camera will take a fraction of a second longer to process before shooting the next image.

Despite the larger file size, many photographers prefer to shoot in Camera Raw because they want an image to be pure and unadulterated.

Once downloaded, rather than work in Photoshop, many workers open the Camera Raw file in the Camera Raw utility. This utility offers many image-adjustment controls that will look familiar to you from Photoshop: Shadows, Highlights, Hue, Saturation, and so forth. It also offers controls you've not seen in Photoshop, such as Temperature, Tint, Clarity, and Dehaze.

As a Photoshop designer, you might initially feel that you want to do all your work, including image adjusting, in Photoshop. That's fine. However, the more and more involved you get working with Photoshop, the more involved you are likely to get with digital photography. In the process of searching out more photography to work with, you will meet photographers, and you will likely purchase your own equipment and start shooting your own images to get exactly what you want for your projects. Once you start working with photographers or with your own camera, you too will be put in the position of choosing to shoot in Camera Raw or in JPEG. You'll also be put into the position of having to sift through dozens, if not hundreds, of images downloaded from your camera, and you might find yourself exploring possibilities with those images quickly in Camera Raw rather than going immediately into Photoshop.

Editing an image in Camera Raw

1. In Photoshop, navigate to where you store your Chapter 7 Data Files, then open PS 7-8.rw2.

   The RW2 file extension indicates that this is a Camera Raw file. The image opens in the Camera Raw utility with an Edit panel on the right side of the image.

   TIP If the Set Up Camera Raw window opens asking you to choose from two user interface (UI) styles, choose a style, then click OK.

2. On the **Edit panel**, drag the **Exposure slider**, under the **Basic section**, to **+1.40**.

   The Exposure setting represents the amount of light that was captured for the photograph. Increased exposure brightens the image overall.

3. Click the **White balance list arrow**, above Temperature, then click **Cloudy**.

   White balance is a process by which unrealistic color casts are removed from areas of an image that are meant to appear as neutral white.

4. Click the **Set zoom level list arrow** in the bottom-left corner, choose **100%**, then use the **Hand tool** to center the eagle's head in the view window.

5. Drag the **Vibrance slider** to **+28**.

6. Expand the **Detail section** on the Edit panel.

7. Drag the **Sharpening slider** to **60**, then drag the **Noise Reduction slider** to **20**.

   Your Camera Raw utility window should resemble Figure 25.

8. At the bottom-right corner of the window, note the two buttons **Done** and **Open**.

9. Click **Done**.

   Clicking Done applies the changes you made in the Camera Raw window and closes the file.

10. Open the file PS 7-8.rw2 again.

    The image reopens in Camera Raw with all the adjustments you made still active. However, these edits were *not* saved with the image file. Instead, another file, followed by an .xmp suffix, was created in the same folder as PS 7-8.rw2. This file contains the code of the edits you made. When you reopen the image file, it references the code to restore your edits in the Camera Raw dialog box.

11. Click **Open**.

The image opens in Photoshop in RGB Color mode.

12. Open the Image Size dialog box.

    The image is roughly 17" × 13" at 300 ppi. Since the file is so large, you won't save a Photoshop version; you always have the Camera Raw data file should you want to do further work.

13. Click **Cancel**, then close the file without saving changes.

You opened an image in Camera Raw and improved it dramatically with the control functions in the utility. You clicked Done, which applied and saved the changes with the file. You reopened the file, noticed the changes were saved, then opened the image in Photoshop.

Figure 25 The Camera Raw utility window

Reduce image size and resolution

1. Open PS 7-9.psd, then save it as **Eagle Comp**.
2. Click Image on the menu bar, then click Image Size. This is a huge digital file. It's roughly 17" × 11" at 300 ppi.
3. Verify that the Resample check box is checked, click the Resample menu, then click Bicubic Sharper (reduction).
4. Change the Width to 8, then change the Resolution to 150.
   Your Image Size dialog box should resemble Figure 26. Note at the top that the new file size will be 2.57M, reduced from 48.1M.
5. Click OK.
   While this is no longer a high-resolution file at this size, there is no interpolated data in the resulting image because Photoshop does not manufacture pixels in a reduction; on the contrary, it discards them.
6. Save your work, then close Eagle Comp.

Figure 26 Image Size dialog box set for reduction

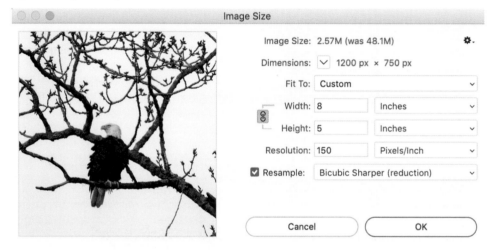

Enlarge image size and increase resolution

1. Open PS 7-10.psd, then save it as **Reflecting Pool**. Imagine your client sent you this image from his website and asks you to use it as an 8" × 10" image to be printed as the cover image on his company's annual report. Right away, you realize that he does not understand anything about image resolution.

2. Click Image on the menu bar, then click Image Size. This image is low resolution. It has just 423 pixels as its width. This image is 6" × 4" at 72 ppi. This makes sense, because it was being used on the client's website, and 72 ppi is the resolution for on-screen images. When you explain to your client that the image can't be used at the large size he wants, he asks you to "res it up" with hopes that it won't look so bad.

3. Verify that the Resample check box is checked, click the Resample menu, then click Bicubic Smoother (enlargement).

4. Change the Width to 10.
   The Height changes to 6.667, which is less than the client needs for an 8" × 10" final image. Not only is this image's resolution too low to work with, it's also not proportional to the client's needs and will need to be cropped.

5. Change the Height to 8.
   The Width increases to 12.

6. Change the Resolution to 300.

Your Image Size dialog box should resemble Figure 27. The Image Size information at the top of the dialog box indicates that the file size will increase from 364.5K to 24.7M. The 423-pixel width that you started with will be interpolated to 3,600 pixels, nearly a 900% increase. This is becoming a mission that cannot succeed.

7. Click OK, click View on the menu bar, then click 100%.

The resulting image is obviously low quality and unacceptable for any professional publication like an annual report. The entire image is blurry and pixelated and lacks any semblance of detail. When your client sees the results of trying to "res up" a file, he finally understands why his original photo will never work for print. He hires a photographer to capture the same image at the correct resolution needed for a high-quality print job, like an annual report.

8. Save your work, then close Reflecting Pool.

Figure 27 Image Size dialog box set for enlargement

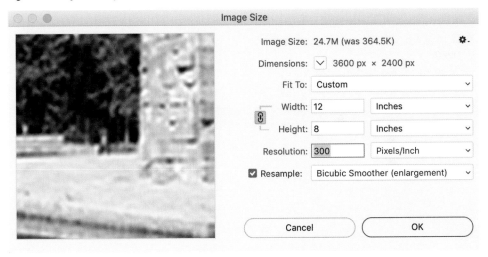

Straighten an image with the Crop tool

1. Open PS 7-11.psd, then save it as **Skyline Straighten**.
2. Press the letter [C] on your keypad to access the Crop tool, then click the Straighten button on the Options panel.
3. Note the line where the buildings meet the water line.
4. Drag the Straighten tool approximately 1 inch along the water line.
   The image is rotated so that the waterline is parallel to the bottom edge of the image.

5. Click [return] (Mac) or [Enter] (Win) to execute the crop.
6. Save the file, then close Skyline Straighten.

Crop images to a specific size and resolution

1. Open the three Construction photos in the Construction folder.
   You will resize each image to 2" × 2" at 300 ppi so they can be positioned side by side as a trio.
2. Click the Crop tool, click the preset aspect ratio list arrow, then click W × H × Resolution on the Options panel.
3. Type **2** in the set the width text box, then press [tab] to set the height.
4. Type **2** in the set the height text box, then press [tab] to set the resolution.

5. Type **300** in the px/in text box.
6. View the Construction 1 image, then crop it in a way that you think looks good.
7. Switch to the Construction 2 image, then crop it in a way that makes it a partner to the first image.
8. Switch to the Construction 3 image, then crop it as the third in the series.
   Figure 28 shows one example of the three crops.
9. Save Construction 1 as **Construction 1 cropped**, then close the file.
10. Save Construction 2 as **Construction 2 cropped**, then close the file.
11. Save Construction 3 as **Construction 3 cropped**, then close the file.

Figure 28 Three crops at 2" × 2" and 300 ppi

Chris Borello

Create and apply an action

1. Open the Patterns folder, then open all seven images in the folder.
2. Click Window on the menu bar, then click Blue at the bottom of the menu to switch to the Blue file.
3. Open the Actions panel, click the Actions panel menu button, then click New Action.
4. Type **Resolution 300 to 72** in the Name text box.
5. Click Record.
6. Click Image on the menu bar, then click Image Size.
7. Verify that the Resample check box is checked, click the Resample menu, then click Bicubic Sharper (reduction).
8. Change the Resolution to 72, then click OK.
9. Click File on the menu bar, then click Save As.
10. Create a new folder, then name it **72 ppi**.
11. Set the file type as Photoshop, then click Save.
12. Click File on the menu bar, then click Close.
13. Click the Stop playing/recording button on the Actions panel.
14. Switch to the Yellow file, then target the Resolution 300 to 72 action on the Actions panel.
15. Click the Play selection button.
    The Yellow file vanishes because the last step in the action is Close.
16. Apply the Resolution 300 to 72 action to the remaining four files.
17. Open the 72 ppi folder.
    The folder contains six files that all have 72 ppi as their resolution.

Batch process an action

1. Click File on the menu bar, point to Automate, then click Batch.
2. In the Play section, click the Action list arrow, then click Resolution 300 to 72.
3. In the Source section, click the Choose button, navigate to the Halftones folder, click to select it, then click Choose.
4. Verify that none of the four check boxes are checked.
5. Click OK.
6. Navigate to the 72 ppi folder in the Patterns folder, then open it.
    As shown in Figure 29, seven files with the name Halftone have been added to the 72 ppi folder with the pattern files.

Figure 29 Seven Halftone images added to the 72 ppi folder

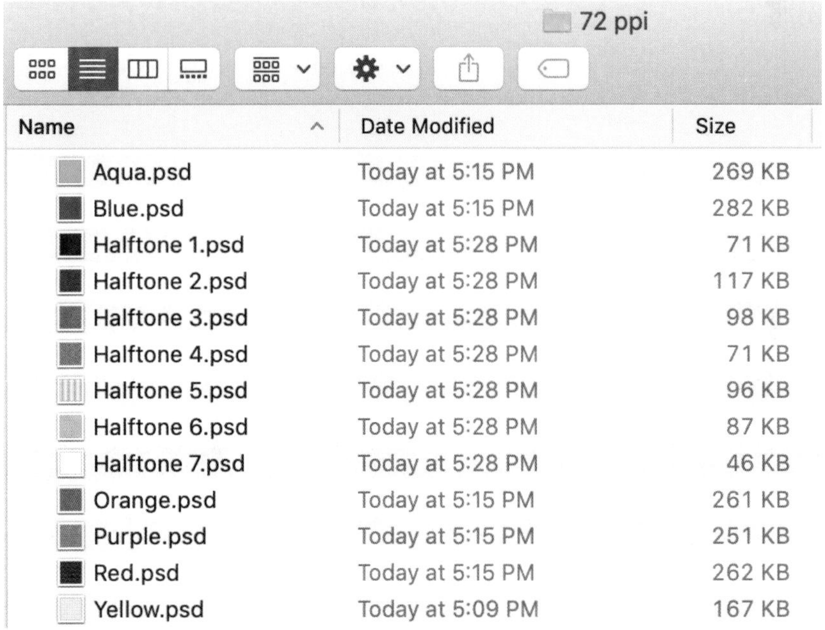

Edit an image in Camera Raw

1. In Photoshop, navigate to where you store your Chapter 7 Data Files, then open PS 7-12.rw2. The image opens in the Camera Raw utility.
2. In the Basic section, drag the Temperature slider to 5300.
3. Drag the Exposure slider to +0.15.
4. Drag the Clarity slider to +24.
5. Drag the Vibrance slider to +33, then drag the Saturation slider to +10.
   Your Camera Raw window should resemble Figure 30.
6. Click Done.

Figure 30 The Camera Raw utility window

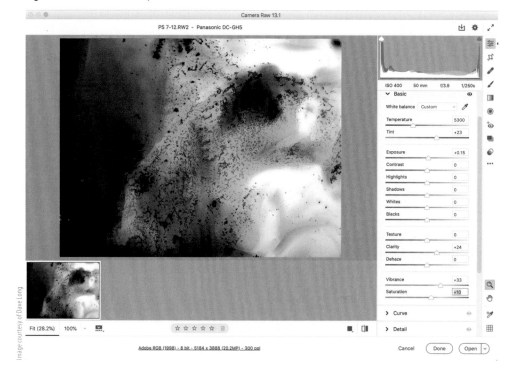

Image courtesy of Dave Long

In this Project Builder, you will create an action for a High Pass sharpening layer, one that you can use over and over in your work. Because you will use the filter at different strengths for different projects, you will use a modal control for the filter step in the action.

1. Open PS 7-13.psd, then save it as **Sharpen Stripes**.
2. Target the Cyan layer on the Layers panel.
3. Open the Actions panel, click the Actions panel menu button, then click New Action.
4. Name the new action **High Pass Sharpen**, then click Record.
5. Click Select on the menu bar, then click All.
6. Click Edit on the menu bar, then click Copy Merged.
7. Click Edit on the menu bar, then click Paste.
8. Click Filter on the menu bar, point to Other, then click High Pass.
9. Type **3** in the Radius text box, then click OK.
10. Set the layer's blending mode to Overlay.
11. Click the Stop playing/recording button on the Actions panel.
12. Click the empty square beside the High Pass step on the Actions panel to add a modal control to that step.
    Your Actions panel should resemble Figure 31.
13. Save your work, then close Sharpen Stripes.
14. Open PS 7-14.psd, then save it as **Violin Sharpened**.
15. Hide the Noise layer, then target the Hue/Saturation 1 adjustment layer.
    When you sharpen, never include a noise layer in the sharpening.
16. Target the High Pass Sharpen action on the Actions panel, then click the Play selection button.
    Because of the modal control, the action stops when the High Pass dialog box opens.
17. Type **2** in the Radius text box, then click OK.
18. Rename the new layer **HP2.0**, then show the Noise layer.
19. Save your work, then close Violin Sharpened.

Figure 31 High Pass Sharpen action on the Actions panel

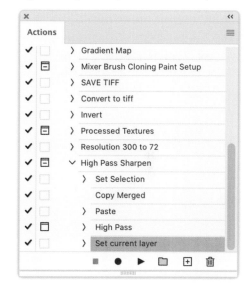

PROJECT BUILDER 2

In this Project Builder, you will create an action for a Noise layer, one that you can use over and over in your work. Because you will want to add noise in different amounts for different images, you will use a modal control for the filter step in the action.

1. Open PS 7-15.psd.
2. Target the Cyan layer on the Layers panel.
3. Open the Actions panel, click the Actions panel menu button, then click New Action.
4. Name the new action **Add Noise Layer**, then click Record.
5. Click the Create new layer button.
6. Click Edit on the menu bar, then click Fill.
7. Fill the layer with 50% Gray.
8. Click Filter on the menu bar, point to Noise, then click Add Noise.
9. Type **8** in the Amount text box, then click OK.
10. Set the layer's blending mode to Overlay.
11. Click the Stop playing/recording button on the Actions panel.
12. Click the empty square beside the Noise step to add a modal control to that step.
    Your Actions panel should resemble Figure 32.
13. Close the file without saving changes.

Figure 32 Add Noise Layer action on the Actions panel

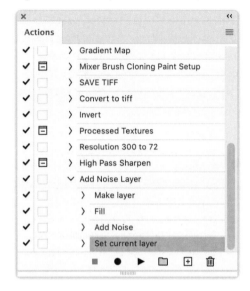

DESIGN PROJECT

This Design Project uses an abstract image to give you the opportunity to explore more artistic aspects of cropping. You will crop one image multiple times at different sizes. There will be no "right" answers. Crop in a way that feels right and looks interesting to you.

1. Open PS 7-16.psd.
   This is the image that you edited in the Camera Raw lesson.
   You will crop the image to be framed at four different sizes, all at 300 ppi.
2. Click Image on the menu bar, then click Duplicate.
3. Repeat Step 2 to make three more duplicate files.
4. Click the Crop tool, then use the W × H × Resolution Ratio setting to crop the first image at 2" wide × 2" high at 300 ppi.
5. Repeat Step 4 to create four more cropped images at the following sizes:
   2" × 8", 3" × 6", 5" × 7", and 6" × 6".
6. When you are done, save all five images, and name them by their size dimensions.
   Figure 33 shows an example of the five cropped images.

Figure 33 One image cropped five different ways

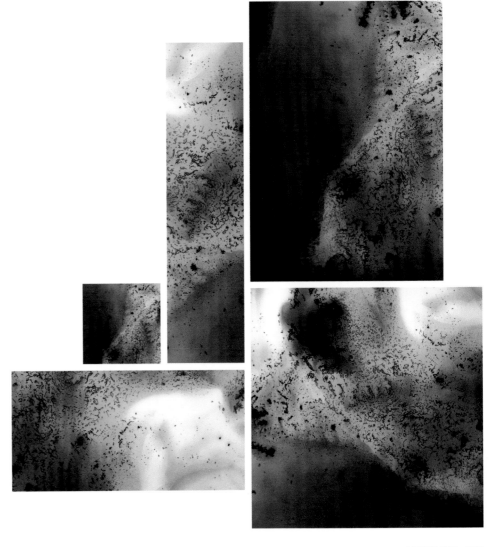

MAKING THE HIDDEN WORLD VISIBLE

Anand Varma, Hummingbird
shaking off water droplets

Science photographer Anand Varma has always found inspiration, stimulation, and wonder in the natural world. During college, he began working as an assistant to *National Geographic* photographer David Liittschwager. He also had his first opportunity to work with a scientist to solve a research question using the medium of photography. These experiences led him to realize he could use a camera as a means of both communication and discovery, to explore scientific observations made by others, and to uncover new information about the natural world.

DEVELOPING THE PROCESS

Anand's first project was a collaboration with Dr. Christopher Clark on his work with hummingbirds. His task was to figure out how to use still photography to capture images of the birds flying inside a wind tunnel. Solving this puzzle was exciting and helped Anand decide he wanted to pursue this type of work for his career.

When Anand starts a project, he works with the researcher to define the question he wants to answer using photography. Then through a trial-and-error process, he uses his camera to gather data about the subject. He evaluates the way light interacts with it and looks for structures, textures, and details that normally go unnoticed or that are not visible without the aid of a camera. He then designs the apparatus and the experiment to recreate conditions that allow him to capture these variables. The process can take months.

CAPTURING THE IMAGE

For this image, Anand worked with researchers who were studying the motions that hummingbirds use to dry themselves off. The movement is so quick, it happens within a fraction of a second, much faster than the eye can see.

From talking with the researchers, Anand knew he could use a tiny misting nozzle from a grocery store produce section to get the bird just wet enough to encourage the natural behavior of shaking its feathers. Then he had to decide how to compose the image. Because he wanted to focus on the behavior, he chose to use a dark background and zoom the shot in tight around the bird.

Next, he had to figure out how to use lighting to shape the viewer's attention and highlight specific details. He wanted to show both the bird and the motion of the water droplets as the bird shook them off. He used a very bright, very fast flash to light the bird from the front and kept the shutter open for 1/15 of a second while lighting the scene from behind to capture the trajectories of the water drops. It took many attempts, but he ultimately was able to capture the bird at exactly the right moment.

THE RESULT

The image perfectly reveals the complexity of motion as the bird shakes itself off. It surprises the viewer by capturing the richness of one tiny moment in time and space. The image inspires a sense of wonder and a joy of discovery and encourages viewers to observe hummingbirds more closely when they see them. According to Anand, a successful image is one that rewards the viewer for paying attention, where the longer you look, the more you see.

ANAND'S POINTS OF INTEREST

1. Circular lines form and surround the beak. These lines communicate the motion in which the beak is moving when the hummingbird shakes.

2. Squiggly and seemingly fast-moving lines spray from the hummingbird's head. These lines demonstrate the speed at which the hummingbird is shaking in an effort to dry itself.

3. The wings of the hummingbird look to be layered and at various opacities. This effect communicates the rapid movement of the bird when it spreads its wings wide and opens up to shake off water.

PROJECT DESCRIPTION

In this project, you will analyze and respond to Anand's image. You'll have the opportunity to investigate the different elements of the image and interpret the story for yourself. Look at the photo closely. Take note of anything that catches your attention. You'll be writing a brief analysis consisting of your observations, your interpretation of the story, any questions that come to mind, and the messages you take away. If you can, talk to your classmates and discuss your ideas. Decide which elements of the photo are impactful to you, and write a brief analysis of your findings.

QUESTIONS TO CONSIDER

What is the story?

What stands out to you?

What would you change? Why?

What questions do you have?

What caught your attention first?

Is there anything that seems confusing?

Do you like the image?

USE SOME OF THESE VOCABULARY WORDS

Hierarchy: Used to communicate the importance of each element on the page by manipulating things like color, size, etc.

Opacity: The transparency of an image or element.

Hue: A color or shade.

Tint: A lighter hue created by adding white. This lightens the hue and makes it less intense.

Texture: The surface characteristic of an element.

Contrast: Occurs when two elements on a page are different.

Color: Combination of hues applied to a line or shape.

GETTING STARTED

Analyze the photo. Look at the bird's wings, and make observations about the overlap and motion. Use a pen to mark the areas that catch your attention.

Follow the lines of motion. Consider the shape of the lines and the direction in which they travel. Think about what this communicates about the movement and motion of the bird.

Organize your thoughts by creating a list of your ideas and findings. Figure out what parts of the image are important for you to point out and how those points influenced your interpretation of the story.

SKILLS YOU'LL PRACTICE

Critical thinking

Giving feedback

Design analysis

Writing

Using design vocabulary

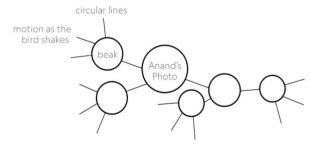

One way to organize your thoughts is with a graphic organizer. Here's an example of how you might use an idea web to capture your thoughts about the photo.

PROJECT DESCRIPTION

In this project, you will be exploring storytelling as a way to learn about science. Using one of the photos provided as a starting point, you will be investigating motion and movement as it relates to an animal.

You'll need to research your chosen animal, examine what kinds of movements it makes, and determine why it makes that particular movement. Once you have found your unique story, you will communicate your findings by creating a composition made up of various design elements, effects, and layers that depict the animal, its motion, and the environment in which the motion occurs.

The goal of this project is to communicate a scientific explanation of an animal's motion in a particular environment using a single composition.

SKILLS TO EXPLORE

- Paint inside selections
- Move selected pixels
- Examine selection edges
- Explore vector selection tools
- Explore shape tools
- Use magic wand selection
- Work with channels panel
- Create and customize gradients

FILES YOU'LL USE

- Ps_u2_hummingbird.JPEG
- Ps_u2_bee.JPEG
- Ps_u2_beaver.JPEG
- Ps_u2_mantisshrimp.JPEG
- Ps_u2_snake.JPEG

You will use Photoshop for this project to create an image that is inspired by Anand's photographic work.

SKILLS CHALLENGE
CREATE AN ACTION ZOOM BLUR EFFECT

Step 1: Create a duplicate background layer.

Step 2: Make sure the layer copy is selected in the Layers panel. On the Filter menu, point to Blur, then choose Radial Blur. A Radial Blur dialog box should appear. Enter the following settings:

Amount: The higher the amount, the more blur is applied. Start at 50, and increase until you reach your desired blur level.

Blur Method: Select Best.

Quality: Select Zoom.

Blur Center: Use this box to set the point from where the blur will appear to be "zooming" out. Click inside the box to set the point. Click OK.

Step 3: Make sure the layer copy is selected. Click on the Layer Mask icon at the bottom of the Layers panel.

Step 4: Make sure the layer mask is selected by looking for a thin white border around the mask.

Step 5: Select the Gradient Tool from the Tools panel. Look at the Options Bar and select Radial Gradient, then apply the gradient by clicking and dragging your mouse.

Step 6: Click on the center of your focal point, and drag the mouse out until you think you have created enough space around the focal point. The area between the start and end points of the gradient will become a smooth transition between the two layers.

1. Think about what new information you can provide. Your composition should give viewers information they probably didn't know before. This is an opportunity for you to teach your viewers something about science in a creative way.

2. Consider this project as a puzzle that needs to be solved. Capturing movement that is often invisible to the naked eye is not an easy task. When conducting your research, look for videos and images that capture motion in a unique way, and see if any of those techniques can be applied to your own work.

3. Decide what needs to be included in the environment to tell the story. Establishing the environment in which your chosen animal conducts its unique motion is a critical element in telling the full story. Think about what causes the animal to make its motion and how those circumstances might be communicated in your composition.

The student spent time exploring the different parts of a bat's anatomy, as well as the bat's common resting position.

GETTING STARTED

1. Do your research. Use what's available to you to learn about the animal you chose. Find videos, images, drawings, blog posts, personal accounts, and other resources that give you information about a critical movement your animal makes in a particular situation.

2. Find some inspiration. Make guesses and predictions about what you might find. Chances are, this is not the first time you have heard of the animal you are working with. Use what you already know about the animal to guide your hunt for information.

3. Sketch out what you're thinking. Use pen, pencils, paper, or notepad, to jot down a few ideas for design elements. Doing this will help guide the development of your composition, and help you build upon your different ideas.

Most interested in the wings, the student experimented with proximity, variety, and foreground to communicate the different position and forms a bat's wings can take.

PROJECT DESCRIPTION

In this project, you will continue your exploration of motion and movement by examining the movement of an animal in your own vicinity. You'll need to make your own observations and research your chosen specimen to learn about how it moves. You will create a composition that communicates an important action and movement in a particular environment.

Take time to figure out what animals are around you. This could be a squirrel in a tree, an ant on the sidewalk, or even a spider on the wall. Using whatever tools are available to you, document your observations.

Create a composition using your taken and/or found images, and visualize your subject in motion. The goal of this project is for you to communicate a scientific description of motion that takes place in a location familiar to you and to encourage people to take a closer look at what's around them.

SKILLS TO EXPLORE

- Create and edit swatches
- Explore tools to repair and reconstruct images
- Create custom layer styles
- Use guides and grids
- Create a stamp visible layer
- Adjust layer opacity and fill opacity
- Use level adjustments
- Explore hue and saturation

THINK LIKE ANAND

1. Embrace trial and error. One of the most effective ways to learn your tools is by experimenting with them and trying new techniques. In this project, you are encouraged to be experimental and to see what you can create without being rigid in your approach.

2. Look for new ideas. Think outside the box with this composition. If your original idea doesn't seem to be working, don't be afraid to go back to the drawing board. Identifying what doesn't work can often be a productive part of the creative process.

3. Reward viewers for paying attention. Make small details a big part of your composition. You want your viewers to learn more about your scientific concept the longer they look at it, so ensure there are plenty of intricate, crucial, and communicative details for them to see.

SKILLS CHALLENGE
CORRECT COLOR CONTRAST

Step 1: On the Layers panel, click the Create new fill or adjustment layer icon, and choose Levels.

Step 2: To make sure the Levels adjustment layer in the Layers panel is selected, go to the Properties panel to access the controls for the adjustment.

Step 3: On the Properties panel, click on the Gray Eyedropper.

Step 4: Click on something in the image that should be a neutral color, such as gray, black, or white. When you click, the other colors in the image will shift.

GETTING STARTED

In this project, you'll get to interact with something in your environment. This can be both exciting and daunting. Being patient and diligent will be key to capturing the different parts of your story. In this section you are encouraged to spend ample time exploring and having conversations before starting your composition.

1. Explore your immediate vicinity and community. Take a walk around town. You may be surprised how many small living creatures exist in your daily life.

The student brainstormed and sketched the key elements needed for a story about honeybees.

2. Take notes of observations and conversations. While exploring your area, use what you have available to you to document your findings. Who might be a good person to talk to about this project? It could be your biology teacher, the janitor who knows the school grounds, or a science enthusiast in your class or family.

3. Consider a collaboration. Maybe your story and your classmate's story are one in the same, and maybe they explore similar ideas. Consider working together and bringing your ideas together in one collaborative project.

4. Always keep safety in mind when working on a project that requires interaction with an object you are unfamiliar with. It is not recommended that you pick up or handle any animals while working on this project. It is best to safely observe from a distance. Use your resources to get a closer look at your subject's different behaviors.

Fascinated by the different types of bees, the student experimented with repetition, shape, and scale to display key distinctions and establish focus.

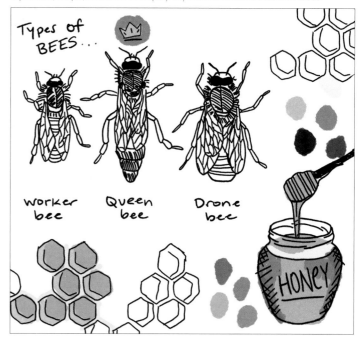

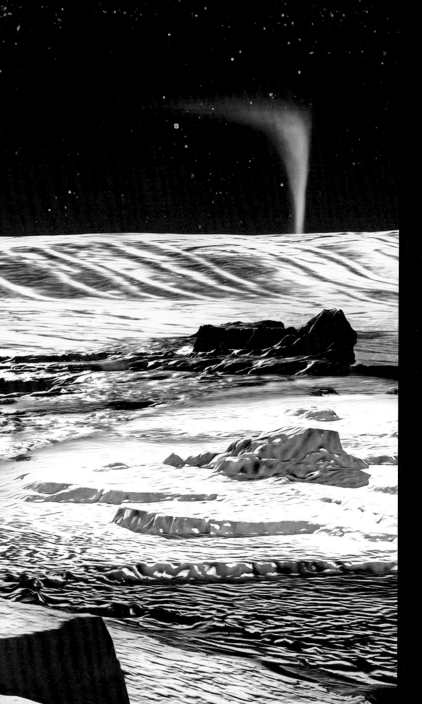

A scientific illustration provides a model to suggest what the surface of Pluto might look like. This "Plutoscape" shows Pluto's largest moon, Charon, in the distance.

Illustration by John Tomanio. From "Pluto at Last." *National Geographic Magazine*, Vol. 228, No. 1, July, 2015

CHAPTER 8

GET STARTED WITH
ILLUSTRATOR

CERTIFIED PROFESSIONAL

Adobe Certified Professional in Graphic Design and Illustration Using Adobe Illustrator

2. Project Setup and Interface

This objective covers the interface setup and program settings that assist in an efficient and effective workflow, as well as knowledge about ingesting digital assets for a project.

2.1 Create a document with the appropriate settings for mobile, web, print, film and video, or art and illustration.
  A Set appropriate document settings for printed and onscreen artwork.
  B Create a new document preset to reuse for specific project needs.

2.2 Navigate, organize, and customize the application workspace.
  A Identify and manipulate elements of the Illustrator interface.
  B Organize and customize the workspace.
  C Configure application preferences.

2.3 Use nonprinting design tools in the interface to aid in design or workflow.
  A Navigate a document.
  B Use rulers.
  C Use guides and grids.
  D Use views and modes to work efficiently with vector graphics.

2.4 Manage assets in a project.
  A Open artwork.
  B Place assets in an Illustrator document.

2.5 Manage colors, swatches, and gradients.
  A Set the active fill and stroke color.

4. Creating and Modifying Visual Elements

This objective covers core tools and functionality of the application, as well as tools that affect the visual appearance of document elements.

4.3 Make, manage, and manipulate selections.
  A Select objects using a variety of tools.
  B Modify and refine selections using various methods.
  C Group or ungroup selections.

4.4 Transform digital graphics and media.
  A Modify artboards.
  B Rotate, flip, and transform individual layers, objects, selections, groups, or graphical elements.

LESSON 1

EXPLORE THE ILLUSTRATOR WORKSPACE

▶ *What You'll Do*

In this lesson, you will start Adobe Illustrator and explore the workspace.

Looking at the Illustrator Workspace

The arrangement of windows and panels that you see on your monitor is called the **workspace**. The Illustrator workspace features the following areas: artboard, pasteboard, menu bar, Control panel, toolbar, and a stack of collapsed panels along the right side of the document window. Figure 1 shows the default workspace, which is called Essentials Classic.

Illustrator offers predefined workspaces that are customized for different types of tasks. Each workspace is designed so that panels with similar functions are grouped together. For example, the Typography workspace shows the many type- and typography-based panels that are useful for working with type. You can switch from one workspace to another by clicking Window on the menu bar, pointing to Workspace, and then choosing a workspace. Or you can click the Switch Workspace button on the menu bar.

Figure 1 Essentials Classic workspace

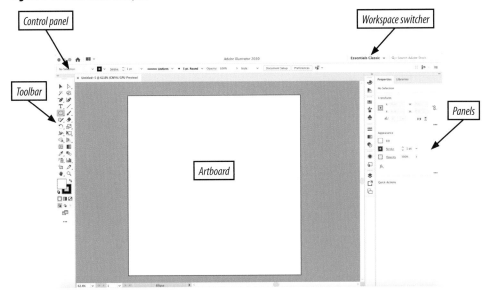

You can customize the workspace to suit your working preferences. For example, you can open and close whatever panels you want and group them as you like and in a way that makes sense for you and your work. You can save a customized workspace by clicking Window on the menu bar, pointing to Workspace, then clicking New Workspace. Once the new workspace is named, it will appear in the Workspace menu.

Exploring the Toolbar

As its name implies, the toolbar houses all the tools that you will work with in Illustrator. The first thing you should note about the toolbar is that not all tools are visible; many are hidden. Look closely and you will see that some tools have small black triangles, indicating that other tools are hidden behind them. To access hidden tools, point to the visible tool on the toolbar, then press and hold the mouse button. This will reveal a menu of hidden tools. The small black square to the left of a tool name in the submenu indicates which tool is currently visible on the toolbar, as shown in Figure 2.

When you expose hidden tools, you can click the small triangle to the right of the menu and create a separate panel for those tools.

You can view the toolbar as a single column or a double column of tools. Simply click the Collapse/Expand panels button at the top of the toolbar to toggle between the two setups. In this book, we will show you the toolbar in double columns.

Figure 3 identifies essential tools that you'll use all the time when you're working with Illustrator. To choose a tool, simply click it. You can also press a shortcut key to access a tool. For example, pressing the letter [P] on your keypad selects the Pen tool. To learn the shortcut key for each tool, point to a tool until a tool tip appears with the tool's name and its shortcut key in parentheses. **Tool tips** are small windows of text that identify various elements of the workspace, such as tool names, buttons on panels, or names of colors on the Swatches panel, for example. Tool tips appear when they are activated in the General preferences dialog box. Click Illustrator (Mac) or Edit (Win) or on the menu bar, point to Preferences, then click General.

Figure 2 Viewing hidden tools

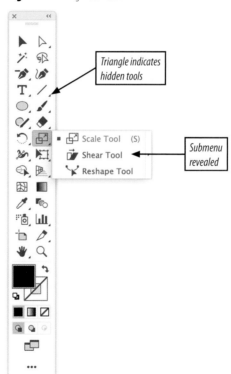

Figure 3 Essential tools

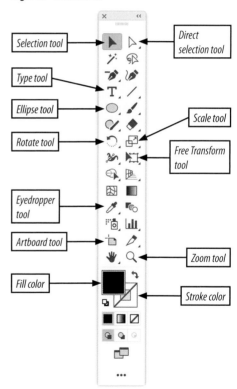

Working with Panels

Working in Illustrator is not only about using tools and menus. Many essential Illustrator functions are grouped into panels. For example, the Paragraph panel is the central location for paragraph editing functions, such as text alignment and paragraph indents. The Swatches panel houses colors that you can access to apply fills and strokes to objects.

You access all panels from the Window menu. You never have to wonder where to find a panel, because all panels are on the Window menu. Some panels are placed within categories on the Window menu. For example, all the text-related panels, such as the Character panel and the Paragraph panel, are listed in the Type category.

When you choose a panel from the Window menu, the panel is displayed in its expanded view. Panels themselves have menus. You can display a panel's menu by clicking the panel menu button at the top right of the panel. Figure 4 shows the Paragraph panel and its menu.

To better manage available workspace, you can reduce the size of a panel by clicking the Collapse to Icons button, which displays a panel only by its name and an icon. Even better, you can group panels strategically to save space and to combine specific functions into one area. Figure 5 shows two essential typography panels grouped together. The Paragraph panel is the active panel—it is in front of the

Character panel in the group and available for use. To activate the Character panel, you would simply click its tab. With this simple grouping, you can do nearly all the text formatting you're likely to do, all in one place. To group panels, drag one by its name onto the name of the other.

Docking panels is another way to organize panels. When you dock panels, you connect the bottom edge of one panel to the top edge of another panel so that both move together. To dock panels, first drag a panel's name tab to the bottom edge of another panel. When the bottom edge of the other panel is highlighted in bright blue, release the mouse button, and the two panels will be docked.

Figure 4 The Paragraph panel menu

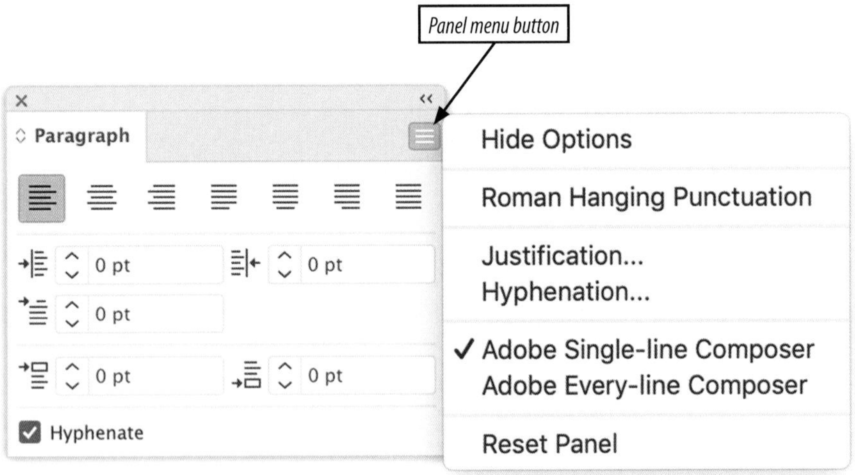

Figure 5 Character and Paragraph panels grouped

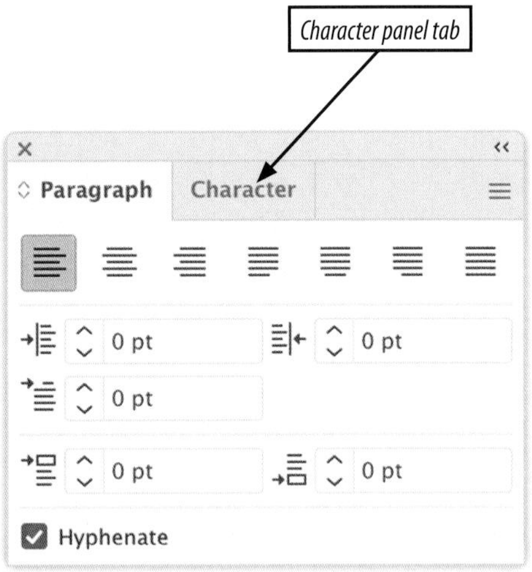

Figure 6 shows an entire dock of panels minimized on the right side of the document window. Clicking a panel thumbnail, or icon, opens the panel as well as any other panels with which it is grouped. In the figure, the Color panel icon has been clicked, and the panel is showing. Docking panels in this manner is a great way to save space on your screen, especially if you're the type of designer who likes to have a lot of panels available at all times.

TIP You can hide all open panels, including the toolbar, by pressing [tab]. Press [tab] again to show the panels. This is especially useful when you want to view artwork and the entire document window without panels in the way.

Creating Customized Toolbars

The ability to create alternative, customized toolbars is a great feature in Illustrator. Over the years, as Illustrator has become more complex and able to do more and more things, the toolbar has become quite crowded. You can create multiple toolbars specified for different functions. For example, you could customize a toolbar just for your favorite drawing tools or just for transforming objects.

To create additional toolbars, click the Window menu, point to Toolbars, then click New Toolbar. Once you've named the toolbar, it appears on the artboard beside the main toolbar. To add tools to the new toolbar, click the three dots at the bottom, then drag and drop tools from the menu. Note that all toolbars you create are listed and accessible on the Window menu.

Figure 6 Multiple panels docked together and minimized as icons

Click icon to expand

Explore the Toolbar

1. Start Adobe Illustrator.

2. Click **File** on the menu bar, click **Open**, navigate to the drive and folder where your Chapter 8 Data Files are stored, then open **AI 1-1.ai**.

3. Click **Window** on the menu bar, point to **Workspace**, then click **Essentials Classic**.

4. Click **Window** on the menu bar, point to **Workspace**, then click **Reset Essentials Classic**.

   Your window should resemble Figure 7.

5. Click the **small double arrow** at the top of the toolbar, then click it again to switch between the two toolbar setups.

All of the figures in this book that show the toolbar will display the panel in two columns.

6. Point to the **Type tool** T, then press and hold the mouse button to see the **Type on a Path tool** .

7. View the **hidden tools** behind the other tools with small black triangles.

8. Click **Illustrator (Mac)** or **Edit (Win)** on the menu bar, point to **Preferences**, click **General**, verify that **Show Tool Tips** is checked, then click **OK**.

9. Position your mouse pointer over the **Selection tool** until its tool tip appears.

10. Press the following keys, and note which tools are selected with each key: **[A]**, **[P]**, **[V]**, **[T]**, **[I]**, **[H]**, and **[Z]**.

11. Press **[tab]** to temporarily hide all open panels, then press **[tab]** again.

    The panels reappear.

12. Keep this file open, and continue to the next set of steps.

You explored different views of the toolbar, revealed hidden tools, used shortcut keys to access tools quickly, hid the panels, and then displayed them again.

OPENING ILLUSTRATOR FILES IN PREVIOUS VERSIONS

Illustrator is "backwards compatible," meaning that Illustrator CC can open files from previous versions. The reverse, however, isn't true; earlier versions can't open newer versions. For example, Illustrator CS6 cannot open Illustrator CC documents. This can become an issue if you send an Illustrator CC file to another designer, client, or vendor who is using an older version. To accommodate, you can "save down" to a previous version when you save the file. When you name the file and click Save, the Illustrator Options dialog box opens. Click the Version list arrow to choose the version to which you want to save it. Note that any new CC features used in your file may be lost when the file is converted to the older format.

Figure 7 The document window

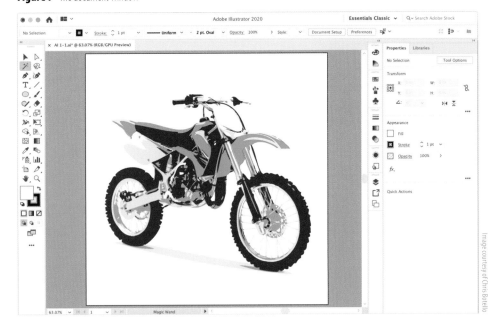

Image courtesy of Chris Botello

Work with panels

1. At the right-hand side of the window, drag the **Properties panel** by its name to the center of the window, then click the **small x** at the upper-left corner of the panel to close it.

2. Drag the **Libraries panel** by its name to the center of the window, then close it.

3. Click the **Swatches panel icon** 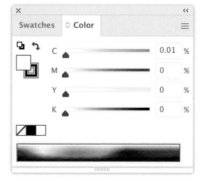 in the dock of collapsed panels to the right of the pasteboard to open the Swatches panel.

   The panel opens but does not detach from the stack of collapsed panels. The Swatches panel is grouped with the Brushes and Symbols panels in this workspace.

4. Drag the **Swatches panel name tab** to the left so it is ungrouped from the stack.

5. Click the **Color panel icon** in the dock of collapsed panels, then drag the **Color panel name tab** to the left so it is ungrouped from the stack.

6. Drag the **Color panel name tab** onto the **Swatches panel name tab**, then release the mouse button.

   The Color panel is grouped with the Swatches panel, as shown in Figure 8.

TIP If you do not see the CMYK sliders on the Color panel, click the Color panel menu button ☰, then click Show Options.

7. Click **Window** on the menu bar, then click **Align**.

   The Align panel appears and is grouped with the Transform and Pathfinder panels.

8. Drag the **entire panel group** to the bottom edge of the Swatches and Color panels group; then, when a blue horizontal line appears, release the mouse button.

   The panel is docked, as shown in Figure 9.

9. Click and drag the **gray bar** at the top of the Swatches and Color panels group around the document window.

Figure 8 Grouped panels

The Align, Transform, and Pathfinder panels group moves with the Swatches and Color panels group because it is docked.

Figure 9 Docked panels

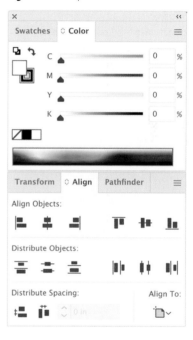

10. Keep this file open, and continue to the next set of steps.

You explored methods for grouping and ungrouping panels, then you docked two panel groups together.

Create and save a customized workspace

1. Using the same methods, create the dock of panels shown in Figure 10.

2. Close all the other panels at the far-right edge of the window.

3. Minimize the dock of panels you created so they appear as icons.

4. Position the dock of icons at the far-right edge of the window.

The right edge of your window should resemble Figure 11.

5. Click **Window** on the menu bar, point to **Workspace**, then click **New Workspace.**

6. In the **Name text box**, type **your last name** in all caps, then click **OK.**

A new workspace is created representing the current layout of the document window.

You docked panels, minimized them to small icons at the right side of the window, and then created a new workspace with the new arrangement.

Figure 10 Seven panels grouped and docked

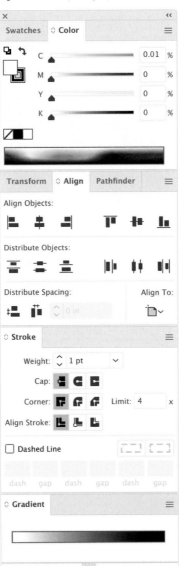

Figure 11 Dock of seven minimized panels

VIEW AND MODIFY ARTBOARD ELEMENTS

▶ *What You'll Do*

In this lesson, you will explore various methods for viewing the document and document elements, such as rulers, guides, grids, and selection marks.

Using the Zoom Tool

Imagine creating a layout on a traditional pasteboard—not on your computer. For precise work, you would bring your nose closer to the pasteboard so you could better see what you're doing. At other times, you would hold the pasteboard away from you at arm's length so you could get a larger perspective of the artwork.

When you're working in Illustrator, the Zoom tool performs these functions for you. When you click the Zoom tool and move it over the document window, the pointer shows a plus sign. When you click the document, the area you click is enlarged. To reduce the view of the document, press and hold [option] (Mac) or [Alt] (Win). When the plus sign changes to a minus sign, click the document, and the document size is reduced.

Using the Zoom tool, you can reduce or enlarge the view of the document from 3.13% to 64,000%. Note that the current magnification level appears in the document tab near the filename and in the Zoom Level text box at the bottom-left corner of the window.

Accessing the Zoom Tool

As you work, you can expect to zoom in and out of the document more times than you can count. The most basic way of accessing the Zoom tool is to click it on the toolbar, but this can get very tiring if you need to access it often.

A better method for accessing the Zoom tool is to use keyboard shortcuts. When you are using other tools, don't switch to the Zoom tool by selecting it from the toolbar. Instead, press and hold [command] [space bar] (Mac) or [Ctrl] [space bar] (Win) to temporarily change the Selection tool into the Zoom tool. When you release the keys, the Zoom tool changes back to whichever tool you were using. To access the Zoom-minus tool, press and hold [command] [option] [space bar] (Mac) or [Ctrl] [Alt] [space bar] (Win).

TIP Double-clicking the Zoom tool on the toolbar changes the document view to 100% (actual size). In addition to the Zoom tool, Illustrator offers other ways to zoom in and out of your document. One of the quickest and easiest ways is to press [command] [+] (Mac) or [Ctrl] [+] (Win) to enlarge the view, and [command] [−] (Mac) or [Ctrl] [−] (Win) to reduce the view. You can also use the Zoom In and Zoom Out commands on the View menu.

Using the Hand Tool

When you zoom in on a document to make it appear larger, eventually the document will be too large to fit in the window. Therefore, you will need to scroll to see other areas of it. You can use the scroll bars along the bottom and the right sides of the document window or you can use the Hand tool to scroll through the document.

The best way to understand the concept of the Hand tool is to think of it as your own hand. Imagine that you could put your hand up to the document on your monitor and move the document left, right, up, or down like a paper on a table or against a wall. This is similar to how the Hand tool works.

Using the Hand tool is often a better choice for scrolling than using the scroll bars because you can access the Hand tool using a keyboard shortcut. Regardless of whatever tool you are using, simply press and hold [space bar] to access the Hand tool. Release [space bar] to return to whatever tool you were using.

TIP Double-clicking the Hand tool on the toolbar changes the document view to fit the page (or the spread) in the document window.

Working with Rulers, Grids, and Guides

Many illustrations involve positioning and aligning objects precisely. Illustrator is well equipped with many features that help you with these tasks.

Rulers are positioned at the top and left sides of the pasteboard to help you align objects. To display or hide the rulers, you can click View on the menu bar, point to Rulers, then click Hide Rulers or Show Rulers, or you can use the keyboard shortcuts [command] [R] (Mac) or [Ctrl] [R] (Win). Rulers can display measurements in different **units**, such as inches, picas, or points. You determine the units with which you want to work in the Preferences dialog box. On the Illustrator (Mac) or Edit (Win) menu, point to Preferences, then click Units to display the dialog box.

TIP In this book, all exercises use inches as the unit of measurement.

Hiding and Showing Selection Marks

All objects you create have visible selection marks or selection edges, and when an object is selected, those edges automatically highlight to show anchor points.

While you're designing your illustration, you might want to work with selection marks hidden so all you see is the artwork. To hide or show selection marks, click the Hide Edges or Show Edges command on the View menu.

Figure 12 shows artwork with selection marks visible and hidden. In both examples, the artwork is selected, but the selection marks are not visible in the example on the right.

Figure 12   Selection marks visible on the left star

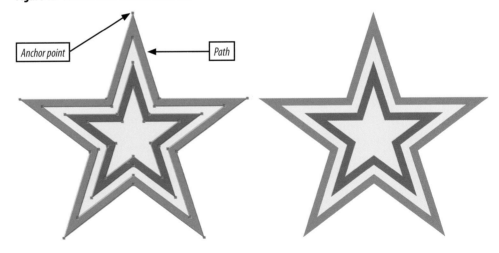

Choosing Screen Modes

Screen modes are options for viewing documents. The two basic screen modes in Illustrator are Preview and Outline. You'll work in Preview mode most of the time. In **Preview** mode, you see all your objects with fills and strokes and effects.

Outline mode displays all your objects as only hollow shapes, with no fills or strokes. Working in Outline mode can sometimes be helpful for selecting various objects that are positioned close together.

Figure 13 shows the motorcycle artwork in Outline mode.

To select objects in Preview mode, simply click anywhere on the object's fill or stroke. In Outline mode, however, you need to click the edge of the object.

Figure 13 Artwork in Outline mode

Understanding Preferences

All Adobe software products come loaded with preferences. **Preferences** are specifications you can set for how certain features of the application behave. The Preferences dialog box houses the multitude of Illustrator preferences. Getting to know available preferences is a smart approach to mastering Illustrator. Many preferences offer important choices that will have significant impact on how you work.

Working with Multiple Open Documents

On many occasions, you'll find yourself working with multiple open documents. For example, let's say you're into scrapbooking. If you're designing a new illustration to highlight a recent trip to Italy, you might also have another file open of an illustration you created last year when you went to Hawaii. Why? For any number of reasons. You might want to copy and paste art elements from the Hawaii document into the new document. Or you might want the Hawaii document open simply as a reference for typefaces, type sizes, image sizes, and effects that you used in the document.

When you're working with multiple open documents, you can switch from one to the other simply by clicking on the title bar of each document.

Illustrator offers a preference for having multiple open documents available as tabs in the document window. This can be useful for keeping your workspace uncluttered. With this preference selected, a tab will appear for each open document, showing the name of the document. When you click the tab, that document becomes active.

Working with tabbed documents can sometimes be inhibiting, because the tabbed option allows you to view only one document at a time. That issue is easily solved, however. All you need to do is drag a tabbed document by its name out of the window, and it will be become a floating window.

The User Interface preferences dialog box is where you specify whether you want open documents to appear as tabs. Click Illustrator (Mac) or Edit (Win) on the menu bar, point to Preferences, then click User Interface. Click to activate the Open Documents As Tabs option, then click OK.

Using Shortcut Keys to Execute View Commands

The most commonly used commands in Illustrator list a shortcut key beside the command name. Shortcut keys are useful for quickly accessing menu commands without stopping work to go to the menu. Make a mental note of helpful shortcut keys and incorporate them into your work. You'll find that using them becomes second nature.

See Table 1 for shortcut keys you will use regularly for manipulating the view of your Illustrator screen.

TABLE 1: SHORTCUT KEYS FOR VIEWING COMMANDS		
	Mac	**Windows**
Hide/Show Guides	command-;	Ctrl-;
Hide/Show Edges	command-H	Ctrl-H
Hide/Show Rulers	command-R	Ctrl-R
Activate/Deactivate Smart Guides	command-U	Ctrl-U
Fit Page in Window	command-0	Ctrl-0
Fit Spread in Window	option-command-0	Alt-Ctrl-0
Toggle Preview and Outline Screen Modes	command-Y	Ctrl-Y
Hide/Show Grid	command-"	Ctrl-"

Use the Zoom tool and the Hand tool

1. Press the **letter [Z]** on your keypad to access the **Zoom tool** 🔍 .

2. Position the **Zoom tool** 🔍 over the **document window**, click twice to enlarge the document, press **[option] (Mac)** or **[Alt] (Win)**, then click twice to reduce the document.

3. Click the **Zoom Level list arrow** in the lower-left corner of the document window, then click **800%**.

   Note that 800% is now listed in the document tab beside the file name.

4. Double-click **800%** in the Zoom Level text box, type **300**, then press **[return] (Mac)** or **[Enter] (Win)**.

5. Click the **Hand tool** 🖐 on the toolbar, then click and drag the **document window** to scroll.

6. Double-click the **Zoom tool** 🔍 .

   Double-clicking the Zoom tool 🔍 changes the view of the document to 100% (actual size).

7. Click the **Selection tool** ▶ , point to the **center of the document window**, then press and hold **[command] [space bar] (Mac)** or **[Ctrl] [space bar] (Win)**.

   The Selection tool ▶ changes to the Zoom tool 🔍 .

8. Click **three times**, then release **[command] [space bar] (Mac)** or **[Ctrl] [space bar] (Win)**.

9. Press and hold **[space bar]** to access the **Hand tool** 🖐 , then scroll around the image.

10. Press and hold **[command] [option] [space bar] (Mac)** or **[Ctrl] [Alt] [space bar] (Win)**, then click the **mouse button** multiple times to reduce the view to 25%.

    Your document window should resemble Figure 14.

11. Keep this file open, and continue to the next set of steps.

You explored various methods for accessing and using the Zoom tool for enlarging and reducing the document. You also used the Hand tool to scroll around an enlarged document.

Figure 14 Viewing the document at 25%

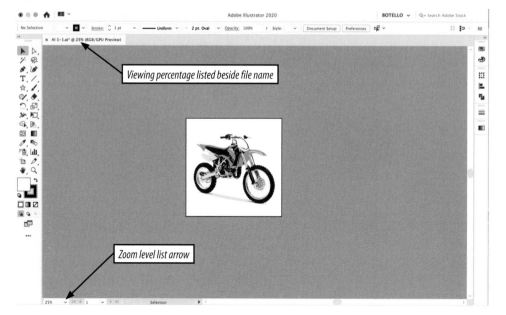

USING THE KEYBOARD SHORTCUTS DIALOG BOX

Shortcuts are keyboard combinations you can use instead of clicking menu items to execute commands. Illustrator lets you view a list of all shortcuts, edit or create shortcuts, define your own sets of shortcuts, change individual shortcuts within a set, and switch between sets of shortcuts in the Keyboard Shortcuts dialog box. To open the Keyboard Shortcuts dialog box, click Edit on the menu bar, then click Keyboard Shortcuts. Choose a set of shortcuts from the Set menu at the top of the Keyboard Shortcuts dialog box, then choose to modify either Menu Commands or Tools from the menu. To activate the set of shortcuts, click OK. To change a shortcut, click in the Shortcut column of the scroll list, type a new shortcut, then click OK.

Hide and show rulers and set units and increments preferences

1. Click **View** on the menu bar, note the shortcut key for the **Fit All in Window command**, then click **Fit Artboard in Window**.

2. Click **View** on the menu bar, point to **Rulers**, then note the **Hide/Show Rulers command** and its shortcut key.

   The Rulers command is listed as either Hide Rulers or Show Rulers depending on the current status.

3. Leave the View menu, then press **[command] [R] (Mac)** or **[Ctrl] [R] (Win)** several times to hide and show rulers, finishing with rulers showing.

4. Note the units on the rulers.

   Depending on the preference you have set, your rulers might be showing inches, picas, or another unit of measure.

5. Click **Illustrator (Mac)** or **Edit (Win)** on the menu bar, point to **Preferences**, then click **Units**.

6. Click the **General list arrow** to see the available measurement options, then click **Picas**.

7. Click **OK**.

   The rulers change to pica measurements. Picas are a unit of measure used in layout design long before the advent of computerized layouts. One pica is equal to 1/6 inch. It's important that you understand that the unit of measure you set as ruler units will affect all measurement utilities in the application, such as those on the Transform panel, in addition to the ruler increments.

8. Reopen the **Units Preferences dialog box**, click the **General list arrow**, then click **Inches**.

   Your dialog box should resemble Figure 15.

9. Click **OK**.

10. Keep this file open and continue to the next set of steps.

You used shortcut keys to hide and show rulers in the document. You used the Units Preferences dialog box to change the unit of measure for ruler units.

Figure 15 Units preferences set to Inches

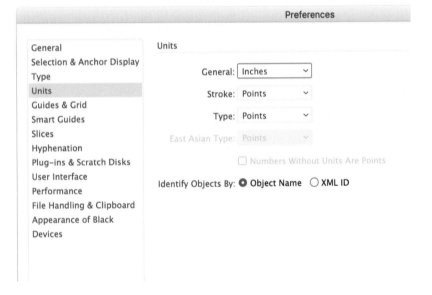

ARRANGING DOCUMENTS

When you're working with multiple documents, you can use the Arrange Documents button ▦ ⌄ on the menu bar. If you have three separate documents open, for example, the 3-UP options in the Arrange Documents panel will tile and display all three documents in a column or a row. The Tile All In Grid option positions all open documents in a single window, allowing you to compare artwork from one file to another and even drag objects across documents.

Hide and show guides, selection marks, and the document grid

1. Click **Select** on the menu bar, then click **All**.

2. Click **View** on the menu bar, then note the **Hide/Show Edges command** and its shortcut key.

   The command is listed as either Hide Edges or Show Edges, depending on the current status.

3. Leave the View menu, then press **[command] [H] (Mac)** or **[Ctrl] [H] (Win)** several times to switch between hiding and showing selection marks, finishing with marks showing.

TIP The Hide Edges shortcut key is easy to remember if you think of *H for Hide*. Remember, though, that this shortcut key only hides and shows selection marks—not other elements, like ruler guides, which use different shortcut keys.

4. Click the **Select** menu, then click **Deselect**.

5. Click **View** on the menu bar, point to **Guides**, then note the **Hide/Show Guides command** and its shortcut key.

   The Guides command is listed as either Hide Guides or Show Guides depending on the current status.

6. Leave the View menu, then press **[command] [;] (Mac)** or **[Ctrl] [;] (Win)** several times to hide and show guides, finishing with guides showing.

   Four guides are shown in Figure 16.

TIP Make note of the difference between the Hide/Show Guides shortcut key and the Hide/Show Edges shortcut key.

7. Click **View** on the menu bar, then click **Show Grid**.

8. Leave the View menu, then press **[command] ["] (Mac)** or **[Ctrl] ["] (Win)** several times to hide and show the grid.

TIP Notice the difference between the Hide/Show Guides shortcut key and the Hide/Show Grid shortcut key—they're just one key away from each other.

9. Hide the grid and the guides.

10. Keep this file open and continue to the next set of steps.

You used shortcut keys to hide and show selection marks, ruler guides, and the document grid.

Figure 16 Four guides showing

Guides

Toggle screen modes and work with multiple documents

1. Click the **View menu**, note the shortcut key command for **Outline mode**, then escape the View menu.

2. Press **[command] [Y] (Mac)** or **[Ctrl] [Y] (Win)** repeatedly to toggle between Outline and Preview mode, finishing in Preview mode.

3. Click **Illustrator (Mac)** or **Edit (Win)** on the menu bar, point to **Preferences**, then click **User Interface.**

4. Verify that the **Open Documents As Tabs check box** is checked, then click **OK.**

5. Click **File** on the menu bar, click **Save As**, type **Motocross** in the File name box, then click the **Save button** to save the file with a new name.

TIP Each time you save a data file with a new name, the Illustrator Options dialog box will open. Click OK to close it.

6. Open AI 1-2.ai, then click the **tabs** of each open document several times to toggle between them, finishing with Motocross.ai as the active document.

7. Drag the **Motocross.ai tab** straight down approximately **½ inch**.

    When you drag a tabbed document down, it becomes a "floating" document.

8. Position your mouse pointer **over the title bar of Motocross.ai**, click and drag to position it at the **top of the window beside the AI 1-2.ai tab**, then release the mouse button when you see a horizontal blue bar.

    The document is tabbed once again.

9. Close AI 1-2.ai without saving changes if you are prompted.

10. Close Motocross.ai without saving changes if you are prompted.

You verified that the Open Documents As Tabs option in the User Interface Preferences dialog box was activated. You removed the document from its tabbed position, resized it, moved it around, then returned it to its tabbed status.

USING THE DOCUMENT INFO PANEL

The Document Info panel, listed on the Window menu, contains useful information about the document and objects in the document. Along with general file information such as filename, ruler units, and color space, the panel lists specific information like the number and names of graphic styles, custom colors, patterns, gradients, fonts, and placed art. To view information about a selected object, choose Selection Only from the panel menu. Leaving this option deselected lists information about the entire document. To view artboard dimensions, click the Artboard tool, choose Document from the panel menu, and then click to select the artboard you want to view.

DEACTIVATING CORNER WIDGETS WHEN USING THE DIRECT SELECTION TOOL

When you select the Direct Selection tool and select an object on the page, it is likely that you will see small icons beside the selected object. These are corner widgets, and they are a new feature in Illustrator Creative Cloud that allows you to modify the corners of objects into round and pointed corners. We cover this extensively in Chapter 11. When doing the many exercises in this book that involve using the Direct Selection tool, it is best that you deactivate corner widgets so they don't distract from your work. To do so, click the View menu, then click Hide Corner Widget.

WORK WITH OBJECTS AND SMART GUIDES

▶ *What You'll Do*

In this lesson, you will work with objects with smart guides.

Working with Preferences

Illustrator features several Preferences dialog boxes. Preferences affect many aspects of the Illustrator interface, including guides, smart guides, and rulers. You can think of preferences as the "ground rules" that you establish before doing your work. For example, you might want to specify your preferences for guide and grid colors or for hyphenation if you're doing a lot of type work.

One tricky thing about preferences is that, if you're just learning Illustrator, preferences refer to things you don't really know about. That's OK. Illustrator's preferences default to a paradigm that makes most of the work you do intuitive. But as you gain experience, it's a good idea to go back through the available preferences and see if there are any changes you want to make or with which you want to experiment.

One more thing about preferences: remember that they're there. Let's say you want to apply a 2 pt. stroke to an object, but the Stroke panel is showing stroke weight in inches. First, you click the Stroke panel options button to show the Stroke panel menu, but you soon find that the menu holds no command for changing the readout from inches to points. That's when you say to yourself, "Aha! It must be a preference."

Resizing Objects

Individual pieces of artwork that you create in Illustrator—such as squares, text, or lines—are called **objects**. All objects you create in Illustrator are composed of paths and anchor points. When you select an object, its paths and anchor points become highlighted.

You have many options for changing the size and shape of an object. One of the most straightforward options is to use the **bounding box**. Select any object or multiple objects, then click Show Bounding Box on the View menu. Eight handles appear around the selected object, as shown in Figure 17. Click and drag the handles to change the shape and size of the object.

When you select multiple objects, a single bounding box appears around all the selected objects. Manipulating the bounding box will affect all the objects. Illustrator offers basic keyboard combinations that you can use when dragging bounding box handles. See Table 2.

Figure 17 Bounding box around selected object

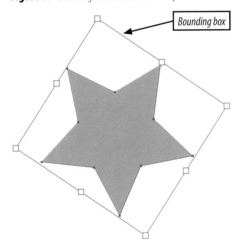

Bounding box

TABLE 2: OBJECT RESIZING COMBINATIONS		
Mac	Windows	Result
Shift-drag a corner handle	Shift-drag a corner handle	The object is resized in proportion; its shape doesn't change
Option-drag a handle	Alt-drag a handle	Resizes the object from its center point
Option-shift-drag a handle	Alt-shift-drag a handle	Resize the object from its center and in proportion

Copying Objects

At any time, you can copy and paste an object. When you paste, the object is pasted at the center of the artboard—regardless of the position of the original. When designing, you'll often find it more desirable for the copy to be pasted in the exact same location as the original. The **Paste in Front** command pastes the copy directly in front of the original. The **Paste in Back** command pastes the copy directly behind the original. Both have quick keys that are easy to remember. The command for Paste in Front is [command] [F] (Mac) or [Ctrl] [F] (Win) and Paste in Back is [command] [B] (Mac) or [Ctrl] [B] (Win).

Be sure to make a note that you can copy objects while dragging them. Press and hold [option] (Mac) or [Alt] (Win), then drag to create a copy of the object. This behavior is referred to as **drag and drop a copy**, and it's something you'll do a lot of in Illustrator and in this book.

TIP In this book, you'll be asked numerous times to paste in front and paste in back. The direction will read, "Copy, then paste in back," or "Copy, then paste in front." It would be a good idea for you to remember the quick keys.

Hiding, Locking, and Grouping Objects

The Hide, Lock, Group, and Ungroup commands on the Object menu are essential for working effectively with layouts, especially complex layouts with many objects. Hide objects to get them out of your way. They won't print, and nothing you do will change the location of them as long as they are hidden. Lock an object to make it immovable—you will not be able to select it. Lock your objects when you have them in a specific location and you don't want to accidentally move or delete them. Don't think this is being overly cautious. Accidentally moving or deleting objects and being unaware that you did so happens all the time in complex layouts. Having objects grouped strategically is also a solution for getting your work done faster.

You group multiple objects with the Group command on the Object menu. Grouping objects is a smart and important strategy for protecting the relationships between multiple objects. When you click on grouped objects with the Selection tool, all the objects are selected. Thus, you can't accidentally select a single object, move it, or otherwise alter it independently from the group. However, you *can* select individual objects within a group with the Direct Selection tool—that's how the tool got its name. Even if you select and alter a single object within a group, the objects are not ungrouped. If you click on any of them with the Selection tool, all members of the group will be selected.

Working with Smart Guides

When aligning objects, you will find **smart guides** to be very effective and, well, really smart. When the Smart Guides feature is activated, smart guides appear automatically when you move objects in the document. They give you visual information for positioning objects precisely in relation to the artboard or other objects. For example, you can use smart guides to align objects to the edges and centers of other objects, and to the horizontal and vertical centers of the artboard.

You can change settings for smart guides using the Smart Guides section of the Preferences dialog box. You use the View menu to turn them on and off. Figure 18 shows smart guides at work.

Figure 18 Smart guides indicate relationships between objects

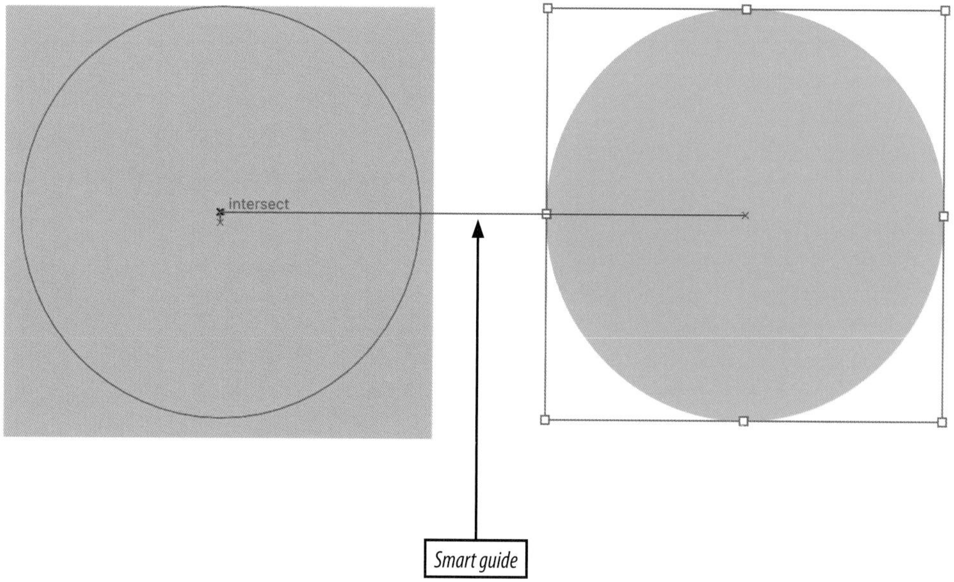

intersect

Smart guide

Set essential preferences

1. Check to make sure you have closed all open documents.

   When changing preference settings, no documents should be open.

2. Click **Illustrator (Mac)** or **Edit (Win)** on the menu bar, point to **Preferences**, then click **General**.

3. Set your General preferences to match Figure 19, then keep the dialog box open until the end of the exercise. You will be making changes to other preference categories.

   The keyboard increment determines the distance a selected object moves when you click an arrow key on your keypad. The measurement entered, .0139" is equivalent to 1 pt. The Show Tool Tips option will reveal a tool's name when you position your cursor over it.

   TIP If you press and hold [shift] while pressing the arrow keys, a selected object moves a distance that is 10× the keyboard increment.

4. Click **Guides & Grid** on the left side of the Preferences dialog box, then verify that your settings match those shown in Figure 20.

   TIP Note that you have options for showing your guides as dots.

Figure 19 General preferences

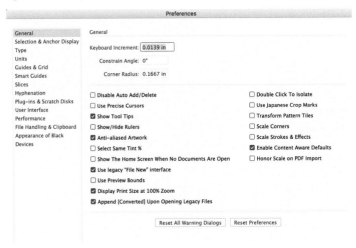

Figure 20 Guides & Grid preferences

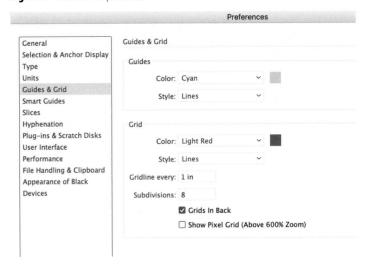

5. Click **Smart Guides** on the left side of the Preferences dialog box, then enter the settings shown in Figure 21.

TIP It's a good idea for your smart guides to be a distinctly different color than your ruler guides and artboard grid.

6. Click **User Interface** on the left side of the Preferences dialog box, then make sure your settings match those shown in Figure 22.

7. Click **OK.**

You specified various essential preferences in different Preferences dialog boxes.

Figure 21 Smart Guides preferences

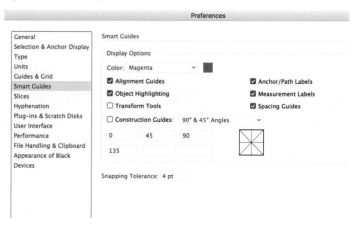

Figure 22 User Interface preferences

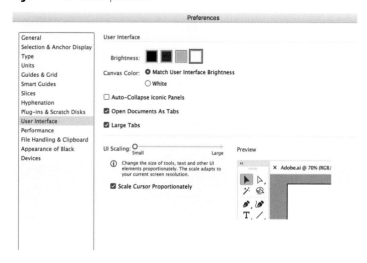

Resize objects

1. Open A1-2.ai, then save it as **Objects**.

2. Click the **Selection tool** ▶, then click the **pink square** to select it.

   As shown in Figure 23, the paths and the anchor points that draw the square are revealed, as is the object's center point.

3. Click **View** on the menu bar, then click **Show Bounding Box**.

   Eight handles appear around the rectangle.

   TIP Make it a point to remember the quick key for showing and hiding the bounding box: [shift] [command] [B] (Mac) or [shift] [Ctrl] [B] (Win).

4. Click and drag **various handles**, and note how the object is resized.

5. When you are done experimenting, undo all the moves you made to the bounding box.

   The Undo command is at the top of the Edit menu.

6. Press and hold down **[shift]** while dragging the **top-left corner handle** toward the edge of the document.

   The object is resized proportionately.

7. Undo the move.

8. Click the **green circle** to select it.

9. Press and hold **[option] (Mac)** or **[Alt] (Win)**, then start dragging **any corner handle**.

   As you drag, the object is resized from its center.

10. While still holding down **[option] (Mac)** or **[Alt] (Win)** and dragging, press and hold **[shift]**.

    The object is resized in proportion from its center.

11. Scale the **circle** to any size.

12. Undo the move.

13. Click **Select** on the menu bar, then click **All**.

    All the objects on the artboard are selected. The bounding box appears around all three objects. Make it a point to remember the quick

    key for Select All: [command] [A] (Mac) or [Ctrl] [A] (Win).

14. Using the skills you learned in this lesson, experiment with resizing all the objects.

15. Click **File** on the menu bar, click **Revert**, then click **Revert** when you are prompted to confirm.

    Reverting a file returns it to its status when you last saved it. You can think of it as a "super undo."

16. Keep this file open and continue to the next set of steps.

You explored various options for resizing objects, then you reverted the file.

Copy and duplicate objects

1. Click **View** on the menu bar, then click **Hide Bounding Box**.

2. Select the **star**, then copy it, using the **[command] [C] (Mac)** or **[Ctrl] [C] (Win)** shortcut keys.

3. Click **Edit** on the menu bar, then click **Paste in Front**.

   The copy is pasted directly in front of the original star.

4. Press the **letter [I]** on your keypad to switch to the **Eyedropper tool** ✎.

   The star remains selected.

5. Click the **pink square**.

   The star takes on the same fill and stroke colors as the square.

6. Press the right arrow key [→] on your keypad 10 times.

   The star moves 10 keyboard increments to the right.

Figure 23 Paths, anchor points, and center point on an object

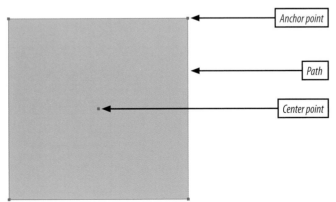

Anchor point

Path

Center point

7. Deselect all, click **Edit** on the menu bar, then click **Paste in Back**.

A copy of the orange star is pasted directly behind the original orange star that was copied.

8. Click the **Eyedropper tool** 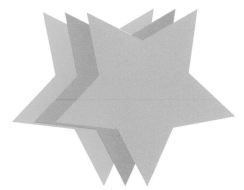 on the **green circle**.

9. Press and hold **[shift]**, then press ← on your keypad one time.

Pressing and holding [shift] when pressing an arrow key moves the selected object(s) 10 keyboard increments.

10. Press and hold **[command] (Mac)** or **[Ctrl] (Win)** so your cursor switches temporarily from the **Eyedropper tool** , to the **Selection tool** , then click the **artboard** with the **Selection tool** to deselect all.

Pressing [command] (Mac) or [Ctrl] (Win) is a quick way to switch temporarily to the Selection tool .

Figure 24 Three stars

11. Compare your artboard to Figure 24.

12. Click the **Selection tool** , then select the **green circle**.

13. Press and hold **[option] (Mac)** or **[Alt] (Win)**, then drag a **copy of the circle** to the **center of the pink square**.

Your artboard should resemble Figure 25.

TIP This method for creating a copy is referred to as "drag and drop a copy."

14. Save your work, then close the file.

You copied and pasted an object, noting that it pasted by default in the center of the artboard. You used the Paste in Front and Paste in Back commands along with arrow keys to make two offset copies of the star. You duplicated the circle with the drag and drop technique.

Figure 25 Dragging and dropping a copy of the circle

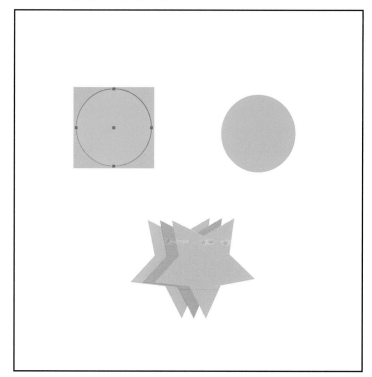

Hide, lock, and group objects

1. Open AI 1-3.ai, then save it as **Groups**.
2. Click **Object** on the menu bar, then click **Show All**.

   This document was originally saved with hidden objects. Three objects appear. They are all selected.
3. Click **Object** on the menu bar, then click **Group**.
4. Click the **Selection tool** ▶, click **anywhere on the pasteboard** to deselect all, then click the **pink circle**.

   All three objects are selected because they are grouped.
5. Click the **pasteboard** to deselect all, click the **Direct Selection tool** ▷, then click the **pink circle**.

   Only the circle is selected, because the Direct Selection tool ▷ selects individual objects within a group.
6. Select all, click **Object** on the menu bar, then click **Ungroup**.
7. Click the **Selection tool** ▶, select the **small square**, click **Object** on the menu bar, point to **Lock**, then click **Selection**.

   The object's handles disappear, and it can no longer be selected.
8. Click **Object** on the menu bar, then click **Unlock All**.

   The small square is unlocked.
9. Select all, click **Object** on the menu bar, point to **Hide**, then click **Selection**.

   All selected objects disappear.

10. Click **Object** on the menu bar, then click **Show All**.

    The three objects reappear in the same location that they were in when they were hidden.

    TIP Memorize the shortcut keys for Hide/Show, Group/Ungroup, and Lock/Unlock. They are easy to remember and extremely useful. You will be using these commands a lot when you work in Illustrator.

11. Hide the **pink circle** and the **small square**.
12. Save your work, then continue to the next set of steps.

You revealed hidden objects, grouped them, then used the Direct Selection tool to select individual objects within the group. You ungrouped, locked, unlocked, and hid objects.

Figure 26 Smart guide aligning square with center of artboard

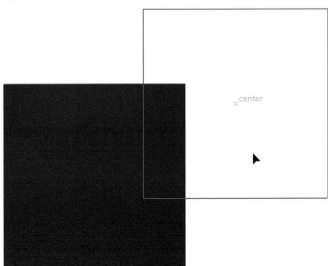

Work with smart guides

1. Click **View** on the menu bar, then click **Smart Guides** if it is not already checked.
2. Click the **large blue square**, then try to center it visually on the page.
3. Release the mouse button when the word **center** appears, as shown in Figure 26.

   Smart guides use the word center to identify when the center point of an object is in line with the center point of the artboard.
4. Show the **hidden objects**, then hide the **small square**.

5. Using smart guides, align the **center of the pink circle** with the **center of the large blue square**.

6. Show the **hidden small square**.

7. Use smart guides to align the **top of the small square** with the **top of the large square**, as shown in Figure 27.

8. Position the **small square** as shown in Figure 28.

9. Save your work, then close the Groups document.

You aligned an object at the center of the document and created precise relationships among three objects using smart guides.

Figure 27 Aligning the tops of two squares

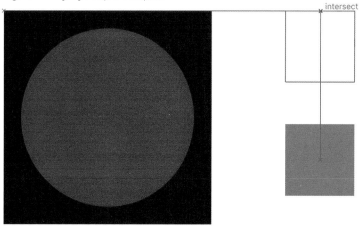

Figure 28 Aligning the bottoms of two squares

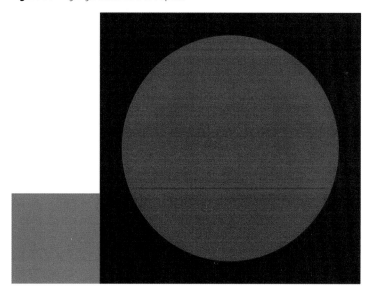

CREATE BASIC SHAPES

In this lesson, you will examine the differences between bitmap and vector graphics. Then you will use the Rectangle tool to examine Illustrator's various options for creating simple vector graphics.

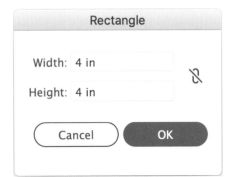

Understanding Bitmap Images and Vector Graphics

Before you begin drawing, you should become familiar with some basic information about computer graphics.

For starters, computer graphics fall into two main categories—bitmap images and vector graphics. **Bitmap images** are created using a square or rectangular grid of colored squares called **pixels**. Because pixels (a contraction of "picture elements") can render subtle gradations of tone, they are the most common medium for continuous-tone images—what you perceive as a photograph.

All scanned images are composed of pixels, and all "digital" images are composed of pixels. Adobe Photoshop is the leading graphics application for working with digital "photos." Figure 29 shows an example of a bitmap image.

Figure 29 Bitmap graphics

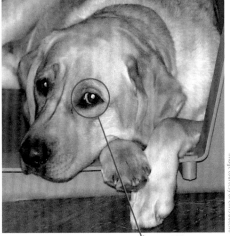

Image courtesy of Chris Botello

Pixels

The number of pixels in each inch is referred to as the image's **resolution**. To be effective, pixels must be small enough to create an image with the illusion of continuous tone. Thus, bitmap images are termed **resolution-dependent**.

The important thing to remember about bitmap images is that any magnification of the image—resizing the image to be bigger—essentially means that fewer pixels are available per inch (the same number of pixels is now spread out over a larger area). This decrease in resolution will have a negative impact on the quality of the image. The greater the magnification, the greater the negative impact.

Graphics that you create in Adobe Illustrator are vector graphics. **Vector graphics** are created with lines and curves and are defined by mathematical objects called vectors.

Vectors use geometric characteristics to define the object. Vector graphics consist of anchor points and line segments, together referred to as paths. Figure 30 shows an example of a vector graphic.

Computer graphics rely on vectors to render bold graphics that must retain clean, crisp lines when scaled to various sizes. Vectors are often used to create logos or "line art," and they are the best choice for typographical work, especially small and italic type.

As mathematical objects, vector graphics can be scaled to any size. Because they are not created with pixels, there is no inherent resolution. Thus, vector graphics are termed **resolution-independent**. This means that any graphic that you create in Illustrator can be output to fit on a postage stamp or on a billboard!

Figure 30 Vector graphics

Use the Rectangle tool

1. Click **File** on the menu bar, click **New**, create a new document that is 8" wide by 8" in height, name the file **Basic Shapes**, then click **OK**.

2. Click **File** on the menu bar, click **Save As**, navigate to the drive and folder where your Data Files are stored, then save the file.

3. Click the **Default Fill and Stroke button** 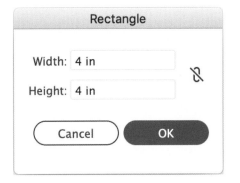 on the toolbar.

4. Click the **Swap Fill and Stroke button** on the toolbar to reverse the default colors.

   Your fill color should now be black, and your stroke color white. The **fill color** is the inside color of an object. The **stroke color** is the color of the object's border or frame.

5. Click the **Rectangle tool** on the toolbar.

6. Click and drag the **Rectangle tool pointer** on the artboard, then release the mouse button to make a rectangle of any size.

7. Press and hold **[shift]**, then create a **second rectangle**.

   As shown in Figure 31, pressing and holding [shift] while you create a rectangle constrains the shape to a perfect square.

8. Create a **third rectangle** drawn from its center point by pressing and holding **[option] (Mac)** or **[Alt] (Win)** as you drag the **Rectangle tool pointer.**

   TIP Use [shift] in combination with [option] (Mac) or [Alt] (Win) to draw a perfect shape from its center.

9. Save your work, then continue to the next set of steps.

You created a freeform rectangle, then you created a perfect square. Finally, you drew a square from its center point.

Use the Rectangle dialog box

1. Click **Select** on the menu bar, then click **All** to select all the objects.

2. Click **Edit** on the menu bar, then click **Cut** to remove the objects from the artboard.

3. Verify that the **Rectangle tool** is still selected, then click **anywhere on the artboard**.

   When a shape tool is selected, clicking once on the artboard opens the tool's dialog box, which allows you to enter precise information for creating the shape. In this case, it opens the Rectangle dialog box.

4. Type **4** in the Width text box, type **4** in the Height text box, as shown in Figure 32, then click **OK**.

5. Save your work, then continue to the next lesson.

You clicked the artboard with the Rectangle tool, which opened the Rectangle dialog box. You entered a specific width and height to create a perfect 4" square.

Figure 31 Creating a rectangle and a square

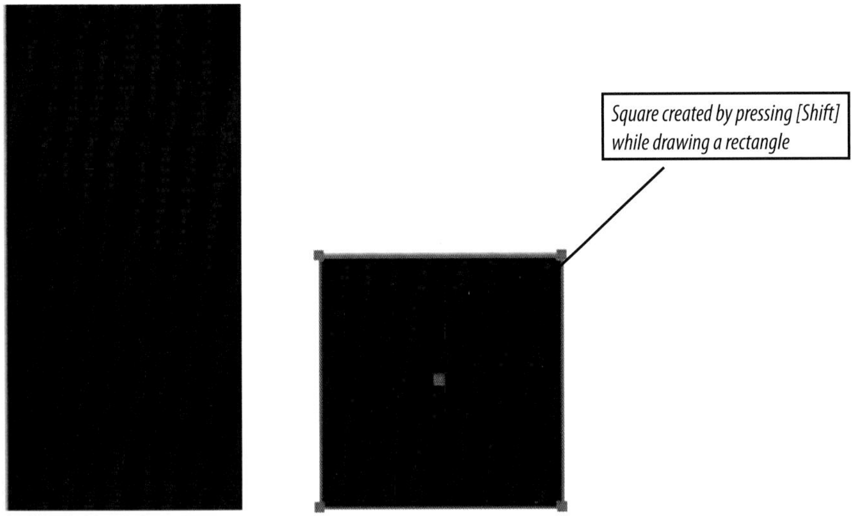

> Square created by pressing [Shift] while drawing a rectangle

Figure 32 Rectangle tool dialog box

Rectangle

Width: 4 in

Height: 4 in

Cancel   OK

APPLY FILL AND STROKE COLORS TO OBJECTS

▶ *What You'll Do*

In this lesson, you will use the Swatches panel to add a fill color to an object and apply a stroke as a border. Then you will use the Stroke panel to change the size of the default stroke.

Activating the Fill or Stroke

The Fill and Stroke buttons are on the toolbar. To apply a fill or stroke color to an object, you must first activate the appropriate button. You activate either button by clicking it, which moves it in front of the other. When the Fill button is in front of the Stroke button, the fill is activated. The Stroke button is activated when it is in front of the Fill button.

As you work, you will often switch back and forth, activating the fill and the stroke. Rather than using the mouse to activate the fill or the stroke each time, simply press [X] to switch between the two modes.

Applying Color with the Swatches Panel

The Swatches panel is central to color management in the application and a main resource for applying fills and strokes to objects.

The Swatches panel has several preset colors, along with gradients, patterns, and shades of gray. The swatch with the red line through it is called [None] and is used as a fill for a "hollow" object. Any object without a stroke will always have [None] as its stroke color.

When an object is selected, clicking a swatch on the panel will apply that color as a fill or a stroke, depending on which of the two is activated on the toolbar. You can also drag and drop swatches onto unselected objects. Dragging a swatch to an unselected object will change the color of its fill or stroke, depending upon which of the two is activated.

Apply fill and stroke colors

1. Verify that the **4" × 4" square** is still selected.
2. Click the **fill color** on the toolbar to verify that it is the active color.

   See Figure 33.

3. Click **any blue swatch** on the Swatches panel to fill the square.

   Note that the Fill button on the toolbar is now also blue.

   TIP When you position the mouse pointer over a color swatch on the Swatches panel, a tool tip appears that shows the name of that swatch.

4. Click the **Selection tool** ▶, then click **anywhere on the artboard** to deselect the blue square.
5. Drag and drop a **yellow swatch** from the Swatches panel onto the blue square on the artboard.

The fill color changes to yellow because the fill button is activated on the toolbar.

6. Press the **letter [X]** to activate the **Stroke button** on the toolbar.
7. Click any **red swatch** on the Swatches panel.

   A red stroke is added to the square because the Stroke button is activated on the toolbar.

8. Open the **Stroke panel**, increase the Weight to **8 pt.**, then compare your artwork to Figure 34.

   TIP By default, Illustrator positions a stroke equally inside and outside an object. Thus, an 8 pt. stroke is rendered with 4 pts. inside the object and 4 pts. outside.

9. Note the **Align Stroke section** on the Stroke panel.
10. Click the **Align Stroke to Inside button** 🔲.

    The entire stroke moves to the inside of the square.

11. Click the **Align Stroke to Outside button** 🔲.

    The entire stroke moves to the outside of the square.

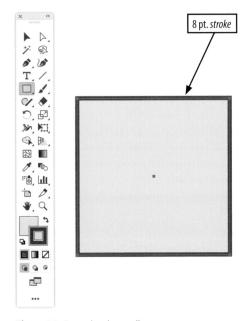

8 pt. *stroke*

Figure 34 8 pt. red stroke on yellow square

12. Click the **Align Stroke to Center button** 🔲.

    The stroke is returned to the default position, equally inside and outside the object.

13. Click ✎ **(None)** on the Swatches panel to remove the stroke from the square.
14. Save your work, then continue to the next set of steps.

You filled the square with blue by clicking a blue swatch on the Swatches panel. You then changed the fill and stroke colors to yellow and red by dragging and dropping swatches onto the square. You used the Stroke panel to increase the weight and change the alignment of the stroke, then removed it by choosing [None] from the Swatches panel.

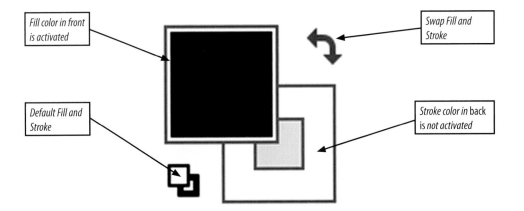

Fill color in front is activated

Swap Fill and Stroke

Default Fill and Stroke

Stroke color in back is *not activated*

Figure 33 Fill color in front and activated on the toolbar

SELECT, MOVE, AND ALIGN OBJECTS

▶ *What You'll Do*

In this lesson, you will use the Selection tool in combination with smart guides to move, copy, and align four squares.

Selecting Objects

Before you can move or modify an Illustrator object, you must select it. When working with simple illustrations that contain few objects, selecting is usually simple, but it can become very tricky in complex illustrations, especially those containing many small objects positioned closely together.

By now you're familiar with using the Selection tool to select objects. You can also use the Selection tool to create a marquee selection, which is a dotted rectangle that disappears as soon as you release the mouse button. Any object that the marquee touches before you release the mouse button will be selected. Marquee selections are useful for both quick selections and precise selections. Make sure you practice and make them part of your skills set.

Moving Objects

When it comes to accuracy, consider that Illustrator can move objects incrementally by fractions of a point—which itself is a tiny fraction of an inch! That level of precision is key when moving and positioning objects.

Two basic ways to move objects are by clicking and dragging or by using the arrow keys, which by default move a selected item in 1 pt. increments. Pressing [shift] when you press an arrow key moves the object in increments of 10 pts. in that direction.

Pressing [shift] when dragging an object constrains the movement to horizontal, vertical, and 45° diagonals. Pressing [option] (Mac) or [Alt] (Win) while dragging an object creates a copy of the object.

Move and position objects with precision

1. Click **View** on the menu bar, then click **Fit Artboard in Window**.

2. Click **View** on the menu bar, then verify that both **Smart Guides** and **Snap to Point** are activated.

   Snap to Point automatically aligns anchor points when they get close together. When dragging an object, you'll see it "snap" to align itself with a nearby object or guide.

   TIP There will be a check next to each if it is activated. If it is not activated, click each option to make it active.

3. Click the **Selection tool** 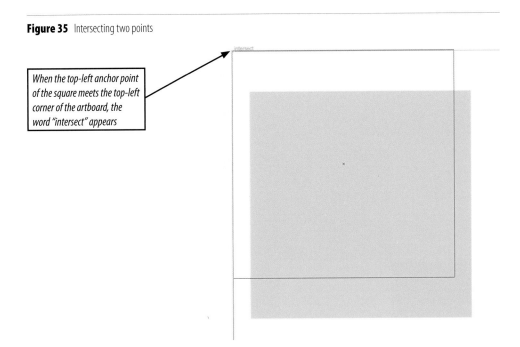 on the toolbar, then click the **yellow square**.

4. Position the pointer over the **top-left anchor point**; click and drag so that the anchor point aligns with the **top-left corner of the artboard**, as shown in Figure 35; then release the mouse button.

   The smart guide changes from "anchor" to "intersect" when the two corners are aligned.

You used the Selection tool in combination with smart guides to position an object exactly at the top-left corner of the artboard.

Figure 35 Intersecting two points

When the top-left anchor point of the square meets the top-left corner of the artboard, the word "intersect" appears

Duplicate objects using drag and drop

1. Press and hold **[shift] [option] (Mac)** or **[shift] [Alt] (Win)**, then click and drag a **copy of the yellow square** immediately below itself, as shown in Figure 36.

   When moving an object, pressing and holding [shift] constrains the movement vertically, horizontally, or on 45° diagonals. Pressing [option] (Mac) or [Alt] (Win) while dragging an object creates a copy of the object.

   TIP When you press [option] (Mac) or [Alt] (Win) while dragging an object, the pointer becomes a double-arrow pointer.

2. With the bottom square still selected, press and hold **[shift]**, then click the **top square** to select both items.

3. Press and hold **[shift] [option] (Mac)** or **[shift] [Alt] (Win)**, then drag a **copy of the two squares** immediately to the right.

4. Change the **fill color** of **each square** to match the colors shown in Figure 37.

5. Save your work, then continue to the next lesson.

You moved and duplicated the yellow square using [shift] to constrain the movement and [option] (Mac) or [Alt] (Win) to duplicate or "drag and drop" copies of the square.

Figure 36 Duplicating the square

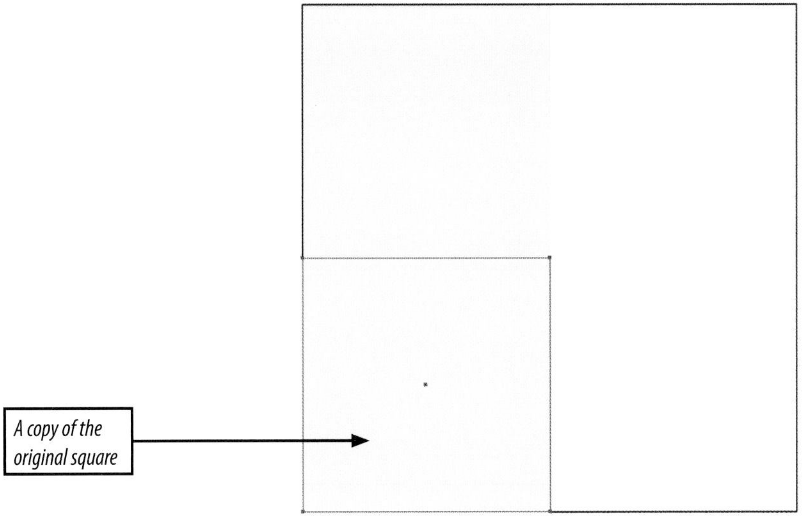

A copy of the original square

Figure 37 Four squares with different fills

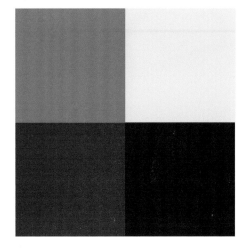

TRANSFORM OBJECTS

In this lesson, you will scale, rotate, and reflect objects, using the basic transform tools. You will also create a star and a triangle.

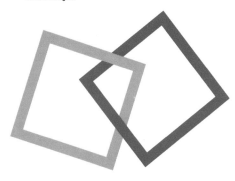

Transforming Objects

The Scale, Rotate, and Reflect tools are the fundamental transform tools. As their names make clear, the Scale and Rotate tools resize and rotate objects, respectively. When you use the tool's dialog box, the objects are transformed from their center points.

Use the Reflect tool to "flip" an object over an imaginary axis. The best way to understand the Reflect tool is to imagine positioning a mirror perpendicular to a sheet of paper with a word written on it. The angle at which you position the mirror in relation to the word is the reflection axis. The reflection of the word in the mirror is the result of what the Reflect tool does. For example, text reflected across a horizontal axis would appear upside down and inverted. Text reflected across a vertical axis would appear to be inverted and running backwards, as shown in Figure 38.

Figure 38 Reflected text

Reflect

- - - - - - - - - - - - - - - - - -

Reflect

Reflect | Reflect

Each transform tool has a dialog box where you enter precise numbers to execute the transformation on a selected object. You can access a tool's dialog box by double-clicking the tool. Click the Copy button in the dialog box to create a transformed copy of the selected object. Figure 39 shows the Scale dialog box.

Repeating Transformations

One of the most powerful commands relating to the transform tools is Transform Again, found on the Object menu. Whenever you transform an object, selecting Transform Again repeats the transformation. For example, if

Figure 39 Scale dialog box

you scale a circle 50%, the Transform Again command will scale the circle 50% again.

The power of the command comes in combination with copying transformations. For example, if you rotate a square 10° and copy it at the same time, the Transform Again command will create a second square rotated another 10° from the first copy. Applying Transform Again repeatedly is handy for creating complex geometric shapes from basic objects.

Use the Scale and Rotate tools

1. Select the **green square**, double-click the **Scale tool** ⌗ , type **50** in the Scale text box, then click **OK**.

2. Click **Edit** on the menu bar, then click **Undo Scale**.

TIP You can also undo your last step by pressing [command] [Z] (Mac) or [Ctrl] [Z] (Win).

3. Double-click the **Scale tool** ⌗ again, type **50** in the Scale text box, then click **Copy**.

   The transformation is executed from the center point; the center points of the original and the copy are aligned.

4. Fill the **new square** created in Step 3 with **blue**.

5. Double-click the **Rotate tool** ↻ , type **45** in the Angle text box, click **OK**, then deselect.

6. Apply a **22 pt. yellow stroke** to the rotated square, deselect, then compare your screen to Figure 40.

7. Save your work, then continue to the next set of steps.

You used the Scale tool to create a 50% copy of the square, then filled the copy with blue. You rotated the copy 45°. You then applied a 22 pt. yellow stroke.

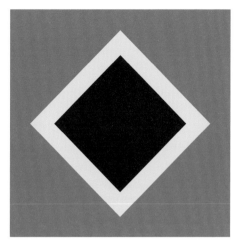

Figure 40 Rotated square

Use the Transform Again command

1. Click the **Ellipse tool** ◯ on the toolbar.

TIP The Ellipse tool ◯ is located behind the Rectangle tool ▢ .

2. Click the **artboard** to open the Ellipse tool dialog box, type **3** in the Width text box and **.5** in the Height text box, then click **OK**.

3. Change the **fill color** to **[None]**, the **stroke color** to **blue**, and the **stroke weight** to **3 pt**.

4. Click the **Selection tool** ▶ , click the **center point of the ellipse**, then drag it to the **center point of the yellow square**.

TIP The center smart guide appears when the two centers meet.

Continued on next page

5. Double-click the **Rotate tool** , type **45** in the Angle text box, then click **Copy**.

6. Click **Object** on the menu bar, point to **Transform**, then click **Transform Again.**

TIP You can also access the Transform Again command by pressing [command] [D] (Mac) or [Ctrl] [D] (Win).

7. Press **[command] [D] (Mac)** or **[Ctrl] [D] (Win)** to create a **fourth ellipse**.

Your screen should resemble Figure 41.

8. Select the **four ellipses**, click **Object** on the menu bar, then click **Group**.

9. Save your work, then continue to the next set of steps.

You created an ellipse, filled and stroked it, and aligned it with the yellow square. You then created a copy rotated at 45°. With the second copy still selected, you used the Transform Again command twice, creating two more rotated copies. You then grouped the four ellipses.

Create a star and a triangle, and use the Reflect tool

1. Select the **Star tool** , then click **anywhere on the artboard**.

The Star tool is hidden beneath the current shape tool.

2. Type **1** in the **Radius 1 text box**, type **5** in the **Radius 2 text box**, type **5** in the **Points text box**, then click **OK**.

A star has two radii; the first is from the center to the inner point, and the second is from the center to the outer point. The **radius** is a measurement from the center point of the star to either point.

TIP When you create a star using the Star dialog box, the star is drawn upside down.

3. Double-click the **Scale tool** , type **25** in the **Scale text box**, then click **OK**.

4. Fill the star with **white**, then apply a **5 pt. blue stroke** to it.

5. Click the **Selection tool** , then move the star so that it is completely within the red square.

6. Double-click the **Reflect tool** , click the **Horizontal option button**, then click **OK**.

The star "flips" over an imaginary horizontal axis.

TIP The Reflect tool , is located behind the Rotate tool .

7. Use the **Selection tool** or the **arrow keys** to position the star roughly in the **center of the red square**.

Your work should resemble Figure 42.

8. Click the **Polygon tool** on the toolbar.

The Polygon tool is hidden beneath the current shape tool on the toolbar.

9. Click **anywhere on the blue square** to open the tool's dialog box.

10. Type **1.5** in the **Radius text box**, type **3** in the **Sides text box**, then click **OK**.

11. Fill the **triangle** with **red**.

12. Change the **stroke color** to **yellow** and the **stroke weight** to **22 pt**.

13. Position the **triangle** so that it is centered within the **blue square**.

Your completed project should resemble Figure 43.

14. Save your work, then close Basic Shapes.

You used the shape tools to create a star and a triangle, then used the Reflect tool to "flip" the star over an imaginary horizontal axis.

Figure 41 Using the Transform Again command

Figure 42 The star with a white fill and blue stroke

Figure 43 The finished project

MAKE DIRECT SELECTIONS

▶ *What You'll Do*

In this lesson, you will use the Direct Selection tool and a combination of menu commands, such as Add Anchor Points and Paste in Front, to convert existing shapes into new designs.

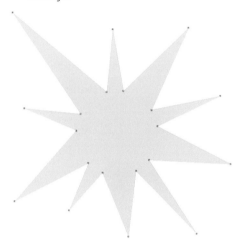

Using the Direct Selection Tool

The Direct Selection tool selects individual anchor points or single paths of an object. Using [shift], you can select multiple anchor points or multiple paths. You can also select multiple points or paths by dragging a direct selection marquee. The tool also selects individual objects within a group, which can be useful for modifying just one object in a complex group.

Clicking the center of an object with the Direct Selection tool selects the entire object. Clicking the edge selects the path segment only; the anchor points on the object all appear white, which means they are not selected.

The Direct Selection tool gives you the power to distort simple objects such as squares and circles into unique shapes. Don't underestimate its significance. While the Selection tool is no more than a means for selecting and moving objects, the Direct Selection tool is in itself a drawing tool. You will use it over and over again to modify and perfect your artwork.

Adding Anchor Points

As you distort basic shapes with the Direct Selection tool, you will often find that to create more complex shapes, you will need additional anchor points.

The Add Anchor Points command creates new anchor points without distorting the object. To add anchor points to an object, click the Object menu, point to Path, then click Add Anchor Points. The new points are automatically positioned exactly between the original anchor points. You can create as many additional points as you wish.

Turning Objects into Guides

Guides are one of Illustrator's many features that help you work with precision. Any object you create can be turned into a guide. With the object selected, click the View menu, point to Guides, then click Make Guides. Guides can be locked or unlocked in the same location. It is a good idea to work with locked guides so they don't interfere with your artwork. Unlock guides only when you want to select them or delete them.

When an object is turned into a guide, it loses its attributes, such as its fill, stroke, and stroke weight. However, Illustrator remembers the original attributes for each guide. To transform a guide back to its original object, first unlock and then select the guide. Click the View menu, point to Guides, then click Release Guides.

Working with the Stacking Order

The **stacking order** refers to the order of how objects are arranged in front and behind other objects on the artboard. Every time you create an object, it is created in front of the existing objects. (Note that this discussion does not include any role of layers and the Layers panel.) You can manipulate the stacking order with the Arrange commands on the Object menu. See Table 3 for descriptions of each Arrange command.

You can also use the **Draw Behind drawing mode** to create an object behind a selected object or at the bottom of the stacking order.

Make guides and direct selections

1. Open AI 1-4.ai, then save it as **Direct Selections**.

2. Click **View** on the menu bar, then deactivate the **Smart Guides feature**.

3. Click the **Selection tool** ▶, then select the **green polygon**.

4. Click **View** on the menu bar, point to **Guides**, then click **Make Guides**.

   The polygon is converted to a guide.

   TIP If you do not see the polygon-shaped guide, click View on the menu bar, point to Guides, then click Show Guides.

5. Convert the **purple starburst** to a guide.

6. Click **View** on the menu bar, point to **Guides**, click **Lock Guides**, then click the **pasteboard** to close the menu.

If you see Unlock Guides on the Guides menu, the guides are already locked.

7. Click the **Direct Selection tool** ▷, then click the **edge of the red square**.

   The four anchor points turn white. If the four anchor points are not white, deselect and try again. You must click the very edge of the square, not inside it.

8. Click and drag the **anchor points** to the **four corners of the guide** to distort the square.

   Your work should resemble Figure 44.

You converted two objects to guides. You then used the Direct Selection tool to create a new shape from a square by moving anchor points independently.

TABLE 3: ARRANGE COMMANDS			
Command	**Result**	**quick key (Mac)**	**quick key (Win)**
Bring Forward	Brings a selected object forward one position in the stacking order	[command] [right bracket]	[Ctrl] [right bracket]
Bring to Front	Brings a selected object to the very front of the stacking order—in front of all other objects	[shift] [command] [right bracket]	[shift] [Ctrl] [right bracket]
Send Backward	Sends a selected object backward one position	[command] [left bracket]	[Ctrl] [left bracket]
Send to Back	Sends a selected object to the very back of the stacking order—behind all the other objects	[shift] [command] [left bracket]	[shift] [Ctrl] [left bracket]

Figure 44 Reshaped red square and guides

Add anchor points

1. Using the **Direct Selection tool** , click the **center of the light blue star**, then note the anchor points used to define the shape.

2. Click **Object** on the menu bar, point to **Path**, then click **Add Anchor Points**.

3. Click the **artboard** to deselect the star, then click the **edge of the star**.

   All the anchor points turn white and are available to be selected independently. If the anchor points are not white, deselect and try again. You must click the very edge of the square, not inside it.

4. Move the **top anchor point on the star** to align with the **top point of the guide** that you made earlier.

5. Working clockwise, move every other anchor point outward to align with the guide, creating a 10-point starburst.

   Your work should resemble Figure 45.

6. Select and move any of the **inner anchor points** to modify the starburst to your liking.

7. Save your work, then continue to the next set of steps.

You used the Add Anchor Points command and the Direct Selection tool to create an original 10-point starburst from a generic five-point star.

Modify the stacking order and use the Draw Behind drawing mode

1. Click the **Selection tool**  on the toolbar, click the **red rectangle**, click **Object** on the menu bar, point to **Arrange**, then click **Send to Back**.

   The red rectangle moves to the back of the stacking order.

2. Select the **yellow path**, click **Object** on the menu bar, point to **Arrange**, then click **Send Backward**.

   The path moves one level back in the stacking order. When discussing the stacking order, it's smart to use the term "level" instead of "layer." In Illustrator, layers are different than the stacking order.

   TIP Click the center of the yellow path to select it.

3. Select the **blue oval**, click **Object** on the menu bar, point to **Arrange**, click **Bring Forward**, then deselect.

   As shown in Figure 46, the blue oval moves one level forward in the stacking order.

Figure 45 Reshaped starburst

Figure 46 Blue oval moved in front of yellow path

4. Verify that the **toolbar** is displayed in two columns.

When the toolbar is displayed in two columns, the three drawing modes are visible as icons at the bottom. When the panel is displayed in a single column, you need to click the Drawing Modes icon to display the tools in a submenu.

5. Note the **four objects** in the bottom-left quadrant of the artboard.

The blue oval is at the back, the purple rectangle is in front of the blue oval, the curvy yellow path is in front of the purple rectangle, and the red rectangle is at the front.

6. Select the **purple rectangle**, then click the **Draw Behind button** at the bottom of the toolbar.

There are three available drawing modes: Draw Normal, Draw Behind, and Draw Inside.

7. Click the **Ellipse tool** on the toolbar, then draw a **circle** at the **center of the blue oval**.

The circle is created behind the purple rectangle, though it still appears to be in front while it is selected. With the Draw Behind drawing mode activated, an object you draw will be positioned one level behind any selected object on the artboard. If no object is selected, the new object will be positioned at the back of the stacking order.

8. Click the **Eyedropper tool**, click the **red rectangle**, then compare your artboard to Figure 47.

The Eyedropper tool samples the fill and stroke colors from the red rectangle and applies them to the selected object.

9. Click the **Draw Normal button**, then save your work.

10. Continue to the next set of steps.

You arranged objects on the artboard, used the Draw Behind feature, then changed the color of the circle you created.

Figure 47 Red circle drawn behind the purple rectangle

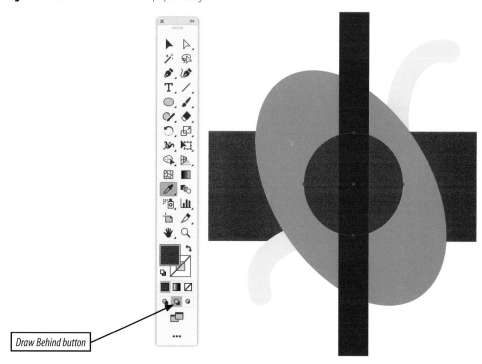

Draw Behind button

Create a simple special effect utilizing the Direct Selection tool

1. Click the **Selection tool** ▶, overlap the **large orange** and **blue squares** so that they resemble the small orange and blue squares, then deselect.

2. Click the **Direct Selection tool** ▷, then select the **top path segment** of the orange square.

    It will look like the whole square is selected, but you will see white anchor points in the four corners.

3. Copy the **path**.

4. Select the **intersecting path segment** on the blue square.

5. Click **Edit** on the menu bar, click **Paste in Front**, then compare your result to Figure 48.

6. Save your work, then close the Direct Selections document.

You performed a classic Illustrator trick using the Direct Selection tool. Selecting only a path, you copied it and pasted it in front of an intersecting object to create the illusion that the two objects were linked.

Figure 48 Illusion of linked squares

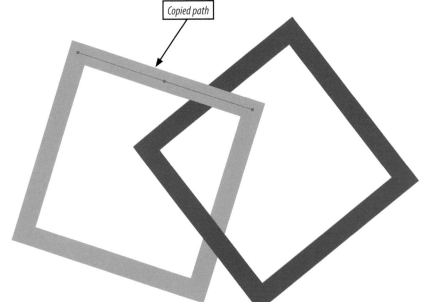

Copied path

WORK WITH MULTIPLE ARTBOARDS

▶ *What You'll Do*

In this lesson, you will explore various options when working with multiple artboards.

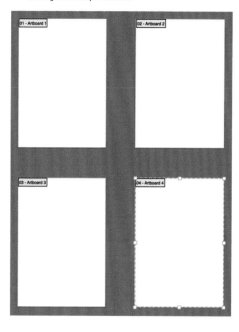

Understanding Multiple Artboards

The artboard is your workspace in an Illustrator document. Sometimes the size of the artboard will be important to your design; sometimes it won't. For example, let's say that you're designing a logo that will be used for a variety of items such as letterhead, business cards, a poster, and a building sign. When you are creating the logo, you're just designing artwork. The size at which you're creating the artwork isn't really important because you can resize it later to use in these different types of layouts.

At other times, the work you do in Illustrator will be at a specific size. Let's say, for example, that you're designing layouts for letterhead, business cards, and promotional postcards for the company for which you made the logo. In this case, you would need to set up your document, or the size of the artboard, at specific sizes, such as 8.5" × 11" for the

letterhead, 3" × 2.5" for the business card, and 4" × 6" for the postcard.

Illustrator allows you to have anywhere from one to 100 artboards in a single document, depending on the size of the artboards. Using the previous example, this means that you could design all three pieces in one document—no need to switch between documents for the letterhead, business card, and postcard.

Beyond this basic convenience, working with multiple artboards offers many important benefits. You won't have to recreate unique swatch colors or gradients in different files; you'll only need to create them once.

Paste commands on the Edit menu allow you to paste an object on multiple artboards in exactly the same location—another example of the consistency that can be achieved by working in a single document.

Managing Multiple Artboards

Creating multiple artboards can be the first thing that you do when beginning a design or one of the last things you do. The New Document dialog box, shown in Figure 49, is where you define the specifics of a document, including the number of artboards.

The Width and Height values define the size of all the artboards you create at this stage, whether single or multiple, but you can resize artboards any time after creating them.

Once you specify the number of artboards, you have controls for the layout of the artboards. The four buttons to the right of the Number of Artboards text box offer basic layout choices—grid by row, grid by column, arrange by row, and arrange by column. The Spacing text box specifies the physical space between artboards, and the Rows value defines the number of rows of artboards in a grid.

When you click the OK button in the New Document dialog box, the document window displays all the artboards you've specified. Regardless of the number, the top-left artboard will be highlighted with a black line. This identifies the artboard as "active." As such, all View menu commands you apply affect this

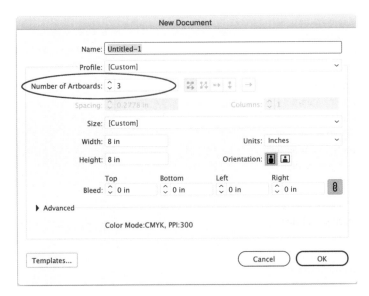

Figure 49 New Document dialog box

artboard. In other words, if you click the Fit Artboard in Window command, the active artboard is resized to fit in the document window. You can also click the Fit All in Window command to view all artboards.

When you create a new document, you can use a preset document profile in the New Document dialog box. The Document Profile menu lists preset values for size, color mode, units, orientation, transparency, and resolution. This can help you set up the basic orientation for your document quickly. For example, the Web profile automatically creates an RGB document with pixels as units. By default, all new document profiles use one artboard, but you can add more in the Number of Artboards text box.

The **Artboard tool** on the toolbar is your gateway to managing multiple artboards. Clicking the Artboard tool takes you to "artboard editing mode." As shown in Figure 50, when you click the tool, all artboards appear numbered against a dark gray background. The "selected" artboard is highlighted with a marquee. When an artboard is selected, you can change settings for it on the Control panel beneath the menu bar, using the following options:

- Click the Presets menu to change a selected artboard to any of the standard sizes listed, such as Letter, Tabloid, or Legal.
- Click the Portrait or Landscape buttons to specify the orientation for the selected artboard.
- Click the New Artboard button to create a duplicate of the selected artboard.
- Click the Delete Artboard button to delete the selected artboard.
- Click the Name text box to enter a name for the selected artboard. This could be useful for managing your own work and for adding clarity when you hand your Illustrator file over to a printer or some other vendor.
- Click the Width and Height text boxes to enter different values and resize the selected artboard.

To exit edit artboards mode, press the Escape key or click any other tool on the toolbar.

Figure 50 Artboard tool selected; artboards can be edited

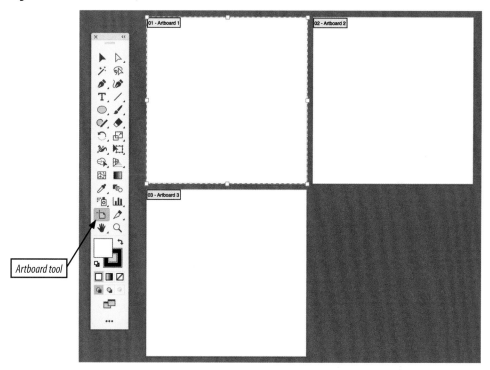

Artboard tool

Creating, Editing, and Arranging Artboards

Once you click the Artboard tool, you have many options for creating, editing, and arranging artboards.

You can click the New Artboard button on the Control panel. When you do, move your cursor over the other artboards and you'll see a transparent artboard moving with the cursor. If you have smart guides activated, green lines will appear to help you align the new artboard with the existing artboards. Click where you want to position the new artboard. Using this method, the new artboard button will create a new artboard at the size specified in the New Document dialog box.

As an alternative, you can simply click and drag with the Artboard tool to create a new artboard. Once you "drag out" the new artboard, you can enter a specific height and width for the artboard on the Control panel. To resize an existing artboard, first select the artboard, then enter values in the Width and Height text boxes.

You can manipulate the layout and positioning of artboards simply by clicking and dragging them as you wish.

Printing Multiple Artboards

When you work with multiple artboards, you can print each artboard individually, or you can compile them into one page. Usually, you'll want to print them individually, and this is easy to do in the Print dialog box. Use the forward and backward arrows in the print preview window to click through each artboard. In the Artboards section, if you click All, all artboards will print. To print only specific artboards, enter the artboard number in the Range field. To combine all artwork on all artboards onto a single page, select the Ignore Artboards option. Depending on how large your artboards are, they'll be scaled down to fit on a single page or tiled over a number of pages.

Using the Artboards Panel

You can use the Artboards panel to perform artboard operations. You can add or delete artboards, reorder and renumber them, and navigate through multiple artboards. When you create multiple artboards, each is assigned a number and is listed with that number on the Artboards panel. If you select an artboard, you can click the up and down arrows to reorder the artboards in the panel. Doing so will renumber the artboard but will not change its name.

Pasting Artwork on Multiple Artboards

The ability to paste copied artwork on multiple artboards is an important function and critical to maintain consistency between layouts. The Edit menu offers two powerful commands: Paste in Place and Paste on All Artboards. Use the Paste in Place command to paste an object from one artboard to the same spot on another. Even if the two artboards are different sizes, the pasted logo will be positioned at exactly the same distance from the top-left corner of the artboard.

The Paste on All Artboards command goes a giant step further, pasting artwork in the same position on all artboards.

Create a new document with multiple artboards

1. Verify that no documents are open and that smart guides are activated.

TIP The Smart Guides command is on the View menu.

2. Click **File** on the menu bar, then click **New**.

The New Document dialog box opens.

3. Type **Winning Business Collateral** in the **Name text box**.

4. Set the number of artboards to **3**, then click the **Grid by Row button** .

5. Set the **Spacing** and **Columns text boxes** to **2**.

6. Verify that the **Units** are set to **Inches**.

7. Set the Width to **6** and the Height to **8.5**, then compare your dialog box to Figure 51.

8. Click **OK**.

When you click OK, the three artboards fit in your document window.

9. Click the **Selection tool** ▶, then click **each artboard** to make each active.

A thin black line highlights each artboard when it is selected.

Figure 51 New Document dialog box set to create three artboards at 6" × 8.5"

10. Click the **top-right artboard** to make it the active artboard, click **View** on the menu bar, then click **Fit Artboard in Window**.

11. Click **View** on the menu bar, then click **Fit All in Window**.

12. Continue to the next set of steps.

You specified settings for a new document with three artboards in the New Document dialog box. You clicked artboards in the document to activate them. You used the Fit in Window and Fit All in Window commands to view artboards.

Create and name artboards

1. Click the **Artboard tool** 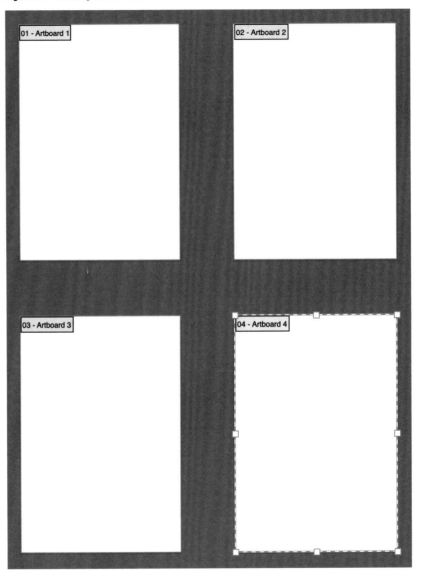 on the toolbar.

   Clicking the Artboard tool switches the interface to the editing artboards mode. The top-right artboard is selected. All the artboards are numbered.

2. Click the **New Artboard button** ⊞ on the Control panel.

   A new artboard with the number 4 is added. The New Artboard button ⊞ creates a new artboard at the specified document size (in this case, 6" × 8.5").

3. Click and drag to position the **new artboard** as shown in Figure 52.

4. Click the **top-right artboard** to select it, then click the **Delete Artboard button** 🗑 on the Control panel.

5. Click the **Artboard tool** on the toolbar, then click and drag to create a **new artboard** approximately the size of a standard business card.

Figure 52 Positioning the new artboard

01 - Artboard 1

02 - Artboard 2

03 - Artboard 3

04 - Artboard 4

6. Press and hold **[option] (Mac)** or **[Alt] (Win),** then drag and drop a **copy of the new artboard** in the space beneath it, as shown in Figure 53.

7. Click the **bottom-left artboard** to select it, then type **Bookmark** in the Name text box on the Control panel.

   The artboard is renamed.

8. Name the **bottom-right artboard Buckslip**.

9. Name the **top-left artboard Letterhead**.

10. Name the **two new artboards Biz Card Front** and **Biz Card Back**, respectively.

11. Save your work, then continue to the next set of steps.

You created a new artboard using three different methods: using the New Artboard button, using the Artboard tool, and dragging and dropping. You named all artboards.

Figure 53 New artboard created by dragging and dropping

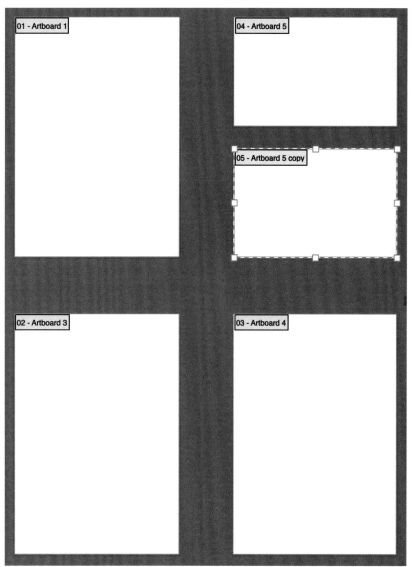

01 - Artboard 1

04 - Artboard 5

05 - Artboard 5 copy

02 - Artboard 3

03 - Artboard 4

Resize and arrange artboards

1. Click the **artboard named Bookmark** to select it, type **2** in the **W Value (width) field** on the Control panel, then press or **[return] (Mac)** or **[Enter] (Win)**.

   The artboard is resized.

2. Resize the artboard named **Buckslip** to **4" wide × 6" high**.

3. Resize the **two business cards** to **3.5" × 2"**.

4. Click the **Letterhead artboard**, click the **Select Preset menu** on the Control panel, then click **Letter**.

   The artboard is resized to 8.5" × 11".

5. Click and drag the **artboards** to arrange them as shown in Figure 54.

6. Click the **Selection tool** 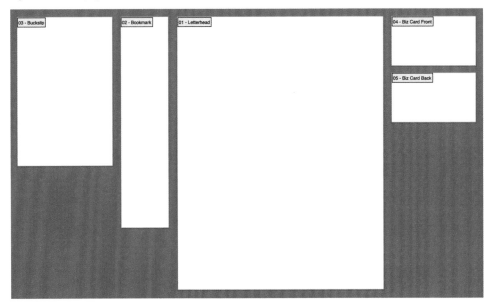 to escape edit artboards mode, then save your work.

7. Continue to the next set of steps.

You resized, renamed, and arranged artboards.

Paste artwork on multiple artboards

1. Open the file named Winning Logo.ai.

2. Click **Select** on the menu bar, click **All**, click **Edit** on the menu bar, then click **Copy.**

3. Close Winning Logo.ai.

4. In the Winning Business Collateral document, click the **Artboard Navigation menu list arrow** in the lower-left corner of the document window, as shown in Figure 55, then click **1 Letterhead**.

   The Letterhead artboard is centered in the window.

TIP The Artboard Navigation menu list arrow is at the lower-left corner of the document window.

Figure 54 Rearranging the artboards

Figure 55 Choosing 1 Letterhead from the Artboard Navigation menu

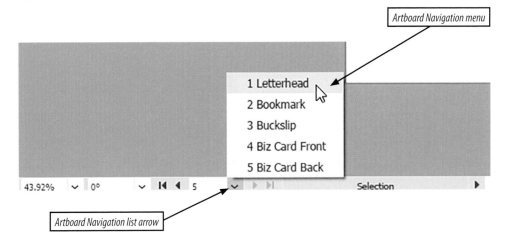

5. Click **Edit** on the menu bar, click **Paste**, then position the artwork as shown in Figure 56.

6. Click **Edit** on the menu bar, then click **Copy**.

Even though the artwork is already copied, you need to copy it again so it is copied from this specific location.

7. Click the **Buckslip artboard** to make it the active artboard.

8. Click **Edit** on the menu bar, then click **Paste in Place**.

The artwork is placed in the same location, relative to the top-left corner of the artboard, on the Buckslip artboard.

9. Click **Edit** on the menu bar, then click **Undo Paste in Place**.

10. Click **Edit** on the menu bar, then click **Paste on All Artboards**.

11. Click **View**, click **Fit All in Window**, then compare your screen to Figure 57.

12. Save and close the Winning Business Collateral document.

You copied artwork, then pasted it in a specific location on one artboard. You used the Paste in Place command to paste the artwork in the same location on another artboard. You then used the Paste on All Artboards command to paste the artwork on all artboards.

Figure 56 Positioning the logo

Figure 57 Artwork pasted on all artboards

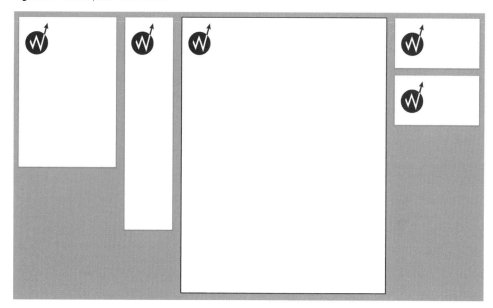

Explore the Illustrator workspace

1. Click File on the menu bar, click Open, navigate to the drive and folder where your Chapter 8 Data Files are stored, click AI 1-5.ai, then click Open.
2. Click Window on the menu bar, point to Workspace, then click Essentials.
3. Click the double arrows on the toolbar to see two setups for the toolbar.
4. Point to the Type tool, then press and hold the mouse button to see the Type on a Path tool.
5. View the hidden tools behind the other tools with small black triangles.
6. Click Illustrator (Mac) or Edit (Win) on the menu bar, point to Preferences, click General, verify that Show Tool Tips is checked, then click OK.
7. Position your mouse pointer over the Direct Selection tool until its tool tip appears.
8. Click the Selection tool, then press the following keys and note which tools are selected with each key: [P], [V], [T], [I], [H], [Z], [A].
9. Press [tab] to temporarily hide all open panels, then press [tab] again.
10. Click the Color panel icon in the stack of collapsed panels to the right of the pasteboard to open the Color panel.
11. Click the Collapse panels button at the top of the panel to minimize the panel, then click Color to open the panel again.
12. Drag the Color panel name tab to the left so it is ungrouped.

13. Click the Swatches panel icon in the stack of collapsed panels to the right of the pasteboard to open the Swatches panel.
14. Drag the Swatches panel name tab to the left so it is ungrouped.
15. Drag the Swatches panel name tab to the blank space next to the Color panel name tab, then release the mouse button.
16. Click Window on the menu bar, then click Info.
17. Drag the Info panel name tab to the bottom edge of the Color and Swatches panels group until you see a blue horizontal line appear, then release the mouse button to dock the Info panel.
18. Click and drag the dark gray bar at the top of the panel group, found above the Color and Swatches panel name tabs, to move the docked panels.
19. Click the Info panel name tab, then drag it away from the other two panels.
20. Click Window on the menu bar, point to Workspace, then click Reset Essentials.
21. Press the letter [Z] on your keypad to access the Zoom tool.
22. Position the Zoom tool over the document window, click twice to enlarge it, press [option] (Mac) or [Alt] (Win), then click twice to reduce the document.
23. Click the Zoom Level list arrow in the lower-left corner of the document window, then click 600%.
24. Note that 600% is now listed in the document tab.
25. Double-click 600% in the Zoom Level text box, type **300**, then press [return] (Mac) or [Enter] (Win).
26. Click the Hand tool on the toolbar, then click and drag the document window to scroll.

27. Double-click the Zoom tool.
28. Click the Selection tool, point to the center of the document window, then press and hold [command] [space bar] (Mac) or [Ctrl] [space bar] (Win).
29. Click three times, then release [command] [space bar] (Mac) or [Ctrl] [space bar] (Win).
30. Press and hold [space bar] to access the Hand tool, then scroll around the image.
31. Press and hold [command] [option] [space bar] (Mac) or [Ctrl] [Alt] [space bar] (Win), then click the artboard multiple times to reduce the view to 25%.

View and modify artboard elements

1. Click View on the menu bar, then click Fit Page in Window.
2. Click View on the menu bar, then note the Rulers command and its shortcut key.
3. Leave the View menu, then press [command] [R] (Mac) or [Ctrl] [R] (Win) several times to hide and show rulers, finishing with rulers showing.
4. Note the units on the rulers.
5. Click Illustrator (Mac) or Edit (Win) on the menu bar, point to Preferences, then click Units.
6. Click the General list arrow to see the available measurement options, then click Picas.
7. Click OK.
8. Reopen the Units Preferences dialog box, click the General list arrow, then click Inches.
9. Click OK.
10. Select all the objects on the artboard.
11. Click View on the menu bar, then note the Hide/Show Edges command and its shortcut key.

12. Leave the View menu, then press [command] [H] (Mac) or [Ctrl] [H] (Win) several times to switch between hiding and showing selection marks, finishing with selection marks showing.

13. Click the View menu, point to Guides, then note the Guides commands and their shortcut keys.

14. Escape the View menu, then press [command] [;] (Mac) or [Ctrl] [;] (Win) several times to hide and show guides, finishing with guides showing.

15. Click View on the menu bar, then click Show Grid.

16. Press [command] ["] (Mac) or [Ctrl] ["] (Win) several times to hide and show the grid.

17. Hide guides and the grid.

18. Click View on the menu bar, then note the quick key command for Outline mode.

19. Enter [command] [Y] (Mac) or [Ctrl] [Y] (Win) repeatedly to toggle between Outline and Preview modes, finishing in Preview mode, as shown in Figure 58.

20. Click Illustrator (Mac) or Edit (Win) on the menu bar, point to Preferences, then click User Interface.

21. Verify that the Open Documents As Tabs check box is checked, then click OK.

22. Save AI 1-5.ai as **Tiger**.

23. Open AI 1-2.ai, then click the tabs of each document several times to toggle between them, finishing with Tiger.ai as the active document.

24. Drag the Tiger.ai tab straight down approximately ½ inch.

25. Position your mouse pointer over the upper-right or bottom-right corner of the document, then click and drag toward the center of the monitor window to reduce the window to approximately half its size.

Figure 58 Skills Review, Part 1

Shutterstock/Bibadash

26. Position your mouse pointer over the title bar of the document, then click and drag to move Tiger.ai halfway down toward the bottom of your monitor.

27. Position your mouse pointer over the title bar of Tiger.ai, click and drag to position it at the top of the window beside the AI 1-2.ai tab, then release the mouse button when you see a horizontal blue bar.

28. Close AI 1-2.ai without saving changes if you are prompted.

29. Close Tiger.ai without saving changes if you are prompted.

(continued)

Work with objects and smart guides.

1. Open AI 1-6.ai, then save it as **Object Skills**.
2. Click View on the menu bar, then verify that the Bounding Box command is set to Show Bounding Box.
3. Click the Selection tool, then click the yellow square to select it.
4. Click View on the menu bar, then click Show Bounding Box.
5. Click and drag various handles, and note how the object is resized.
6. When you are done experimenting, undo all the moves you made.
7. Click to select the purple circle.
8. Press and hold down [option] (Mac) or [Alt] (Win), then start dragging any corner handle.
9. While still dragging, press and hold [shift].
10. Scale the circle to any size.
11. Undo the move.
12. Select all.
13. Using the skills you learned in this lesson, reduce the size of the objects in proportion so they are much smaller on the artboard, then click the artboard to deselect the objects.
14. Click File on the menu bar, click Revert, then click Revert when you are prompted to confirm.
15. Click View on the menu bar, then click Hide Bounding Box.
16. Select the star, then copy it, using the [command] [C] (Mac) or [Ctrl] [C] (Win) shortcut keys.
17. Click Edit on the menu bar, then click Paste to place a copy of the star at the center of the artboard.

18. Undo the paste.
19. Click Edit on the menu bar, then click Paste in Front.
20. Press the letter [I] on your keypad to switch to the Eyedropper tool, then click the yellow square.
21. Press the right arrow key on your keypad 10 times.
22. Deselect all, click Edit on the menu bar, then click Paste in Back.
23. Click the Eyedropper tool on the purple circle.
24. Press and hold [shift], then press the ← on your keypad one time.
25. Press and hold [command] (Mac) or [Ctrl] (Win) so your cursor switches temporarily from the Eyedropper tool to the Selection tool, then click the artboard with the Selection tool to deselect all.

26. Click the Selection tool, then select the purple circle.
27. Press and hold [option] (Mac) or [Alt] (Win), then drag a copy of the circle to the center of the square. Your screen should resemble Figure 59.
28. Save your work, then close the file.
29. Open AI 1-7.ai, then save it as **Group Skills**.
30. Click Object on the menu bar, then click Show All.
31. Click Object on the menu bar, then click Group.
32. Click the Selection tool, click anywhere on the pasteboard to deselect all, then click the largest blue square.
33. Click the pasteboard to deselect all, click the Direct Selection tool, then click the same square.

Figure 59 Skills Review, Part 2

34. Select all, click Object on the menu bar, then click Ungroup.
35. Deselect all.
36. Click the Selection tool, select the smallest square, click Object on the menu bar, click Lock, then click Selection.
37. Click Object on the menu bar, then click Unlock All.
38. Select the three blue squares, click Object on the menu bar, then click Hide.
39. Click Object on the menu bar, then click Show All.
40. Click View on the menu bar, then verify that Smart Guides is checked.
41. Click the large blue square, then drag it by its center point toward the center of the artboard.
42. Release the mouse button when the word center appears.

Figure 60 Skills Review, Part 3

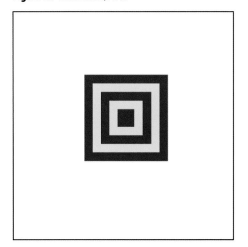

43. Using the same steps, align all the squares so that your artboard resembles Figure 60.
44. Save your work and close the file.

Create and basic shapes and apply color.

1. Open AI 1-8.ai, then save it as **Flag**.
2. Select the black rectangle, then change its fill to a dark blue swatch on the Swatches panel.
3. Select the gray rectangle, then change its fill to a light blue swatch.
4. Select the two blue rectangles, press and hold [option] (Mac) or [Alt] (Win), then drag copies of the squares immediately above them.

5. Select all four squares, copy them, click Edit on the menu bar, then click Paste in Front.
6. Drag the new squares immediately to the right of the existing four squares.
7. With the four new squares still selected, double-click the Reflect tool, click the Horizontal option button, click Copy, then deselect the squares.
   Your artboard should resemble Figure 61.
8. Save your work.

Make direct selections.

1. Select the four light blue squares, then lock them.
2. Click the Direct Selection tool.

Figure 61 Positioning four squares

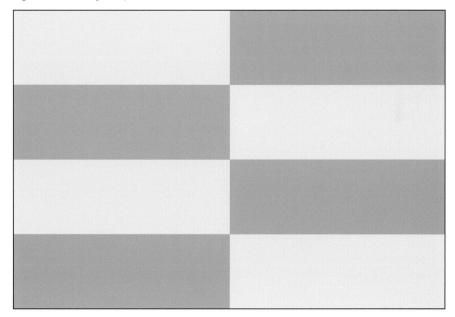

3. Select only the top-right corner of the top-left dark blue rectangle, then drag the point straight up to the top edge of the artboard.

4. Select only the bottom-left corner of the bottom-right dark blue rectangle, then drag the point straight down to the bottom edge of the artboard.
   Your artboard should resemble Figure 62.

5. Save your work.

Stroke and transform shapes

1. Click the Rectangle tool, click the artboard to open its dialog box, then create a rectangle that is 2.5" × 2.5".

2. Center the rectangle on the artboard.

3. Apply a None ✎ fill to the rectangle and a 2 pt. black stroke.

4. Double-click the Rotate tool to open its dialog box, type **12** in the Angle text box, then click Copy.

5. Enter [command] [D] (Mac) or [Ctrl] [D] (Win) 13 times to repeat the transformation 13 times.

6. Select all of the black rectangles, click Object on the menu bar, then click Group.

7. Deselect all, then set the fill color to the dark blue color and the stroke color to None ✎ .

8. Click the Ellipse tool, then position the crosshair exactly at the center of the artboard.

9. Press and hold [option] (Mac) or [Alt] (Win), begin dragging out an ellipse from its center, add the [shift] key to constrain it to a perfect circle, then size the circle so that extends out to the exact edge of the shape created by the rectangles.

10. Change the stacking order so the dark blue circle is behind all the black rectangles.
    Your artboard should resemble Figure 63.

11. Save your work, then close Flag.ai.

Figure 62 Changing the shape of two rectangles

Figure 63 The final flag artwork

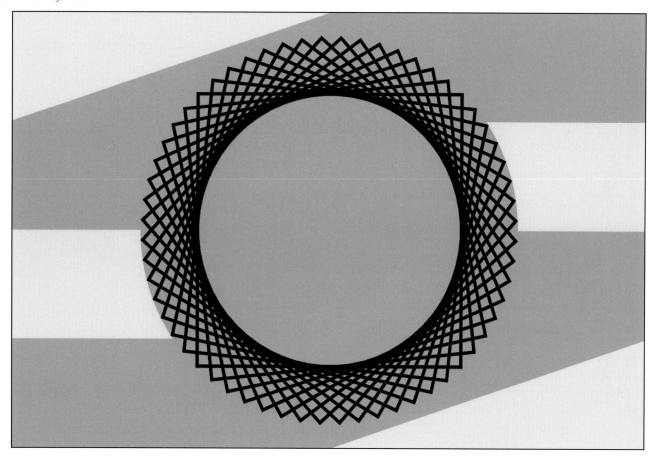

Work with multiple artboards.

1. Open AI 1-9. ai, then save it as **Artboard Skills**.
2. Click the Artboard tool.
3. Click the New Artboard button on the Control panel.
4. Float your cursor over the artboard, then position the new artboard to the right of the original.
5. Scroll to the right of the newest artboard.
6. Click and drag with the Artboard tool to create a new artboard of any size to the right of the new artboard.
7. Click the original artboard and name it **Stationery**.
8. Type **8** in the W Value (width) text box on the Control panel, type **10** in the H Value (height) text box, then press [return] (Mac) or [Enter] (Win).
9. Name the second artboard **Envelope**, then resize it to 9" wide × 3" high.
10. Name the third artboard **Business Card**, then resize it to 3.5" × 2".
11. Click View on the menu bar, then click Fit All in Window.
12. Click and drag the artboards to arrange them as shown in Figure 64.
13. Save your work, then close the Artboard Skills document.

Figure 64 Completed Skills Review

This project builder will reinforce making stars and using the Direct Selection tool to modify basic shapes. Rather than work with a conventionally shaped star, you will create something original. This exercise is also very instructive for using copies as shadows and overlapping fills in a way that creates the look of one object from many. If you like, you can imagine that the exercise is for a logo for a restaurant.

1. Open AI 1-10.ai, then save it as **Window Sign**.
2. Click the Direct Selection tool, then click the edge of the star.
3. Move two of the outer anchor points of the star farther from its center.
4. Move four of the inner points toward the center.
5. Select the entire star.
6. Reflect a copy of the star across the horizontal axis.
7. Fill the new star with an orange swatch, and reposition it to your liking.
8. Group the two stars.
9. Copy the group, then paste in back.
10. Fill the copies with black.
11. Using your arrow keys, move the black copies five increments to the right and five increments down.
12. Select only the orange star using the Direct Selection tool.
13. Copy the orange star, then paste in back.
14. Fill the new copy with black.
15. Rotate the black copy 8°.
16. Apply a yellow fill to the orange star, then apply a 1 pt. black stroke to both yellow stars.
17. Remove the black stroke from the front-most star.
18. Save your work, then compare your illustration to Figure 65 on the following page.
    What's interesting about the result is that there's a black shadow between the two yellow stars. You would expect both black stars to be behind the two yellow stars, performing the role of shadows. In that case, the two yellow stars would overlap in a way that they would appear as a single star. In this case, the black star between them is unexpected and creates a more complex effect for the illustration.
19. Close the Window Sign document.

Figure 65 Final Project Builder 1

This is a great exercise with a stunning result that shows the power of executing multiple transformations and, in this case, alternating colors. You can imagine that this result would make for a great illustration for an optometrist or any entity that works with eyes or with vision.

1. Create a new document that is 6" × 6".
2. Save the document as **Iris Vision Design**.
3. Create an ellipse that is 1" wide × 4" in height, and position it at the center of the artboard.
4. Fill the ellipse with [None] and add a 1 pt. blue stroke.
5. Create a copy of the ellipse rotated at 15°.
6. Apply the Transform Again command 10 times.
7. Select all and group the ellipses.
8. Create a copy of the group rotated at 5°.
9. Apply a red stroke to the new group.
10. Transform again one time.
11. Apply a bright blue stroke to the new group.
12. Select all.
13. Rotate a copy of the ellipses 2.5°.
14. Create a circle that is 2" × 2".
15. Fill the circle with black, and give it no stroke.
16. Position the black-filled circle in the center of the ellipses.
17. Cut the circle.
18. Select all.
19. Paste in back.
20. Save your work, then compare your illustration to Figure 66.
21. Close the Iris Vision Design document.

Figure 66 Completed Project Builder 2

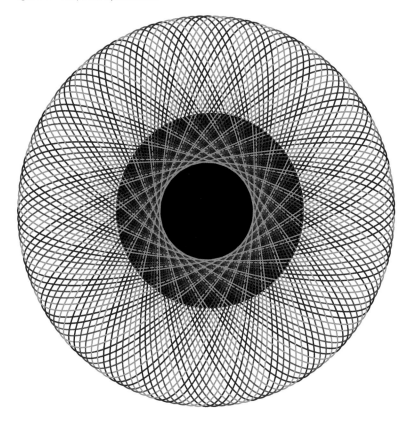

The owner of Emerald Design Studios has hired you to design an original logo for her new company. She's a beginner with Illustrator, but has created a simple illustration of what she has in mind. She tells you to create something "more sophisticated." The only other information she offers about her company is that they plan to specialize in precise, geometric design.

1. Open AI 1-11.ai, then save it as **Emerald Logo**.
2. Select all four diamonds and group them.
3. Use the Scale tool to create a copy at 75%.
4. Use the Transform Again command five times.
5. Use smart guides or Outline mode to help you identify each of the seven groups.
   Smart guides will appear as you mouse over each group. Outline mode will show you the black outlines of all seven groups.
6. Rotate all the groups in relation to one another so that no two groups are on the same angle.
7. Apply a dark green stroke to all groups.
   Figure 67 shows one possible result of multiple transformations. Your illustration may differ.
8. Save your work, then close the Emerald Logo document.

Figure 67 One result for the Design Project

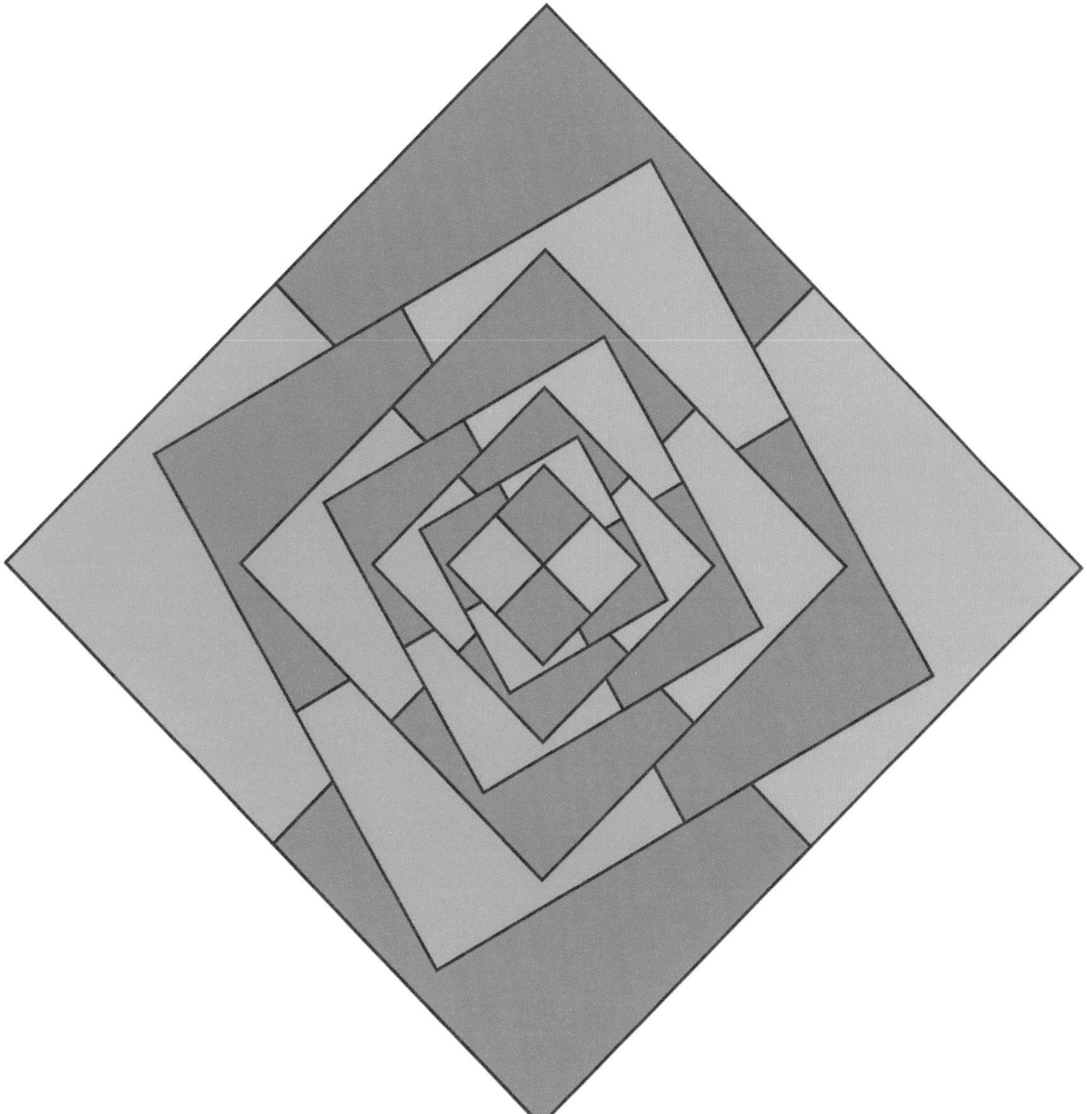

CREATE TEXT
AND GRADIENTS

1. Create Point Text
2. Flow Text into an Object
3. Position Text on a Path
4. Manipulate Text with the Touch Type Tool
5. Create Gradients
6. Adjust Gradients in Text and Objects
7. Apply Gradients to Strokes

Adobe Certified Professional in Graphic Design and Illustration Using Adobe Illustrator

1. Working in the Design Industry

This objective covers critical concepts related to working with colleagues and clients, as well as crucial legal, technical, and design-related knowledge.

1.5 Demonstrate knowledge of basic design principles and best practices employed in the design industry.
  B Identify and use common typographic adjustments to create contrast, hierarchy, and enhanced readability/legibility.

2. Project Setup and Interface

This objective covers the interface setup and program settings that assist in an efficient and effective workflow, as well as knowledge about ingesting digital assets for a project.

2.2 Navigate, organize, and customize the application workspace.
  C Configure application preferences.
2.4 Manage assets in a project.
  B Place assets in an Illustrator document.
2.5 Manage colors, swatches, and gradients.
  B Create and customize gradients.
  C Create, manage, and edit swatches and swatch libraries.

4. Creating and Modifying Visual Elements

This objective covers core tools and functionality of the application, as well as tools that affect the visual appearance of document elements.

4.2 Add and manipulate text using appropriate typographic settings.
  A Use type tools to add typography.
  B Use appropriate character settings.
  C Use appropriate paragraph settings.
  D Convert text to graphics.
  E Manage text flow.

CREATE POINT TEXT

▶ *What You'll Do*

In this lesson, you will use the Type tool to create the word BERRY as display text. You will use the Character panel to format the text and perfect its appearance. You will also create a vertical version of the text.

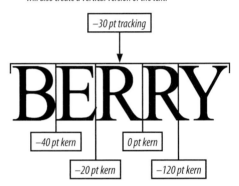

Creating Text

You can create text anywhere on the artboard. Select the Type tool, click the artboard, then begin typing. You can enter text horizontally or vertically. The ability to type vertically is rather unusual; most text-based applications don't offer this option.

Text generated by the Type tool is positioned on a path called the **baseline**. You can select text by clicking anywhere on the text or by clicking on the baseline, depending on how your Type preferences are set.

Formatting Text

The Character and Paragraph panels neatly contain all of the classic commands for formatting text. Use the Character panel to modify text attributes such as font and type size, tracking, and kerning. You can adjust the **leading**, which is the vertical space between baselines, or apply a horizontal or vertical scale, which compresses or expands selected type, as shown in Figure 1. The Paragraph panel applies itself to more global concerns, such as text alignment, paragraph indents, and vertical spaces between paragraphs.

Figure 1 Examples of text formatting

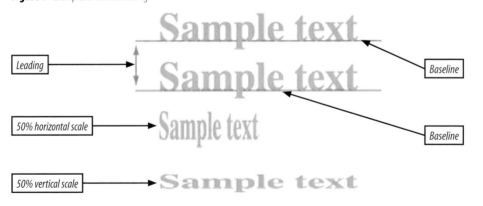

Tracking and kerning are essential, but often overlooked, typographic operations. **Tracking** inserts uniform spaces between characters to affect the width of selected words or entire blocks of text. **Kerning** is used to affect the space between any two characters and is particularly useful for improving the appearance of headlines and other display text. Positive tracking or kerning values move characters farther apart; negative values move them closer together.

Illustrator can track and kern type down to 1/1000 of a standard em space. The width of an em space is dependent on the current type size. In a 1-point font, the em space is 1 point. In a 10-point font, the em space is 10 points. With kerning units that are 1/1000 of an em, Illustrator can manipulate a 10-point font at increments of 1/100 of 1 point! Figure 2 shows examples of kerning and tracking values.

Figure 2 Examples of kerning and tracking

kern
−30/1000

kern
0/1000

kern
30/1000

track
staying on
−30/1000

track
staying on
0/1000

track
staying on
30/1000

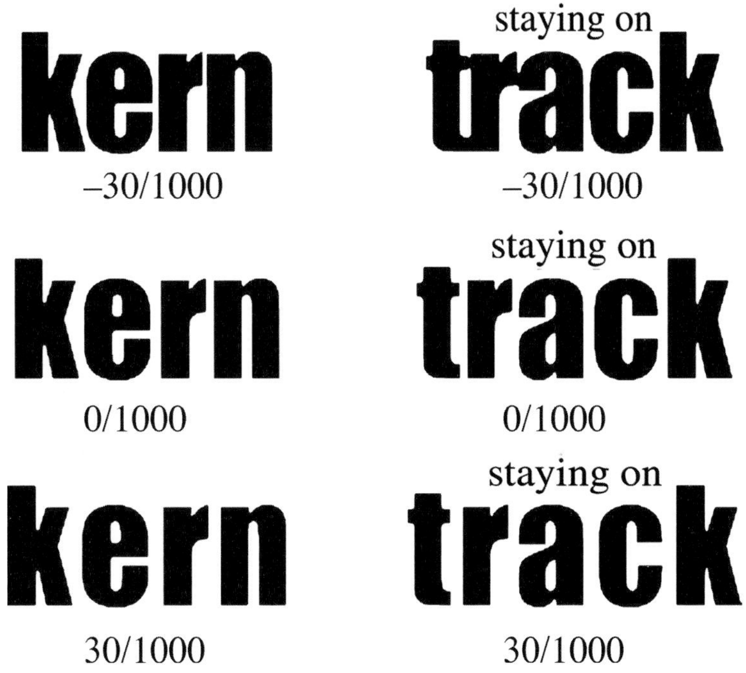

Adjusting and Applying Hyphenation

When working with large blocks of text, you can decide whether or not you want to hyphenate the text. Illustrator has a Preferences panel dedicated to hyphenation. Click Illustrator (Mac) or Edit (Win) on the menu bar, point to Preferences, then click Hyphenation. Hyphenation in Illustrator is applied automatically based on the language dictionary that is in use. You can turn automatic hyphenation on and off or change the hyphenation default settings in the Hyphenation dialog box. To access the Hyphenation dialog box, click the Paragraph panel menu button, then click Hyphenation. To turn hyphenation off, remove the check mark in the Hyphenation check box.

Hiding Objects While Working with Text

Two factors that make selecting text and other objects difficult are the number and proximity of objects in the document. When you have many objects positioned closely together, selecting an individual object can sometimes be tricky.

Hiding objects is a simple way to avoid this problem, just don't forget they are there—they won't print if they are hidden.

The Hide Selection command is on the Object menu—as is the Show All command, which reveals all hidden objects. When hidden objects are revealed, they are all selected.

Create text

1. Open AI 2-1.ai, then save it as **Berry**.

2. Click **View** on the menu bar, then click **Hide Bounding Box** if the bounding box is showing.

   If the bounding box is already hidden, you won't see the Hide Bounding Box command.

3. Click the **Type tool** T, then click **anywhere on the artboard**.

   When you click, type is created. The type is 12 pt. by default and is selected, so you can type over it.

4. Type **BERRY** using all capital letters.

   The word BERRY will be interesting for you to work with because the letter combinations will require you to kern them in relation to one another.

TIP By default, new text is generated with a black fill and no stroke. Text you create by clicking the artboard is called point text.

5. Click the **Selection tool** ▶, then drag the **text** to the center of the artboard.

TIP Verify that Smart Guides are not activated.

6. Click **Window** on the menu bar, point to **Type**, then click **Character** to show the Character panel.

7. Click the **Character panel menu button** ≡, then click **Show Options** to view the entire panel as shown in Figure 3.

8. Save your work, then continue to the next set of steps.

You used the Type tool to create the word BERRY, showed the Character panel, then expanded the view of the Character panel.

Figure 3 Character panel with all options showing

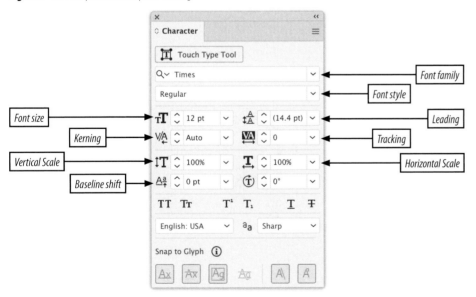

TRACKING AND KERNING

Typography, the art of designing letterforms, has a long and rich history that extends back to the Middle Ages. With the advent of desktop publishing in the mid-1980s, many conventional typographers and typesetters declared "the death of typography." They claimed that unskilled computer users would be careless with type and that computers would reduce typography to ugly, bitmap fonts. More optimistic mindsets have since prevailed. The personal computer and software, such as Adobe Illustrator, have made available libraries of typefaces that are far more extensive than what has ever been available before. Contrast this with the days when the typewriter ruled, with its single typeface and two point sizes as the standard for literally millions of documents, and you get a sense of the typographic revolution that has occurred in the last 30 years.

Many designers are so eager to tackle the "artwork" that they often overlook the type design in an illustration. Tracking and kerning, which are the manipulation of space between words and letters, are essential elements to good type design and are often woefully ignored.

Illustrator's precise tracking and kerning abilities are of no use if they are ignored. One good way of maintaining awareness of your tracking and kerning duties is to take note of others' oversights. Make it a point to notice tracking and kerning, or the lack thereof, when you look at magazines, posters, and especially billboards. You'll be amazed at what you'll see.

Format text

1. On the Character panel, click the **Font family list arrow**, point to **Times New Roman** or a similar font, then click **Regular** from the Font style list arrow.

2. Click the **Font size text box** ⊤T , type **142**, then press **[return] (Mac) or [Enter] (Win)**.

3. Click the **Horizontal Scale text box** ⊥T , type **90**, then press **[return] (Mac) or [Enter] (Win)**.

4. Deselect the text.

5. Save your work, then continue to the next set of steps.

You used the Character panel to modify the font, font size, and horizontal scaling of the word BERRY.

Track and kern text

1. Compare your text to Figure 4.

   The spatial relationships between the letters are inconsistent and challenging. The two Rs are the only two letters that are almost touching. The E is closer to the first R than it is to the B, and the Y is too far away from the second R.

2. Select the **text** with the **Selection tool** ▶ .

3. On the Character panel, enter **−30** in the **Tracking text box** 🗚 .

4. Click the **Type tool** T , then click **between the B and the E**.

5. On the Character panel, click the **up and down arrows** in the **Kerning text box** 🗛 to experiment with higher and lower kerning values, then change the Kerning value to **−40**.

6. Using Figure 5 as a guide, change the Kerning values to **−20**, **0**, and **−120** between the next three letter pairs.

   The two Rs are kerned so they are touching. When two letters touch in this way, it is called a **ligature** in typography lingo.

Continued on next page

Figure 4 Formatted text

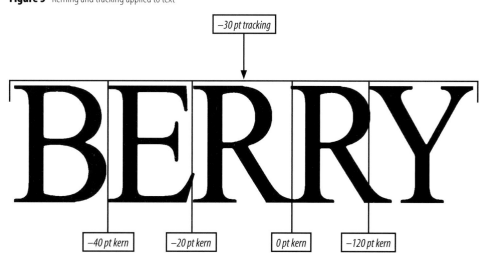

Figure 5 Kerning and tracking applied to text

−30 pt tracking

−40 pt kern   −20 pt kern   0 pt kern   −120 pt kern

7. Click the **Selection tool** , open the **Paragraph panel**, then click the **Align center button** , as shown in Figure 6.

When text is center aligned, its anchor point is centered on its baseline. This can be handy for aligning its center with the center of other objects.

8. Click **Object** on the menu bar, point to **Hide**, then click **Selection**.

9. Save your work, then continue to the next set of steps.

You used the Character panel to change the tracking of the word BERRY, then you entered different Kerning values to affect the spacing between the four letter pairs. You center-aligned the text, then hid the text.

Create vertical type

1. Click the **Vertical Type tool** , then click **anywhere on the artboard**.

TIP The Vertical Type tool is hidden beneath the Type tool .

Align center button

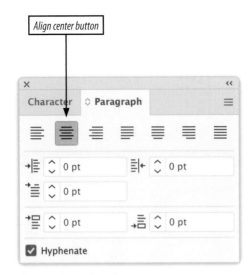

Figure 6 Paragraph panel

2. Type the word **BERRY** using all capital letters.

TIP The Type tools retain the formatting attributes that were previously chosen. Therefore, the new text has the same Tracking value of −30, and the Horizontal Scale is set to 90%.

3. Click the **Selection tool** , select the **text**, then move it to the center of the artboard.

TIP When any tool other than the Selection tool is selected on the toolbar you can press [command] (Mac) or [Ctrl] (Win) to switch to the Selection tool . When you release [command] (Mac) or [Ctrl] (Win), the last chosen tool will be active again.

4. Change the **font size** to **84 pt**.

5. Change the **Tracking value** to **−160**.

6. Verify that both the **Horizontal** and **Vertical Scales** are set to **100%**, then deselect the text.

Your screen should resemble Figure 7.

7. Save your work, then close the Berry document.

You used the Vertical Type tool to create a vertical alternative to the first word you typed. You adjusted the tracking to better suit a vertical orientation.

Figure 7 Vertical text

FLOW TEXT INTO AN OBJECT

▶ *What You'll Do*

In this lesson, you will explore options for formatting text flowed into objects.

Filling an Object with Text

Using the Area Type tool, you can flow text into any shape you can create, from circles to birds to bumblebees! Text in an object can be formatted as you would format text in a basic rectangular box. You can change such attributes as fonts, font size, and alignment, and the text will reflow in the object as you format it. Text that you create inside an object is called **area text**.

Figure 8 shows an example of an object filled with text. Note the blue background in the figure. When you first flow text into an object using the Area Type tool, the object loses any fill or stroke color applied to it. However, you can add different colors to the object and the text after you enter the text. When you select the object with the Selection tool, any fill or stroke you choose will be applied to the text. When you select the object with the Direct Selection tool, the fill or stroke will be applied to the object.

Figure 8 An object filled with text

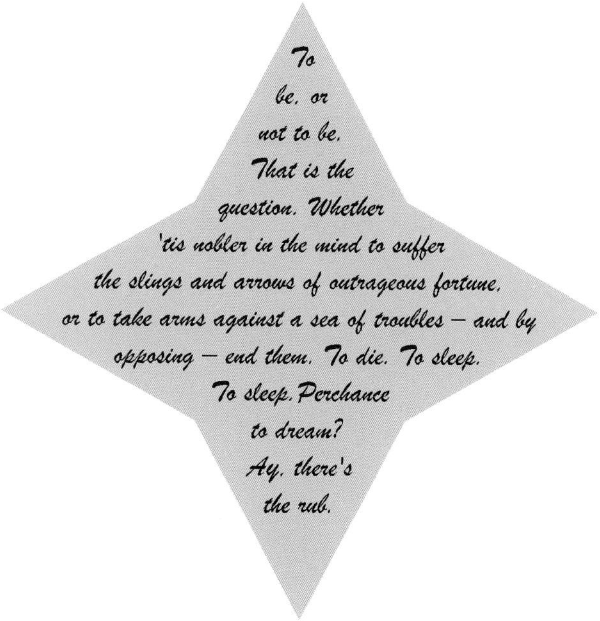

After the text is flowed into the object, you can use the Direct Selection tool to modify the object; the text will reflow within the modified shape.

You'll often find that centering text in an object is the best visual solution. Figure 9 shows text aligned left and flowed into an odd-shaped object. In Figure 10, the same text is centered and fills the object in a way that is more visually pleasing.

TIP You can underline text and strike through text using the Underline and Strikethrough buttons at the bottom of the Character panel.

Figure 9 Text aligned left

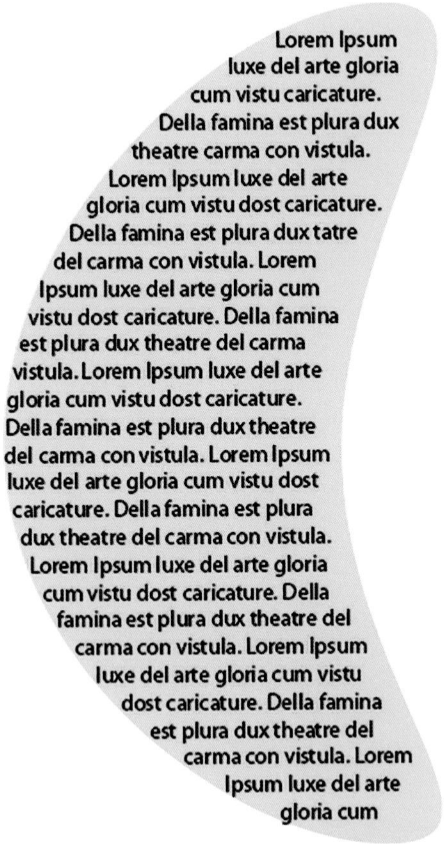

Lorem Ipsum
luxe del arte gloria
cum vistu caricature.
Della famina est plura dux
theatre carma con vistula.
Lorem Ipsum luxe del arte
gloria cum vistu dost caricature.
Della famina est plura dux tatre
del carma con vistula. Lorem
Ipsum luxe del arte gloria cum
vistu dost caricature. Della famina
est plura dux theatre del carma
vistula. Lorem Ipsum luxe del arte
gloria cum vistu dost caricature.
Della famina est plura dux theatre
del carma con vistula. Lorem Ipsum
luxe del arte gloria cum vistu dost
caricature. Della famina est plura
dux theatre del carma con vistula.
Lorem Ipsum luxe del arte gloria
cum vistu dost caricature. Della
famina est plura dux theatre del
carma con vistula. Lorem Ipsum
luxe del arte gloria cum vistu
dost caricature. Della famina
est plura dux theatre del
carma con vistula. Lorem
Ipsum luxe del arte
gloria cum

Figure 10 Text centered in the object

Lorem Ipsum
luxe del arte gloria
cum vistu caricature.
Della famina est plura dux
theatre carma con vistula.
Lorem Ipsum luxe del arte
gloria cum vistu dost caricature.
Della famina est plura dux tatre
del carma con vistula. Lorem
Ipsum luxe del arte gloria cum
vistu dost caricature. Della famina
est plura dux theatre del carma
vistula. Lorem Ipsum luxe del arte
gloria cum vistu dost caricature.
Della famina est plura dux theatre
del carma con vistula. Lorem Ipsum
luxe del arte gloria cum vistu dost
caricature. Della famina est plura
dux theatre del carma con vistula.
Lorem Ipsum luxe del arte gloria
cum vistu dost caricature. Della
famina est plura dux theatre del
carma con vistula. Lorem Ipsum
luxe del arte gloria cum vistu
dost caricature. Della famina
est plura dux theatre del
carma con vistula. Lorem
Ipsum luxe del arte
gloria cum

FORMATTING A STORY

You can use any of the shapes you create as text boxes, and you can thread, or flow, text from one object to another. When you add text to an object, it becomes a text object with an in port and an out port. To thread text, click the out port of an object that contains text; then click the in port of the object to which you want to thread the text. If the object isn't already defined as a text object, click on the path of the object.

You can also thread text by selecting an object that has type in it and then selecting the object or objects to which you want to thread the text. Click Type on the menu bar, point to Threaded Text, then click Create. You will see icons representing threads. To view threads, choose View on the menu bar, point to Show Text Threads, then select a linked object.

Fill a rectangle with text

1. Open AI 2-2.ai, then save it as **Newspaper Column**.

2. Open the file named Dummy text.ai.

3. Click the **Type tool** T , click anywhere in the text, then press **[command] [A] (Mac)** or **[Ctrl] [A] (Win)** to select all the text.

4. Copy the text, then close the Dummy text file.

5. In the Newspaper Column file, click the **Rectangle tool** .

6. Draw a **rectangle** that corresponds exactly to the blue guides.

   It doesn't matter if your rectangle has a fill or a stroke.

7. Click the **Area Type tool** .

8. Position the **Area Type tool** on the **top path of the rectangle**, then click.

   The rectangle automatically fills with dummy placeholder text that is selected and highlighted. It's important to understand that this is not the text you copied from the other file. It is default text that fills an object whenever you click the Area Type tool on the object.

TIP This default placeholder text feature is a preference that can be disabled. To do this, go to the Type Preferences dialog box, then disable the Fill New Type Objects With Placeholder Text option.

9. Click **Edit** on the menu bar, then click **Paste**.

   The text you copied replaces the default placeholder text.

10. Select all the **text**, then change the font to **Times New Roman** on the Character panel.

    If your computer doesn't have Times New Roman, use something similar.

11. Set the **font size** to **12**, then set the **leading** to **13.5**.

12. On the Paragraph panel, set the **Space after paragraph value** to **5 pt**.

13. Set the **First-line left indent** to **8 pt**.

14. Click the **Justify with last line aligned left button** .

    Your Paragraph panel should resemble Figure 11.

Continued on next page

Figure 11 Settings on the Paragraph panel

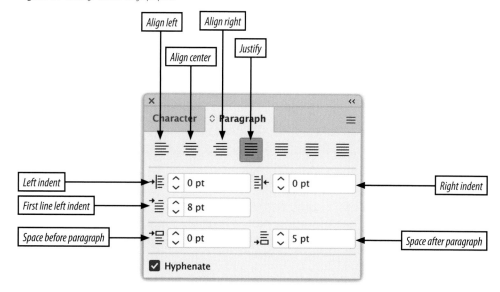

15. Deselect the text, hide guides, then compare your results to Figure 12.

TIP To hide guides, click View on the menu bar, point to Guides, then click Hide Guides.

16. Save your work, then close the Newspaper Column document.

You drew a rectangle, then used the Area Type tool to fill the rectangle with copied text. You used the Character and Paragraph panels to modify the text to fit the rectangle to the format of a traditional newspaper column.

Fill an irregular shaped object with text

1. Open AI 2-3.ai, then save it as **California**.

2. Open the file named Dummy text.ai, click the **Type tool** 🄣 , then click and drag to select only the **first two paragraphs**.

3. Copy the selected text, then close the Dummy text file.

4. Click the **Selection tool** ▶ , then click the **outline of California** to select it.

5. Click the **Area Type tool** 🄣 .

6. Position the **Area Type tool** 🄣 on the **top of the path**, then click.

The outline of the California graphic loses its black stroke.

7. Click **Edit** on the menu bar, then click **Paste**.

The copied text replaces the default placeholder text.

8. Select all the text.

9. On the Character panel, set the **font size** to **12**, then set the **leading** to **13**.

10. On the Paragraph panel, set the **Space after paragraph value** 🄣 to **7 pt**.

11. Click the **Align center button** ☰ .

12. Set the **Left indent** 🄣 and the **Right indent** 🄣 to 8 pt.

13. Click the **type cursor** before the **letter S** in the first line of text.

14. Press **[return] (Mac)** or **[Enter] (Win)**.

15. Click the **Selection tool** ▶ , then click a **gold or yellow swatch** on the Swatches panel.

The text changes to the color you click.

16. Click the **artboard** to deselect.

17. Click the **Direct Selection tool** ▷ , then click the **edge of the outine of California**.

Since the object has no fill or stroke, you can't see the edge when it's not selected. You can guess where the edge is to select it, or you can switch to Outline mode to see it and select it.

18. Verify that the **fill color** is active on the toolbar, then click a **dark red swatch** on the Swatches panel.

19. Activate the **stroke color** on the toolbar, then apply a **black stroke** to the object.

20. Show the Stroke panel, then change the **Weight** to **3 pt**.

21. Deselect.

Figure 12 Newspaper column formatted

Newspaper headline goes here in 24 point bold text

by J. Q Reporter

Sed ut perspiciatis unde omnis iste natus error sit voluptatem accusantium doloremque laudantium, totam rem aperiam, eaque ipsa quae ab illo inventore veritatis et quasi architecto beatae vitae dicta sunt explicabo. Nemo enim ipsam voluptatem quia voluptas sit aspernatur aut odit aut fugit, sed quia consequuntur magni dolores eos qui ratione voluptatem sequi nesciunt. Neque porro quisquam est, qui dolorem ipsum quia dolor sit amet, consectetur, adipisci velit, sed quia non numquam eius modi tempora incidunt ut labore et dolore magnam aliquam quaerat voluptatem. Ut enim ad minima veniam, quis nostrum exercitationem ullam corporis suscipit laboriosam, nisi ut aliquid ex ea commodi consequatur? Quis autem vel eum iure reprehenderit qui in ea voluptate velit esse quam nihil molestiae consequatur, vel illum qui dolorem eum fugiat quo voluptas nulla pariatur?

At vero eos et accusamus et iusto odio dignissimos ducimus qui blanditiis praesentium voluptatum deleniti atque corrupti quos dolores et quas molestias excepturi sint occaecati cupiditate non provident, similique sunt in culpa qui officia deserunt mollitia animi, id est laborum et dolorum fuga. Et harum quidem rerum facilis est et expedita distinctio. Nam libero tempore, cum soluta nobis est eligendi optio cumque nihil impedit quo minus id quod maxime placeat facere possimus, omnis voluptas assumenda est, omnis dolor repellendus. Temporibus autem quibusdam et aut officiis debitis aut rerum necessitatibus saepe eveniet ut et voluptates sint et molestiae non recusandae. Itaque earum rerum hic tenetur a sapiente delectus, ut aut reiciendis voluptatibus maiores alias consequatur aut perferendis doloribus asperiores repellat.

Nemo enim ipsam voluptatem quia voluptas sit aspernatur aut odit aut fugit, sed quia consequuntur magni dolores eos qui ratione voluptatem sequi nesciunt. Neque porro quisquam est, qui dolorem ipsum quia dolor sit amet, consectetur, adipisci velit, sed quia non numquam eius modi tempora incidunt ut labore et dolore magnam aliquam quaerat voluptatem. Ut enim ad minima veniam, quis nostrum exercitationem ullam corporis suscipit laboriosam, nisi ut aliquid ex ea commodi consequatur? Temporibus autem quibusdam et aut officiis debitis aut rerum necessitatibus saepe eveniet ut et voluptates repudiandae sint et molestiae non recusandae.

22. Click the **Selection tool** ▶, click the **text** to select it, then click the **white swatch** on the Swatches panel.

Your artwork should resemble Figure 13.

23. Save your work, then close the California document.

You used the Area Type tool to paste text into an object the shape of the state of California. You used the Character and Paragraph panels to format the text to fit the object in a way that was most visually appealing. You then changed the color of the text and applied a fill and stroke to the object.

Figure 13 Completed California artwork

Sed ut perspiciatis unde omnis iste natus error sit voluptatem accusantium doloremque laudantium, totam rem aperiam, eaque ipsa quae ab illo inventore veritatis et quasi architecto beatae vitae dicta sunt explicabo. Nemo enim ipsam voluptatem quia voluptas sit aspernatur aut odit aut fugit, sed quia consequuntur magni dolores eos qui ratione voluptatem sequi nesciunt. Neque porro quisquam est, qui dolorem ipsum quia dolor sit amet, consectetur, adipisci velit, sed quia non numquam eius modi tempora incidunt ut labore et dolore magnam aliquam quaerat voluptatem. Ut enim ad minima veniam, quis nostrum exercitationem ullam corporis suscipit laboriosam, nisi ut aliquid ex ea commodi consequatur? Quis autem vel eum iure reprehenderit qui in ea voluptate velit esse quam nihil molestiae consequatur, vel illum qui dolorem eum fugiat quo voluptas nulla pariatur?

At vero eos et accusamus et iusto odio dignissimos ducimus qui blanditiis praesentium voluptatum deleniti atque corrupti quos dolores et quas molestias excepturi sint occaecati cupiditate non provident, similique sunt in culpa qui officia deserunt mollitia animi, id est laborum et dolorum fuga. Et harum quidem rerum facilis est et expedita distinctio. Nam libero tempore, cum soluta nobis est eligendi optio cumque nihil impedit quo minus id quod maxime placeat facere possimus, omnis voluptas assumenda est, omnis dolor repellendus. Temporibus autem quibusdam et aut officiis debitis aut rerum necessitatibus saepe eveniet ut et voluptates repudiandae sint et molestiae non recusandae. Itaque earum rerum hic tenetur a sapiente delectus, ut aut reiciendis voluptatibus maiores alias consequatur aut perferendis doloribus asperiores repellat.

CALIFORNIA

POSITION TEXT ON A PATH

▶ **What You'll Do**

In this lesson, you will explore the many options for positioning text on a path.

Using the Path Type Tools

Using the Type on a Path tool or the Vertical Type on a Path tool, you can type along a straight or curved path. This is the most compelling of Illustrator's text effects, and it opens up a world of possibilities for the designer and typographer.

You can move text along a path to position it where you want. You can "flip" the text to make it run in the opposite direction, on the opposite side of the path. You can also change the baseline shift to modify the distance of the text's baseline in relation to the path. A positive value "floats" the text above the path, and a negative value moves the text below the path. You can modify text on a path in the same way you would modify any other text element. Figure 14 shows an example of text on a path, whereas Figure 15 shows an example of text flipped across a path.

Figure 14 Text on a path

Figure 15 Text flipped across a path

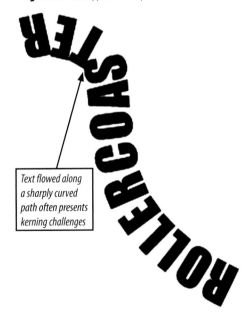

Text flowed along a sharply curved path often presents kerning challenges

You can replace a given font in a document with another font using the Find Font utility. Click Type on the menu bar, then click Find Font. All the fonts used in the document are listed. Select the name of the font you want to find; the first occurrence of the font is highlighted in the document window. Select a replacement font from the Replace with Font From list arrow. You can click Change to change just one occurrence of the selected font, or you can click Change All to change all occurrences of the selected font. Note that when you replace a font using the Find Font command, all other type attributes applied to the original remain applied to the replacement font.

A style is a group of formatting attributes—such as font, font size, color, and tracking—that you apply to text. You use the Character Styles panel to create and apply styles for individual words or characters, such as a footnote. You use the Paragraph Styles panel to apply a style to a paragraph. Paragraph styles include formatting options such as indents and drop caps. Using styles saves you time and keeps your work consistent. If you create styles for an Illustrator document, the styles are saved with the document and are available to be loaded for use in other documents.

Flow text on a path

1. Open AI 2-4.ai, then save it as **Type on a Path Intro**.

TIP Turn off the Bounding Box when you work with the Type tools.

2. Click the **Selection tool** ▶, then select the **path**.

3. Click the **Type on a Path tool** ⤳, click the **path** close to the leftmost anchor point.

4. Type **ROLLERCOASTER** in all caps.

5. Click **the Selection tool** ▶, change the **typeface** to **Impact**, then change the **font size** to **22 pt**.

Three light blue brackets appear on the path, as shown in Figure 16. The brackets are used for dragging the text along the path. The left and right brackets represent the space in which the text is visible on the panel. In other words, the text can be visible on the path only in the space between the two outer brackets.

Continued on next page

Figure 16 Identifying the three brackets on the path

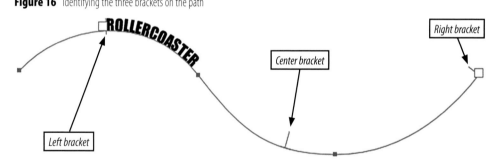

6. Click and drag the **left bracket** to the right to move the type along the entire path.

7. Click and drag the **left bracket** to the left to return the type to the beginning of the path.

8. On the Paragraph panel, click the **Align center button** 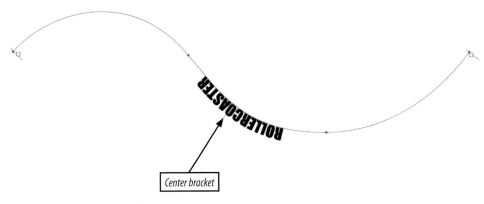 .

   The center bracket indicates the center point between the two other brackets. The text is now centered at the center bracket.

9. Click and drag the **center bracket** down across the path so your text flips onto the other side of the path, as shown in Figure 17.

10. Click and drag the **left bracket** to the right to move the text along the bottom side of the path.

11. Click and drag the **left bracket** to the left to return the text to the center of the path.

12. Click and drag the **center bracket** across the path again so the text is once again positioned on the top of the path and reads right to left.

Center bracket

Figure 17 Flipping text across a path

13. On the Character panel, enter **–18** in the **baseline shift text box** .

    The baseline shift value indicates the distance between the baseline of the text and the path. At a value of 0, the bottom of the text sits on the path. With a negative value, the text moves below the path. In this case, with a –18 baseline shift, the text is completely below the path.

14. Save your work, then close the Type on a Path Intro document.

You used the Type on a Path tool to type on a path. You formatted the text, then used the left bracket to move the type along the path. You used the center bracket to flip the type back and forth across the path. You then changed the baseline shift to move the text in relation to the path.

Flow text on a path

1. Open AI 2-5.ai, then save it as **Type on a Circle**.
2. Click the **Selection tool** ▶, select the **inner circle**, then copy it.

   You will paste the copy of the inner circle in a later step.
3. Select **both circles**, then **lock** them.
4. Enter **[command] [F] (Mac)** or **[Ctrl] [F] (Win)** to paste in front.

   The copied circle pastes in front the original. When you put type on a path, the path loses its fill and stroke. Therefore, you will place the type on this copied path.
5. Click the **Type on a Path tool** 〜, position it at **10 o'clock on the small circle**, then click.
6. Type **MELROSE AVENUE** in all caps.
7. Click the **Align center button** ≣ on the Paragraph panel.
8. On the Character panel, set the **font** to **Impact**, set the **font size** to **45**, then verify that all other text boxes on the Character panel are set to their default settings (0 or 100%).

   As shown in Figure 18, the left and right brackets are very close together.

Continued on next page

Figure 18 Preparing to drag handles

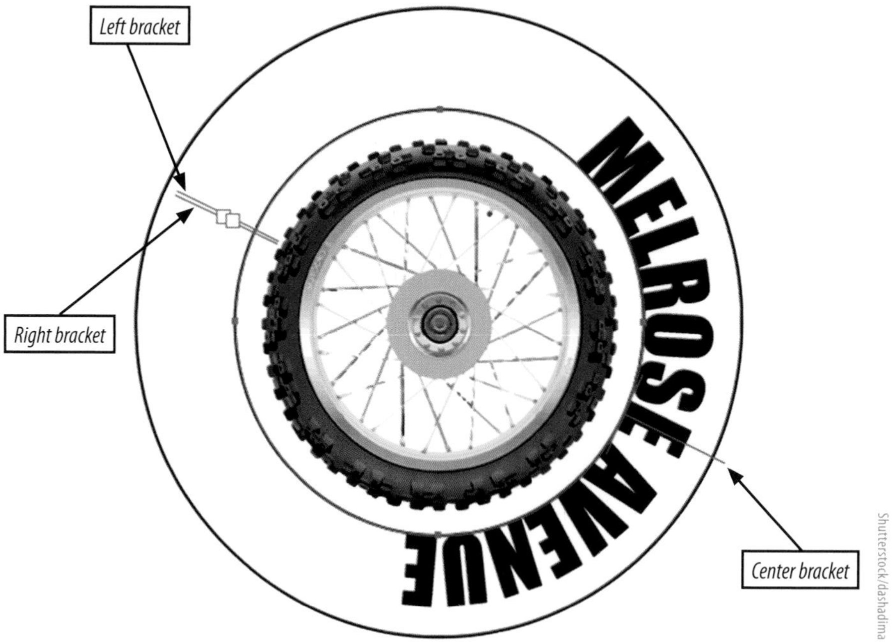

Left bracket

Right bracket

Center bracket

Shutterstock/dashadima

9. With the **Selection tool** ▶, position the **left bracket** and **right bracket** at **9 o'clock** and **3 o'clock**, respectively.

The text needs to be positioned vertically between the two circles.

10. On the Character panel, enter **7 pt**. in the baseline shift text box △▲ .

Your artwork should resemble Figure 19.

11. Click **Object** on the menu bar, then click **Lock**.

The path and the text on the path are locked.

12. Click **Edit** on the menu bar, then click **Paste in Front**.

A third circle is pasted. You will use this new circle to place the text at the bottom of the illustration.

13. Position the **left bracket** at **3 o'clock** and the **right bracket** at **9 o'clock**.

Your artwork should resemble Figure 20.

14. Drag the **center bracket** straight across the circle path so the type flips across the path. On the Character panel enter **–44** in the baseline shift text box, then enter **–140** in the tracking text box.

Because the baseline shift and tracking values are so extreme, the text requires kerning between the letter pairs in many instances. Particularly problematic is that the space between "MOTORCYCLE" and "SHOP" needs to be increased so they appear as two separate words.

15. Kern character pairs as you see fit to best improve the appearance of the text.

16. Click the **Rectangle tool** ▢ , create a **small rectangle**, then rotate it to make a diamond shape positioned at **9 o'clock**.

TIP Rotate the rectangle using the Rotate tool ↻ or show the bounding box and rotate using a handle.

17. Create a copy of the **diamond**, position it at **3 o'clock**, then compare your results to Figure 21.

18. Save your work, then close the Type on a Circle document.

You created artwork with text wrapping over and under the same circle. You used two circles to achieve the effect—one for the text at the top and another for the text at the bottom. You changed the baseline shift to position the text vertically centered in the space between the two circles. You flipped the bottom text across the path so it reads left to right. You then adjusted the baseline shift, tracking, and kerning values to perfect its appearance.

Figure 19 Positioning the text on the circle

Figure 20 Text at the bottom is upside down

Figure 21 Final artwork

MANIPULATE TEXT WITH THE TOUCH TYPE TOOL

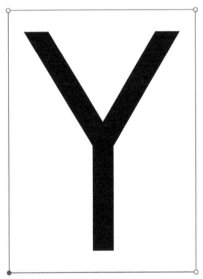

Using the Touch Type Tool

The Touch Type tool has the power to truly allow designers to do what they want do with type in Illustrator. Illustrator has long held the unofficial but widely accepted title of best application for designing and manipulating type—but, nevertheless, there were limitations. To best understand the benefits of the Touch Type tool, it helps first to examine those limitations.

Figure 22 shows the word "bounce" set in Illustrator text. Note by the selection marks that the word is a single object. If you wanted to manipulate the text to appear as shown in Figure 23, you'd have to use the Character panel and apply baseline shifts and rotations to each character. If you then wanted to manipulate the space between the characters, as shown in Figure 24, you'd need to kern each letter pair. Because of the tedious and time-consuming challenges of working with individual characters, many designers instead choose to set each character as a single object, as shown in Figure 25.

Figure 22 A single text object

Figure 23 Text characters manipulated individually

Figure 24 Kerning manipulated individually

Figure 25 A work-around; each character is an individual object

The Touch Type tool allows you to scale, rotate, and move each character in a type object independently of the other characters. Rather than have to input values in the Character panel, you can manipulate individual characters by hand, scaling and repositioning by hand. It is truly revolutionary to Illustrator.

Working with the Touch Type Tool

After you've typed a word, click the Touch Type tool, then click a letter. When you do, a rectangle with five points—one on each corner and one centered at the top—appears around the character. Clicking and dragging these five points, you can scale the character uniformly, scale vertically, scale horizontally, rotate, and move the character. Figure 26 identifies what each point does to the type.

TIP You can use the Touch Type tool to quickly select and change the color of each character in a type object.

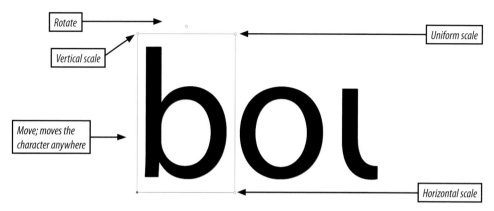

Figure 26 Transform options with the Touch Type tool

What's truly brilliant about the Touch Type tool is that the other letters in the word move to accommodate any transformation you make. What's more, you can freely move type characters closer together or farther apart as you transform them. The Touch Type tool brings enormous freedom for working with type and opens the door to new possibilities and new ideas for typographical illustrations.

Use the Touch Type tool

1. Open AI 2-6 save it as **Touch Type**, then verify that the Swatches panel is showing.

2. Click the **Touch Type tool** , then click the **first letter T**.

   A bounding box appears around the letter.

   TIP The Touch Type tool is located behind the Type tool **T**, with the other type tools.

3. Click and drag the **top-right handle** of the bounding box.

   As you drag, the letter is scaled in proportion.

4. Drag until the type resembles Figure 27.

   As you drag, notice that the space between the bounding box around the letter T and the letter o next to it does not change.

5. Position the **Touch Type tool** over the left center of the **letter T** then drag.

   The letter moves independently from the other letters. No matter how far you drag the letter T vertically, the horizontal space between the letter T and the o is maintained.

6. Undo your steps as necessary so the type still resembles Figure 27.

7. Select the **letter o** with the **Touch Type tool**, then drag it closer to the **letter T**, as shown in Figure 28.

   Now that both the letter T and the letter o have been manipulated by the Touch Type tool, you are able to move the letter o as close or as far apart to the letter T as you like—even overlap them.

8. Click the **letter u**, then click and drag the **lower-right handle**.

   The character is scaled on the horizontal axis only.

9. Click the **letter c**, then click and drag the **upper-left handle**.

   The character is scaled on the vertical axis only.

10. Click the **letter h**, then click and drag the **point centered above it**.

    The character is rotated as you drag.

11. Select the **letter T** with the **Touch Type tool**, then change its **fill color** on the Swatches panel to a color of your choice.

12. Use the **Touch Type tool** to re-create the illustration shown in Figure 29.

13. Save your work, then close the Touch Type document.

You used the Touch Type tool to scale, rotate, and change the color of individual characters on a text object.

Figure 27 Scaling the "T"

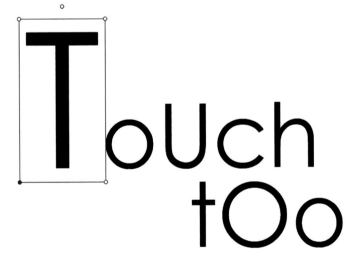

Figure 28 Moving the "o" closer to the "T"

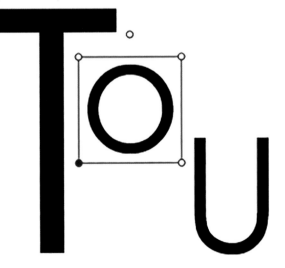

Figure 29 The final illustration

CREATE GRADIENTS

▶ **What You'll Do**

In this lesson, you will use the Color panel, Gradient panel, and Swatches panel to create, name, modify, and save gradients.

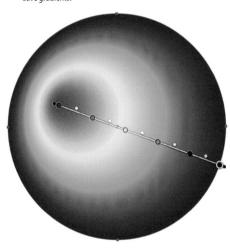

Using the Gradient Panel

A **gradient** is a graduated blend between colors. The Gradient panel is the command center for creating and adjusting gradients. In the panel, you will see a slider that represents the gradient you are creating or using. The slider has at least two colors. The leftmost color is the starting color, and the rightmost color is the ending color.

The colors used in a gradient are represented on the Gradient panel by small circle icons called **color stops**. The Gradient panel shown in Figure 30 shows a two-color gradient.

The point at which two colors meet in equal measure is called the **midpoint** of the gradient. The midpoint is represented by the diamond above the slider. The midpoint does not necessarily need to be positioned evenly between the starting and ending colors. You can change the appearance of a gradient by moving the midpoint.

Figure 30 Gradient panel

Linear gradient

Radial gradient

Reverse gradient

Gradient slider

Color stop

◇ Gradient

Type:

Edit Gradient

Stroke:

0°

Opacity:

Location:

The Swatches panel contains standard gradients that come with the software. To create your own original gradients, start by clicking an object filled with an existing gradient. You can then modify that existing gradient on the Gradient panel. You can change either or both the beginning and ending colors. You can change the location of the midpoint. You can also add additional colors into the gradient or remove existing colors.

> **TIP** As you work to perfect a gradient, you can see how your changes will affect the gradient by filling an object with the gradient you are modifying. As you make changes on the Gradient panel, the changes will be reflected in the object.

You can define a gradient as linear or radial. A linear gradient can be positioned left to right, up and down, or on any angle. You can change the angle of the gradient by entering a new value in the Angle text box on the Gradient panel.

Think of a radial gradient as a series of concentric circles. With a radial gradient, the starting color appears at the center of the gradient. The blend radiates out to the ending color. By definition, a radial gradient has no angle ascribed to it.

Using the Color Panel

The Color panel, shown in Figure 31, is where you move sliders to mix new colors for fills, strokes, and gradients. You can also use the panel to adjust the color in a filled object.

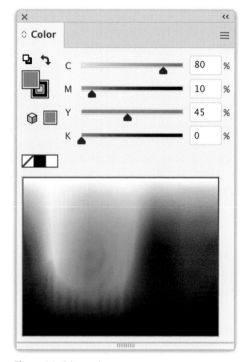

Figure 31 Color panel

The panel has five color modes: CMYK, RGB, Grayscale, HSB, and Web Safe RGB. The panel will default to CMYK or RGB, depending on the color mode you choose when creating a new document.

Rather than use the sliders, you can also type values directly into the text boxes. For example, in CMYK mode, a standard red color is composed of 100% Magenta and 100% Yellow. The notation for this callout would be

100M/100Y. Note that you don't list the zero values for Cyan (C) and Black (K)—you don't list the color as 0C/100M/100Y/0K. In RGB mode (0–255), a standard orange color would be noted as 255R/128G.

Changing Color Stops

The best way to change a color stop on the Gradient panel is to double-click the color stop. Doing so opens a dual Color/Swatches panel that allows you to toggle between the two by clicking the appropriate panel icon on the left edge. Choose the Color panel icon to create a new color or adjust an existing color. Use the Swatches panel icon to choose an already-named color.

Adding Colors and Gradients to the Swatches Panel

Once you have defined a color or a gradient to your liking, it's a smart idea to save it by dragging it into the Swatches panel or click the Color panel menu button and select Create New Swatch. Once a color or gradient is moved into the Swatches panel, you can name it by double-clicking it and then typing a name in the Swatch Options dialog box. You cannot modify it, however. For example, if you click a saved gradient and adjust it on the Gradient panel, you can apply the new gradient to an object, but the original gradient on the Swatches panel remains unaffected. You can save the new and altered gradient to the Swatches panel for future use.

Create a gradient

1. Open AI 2-7.ai, then save it as **Gradient fills**.

2. Create a **4" circle** at the center of the artboard, then apply a **yellow fill** to the circle.

3. Click the **Swatches panel menu button** ☰, point to **Open Swatch Library**, point to **Gradients**, then click **Spectrums**.

   The Spectrums panel opens.

4. Click the **swatch named Spectrum**.

   The yellow fill changes to the Spectrum fill.

5. Open the **Gradient panel**.

6. Click the **Gradient panel menu button** ☰, then click **Show Options** if they are not already showing.

7. Click the **yellow color stop** on the gradient slider, and drag it straight down off the panel to delete it.

8. Delete all the **color stops** *except* for the first and last color stops.

   TIP The changes you make to the gradient slider are reflected in the selected circle.

9. Click the **leftmost color stop** to select it, press and hold **[option] (Mac)** or **[Alt] (Win)**, then click the **red swatch** in the top row of the Swatches panel.

10. Double-click the **rightmost color stop**.

    The Color/Swatches panel opens at the bottom of the Gradient panel.

11. Click a **purple swatch** on the Swatches panel.

    It's not necessary to press and hold [option] (Mac) or [Alt] (Win) when using *this* Swatches panel to change a color stop. For that reason, this is the easiest and fastest way to change a color stop.

12. Float the **mouse pointer** just below the **bottom edge of the gradient slider** on the Gradient panel until a **white arrowhead with a plus sign** appears, then click to add a **new color stop** between the red and purple stops.

13. Double-click the **new color stop**, change its color to **orange**, then drag it to the immediate right of the red color stop.

14. Click to add a **new color stop** between the orange and purple stops.

15. Change its color to **yellow**.

16. Add a **new color stop** between the yellow and purple stops, then change its color to **green**.

17. Add a **blue color stop** between the green and purple stops.

18. Spread the **color stops** out evenly so your Gradient panel resembles Figure 32.

Figure 32 Six color stops on the Gradient panel

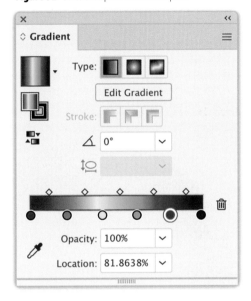

19. Click the **Selection tool** ▶, then click the **Radial Gradient button** ▦ on the Gradient panel.

As shown in Figure 33, the fill in the circle becomes a radial gradient from red in the center to purple at the outer edge.

20. Click the **Color panel menu button** ≡, then click **Create New Swatch**.

21. Name the new swatch **Custom Rainbow**, then click **OK**.

The Custom Rainbow swatch is added to the Gradients section of the Swatches panel.

22. Click the **Gradient tool** ▮ on the toolbar.

The Gradient tool is used to manipulate gradient fills that are already applied to objects. The gradient control bar appears directly on the selected circle. You can change the length, angle, and direction of the gradient by dragging the gradient control bar. You can manipulate the color stops to position them exactly where you want them on the circle.

23. Click the **black button** on the far left of the **gradient control bar**, then drag it in any direction to any length.

Figure 34 shows one possibility.

24. Save your work, then continue to the next lesson.

You applied the Spectrum gradient to the yellow circle. You modified the gradient by deleting color stops and adding new color stops. You changed the color of the new stops, then applied the gradient as a radial gradient. You clicked the Gradient tool, then moved the gradient control bar to modify how the radial gradient fills the circle.

Figure 33 Gradient applied as a radial gradient

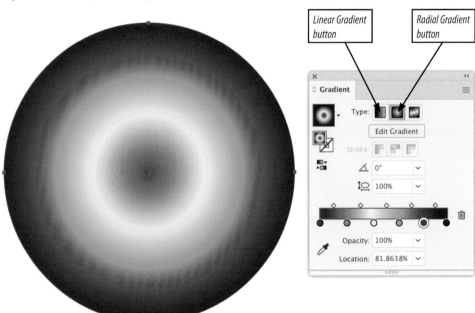

Figure 34 Modified gradient fill

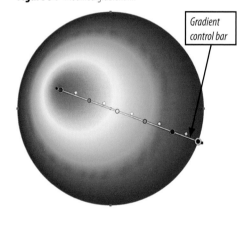

ADJUST GRADIENTS IN TEXT AND OBJECTS

GRADIENT
GRADIENT
GRADIENT

Applying Fills and Strokes to Text

Regardless of the fill and stroke colors shown on the toolbar, new text is generated by default with a black fill and no stroke. To change the color of text, you must select the text with a Selection tool or by highlighting it with a Type tool. When you switch to a Selection tool, the text is selected as a single object (a blue baseline and anchor point are revealed), and any color changes you make will affect the text globally. If you want to change the fill or the stroke of an individual character, you must select that character with a Type tool.

Converting Text to Outlines

About the only thing you can't do to Illustrator text is fill it with a gradient. To create that effect, you first need to convert the text into objects. You can do this by selecting the text, then using the Create Outlines command on the Type menu. The letterforms, or outlines, become standard Illustrator objects with anchor points and paths that you can modify like any other object. Figure 35 shows an example of text converted to outlines.

Create Outlines is a powerful feature. Beyond allowing you to fill text with a gradient, it allows you to modify the letter forms as you would any other object. It also makes it possible to create a document with text and without fonts. This can save you time in document management when sending files to a printer by circumventing potential problems with missing fonts or font conflicts.

Once text is converted to outlines, you can no longer change the typeface. Also, the type loses its font information, including sizing "hints" that optimize letter shape at different sizes. Therefore, if you plan to scale type substantially, change its font size on the Character panel before converting it to outlines.

Figure 35 Text converted to outlines

Using the Gradient Tool with Linear Gradient Fills

As you saw with the radial gradient in the previous lesson, the Gradient tool is used to manipulate gradient fills that are already applied to objects, and it only affects the way a gradient fills an object.

To use the Gradient tool, you first select an object with a gradient fill. When you click the Gradient tool, the **gradient control bar** appears in the object itself, as shown in Figure 36. For linear gradients, the gradient control bar begins at the left edge and ends at the right edge by default.

You can change the length, angle, and direction of the gradient by dragging the gradient control bar.

Figure 36 Gradient control bar

Figure 37 shows the gradient control bar starting outside the object at the top and ending below it. Where you begin dragging and where you end dragging determine the length of the gradient from the beginning color to the ending color, even if it's outside the perimeter of the object.

You can further modify how the gradient fills the object by modifying the gradient control bar itself. Click and drag the diamond-shaped endpoint of the bar to lengthen or shorten the gradient. You can also click and drag the

Figure 37 Changing the position of the gradient control bar

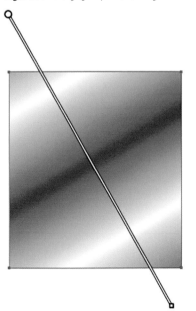

circle-shaped starting point to move the entire bar to a different location.

When you click the gradient control bar, the color stops that compose the gradient appear, as shown in Figure 38. You can click and drag the color stops right there, on the object, for precise control of how the gradient fills the object. You can change the color of the stops on the gradient control bar and even add or delete color stops. To change the color of a stop, simply double-click it; the Color/Swatches panel will appear at the bottom of the Gradient panel.

Figure 38 Color stops on the gradient control bar

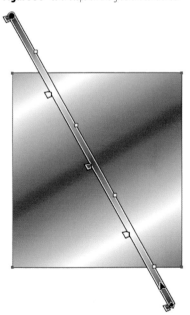

Perhaps the best method for working with the gradient control bar is to first click and drag the Gradient tool as close as possible to where you want it to begin and end. Then use the gradient control bar for tweaking the position of the gradient and the position of the color stops within the object.

When you float the cursor near the endpoint of the gradient control bar, the rotate icon appears, as shown in Figure 39. Click and drag to rotate the gradient control bar and the gradient within the object.

Applying Gradient Fills to Multiple Objects

If you select multiple objects and then click a gradient swatch on the Swatches panel, the gradient will fill each object individually. However, with all the objects selected, you can use the Gradient control bar to extend a single gradient across all of them.

When you convert text to outlines and apply a gradient fill, the gradient automatically fills each letter individually. In other words, if you fill a five-letter word with a rainbow gradient, each of the five letters will contain the entire spectrum. To extend the gradient across all the letters, drag the Gradient tool from the left edge of the word to the right edge, or vice versa.

Using the Gradient Tool with Radial Gradient Fills

With radial gradients, the gradient control bar shows the length of the gradient from the center of the circle to the outermost circle. Figure 40 shows the gradient control bar for three radial gradients.

Figure 40 Three radial gradients

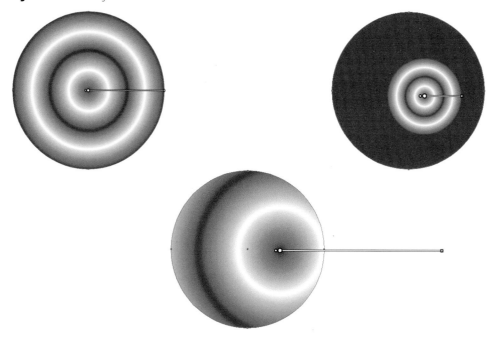

Figure 39 Rotating the gradient control bar

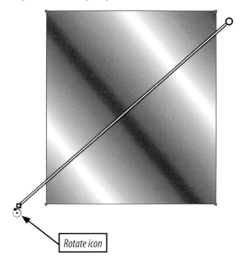

Rotate icon

When you click the gradient control bar on a radial gradient, a dotted line appears, showing you the perimeter of the gradient, whether that's within or outside the actual object. In Figure 41, the dotted line indicates that more of the gradient is actually outside of the object than visible within the object.

Radial gradients are not limited to concentric circles: You can also create radial gradients with concentric ellipses. To do so, click and drag the black circle on the dotted line of the radial gradient. As shown in Figure 42, doing so will distort the concentric circles into ellipses.

Figure 41 Dotted line shows the perimeter of the radial gradient

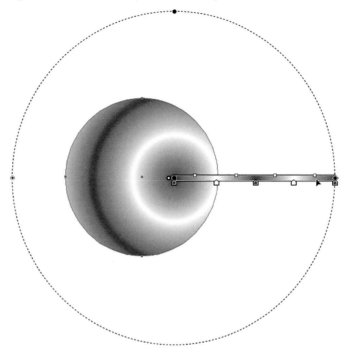

Figure 42 Distorting the gradient

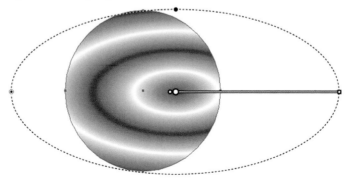

Apply a gradient fill to text

1. Open the Gradient fills.ai document from the previous lesson, if necessary.

2. Click **Object** on the menu bar, then click **Show All**.

3. Click the **Selection tool** ▶, select the **circle with the gradient**, click **Object**, point to **Hide**, then click **Selection**.

4. Select all **six lines of text**, click **Type** on the menu bar, then click **Create Outlines**.

   The type is converted to shapes and is no longer editable as type.

5. Click **View** on the menu bar, then click **Hide Edges**.

6. Click the **Custom Rainbow swatch** you created and saved to the Swatches panel.

7. On the Gradient panel, click the **Linear Gradient button** ▣.

   The gradient fills each letter form individually. In other words, the gradient runs from red to violet from left to right in each letterform on the page.

8. Click the **Selection tool** ▶, then click to select the **second word from the top**.

   Because selection edges are hidden, you won't see selection marks.

9. Click the **Gradient tool** ▣ on the toolbar.

When you select the Gradient tool ▣, gradient control bars appear on each letter. You will use the Gradient tool ▣ on the toolbar to manipulate the gradient fills.

10. Press and hold **[shift]**, then click and drag the **Gradient tool** ▣ from the **top of the letter T to the bottom of the letter T**.

TIP Introducing the [shift] key constrains the drag to a straight line.

11. Select the **third word**, then click and drag the **Gradient tool** ▣ from the left edge of the letter G to the right edge of the letter T.

12. Select the **fourth word**, then click and drag the **Gradient tool** ▣ from the left edge of the artboard to the right edge of the artboard.

13. Select the **fifth word**, then click and drag the **Gradient tool** ▣ from the left edge of the letter D to the right edge of the letter D.

14. Select the **sixth word**, then click and drag the **Gradient tool** ▣ from the top-left corner of the letter A diagonally down to the bottom-right edge of the letter I.

   Your artwork should resemble Figure 43.

15. Save your work, then close the Gradient fills document.

You filled the same text objects six different ways using the Gradient tool at different lengths and angles.

Figure 43 Six different gradient fills

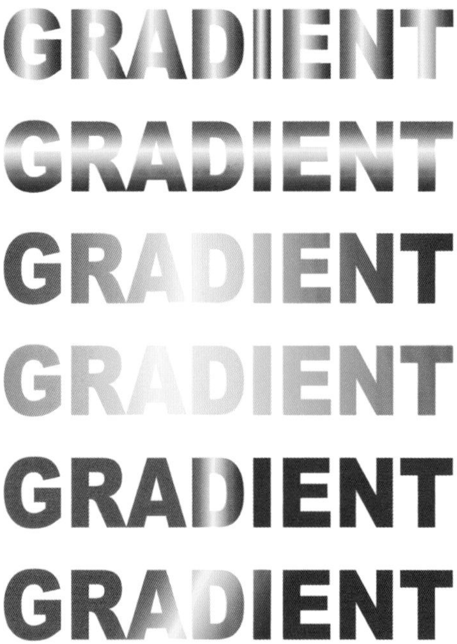

Adjust a radial gradient fill

1. Open AI 2-8.ai, then save it as **Motorcycle Radial**.
2. Select the **small circle**, then change its **stroke color to red**.
3. On the Stroke panel, change the **Weight** to **12 pt**.
4. On the Stroke panel, click the **Align Stroke to Outside button** 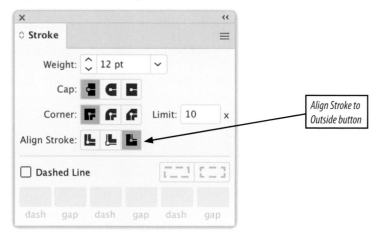.

   Your Stroke panel should resemble Figure 44.
5. Increase the **stroke weight** to **51 pt**.

   At 51 pt., the stroke is the same size as the space between the two circles, no larger.
6. Click **Object** on the menu bar, point to **Path**, then click **Outline Stroke**.

The Outline Stroke command converts a stroked path into an object at the current size of the stroke. The object is now like a donut: a large circle with a smaller circle cut out of its center.

7. Verify that the **fill color** is activated on the toolbar.
8. On the Gradient panel, click the **black and white gradient square** directly under the panel name.

   The linear gradient fills the selected object.
9. On the Gradient panel, click the **Radial Gradient button** .

   The object is filled with a radial gradient. The result is a bit tricky, because it appears mostly black. With a radial gradient, the start color (in this case, white) is at the center of the object. This object's center is a negative space, so we can't see the

white color at its center. Nevertheless, the gradient is radiating from white at the object's center to black at its outer edge.

10. On the Gradient panel, drag the **white color stop** to the right to the midpoint of the gradient slider.
11. Add a **new color stop** to the left of the gradient slider.
12. Change the color of the **leftmost color stop** and the **rightmost color stop** to **green**.

   Your Gradient panel should resemble Figure 45.

   TIP Note that the rightmost color stop represents the outer edge of the circular object.

Continued on next page

Figure 44 Stroke panel set to Align Stroke to Outside

Figure 45 Three color stops on the Gradient panel

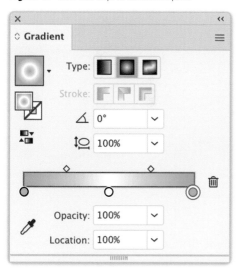

13. Reposition the **color stops** as shown in Figure 46.

With the three color stops in this far-right position, the three-color gradient is visible at the outer edges of the object.

14. Click **Object** on the menu bar, point to **Arrange**, then click **Send to Back**.

15. Deselect, then compare your artwork to Figure 47.

16. Save your work, then close the Motorcycle Radial document.

You applied a heavy weight stroke to the outside of a circle then converted the stroke to an object. You then applied a radial gradient to the object and moved the color stops so the gradient was visible inside the object.

Figure 46 Positioning the color stops so the gradient is visible in the object

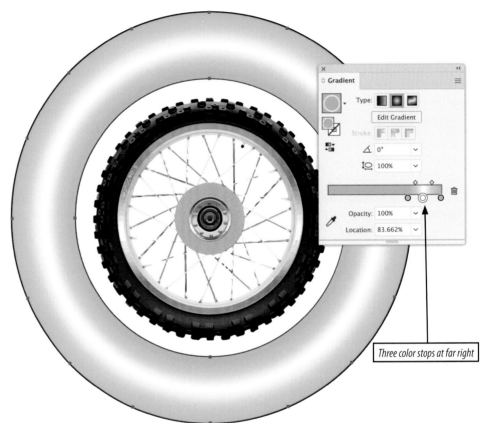

Three color stops at far right

Figure 47 Final artwork

APPLY GRADIENTS TO STROKES

What You'll Do

In this lesson, you will apply gradients to strokes on objects and use the Gradient panel to determine how the gradient strokes the object.

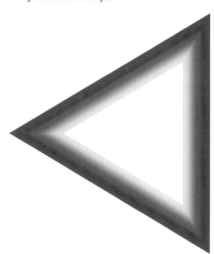

Applying a Gradient to a Stroke

You can use the Gradient panel to apply a gradient to a stroked object and to determine how the gradient is applied. To apply the stroke, simply select the object and, with the Stroke icon activated, choose a gradient to apply to the object.

The Gradient panel offers three buttons you can use to determine how the gradient is applied to the stroke. The three options are as follows:

Within Stroke: As shown in Figure 48, the gradient moves left to right across the object.

Figure 48 The within stroke option for the gradient

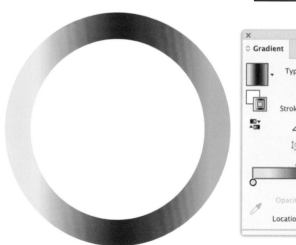

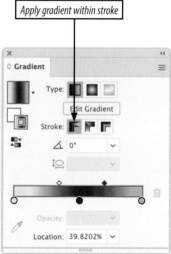

Apply gradient within stroke

Along Stroke: As shown in Figure 49, the gradient moves clockwise around the object.

Across Stroke: As shown in Figure 50, the gradient radiates from the outside to the inside of the stroke.

If you want to specify how the stroke aligns to the object—inside, center, or outside—use the align stroke options on the Stroke panel before using the Gradient panel to apply a gradient to the stroke.

You cannot apply a gradient to a stroke on live type. You must first convert the type to outlines, then you will be able to apply a gradient to the stroke.

Figure 49 The along stroke option for the gradient

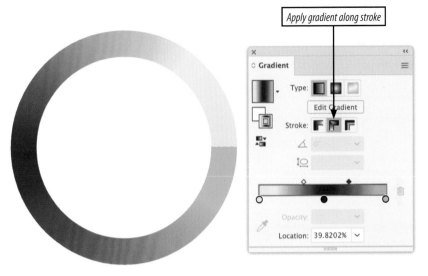

Figure 50 The across stroke option for the gradient

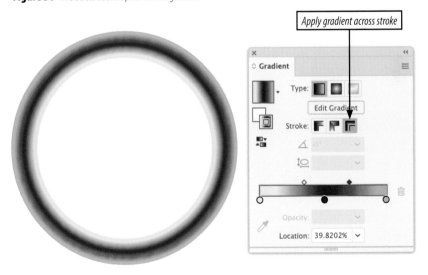

Apply gradients to strokes

1. Open AI 2-9.ai, then save it as **Gradient Strokes**.

2. Select the **triangle**, then verify that the **stroke icon** is activated on the toolbar.

3. Click the **Yellow**, **Orange**, **Blue gradient swatch** on the Gradient panel.

   The gradient is applied to the triangle.

4. Note the **three stroke buttons** on the Gradient panel.

   By default, the first button—Apply gradient within stroke—is selected. As shown in Figure 51, the gradient moves from left to right across the triangle.

TIP In the figure, the selection marks on the triangle are hidden.

5. Click the **second** of the **three stroke buttons**.

   As shown in Figure 52, the Apply gradient along stroke option is applied, and the gradient moves clockwise around the stroke.

Figure 51 Gradient applied within stroke

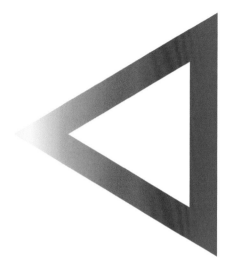
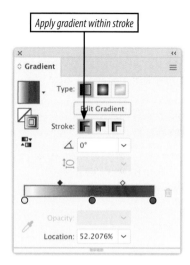

Figure 52 Gradient applied along stroke

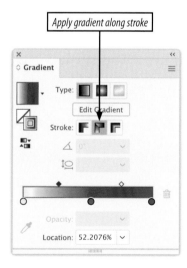

6. Click the **third** of the **three stroke buttons**.

   As shown in Figure 53, the Apply gradient across stroke option is applied, and the gradient radiates outward from the center of the stroke.

7. Click the **Reverse Gradient button** 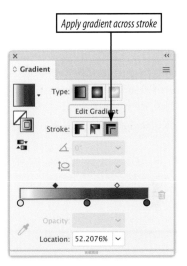 on the Gradient panel, then compare your screen to Figure 54.

8. Save your work, then close the Gradient Strokes document.

You applied a gradient to the stroke on an object, then applied two different options for how the stroke is applied. You clicked the Reverse Gradient button to reverse how the across stroke option applied the gradient.

Figure 53 Gradient applied across stroke

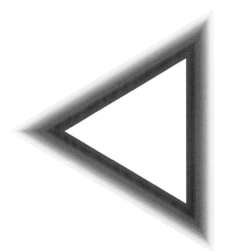

Apply gradient across stroke

Figure 54 Reversing the gradient on the stroke

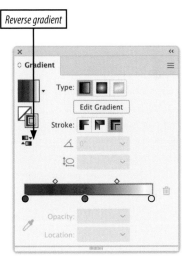

Reverse gradient

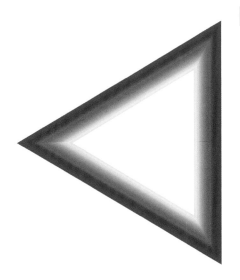

Create point text

1. Open AI 2-10.ai, then save it as **Restaurant Logo**.
2. Using a bold font, type **NOW OPEN** on two lines anywhere on the artboard, using all capital letters.

TIP   The font used in Figure 55 is Impact.

3. Change the font size to 29 pt. and the leading to 25 pt.
4. Verify that the baseline shift is set to 0.
5. Change the alignment to center and the horizontal scale to 75%.
6. Position the text in the center of the white circle.
7. Hide the text.
8. Save your work.

Flow text into an object

1. Copy the beige circle.
2. Paste the copy in front of it.
3. Click the Type tool, then select all of the green text at the bottom of the artboard, with the Type tool.
4. Copy the green text.
5. Click the Selection tool, then click the top beige circle.
6. Click the Area Type tool, click the edge of the top beige circle, then paste.
7. Center-align the text in the circle.
8. Change the baseline shift to −4 pt.
9. Fill the selected text with the same fill color as the beige circle (50% Orange).
10. On the Color panel, drag the Magenta slider to 40% to darken the text.
11. Hide the text.
12. Save your work.

Figure 55   Completed Skills Review

Position text on a path

1. Select the dark gray circle.
2. Click the Type on a Path tool, then click the top of the circle.
3. Using a bold font, type **THE HOLE-IN-ONE** in all capital letters across the top of the circle

TIP The font in Figure 55 is Arial Black. If your type appears at the bottom of the circle, drag the start or end bracket to position the type at the top of the circle. Zoom in so you can clearly see the brackets. If you move the circle instead of the type, undo your last step and try again.

4. Change the font size to 36 pt., and set the horizontal scale to 75% and the fill color to White.

TIP You may need to use a different font size, depending on the font you choose.

5. Click the Selection tool, click Edit on the menu bar, click Copy, click Edit on the menu bar, click Paste in Front, then move the center bracket clockwise to position the copied text across the bottom of the circle.
6. Select the copied text with the Type tool, then type **RESTAURANT**.
7. Drag the RESTAURANT text across the path to flip its direction.
8. Apply a negative baseline shift to move the text below the path.

TIP The baseline shift used in Figure 55 is −26 pt.

9. Copy both text objects, click Edit on the menu bar, then click Paste in Back.
10. Fill the back copies of the text with Black, then move them 2 pt. up and 2 pt. to the right.
11. Save your work.

Create and apply gradients

1. Apply the White, Black Radial gradient to the small white circle.
2. Change the ending color stop on the gradient slider to Smoke.
   Each swatch has a color name that you will see when you hover the mouse pointer over the swatch.

TIP Press [option] (Mac) or [Alt] (Win) while you select Smoke from the Swatches panel.

3. Save the new gradient to the Swatches panel.
4. Name it **Golf Ball**.
5. Fill the large green circle with the Golf Ball gradient.
6. Change the starting color stop to Pure Yellow.
7. Change the ending color stop to Little Sprout Green.
8. Move the midpoint to the 80% location on the gradient slider.
9. Save the new gradient as **The Rough**.
10. Apply a 2 pt. black stroke to the large circle and the smaller peach circle.
11. Save your work.

Adjust a gradient and create a drop shadow

1. Click Object on the menu bar, then click Show All.
2. Deselect all by clicking the artboard.
3. Select NOW OPEN and convert the text to outlines.
4. Fill the text with the white to black linear gradient.
5. Change the starting color stop to Black.
6. Create an intermediary white color stop at the 50% mark on the gradient slider.
7. Drag the Gradient tool starting at the top of the word NOW to the bottom of the word OPEN.
8. Change the middle color stop of the gradient to Latte.

9. Save the new gradient as **Flash**.
10. Deselect the text.
11. Delete the green text from the bottom of the artboard.
12. Convert the remaining text objects into outlines.
13. Apply a 2 pt. black stroke to the two circles in the illustration.
14. Select all, then lock all objects.
15. Save your work, compare your illustration to Figure 55, then close the Restaurant Logo document.

Apply gradients to strokes

1. Open AI 2-11.ai, then save it as **Gradient Strokes to Text**.
2. Select the letter Z with the Selection tool, then verify that the stroke icon is activated on the toolbar.
3. Click Type on the menu bar, then click Create Outlines.
4. Click the White to Cyan gradient swatch on the Swatches panel.
   The gradient is applied to the stroke.
5. Note the three stroke buttons on the Gradient panel.
6. Click the third of the three stroke buttons.
7. Click the Reverse Gradient button on the Gradient panel.
8. Save your work, then close the Gradient Strokes to Text document.

An eccentric California real-estate mogul hires your design firm to "create an identity" for La Mirage, his development of high-tech executive condominiums in Palm Springs. Since he's curious about what you'll come up with on your own, the only creative direction he'll give you is to tell you that the concept is "a desert oasis."

1. Create a new 6" × 6" document, then save it as **Desert Oasis**.
2. Using a bold font and 80 pt. for a font size, type **LA MIRAGE** in all capitals.

TIP The font shown in Figure 56 is Impact.

3. Change the horizontal scale to 80%.
4. Change the baseline shift to 0.
5. Apply a −100 Kerning value between the two words.
6. Convert the text to outlines, then click the linear gradient swatch on the Swatches panel that fades white to black.
7. Using the Color panel, change the first color stop to 66M/100Y/10K.
8. Create an intermediary color stop that is 25M/100Y.
9. Position the intermediary color stop at 70% on the slider.
10. Save the gradient on the Swatches panel, and name it **Desert Sun**.

11. Drag the Gradient tool from the exact top to the exact bottom of the text.
12. Create a rectangle around the text, and fill it with the Desert Sun gradient.
13. Drag the Gradient tool from the bottom to the top of the rectangle.
14. Send the rectangle to the back of the stack.
15. Apply a 1 pt. black stroke to LA MIRAGE.
16. Type the tagline, a **desert oasis**, in 14 pt. lowercase letters.
17. Apply a Tracking value of 500 or more to the tagline, then convert it to outlines.
18. Save your work, compare your image to Figure 56, then close the Desert Oasis document.

Figure 56 Completed Project Builder 1

Your friend owns Loon's Balloons. She stops by your studio with a display ad that she's put together for a local magazine and asks if you can make all the elements work together better. Her only direction is that the balloon must remain pink.

1. Open AI 2-12.ai, then save it as **Balloons**.
2. Save the pink fill on the balloon to the Swatches panel, and name it **Hot Pink**.
3. Fill the balloon shape with the White, Black Radial gradient from the Swatches panel.
4. Change the black color stop on the gradient slider to Hot Pink.
5. Using the Gradient tool, change the highlight point on the balloon shape so it is no longer centered in the balloon shape.
6. Copy the balloon, then paste it in front.
7. Click the Selection tool on the block of text that begins with "specializing in . . ." and then cut the text.
8. Click the top balloon with the Selection tool, then switch to the Area Type tool.
9. Click the top edge of the top balloon, then paste.
10. Center the text and apply a –4 baseline shift.
11. Adjust the layout of the text as necessary.

TIP You can force a line of text to the next line by clicking before the first word in the line you want to move, then pressing [shift] [return] (Mac) or [shift] [Enter] (Win).

12. Move the headline LOON'S BALLOONS so each word is on a different side of the balloon string.
13. Apply a 320 Kerning value between the two words.
14. Save your work, compare your screen to Figure 57, then close the Balloons document.

Figure 57 Completed Project Builder 2

specializing in all your balloon needs - for birthdays, weddings, anniversaries, graduations, halloween, new year's eve parties, or just to say hello - we've got the balloon for you. call 555-7717

LOON'S BALLOONS

You work in the marketing department of a major movie studio, where you design movie posters and newspaper campaigns. You are respected for your proficiency with typography. Your boss asks you to come up with a "teaser" campaign for the movie *Vanishing Point*, a spy thriller. The campaign will run on billboards in 10 major cities and will feature only the movie title, nothing else.

1. Create a new 6" × 6" document, then save it as **Vanish**.
2. Type **VANISHING POINT**, using 100 pt. and a bold font.

TIP The font used in Figure 56 is Impact.

3. Change the Horizontal Scale to 55%.
4. Convert the text to outlines.
5. On the Swatches panel, click the white to black linear gradient swatch.
6. Drag the Gradient tool from the exact bottom to the exact top of the letters.
7. Copy the letters, then paste them in front.
8. Fill the copied letters in front with White.
9. Using your arrow keys, move the white letters 2 pt. to the left and 8 pt. up.
10. Save your work, then compare your text with Figure 58.
11. Close the Vanish document.

Figure 58 Completed Design Project

ALEX
VON DALLWITZ
ART DIRECTOR

Alex von Dallwitz has been drawing for as long as he can remember. His love of cityscapes and design initially propelled him into architecture. But after experiencing the restrictive codes and regulations of the field, Alex decided to switch gears and study graphic design.

As a student, Alex drew inspiration from his art and design teachers, as well as professional graphic artists like Saul Bass and Armin Hofmann. Studying and emulating their work helped Alex find his own unique style. After working in various design studios, Alex took on the role of Art Director at National Geographic Learning. In addition to providing artistic direction for both print and digital education products, Alex designs page layouts and covers, combining imagery and typography to create engaging user experiences. Along with his team, Alex sees a project through every stage of the process, from research and prototyping to final publication.

This role often comes with a busy schedule and looming deadlines. Even so, Alex sees the value in taking short breaks to clear his head. For Alex, nature is more than just rejuvenating—it's inspiring.

Hiking, biking, and kayaking help Alex get his creative juices flowing. In addition, with many people working remotely, the interaction between colleagues and vendors is critical and often helps Alex to see his project from a new perspective. Alex shares, "Whether you're collaborating with a colleague or you're engaged with a National Geographic Explorer, there are such great interactions that happen… these are the people that help bring the story to life."

PROJECT DESCRIPTION

In this project, you will create a new or updated logo for a school club or team. You will have the opportunity to think through the different aspects of the organization and reflect on its goals and mission. You will then decide which elements of the club or team are most important to capture in the revised logo. The goal of this project is to create or enhance a logo to capture people's attention and visually represent the personality and culture of the organization.

QUESTIONS TO CONSIDER

What stands out to you?

What questions would you ask?

What is important to convey in the logo?

Supervised Agricultural Experience logo
© Cengage Learning, Inc.

GETTING STARTED

A logo should clearly communicate the mission of an organization. It should also grab the reader in an instant. Research the dos and don'ts of logo design. Look at examples of logos for businesses you admire. Are they simple or more elaborate? How many colors are used in the design? How do the visual elements interact with the typography?

Then talk to some members of the school club or team you have chosen. What do they feel are the most important aspects of their organization? What colors, symbols, or images would best represent this group? As you reflect on the logos you are drawn to and the mission of the organization, draw simple sketches of your ideas and refine your design. Does your sketch clearly represent the club or team? Would an outsider to the organization know what this logo represents?

CHAPTER **10**

DRAW AND COMPOSE
AN ILLUSTRATION

1. Draw Straight Lines
2. Draw Curved Lines
3. Draw Elements of an Illustration
4. Apply Attributes to Objects
5. Assemble an Illustration
6. Stroke Objects for Artistic Effect
7. Use Image Trace
8. Use the Live Paint Bucket Tool
9. Explore Alternate Drawing Techniques

Adobe Certified Professional in Graphic Design and Illustrations Using Adobe Illustrator

2. Project Setup and Interface

This objective covers the interface setup and program settings that assist in an efficient and effective workflow, as well as knowledge about ingesting digital assets for a project.

2.4 Manage assets in a project.
    B Place assets in an Illustrator document.
    C Use the Links panel.

4. Creating and Modifying Visual Elements

This objective covers core tools and functionality of the application, as well as tools that affect the visual appearance of document elements.

4.1 Use core tools and features to create visual elements.
    A Create graphics or artwork to create visual elements.

4.3 Make, manage, and manipulate selections.
    B Modify and refine selections using various methods.

4.5 Use basic reconstructing and editing techniques to manipulate digital graphics and media.
    A Apply basic autocorrection methods and tools.
    B Repair and reconstruct graphics.
    D Use Image Trace to create vectors from bitmap images.

DRAW STRAIGHT LINES

▶ *What You'll Do*

In this lesson, you will create three new views, then explore basic techniques for using the Pen tool as you prepare to draw a complex illustration.

Drawing in Illustrator

You can create any shape using the Pen tool, which is why it's often called "the drawing tool." More precisely, the pen is a tool for drawing straight lines, curved lines, polygons, and irregularly shaped objects. It is, however, no *more* of a drawing tool than any of the shape tools but, rather, simply more versatile. Make note that *to master Illustrator, you must master the Pen tool.*

The challenges of the Pen tool are finite and can be grasped with no more than 30 minutes' study. As with many aspects of graphic design (and of life!), mastery comes with practice. So make it a point to learn Pen tool techniques. Don't get frustrated. Use the Pen tool often, even if it's just to play around making odd shapes.

All artists learn techniques for using tools such as brushes, chalk, and palette knives. Once learned, those techniques become second nature, subconscious and unique to the artist. Much the same goes for Illustrator's Pen tool. When you are comfortable and confident, you will find yourself effectively translating design ideas from your imagination straight to the artboard, without even thinking about the tool!

Viewing Objects on the Artboard

If you are drawing on paper and you want to see your work up close, you move your nose closer to the paper. Computers offer more effective options. As you have already seen, the Zoom tool is used to enlarge areas of the artboard for easier viewing. When you are working with the Pen tool, your view of the board becomes more critical as anchor points are tiny, and you will often move them in 1-point increments.

Instead of clicking the Zoom tool to enlarge the artboard, you can click and drag a marquee around the specific area you want to enlarge. The **marquee,** which is a dotted rectangle surrounding the area, will disappear when you release the Zoom tool, and whatever was in the marquee will be magnified as much as possible while still fitting in the window.

The New View command allows you to save any view of the artboard. Let's say you zoom in on an object. You can save that view and give it a descriptive name, using the New View command. The name of the view is then listed at the bottom of the View menu, so you can return to it at any time by selecting it. Saving views is an effective way to increase your productivity.

Drawing Straight Segments with the Pen Tool

You can use the Pen tool to make lines, also known as **paths**. You can also use it to create a closed shape, such as a triangle or a pentagon. When you click the Pen tool to make anchor points on the artboard, straight segments are automatically placed between the points. When the endpoints of two straight segments are united by a point, that point is called a **corner point**. Figure 1 shows a simple path drawn with five anchor points and four segments.

Perfection is an unnecessary goal when you are using the Pen tool because you can move and reposition anchor points and segments, as well as add and delete new points. You can use the Pen tool to create the general shape you have in your mind. Once the object is complete, you can use the Direct Selection tool to perfect or tweak the points and segments. Tweaking a finished object is always part of the drawing process.

TIP When the Pen tool is positioned over an anchor point on a selected path, the Delete Anchor Point tool appears. To remove a point from a path, use the Delete Anchor Point tool . If you select a point and cut it, the path becomes broken.

Aligning and Joining Anchor Points

Often, you will want to align anchor points precisely. For example, if you have drawn a diamond-shaped object with the Pen tool, you may want to align the top and bottom points on the same vertical axis and then align the left and right points on the same horizontal axis to perfect the shape.

The **Average** command is a simple and effective choice for aligning points. With two or more points selected, you can use the Average command to align them on the horizontal axis, on the vertical axis, or on both the horizontal and vertical axes. Two points aligned on both the horizontal and vertical axes are positioned one on top of the other.

Why is this command named "Average"? The name is appropriate because when the command moves two points to line them up on a given axis, that axis is positioned at the average distance between the two points. Thus, each point moves the same distance.

Figure 1 Elements of a path composed of straight segments

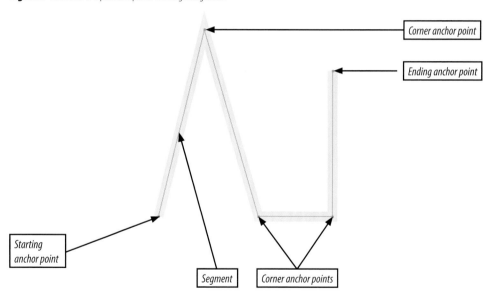

Corner anchor point

Ending anchor point

Starting anchor point

Segment

Corner anchor points

The **Join** command unites two anchor points. When two points are positioned in different locations on the artboard, the Join command creates a segment between them. When two points are aligned on both the horizontal and vertical axes and are joined, the two points become one. Applying the Join command always results in a corner point.

You will often use the Average and Join commands in tandem. Figure 2 shows two pairs of points that have each been aligned on the horizontal axis, then joined with the Join command.

Create new views

1. Open AI 3-1.ai, then save it as **Straight Lines**.

2. Choose the **Essentials workspace**, click the **Zoom tool** 🔍 on the toolbar, then position it at the **upper-left corner of the artboard**.

3. Click and drag a **marquee** that encompasses the **entire yellow section**, as shown in Figure 3.

   The area within the selection box is now magnified.

   TIP If the Zoom tool does not offer a marquee selection, click Illustrator (Mac) or Edit (Win) on the menu bar, click Preferences, click the Selection & Anchor Display, then remove the check mark next to Zoom to Selection.

4. Click **View** on the menu bar, then click **New View**.

5. Name the new view **yellow**, then click **OK**.

6. Press and hold **[space bar]** to access the **Hand tool** 🖐, then drag the **artboard** upward until you have a view of the **entire pink area**.

7. Create a **new view** of the **pink area**, and name it **pink**.

   TIP If you need to adjust your view, you can quickly switch to a view of the entire artboard by pressing [command] [0] (Mac) or [Ctrl] [0] (Win), then create a new marquee selection with the Zoom tool 🔍.

8. Create a **new view** of the **green area**, named **mint**.

Figure 2 Join command unites open points

Figure 3 Drag the Zoom tool to select what will be magnified

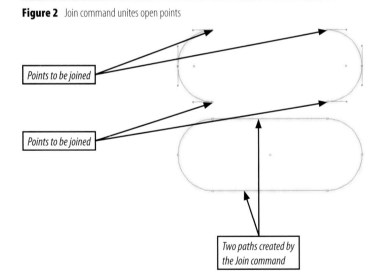

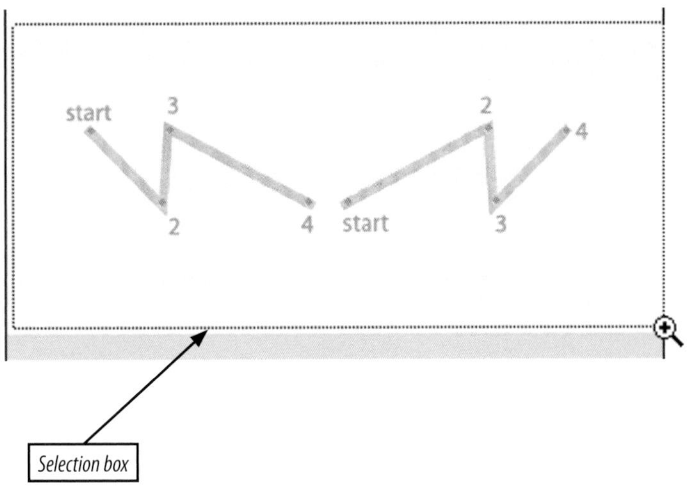

Points to be joined

Points to be joined

Two paths created by the Join command

start   3   2   4

2   4   start   3

Selection box

9. Click **View** on the menu bar, then click **yellow** at the bottom of the menu.

The Illustrator window changes to the yellow view.

TIP You can change the name of a view by clicking View on the menu bar, then clicking Edit Views.

You used the Zoom tool to magnify an area of the artboard. You named the view yellow and then made two more views named pink and mint.

Draw straight lines

1. Verify that you are still in the **yellow view**, then click the **Pen tool** ✐.

2. Open the **Swatches panel**, set the **fill color** to **[None]** ╱ and the **stroke color** to **Black**,

then open the **Stroke panel** and set the **stroke weight** to **1 pt**.

3. Using Figure 4 as a reference, click **position 1 (start)**.

4. Click **position 2**, then note how a segment is automatically drawn between the two anchor points.

5. Click **position 3**, then click **position 4**.

TIP If you become disconnected from the current path you are drawing, undo your last step, then click the last anchor point with the Pen tool ✐. and continue.

6. Press and hold **[command] (Mac)** or **[Ctrl] (Win)** to switch to the **Selection tool** ▶, then click the **artboard** to stop drawing the path and to deselect it.

You need to deselect one path before you can start drawing a new one.

7. Release **[command] (Mac)** or **[Ctrl] (Win)**, click **position 1 (start)** on the next path, then click **position 2**.

8. Skip over position 3 and click **position 4.**

9. Using Figure 5 as a guide, position the **Pen tool** ✐ anywhere on the segment **between points 2 and 4**, then click to add a **new anchor point**.

TIP When the Pen tool ✐ is positioned over a selected path, the Add Anchor Point tool ✐₊ appears.

10. Click the **Direct Selection tool** ▷, **then drag the new anchor point** to **position 3**, as shown in Figure 6.

Using the Pen tool, you created two straight paths.

Figure 4 Four anchor points and three segments

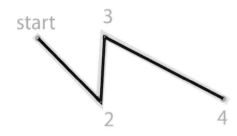

Figure 5 Click the path with the Pen tool to add a new point

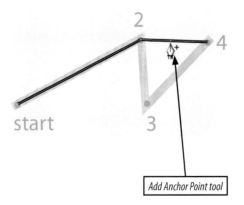

Add Anchor Point tool

Figure 6 Move an anchor point with the Direct Selection tool

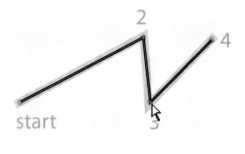

Close a path and align the anchor points

1. Click **View** on the menu bar, then click **pink**.

2. Click the **Pen tool** ✒️, click the **start/end position** at **the top of the polygon**, then click **positions 2 through 6**.

3. Position the **Pen tool** ✒️ over the **first point** you created, then click to close the path, as shown in Figure 7.

4. Switch to the **Direct Selection tool** ▷, click **point 3**, press and hold **[shift]**, then click **point 6**.

TIP You use the [shift] key to select multiple points. Anchor points that are selected appear as solid blue squares; anchor points that are not selected are white or hollow squares.

5. Click **Object** on the menu bar, point to **Path**, then click **Average**.

6. Click the **Horizontal option button** in the Average dialog box, then click **OK**.

    The two selected anchor points align on the horizontal axis, as shown in Figure 8.

7. Select both the **start/end point** and **point 4**.

8. Use the **Average command** to align the points on the vertical axis.

Figure 7 Close a path at its starting point

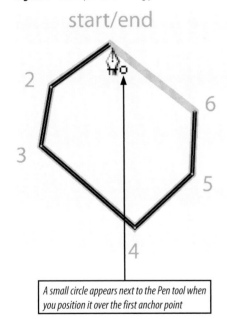

A small circle appears next to the Pen tool when you position it over the first anchor point

Figure 8 Two points aligned on the horizontal axis

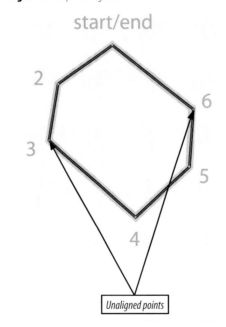

Unaligned points

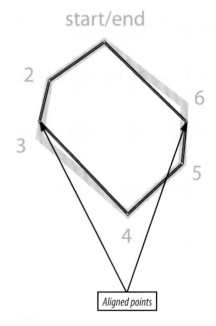

Aligned points

9. Select both **point 2** and **point 5**, then use the **Average command** to align the points on both axes, as shown in Figure 9.

You drew a closed path, then used the Average command to align three sets of points. You aligned the first set on the horizontal axis, the second on the vertical axis. You aligned the third set of points on both axes, which positioned them one on top of the other.

Join anchor points

1. Switch to the **mint view** of the artboard.

2. Use the **Pen tool** 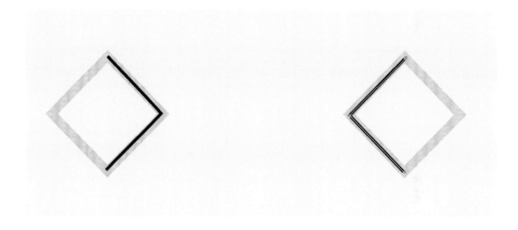 to trace the **two diamond shapes**.

TIP Remember to deselect the first diamond path with the Selection tool before you begin tracing the second diamond.

3. Click the **left anchor point** of the **first diamond** with the **Direct Selection tool**, click **Edit** on the menu bar, then click **Cut**.

Cutting points also deletes the segments attached to them.

4. Cut the **right point** on the **second diamond**.

Your work should resemble Figure 10.

Continued on next page

Figure 9 Averaging two points on both the horizontal and vertical axes

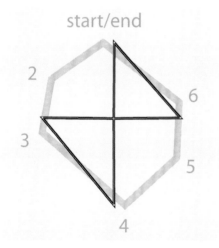

Figure 10 Cutting points also deletes the segments attached to them

---

5. Select the **top point** on each path.

6. Click **Object** on the menu bar, point to **Path**, then click **Join**.

The points are joined by a straight segment, as shown in Figure 11.

TIP The shortcut key for Average is [command] [option] [A] (Mac) or [Ctrl] [Alt] [A] (Win). The shortcut key for Join is [command] [J] (Mac) or [Ctrl] [J] (Win).

7. Join the **two bottom points**.

8. Apply a **yellow fill** to the object, then save your work.

Your work should resemble Figure 12.

9. Close the Straight Lines document.

You drew two closed paths. You cut a point from each path, which deleted the points and the segments attached to them, creating two open paths. You used the Join command, which drew a new segment between the two top points and the two bottom points on each path. You then applied a yellow fill to the new object.

Figure 11 Join command unites two distant points with a straight segment

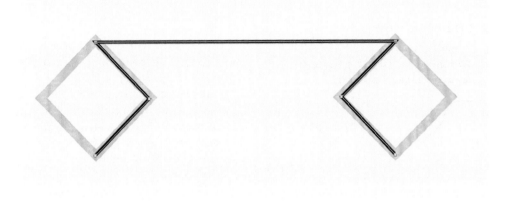

Figure 12 Joining the two open anchor points on an open path closes the path

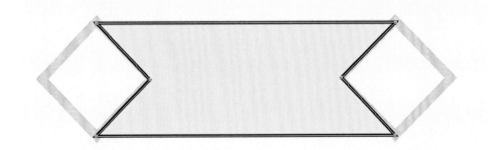

DRAW CURVED LINES

▶ **What You'll Do**

In this lesson, you will use the Pen tool to draw and define curved paths, and you will learn techniques to draw lines that abruptly change direction.

Defining Properties of Curved Lines

When you click to create anchor points with the Pen tool, the points are connected by straight segments. You can "draw" a curved path between two anchor points by *clicking and dragging* the Pen tool to create the points instead of just clicking. Anchor points created by clicking and dragging the Pen tool are known as **smooth points**.

When you use the Direct Selection tool to select a point connected to a curved segment, you will expose the point's **direction lines**, as shown in Figure 13. The angle and length of the direction lines determine the arc of the curved segment. Direction lines are editable. You can click and drag the **direction points**, or handles, at the end of the direction lines to reshape the curve. Direction lines function only to define curves and do not appear when a document is printed.

Figure 13 Direction lines define a curve

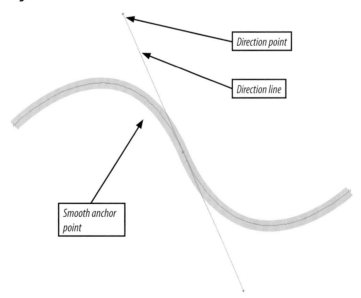

Direction point

Direction line

Smooth anchor point

A **smooth point** always has two direction lines that move together as a unit. The two curved segments attached to the smooth point are both defined by the direction lines. When you manipulate the direction lines on a smooth point, you change the curve of both segments attached to the point, always maintaining a *smooth* transition through the anchor point.

> **TIP** You can change the appearance of anchors and handles in the Selection & Anchor Display section of the Preferences dialog box. One key preference is "Highlight anchors on mouse over." With this activated, anchor points are enlarged when you float a selection tool over them, making them easier to select.

When two paths are joined at a corner point, the two paths can be manipulated independently. A corner point can join two straight segments, one straight segment and one curved segment, or two curved segments. That corner point would have zero, one, or two direction lines, respectively. Figure 14 shows examples of smooth points and corner points.

When a corner point joins one or two curved segments, the direction lines are unrelated and are often referred to as "broken." When you manipulate one, the other doesn't move.

Converting Anchor Points

The Anchor Point tool changes corner points to smooth points and changes smooth points to corner points.

To convert a corner point to a smooth point, you click and drag the Anchor Point tool on the anchor point to *pull out* direction lines. See Figure 15.

Figure 14 Smooth points and corner points

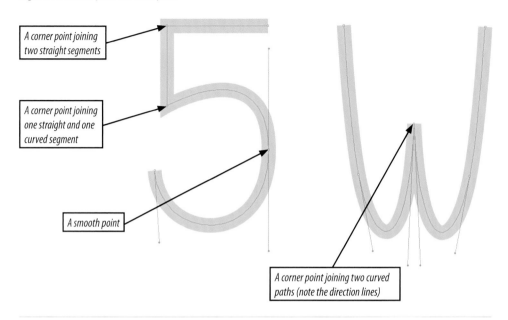

A corner point joining two straight segments

A corner point joining one straight and one curved segment

A smooth point

A corner point joining two curved paths (note the direction lines)

Figure 15 Converting a corner point to a smooth point

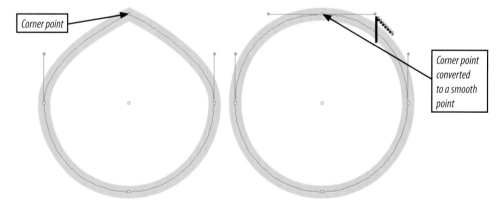

Corner point

Corner point converted to a smooth point

The Anchor Point tool works two ways to convert a smooth point to a corner point, and both are very useful when drawing.

When you click directly on a smooth point with the Anchor Point tool, the direction lines disappear. The two attached segments lose whatever curve defined them and become straight segments, as shown in the middle circle in Figure 16.

You can also use the Anchor Point tool on one of the two direction lines of a smooth point. The tool "breaks" the direction lines and allows you to move one independently of the other, as shown in the third circle in Figure 16. The smooth point is converted to a corner point that now joins two unrelated curved segments. Once the direction lines are broken, they remain broken. You can manipulate them independently with the Direct Selection tool; you no longer need the Anchor Point tool to do so.

Toggling Between the Pen Tool and Selection Tools

Drawing points and selecting points go hand in hand, and you will often need to switch back and forth between the Pen tool and one of the selection tools. Clicking from one tool to the other on the toolbar is unnecessary and will impede your productivity. To master the Pen tool, you must incorporate the keyboard command for "toggling" between the Pen tool and the selection tools. With the Pen tool selected, press [command] (Mac) or [Ctrl] (Win), which will switch the Pen tool to the Selection tool or the Direct Selection tool, depending on which tool you used last.

Figure 16 Converting smooth points to corner points

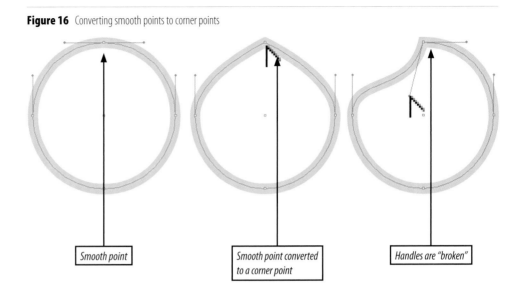

Smooth point

Smooth point converted to a corner point

Handles are "broken"

Draw and edit a curved line

1. Open AI 3-2.ai, then save it as **Curved Lines 1**.

2. On the toolbar, verify that the **fill color** is **[None]** and the **stroke color** is **Black**.

3. Click the **Pen tool** , then position it over the **first point position** on the line.

4. Click and drag upward until the pointer is at the **center of the purple star**, then release the mouse button.

5. Position the **Pen tool** over the **second point position.**

6. Click and drag down to the **red star**, then release the mouse button.

7. Using the same method, trace the remainder of the **blue lines**, as shown in Figure 17.

8. Click the **Direct Selection tool** on the toolbar.

9. Select the **second anchor point.**

   When you click an anchor point with the Direct Selection tool , the anchor points' two direction lines with direction handles appear. Direction handles can be dragged to manipulate the path.

10. Click and drag the **direction handle** of the **top direction line** to the **second purple star**, as shown in Figure 18, then release the mouse button.

    The move changes the shape of both segments attached to the anchor point.

11. Select the **third anchor point** with the **Direct Selection tool** .

12. Drag the **bottom direction handle** to the **second red star**, as shown in Figure 19, then release the mouse button.

13. Manipulate the direction lines to restore the curves to their appearance in Figure 17.

14. Save your work, then close the Curved Lines 1 document.

You traced a curved line by making smooth points with the Pen tool. You used the Direct Selection tool to manipulate the direction lines of the smooth points and adjust the curves. You then used the direction lines to restore the line to its original curves.

Figure 17 Smooth points draw continuous curves

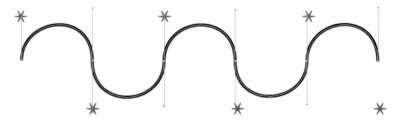

Figure 18 Moving one direction line changes two curves

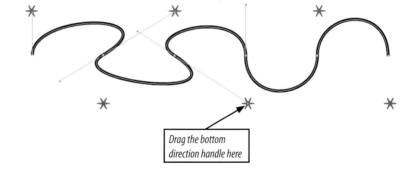

Click the Direct Selection tool on any smooth point to expose its direction lines

Figure 19 Round curves are distorted by moving direction lines

Drag the bottom direction handle here

Convert anchor points

1. Open AI 3-3.ai, then save it as **Curved Lines 2**.

2. Click **View** on the menu bar, then click **View #1**.

3. Click the **Direct Selection tool** ▷, anywhere on the **black line**.

   Make note of the location of the six existing anchor points that become visible.

4. Click **Object** on the menu bar, point to **Path**, then click **Add Anchor Points**.

   Five anchor points are added. They do not change the shape of the line.

5. Click the **Anchor Point tool** ▷, then click **each of the five new anchor points**.

   The smooth points are converted to corner points, as shown in Figure 20.

   TIP The Anchor Point tool ▷ is hidden beneath the Pen tool ✒.

6. Click the **six original anchor points** with the **Anchor Point tool** ▷.

7. Position the **Anchor Point tool** ▷, over the **sixth anchor point** from the left.

8. Click and drag the **anchor point** to the **purple star**.

   The corner point is converted to a smooth point.

9. Using Figure 21 as a guide, convert the **corner points** to the left and right of the new curve.

You added five new anchor points to the line, then used the Anchor Point tool to convert all 11 points from smooth points to corner points. You then used the Anchor Point tool to convert three corner points to smooth points.

Figure 20 Smooth points converted to corner points

Figure 21 Smooth points restored from corner points

Draw a line with curved and straight segments

1. Click **View** on the menu bar, then click **View #2**.

2. Click the **Pen tool** ✎, position it over the **first point position**, then click and drag down to the **green star**.

3. Position the **Pen tool** ✎ over the **second point position**, then click and drag up to the **purple star**, as shown in the top section of Figure 22.

4. Click the **second anchor point** with the **Pen tool** ✎.

   The direction line you dragged is deleted, as shown in the lower section of Figure 22. Deleting the direction line allows you to change the direction of the path.

5. Click the **third point position** to create the third anchor point.

6. Position the **Pen tool** ✎ over the **third anchor point**, then click and drag a **direction line** up to the **green star**.

7. Position the **Pen tool** ✎ **over the fourth point position**, then click and drag down to the **purple star**.

8. Click the **fourth anchor point**.

9. Position the **Pen tool** ✎ over the **fifth position**, then click.

10. While the **Pen tool** ✎ is still positioned over the **fifth anchor point**, click and drag a **direction line** down to the **green star.**

11. Finish tracing the line, then deselect the path.

12. Save your work, then continue to the next set of steps.

You traced a line that has three curves joined by two straight segments. You used the technique of clicking the previous smooth point to convert it to a corner point, allowing you to change the direction of the path.

Figure 22 Click to convert an open smooth point to a corner point

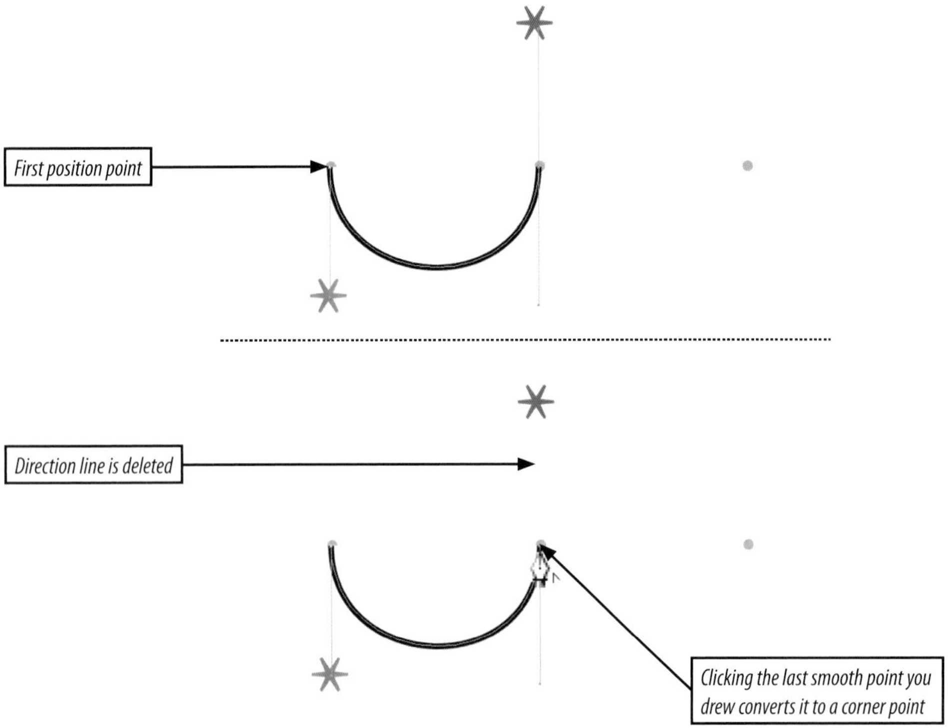

First position point

Direction line is deleted

Clicking the last smooth point you drew converts it to a corner point

THE PENCIL, SMOOTH, AND PATH ERASER TOOLS

When drawing paths, be sure to experiment with the Pencil, Smooth, and Path Eraser tools, which are grouped together on the toolbar. You can draw freehand paths with the Pencil tool and then manipulate them using the Direct Selection tool, the Smooth tool, the Path Eraser tool, or the Path Reshape feature on the Pen tool or Anchor Point tool. The Smooth tool is used to smooth over line segments that are too bumpy or too sharp. The Path Eraser tool looks and acts just like an eraser found at the end of a traditional pencil; dragging it over a line segment erases that part of the segment from the artboard. The Pencil tool draws freehand lines or straight lines. Press and hold [shift] while dragging the Pencil tool to draw horizontal and vertical straight lines and diagonal lines with a 45° angle.

Reverse direction while drawing

1. Click **View** on the menu bar, then click **View #3**.

2. Click the **Pen tool** , position it over the **first point position**, then click and drag down to the **purple star**.

3. Position the **Pen tool** over the **second point position**, then click and drag up to the **red star**, as shown in the top section of Figure 23.

4. Press and hold **[option] (Mac)** or **[Alt] (Win)** to switch to the **Anchor Point tool**, then click and drag the **direction handle** on the **red star** down to the **second purple star**, as shown in the lower section of Figure 23.

   TIP Press [option] (Mac) or [Alt] (Win) to toggle between the Pen tool and the Anchor Point tool.

5. Release **[option] (Mac)** or **[Alt] (Win)**, then continue to trace the line using the same method.

   TIP If you switch between the Pen tool and the Anchor Point tool using the toolbar instead of using [option] (Mac) or [Alt] (Win), you will disconnect from the current path.

6. Save your work, then close the Curved Lines 2 document.

You used the Anchor Point tool to break the direction lines of a smooth point, converting it to a corner point in the process. You used the redirected direction line to define the next curve in the sequence.

Figure 23 Use the Anchor Point tool to "break" the direction lines and redirect the path

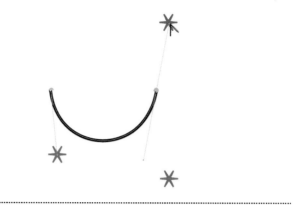

DRAW ELEMENTS OF AN ILLUSTRATION

▶ *What You'll Do*

In this lesson, you will draw 14 elements of an illustration. By tracing previously drawn elements, you will develop a sense of where to place anchor points when drawing a real-world illustration.

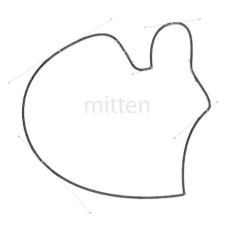

Starting an Illustration

Getting started with drawing an illustration is often the hardest part. Sometimes the illustration will be an image of a well-known object or a supplied sketch or a picture. At other times, the illustration to be created will exist only in your imagination. In either case, the challenge is the same: How do you translate the concept from its source to the Illustrator artboard?

Drawing from Scratch

Drawing from scratch means that you start with a new Illustrator document and create the illustration, using only the Illustrator tools. This approach is common, especially when the goal is to draw familiar items such as a daisy, fish, or sun.

Illustrator's shape tools (such as the Ellipse tool) combined with the transform tools (such as the Rotate tool) make the program powerful for creating geometric designs from scratch. The Undo and Redo commands allow you to experiment and create surprising designs.

Typographic illustrations—even complex ones—are often created from scratch.

Many talented illustrators and designers can create complex graphics off the cuff. It can be an astounding experience to watch an illustrator start with a blank artboard and, with no reference material, produce sophisticated graphics with attitude, expression, and emotion, as well as unexpected shapes and subtle relationships between objects.

Tracing a Scanned Image

Using the Place command, it is easy to import a scanned image into Illustrator. For complex illustrations—especially those of people or objects with delicate relationships, such as maps or blueprints—many designers find it easier to scan a sketch or a photo and import it into Illustrator as a guide or a point of reference.

Tracing a scanned image is not "cheating." An original drawing is an original drawing, whether it is first created on a computer or on a piece of paper. Rather than being a negative, the ability to use a computer to render a sketch is a fine example of the revolutionary techniques that illustration software has brought to the art of drawing. Figure 24 shows an illustration created from scratch in Illustrator, and Figure 25 shows a scanned sketch that will be the basis for the illustration you will create throughout this chapter.

Figure 24   An illustration created from scratch

Figure 25   Place a scanned sketch in Illustrator, and you can trace it or use it as a visual reference

Draw a closed path using smooth points

1. Open AI 3-4.ai, then save it as **Snowball Parts**.

2. Click **View** on the menu bar, then click **Arm**.

3. Verify that the **fill color** is set to **[None]** and the **stroke color** is set to **Black**.

4. Click the **Pen tool** 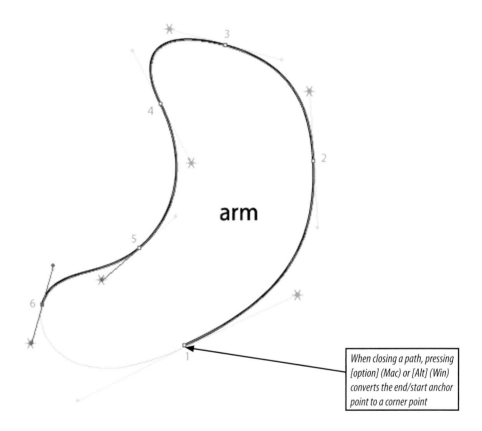, position it over **point 1**, then click and drag a **direction line** to the **green star on the right side of the 1**.

5. Go to **position 2**, then click and drag a **direction line to the next green star**.

TIP Watch the blue preview of the new segment fall into place as you drag the Pen tool. This will help you understand when to stop dragging the direction line.

6. Using the same method, continue to draw **points 3 through 6**, then compare your screen to Figure 26.

7. Position the **Pen tool** over **point 1.**

8. Press and hold **[option] (Mac)** or **[Alt] (Win)**, then click and drag to position the **ending segment** and close the path.

You drew a curved path. To close the path, you used a corner point, which allowed you to position the ending segment without affecting the starting segment.

Figure 26 Points 1 through 6 are smooth points

> When closing a path, pressing [option] (Mac) or [Alt] (Win) converts the end/start anchor point to a corner point

Begin and end a path with a corner point

1. Click **View** on the menu bar, then click **Hatband** at the very bottom of the menu.

2. Verify that the **fill color** is set to **[None]** and the **stroke color** is set to **Black**.

3. Click the **Pen tool** , then click **position 1** to create a corner point.

4. Draw the next two curved segments for **positions 2** and **3**, using the green stars as guides.

5. Position the **Pen tool** over **position 4**, then click and drag to the **green star**.

6. Click **position 5** to create a corner point, as shown in Figure 27.

7. Position the **Pen tool** over **position 6**, then click and drag to the **green star**.

8. Click **position 1** to close the path with a corner point.

9. Click the **Selection tool** , then deselect the path.

You began a path with a corner point. When it was time to close the path, you simply clicked the starting point. Since the point was created without direction lines, there were no direction lines to contend with when closing the path.

Figure 27   Point 5 is a corner point

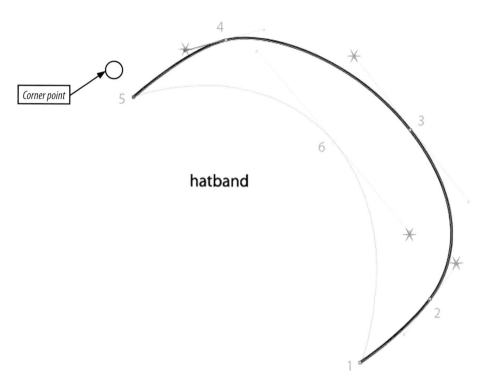

Corner point

hatband

Redirect a path while drawing

1. Click **View** on the menu bar, then click **Nose**.

   The Nose view includes the nose, mouth, eyebrow, and teeth.

2. Click the **Pen tool** , then click **point 1** on the nose to start the path with a corner point.

3. Create smooth points at **positions 2** and **3**.

The direction of the nose that you are tracing abruptly changes at point 3.

4. Press and hold **[option] (Mac)** or **[Alt] (Win)** to switch to the **Anchor Point tool** , then move the **top direction handle** of **point 3** down to the **red star**, as shown in Figure 28.

5. Release **[option] (Mac)** or **[Alt] (Win)** to switch back to the **Pen tool** , click and drag **position 4** to finish drawing the path, click the **Selection tool** , then deselect the path.

The nose element, as shown in Figure 29, is an open path.

6. Save your work, then continue to the next set of steps.

Tracing the nose, you encountered an abrupt change in direction, followed by a curve. You used the Anchor Point tool to redirect the direction lines on point 3, simultaneously converting point 3 from smooth to corner and defining the shape of the curved segment that follows.

Figure 28 Use the Anchor Point tool to redirect the path

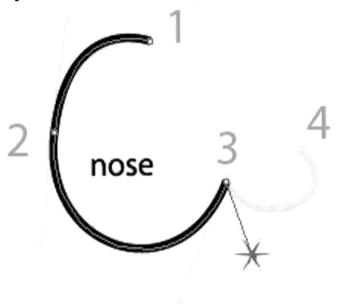

Figure 29 Nose element is an open path

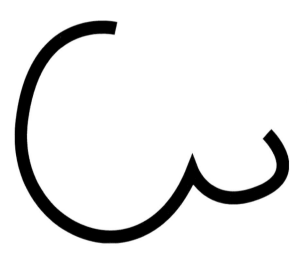

Place a scanned image

1. Click **View** on the menu bar, then click **Fit All in Window**.

2. Click **File** on the menu bar, then click **Place**.

3. Navigate to the drive and folder where your Chapter 10 Data Files are stored.

4. Click **Snowball Sketch.tif**, then click **Place**.

5. Click anywhere on the artboard to place the file.

6. Use the **Scale tool** , to scale the placed file **115%**.

TIP You can apply all the transform tools to placed files.

7. Click the **Selection tool** , move the placed file to the right of the artboard, then lock it.

8. Draw the remaining elements of the illustration, using the sketch or Figure 30 as a reference. Save your work after you complete each element.

TIP The mouth, eyebrow, and teeth are in the Nose view.

You placed a file of a scanned sketch to use as a reference guide. You scaled the object, dragged it to the right of the artboard, locked it, and then drew the remaining elements of the illustration.

Figure 30 Use a scanned sketch as a reference or for tracing

APPLY ATTRIBUTES TO OBJECTS

▶ ### *What You'll Do*

You will create four new colors on the Color panel and apply each to one of the illustration elements. Using the Eyedropper tool, you will paint the remaining items quickly and easily.

Using the Eyedropper Tool

In Illustrator, **attributes** are formatting that you have applied to an object to affect its appearance. Typographic attributes, for example, would include font, leading, and horizontal scale. Artistic attributes include the fill color, stroke color, and stroke weight.

The Eyedropper tool is handy for applying *all* attributes of an object to another object. Its icon is particularly apt. The Eyedropper tool "picks up" an object's attributes, such as fill color, stroke color, and stroke weight.

| **TIP** You can think of the Eyedropper tool as taking a sample of an object's attributes.

The Eyedropper tool is particularly useful when you want to apply one object's attributes to another. For example, if you have applied a blue fill with a 3.5 pt. orange stroke to an object, you can easily apply those attributes to new or already-existing objects. Simply select the object that you want to format, then click the formatted object with the Eyedropper tool.

This is a simple example, but don't underestimate the power of the Eyedropper tool. As you explore more of Illustrator, you will find that you are able to apply a variety of increasingly complex attributes to objects. The more complex the attributes, the more the Eyedropper tool reveals its usefulness.

You can also use the Eyedropper tool to copy type formatting and effects between text elements. This can be especially useful when designing display type for headlines.

Adding a Fill to an Open Path

You can think of the letter O as an example of a closed path and the letter U as an example of an open path. Although it seems a bit strange, you can add a fill to an open path just as you would to a closed path. The program draws an imaginary straight line between the endpoints of an open path to define where the fill ends. Figure 31 shows an open path in the shape of a U with a red fill. Note where the fill ends. For the most part, avoid applying fills to open paths. Though Illustrator will apply the fill, an open path's primary role is to feature a stroke. Any effect that you can create by filling an open path you can also create with a more effective method by filling a closed path.

Figure 31 A fill color applied to an open path

Apply new attributes to closed paths

1. Verify that nothing is selected on the artboard.
2. Open the **Color panel**, then create a **royal blue color** on the Color panel.
3. Fill the **arm** with the royal blue color, then change its **stroke weight** to **6 pt**.

TIP Use the views at the bottom of the View menu to see and select each element with which you need to work. The mouth, eyebrow, and teeth are in the Nose view.

4. Deselect the arm, then create a **deep red color** on the Color panel.
5. Fill the **hatband** with the **deep red color**, then change its **stroke weight** to **3 pt**.

6. Deselect the **hatband**, then create a **flesh-toned color** on the Color panel that is **20% Magenta** and **56% Yellow**.
7. Fill the **head** with the **flesh tone**; don't change the stroke weight.
8. Fill the **pom-pom** with **White**; don't change the stroke weight.
9. Fill the **mouth** with **Black**; don't change the stroke weight.
10. Compare your work with Figure 32.
11. Save your work, then continue to the next set of steps.

You applied new attributes to five closed paths by creating three new colors, using them as fills, then changing the stroke weight on two of the objects.

Figure 32 New attributes applied to five elements

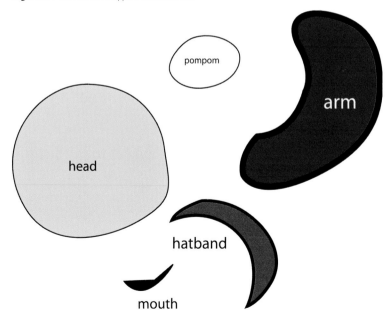

Copy attributes with the Eyedropper tool

1. Select the **torso**.

2. Click the **Eyedropper tool** 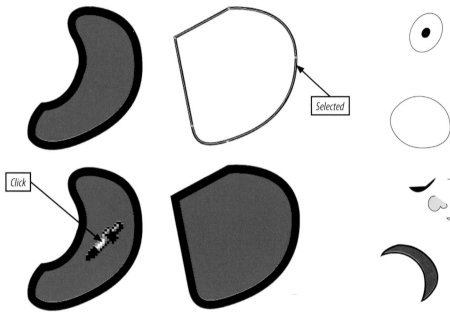, then click the **blue arm**.

   As shown in Figure 33, the torso takes on the same fill and stroke attributes as the arm.

3. Switch to the **Selection tool** ▶, select the **hat**, click the **Eyedropper tool** ✎, then click the **hatband**.

4. Using any method you like, fill and stroke the remaining objects using the colors shown in Figure 34.

5. Save your work, then continue to the next set of steps.

You applied the attributes of one object to another by first selecting the object to which you wanted to apply the attributes, then clicking the object with the desired attributes using the Eyedropper tool.

Figure 33 Use the Eyedropper tool to apply the attributes of one object to another with one click

Selected

Click

Figure 34 All elements ready to be assembled

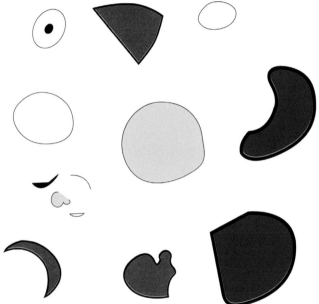

ASSEMBLE AN ILLUSTRATION

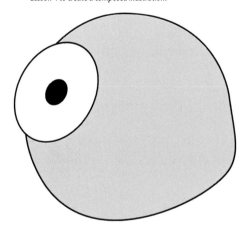

Assembling an Illustration

Illustrator's basic stacking order design is sophisticated enough to compose any illustration. Assembling an illustration with multiple objects will test your fluency with the stacking order commands: Bring to Front, Send to Back, Bring Forward, Send Backward, Paste in Front, Paste in Back, Group, Lock, Unlock All, Hide, and Show All. The sequence in which you draw the elements determines the stacking order (newer elements are in front of older ones), so you'll almost certainly need to adjust the stacking order when assembling the elements. Locking and hiding placed elements will help you to protect the elements when they are positioned correctly.

Assemble the illustration

1. Select and copy **all the elements** on the artboard.
2. Create a **new CMYK Color document** that is **9" × 9"**, then save it as **Snowball Assembled**.
3. Paste the **copied elements** into the Snowball Assembled document.
4. Deselect all objects, select the **head**, click **Object** on the menu bar, point to **Arrange**, then click **Send to Back**.
5. Group the **eye and the iris**, then position the **eye on the head** as shown in Figure 35.
6. Click the **eye**, press **[option] (Mac)** or **[Alt] (Win)**, then drag to create a copy of it, as shown in Figure 36.

Continued on next page

Figure 35 Eye positioned on the head

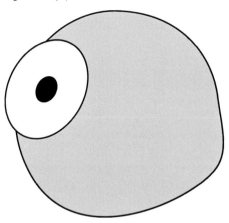

Figure 36 Second eye is a copy of the first

7. Position the **nose on the face**, cut the **nose**, select the **left eye**, then paste in front.

The nose is pasted in the same position, but now it is in front of the eye, as shown in Figure 37.

8. Select the **teeth**, then bring them to the front.

9. Position the **teeth over the mouth**, then group them.

10. Position the **mouth and the teeth on the head**, and the **eyebrow over the right eye**, as shown in Figure 38.

11. Finish assembling the illustration, using Figure 39 as a guide.

12. Save your work, then continue to the next set of steps.

TIP Use the Arrange commands on the Object menu to change the stacking order of objects as necessary.

You assembled the illustration utilizing various commands to change the stacking order of the individual elements.

Figure 37 Nose pasted in front of the left eye

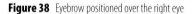

The nose behind the left eye

The nose in front of the left eye

Figure 38 Eyebrow positioned over the right eye

Figure 39 All elements in position

STROKE OBJECTS FOR ARTISTIC EFFECT

▶ *What You'll Do*

In this lesson, you will experiment with strokes of varying weight and attributes using options on the Stroke panel. You will then apply pseudo-strokes to all of the objects to create dramatic stroke effects.

Defining Joins and Caps

In addition to applying stroke weights, you use the Stroke panel to define other stroke attributes, including joins and caps, and whether a stroke is solid or dashed. Figure 40 shows the Dashed Line utility and Cap options on the Stroke panel.

Caps are applied to the ends of stroked paths. The Stroke panel offers three choices: Butt Cap, Round Cap, and Projecting Cap. Choose Butt Cap for squared ends and Round Cap for rounded ends. Generally, rounded caps are more appealing to the eye.

Figure 40 Stroke panel

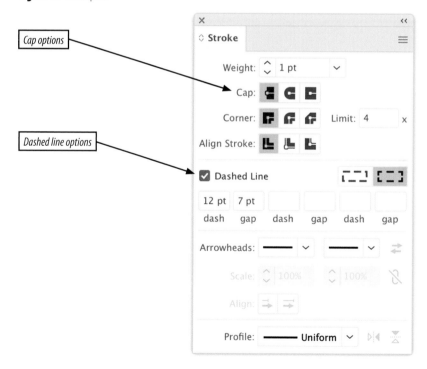

The Projecting Cap applies a squared edge that extends the anchor point at a distance that is one-half the weight of the stroke. With a Projecting Cap, the weight of the stroke is equal in all directions around the line. The Projecting Cap is useful when you align two anchor points at a right angle, as shown in Figure 41.

When two stroked paths form a corner point, **joins** define the appearance of the corner. Miter Join is the default join and produces stroked lines with pointed corners. The Round Join produces stroked lines with rounded corners, and the Bevel Join produces stroked lines with squared corners. The greater the weight of the stroke, the more apparent the join will be, as shown in Figure 42.

Defining the Miter Limit

The **miter limit** determines when a miter join will be squared off to a beveled edge. The miter is the length of the point from the inside to the outside. The length of the miter is not the same as the stroke weight. When two stroked paths are at an acute angle, the length of the miter will greatly exceed the weight of the stroke, which results in an extreme point that can be very distracting.

| **TIP** You can align a stroke to the center, inside, or outside of a path using the Align Stroke buttons on the Stroke panel.

The default miter limit is 4, which means that when the length of the miter reaches 4 times the stroke weight, the program will automatically square it off to a beveled edge. Generally, you will find the default miter limit satisfactory, but you should remain conscious

of it when you draw objects with acute angles, such as stars and triangles. Figure 43 shows the impact of a miter limit on a stroked star with acute angles.

Figure 41 Projecting caps are useful when segments meet at right angles

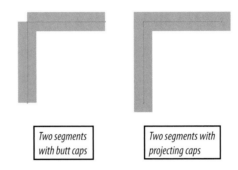

Two segments with butt caps

Two segments with projecting caps

Figure 42 Three types of joins

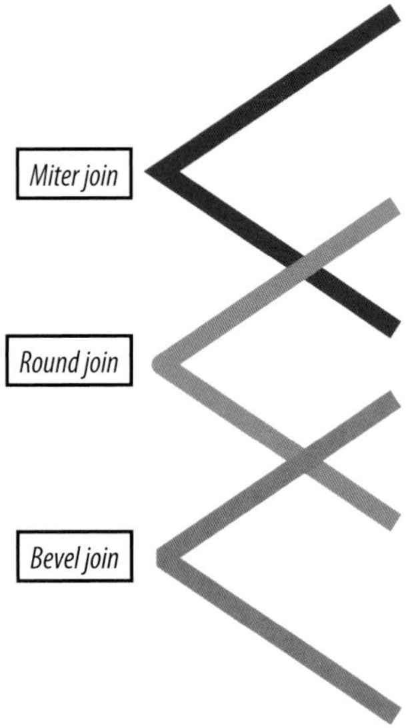

Miter join

Round join

Bevel join

Figure 43 Miter limit affects the length of stroked corner points

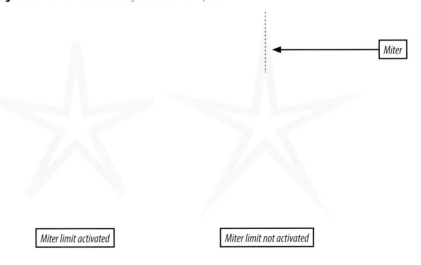

Miter

Miter limit activated

Miter limit not activated

Creating a Dashed Stroke

A dashed stroke is like any other stroked path in Illustrator, except that its stroke has been broken up into a sequence of dashes separated by gaps. The Stroke panel offers you the freedom to customize dashed or dotted lines by entering the lengths of the dashes and the gaps between them in the six dash and gap text boxes. You can create a maximum of three different sizes of dashes separated by three different sizes of gaps. The pattern you establish will be repeated across the length of the stroke.

When creating dashed strokes, remain conscious of the cap choice on the Stroke panel. **Butt caps** create familiar square dashes, and **round caps** create rounded dashes.

Creating a dotted line requires round caps. Figure 44 shows three dashed lines using the same pattern but with different caps applied. The red line is formatted with butt caps. The blue line is formatted with round caps. The green line is a dotted path. Dotted paths are formatted with round caps and a dash width of 0 pts.

Improving the Appearance of a Dashed Stroke

The Stroke panel offers two helpful settings for working with dashed lines—"Preserves exact gap and dash lengths" (Exact dashes) and "Aligns dashes and corners to path ends, adjusting lengths to fit" (Adjust dashes). These settings affect how dashes are distributed along a stroked path or the edge of a stroked object. Figure 45 shows each option. The red rectangle is an

example of the Exact dashes option. The dashes are distributed around the edge of the rectangle with the exact measurements input in the Stroke panel, regardless of the resulting appearance. In this case, the appearance leaves a bit to be desired. Each of the four corners looks different from the others, which is a bit disconcerting.

The blue rectangle is an example of the Adjust dashes option. Though the measurements for the dashed stroke are the same as those input for the red rectangle, here the Adjust dashes option automatically adjusts the position and gaps of the dash so the corners all look the same and the overall dashed effect is balanced.

Creating Pseudo-stroke Effects

Strokes around objects, especially black strokes, often contribute much to an illustration in terms of contrast, dimension, and dramatic effect. A classic technique that designers have used since the early versions of Illustrator is the "pseudo-stroke," or false stroke. Basically, you place a black-filled copy behind an illustration element, then distort the black element with the Direct Selection tool so it "peeks" out from behind the element in varying degrees.

This technique, as shown in Figure 46, is relatively simple to execute and can be used for dramatic effect in an illustration.

Figure 44 Caps are an important factor in determining the appearance of a dotted line

Figure 45 Gap and dash options applied to a stroke

Figure 46 The "pseudo-stroke" effect

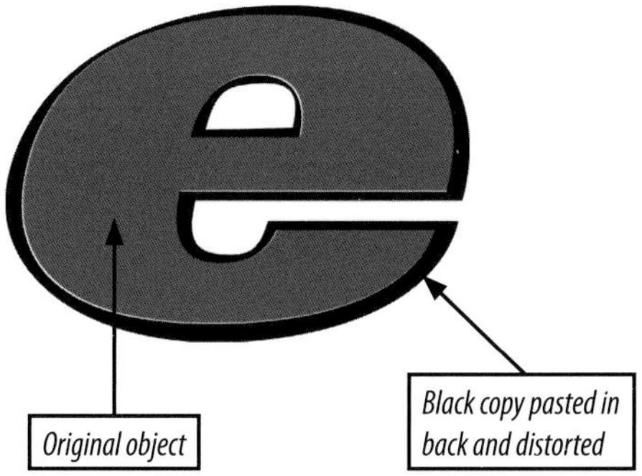

Original object

Black copy pasted in back and distorted

Modify stroke attributes

1. Select the **eyebrow**, the **nose**, and the **mouth**.

2. Click **Select** on the menu bar, then click **Inverse**.

   The selected items are now deselected, and the deselected items are selected.

3. Hide the selected items, then open the **Stroke panel**.

4. Select all, then change the **stroke weight** to **3 pt**.

5. Click the **Stroke panel menu button** ≡ , click **Show Options** if options are hidden, then click the **Round Cap button** ◖ .

   The caps on open paths are rounded.

6. On the Stroke panel, click the **Bevel Join button** ┏ .

   The miter joins on the mouth and nose change to bevel joins, as shown in Figure 47.

7. On the **Stroke panel**, click the **Round Join button** ┏ .

The bevel joins on the mouth and nose change to round joins, as shown in Figure 48.

8. Remove the stroke from the teeth.

TIP Use the Direct Selection tool ▷. to select the teeth, since they are grouped with the mouth.

You hid elements so you could focus on the eyebrow, nose, and mouth. You applied round caps to the open paths and round joins to the corner points.

Figure 47 Bevel joins applied to paths

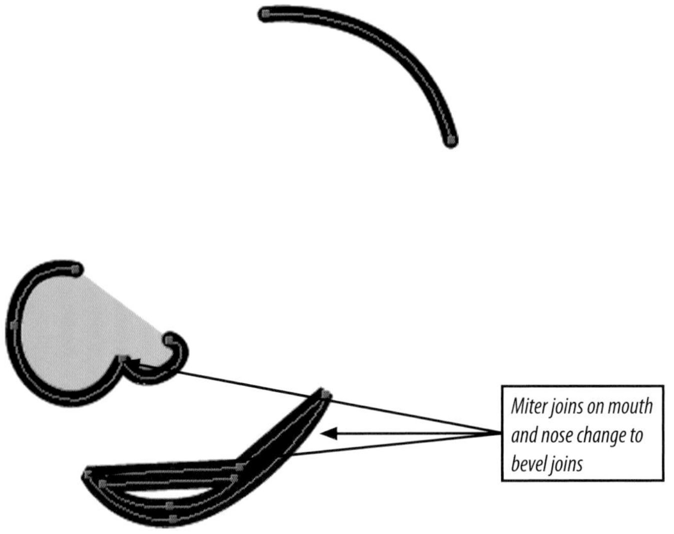

Miter joins on mouth and nose change to bevel joins

Figure 48 Round joins applied to paths

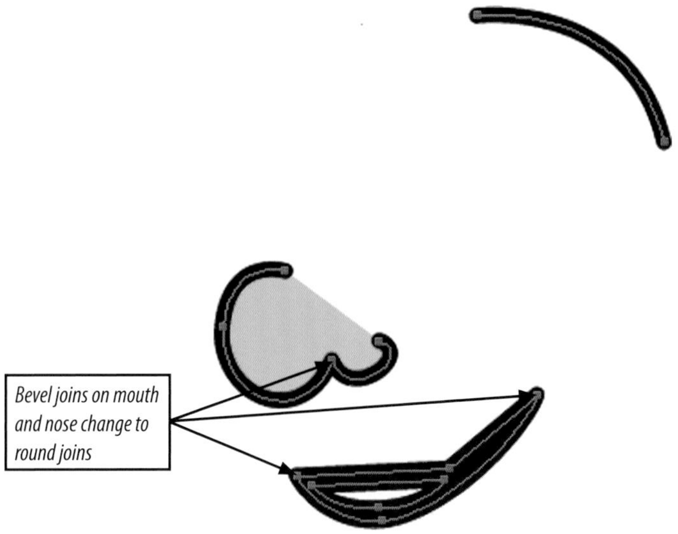

Bevel joins on mouth and nose change to round joins

Create a dashed and dotted stroke

1. Show all objects, then select all.

2. Deselect the snowball, then hide the selected items.

   The snowball should be the only element showing.

3. Select the **snowball**, then change the **stroke weight** to **4 pt**.

4. Click the **Dashed Line check box** on the Stroke panel.

5. Experiment with different dash and gap sizes.

6. Toggle between Butt and Round Caps.

   The dashes change from rectangles to ovals.

7. Enter **1 pt. dashes** and **4 pt. gaps**.

8. Click the **Round Cap button** , verify that the **Adjust dashes option** is activated, then compare your snowball to the one shown in Figure 49.

9. Show all the objects that are currently hidden.

10. Save your work, then continue to the next set of steps.

You applied a dashed stroke to the snowball object and noted how a change in caps affected the dashes.

Figure 49 Creating a dotted stroke using the Stroke panel

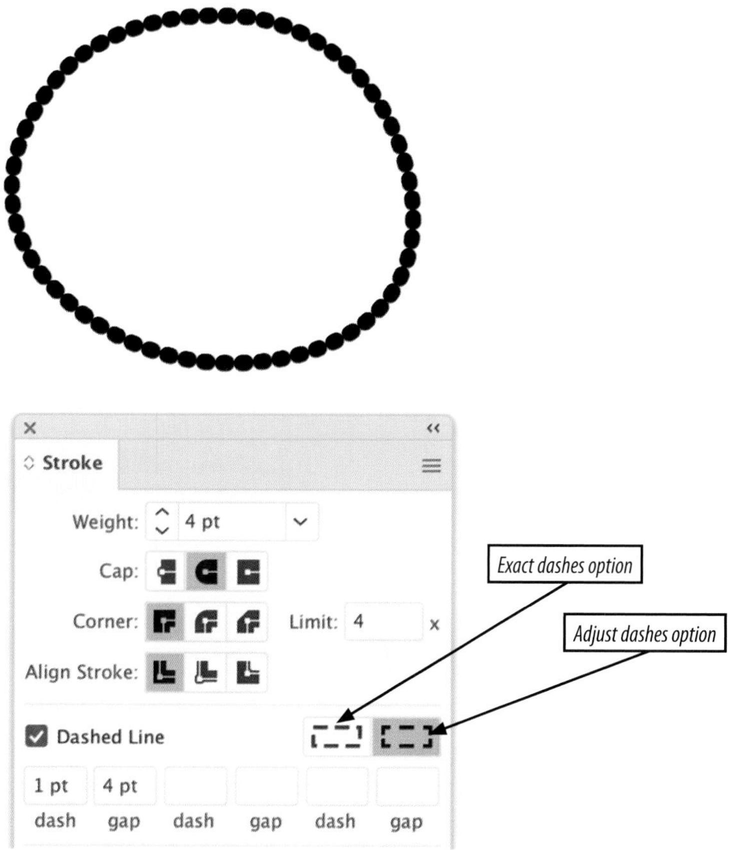

Create pseudo-strokes

1. Select the **pom-pom**, copy it, then paste in back.

2. Apply a **black fill** to the copy.

TIP The copy is still selected behind the original white pom-pom, making it easy to apply the black fill.

3. Click the **white pom-pom**, then remove the stroke.

4. Lock the **white pom-pom**.

5. Using the **Direct Selection tool** 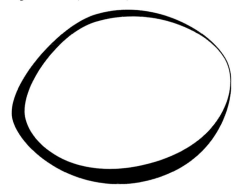, select the **bottom anchor point** on the black copy.

6. Use the **arrow keys** on your keypad to move the **anchor point 5 pts. down**.

    More and more of the black copy is revealed as its size is increased beneath the locked white pom-pom.

7. Move the **left anchor point 4 pts. to the left**.

8. Move the **top anchor point 2 pts. up**, then deselect.

    Your work should resemble Figure 50.

9. Using the same methods and Figure 51 as a reference, create distorted black copies behind all the remaining elements except the torso, the mouth, and the eyebrow.

10. Save your work, then close the Snowball Assembled document.

You created black copies behind each element, then distorted them, using the Direct Selection tool and the arrow keys, to create the illusion of uneven black strokes around the object.

Figure 50 Pom-pom with the pseudo-stroke effect

Figure 51 Completed illustration

USE IMAGE TRACE

Using Image Trace

Image Trace is a feature that converts a bitmap image into a vector image so you can modify it as you would a vector graphic. When you place and select an image, the Image Trace button becomes available on the Control panel. Click the triangle beside the Image Trace button to expose the Image Trace menu, shown in Figure 52. Image Trace offers many tracing presets that give you different results. These presets include Line Art, Sketched Art, Black and White Logo, and 16 Colors.

In addition to the options in the Image Trace menu, you can use the Image Trace panel, shown in Figure 53. Here you can click the Preset list arrow to choose which type of preset you want to use to trace the bitmap. Click the Preview check box to see a preview of your image as you click on different presets.

Figure 52 Tracing presets in the Image Trace menu

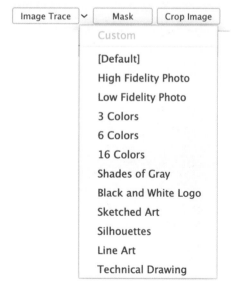

Figure 53 Image Trace panel

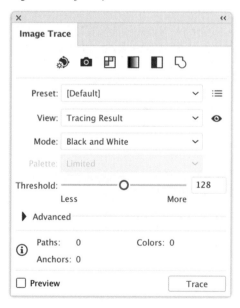

The Image Trace panel is dynamic if the Preview option is activated. The selected image will update with any changes you make in the panel. Click the View menu to see the Tracing Results, or switch to Outline view to see just the paths being created by the tracing utility. Drag the Colors slider to increase or decrease the number of colors available for the resulting trace. Figure 54 shows the traced image reduced to six colors.

TIP The Colors slider is called the Threshold slider when you are working with black and white only.

Tracing a Line Art Sketch

Figure 55 shows a magic marker sketch of a dog that has been scanned into Photoshop and placed in Illustrator. Figure 56 shows the artwork after it has been traced using the Sketched Art preset in the Image Trace panel. Not much difference, you say? Images can be deceiving. Though the images in Figures 55 and 56 appear to be similar, they couldn't be more different because the artwork in Figure 56 is a vector graphic that has been traced from the bitmap graphic shown in Figure 55.

Figure 54 Traced image

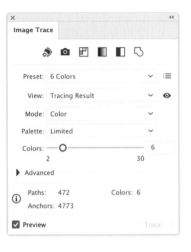

Figure 55 Bitmap graphic placed in Illustrator

Figure 56 Traced graphic

Tracing a Photograph

You use Image Trace to trace a bitmap photo the same way you trace a sketch. With photographic images especially, the presets list can be used to create some really interesting illustration effects. Figure 57 shows four different vector graphics, each traced with a different preset and with different color settings.

Expanding a Traced Graphic

After Image Trace has been executed, the Expand button becomes available on the Control panel. To select and modify the paths and points that make up the new vector graphic, you must first click the Expand button. Once expanded, the illustration is available to be selected and modified, as shown in Figure 58.

Especially when tracing photographs, the Image Trace utility creates illustrations with complex relationships between different paths. Working with expanded tracing results will often test your skills for working with paths.

Figure 57 Four traced graphics

Figure 58 Expanded artwork with selectable components

Whenever you link to or embed artwork from another file, such as a TIF file from Photoshop, that file will be listed on the Links panel along with any metadata that has been saved with the file. The Links panel shows a thumbnail of the artwork and the filename to help you identify the file. The Links panel also uses icons to indicate the artwork's status, such as whether the link is up to date, the file is missing, or the file has been modified since you placed it. You can use the Links panel to see and manage all linked or embedded artwork. To select and view a linked graphic, select a link and then click the Go To Link button, or choose Go To Link on the Links panel menu. The file will appear centered in the window.

When you place an image, the Control panel lists the name of the placed file, its color mode (usually RGB, CMYK, or Grayscale), and its resolution in PPI (pixels per inch). The resolution listing is the effective resolution—in other words, the resolution of the file as its size in Illustrator. If you scale up a placed image, its effective resolution goes down, and the resolution listing on the Control panel will update to show the decrease. In the converse, if you scale down a placed image, its effective resolution increases.

Click on the filename on the Control panel to reveal a menu of options, shown in Figure 59. These commands help you to manage the link to the placed file. For example, click Go To Link, and the placed file will be centered in your window; this can be very helpful when working with many images. Click Edit Original to open the placed file in its native application. Click Relink to reestablish the link to the placed image if you've moved it to a different location on your computer or server.

These commands are all available on the Links panel, shown in Figure 60. Note the yellow triangle with the exclamation point, which indicates that the placed file has been modified in its native application since being placed. In other words, the original is different from the placed file. Click the Update Link icon on the Links panel or on the Control panel to update the link and bring the placed file in sync with the original file.

Figure 59 Link options on the Control panel

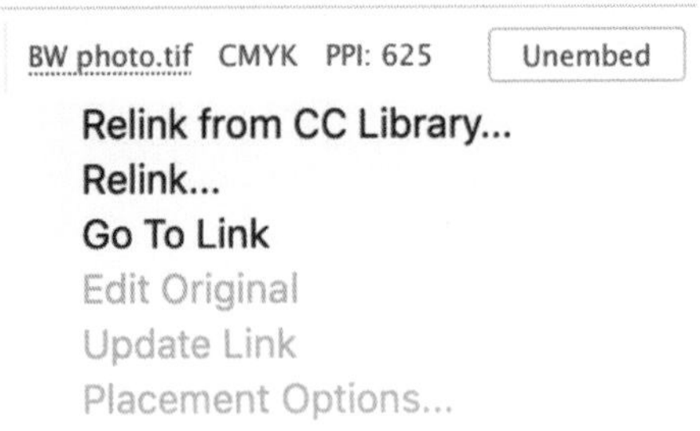

BW photo.tif   CMYK   PPI: 625   [Unembed]

Relink from CC Library...
Relink...
Go To Link
Edit Original
Update Link
Placement Options...

Embedding Placed Images

Another important option on the Control panel is the **Embed** button. When you place a file, that file is not automatically a part of the Illustrator file. Instead, a link is created from Illustrator to that file. If you were to move the Illustrator file to a different computer—or email it to a friend—the placed image would not be available when the file is opened on the

Figure 60 Links panel

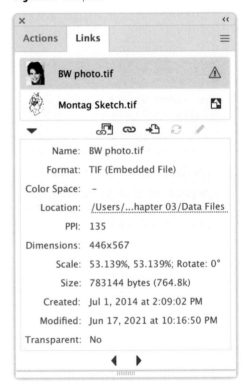

other computer. The link would be broken. For this reason, many designers choose to click the Embed button; doing so is like copying and pasting the placed file into the Illustrator document. The placed image no longer links to an original; it is in the Illustrator document and saved with the Illustrator document.

TIP To unembed an image, click Unembed on the Control panel or click the Links panel menu button, then click Unembed. You will be prompted to save the image to your hard drive.

Use Image Trace to trace a sketch

1. Open AI 3-5.ai, then save it as **Image Trace Sketch**.

The file contains a placed marker sketch that was scanned in Photoshop.

2. Click the **Selection tool** ▶, then click the **placed graphic**.

When the placed graphic is selected, the Image Trace button on the Control panel becomes visible.

3. On the Control panel, click **Image Trace**.

A progress bar appears while the placed image is being traced. Once completed, the Expand button appears on the Control panel.

4. On the Control panel, click **Expand**.

As shown in Figure 61, the traced graphic is expanded into vector objects.

5. Deselect all; then, using the **Direct Selection tool** ▷, select and fill the illustration with whatever colors you like. Figure 62 shows one example.

6. Save your work, then close the Image Trace Sketch document.

You used the Image Trace utility on the Control panel to convert a placed sketch into vector objects.

Figure 61 Expanded artwork

Use Image Trace to trace a photo

1. Open AI 3-6.ai, then save it as **Image Trace Photo**.

The file contains a placed image that was scanned into Photoshop.

2. Zoom in on the photo, click the **Selection tool** ▶, select the **graphic**, then open the **Image Trace panel** from the Window menu.

3. Click the **Preset list arrow**, then click **Line Art**.

Continued on next page

Figure 62 One example of the painted illustration

4. Click the **Mode list arrow**, then click **Grayscale**.

5. Click the **Preview check box** if necessary.

   Your panel and image should resemble Figure 63.

6. Click the **Mode list arrow**, then click **Color**.

7. Drag the **Colors slider** to **4**, then compare your result to Figure 64.

8. Click **Expand** on the Control panel, then deselect all.

9. Click the **Direct Selection tool** 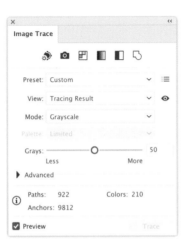, then select and fill the objects that make up the illustration. Figure 65 shows one example.

10. Save your work, then close Image Trace Photo.

You used the Image Trace panel to explore various tracing and color options, watching the result update dynamically.

Figure 63 Previewing the Image Trace results

Figure 64 Changing the results to four colors only

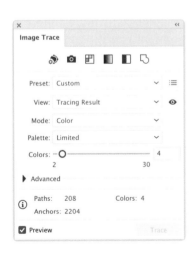

Figure 65 Coloring the expanded artwork

USE THE LIVE PAINT BUCKET TOOL

▶ *What You'll Do*

In this lesson, you will use the Live Paint Bucket tool and the Live Paint Selection tool, learn about regions and edges, and paint live paint groups

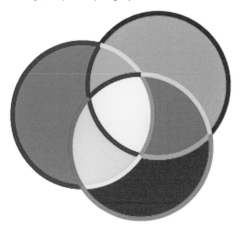

Using the Live Paint Features

When Adobe launched the Live Paint Bucket tool, they called it "revolutionary," and that was not an overstatement. The Live Paint Bucket tool breaks all the fundamental rules of Illustrator and creates some new ones. For that reason, when you are working with the Live Paint Bucket tool, it's a good idea to think of yourself as working in Live Paint mode because Illustrator will function differently with this tool than it will with any other. Essentially, the Live Paint Bucket tool is designed to make painting easier and more intuitive. It does this by changing the basic rules of Illustrator objects. In Live Paint mode, the concept of "objects" no

longer applies—you can fill and stroke negative spaces. The Live Paint Bucket tool uses two object types called regions and edges. **Regions** and **edges** are comparable to fills and strokes, but they are "live." As shown in Figure 66, where two regions overlap, a third region is created and can be painted with its own color.

Adobe likes to say that Live Paint is intuitive—something that looks like it should be able to be filled with its own color can indeed be filled with its own color. As long the Live Paint Bucket tool is selected, selected objects can be filled using the new rules of Live Paint mode. Once you leave Live Paint mode, the paint that you have applied to the graphic remains part of the illustration.

Figure 66 Identifying regions and edges in an illustration

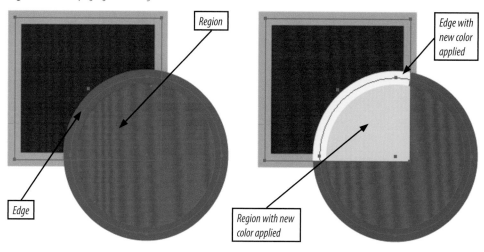

Live Painting Regions

Figure 67 shows three selected rectangles that overlap each other. The selection marks show various shapes created by the overlap. As stated earlier, these overlapping areas or shapes are called regions. To fill the regions, you must first select all the objects that you want to paint. Click the Live Paint Bucket tool, click a color on the Swatches panel, then click a region that you want to fill. As shown in Figure 68, when you position the Live Paint Bucket tool pointer over a region, that region is highlighted. Then when you click the Live Paint Bucket tool, the region is filled, as shown in Figure 69.

As shown in Figure 70, each region can be filled with new colors. But that's not all that the Live Paint Bucket tool has to offer. The "live" part of Live Paint is that these regions are now part of a **Live Paint group**, and they maintain a dynamic relationship with each other. This means that when any of the objects is moved, the overlapping area changes shape and fill accordingly. For example, in Figure 71, the tall, thin rectangle has been moved to the left. Note how the overlapping regions have been redrawn and how their fills have updated with the move.

TIP To select multiple regions in a Live Paint group, click the **Live Paint Selection tool** 🖫, on the toolbar, click the first region, press and hold [shift], then click the remaining regions. The selected regions appear with a gray dotted fill pattern until you click a new color on the Swatches panel and deselect the artwork.

Figure 67 Three overlapping selected rectangles

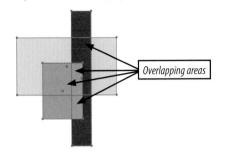

Overlapping areas

Figure 68 Positioning the Live Paint Bucket tool pointer

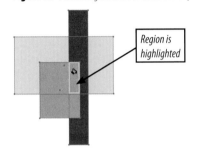

Region is highlighted

Figure 69 Filling a region with a new color

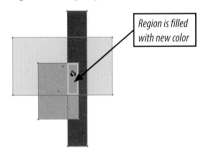

Region is filled with new color

Figure 70 Filling multiple regions

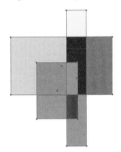

Figure 71 Moving an object in a Live Paint group

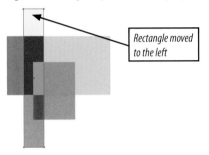

Rectangle moved to the left

Painting Virtual Regions

The intuitive aspect of Live Paint mode goes one step further with virtual regions. Figure 72 shows six Illustrator paths; each path is selected and has a 1 pt. black stroke and no fill. This simple illustration provides a perfect example of the powers of the Live Paint Bucket tool.

Imagine trying to fill the four center polygons created by the overlapping strokes in "classic"

Illustrator without the Live Paint Bucket tool. This seemingly simple goal would be a very tough challenge. You would need to create four polygons that align perfectly with the shapes created by the overlapping strokes because without the shapes, you'd have nothing to fill. And because the strokes are so thin, you'd need those polygons to align exactly with the strokes. Finally, if you moved any of the strokes, you'd need to modify the polygons to match the new layout.

With the Live Paint Bucket tool, the regions that are created by the intersection of the paths can be filled as though they were objects. Figure 73 shows four regions that have been filled with the Live Paint Bucket tool.

In this case, as in the case of the overlapping rectangles, the dynamic relationship is maintained. Figure 74 shows the paths moved, the filled regions redrawn, and their fills updated.

Figure 72 Six paths

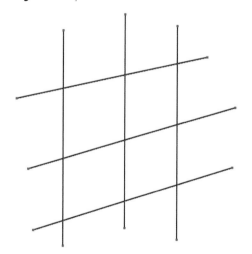

Figure 73 Four filled regions between paths

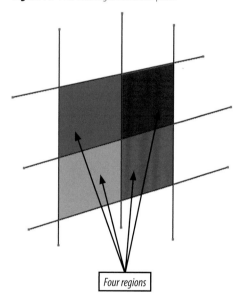

Four regions

Figure 74 Moving paths in a Live Paint group

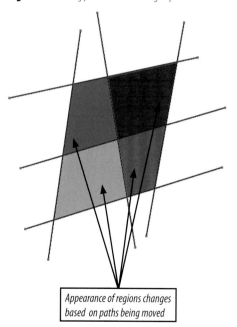

Appearance of regions changes based on paths being moved

Inserting an Object into a Live Paint Group

New objects can be inserted into a Live Paint group. To do so, switch to the Selection tool, then double-click inside any of the regions of the group. As shown in Figure 75, a gray rectangle appears around the group, indicating that you are in insertion mode. Once in **insertion mode**, you can then add an object or objects to the group.

As shown in Figure 76, another tall rectangle has been added to the group. It can now be painted with the Live Paint Bucket tool as part of the Live Paint group. Once you've added all that you want to the Live Paint group, exit insertion mode by double-clicking the Selection tool outside of the Live Paint group.

Expanding a Live Paint Group

When you are done colorizing a Live Paint group, you have the option of using the Expand command to release the Live Paint group into its component regions. Simply select the Live Paint group, then click the Expand button on the Control panel. Each region will be converted to an ordinary Illustrator object.

Figure 75 Viewing the art in insertion mode

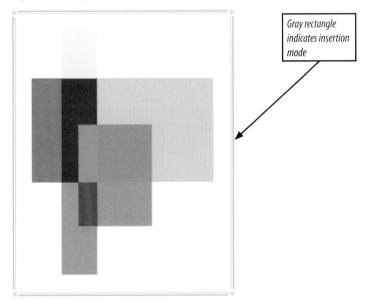

Gray rectangle indicates insertion mode

Figure 76 Adding an object to the Live Paint group

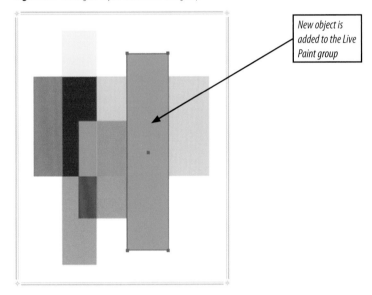

New object is added to the Live Paint group

Live Painting Edges

In Live Paint mode, just as regions are akin to fills, edges are akin to strokes. With the Live Paint Bucket tool, you can paint edges as well as regions.

Figure 77 shows two overlapping objects, each with a 6 pt. stroke. To paint edges (strokes), you must first double-click the Live Paint Bucket tool, then activate the Paint Strokes check box in the Live Paint Bucket Options dialog box, as shown in Figure 78. When activated, the Live Paint Bucket tool will paint either regions or edges, depending on where it's positioned.

When you position the Live Paint Bucket tool over an edge, its icon changes to a paintbrush icon. The edge is highlighted and paintable as though it were its own object, as shown in Figure 79.

Figure 77 Two overlapping rectangles

Figure 78 Choosing the Paint Strokes option

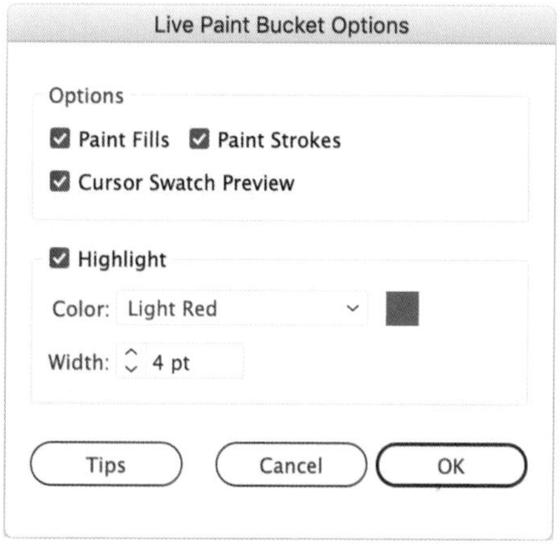

Figure 79 Painting edges

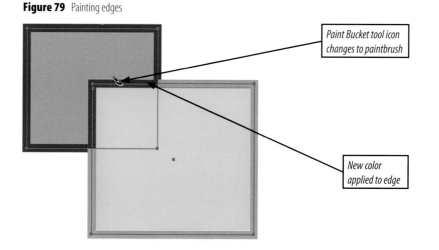

Paint Bucket tool icon changes to paintbrush

New color applied to edge

Use the Live Paint Bucket tool

1. Open AI 3-7.ai, then save it as **Live Paint Circles**.

2. Open the **Swatches panel**, fill the **top circle** with **red**, fill the **left circle** with **green**, then fill the **right circle** with **blue**.

3. Select all, double-click the **Live Paint Bucket tool** 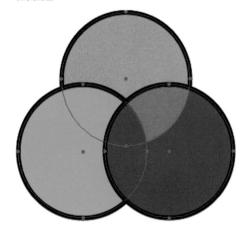 to open the Live Paint Bucket Options dialog box, verify that both the **Paint Fills** and **Paint Strokes check boxes** are checked, then click **OK**.

   TIP The Live Paint Bucket tool 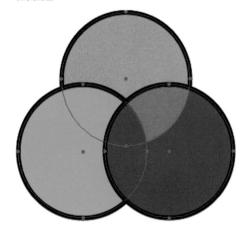 is located behind the Shape Builder tool 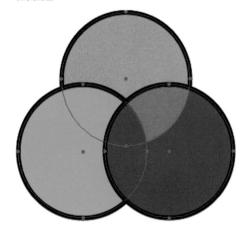 .

4. Click any of the **orange swatches** on the Swatches panel.

   Note that because you are in Live Paint mode, none of the selected objects change to orange when you click the orange swatch.

5. Position the **Live Paint Bucket tool pointer** over the **red fill of the red circle**, then click.

6. Click any **pink swatch** on the Swatches panel, position the **Live Paint Bucket tool pointer** over the area where the **orange circle overlaps the blue circle**, then click.

   As shown in Figure 80, the region of overlap between the two circles is filled with pink.

7. Using any colors you like, fill all seven regions so your artwork resembles Figure 81.

8. Click the **stroke button** on the toolbar to activate the stroke, then choose any **purple swatch** on the Swatches panel, position the **Live Paint Bucket tool pointer** over any of the **black strokes** in the artwork, then click.

   When positioned over a stroke, the Live Paint Bucket tool pointer changes to a paintbrush icon.

9. Using any color you like, change the color of all 12 edges, then deselect all so your artwork resembles Figure 82.

Figure 80 Painting the region that is the overlap between two circles

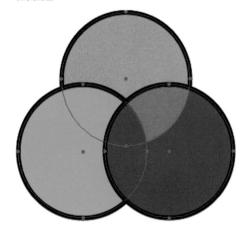

Figure 81 Viewing seven painted regions

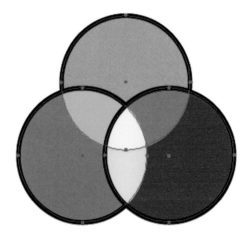

Figure 82 Viewing 12 painted edges

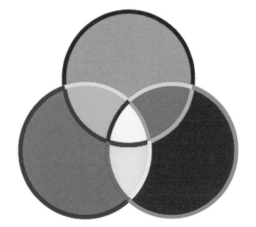

10. Deselect all; click the **Direct Selection tool** ; then, without pulling them apart, drag the **circles** in different directions, noting that the components of the Live Paint group maintain a dynamic relationship as shown in Figure 83.

11. Select all, click **Expand** on the Control panel, deselect all, then pull out all the regions so your artwork resembles Figure 84.

The illustration has been expanded into multiple objects.

12. Save your work, then close the Live Paint Circles document.

You used the Live Paint Bucket tool to fill various regions and edges of three overlapping circles. You then moved various components of the Live Paint group, noting that they maintain a dynamic relationship. Finally, you expanded the Live Paint group, which changed your original circles into multiple objects.

Figure 83 Exploring the dynamic relationship between regions in a Live Paint group

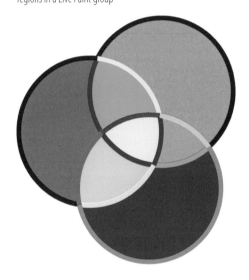

Figure 84 Dissecting the expanded Live Paint group

Use the Live Paint Bucket tool to paint an illustration

1. Open AI 3-8.ai, then save it as **Live Paint Dog**.

2. Click the **Selection tool** 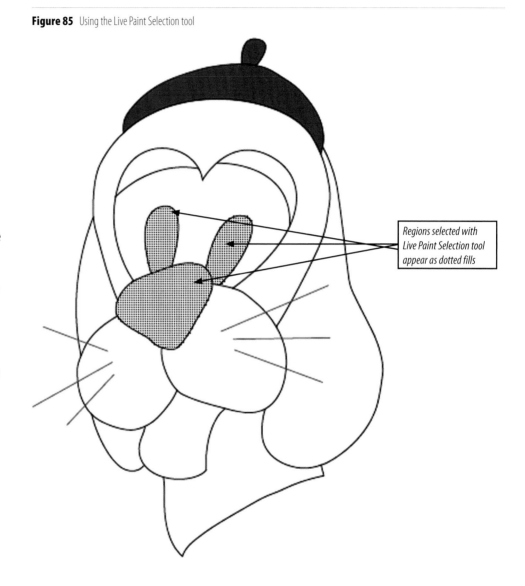, then click the **different colored strokes** so you understand how the illustration has been drawn.

   The illustration has been created with a series of open paths. The only closed path is the nose.

3. Select all, then change the **stroke color** of all the **paths** to **Black**.

4. Click the **Live Paint Bucket tool**, then click a **red swatch** on the Swatches panel.

   Note that because you are in Live Paint mode, none of the selected objects changes to red when you click the red swatch.

5. Press **[command] (Mac)** or **[Ctrl] (Win)** to switch to the **Selection tool**, click the **artboard** to deselect all, then release **[command] (Mac)** or **[Ctrl] (Win)** to return to the **Live Paint Bucket tool**.

6. Fill the **hat** and the **knot** at the top of the hat with **red**, then click **Black** on the Swatches panel.

7. Click the **Live Paint Selection tool**, click the **nose**, press and hold **[shift]**, click the **left eye**, then click the **right eye**.

   Your illustration should resemble Figure 85.

   TIP When you select multiple areas with the Live Paint Selection tool, the areas are filled with a dot pattern until you apply a color.

Figure 85 Using the Live Paint Selection tool

Regions selected with Live Paint Selection tool appear as dotted fills

8. Click **Black** on the Swatches panel.

9. Using the same method, select **both eyelids**, then fill them with a **lavender swatch**.

10. Click the **Live Paint Bucket tool** , click a **yellow swatch** on the Swatches panel, then paint the illustration so your illustration resembles Figure 86.

    Note the small areas between the whiskers that must be painted yellow.

11. Using the **Live Paint Bucket tool** , paint the **right jowl light brown**, paint the **left jowl a darker brown**, then paint the **tongue pink**.

12. Click the **stroke button** on the toolbar to activate the stroke, then click a **gray swatch** on the Swatches panel.

13. Double-click the **Live Paint Bucket tool** , click the **Paint Stroke check box** in the Live Paint Bucket Options dialog box if it is not already checked, then click **OK**.

14. Click the **Live Paint Bucket tool** on **each line segment that makes up the dog's whiskers**.

TIP You will need to click 14 times to paint the six whiskers because each whisker is made from more than one line segment.

Continued on next page

Figure 86 Painting the yellow regions

15. Deselect, compare your work to Figure 87, save your work, then close the Live Paint Dog document.

You used the Live Paint Bucket tool to fill regions created by the intersection of a collection of open paths. You also used the tool to paint edges.

Figure 87 Viewing the finished artwork

EXPLORE ALTERNATE DRAWING TECHNIQUES

In this lesson, you will learn some new and fun drawing techniques including how to reshape a path with the Anchor Point tool and how to change Pencil tool settings to draw the way you want to.

Reshaping Path Segments with the Anchor Point Tool

Along with its ability to convert smooth anchor points to corner anchor points and vice versa, the Anchor Point tool can also convert path segments from straight to curved. In fact, the Anchor Point tool is so powerful that you can use it as an alternate to dragging directional handles to modify a curve. Instead, you can click and drag any segment with the Anchor Point tool to reshape it and position it as you like.

Figure 88 shows a shape created from a simple rectangle. No directional handles were manipulated to create these curves. Instead, the original straight segments were curved and reshaped using the Anchor Point tool.

When you're creating paths with the Pen tool, you can access the Anchor Point tool and the path segment reshape function simply by pressing [option] (Mac) or [Alt] (Win).

In practice, you'll likely use a combination of both methods—dragging directional handles

and dragging path segments—but you'll find that the Anchor Point tool adds a more freehand, intuitive option.

Drawing with the Pencil Tool

With the widespread use of tablets and pen styluses, advances in Illustrator's Pencil tool are making the tool a great option for drawing by hand. For many designers, it's become a real alternative to the Pen tool.

Figure 88 A curved object reshaped from a simple rectangle

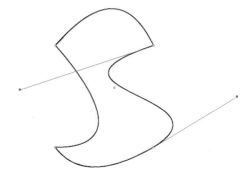

Setting specific options is important for making the tool practical for drawing. In Figure 89, note that the Fidelity slider is set to Smooth. At this setting, relatively uneven lines you draw using your stylus and tablet will smooth out automatically.

Figure 90 shows a relatively uneven line being drawn with the Pencil tool. Figure 91 shows the same path once the Pencil tool is lifted. The path is automatically smoothed out and anchor points are added at necessary locations.

Note the Keep selected option in Figure 89. When this option is activated, you can add to a path you've already drawn by floating over an open anchor point and continuing your drawing with the Pencil tool. Essentially, this allows you to draw on your screen with the Pencil tool as you would draw on a piece of paper with a real pencil.

The Edit selected paths option is a critical one that has a big effect on how the Pencil tool works. It's one you might have to activate and deactivate to draw certain types of artwork.

Figure 89 Pencil Tool Options dialog box

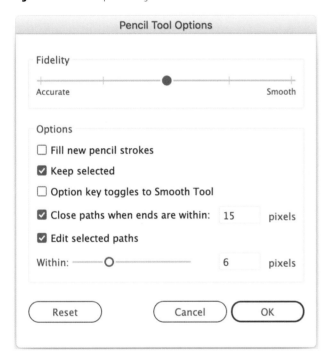

Figure 90 Rough line being drawn

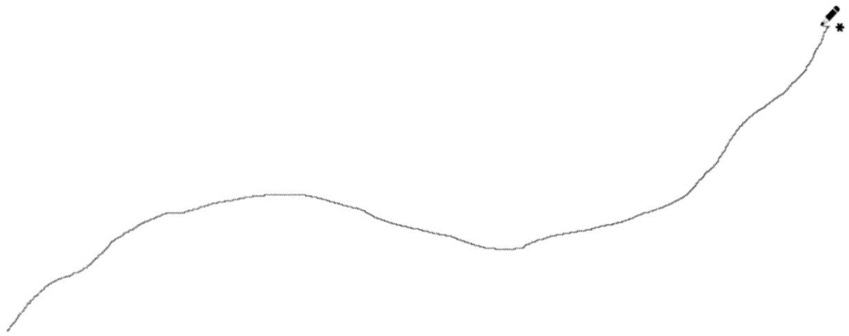

Figure 91 Rough line smoothed automatically

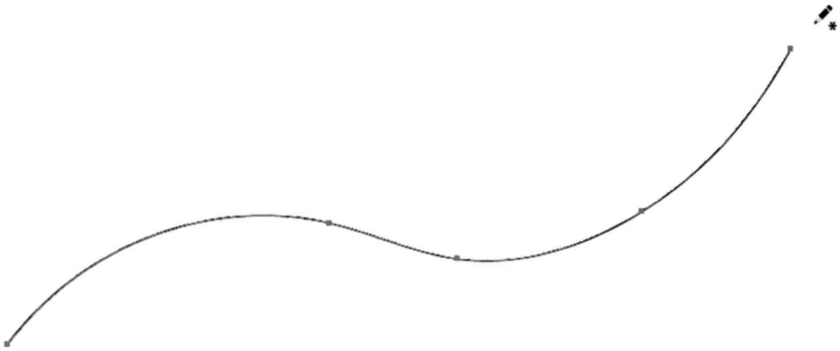

Figure 92 shows a simple, hand-drawn circle done with the Pencil tool. If you want to draw a line across the circle, as shown in Figure 93, you must do so with the Edit selected paths option *deactivated*. If the Edit selected paths option is activated, drawing the line across the circle will edit the circle and redraw it with the new line, as shown in Figure 94.

On the other hand, the Edit selected paths option can be very useful for doing just that—editing paths while you draw. If you want to tweak a line, simply draw over it and the path will redraw with the new line.

TIP Press [shift] while drawing with the Pencil tool  to draw in straight lines.

Figure 92 Simple circle

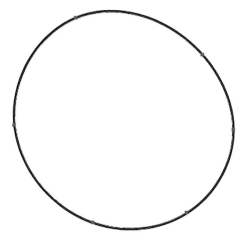

Figure 93 Circle with line drawn across it

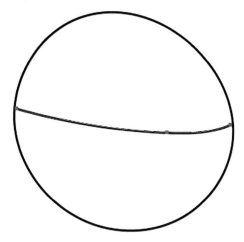

Figure 94 Circle redrawn with new line

Reshape path segments with the Anchor Point tool

1. Open AI 3-9.ai, then save it as **Reshape Path**.

2. Click the **Anchor Point tool** 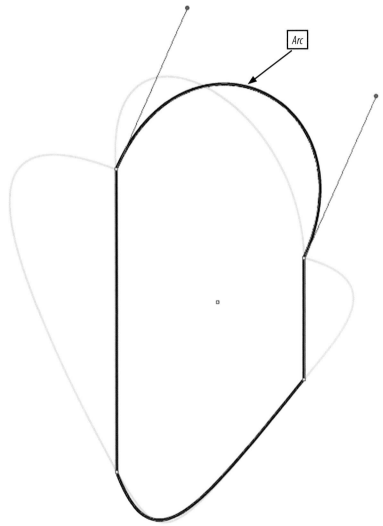.

   The Anchor Point tool is behind the Pen tool.

   TIP You can access the Anchor Point tool by pressing [shift] [C] on your keypad. If you are drawing with the Pen tool, you can press [option] (Mac) or [Alt] (Win) to quickly switch to the Anchor Point tool.

3. Drag the **bottom black path segment** as many times as necessary to align it to the blue line.

   In this exercise, you will drag only path segments; don't drag any anchor points or any directional handles. This exercise is intended to show that you can use the Anchor Point tool alone to reshape any path. Depending on where you click, you can eventually modify a path into any shape.

4. Drag the **right black segment** to align it to the blue line.

5. Using Figure 95 as a reference, drag the **top black segment** up then, as you're dragging, press the **[shift] key** and keep dragging to make the **arc** shown in the figure.

   With the [shift] key pressed, the directional handles are even and the arc is balanced on both sides.

6. Drag the **arc** left so it aligns with the top blue path.

7. Reshape the remaining paths to match the blue shape.

8. Save your work, then close Reshape Path.

You used the Anchor Point tool to reshape an object.

Figure 95 Reshaping the segment with the [shift] key in play

Arc

Draw with the Pencil tool

1. Open AI 3-10.ai, then save it as **Pencil Tool**.

2. Set the **fill color** to **[None]**, set the **stroke color** to **Black**, then set the **stroke weight** to **2 points**.

3. Double click the **Pencil tool** , then compare your Pencil Tool Options dialog box to Figure 96.

   Note that Fidelity is set to Smooth and that the Keep selected and Edit selected paths options are both activated.

Continued on next page

Figure 96 Pencil Tool Options dialog box

4. Click **OK**, then zoom in on the **top path** on the artboard.

5. Trace the **first half-circle** slowly, then release the mouse button.

   As you draw, the path is very jagged and rough, but when you release the mouse button, the path is smoothed out. As shown in Figure 97, the path is created with the minimum number of anchor points necessary.

6. Float over the **end point**, then draw the **second half-circle**.

   Because the Keep selected option is activated, the second segment you draw is connected to the first to create a single path.

7. Finish drawing the **top path**.

8. Zoom in on the **middle path** on the artboard.

9. Trace the **first half-circle**, then, *without releasing your finger from the mouse pointer*, press and hold **[shift]**, then trace the **straight horizontal line** so your path resembles Figure 98.

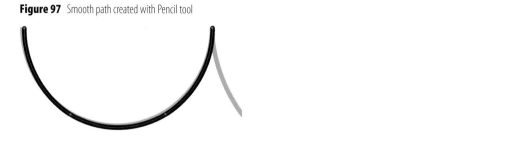

Figure 97 Smooth path created with Pencil tool

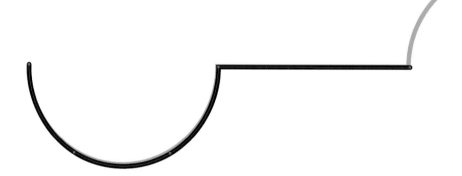

Figure 98 Straight segment added to curved segment

10. Using the same method, complete the trace in one move.

11. Zoom in on the path at the **bottom of the artboard**, then select it with the **Selection tool** 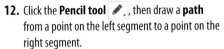 .

The path was drawn with the Pencil tool .

12. Click the **Pencil tool** , then draw a **path** from a point on the left segment to a point on the right segment.

As shown in Figure 99, because the Edit selected paths option is activated, the object is edited and redrawn with the new path.

13. Save your work, then close the Pencil Tool document.

You used the Pencil tool to trace different paths. You introduced the [shift] key to trace straight paths along with curved paths. With the Edit selected paths option activated, you edited a path by drawing a segment across an existing object.

Figure 99 Editing the path with the Pencil tool

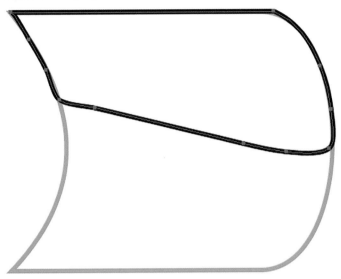

Draw straight lines

1. Open AI 3-11.ai, then save it as **Mighty Montag**.
2. Place the Montag Sketch.tif into the Mighty Montag document; you will need to navigate to the drive and folder where your Chapter 10 Data Files are stored to find it.
3. Position the sketch in the center of the artboard, then lock it.
4. Set the fill color to [None] and the stroke to 1 pt. Black.
5. Click the Pen tool, then starting with the two lines that represent the dog's neck, create a 4-sided shape for the neck.
   Don't worry that the shape is in front of the dog's tongue, ears, and jowls. It will eventually be placed behind them when you assemble the illustration.
6. Draw six whiskers.
7. Save your work.

Draw curved lines

1. Using the Pen tool, draw an oval for the eye.
2. Draw a crescent moon shape for the eyelid.
3. Draw an oval for the iris.
4. Save your work.

Draw elements of an illustration

1. Trace the left ear.
2. Trace the hat.
3. Trace the nose.
4. Trace the left jowl.
5. Trace the right jowl.
6. Trace the tongue.
7. Trace the right ear.
8. Trace the head.
9. Save your work.

Apply attributes to objects

1. Unlock the placed sketch and hide it.
2. Fill the hat with a red swatch.
3. Fill the right ear with 9C/18M/62Y.
4. Fill the nose with Black.
5. Fill the eye with White.
6. Fill the tongue with Salmon.
7. Using Figure 100 as a guide, use the colors on the Swatches panel to finish the illustration.
8. Save your work.

Assemble an illustration

1. Send the neck to the back of the stacking order, then lock it.
2. Send the head to the back, then lock it.
3. Send the left ear to the back, then lock it.
4. Bring the hat to the front.
5. Bring the right ear to the front.
6. Select the whiskers, group them, then bring them to the front.
7. Select the tongue, then cut it.
8. Select the right jowl, then apply the Paste in Back command.
9. Bring the nose to the front.
10. Select the eye, the eyelid, and the iris; then group them.
11. Drag and drop a copy of the eye group.

TIP Press and hold [option] (Mac) or [Alt] (Win) as you drag the eye group.

12. Select the right jowl.
13. On the Color panel add 10% K to darken the jowl.
14. Use the Color panel to change the fills on other objects to your liking.
15. Save your work.

Stroke objects for artistic effect

1. Make the caps on the whiskers round.
2. Change the whiskers' stroke weight to .5 pt.
3. Unlock all.
4. Select the neck and change the joins to round.
5. Apply pseudo-strokes to the illustration.

TIP Copy and paste the elements behind themselves, fill them with black, lock the top objects, then use the Direct Selection tool to select anchor points on the black-filled copies. Use the arrow keys on the keyboard to move the anchor points. The black copies will peek out from behind the elements in front.

6. Click Object on the menu bar, then click Unlock All.
7. Delete the Montag Sketch file behind your illustration.
8. Save your work, compare your illustration to Figure 100, then close the Mighty Montag document.

Figure 100 Completed Skills Review, Part 1

Use Image Trace

1. Open AI 3-12.ai, then save it as **Skills Trace Photo**.
2. Zoom in on the photo, click the Selection tool, select the graphic, then open the Image Trace panel.
3. Click the Preset list arrow on the Image Trace panel, then click Line Art.
4. Click the Mode list arrow, then click Grayscale.
5. Click to activate the Preview option if necessary.
6. Click the Mode list arrow, then click Color.
7. Drag the Colors slider to 6.
8. Click the Expand button on the Control panel, then deselect all.
9. Click the Direct Selection tool, then select and fill the objects that make up the illustration.
10. Figure 101 shows one example.
11. Save your work, then close the Skills Trace Photo document.

Figure 101 Completed Skills Review, Part 2

Morguefile

Use the Live Paint Bucket tool

1. Open AI 3-13.ai, then save it as **Live Paint Skills**.
2. Open the Swatches panel, fill the top circle with any orange swatch, fill the left circle with any blue swatch, then fill the right circle with any purple swatch.
3. Select all, then double-click the Live Paint Bucket tool to open the Live Paint Bucket Options dialog box, verify that both the Paint Fills and Paint Strokes check boxes are checked, then click OK.
4. Click any yellow swatch on the Swatches panel.
5. Position the Live Paint Bucket tool pointer over the orange fill of the orange circle, then click.
6. Click any pink swatch on the Swatches panel, position the Live Paint Bucket tool pointer over the area where the yellow circle overlaps the purple circle, then click.
7. Using any colors you like, fill the remaining five regions with different colors.
8. Click the stroke button on the toolbar, click any blue swatch on the Swatches panel, position the Live Paint Bucket tool pointer over any of the black strokes in the artwork, then click.
9. Using any color you like, change the color of all 12 edges, then deselect all.
10. Click the Direct Selection tool; then, without pulling them apart, drag the circles in different directions noticing that they stay grouped, as shown in Figure 102.
11. Save your work, then close the Live Paint Skills document.

Figure 102 Completed Skills Review, Part 3

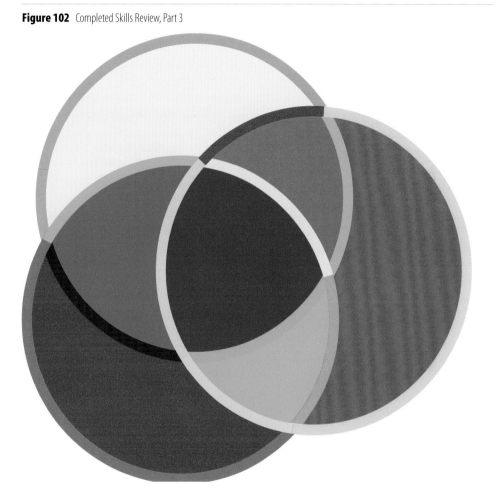

PROJECT BUILDER 1

The owner of The Blue Peppermill Restaurant has hired your design firm to take over all its marketing and advertising, saying it needs to expand its efforts. You request all The Blue Peppermill's existing materials, such as slides, prints, digital files, brochures, and business cards. Upon examination, you realize that the restaurant has no vector graphic version of its logo. Deciding that this is an indispensable element for future design and production, you scan in a photo of its signature peppermill, trace it, and apply a blue fill to it.

1. Create a new 6" × 6" document, then save it as **Peppermill**.
2. Place the Peppermill.tif file into the Peppermill document.

The Peppermill.tif file is in the Chapter 10 Data Files folder.

3. Scale the placed image 150%, then lock it.
4. Set the fill color to [None] and the stroke to 2 pt. Black.
5. Using the Zoom tool, create a selection box around the round element at the top of the peppermill to zoom in on it.
6. Using the Pen tool, trace the peppermill, adjusting your view as necessary to see various sections of the peppermill as you trace, then fill it with a blue swatch.
7. When you finish tracing, tweak the path, if necessary, then save your work.
8. Unlock the placed image and cut it from the document.
9. Save your work, compare your illustration to Figure 103, then close the Peppermill document.

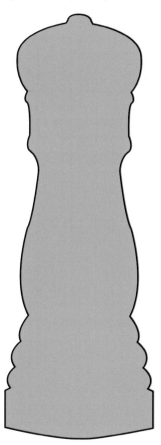

Figure 103 Completed Project Builder 1

PROJECT BUILDER 2

You work at a children's library that has recently been remodeled. The staff has asked you to create a mural theme with interesting shapes of bright colors for the freshly painted walls. You create a sample in Illustrator to present to the staff—a single theme that can be modified to create multiple versions of the artwork.

1. Open AI 3-14.ai, then save it as **Tic Tac Toe**.
2. Select all, then change the stroke colors to Black.
3. Click the Live Paint Bucket tool, select a fill color, then click in any of the squares.
4. Fill each of the squares with a different color, then deselect all.
5. Click the Direct Selection tool, then change the angles of the black paths. Figure 104 shows one possible result.
6. Save your work, then close Tic Tac Toe.

Figure 104 Completed Project Builder 2

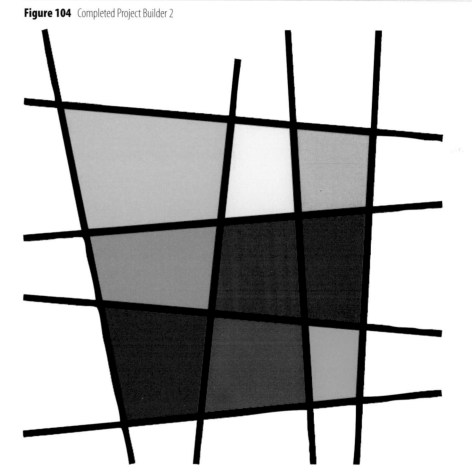

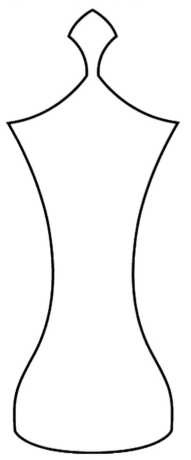

DESIGN PROJECT 1

Your design firm is contacted by a company called Stratagem with a request for a proposal. Stratagem manufactures molds for plastic products. The terms of the request are as follows: You are to submit a design for the shape of the bottle for a new dishwashing liquid. You are to submit a single image that shows a black line defining the shape. The line art should also include the nozzle. The size of the bottle is immaterial. The design is to be "sophisticated, so as to be in visual harmony with the modern home kitchen." The name of the product is "Sleek."

1. Go to the grocery store and purchase bottles of dishwashing liquid whose shape you find interesting.

2. Use the purchases for ideas and inspiration.
3. Sketch your idea for the bottle's shape on a piece of paper.
4. Take a picture of the sketch or scan it and save it as a TIF file.
5. Create a new Illustrator document, then save it as **Sleek Design**.
6. Place the scan in the document, then lock it.
7. Trace your sketch, using the Pen tool.
8. When you are done tracing, delete the sketch from the document.
9. Tweak the line to define the shape to your specifications.
10. Use the Average dialog box to align points to perfect the shape.
11. Save your work, compare your illustration to Figure 105, then close the Sleek Design document.

Figure 105 Completed Design Project 1

The classic sci-fi movie, *2001: A Space Odyssey*, includes a 20-minute "Dawn of Man" sequence that begins millions of years ago with a group of apes, presumably on the African plains. One day, *impossibly*, a tall, black, perfectly rectangular slab appears out of nowhere on the landscape. At first the apes are afraid of it, afraid to touch it. Eventually, they accept its presence.

Later, one ape looks upon a femur bone from a dead animal. With a dawning understanding, he uses the bone as a tool, first to kill for food and then to kill another ape from an enemy group. Victorious in battle, the ape hurls the bone into the air. The camera follows it up, up, up, and—in one of the most famous cuts in film history—the image switches from the white bone in the sky to the similar shape of a white spaceship floating in space.

1. How do you feel upon first seeing the "monolith" (the black rectangular slab)? Were you frightened? Do you sense that the monolith is good, evil, or neutral?
2. How would you describe the sudden appearance of the straight-edged, right-angled monolith against the landscape? What words describe the shapes of the landscape in contrast to the monolith?
3. Do you think perfect shapes exist in nature, or are they created entirely out of the imagination of human beings?
4. If perfect shapes exist—if they are real—can you name one example? If they are not real, how is it that humankind has proven so many concepts in mathematics that are based on shapes, such as the Pythagorean theorem?
5. What advancements and achievements of humankind have their basis in peoples' ability to conceive of abstract shapes?
6. Can it be said legitimately that the ability to conceive abstract shapes is an essential factor that distinguishes humankind from all the other species on the planet?
7. Create a new document, then save it as **Shape**.
8. In Adobe Illustrator, draw any shape you remember from the opening sequence, except the monolith.

Figure 106 A stamp printed in Great Britain for the Great British Film series shows 2001: *A Space Odyssey*; circa 2014

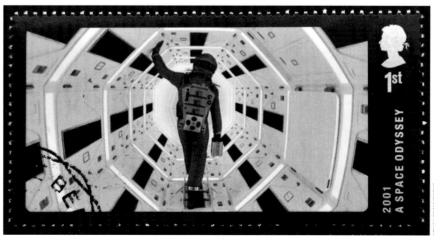

TRANSFORM AND DISTORT OBJECTS

CERTIFIED PROFESSIONAL

Adobe Certified Professional in Graphic Design and Illustration Using Adobe Illustrator

3. Organize Documents

This objective covers document structure such as layers and tracks, for efficient workflows.

3.2 Modify layer visibility using opacity and masks.

 B Create, apply, and manipulate clipping masks.

4. Creating and Modifying Visual Elements

This objective covers core tools and functionality of the application, as well as tools that affect the visual appearance of document elements.

4.4 Transform digital graphics and media.

 B Rotate, flip, and transform individual layers, objects, selections, groups, or graphical elements.

4.5 Use basic reconstructing and editing techniques to manipulate digital graphics and media.

 B Repair and reconstruct graphics.

 C Evaluate or adjust the appearance of objects, selections, or layers.

TRANSFORM OBJECTS

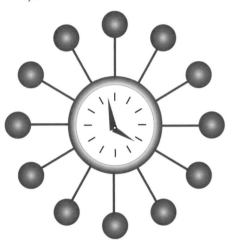

Mastering Illustrator Tools

Think about a conventional toolbox. You've got a hammer, nails, a few different types of screwdrivers, screws, nuts, bolts, a wrench, and probably some type of measuring device. That set of tools could be used to build anything from a birdhouse to a dollhouse to a townhouse to the White House.

A carpenter uses tools in conjunction with one another to create something, and that something is defined far less by the tools than by the imagination of the carpenter. But even the most ambitious imagination is tempered by the demands of knowing which tool to use and when.

Illustrator offers many sophisticated transform "tools" on the toolbar, and the metaphor is apt. Each tool provides a basic function, such as a rotation, scale, reflection, precise move, or precise offset. It is you, the designer, who uses those tools in combination with menu commands and other features to realize your vision. And like the carpenter, your ability to choose the right tool at the right time will affect the outcome of your work.

This is one of the most exciting aspects of working in Illustrator. After you learn the basics, there's no blueprint for building an illustration. It's your skills, your experience, your smarts, and your ingenuity that lead you toward your goal. No other designer will use Illustrator's tools quite the same way you do. People who appreciate digital imagery understand this significant point: Although the tools are the same for everyone, the result is personal—it's *original*.

Defining the Transform Tools

When you change an object's size, shape, or position on the artboard, Illustrator defines that operation as a transformation. Transforming objects is a fundamental operation in Illustrator, one you will perform countless times.

Because transformations are so essential, Illustrator provides a number of methods for doing them. As you gain experience, you will naturally adopt the method that you find most comfortable or logical.

The toolbar contains five transform tools: Rotate, Scale, Reflect, Shear, and Free Transform. The Rotate tool rotates an object or a group of objects around a fixed point. The Scale tool enlarges and reduces the size of objects. The Reflect tool "flips" an object across an imagined axis, usually the horizontal or the vertical axis; however, you can define any diagonal as the axis for a reflection. In Figure 1, the illustration has been flipped to create the illusion of a reflection in a mirror.

TIP The Reflect tool comes in very handy when you are drawing or tracing a symmetrical object, such as a spoon. Simply draw or trace half of the drawing, then create a flipped copy—a mirror image. Join the two halves, and you have a perfectly symmetrical shape...in half the time!

The Shear tool slants—or skews—an object on an axis that you specify. By definition, the Shear tool distorts an object. Of the five transform tools, you will probably use the Shear tool the least, although it is useful for creating a cast shadow or the illusion of depth.

Finally, the Free Transform tool offers you the ability to perform quick transformations and distort objects in perspective.

Figure 1 The Reflect tool flips an image horizontally or vertically

Defining the Point of Origin

All transformations are executed in relation to a fixed point. In Illustrator, this point is called the **point of origin**. For each transform tool, the default point of origin is the selected object's center point. However, you can change that point to another point on the object or to a point elsewhere on the artboard. For example, when a majorette twirls a baton, that baton is essentially rotating on its own center. By contrast, the petals of a daisy rotate around a central point that is not positioned on any of the petals themselves, as shown in Figure 2.

There are four basic methods for making transformations with the transform tools. First, select an object, then do one of the following:

- Click a transform tool, then click and drag anywhere on the artboard. The object will be transformed using its center point as the default point of origin.
- Double-click the transform tool, which opens the tool's dialog box. Enter the values you want to use to execute the transformation, then click OK. You may also click Copy to create a transformed copy of the selected object. The point of origin for the transformation will be the center point of the selected object.
- Click a transform tool, then click the artboard. Where you click the artboard defines the point of origin for the transformation. Click and drag anywhere on the artboard, and the selected object will be

transformed from the point of origin that you clicked.
- Click a transform tool, press [option] (Mac) or [Alt] (Win), then click the artboard. The tool's dialog box opens, allowing you to enter precise values for the transformation. When you click OK or Copy, the selected object

will be transformed from the point of origin that you clicked.

TIP If you transform an object from its center point and then select another object and apply the Transform Again command, the point of origin has not been redefined, and the second object will be transformed from the center point of the first object.

Figure 2 All transformations are executed from a point of origin

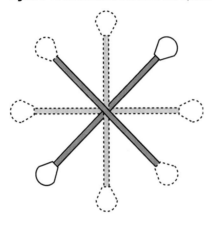

A baton rotating around its own center

Petals of a daisy rotate around a central point

Working with the Transform Again Command

An essential command related to transformations is Transform Again. Whenever you execute a transformation, such as scale or rotate, you can repeat the transformation quickly by using the Transform Again command. This is also true for moving an object. Using the Transform Again command will move an object the same distance and angle entered in the last step. The quickest way to use the Transform Again command is to press [command] [D] (Mac) or [Ctrl] [D] (Win). To remember this quick key command, think "D for *duplicate*."

A fine example of the usefulness of the Transform Again command is the ease with which you can make incremental transformations. For example, let's say you have created an object to be used in an illustration, but you haven't decided how large the object should be. Simply scale the object by a small percentage—say 5%—then press the quick key for Transform Again repeatedly until you are happy with the results. The object gradually gets bigger, and you can choose the size that pleases your eye. If you transform again too many times, and the object gets too big, simply undo repeatedly to decrease the object's size in the same small increments.

Using the Transform Each Command

The Transform Each command allows you to transform multiple objects individually, as shown in Figure 3. The Transform Each dialog box offers options to move, scale, rotate, or reflect an object, among others. All of them will affect an object independent of the other selected objects.

Without the Transform Each command, applying a transformation to multiple objects simultaneously will often yield an undesired effect. This happens because the selected objects are transformed as a group in relation to a single point of origin and are repositioned on the artboard.

Using the Free Transform Tool

When you click the Free Transform tool, an eight-handle bounding box appears around the selected object or objects. You can move the handles to scale or distort the object. You can click and drag outside the bounding box to rotate the selection. With the Free Transform tool, transformations always use the selected object's center point as the point of origin for the transformation.

Figure 3 Multiple objects rotated individually

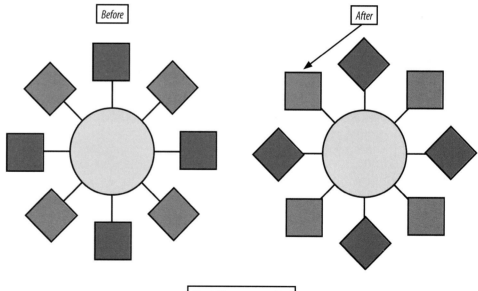

Before

After

The eight squares are rotated on their own center points

In general, the role of the Free Transform tool is to make quick transformations by clicking and dragging; some designers prefer it to the individual Scale and Rotate tools, especially for making inexact transformations. However, the Free Transform tool has a powerful ability to distort objects in very interesting ways.

Moving the handles on the Free Transform tool in conjunction with certain keyboard commands allows you to distort an object or distort in perspective, as shown in Figure 4. You start by dragging any handle on the bounding box; then, to distort in perspective, you must apply the following *after* you start dragging a handle:

- Press and hold [shift] [option] [command] (Mac) or [shift] [Alt] [Ctrl] (Win) to distort in perspective.
- Press and hold [shift] [command] (Mac) or [shift] [Ctrl] (Win) to distort the selection.

When you click the Free Transform tool, the Free Transform toolbar appears, shown in Figure 5. The Free Transform toolbar offers four button controls to execute the transformations described before. If you click the top button, named Constrain, the object will be scaled in proportion. Note, however, that you can just hold the [shift] key when transforming to achieve the same result.

Figure 4 Use the Free Transform tool to distort objects in perspective

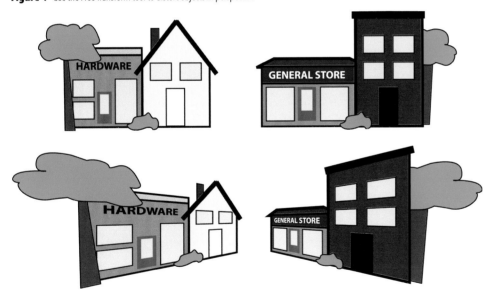

Figure 5 Free Transform toolbar

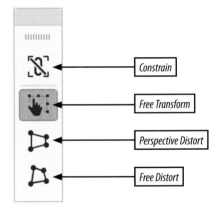

Constrain

Free Transform

Perspective Distort

Free Distort

The second button, Free Transform, is the default setting. With this button selected, the Free Transform tool works as normal. The third button is Perspective Distort. When it is activated, the object will scale in perspective. The fourth button is called Free Distort. When it is activated, all four corner points move independently, allowing you to distort the object at will.

The method you use is up to you. Some designers like the simple ease of use that the tool buttons offer, while others like the hands-on use of alternating keyboard commands. In this lesson, you'll practice the keyboard commands, since that is the trickier method of the two.

Using the Transform Panel

The Transform panel displays information about the size, orientation, and location of one or more selected objects. You can type new values directly into the Transform panel to modify selected objects. All values on the panel refer to the bounding boxes of the objects, whether the bounding box is visible or not.

The Reference Point grid at the top-left corner of the panel determines the point of origin for any transformation you make. For example, if you click the center point on the grid and then scale a circle 200%, the circle will enlarge from its center point. Keep an eye on the Reference Point grid whenever you are using the Transform panel.

To flip an object vertically or horizontally using the Transform panel, click the Transform panel menu button, shown in Figure 6.

Figure 6 Transform panel

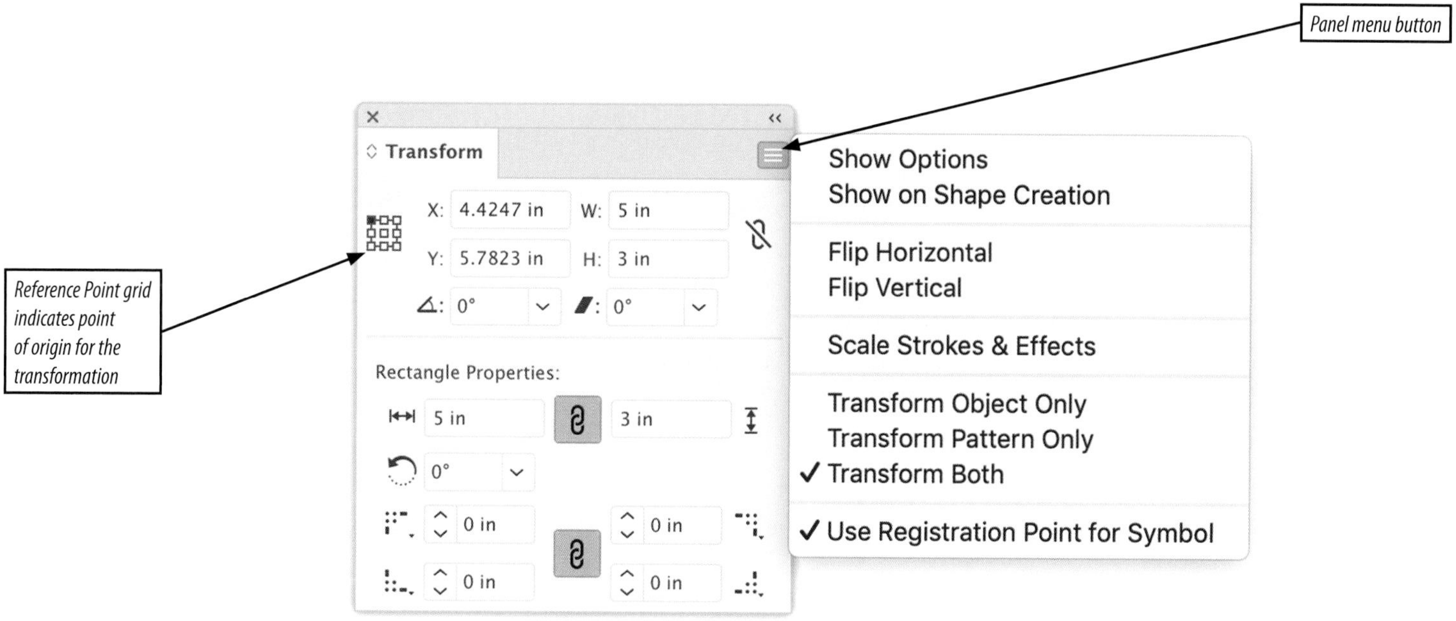

Panel menu button

Reference Point grid indicates point of origin for the transformation

Rotate an object around a defined point

1. Open AI 4-1.ai, then save it as **Mod Clock**.

2. Click the **Selection tool** ▶ on the toolbar, click the **brown line**, then click the **Rotate tool** ↻.

3. Press and hold **[option] (Mac)** or **[Alt] (Win)**, then click the **bottom anchor point of the brown line** to set the point of origin for the rotation.

With a transform tool selected, pressing [option] (Mac) or [Alt] (Win) and clicking the artboard defines the point of origin and opens the tool's dialog box.

4. Enter **30** in the **Angle text box**, then click **Copy**.

5. Press **[command] [D] (Mac)** or **[Ctrl] [D] (Win)** 10 times so your screen resembles Figure 7.

TIP [command] [D] (Mac) or [Ctrl] [D] (Win) is the quick key for the Transform Again command.

6. Select all **12 lines**, group them, send them to the back, then hide them.

7. Select the **small orange circle**, click **View** on the menu bar, then click **Outline**.

8. Click the **Rotate tool** ↻ on the toolbar, press and hold **[option] (Mac)** or **[Alt] (Win)**, then click the **center point of the larger circle** to set the point of origin for the next rotation.

   The small circle will rotate around the center point of the larger circle.

TIP Outline mode is especially useful for rotations because center points are visible and easy to target as points of origin.

Figure 7 12 paths rotated at a point

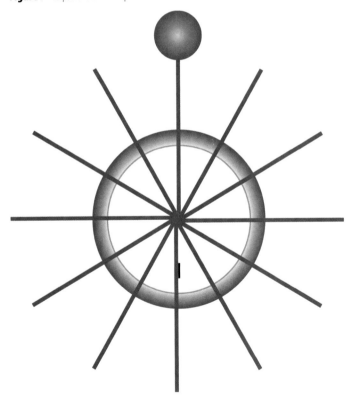

UNDERSTANDING X AND Y COORDINATES

The X and Y coordinates of an object indicate the object's horizontal (X) and vertical (Y) locations on the artboard. These numbers, which appear on the Transform panel and the Control panel, represent the horizontal and vertical distance from the upper-left corner of the artboard. The current X and Y coordinates also depend on the specified reference point. Nine reference points are listed to the left of the X and Y Value text boxes on the Transform panel. Reference points are those points of a selected object that represent the four corners of the object's bounding box, the horizontal and vertical centers of the bounding box, and the center point of the bounding box.

9. Enter **30**, click **Copy**, apply the **Transform Again command** 10 times, then switch to **Preview mode**.

Your screen should resemble Figure 8.

10. Select the **small black vertical dash**, then apply the **Transform Again command** 11 times.

The dash is also rotated around the center point of the larger circle, since a new point of origin has not been set.

11. Unlock the **clock hands in the scratch area**, then move them onto the clock face.

12. Show all, then deselect all to reveal the 12 segments, as shown in Figure 9.

13. Save your work, then close the Mod Clock document.

You selected a point on the brown line, then rotated 11 copies of the object around that point. Second, you defined the point of origin for a rotation by clicking the center point of the larger circle, then rotated 11 copies of the smaller circle and the dash around that point.

Figure 8 12 circles rotated around a central point of origin

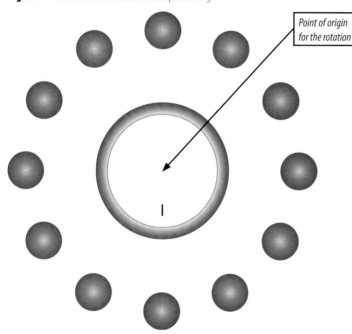

Point of origin for the rotation

Figure 9 Completed illustration

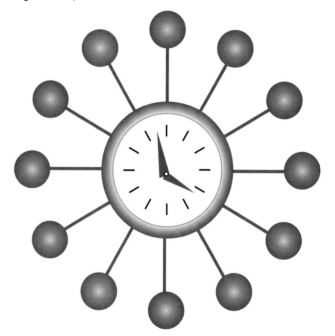

Use the Shear tool

1. Open AI 4-2.ai, then save it as **Shear**.

2. Select all, copy, paste in front, then fill the copy with the swatch named **Graphite**.

3. Click the **Shear tool** 🖋, on the toolbar.

TIP The Shear tool 🖋, is hidden behind the Scale tool 🔲.

4. Press and hold **[option] (Mac)** or **[Alt] (Win)**, then click the **bottom-right anchor point** of the **letter R** to set the origin point of the shear and open the Shear dialog box.

5. Enter **45** in the **Shear Angle text box**, verify that the **Horizontal option button** is checked, then click **OK**.

   Your screen should resemble Figure 10.

6. Click the **Scale tool** 🔲, on the toolbar.

7. Press **[option] (Mac)** or **[Alt] (Win)**, then click **any bottom anchor point** or **segment** on the **sheared objects** to set the point of origin for the scale and open the Scale dialog box.

8. Click the **Non-Uniform option button**, enter **100** in the **Horizontal text box**, enter **50** in the **Vertical text box**, then click **OK**.

9. Send the sheared objects to the back.

10. Apply a **1 pt. black stroke** to the **orange letters**, deselect, then compare your screen to Figure 11.

11. Save your work, then close the Shear document.

You created a shadow effect using the Shear tool.

Figure 10 Letterforms sheared on a 45° angle

The objects are sheared on a 45° angle in relation to a horizontal axis

Figure 11 Shearing is useful for creating a cast-shadow effect

The shadow is "cast" from the letters in the foreground

Use the Reflect tool

1. Open AI 4-3.ai, then save it as **Reflect**.
2. Select all, then zoom in on the **top anchor point**.
3. Click the **Reflect tool** ▷◁ on the toolbar.

   The Reflect tool ▷◁ is hidden behind the Rotate tool ↻.
4. Press **[option] (Mac)** or **[Alt] (Win)**, then click the **top anchor point** to set the point of origin for the reflection.
5. Click the **Vertical option button**, then click **Copy**.

   A copy is positioned, reflected across the axis that you defined, as shown in Figure 12.
6. Deselect all, then click the **Direct Selection tool** ▷. on the toolbar.
7. Using Figure 13 as a guide, drag a **selection box** around the **top two anchor points** to select them.

   TIP One of the anchor points is directly on top of the other because of the reflected copy.
8. Click **Object** on the menu bar, point to **Path**, click **Average**, click the **Both option button**, then click **OK**.
9. Click **Object** on the menu bar, point to **Path**, then click **Join**.
10. Select the **bottom two anchor points**, average them on both axes, then join them to close the path.
11. Save your work, then close the Reflect document.

You created a reflected copy of a path, then averaged and joined two pairs of open points.

Figure 12 Use the Reflect tool for illustrations that demand exact symmetry

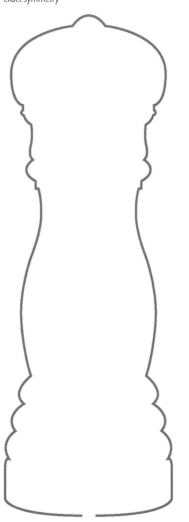

Figure 13 Selecting two anchor points with the Direct Selection tool

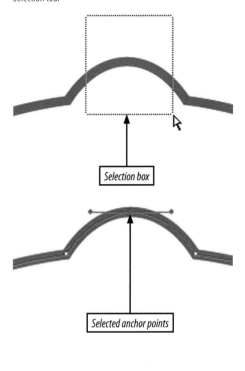

Selection box

Selected anchor points

Use the Free Transform tool to distort in perspective

1. Open AI 4-4.ai, then save it as **Distort in Perspective**.

2. Press **[command] [A] (Mac)** or **[Ctrl] [A] (Win)** to select all, then click the **Free Transform tool**  on the toolbar.

3. Click and begin dragging the **upper-right handle** directly **to the right**; then, while still dragging, press and hold **[shift] [command] (Mac)** or **[shift] [Ctrl] (Win)** and continue dragging, releasing the mouse button when you are halfway to the edge of the artboard.

4. Compare your result to Figure 14.

   The illustration is distorted; the upper-right corner is moved to the right. The other three corners do not move.

5. Press **[command] [Z] (Mac)** or **[Ctrl] [Z] (Win)** to undo the last step.

Figure 14 Distorting the illustration

6. Click and start dragging the **upper-right handle** directly **to the right**; then, while still dragging, press and hold **[shift] [command] [option]** (Mac) or **[shift] [Ctrl] [Alt]** (Win) and continue dragging.

7. Release the mouse button when you are halfway to the edge of the artboard, then compare your result to Figure 15.

   The illustration is distorted with a different perspective.

8. Click and drag the **upper-left corner straight down**; then, while dragging, press and hold **[shift] [command] [option]** (Mac) or **[shift] [Ctrl] [Alt]** (Win) and continue dragging until your illustration resembles Figure 16.

9. Save your work, then close the Distort in Perspective document.

You used keyboard combinations first to distort the illustration, then to distort it in perspective.

Figure 15   Distorting the illustration in perspective

Figure 16   Illustration distorted in complex perspective

LESSON 2

OFFSET AND OUTLINE PATHS

▶ ## *What You'll Do*

In this lesson, you will use the Offset Path command to create concentric squares and the Outline Stroke command to convert a stroked path into a closed path.

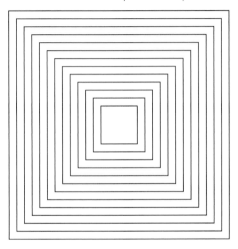

Using the Offset Path Command

Simply put, the Offset Path command creates a copy of a selected path set off by a specified distance. The Offset Path command is useful when working with closed paths—making concentric shapes or making many copies of a path at a regular distance from the original.

Figure 17 shows two sets of concentric circles. **Concentric** refers to objects that share the same center point, as the circles in both sets do. The set on the left was made with the Scale tool, applying an 85% scale and copy to the outer circle, then repeating the transformation 10 times. Note that with each successive copy, the distance from the copy to the previous circle decreases. The set on the right was made by offsetting the outside circle –.125", then applying the same offset to each successive copy. Note the different effect.

When you offset a closed path, a positive value creates a larger copy outside the original; a negative value creates a smaller copy inside the original.

Figure 17 Two sets of concentric circles

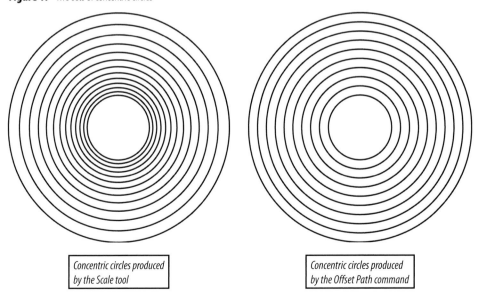

Concentric circles produced by the Scale tool

Concentric circles produced by the Offset Path command

Using the Outline Stroke Command

The Outline Stroke command converts a stroked path into a closed path that is the same width as the original stroked path.

This operation is useful if you want to apply a gradient to a stroke. It is also a useful design tool, allowing you to modify the outline of an object more than if it were just a stroke. Also, it is often easier to create an object with a single heavy stroke and then convert it to a closed path than it is to try to draw a closed path directly, as shown with the letter S in Figure 18.

Offset a path

1. Open AI 4-5.ai, then save it as **Squares**.

2. Select the **square**.

3. Click **Object** on the menu bar, point to **Path**, then click **Offset Path**.

4. Enter **–.125** in the **Offset text box**, then click **OK**.

   A negative value reduces the area of a closed path; a positive value increases the area.

TIP Be sure that your Units preference is set to Inches in the General section of the Units Preferences.

5. Apply the **Offset Path command** with the same value four more times.

TIP The Transform Again command does not apply to the Offset Path command because it is not one of the transform tools.

6. Deselect all, save your work, compare your screen to Figure 19, then close the Squares document.

You used the Offset Path command to create concentric squares.

Figure 18 The Outline Stroke command converts a stroked path to a closed object

Figure 19 Concentric squares created with the Offset Path command

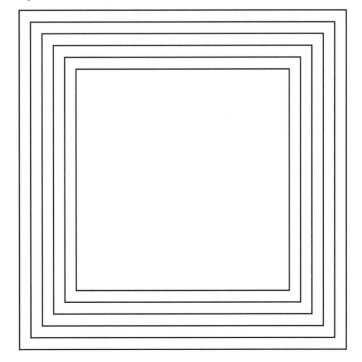

Convert a stroked path to a closed path

1. Open AI 4-6.ai, then save it as **Outlined Stroke**.
2. Select the **path**, then change the **weight** to **36 pt**.
3. Click **Object** on the menu bar, point to **Path**, then click **Outline Stroke**.

   The full weight of the stroke is converted to a closed path, as shown in Figure 20.
4. Save your work, then close the Outlined Stroke document.

You applied a heavy weight to a stroked path, then converted the stroke to a closed path, using the Outline Stroke command.

Figure 20   The Outline Stroke command converts any stroked path into a closed path

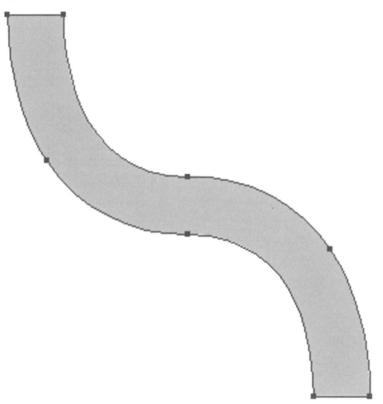

CREATE COMPOUND PATHS

Defining a Compound Path

Practically speaking, you make a compound path to create a "hole" or "holes" in an object. As shown in Figure 21, if you were drawing the letter D, you would need to create a hole in the outlined shape, through which you could see the background. To do so, select the object in back (in this case, the black outline that defines the letter) and the object in front (the yellow object that defines the hole), and apply the Make Compound Path command. When compounded, a "hole" appears where the two objects overlap.

Figure 21   The letter D is an example of a compound path

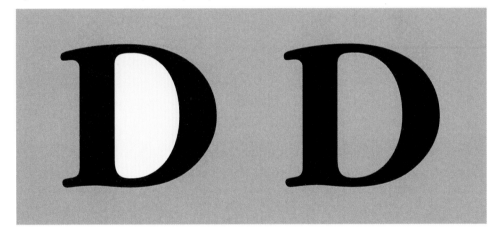

The overlapping object still exists, however. It is simply *functioning* as a transparent hole in conjunction with the object behind it. If you move the front object independently, as shown in Figure 22, it yields an interesting result. Designers have seized upon this effect and have run with it, creating complex and eye-catching graphics, which Illustrator calls compound shapes.

It is important to understand that when two or more objects are compounded, Illustrator defines them as *one* object. This sounds strange at first, but the concept is as familiar to you as the letter D. You identify the letter D as a single object although it is drawn with two paths—one defining the outside edge, the other defining the inside edge.

Compound paths function as groups. You can select and manipulate an individual element with the Direct Selection tool, but you cannot change its appearance attributes independently. Compound paths can be released and returned to their original component objects by applying the Release Compound Path command.

Create compound paths

1. Open AI 4-7.ai, then save it as **Simple Compound**.
2. Cut the **red circle** in the middle of the illustration, then undo the cut.

   The red circle creates the illusion that there's a hole in the life-preserver ring.

3. Select the **red background object**, then change its fill to the **Ocean Blue gradient** on the Swatches panel.

   The illusion is lost; the red circle no longer seems to be a hole in the life preserver.

4. Select both the **white "life preserver" circle** and the **red circle** in the center.
5. Click **Object** on the menu bar, point to **Compound Path**, then click **Make**.

   As shown in Figure 23, the two circles are compounded, with the top circle functioning as a "hole" in the larger circle behind it.

Figure 22 Manipulating compound paths can yield interesting effects

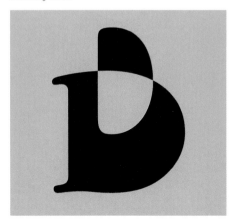

Figure 23 A compound path creates the effect of a hole where two or more objects overlap

6. Move the **background object left and right** and **up and down** behind the circles.

   The repositioned background remains visible through the compounded circles.

7. Deselect all, save your work, then close the Simple Compound document.

You selected two concentric circles and made them into one compound path, which allowed you to see through to the gradient behind the circles.

Create special effects with compound paths

1. Open AI 4-8.ai, then save it as **Compound Path Effects**.

2. Select all.

   The light blue square is locked and does not become part of the selection.

3. Click **Object** on the menu bar, point to **Compound Path**, then click **Make**.

4. Deselect, click the **Direct Selection tool** on the toolbar, then click the **edge** of the **large blue circle**.

5. Click the **center point** of the circle, then scale the **circle 50%** so your work resembles Figure 24.

6. Click **Select** on the menu bar, then click **Inverse**.

7. Click **Object** on the menu bar, point to **Transform**, then click **Transform Each**.

8. Enter **225** in the **Horizontal** and **Vertical text boxes** in the Scale section of the Transform Each dialog box, click **OK,** then deselect all.

   Your work should resemble Figure 25.

9. Using the **Direct Selection tool**, click the **edge of the center circle**, click its **center point** to select the entire circle, then scale the circle **120%**.

10. Apply the **Transform Again command** twice, then compare your screen to Figure 26.

11. Deselect all, save your work, then close the Compound Path Effects document.

You made a compound path out of five small circles and one large circle. You then manipulated the size and location of the individual circles to create interesting designs.

Figure 24 A simple compound path

Figure 25 A more complex compound path

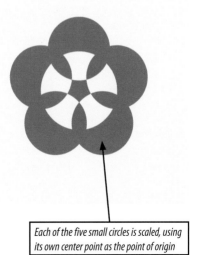

Each of the five small circles is scaled, using its own center point as the point of origin

Figure 26 Simple compound paths can yield stunning visual effects

WORK WITH THE PATHFINDER PANEL

▶ *What You'll Do*

In this lesson, you will use shape modes and pathfinders to create compound shapes from simple shapes.

Defining a Compound Shape

Like a compound path, a **compound shape** is two or more paths that are combined in such a way that "holes" appear wherever paths overlap.

The term "compound shape" is used to distinguish a complex compound path from a simple one. Compound shapes generally assume an artistic rather than a practical role. To achieve the effect, compound shapes tend to be composed of multiple objects. You can think of a compound shape as an illustration composed of multiple compound paths.

Understanding Essential Shape Modes and Pathfinders

Shape modes and **pathfinders** are preset operations that help you combine paths in a variety of ways. They are useful operations for creating complex or irregular shapes from basic shapes. In some cases, they are a means to an end in creating an object. In others, the operation they provide will be the end result you want to achieve. Shape modes and pathfinders can be applied to overlapping objects using the Effect menu or the Pathfinder panel.

For the purposes of drawing and creating new objects, familiarize yourself with the five essential shape modes and pathfinders shown in Figure 27.

Figure 27 Five essential shape modes and pathfinders

Two Objects / No Filter

Unite

Divide

Minus Front

Minus Back

Intersect

Unite shape mode Converts two or more overlapping objects into a single merged object.

Minus Front shape mode Where objects overlap, deletes the frontmost object(s) from the backmost object in a selection of overlapped objects.

Intersect shape mode Creates a single merged object from the area where two or more objects overlap.

Minus Back pathfinder The opposite of Minus Front; deletes the backmost object(s) from the frontmost object in a selection of overlapped objects.

Divide pathfinder Divides an object into its component-filled faces. Illustrator defines a "face" as an area undivided by a line segment.

Using the Pathfinder Panel

The Pathfinder panel contains 10 buttons for creating compound shapes, as shown in Figure 28. As you learned earlier, a compound shape is a complex compound path. You can create a compound shape by overlapping two or more objects, then clicking one of the four shape mode buttons in the top row of the Pathfinder panel, or clicking the Pathfinder panel list arrow, then clicking Make Compound Shape. The four shape mode buttons are Unite, Minus Front, Intersect, and Exclude. When you apply a shape mode button, the two overlapping objects are combined into one object with the same formatting as the topmost object in the group before the shape mode button was applied. After applying a shape mode button, the resulting objects in the compound shape can be selected and formatted using the Direct Selection tool. You can also press [option] (Mac) or [Alt] (Win) when you click a shape mode button. Doing so results in a compound shape whose original objects can be selected and formatted using the Direct Selection tool.

Figure 28 Pathfinder panel

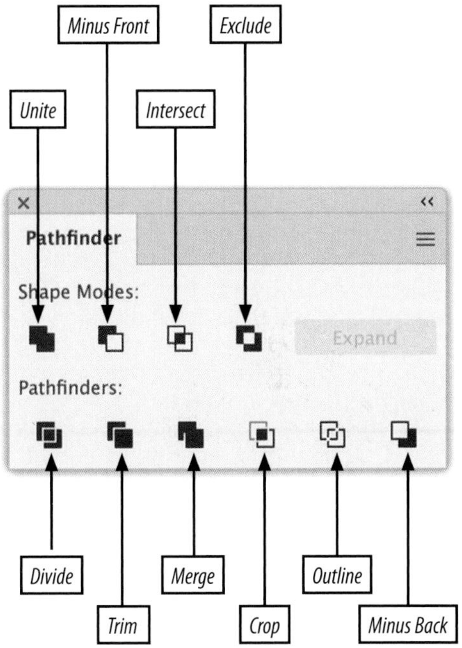

Applying Shape Modes

Figure 29 shows a square overlapped by a circle.

If you apply the Minus Front shape mode button, the resulting object is a compound shape, as shown in Figure 30. Notice the overlapped area is deleted from the square. The circle, too, is deleted. The result is a simple reshaped object.

If you took the same two overlapping shapes shown in Figure 29, but this time pressed [option] (Mac) or [Alt] (Win) when applying

the Minus Front shape mode button, the circle would not be deleted but would function as a hole or a "knockout" wherever it overlaps the square, as shown in Figure 31. The relationship is dynamic: You can move the circle independently with the Direct Selection tool to change its effect on the square and the resulting visual effect.

Releasing and Expanding Compound Shapes

You can release a compound shape, which separates it back into individual objects.

To release a compound shape, click the Pathfinder panel menu button, then click Release Compound Shape. Expanding a compound shape is similar to releasing it, except that it maintains the shape of the compound object. You cannot select the original individual objects. You can expand a compound shape by selecting it, and then clicking the Expand button on the Pathfinder panel.

Figure 29 Two overlapping objects

Figure 30 Applying the Minus Front shape mode without [option] (Mac) or [Alt] (Win)

Figure 31 Applying the Minus Front shape mode with [option] (Mac) or [Alt] (Win)

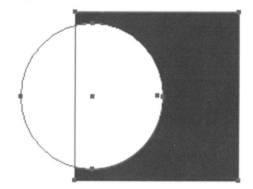

Apply the Unite shape mode

1. Open AI 4-9.ai, then save it as **Heart Parts**.

2. Click **Window** on the menu bar, then click **Pathfinder**.

3. Select **both circles**, then click the **Unite button** on the Pathfinder panel.

   The two objects are united.

4. Move the **diamond shape** up so it overlaps the united circles, as shown in Figure 32.

5. Click the **Delete Anchor Point tool** on the toolbar, then delete the **top anchor point of the diamond**.

6. Select all, press and hold **[option] (Mac)** or **[Alt] (Win)**, click the **Unite button** on the Pathfinder panel, then deselect all.

   Your screen should resemble Figure 33.

7. Remove the **black stroke**, then apply a **red fill** to the new object.

8. Draw a **rectangle** that covers the "hole" in the heart, then fill it with **black**, as shown in Figure 34.

9. Select all, press **[option] (Mac)** or **[Alt] (Win)**, then click the **Unite button** .

   The heart turns black.

10. Double-click the **Scale tool** , then apply a **non-uniform scale** of **90%** on the **horizontal axis** and **100%** on the **vertical axis**.

11. Save your work, then continue to the next set of steps.

You created a single heart-shaped object from two circles and a diamond shape using the Unite shape mode.

Figure 32   A diamond shape in position

Figure 33   The diamond shape and the object behind it are united

Figure 34   A heart shape created by applying the Unite shape mode to three objects

Apply the Minus Front shape mode

1. Rotate the **black heart shape 180°**, then hide it.

2. Create a **square** that is **1.5" × 1.5"** without a fill color and with a **1 pt. black stroke**.

3. Create a **circle** that is **1.75"** in width and height.

4. Switch to **Outline mode**.

5. Move the **circle** so it overlaps the square, as shown in Figure 35.

6. Verify that the **circle** is still selected, click the **Reflect tool** ▷◁ , press **[option] (Mac)** or **[Alt] (Win)**, then click the **center point** of the **square**.

7. Click the **Vertical option button**, click **Copy**, then arrange the three objects so your work resembles Figure 36.

8. Select all, then click the **Minus Front button** ▣ on the Pathfinder panel.

9. Switch to **Preview mode**, then apply a **black fill** to the **new object**.

10. Show all, then overlap the **new shape** with the **black heart shape** to make a spade shape.

11. Select all, click the **Unite button** ▣ on the Pathfinder panel, then deselect.

    Your work should resemble Figure 37.

12. Save your work, then continue to the next set of steps.

You overlapped a square with two circles, then applied the Minus Front shape mode to delete the overlapped areas from the square. You used the Unite button to unite the new shape with a heart-shaped object to create a spade shape.

Figure 35 Circle overlaps the square

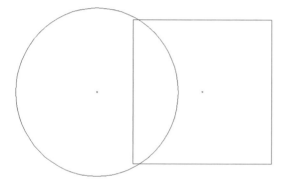

Figure 36 Right circle is a reflected copy of the left one

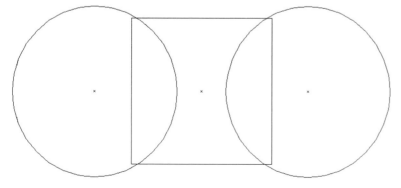

WORKING WITH THE ALIGN PANEL

The Align panel offers a quick and simple solution for aligning selected objects along the axis you specify. Along the vertical axis, you can align selected objects by their rightmost, leftmost, or center point. On the horizontal axis, you can align objects by their topmost, center, or bottommost point. You can also use the panel to distribute objects evenly along a horizontal or vertical axis. In contrasting the Align panel with the Average command, think of the Average command as a method for aligning anchor points and the Align panel as a method for aligning entire objects.

When you align and distribute objects, you have the choice of aligning them to a selection, a key object, or the artboard. If you want to align or distribute objects using the artboard, you must first define the artboard area using the Artboard tool on the toolbar. Click the Align To list arrow on the Align panel, then click Align to Artboard. Resize the artboard as desired. Finally, choose the alignment setting you need on the Align panel.

Figure 37 The final shape with all elements united

Apply the Intersect shape mode

1. Click the **Star tool**  on the toolbar, then click the **artboard**.

2. Enter **1** in the **Radius 1 text box**, **3** in the **Radius 2 text box**, and **8** in the **Points text box**, then click **OK**.

3. Apply a **yellow fill** and no stroke to the **star**.

4. Use the **Align panel** to align the **center points of the two objects** so they resemble Figure 38.

5. Copy the **black spade**, then paste in front.

   Two black spades are now behind the yellow star; the top one is selected.

6. Press and hold **[shift]**, then click to add the **star** to the selection.

7. Click the **Intersect shape mode button** on the Pathfinder panel.

   The intersection of the star and the copied spade is now a single closed path. Your work should resemble Figure 39.

8. Save your work, then close Heart Parts.

You created a star, then created a copy of the black spade-shaped object. You used the Intersect shape mode button to capture the intersection of the two objects as a new object.

Figure 38 Use the Align panel to align objects precisely

Figure 39 Yellow shape is the intersection of the star and the spade

Apply the Divide pathfinder

1. Open AI 4-10.ai, then save it as **Divide**.

2. Select the **red line**, then double-click the **Rotate tool** 🔄.

3. Enter **30** in the **Angle text box**, then click **Copy**.

4. Repeat the transformation four times.

5. Select all, then click the **Divide button** ▣ on the Pathfinder panel.

   The blue star is divided into 12 separate objects, as defined by the red lines, which have been deleted. See Figure 40.

6. Deselect, click the **Direct Selection tool** ▷, select the **left half of the top point**, press **[shift]**, then select **every other object**, for a total of six objects.

7. Apply an **orange fill** to the selected objects.

8. Select the **inverse**, then apply a **yellow fill** so your work resembles Figure 41.

9. Save your work, then close the Divide document.

You used six lines to define a score pattern, then used those lines and the Divide pathfinder to break the star into 12 separate objects.

Figure 40 Blue star is divided into 12 objects by the Divide pathfinder

Figure 41 Divide pathfinder is useful for adding dimension

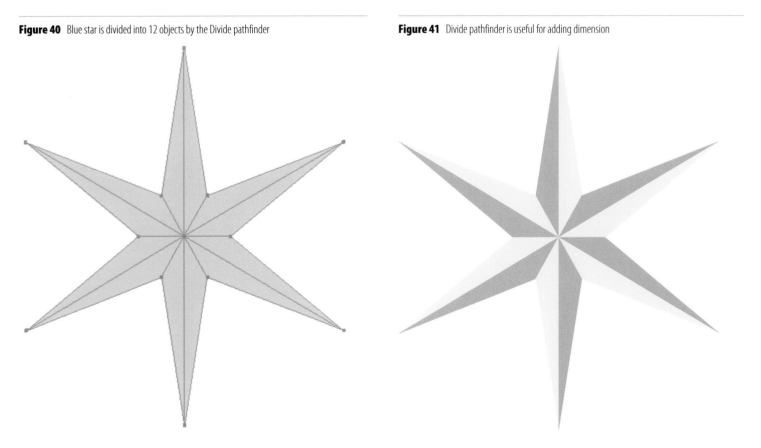

Create compound shapes using the Pathfinder panel

1. Open AI 4-11.ai, then save it as **Compound Shapes**.

2. Click **View** on the menu bar, then click **Yellow**.

3. Select the **two yellow circles**, press **[option] (Mac)** or **[Alt] (Win)**, then click the **Exclude button** on the Pathfinder panel.

   The area that the top object overlaps becomes transparent.

4. Deselect, click the **Direct Selection tool**, then move **either circle** to change the shape and size of the filled areas.

   Figure 42 shows one effect that can be achieved.

5. Click **View** on the menu bar, click **Green**, select the **two green circles**, press **[option] (Mac)** or **[Alt] (Win)**, then click the **Intersect button** on the Pathfinder panel.

   The area not overlapped by the top circle becomes transparent.

6. Deselect, then use the **Direct Selection tool** to move **either circle** to change the shape and size of the filled area.

   Figure 43 shows one effect that can be achieved.

7. Save your work, then close the Compound Shapes document.

You applied shape modes to two pairs of circles, then moved the circles to create different shapes and effects.

Figure 42 An example of the Exclude shape mode

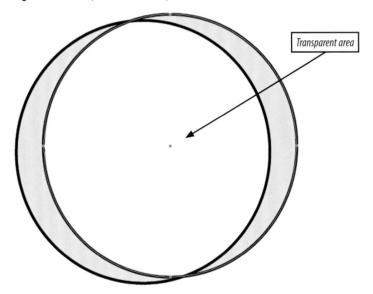

Transparent area

Figure 43 An example of the Intersect shape mode

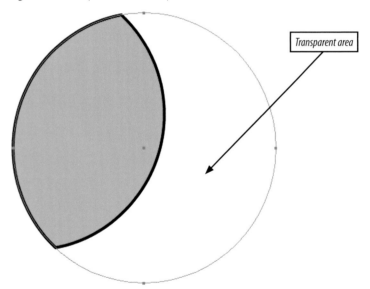

Transparent area

Create special effects with compound shapes

1. Open AI 4-12.ai, then save it as **Compound Shape Effects**.

2. Select all, press **[option] (Mac)** or **[Alt] (Win)**, then click the **Exclude button** ▢ on the Pathfinder panel.

   Your work should resemble Figure 44.

3. Deselect all, click the **Direct Selection tool** ▷ on the toolbar, select the **three squares**, then move them **to the right**, as shown in Figure 45.

4. Drag and drop a **copy of the three squares**, as shown in Figure 46.

TIP Use [shift] [option] (Mac) or [shift] [Alt] (Win) to drag and drop a copy at a 45° angle or in straight vertical or horizontal lines.

5. Scale **each circle 150%** using the **Transform Each command**.

6. Scale the **center circle 200%,** then bring it to the front of the stacking order.

7. Press **[option] (Mac)** or **[Alt] (Win)**, then click the **Intersect button** ▢ on the Pathfinder panel.

   Figure 47 shows the results of the intersection. Your final illustration may vary slightly.

TIP The topmost object affects all the objects behind it in a compound shape.

8. Save your work, then close the Compound Shape Effects document.

You made three squares and three circles into a compound shape by excluding overlapping shape areas. You then manipulated the size and location of individual elements to create different effects. Finally, you enlarged a circle, brought it to the front, then changed its mode to Intersect. Only the objects that were overlapped by the circle remained visible.

Figure 44 A compound shape

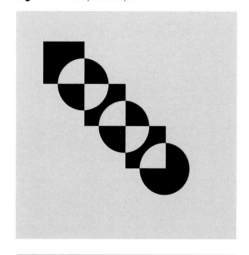

Figure 46 A compound shape

Figure 45 A compound shape

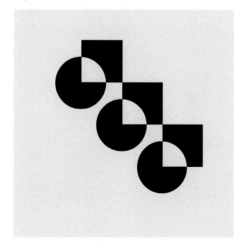

Figure 47 A compound shape

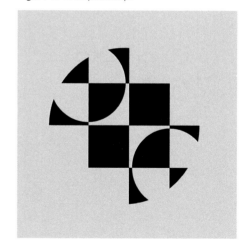

APPLY ROUND CORNERS TO OBJECTS

▶ *What You'll Do*

In this lesson, you will apply round corners to the artwork using the Corners dialog box. You will also learn about the options in the Corners dialog box.

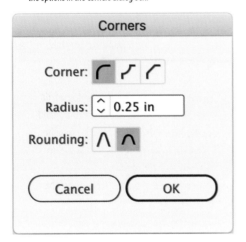

Applying Round Corners

Round corners are an essential component of any designer's tool kit. Figure 48 shows a five-point star, like one you'd see on the American flag. Note the five pointy points. This star is serious, and its points say "don't mess with me." With its mathematical basis and sharp points, a star is regal, which is why it's often used to convey majesty and supremacy.

Figure 49 shows the same star with round corners. The emotional effect of changing an object's corners from pointed to rounded is remarkable. Suddenly, the object is cute and playful. It's almost cartoonish, like an animated character or a sponge toy a child could play with in the bathtub.

Figure 48 Star with pointy points

Figure 49 Star with round corners

Round corners make objects fun, playful, comical, and cute. When you round corners in Illustrator, you are working with widgets, small circles that appear at every corner, as shown in Figure 50. To view widgets, you must select the object with the Direct Selection tool. If you do not see widgets, click the View menu and choose Show Corner Widget.

When you click and drag the widget, all the corners of the object are rounded as you drag. You may have a situation in which you only want to round one corner, not all of them, on a given object. To do so, first select *only* the anchor point of the corner you wish to round with the Direct Selection tool, then drag its associated widget. Using this method, you can apply differently rounded corners to every point on the object.

If you want to apply a specific corner radius to a point, rather than click and drag to create the rounded corner, simply double-click the widget. This opens the Corners dialog box, where you can enter a specific radius, as shown in Figure 51. You can also specify two other types of corners: Inverted Round and Chamfer.

Don't forget that you can apply round corners to type after you've converted the text to outlines. This is a great option for creating fun, friendly letter shapes.

| **TIP** You can also enter a specific radius for a corner by clicking Corners on the Control panel.

Apply corners to an object

1. Open AI 4-13.ai, save it as **Round Corners**, click **View** on the menu bar, then click **Show Corner Widget**.

   If the command reads Hide Corner Widget, do nothing; the corner widget is already showing.

2. Click the **Direct Selection tool** 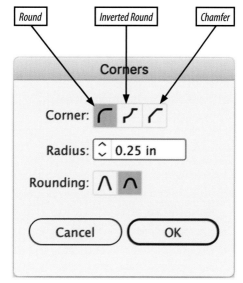 on the toolbar, then click the **interior of the blue shape** to select the object.

   Corner widgets appear at every corner of the selected object.

   TIP If you find corner widgets distracting, you can hide them by using the Hide Corner Widget command on the View menu.

3. Click and drag the **topmost corner widget** toward the center of the object.

   As you drag, all the corners on the object become increasingly rounded.

   Continued on next page

Figure 50 Corner widgets visible on objects

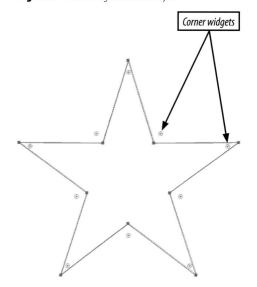

Figure 51 Corners dialog box with options for corners

4. Drag until the object resembles Figure 52.

5. Press and hold **[option] (Mac)** or **[Alt] (Win)**, then click **any corner widget**.

   The round corners change to inverted round corners.

6. While still holding **[option] (Mac)** or **[Alt] (Win)**, click the **corner widget** again.

   As shown in Figure 53, the inverted round corners change to chamfer corners. Each time you press and hold [option] (Mac) or [Alt] (Win), and click a corner widget, the corner cycles through the three types of corner options in the Corners dialog box.

   TIP The word chamfer refers to a cut made in woodcutting and is similar to a beveled edge.

7. While still holding **[option] (Mac)** or **[Alt] (Win)**, click the **corner widget** again.

   The chamfer corners change to round corners.

8. Drag the **corner widget** away from the center of the object.

   The object is restored to its original shape.

9. Save your work, then continue to the next set of steps.

You dragged corner widgets with the Direct Selection tool to create round corners, then modified the corners from round to inverted round to chamfer. You then removed the specialized corners from the object.

Apply specific corner measurements to individual points on an object

1. Deselect all, then select the **top anchor point** on the **blue object** with the **Direct Selection tool** ▷.

2. Click and drag the **top corner widget** toward the center of the object to create a round corner.

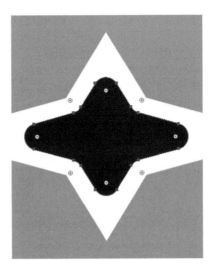

Figure 52 Round corners applied to the object

Note that the radius of the corner is identified in the Corners section of the Control panel.

3. Double-click the **top corner widget**.

   The Corners dialog box opens.

4. Enter **25** in the **Radius text box**, then click **OK**.

5. Select the **anchor point** at the **bottom of the blue object** with the **Direct Selection tool** ▷.

6. Double-click the **corner widget**, enter **25** in the **Radius text box**, then click **OK**.

7. Select both the **orange objects**.

8. On the Control panel, enter **25** in the **Corners text box**, then press **[return] (Mac)** or **[Enter] (Win)**.

   All corners on the orange objects are rounded.

9. Select the **far left** and **far right anchor points** on the **blue object** with the **Direct Selection tool** ▷.

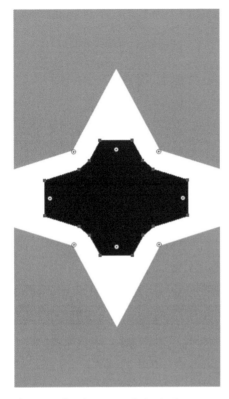

Figure 53 Chamfer corners applied to the object

10. On the Control panel, click the word **Corners** to open the Corners dialog box, click the **Inverted Round option** ⌐, then enter **25** in the **Radius text box**.

11. Deselect all, then compare your artwork to Figure 54.

12. Save your work, then close the Round Corners document.

You applied a corner to individual points on an object, then used the Corners dialog box to apply the exact same corner style to other points on the object and to other objects.

Figure 54 Final artwork with corners applied to all anchor points

LESSON 6

USE THE SHAPE BUILDER TOOL

▶ **What You'll Do**

In this lesson, you will use the Shape Builder tool to create new shapes from overlapping objects.

Understanding the Shape Builder Tool

The Shape Builder tool is grouped on the toolbar with the Live Paint Bucket. This makes sense because the tool functions in a similar manner to the Live Paint Bucket.

The Shape Builder tool is designed to help you create new objects from overlapping objects. Comparing it to the Live Paint Bucket (covered in Chapter 10) can help you understand its role. Where the Live Paint Bucket fills closed paths created by overlapping objects, the Shape Builder tool creates new closed paths from overlapping objects. From this perspective,

you can think of the Shape Builder tool as a combination of the Live Paint Bucket and the Pathfinder tools.

Figure 55 shows eight orange-filled circles overlapping. The Shape Builder tool is selected on the toolbar, and a pink fill and black stroke have been chosen on the toolbar. When the Shape Builder tool is selected, changing the fill or stroke color on the toolbar won't change the color of the selected objects. In the figure, closed objects are highlighted and outlined in red when the Shape Builder tool is dragged across them.

Figure 55 Specifying objects to be created with the Shape Builder tool

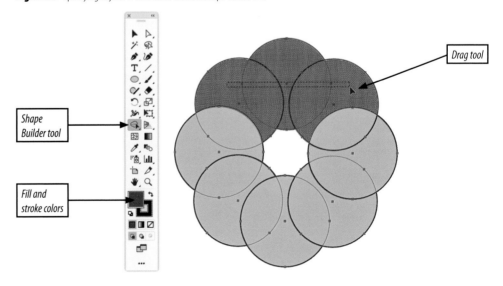

Shape Builder tool

Fill and stroke colors

Drag tool

In Figure 56, those objects are united into a single object with the pink fill and a black stroke. Note that this is not something you could do with the Unite pathfinder. The Unite pathfinder would have united the three whole circles, but, as shown in this example, the Shape Builder tool created a single object from overlapping components of the circles.

In Figure 57, the Shape Builder tool has been dragged to the negative space in the center so it will be added to the merged object.

Figure 56 New object created with the Shape Builder tool

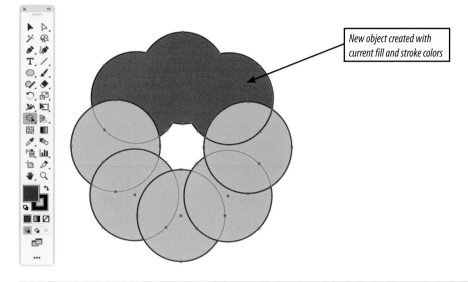

New object created with current fill and stroke colors

Figure 57 Adding the negative space to the object

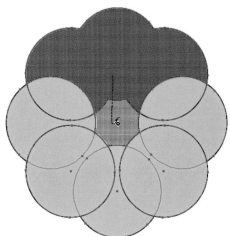

In addition to creating new objects, the Shape Builder tool also deletes closed paths from overlapping objects. To delete an object with the Shape Builder tool, press and hold [option] (Mac) or [Alt] (Win), then click or drag over the objects you want to delete. Note the minus sign beside the Shape Builder tool icon in Figure 58. Upon release, the objects are deleted, as shown in Figure 59.

Figure 58 Specifying objects to be deleted

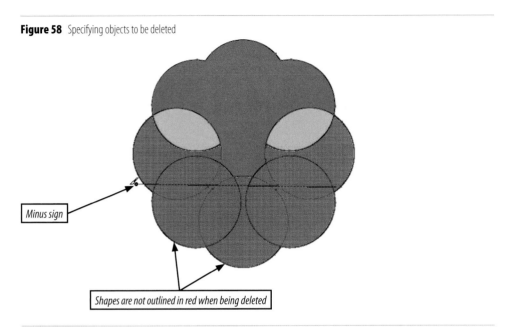

Minus sign

Shapes are not outlined in red when being deleted

Figure 59 Illustration after deletion

Create objects with the Shape Builder tool

1. Open AI 4-14.ai, then save it as **Shape Builder**.
2. Select all, then click the **Shape Builder tool** 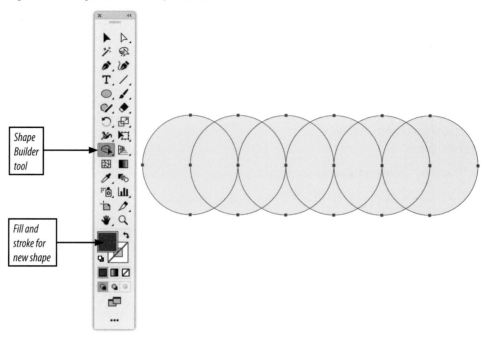 on the toolbar.
3. Set the **fill** and **stroke color** to **Pink** and **[None]**, respectively.

   Your artboard should resemble Figure 60. Even though the yellow circles are selected, when you set the foreground color to a different color, the circles don't change color.

4. Click and drag to highlight the **objects shown in Figure 61**.

   When you release the mouse button, the objects are united as a single object.

   Continued on next page

Figure 60 Selecting a fill color for the Shape Builder tool

Shape Builder tool

Fill and stroke for new shape

Figure 61 Highlighting objects to be merged into a new object

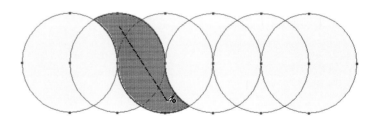

5. Click and drag to highlight the **objects shown in Figure 62**.

Because you included the first pink object, the objects are united into a single object, as shown in Figure 63.

6. Save your work, then continue to the next set of steps.

You dragged with the Shape Builder tool to create a new object.

Delete objects with the Shape Builder tool

1. Verify that the **entire illustration** is selected.

2. Press and hold **[option] (Mac)** or **[Alt] (Win)**, then drag the **Shape Builder tool**

over the objects shown in Figure 64.

When you release, the objects are deleted.

3. Press and hold **[shift] [option] (Mac)** or **[shift] [Alt] (Win)**, then drag the **Shape Builder tool** over all the **yellow objects** to the right of the pink shape.

Adding the [shift] key to the combination allows you to drag a selection marquee to highlight more objects.

4. Press and hold **[option] (Mac)** or **[Alt] (Win)**, then click the **last remaining yellow object**.

Your result should resemble Figure 65.

5. Save your work, then close the Shape Builder document.

You used the Shape Builder tool to delete objects.

Figure 62 Adding more objects to the new shape

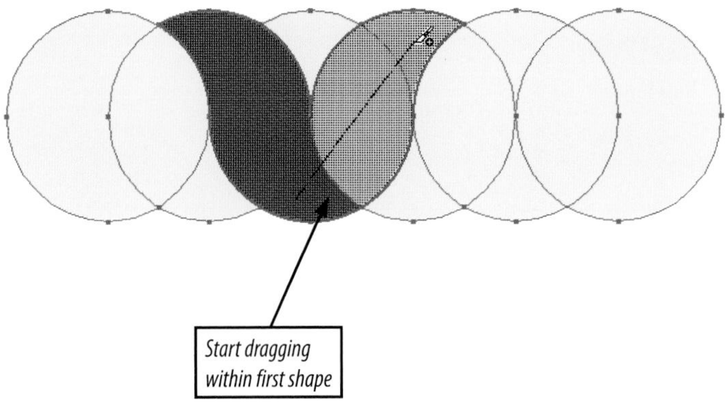

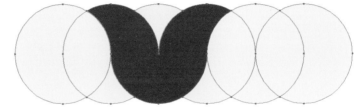

Start dragging within first shape

Figure 63 The new shape

Figure 64 Highlighting shapes to be deleted

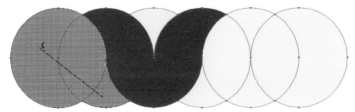

Figure 65 The final shape

CREATE CLIPPING MASKS

What You'll Do

In this lesson, you will explore the role of clipping masks for practical use and for artistic effects

Defining a Clipping Mask

Clipping masks are used to yield a practical result. And as with compound paths, that practical result can be manipulated to create interesting graphic effects.

Practically speaking, you use a clipping mask as a "window" through which you view some or all the objects behind the mask in the stacking order. When you select any two or more objects and apply the Make Clipping Mask command, the *top object* becomes the mask and the object behind it becomes "masked." You will be able to see only the parts of the masked object that are visible *through* the mask, as shown in Figure 66. The mask crops the object behind it.

Figure 66 Clipping mask crops the object behind it

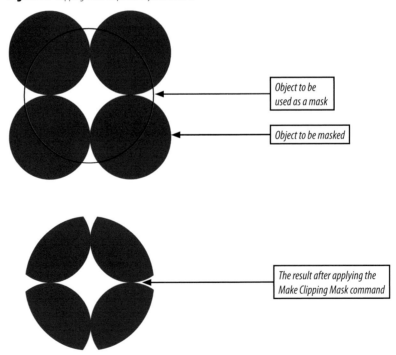

Object to be used as a mask

Object to be masked

The result after applying the Make Clipping Mask command

Using Multiple Objects as a Clipping Mask

When you select multiple objects and apply the Make Clipping Mask command, the top object becomes the mask. Since every object has its own position in the stacking order, it stands to reason that there can be only one top object.

If you want to use multiple objects as a mask, you can do so by first making them into a compound path because Illustrator regards compound paths as a single object. Therefore, a compound path containing multiple objects can be used as a single mask.

Creating Masked Effects

Special effects with clipping masks are, quite simply, fun! You can position as many objects as you like behind the mask and position them in such a way that the mask crops them in visually interesting (and eye-popping!) ways.

Using the Draw Inside Drawing Mode

The Draw Inside drawing mode does just what its name implies: it allows you to create one object within the perimeter of another object. For example, you can draw a square, click the Draw Inside button on the toolbar, then draw a circle that appears only inside the square. Drawing one object inside another is essentially the same thing as creating a clipping mask. The object that's drawn inside is clipped by the object that contains it. If you've drawn an object inside another and you want to remove the relationship between them, click Object on the menu bar, point to Clipping Mask, then click Release.

Create a clipping mask

1. Open AI 4-15.ai, then save it as **Simple Masks**.
2. Click **View** on the menu bar, then click **Mask 1**.
3. Move the **rectangle** so it overlaps the **gold spheres** as shown in Figure 67.
4. Apply the **Bring to Front command** to verify that the rectangle is in front of all the spheres.
5. Select the **seven spheres** and the **rectangle**.
6. Click **Object** on the menu bar, point to **Clipping Mask**, then click **Make**.
7. Deselect, then compare your screen to Figure 68.

Continued on next page

Figure 67 Masking objects must be in front of objects to be masked

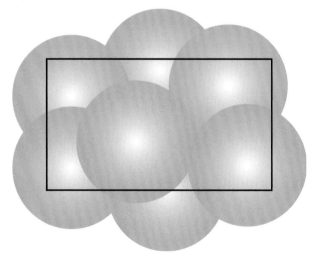

Figure 68 The rectangle masks the gold spheres

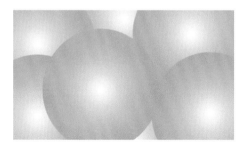

8. Click **View** on the menu bar, then click **Mask 2**.

9. Select the **three circles**, then move them over the "gumballs."

   The three circles are a compound path.

10. Select the **group of gumballs** and the **three circles**, click **Object** on the menu bar, point to **Clipping Mask**, then click **Make**.

11. Deselect, click **Select** on the menu bar, point to **Object**, then click **Clipping Masks**.

12. Apply a **1 pt. black stroke** to the masks.

    Your work should resemble Figure 69.

13. Save your work, then close the Simple Masks document.

You used a rectangle as a clipping mask. Then, you used three circles to mask a group of small spheres and applied a black stroke to the mask.

Apply a fill to a clipping mask

1. Open AI 4-16.ai, then save it as **Magnify**.

2. Move the **large text** over the **small text** so both **letters g** align as shown in Figure 70.

3. Select the **smaller text**, then hide it.

4. Select the **magnifying glass (circle)** and the **handle**, then drag them **over the letter g**, as shown in Figure 71.

Figure 69 A compound path used as a mask

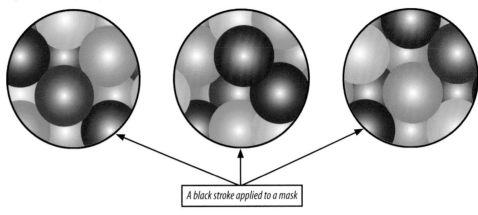

A black stroke applied to a mask

Figure 70 Lining up the letter g

Figure 71 Positioning the magnifying glass

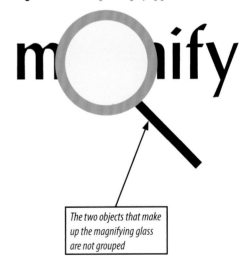

The two objects that make up the magnifying glass are not grouped

5. Deselect all, select only the **circle** and the **text**, click **Object** on the menu bar, point to **Clipping Mask**, then click **Make**.

   The circle is the masking object. The blue fill disappears.

6. Deselect, click **Select** on the menu bar, point to **Object**, then click **Clipping Masks**.

7. Use the **Swatches panel** to apply a **light blue fill** and a **gray stroke** to the mask.

8. Change the **weight** of the stroke to **8 pt**. so your work resembles Figure 72.

9. Show all, deselect, then compare your screen to Figure 73.

10. Select the **mask** only, press and hold **[shift]**, then click the **magnifying glass handle.**

11. Press the **arrow keys** to move the magnifying glass.

   As you move the magnifying glass left and right, it gives the illusion that the magnifying glass is enlarging the text. This would make for an interesting animation in a PDF or on a web page.

12. Save your work, then close the Magnify document.

You used the circle in the illustration as a clipping mask in combination with the large text. You added a fill and a stroke to the mask, creating the illusion that the small text is magnified in the magnifying glass.

Use text as a clipping mask

1. Open AI 4-17.ai, then save it as **Mask Effects**.

2. Select the **four letters** that make the word MASK.

3. Make the **four letters** into a **compound path**.

4. With the compound path still selected, select the **rectangle** behind it.

5. Apply the **Make Clipping Mask command**, then deselect.

6. Save your work, then continue to the next set of steps.

You converted outlines to a compound path, then used the compound path as a mask.

Figure 72 A fill and stroke are applied to a mask

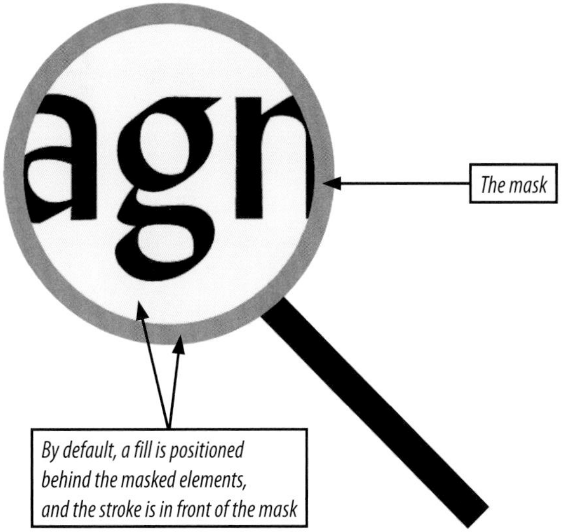

The mask

By default, a fill is positioned behind the masked elements, and the stroke is in front of the mask

Figure 73 Large text is masked by the magnifying glass

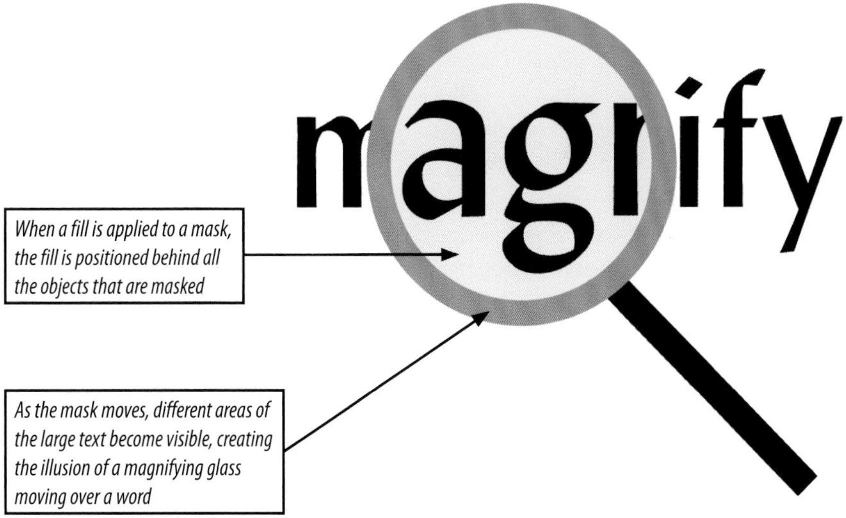

When a fill is applied to a mask, the fill is positioned behind all the objects that are masked

As the mask moves, different areas of the large text become visible, creating the illusion of a magnifying glass moving over a word

Use a clipping mask for special effects

1. Position the **curvy object** with the gradient fill over the mask, as shown in Figure 74.

2. Cut the **curvy object**.

3. Click **Select** on the menu bar, point to **Object**, then click **Clipping Masks**.

   The mask is selected.

4. Click **Edit** on the menu bar, click **Paste in Back**, then deselect so your screen resembles Figure 75.

   The object is pasted behind the mask and in front of the masked rectangle.

5. Click the **Selection tool** ▶ on the toolbar, select the **purple dotted line**, position it over the **letter K**, then cut the **purple dotted line**.

6. Click **Select** on the menu bar, point to **Object**, then click **Clipping Masks**.

7. Click **Edit** on the menu bar, then click **Paste in Back**.

8. Using the same technique, mask the other objects on the artboard in any way that you choose.

   When finished, your mask should contain all the objects, as shown in Figure 76.

TIP Add a stroke to the mask if desired.

9. Save your work, then close the Mask Effects document.

You created visual effects by pasting objects behind a mask.

Figure 74 Curvy object in position to be masked by the letters

Figure 75 Curvy object is masked by the letters

Figure 76 Pasting multiple objects behind a mask yields interesting effects

Use the Draw Inside drawing mode

1. Open AI 4-18.ai, save it as **Draw Inside**, click the **Selection tool** , then select the **blue square** at the top of the document.

   When you select the blue square, by default the fill and stroke buttons on the toolbar take on the object's colors, which, in this case, are Blue and [None].

2. Click the **Draw Inside button** at the bottom of the toolbar, then click the **Ellipse tool** .

   Because you must have an object selected to use the Draw Inside drawing mode, the object you draw will always be the same fill and stroke color as the object you're drawing into. You can make them different colors only after you draw inside.

3. Draw an **ellipse** that overlaps the **blue square**, making it approximately the same size as the **pink ellipse** already on the artboard.

4. With the **ellipse** still selected, change its **fill color** to **yellow**.

   Figure 77 shows one example of how the ellipse is drawn within the blue square. Dotted lines around the four corners of the blue square indicate that it is functioning as a mask for the ellipse. As long as you stay in Draw Inside drawing mode, any object you create will be drawn inside the blue square.

5. Click the **Draw Normal button** on the toolbar, select the word **MASK**, click **Type** on the menu bar, then click **Create Outlines**.

6. With the **outlines** still selected, click **Object** on the menu bar, point to **Compound Path**, click

Make, then fill them with any **green swatch** on the Swatches panel.

Defined as a compound path, the letter outlines are now a single object into which you can draw.

7. Select the **pink ellipse**, cut it, select the **MASK outlines**, then click the **Draw Inside button** .

Dotted lines appear around the MASK outlines, indicated they can be drawn into.

8. Click **Edit** on the menu bar, click **Paste**, then move the **ellipse** so it overlaps the MASK outlines as shown in Figure 78.

9. Save your work, then close the Draw Inside document.

You used the Draw Inside drawing mode to create objects within other objects and within outlined text.

Figure 77 Drawing the yellow ellipse inside the blue square

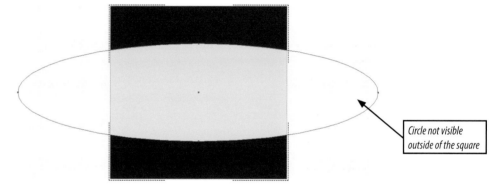

Circle not visible outside of the square

Figure 78 Drawing the pink ellipse inside the outlines via the Paste command

Transform objects

1. Open AI 4-19.ai, then save it as **Transform Skills**.
2. Select "DIVIDE."
3. Scale the text objects non-uniformly: Horizontal = 110% and Vertical = 120%.
4. Rotate the text objects 7°.
5. Shear the text objects 25° on the horizontal axis.
6. Save your work.

Offset and outline paths

1. Ungroup the text outlines.
2. Using the Offset Path command, offset each letter −.05".
3. Save your work.

Work with the Pathfinder panel

1. Select all.
2. Apply the Divide pathfinder.
3. Fill the divided elements with different colors, using the Direct Selection tool.
4. Select all, then apply a 2 pt. white stroke. Enlarge the view to see the effect better.
5. Save your work, compare your image to Figure 79, then close the Transform Skills document.

Create compound paths

1. Open AI 4-20.ai, then save it as **Compounded**.
2. Select all, press [option] (Mac) or [Alt] (Win), then click the Exclude button on the Pathfinder panel.
3. Deselect, then click the center of the small square with the Direct Selection tool.
4. Rotate a copy of the small square 45°.
5. Save your work, compare your image to Figure 80, then close the Compounded document.

Use the Shape Builder tool

1. Open AI 4-21.ai, then save it as **Shape Builder Skills**.
2. Select all, then set the fill color on the objects to [None] so you can see the shapes being created by the overlapping.
3. Click the Shape Builder tool.
4. Set the fill and stroke color to a shade of light blue and [None], respectively.
   Even though the circles are selected, when you set the foreground color to a different color with the Shape Builder tool, the circles don't change color.

Figure 79 Completed Skills Review, Part 1

Figure 80 Completed Skills Review, Part 2

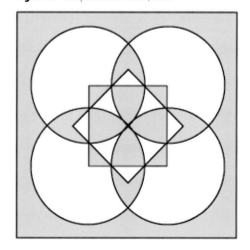

5. Click and drag to highlight the objects shown in Figure 81.

   When you release the mouse button, the objects are united as a single object.
6. Change the fill color on the toolbar to a shade of red.
7. Click and drag to highlight the remaining objects shown in Figure 82.
8. Click the Selection tool, then click the artboard to deselect both objects.
9. Click the top blue object, then drag it away from the red object.
10. Save your work, then close Shape Builder Skills.

Create clipping masks

1. Open AI 4-22.ai, then save it as **Masked Paths**.
2. Position any three of the letters on the right side of the canvas over the artwork on the left.
3. Hide the three letters you didn't choose.
4. Select the three letters over the artwork, click Object on the menu bar, point to Compound Path, then click Make.
5. Select everything on the artboard.
6. Click Object on the menu bar, point to Clipping Mask, then click Make.
7. Deselect all.
8. Click Select on the menu bar, point to Object, then click Clipping Masks.
9. Add a 1.5 pt. black stroke to the selection.
10. Compare your results to Figure 83, which shows one potential result.
11. Save your work, then close Masked Paths.

Figure 81 Highlighting with the Shape Builder tool

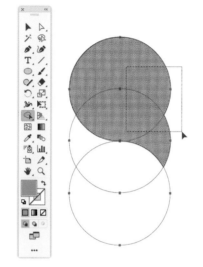

Figure 82 Highlighting the remaining shapes

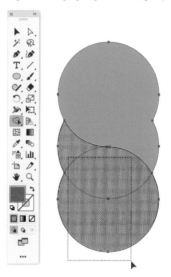

Figure 83 Completed Skills Review, Part 3

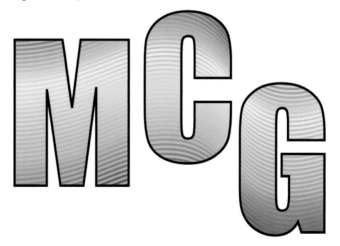

You are entering a contest to design a new stamp. You have decided to use a picture of Mark Twain, which you have placed in an Illustrator document. You have positioned text over the image. Now, to complete the effect, you want to mimic the perforated edges of a stamp.

1. Open AI 4-23.ai, then save it as **Mark Twain Stamp**.
2. Select all the circles, then make them into a compound path.
3. Add the rectangle to the selection. The rectangle is behind the circles in the stacking order.
4. Apply the Minus Front shape mode, then deselect all.
5. Save your work, compare your image to Figure 84, then close the Mark Twain Stamp document.

Figure 84 Completed Project Builder 1

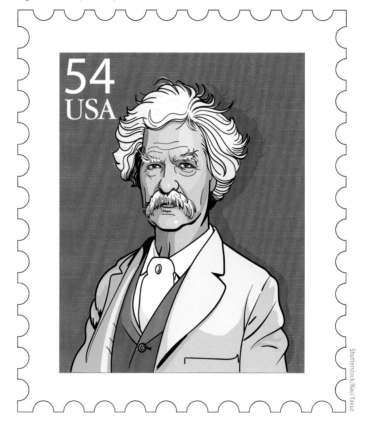

Shutterstock/Naci Yavuz

You have been contracted to design the logo for Wired Gifts, which is an online gift site. Your concept is of a geometric red bow. You feel your idea will simultaneously convey the concepts of gifts and technology.

1. Open AI 4-24.ai, then save it as **Wired**.
2. Switch to Outline mode.
3. Select the small square, click the Rotate tool, press and hold [option] (Mac) or [Alt] (Win), then click the center of the large square.
4. Type **15** in the Angle text box, then click Copy.
5. Repeat the transformation 22 times.
6. Delete the large square at the center.
7. Switch to Preview mode.
8. Select all, then fill all the squares with Caribbean Blue.
   The color swatches on the Swatches panel in this file have been saved with names.
9. Apply the Divide pathfinder to the selection.
10. Fill the objects with the Red Bow gradient.
11. Delete the object in the center of the bow.
    Use the Direct Selection tool to select the object.
12. Select all, then remove the black stroke from the objects.
13. Save your work, compare your illustration with Figure 85, then close the Wired document.

Figure 85 Completed Project Builder 2

DESIGN PROJECT 1

You are an illustrator for a small-town quarterly magazine. You're designing an illustration to accompany an article titled "A Walk Down Main Street." You decide to distort the artwork in perspective to make a more interesting illustration.

1. Open AI 4-25.ai, then save it as **Main Street Perspective**.
2. Select all the buildings on the left, then click the Free Transform tool.
3. Click and begin dragging the upper-right handle straight down.
4. While still dragging, press and hold [shift] [Ctrl] [Alt] (Win) or [shift] [command] [option] (Mac) and continue dragging until you like the appearance of the artwork.
5. Release the mouse button.
6. Click and drag the middle-left handle to the right to reduce the depth of the distortion.
   Figure 86 shows one possible result.
7. Using the same methodology, distort the buildings on the right in perspective.
   Figure 87 shows one possible solution.
8. Save your work, then close the Main Street Perspective document.

Figure 86 Distorting the left of the illustration

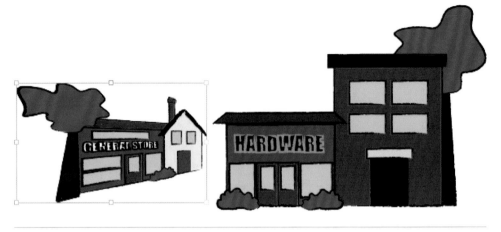

Figure 87 Completed Design Project

You are the design department manager for a toy company, and your next project is to design a dartboard that will be part of a package of "Safe Games" for kids. The target market is boys and girls ages six to adult. You will design the board but not the darts.

1. Create a new document and name it **Dartboard**.
2. Search the Internet for pictures of dartboards.
3. Research the sport of throwing darts. What are the official dimensions of a dartboard? Is there an official design? Are there official colors?
4. Decide which colors should be used for the board, keeping in mind that the sales department plans to position it as a toy for both girls and boys.
5. Using the skills you learned in this chapter and Figure 88 as a guide, design a dartboard.
6. Save your work, compare your image to Figure 88, then close Dartboard.

Figure 88 Completed Design Project 2

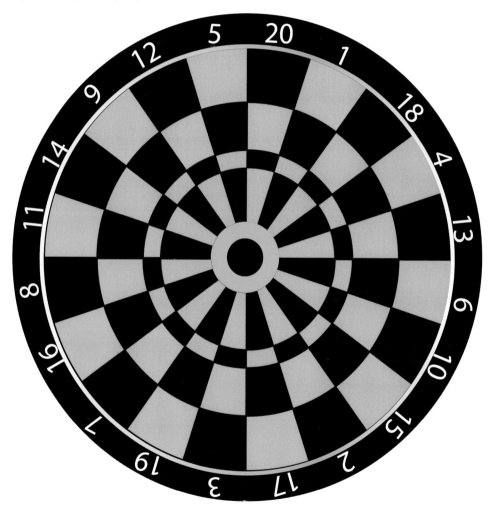

CAPTURING COMPLEXITY

Strangler Fig, a watercolor painting by Nirupa Rao, highlights the plant's unique role in its ecosystem.

Images courtesy of Nirupa Rao

DEVELOPING AN APPRECIATION

Growing up in Bengaluru, India, Nirupa Rao spent much of her childhood exploring the nearby jungle with her family. Their walks through the wild, tropical forest cultivated Nirupa's fondness for and appreciation of nature. Her granduncle, a field botanist, collected plant specimens from the jungle surrounding her grandfather's farm. Her mother's stories of this research inspired an air of adventure and excitement. A storyteller at heart, Nirupa enjoyed putting on plays for her family and also took an interest in creating handcrafted items, such as toys and books. Nirupa has carried her artistic talent and passion for nature into her career as a botanical illustrator. Her detailed works depict impactful stories about the unique behaviors of plants in India.

EDUCATION AND EARLY CAREER

With the exception of one online course, Nirupa is mostly a self-taught artist. While studying in Singapore, Nirupa had the opportunity to learn from other creatives and experiment with different mediums. Her interest grew when her cousin, a botanical researcher, shared photographs of plants and flowers with her. This inspired Nirupa to begin painting. She then took an internship in the children's division of a publishing house in the United Kingdom. While there, she learned about media research and further developed her creative skills using software programs such as Adobe Creative Suite. This helped Nirupa visualize her next step—providing children in India with similar content, so they, too, could learn about plants native to India.

CREATIVE PROJECTS AND PUBLICATIONS

In 2016, *National Geographic* awarded Nirupa a Young Explorers Grant to create an illustrated book of plant life in the Western Ghats of India. Published in 2019, *Hidden Kingdom—Fantastical Plants of the Western Ghats* sets Nirupa's colorful and intricately detailed illustrations to rhyme and helps open children's minds to the magical plants that exist in their own backyard. In addition to publishing other pieces, Nirupa's work has been displayed in the museum at Harvard's Dumbarton Oaks Museums. She collaborates with botanists and naturalists to ensure scientific accuracy in every illustration.

In Nirupa's book, *Hidden Kingdom*, she shares this watercolor painting titled *Strangler Fig*. The painting shows a tropical wild fig tree, which is part of the Ficus genus. This particular fig is often referred to as a strangler fig because of its unique behavior. This keystone species produces fruit throughout the year, providing food for birds, bats, and small mammals. In turn, birds drop strangler fig seeds on the branches of grown trees. The seeds germinate upon existing trees as a means to access sunlight more quickly. Over time, the roots of the strangler fig engulf the host tree, cutting off its access to sunlight and eventually strangling it to death with its roots.

Looking to capture this unique plant behavior, Nirupa created a watercolor painting of the strangler fig. Sitting low on the ground, she sketched the fig from below to capture the shapes of the branches, which she has described as "a hand grasping for sunlight." Nirupa often uses notes, photographs, and detailed sketches of the plants, which she then brings back to her studio to paint, scan, and manipulate using different software. Nirupa's process is very detail-oriented and thorough. She believes if you take the time to comprehend the complexity of an ecosystem, you can begin to understand how individual plants evolve, and what that communicates about the ecology of a place as a whole.

PROJECT DESCRIPTION

In this project, you will explore a plant within your community. Using pencil, paper, paints, or any art supplies available to you, you will create an illustration. Focus on capturing the details of the plant, such as the colors and textures. Include elements of the environment in which it grows. The goal of this project is to create a detailed botanical illustration of a plant and its environment within your community.

SKILLS TO EXPLORE

- Scribbling
- Smoothing and Shading
- Hatching and Cross-Hatching
- Creating Highlights
- Rough Sketching
- Finger Blending
- Stippling
- Working with Pencil, Pen, Paint
- Observation and Patience

SOFT SKILLS CHALLENGE

Host a round-table discussion with at least three classmates. The roundtable should focus on plant life in your community and the local environment as a whole. You will need to recruit classmates to take part in the discussion, write a script introducing the round-table topic and the people participating, and create an outline of the questions and talking points. It will be your job to facilitate the discussion, keep the conversation moving, and ensure everyone's opinion is being respected. The goals of this challenge are to think critically about the plant life in your community and connect it to a bigger picture. Find out what your peers think about the topic and use collaboration and conversation as a way to better understand the complexities of the topic.

ROUND-TABLE CHECKLIST

1. Group of three or more peers

2. Written script introducing the topic and each participant

3. Outline of questions and talking points

4. Safe space to facilitate respectful conversation

FOLLOW NIRUPA'S EXAMPLE

One of the many reasons Nirupa enjoys sketching is that it slows down your eye and helps you pick out small details of the subject you are looking at. This is very important when grasping the complexity of a plant and understanding how it behaves and interacts with other plants and wildlife in its natural environment.

Once you've chosen a plant to sketch, walk around it and look at it from different angles. Think about how much of the plant is visible and which vantage point gives you the best view. Keep your focus on the plant, but make sure you capture relevant surrounding plants and wildlife. Incorporate your prior knowledge about the plant as well. For example, if you were illustrating a purple coneflower, you might wait for a bee to land on the flower and sketch that as well, as the purple coneflower is a favorite for many pollinators.

Create a note-taking system. Consider a grid of notes so you can organize your observations and keep track of important details. Some categories could include: colors, textures, surrounding plant life, observed wildlife, movement over time, etc.

Color	Texture	Movement	Location
Intense red color. Almost looks neon when sun is diectly on them. White tip in the middle of some flowers.		Petals don't move as loosely as they look like they would.	They don't seem to be by a lot of other flowers. Mostly by a lot of tall grass or Cardinals.
The buds and small/new petals look more pinkish. Some of the petals toward the bottom have turned a violet and light purple shade.	The fully bloomed petals look very soft like velvet, but the bud looks sharp. Almost like little spikes.	Petals are tightly held by the stem. With wind or when touched, whole flower moves together in a stiff motion. Looks delicate but holds well.	

To keep organized, the student created a grid system for notes. The student focused on the petals of the flower and how they compared to other flowers around it.

The student focused on illustrating the tree's leaves by experimenting with different lines and shading. The student then took photographs of the entire tree and surrounding environment for later reference.

PROJECT DESCRIPTION

In this project, you will use your plant illustration from the Design Project to create an infographic describing the different parts of the plant. You will need to either photograph and upload, or scan your illustration to your computer. Once you have your botanical illustration available on your computer, you will use Adobe Illustrator to refine, enhance, and add information to it. The goal of this project is to create a comprehensive infographic that educates viewers about the appearance, behavior, and environment of a local plant.

SKILLS TO EXPLORE

- Work with Basic Shapes
- Apply Fill and Stroke Colors to Objects
- Make Direct Selections
- Create Point Text
- Manipulate Text with the Touch Type Tool
- Create Gradients
- Draw Straight and Curved Lines
- Draw Elements of an Illustration
- Apply Attributes to Objects
- Use Image Trace
- Use the Live Paint Bucket Tool
- Transform Objects
- Offset and Outline Paths
- Create Compound Paths
- Work With the Pathfinder Panel
- Apply Round Corners to Objects
- Use the Shape Builder Tool
- Create Clipping Masks

SOFT SKILLS CHALLENGE

Write a blog post about the work you created and share it to a social media account. In your blog, include basic background information about your chosen plant, such as its behavior and characteristics. You will also want to write about why you chose the plant, what your creative process was when creating your composition, and some details of your illustration that a viewer might miss upon first glance. This is a great opportunity to explain your work to a wider audience and tell why you made some of your creative choices.

Don't forget to keep the conversation going. Respond to comments and interactions with your post. The goal of this challenge is for you to present your designs and use your work as a steppingstone to bigger conversations.

FOLLOW NIRUPA'S EXAMPLE

Take photographs. It can be hard to capture every detail in a sketch and even harder to remember the details once you've left the scene. Photographs are a great way to record a moment and refer back to it later. Sometimes photographs can even document elements you did not notice initially; for example, a nearby ant hill or the plant's shadow on the ground.

Use your resources. It can be helpful to know what you are looking for before you get there. Research local plants online, or better yet, find someone in your community to talk to. You might interview your science teacher or a friendly neighbor who enjoys gardening. Plants often have small details, such as colors and textures, that go unnoticed but communicate a lot about their behavior and health. If you do your research ahead of time, you will know what types of organisms are commonly found in your environment, and which are not. This will help you determine whether the plants you are seeing naturally occur in this ecosystem.

GETTING STARTED

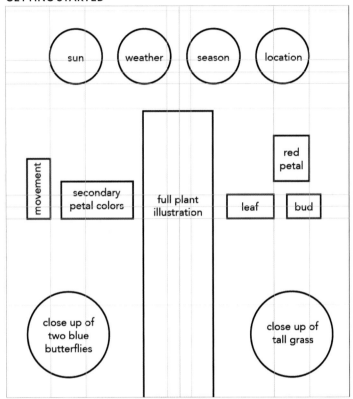

The student has a lot of information to include and fit into a single infographic. To keep it organized and cohesive, the student mapped out where each piece of information will go and eliminated information deemed less important to the story.

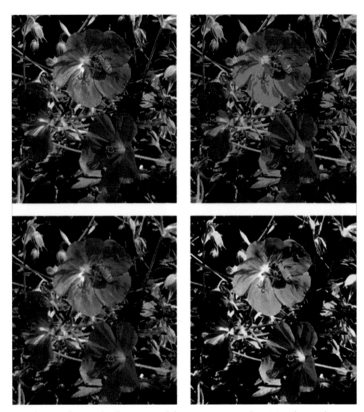

In order to enhance the illustration while maintaining authenticity, the student experimented with several techniques and effects in Illustrator to figure out which one felt the most authentic and original.

As the sun rises above the Tibetan Plateau, Pasang Kaji Sherpa (front) and Lhakpa Tenje Sherpa pass 28,700 feet on Mount Everest. The big question: Did George Mallory and Sandy Irvine get this far—or perhaps reach the top—in 1924?

THE ROOF OF THE WORLD

THE
PAGE
42

JULY
2020

ISSUE

THE GREAT MYSTERY OF
EVEREST

BY **MARK SYNNOTT**   PHOTOGRAPHS BY **RENAN OZTURK**

This dramatic photograph is paired with a visually engaging layout, compelling typography, and bold color to add intrigue to the article.

Photograph by Renan Ozturk. From "The Great Mystery of Everest." *National Geographic Magazine*, Vol. 238, No. 1, July, 2020

$7.95

Lemon-poppyseed
vacherin, huckleberries
and lemon curd

Dessert Menu

$6.50

Orange tea cakes with
honey, pine nut brittle ice
cream and figs

$7.95

Chocolate Genoise cake
with a truffle center and
cocoa nutmeg glaze

12

GET STARTED WITH INDESIGN

1. Explore the InDesign Workspace
2. View and Modify Page Elements
3. Navigate Through a Document
4. Work with Objects and Smart Guides

 CERTIFIED PROFESSIONAL

Adobe Certified Professional in Print & Digital Media Publication Using Adobe InDesign

2. Project Setup and Interface

This objective covers the interface setup and program settings that assist in an efficient and effective workflow, as well as knowledge about ingesting digital assets for a project.

2.2 Navigate, organize, and customize the application workspace.
    A Identify and manipulate elements of the InDesign interface.
    B Organize and customize the workspace.
    C Configure application preferences.

2.3 Use nonprinting design tools in the interface to aid in design or workflow.
    A Navigate a document.
    B Use rulers.
    C Use guides and grids.
    D Use views and modes to work efficiently.

4. Creating and Modifying Document Elements

This objective covers core tools and functionality of the application, as well as tools that affect the visual appearance of document elements.

4.3 Make, manage, and edit selections.
    A Make selections using a variety of tools.
    B Modify and refine selections using various methods.

4.4 Transform digital graphics and media within a publication.
    A Modify frames and frame content.
    B Rotate, flip, and transform individual frames or content.

EXPLORE THE INDESIGN WORKSPACE

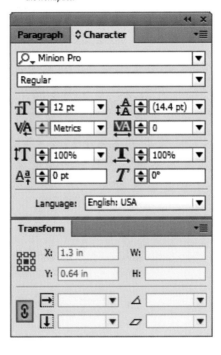

Looking at the InDesign Workspace

The arrangement of windows and panels that you see on your monitor is called the **workspace**. The InDesign workspace features the following areas: the document window, the pasteboard, the menu bar, the Control panel, the toolbar, and a stack of collapsed panels along the right side of the pasteboard. Figure 1 shows the default workspace, which is called Essentials, along with the Control panel along the top. The Control panel lists available options when you click a tool on the toolbar.

InDesign offers many predefined workspaces that are customized for different types of tasks. Each workspace is designed so panels with similar functions are grouped together. For example, the Typography workspace shows the many type- and typography-based panels that are useful for working with type. You can switch from one workspace to another by clicking Window on the menu bar, pointing to Workspace, and then clicking one of the available workspaces. Or you can use the workspace switcher on the menu bar.

You can (and should) customize the workspace to suit your working preferences. For example, you can open and close whatever panels you want and group them as you like and in a way that makes sense for you and your work. You can save a customized workspace by clicking Window on the menu bar, pointing to Workspace, then clicking New Workspace. Once the new workspace is named, it will appear in the Workspace menu.

TIP You can restore the default arrangement of a given workspace by clicking Window on the menu bar, pointing to Workspace, then clicking the Reset command for that workspace's name.

You determine the size of the document, or the page size, when you create the file. A document page is displayed as a white rectangle with a black border and shadow. The **pasteboard** is the area surrounding the document. The pasteboard provides space for extending objects past the edge of the page (known as "creating a bleed"), and it also provides space for storing objects that you may or may not use in the document. Objects that are positioned wholly on the pasteboard do not print, but they are there if you choose to use them in the future.

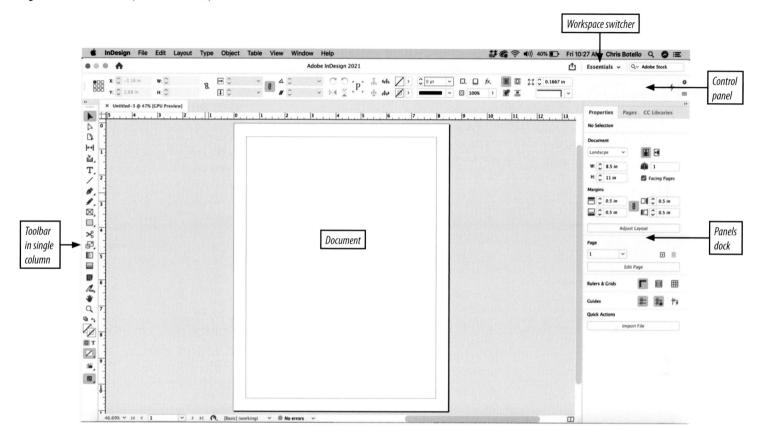

Workspace switcher

Control panel

Toolbar in single column

Document

Panels dock

Exploring the Toolbar

As its name implies, the toolbar houses all the tools that you will work with in InDesign. Simply click a tool to access it.

The first thing that you should note about the toolbar is that not all tools are visible; many are hidden. Look closely and you will see that some tools have small black triangles beside them. These triangles indicate that other tools are hidden behind them. To access hidden tools, point to the visible tool on the toolbar, then press and hold the mouse button; this will reveal a menu of hidden tools. The small black square to the left of a tool name in the menu indicates the tool that is currently visible on the toolbar, as shown in Figure 2.

You can choose to view the toolbar as a single column, a double column, or even a horizontal row of tools. Simply click the two black carats ►► at the top of the toolbar to toggle between the different setups. We recommend that you work with the toolbar in two columns of tools, so that is how we will display the toolbar in this book.

Light gray horizontal lines divide the toolbar into five sections. The top section contains the selection tools. The section beneath that contains item creation tools, such as the drawing, shape, and type tools. Next is a section that contains transform tools, such as the Rotate and Scale tools. The next section contains navigation tools. Here you can find the Hand tool—used to scroll through a document, and the Zoom tool, used to magnify your view of a document.

The bottom-most sections of the toolbar contain functions for applying colors and gradients to objects and choosing different modes for viewing documents, such as the commonly used Preview mode.

To choose a tool, simply click it; you can also press a shortcut key to access a tool. For example, pressing [P] selects the Pen tool. You can have some fun learning the shortcut key for tools you use; some of them are predictable, and some are unexpected. To learn the shortcut key for each tool, point to a tool until a tooltip appears with the tool's name and its shortcut key in parentheses.

Figure 2 Hidden tools on the toolbar

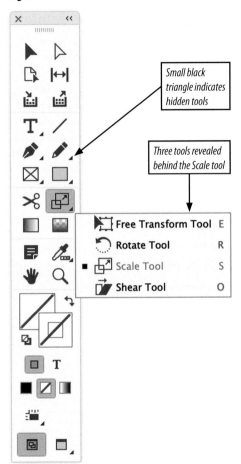

Small black triangle indicates hidden tools

Three tools revealed behind the Scale tool

	Free Transform Tool	E
Rotate Tool	R
Scale Tool	S
Shear Tool	O

Working with Panels

Many InDesign functions are housed on panels. For example, the Paragraph panel contains paragraph editing functions such as text alignment, space before and after paragraphs, and indents. The Character panel, shown in Figure 3, offers controls for changing the font, font size, and leading. Note the panel menu button. Panels contain not only the functions that are displayed; there's also a menu of options you can access. Be sure to investigate panel menus, especially on the Character and Paragraph panels, which offer many type formatting choices.

All panels can be accessed on the Window menu. This is such an important fact that we will repeat it: All panels can be accessed on the Window menu. This means that you never have to wonder how to find a panel; it's on the Window menu.

Some panels are placed within categories on the Window menu. For example, all the text- and table-related panels, such as the Character panel and the Table panel, are listed in the Type & Tables category. The Swatches, Gradient, and Color panels are all categorized under Color. Make note of the Object & Layout category, which contains three powerful panels: Align, Pathfinder, and Transform.

When you choose a panel from the Window menu, the panel appears in its expanded view. To reduce the size of a panel, click the two black carats, which collapses the panel to a named icon.

To better manage available workspace, it's a good idea to group panels; do so strategically, based on their function. Figure 4 shows the Character and Paragraph panels grouped together. The Paragraph panel is the active panel—it is in front of the others in the group and available for use. The Character panel appears as a tab; click it to make it active.

Figure 3 Character panel

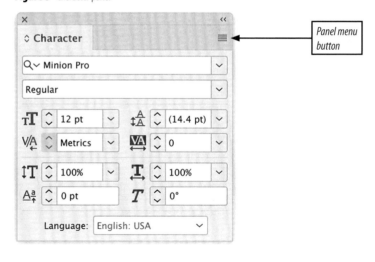

Panel menu button

Figure 4 Two grouped panels

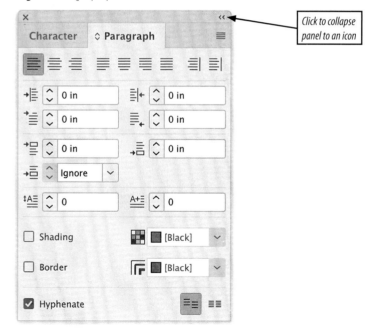

Click to collapse panel to an icon

To group panels, drag one panel by its name onto another panel's name. Ungroup panels by dragging a panel's name tab away from the other panels in the group.

Grouping panels is not the same as docking panels. Docking panels is a different function. When you **dock** panels, you connect the bottom edge of one panel to the top edge of another panel so both move together. To dock panels, drag a panel's name tab to the bottom edge of another panel. When the bottom edge of the other panel is highlighted in bright blue, release the mouse button and the two panels will be docked. To undock a panel, simply drag it away from the other panels.

RESPONDING TO LINKS AND FONT WARNINGS

InDesign documents often contain support files, such as graphics created in other programs like Photoshop and Illustrator. In creating this book, we included all such support files in the same folder as the InDesign data files with which you will be working. By doing so, InDesign will be able to locate those files and update the InDesign document when you open it. When you open a document, however, you will often see a warning about missing or modified links. Unless you are instructed otherwise, you should always click Update Links when you see this warning. Likewise, we have used common fonts in the data files to minimize warnings about missing fonts. However, if you encounter a layout that uses a font not currently loaded on your computer, you can accept the replacement font InDesign offers as an automatic replacement, or if you prefer, you can use the Find Font command on the Type menu to choose another font.

OPENING INDESIGN CC FILES IN EARLIER VERSIONS OF INDESIGN

InDesign CC documents cannot be opened in earlier versions of InDesign, such as CS5 or CS6. To open an InDesign CC document in an earlier version of InDesign, you must export the CC document in the InDesign Markup Language (IDML) format. Click File on the menu bar, click Export, then choose InDesign Markup (IDML) as the file format. The exported document can be opened in earlier versions of InDesign. Note, however, that any new CC features applied to your document will be lost when the file is converted to the older version.

Explore the toolbar

1. Launch Adobe InDesign.

2. Click **File** on the menu bar, click **Open**, navigate to the drive and folder where your Chapter 12 data files are stored, click **ID 1-1.indd**, then click **Open**.

   TIP If you see a warning about missing or modified links, click Update Links. If you see the Missing Fonts dialog box, you can use the font chosen by InDesign by clicking OK, or you can click Find Font and choose another font in the Find Font dialog box. For more information, see the Sidebar titled *Responding to Links and Font Warnings*.

3. Click **Window** on the menu bar, point to **Workspace**, then click **[Typography]**.

4. Click **Window** on the menu bar, point to **Workspace**, then click **Reset Typography** to load the default Typography workspace settings.

5. Point to the **Type tool** T , then press and hold the mouse button to see the **Type on a Path tool** .

6. Using the same method, view the **hidden tools** behind the other tools with small black triangles, shown in Figure 5.

   Your visible tools may differ from the figure.

7. Position your mouse pointer over the **Selection tool** ▶ until its tooltip appears.

8. Press the following keys, and note which tools are selected with each key: **[A]**, **[P]**, **[V]**, **[T]**, **[I]**, **[H]**, **[Z]**.

9. Press **[tab]** to temporarily hide all open panels, then press **[tab]** again.

   The panels reappear.

10. Continue to the next set of steps.

You explored the toolbar, revealed hidden tools, used shortcut keys to access tools quickly, hid the panels, then displayed them again.

Figure 5 Tools that conceal hidden tools

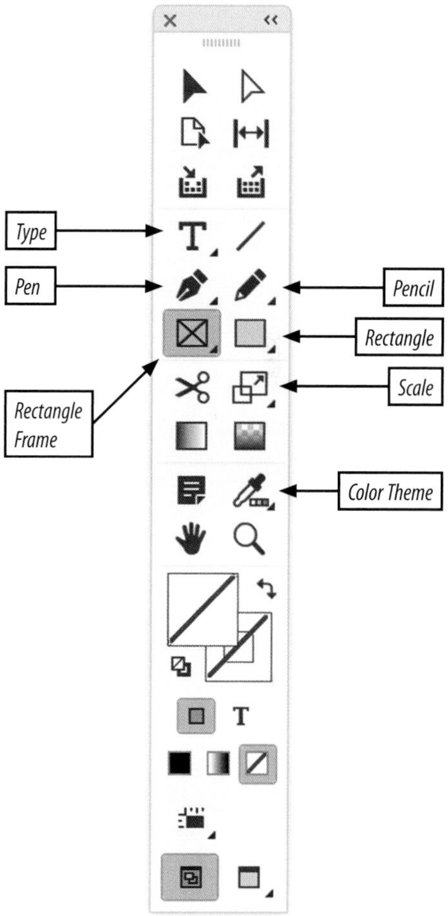

Create a custom workspace

1. Click **Window** on the menu bar, point to **Workspace**, then click **[Essentials Classic]**.

2. Click **Window** on the menu bar, point to **Workspace**, then click **[Reset Essentials Classic]**.

   The Essentials Classic workspace is a practical workspace with many core panels showing. However, it's missing some other important panels, which you will now open.

3. Press and hold **[command] (Mac)** or **[Ctrl] (Win)**, then press the **letter [T]** on your keypad.

   The Character panel appears.

4. Press and hold **[command] [option] (Mac)** or **[Ctrl] [Alt] (Win)**, then press the **letter [T]** on your keypad.

   The Paragraph panel appears.

5. Drag the **Paragraph panel** by its name onto the name of the **Character panel**.

   The two panels are grouped.

6. Click the ◂▸ **button** at the top-right corner of the grouped panel.

   The panel is minimized.

7. Drag the **minimized panel** by the **gray bar** at the top below the Swatches panel in the panels dock at the right edge of the window.

   The Character and Paragraph panels are listed on the dock.

8. Using the Window menu, open the **Align**, **Pathfinder**, and **Transform panels**.

   Align, Pathfinder, and Transform are submenus under the Object & Layout menu.

9. Group the Align, Pathfinder, and Transform panels.

10. Drag the grouped panels into the panels dock below the Character and Paragraph panels.

    Your panels dock should resemble Figure 6. To access any of the panels, simply click on its name.

11. Click **Window** on the menu bar, point to **Workspace**, then click **New Workspace**.

    The New Workspace dialog box opens.

12. Verify that both **Capture options** are checked, type your **last name** in all caps in the **Name text box**, then click **OK**.

    The customized workspace is saved and available on the Window menu under Workspace. You should use this workspace for the remainder of the book.

13. Save your work, then continue to the next lesson.

You grouped panels, minimized them, and added them to the panels dock. You then created a new workspace based on the new arrangement of panels.

Figure 6 The panels dock

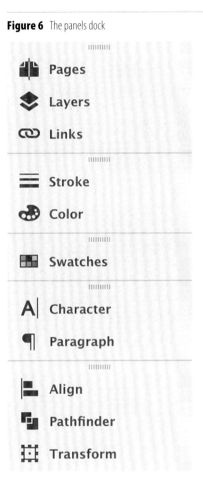

VIEW AND MODIFY PAGE ELEMENTS

▶ What You'll Do

In this lesson, you will explore various methods for viewing the document and page elements like rulers, guides, grids, and frame edges.

Using the Zoom Tool

Imagine creating a layout on a traditional pasteboard—not on your computer. For precise work, you would bring your nose closer to the pasteboard so you could better see what you were doing. At other times, you would hold the pasteboard away from you, at arm's length, so you could get a larger perspective of the artwork.

When you're working in InDesign, the Zoom tool performs these functions for you.

When you click the Zoom tool and move the pointer over the document window, the pointer becomes the Zoom pointer with a plus sign; when you click the document with the Zoom pointer, the document area you clicked is enlarged. To reduce the view of the document, press and hold [option] (Mac) or [Alt] (Win). When the plus sign changes to a minus sign, click the document with this Zoom pointer, and the document size is reduced.

Using the Zoom tool, you can reduce or enlarge the view of the document from 5% to 4000%. Note that the current magnification level appears in the document tab and in the Zoom Level text box at the bottom-left corner of the document window.

Accessing the Zoom Tool

As you work, you can expect to zoom in and out of the document more times than you can count. The most basic way of accessing the Zoom tool is simply to click its icon on the toolbar, but that is most definitely not the way you want to work: switching constantly to click the Zoom tool will slow you down to a snail's pace.

A better method for accessing the Zoom tool is to use keyboard shortcuts. When you are using the Selection tool, for example, don't switch to the Zoom tool. Instead, press and hold [space bar] [command] (Mac) or [space bar] [Ctrl] (Win) to temporarily change the Selection tool into the Zoom Plus tool. Click the document to zoom in. When you release the keys, the Zoom tool changes back to the Selection tool.

To access the Zoom Minus tool, press [space bar] [command] [option] (Mac) or [space bar] [Ctrl] [Alt] (Win).

In addition to the Zoom tool, InDesign offers other ways to zoom in and out of your document. One of the quickest and easiest is to press [command] [+] (Mac) or [Ctrl] [+] (Win) to enlarge the view and [command] [-] (Mac) or [Ctrl] [-] (Win).

TIP Note that if you press the Zoom tool access keys simultaneously, they sometimes won't access the Zoom tool. Instead of pressing simultaneously, press [space bar] first, then add in the one or two other keys. With practice, you'll learn to do this very quickly.

Using the Hand Tool

When you zoom in on a document—when you make it appear larger—the document eventually will be too large to fit in the window. Therefore, you will need to scroll to see other areas of it. You can use the scroll bars along the bottom and the right sides of the document window, but using the Hand tool is quicker.

The best way to understand the concept of the Hand tool is to think of it as your own hand. Imagine that you could put your hand up to the document on your monitor; then move the document left, right, up, or down, like a paper on a table or against a wall. This is analogous to how the Hand tool works.

The Hand tool is a better choice for scrolling than the scroll bars because you can access the Hand tool using a keyboard shortcut. Simply press and hold [space bar] to access the Hand tool. Release [space bar] to return to the tool you were using, without having to choose it again.

> **TIP** A word of caution: You can't use the [space bar] to access the Zoom tool or the Hand tool if your Type tool is active on the toolbar. If you press the [space bar], the software will behave as if you are typing a space.

Working with Rulers, Grids, and Guides

Designing and working with page layouts involves using measurements to position and align elements in your documents.

You will find that InDesign is well-equipped with many features that help you with these tasks.

Figure 7 shows various measurement utilities. **Rulers** are positioned at the top and left side of the pasteboard to help you align objects. Click Show Rulers/Hide Rulers on the View menu to access rulers.

Rulers (and all other measurement utilities in the document) can display measurements in different units, such as inches, picas, or points. You determine the units and increments with which you want to work in the Preferences dialog box. On the Edit menu, point to Preferences, then click Units & Increments to display the dialog box shown.

Figure 7 Various measurement utilities

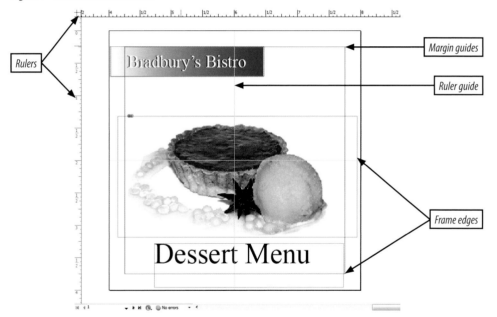

Ruler guides are horizontal and vertical rules that you can position anywhere in a layout as a reference for positioning elements. **Margin guides** are guides you can specify to appear at a given distance within the page, usually to maintain visual consistency from page to page or as a reminder to keep text or other important elements from getting too close to the edge of the page. In addition to guides, InDesign offers a **document grid** for precise alignment. With the "snap" options on, objects that you move around on the page automatically align themselves with guides or with the grid quickly and easily.

Choosing Screen Modes

Screen modes are options for viewing your documents. The two basic screen modes in InDesign are Normal and Preview. You'll work in Normal mode most of the time. In **Normal mode**, you can see all page elements, including margin guides, ruler guides, frame edges, and the pasteboard.

Preview mode shows you what your page would look like with all nonprinting elements removed. When you switch to Preview mode, all guides, grids, and frame edges become invisible to give you an idea of what your document would look like printed or as a PDF file. Even the pasteboard is hidden and becomes gray; thus, any objects on the pasteboard—or any objects that extend off your document page—become invisible. You can think of Preview mode as showing you a "cropped" view of your page—only that which is on the page is visible. However, Preview mode does not hide panels or the menu bar.

TIP The View menu offers commands for switching between Normal and Preview modes, but it's much faster and easier to press the [W] key on your keypad to toggle between the two modes.

Presentation mode presents a view of your document as though it were being showcased on your computer monitor. To toggle Presentation mode on and off, press [shift] [W] on your keypad.

In Presentation mode, your document goes full screen against a black background and is centered and sized so the entire document fits in your monitor window. All other InDesign elements, including panels and the menu bar, disappear. It's a great way to see a "clean" view of the current state of your document and when you think you're done working, a great way to see a "final" view.

When in Presentation mode, you'll have no tools or menus whatsoever to navigate through a multipage document. Instead, use the arrow keys on your keypad to move from page to page. You can also use the [esc] key to leave presentation mode.

Working with Multiple Open Documents

On many occasions, you'll find yourself working with multiple open documents. For example, let's say you're into scrapbooking. If you were designing a new document to showcase a recent trip to Italy, you might also have the file open for the scrapbook you created last year when you went to Hawaii. Why? For any number of reasons. You might want to copy and paste layout elements from the Hawaii document into the new document. Or you might want the Hawaii document open simply as a reference for typefaces, type sizes, image sizes, and effects like drop shadows that you used. When you're working with multiple open documents, you can switch from one to the other simply by clicking on the title bar of each document.

InDesign offers a preference for having multiple open documents available as tabs in the document window. With this preference selected, a tab will appear for each open document showing the name of the document. Simply click the tab and the document becomes active. This can be useful for keeping your workspace uncluttered. However, at times, it might be inhibiting because when working with multiple documents, the tabbed option allows you to view only one document at a time.

You indicate in the Interface Preferences dialog box whether you want open documents to appear as tabs. Click InDesign (Mac) or Edit (Win) on the menu bar, point to Preferences, then click Interface. Click the Open Documents as Tabs check box to select it, as shown in Figure 8, then click OK.

Figure 8 Interface Preferences dialog box

Use the Zoom tool and the Hand tool

1. Press **[Z]** to access the **Zoom tool** 🔍 .

2. Position the **Zoom tool** 🔍 over the document window, click twice to enlarge the document, press **[option] (Mac)** or **[Alt] (Win)**, then click twice to reduce the document.

3. Click the **Zoom Level list arrow** on the status bar, then click **800%**.

   Note that 800% is now listed in the document tab.

4. Double-click **800%** in the **Zoom Level text box**, type **300**, then press **[return] (Mac)** or **[Enter] (Win)**.

5. Click the **Hand tool** 🖐 on the toolbar, then click and drag the **document window** so the image in the window appears as shown in Figure 9.

6. Double-click the **Zoom tool** 🔍 on the toolbar. The magnification changes to 100% (actual size).

7. Click the **Selection tool** ▶ , point to the **center of the document window**, then press and hold **[command] [space bar] (Mac)** or **[Ctrl] [space bar] (Win)**.

   The Selection tool ▶ changes to the Zoom tool 🔍 .

8. Click three times, then release the keyboard keys.

9. Press and hold **[space bar]** to access the **Hand tool** 🖐 , then scroll around the image.

TIP Double-clicking the Hand tool 🖐 on the toolbar changes the document view to fit the page (or the spread) in the document window.

Continued on next page

Figure 9 Scrolling with the Hand tool

Bradbury's Bistro

Dessert Menu

The Hand tool will become a fist when you click and drag.

10. Press and hold **[option] [command] [space bar] (Mac)** or **[Ctrl] [Alt] [space bar] (Win)**, then click the **pasteboard** multiple times to reduce the view to 25%.

Your document window should resemble Figure 10.

11. Save your work, then continue to the next set of steps.

You explored various methods for accessing and using the Zoom tool for enlarging and reducing the document. You also used the Hand tool to scroll around an enlarged document.

Figure 10 A reduced view of the document

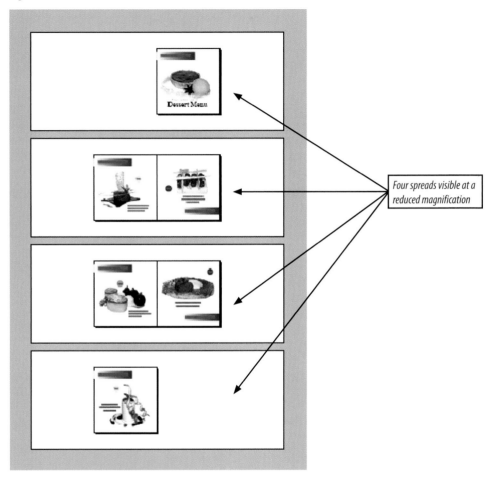

Four spreads visible at a reduced magnification

Hide and show rulers and set units and increments preferences

1. Click **View** on the menu bar, note the shortcut key for the **Fit Page in Window command**, then click **Fit Page in Window**.

   The most commonly used commands in InDesign list a shortcut key beside the command name. Shortcut keys are useful for quickly accessing commands without stopping work to go to the menu. Make a mental note of helpful shortcut keys and incorporate them into your work. You'll find that using them becomes second nature.

2. Click **View** on the menu bar, then note the **Rulers command** and its shortcut key.

   The Rulers command is set to either Hide Rulers or Show Rulers, depending on whether they are showing or not. Click the **pasteboard** to escape the View menu, then press **[command] [R] (Mac)** or **[Ctrl] [R] (Win)** several times to hide and show rulers, finishing with rulers showing.

3. Note the units on the rulers.

   Depending on the preference you have set, your rulers might be showing inches, picas, or another unit of measure.

4. Click **InDesign (Mac)** or **Edit (Win)** on the menu bar, point to **Preferences**, then click **Units & Increments**.

5. In the **Ruler Units section**, click the **Horizontal list arrow** to see the available measurement options.

6. Set the **Horizontal** and **Vertical fields** to **Inches** as shown in Figure 11, then click **OK**.

   The horizontal and vertical rulers change to inches for measurements. Note that when you create a new document, you can specify measurements in the New Document dialog box. It's important to understand that the unit of measure you set in the Preferences dialog box is a global choice. It will affect all measurement utilities in the application, such as those on the Transform panel, in addition to the ruler increments.

TIP Prior to the advent of using computers for layout, graphic designers and layout artists used specific measurements called picas as industry-standard measurements for layouts. (A pica equals $1/6$ of an inch.) Those days are long in the past, however. We advise you to use inches as your measurements simply because they are standard and easily understood. (If you're in Europe or anywhere else that uses the metric system, you are advised to use centimeters.) In this book, page measurements will be in inches. Note, however, that it remains standard to use points as the measurement for type size. One point is equal to $1/72$ of an inch. To give you an example, most body copy in books and magazines use type that is 12 points, or $1/6$ of an inch.

7. Save your work, then continue to the next set of steps.

You used shortcut keys to hide and show rulers in the document. You used the Units & Increments Preferences dialog box to change the unit of measure for the document.

Figure 11 Ruler Units set to Inches

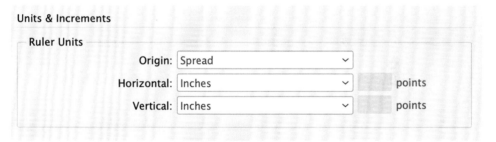

Hide and show ruler guides and the document grid

1. Click **View** on the menu bar, point to **Grids & Guides**, then note the **Show/Hide Guides command** and its shortcut key.

   The command is set to either Hide Guides or Show Guides depending on whether they are showing or not.

2. Click the **pasteboard** to escape the View menu, then press **[command] [;] (Mac)** or **[Ctrl] [;] (Mac)** several times to toggle between hiding and showing guides, finishing with guides showing.

   Showing and hiding guides is easy when you use the shortcut keys. Figure 12 identifies ruler guides and margin guides, which you will learn to create and modify in Chapter 14.

3. Click **View** on the menu bar, point to **Grids & Guides**, then note the **Show/Hide Document Grid** command and its shortcut key.

   The Document Grid command is set to either Hide Document Grid or Show Document Grid depending on whether it is showing or not.

Figure 12 Viewing frame edges and guides

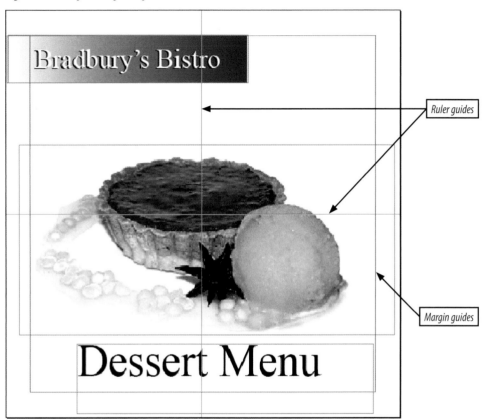

Ruler guides

Margin guides

4. Click the **pasteboard** to escape the View menu, then press **[command] [']** (Mac) or **[Ctrl] [']** (Win) several times to toggle between hiding and showing the document grid.

   Table 1 includes frequently used viewing command shortcut keys.

   TIP Make note of the difference between the Hide/Show Guides shortcut key and the Hide/Show Document Grid shortcut key—they're just one key away from each other.

5. Click **View** on the menu bar, point to **Grids & Guides**, then note the **Snap to Guides** and **Snap to Document Grid commands**.

   The Snap to Guides and Snap to Document Grid commands are on/off commands. When they're active, a check mark is visible to the left of the command.

6. Click the **pasteboard** to escape the View menu.

   You used shortcut keys to hide and show frame edges, ruler guides, and the document grid. You noted the location of the Snap to Guides and Snap to Document Grid commands in the View menu.

TABLE 1: SHORTCUT KEYS FOR VIEW COMMANDS

	Mac	Windows
Hide/Show Guides	[command] [;]	[Ctrl] [;]
Hide/Show Edges	[command] [H]	[Ctrl] [H]
Hide/Show Rulers	[command] [R]	[Ctrl] [R]
Activate/Deactivate Smart Guides	[command] [U]	[Ctrl] [U]
Fit Page in Window	[command] [0]	[Ctrl] [0]
Fit Spread in Window	[option] [command] [0]	[Alt] [Ctrl] [0]
Toggle Normal and Preview	[W]	[W]
Toggle Presentation Mode On/Off	[shift] [W]	[Shift] [W]

SETTING UP DOCUMENT AND FRAME-BASED GRIDS

Sometimes ruler guides just aren't enough, so designers choose to work with grids. Grids are multiple guides positioned to create a grid pattern across the layout. Grids help you align objects quickly and precisely. Every InDesign file you create has a default Document Grid, which you can hide or show using the Hide or Show Document Grid command in the Guides & Grids options on the View menu. You can modify the color and spacing increments of the default document grid using the Grids command in the Preferences dialog box. Choose Snap to Document Grid in the Grids and Guides options on the View menu to force objects to align to the Document Grid.

Sometimes you'll want to use a grid in a specific text frame as opposed to across the entire document. You can set up a grid for a text frame in the Text Frame Options dialog box. Select the frame, click the Object menu, then click Text Frame Options. Click the Baseline Options tab at the top of the dialog box, then enter specifications for the frame-based grid.

Toggle between screen modes

1. Click **View** on the menu bar, point to **Screen Mode**, then click **Preview**.

   All guides and frame edges are hidden, and the pasteboard is now gray. The menu bar and panels remain visible.

2. Press the **letter [W]** on your keypad several times to toggle between Preview and Normal modes, finishing with your document in Normal mode.

3. Click **View** on the menu bar, point to **Screen Mode**, then click **Presentation**.

   The window changes to full-screen, and the full document appears against a black background. Guides, grids, frame edges, panels, and the menu bar are no longer visible.

4. Press the ↓ on your keypad to scroll through the document to the last page.

5. Press the ↑ on your keypad to scroll up to the first page.

6. Press **[esc]** to leave Presentation mode.

7. Press **[shift] [W]** to switch to Presentation mode.

8. Press **[shift] [W]** again to return to Normal mode.

You used menu commands and keyboard keys to toggle among Normal, Preview, and Presentation modes. When in Presentation mode, you used keyboard keys to navigate through the document.

Work with multiple documents

1. Click **InDesign (Mac)** or **Edit (Win)** on the menu bar, point to **Preferences**, click **Interface,** click the **Open Documents as Tabs check box** to select it if it is unchecked, then click **OK**.

2. Save ID 1-1.indd as **Dessert Menu**.

3. Open ID 1-2.indd, then click the **tabs** of each document several times to toggle between them, finishing with Dessert Menu as the active document.

4. Drag the **Dessert Menu tab** straight down approximately ½ inch.

   When you drag a tabbed document down, it becomes a "floating" document.

5. Position the **mouse pointer** over the **bottom-right corner** of the document window, then click and drag **toward the center** of

the monitor window to reduce the window to approximately half its size.

6. Position the **mouse pointer** over the **title bar of the document**, then click and drag to move **Dessert Menu halfway down** toward the bottom of your monitor screen.

   A "floating" document window can be positioned so part of it is offscreen.

7. Position the **mouse pointer** over the **title bar of Dessert Menu**, click and drag to position it at the **top of the window** beside the **ID 1-2.indd tab**, then release the mouse button when you see a horizontal blue bar.

   The document is tabbed once again.

8. Close ID 1-2.indd without saving changes if you are prompted to do so.

You selected the Open Documents as Tabs option in the Preferences dialog box. You opened a second document and noted that it was tabbed. You removed the document from its tabbed position, resized it, moved it around, then returned it to its tabbed status.

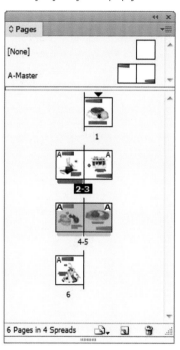

LESSON 3

NAVIGATE THROUGH A DOCUMENT

▶ *What You'll Do*

In this lesson, you will use various methods for navigating through a multiple-page document.

Navigating to Pages in a Document

When you create a layout for a magazine, book, or brochure, you create a document that has multiple pages. A **spread** is two pages that face each other—a left page and a right page—in a multipage document. If you imagine laying an open book on a table, you'd be looking at a spread in the book. Some documents you build will be built with spreads, while others will be just a series of single pages.

You have a variety of methods at your disposal for navigating to pages or spreads in your document. The Go to Page command in the Layout menu offers you the option to enter the page to which you want to go. You can also use the scroll bars on the bottom and right sides of the document window or choose a page from the Page menu in the lower-left corner of the document window. There are also First Page, Previous Page, Next Page, and Last Page buttons at the bottom left of the document window, which you can click to navigate to the document.

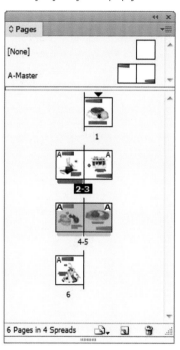

The Pages panel, shown in Figure 13, is a comprehensive solution for working with pages and for moving from page to page in your document. The Pages panel shows icons for all of the pages in the document. Double-clicking a single-page icon brings that page into view. The icon representing the currently visible page appears in blue on the panel. Click the Pages panel menu button to display the Pages panel menu. This menu contains powerful commands that you can use to control all page navigation in InDesign.

Applying Thumbnail Color Labels

You can apply one of 15 color labels to a page thumbnail on the Pages panel. Color labels can be useful for organizing your own work or for working with others on a document. For your own work, you might want to assign color labels to different types of pages. For example, you might want to assign a color label to pages in a document that contain imported Photoshop graphics. Or you might want to assign a specific color to pages that have been approved by your client. When working with others, color labels can be effective as status codes. For example, you can apply a specific color to all pages that are proofed and approved. This way, your whole team can see what is done and what needs to be done at a glance.

To apply color labels, click the Pages panel menu button, point to Page Attributes, point to Color Label, then choose a color. The color that you choose will appear as a small solid rectangle beneath the thumbnail.

Figure 13 Pages panel

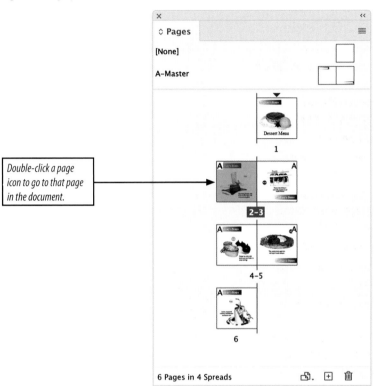

Double-click a page icon to go to that page in the document.

Navigate to pages in a document

1. Click the **Page menu list arrow** at the **bottom left of the document window**, then click **3.**

   The document view changes to page 3.

2. Click **View** on the menu bar, then click **Fit Spread in Window.**

3. At the **bottom-left corner of the document window**, click the **Next Page button** ▶ .

4. Click the **Previous Page button** ◀ twice.

5. Display the **Pages panel**, then double-click the **page 6 icon** on the Pages panel.

   The document view changes to page 6, and the page 6 icon on the Pages panel becomes highlighted, as shown in Figure 14.

6. Double-click the **page 3 icon** on the Pages panel.

   The right half of the spread—page 3—is centered in the document window.

7. Click **Layout** on the menu bar, then click **First Page**.

8. Press **[command] [J] (Mac)** or **[Ctrl] [J] (Win)** to open the Go to Page dialog box, enter **5**, then press **[return] (Mac)** or **[Enter] (Win)**.

TIP Make a point of remembering this command—*J for Jump*. It is one of the fastest ways to jump to a specific page, especially in long documents with a lot of pages on the Pages panel.

You navigated to pages using the Page menu, the Next Spread and Previous Spread buttons, page icons on the Pages panel, the Layout menu, and the Go to Page dialog box.

Figure 14 Targeting page 6 on the Pages panel

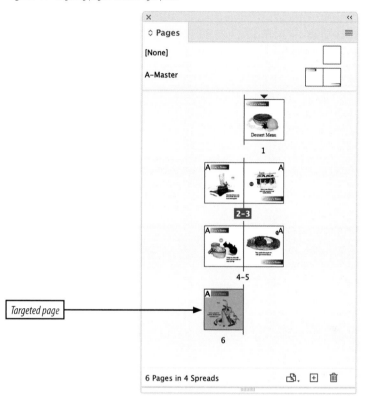

Apply color labels to page thumbnails

1. Click the **page 2 thumbnail** on the Pages panel.
2. Click the **Pages panel menu button** ≡ point to **Page Attributes**, point to **Color Label**, then click **Red**.

   A red bar appears beneath the page thumbnail.

3. Click the **page numbers 4–5** on the Pages panel to select both thumbnails.
4. Click the **Pages panel menu button** ≡, point to **Page Attributes**, point to **Color Label**, then click **Green**.

   Your Pages panel should resemble Figure 15.

5. Save the file, then close the Dessert Menu document.

You applied a color label to a single page thumbnail and a spread thumbnail.

Figure 15 Color labels on the Pages panel

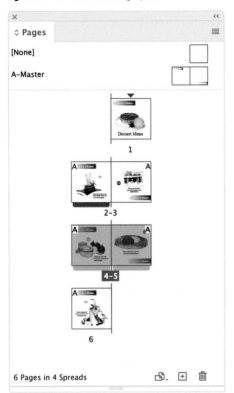

PAGES PANEL OPTIONS

To customize the Pages panel, click the Pages panel menu button, then click Panel Options. This opens the Panel Options dialog box. In the Pages and Masters sections of the dialog box, you can choose a size for page and master icons by clicking the Size list arrow. The Show Vertically and Show Thumbnails check boxes in the Pages and Masters sections control how the icons on the panel are displayed. If you remove the Show Vertically check mark, the page icons on the Pages panel will be displayed horizontally, and you will only be able to resize the width of the Pages panel, not the height. If you remove the Show Thumbnails check mark, the page icons will be blank on the Pages panel. The Icons section of the dialog box defines which additional icons appear next to the page icons. For example, if the Transparency check box is checked, a small transparency icon, that looks like a checkerboard, appears next to the page icon where transparency has been applied to master items. In the Panel Layout section, you can choose whether you want masters on top or document pages on top of the Pages panel.

WORK WITH OBJECTS AND SMART GUIDES

▶ What You'll Do

In this lesson, you will work with objects with smart guides.

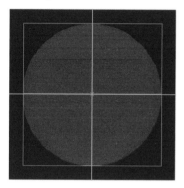

Resizing Objects

Working in InDesign, the term **object** is used to refer to any element on the page. Text, text frames, or graphic elements such as images, blocks of color, or simple lines are all objects on the page. All objects in InDesign are in frames. **Frames** are rectangular, oval, or polygonal shapes used for creating a colored area on the document or placing text and graphics.

When you select an object's frame, its handles become highlighted, as shown in Figure 16.

You can click and drag the handles to change the shape and size of the frame. InDesign offers three important keyboard combinations that you can use when dragging frame handles to affect the frame and its contents. These are listed in Table 2. Be sure to practice all three and incorporate them into your skills set.

You can resize multiple objects just as easily. Simply select multiple objects, and handles will appear around all the selected objects. You can then drag those handles to affect all the objects simultaneously.

Figure 16 Viewing frame handles on a text frame

TABLE 2: DRAGGING FRAME HANDLES WITH KEYBOARD COMBINATIONS		
Mac	**Windows**	**Result**
[shift]-drag a handle	[Shift]-drag a handle	The frame is resized in proportion; contents of the frame are not scaled.
[shift] [command]-drag a handle	[Shift] [Ctrl]-drag a handle	Both the frame and the contents of the frame are scaled.
[shift] [option] [command]-drag a handle	[Shift] [Alt] [Ctrl]-drag a handle	Both the frame and the contents of the frame are scaled from their centers.

Copying Objects

Copying and pasting an object is standard for most software packages. InDesign also offers the Paste in Place command on the Edit menu. This is useful for placing a copy of an object exactly in front of the original object. Select an object, copy it, then click the Paste in Place command.

The Paste in Place command is also useful when pasting objects from page to page. With Paste in Place, copied objects will paste in the exact same location from one page to another.

You can also copy objects while dragging them. Press and hold [option] (Mac) or [Alt] (Win), then drag to create a copy of the object.

Hiding, Locking, and Grouping Objects

The Hide, Lock, Group, and Ungroup commands on the Object menu are essential for working effectively with layouts, especially complex layouts with many objects. Hide objects to get them out of your way. They won't print, and nothing you do changes the location of them as long as they are hidden. Lock objects when you have them in a specific location and you don't want them accidentally moved or deleted. Locking an object makes it immovable—you will not even be able to select it. Don't think this is being overly cautious; accidentally moving or deleting objects—and being unaware that you did so—happens all the time in complex layouts and creates all kinds of problems.

Grouping objects is a smart and important strategy for protecting the relationships between multiple objects. When you select multiple objects and group them, clicking on one object with the Selection tool selects all the objects in the group. Thus, you can't accidentally select a single object and move or otherwise alter it independently from the group. However, you *can* select individual objects using the Direct Selection tool—that's how the tool got its name. Even if you select and alter a single object within a group, the objects are not ungrouped.

To group multiple objects, select them and click the Group command on the Object menu.

Working with Smart Guides

When aligning objects, you will find smart guides to be really effective and, yes, really smart. **Smart guides** are guides that appear automatically when objects are moved in a document and provide information to help position objects precisely in relation to the page or other objects.

For example, smart guides tell you when objects are aligned to each other or to specific areas of the page. Smart guides will tell you when the center of an object is aligned to the horizontal and vertical centers of the page.

Use the View menu to turn smart guides on and off. Figure 17 shows smart guides at work.

Figure 17 Smart guides aligning the top edges of two objects

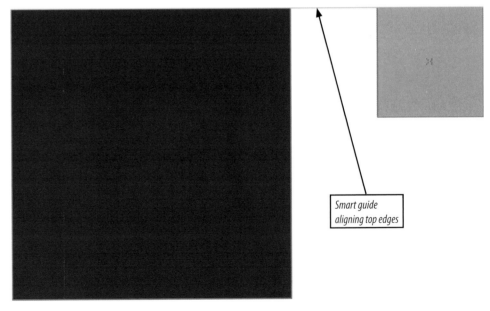

Smart guide aligning top edges

Resize a text object

1. Open ID 1-2.indd, then save it as **Objects**.
2. Click the **Selection tool** 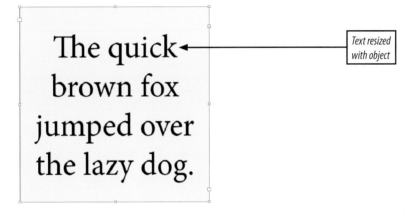, then click the **yellow text box** to select it.
3. Click and drag **various handles** and note how the object is resized.
4. When you are done experimenting, undo all the moves you made.

   The Undo command is at the top of the Edit menu.
5. Press and hold **[shift]**, then drag the **top left corner handle** toward the top-left corner of the document.

   The object is resized proportionately. The text reflows within the resized object, but the text itself is not enlarged.
6. Undo your last step.
7. Press and hold **[option] (Mac)** or **[Alt] (Win)**, then click and drag **any corner handle**.

   The object is resized from its center. The text is not resized.

8. Undo your last step.
9. Press and hold **[shift] [command] [option] (Mac)** or **[shift] [Ctrl] [Alt] (Win)**, then drag **any corner handle**.

   As shown in Figure 18, the object and the text in the object are resized proportionately from the object's center.

10. Click **File** on the menu bar, click **Revert**, then click **Revert (Mac)** or **Yes (Win)** if you are prompted to confirm.

    Reverting a file returns it to its status when you last saved it.

You explored various options for resizing an object and its contents, then you reverted the file.

Figure 18 Resized object and contents

The quick ← Text resized with object
brown fox
jumped over
the lazy dog.

Copy and duplicate objects

1. Select the **text frame**, then press **[command] [C]** **(Mac)** or **[Ctrl] [C] (Win)** to copy it.

2. Click **Edit** on the menu bar, then click **Paste in Place**.

   A copy of the text frame is placed in front of the original in the exact location.

3. Drag the **copy** to the right so the two are side by side.

4. Select the **left object**.

5. Press and hold **[option] (Mac)** or **[Alt] (Win)**, then drag a **copy of the object** to the left so your screen resembles Figure 19.

   TIP This method for creating a copy is referred to as "drag and drop" a copy.

6. Select **all three objects**.

   Handles appear around all three objects.

7. Click and drag **various handles** to resize all three objects.

8. Click **Edit** on the menu bar, then click **Cut**.

9. Save your work, then continue to the next set of steps.

   You duplicated an object in two different ways, first with the Copy and Paste in Place command combination and then with the drag-and-drop technique. You resized multiple objects, then cut them from the document.

Figure 19 Dragging a copy

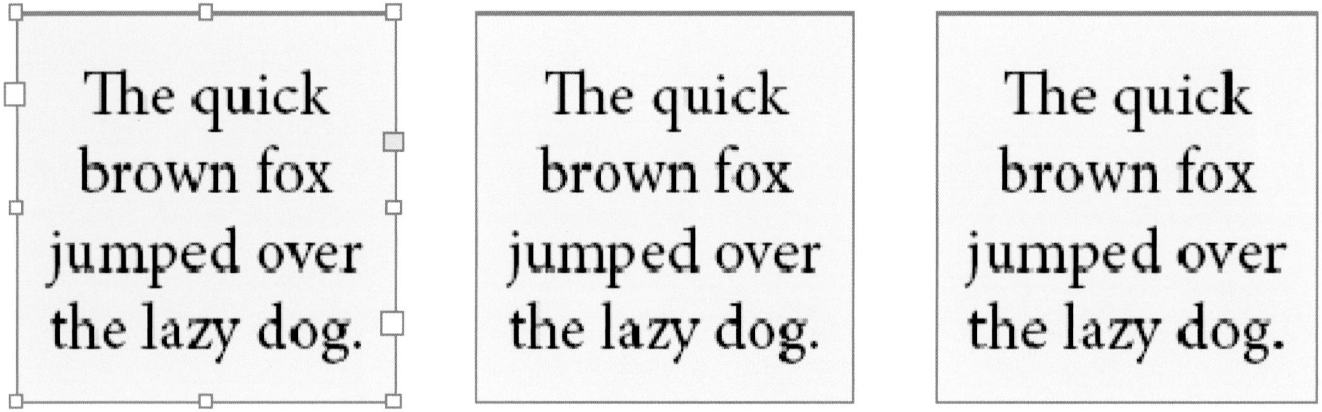

Hide, lock, and group objects

1. Click **Object** on the menu bar, then click **Show All on Spread**.

   This document was originally saved with hidden objects. Three objects appear. They are unselected.

2. Select all three objects, click **Object** on the menu bar, then click **Group**.

3. Click the **Selection tool** ▶, click the **pasteboard** to deselect all, then click the **pink circle**.

   As shown in Figure 20, all three objects are selected because they are grouped. The dotted line around the objects is a visual indication that they are grouped.

4. Click the **pasteboard** to deselect all, click the **Direct Selection tool** ▷, then click the **pink circle**.

Only the circle is selected because the Direct Selection tool ▷ selects individual objects within a group.

5. Select all, click **Object** on the menu bar, click **Ungroup**, then click the **pasteboard** to deselect all.

6. Click the **Selection tool** ▶, select **the small square**, click **Object** on the menu bar, then click **Lock**.

   The object's handles disappear, and a lock icon appears indicating that the object can no longer be selected.

7. Click **Object** on the menu bar, then click **Unlock All on Spread**.

   The small square is unlocked.

8. Select all, click **Object** on the menu bar, then click **Hide**.

All selected objects disappear.

9. Click **Object** on the menu bar, then click **Show All on Spread**.

   The three objects reappear in the same location that they were in when they were hidden.

TIP Memorize the shortcut keys for Hide/Show, Group/Ungroup, and Lock/Unlock. They are fairly easy to remember and extremely useful. You will be using these commands over and over again when you work in InDesign.

10. Hide the **pink circle** and the **small square**.

11. Save your work, then continue to the next set of steps.

You revealed hidden objects, grouped them, then used the Direct Selection tool to select individual objects within the group. You ungrouped the objects, locked them, unlocked them, and hid them.

Figure 20 Three grouped objects

Work with smart guides

1. Click **Edit** on the menu bar, point to **InDesign (Mac)** or **Preferences (Win)**, then click **Guides & Pasteboard**.

2. Verify that your **Smart Guide Options section** matches Figure 21, then click **OK**.

3. Click **View** on the menu bar, point to **Grids & Guides**, then click **Smart Guides**, if necessary, to activate it.

4. Click the **blue rectangle**, then try to center it visually on the page.

5. Release the mouse button when both the **horizontal and vertical smart guides** appear, as shown in Figure 22.

   Both the horizontal and the vertical pink smart guides appear when the object's center point is aligned with the center point of the document. By default, smart guides that show the relationship between objects and the document are pink.

TIP The gray box beside the cursor shows the location coordinates of the object on the page. You will learn a lot more about location coordinates in Chapter 14.

6. Show the **hidden objects**, then hide the **small blue square**.

7. Using the same method, align the **center of the pink circle** with the **center of the large blue square**.

   When the center points of the two objects are aligned, your smart guides will resemble Figure 23.

Figure 21 Smart Guide Options in the Guides & Pasteboard Preferences dialog box

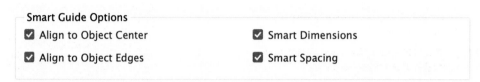

Figure 22 Centering the square on the page

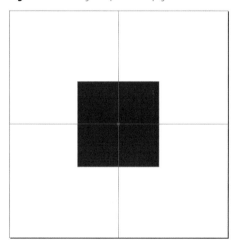

Figure 23 Centering the circle on the square

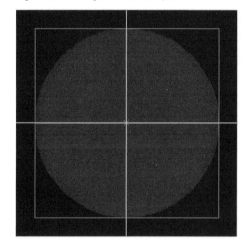

8. Show the **hidden small square**.

9. Use smart guides to align the **top of the small square** with the **top of the large square**, as shown in Figure 24.

10. "Snap" the **left edge of the small square** to the **right edge of the large square**.

11. Position the **small square** as shown in Figure 25.

12. Save your work, then close the Objects document.

You aligned an object at the center of the document and created precise relationships among three objects, using smart guides.

Figure 24 Aligning the top edges of the two squares

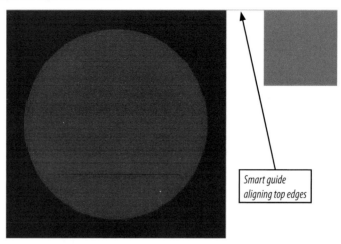

Smart guide
aligning top edges

Figure 25 Aligning the bottom edges of the two squares

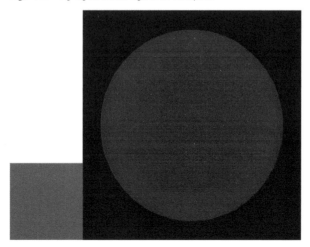

Explore the InDesign workspace

1. Launch Adobe InDesign.
2. Click File on the menu bar, click Open, navigate to the drive and folder where your Chapter 12 Data Files are stored, click ID 1-3.indd, then click Open.
3. Save the file as **Hana.indd**.
4. Click Window on the menu bar, point to Workspace, then click [Essentials Classic].
5. Click Window on the menu bar, point to Workspace, then click Reset Essentials Classic.
6. Point to the Type tool, then press and hold the mouse button to see the hidden tools behind the Type tool.
7. Using the same method, view the hidden tools behind the other tools with small black triangles.
8. Position your mouse pointer over the Selection tool until its tooltip appears.
9. Press the following keys and note which tools are selected with each key: [A], [P], [V], [T], [I], [H], [Z].
10. Press [tab] to temporarily hide all open panels, then press [tab] again.

Work with panels

1. Click the Color panel icon in the stack of collapsed panels on the right of the workspace to expand the Color panel.
2. Drag the Color panel name tab to the left so it is ungrouped from the Stroke panel.
3. Drag the Swatches panel out of the dock, then group it with the Color panel.
4. Click Window on the menu bar, point to Object & Layout, then click Transform.

5. Drag the Transform panel name tab to the bottom edge of the Swatches and Color panels group, then release the mouse button.
   The Transform panel is docked at the bottom of the Swatches and Color group.
6. Click and drag the dark gray bar at the top of the panel group, above the Color and Swatches panel tabs, to move the group of panels.
7. Click the Transform panel name tab, then drag it away from the other two panels to undock it.

Work with the Zoom tool and the Hand tool

1. Press [Z] to access the Zoom tool.
2. Position the Zoom tool over the document window, click three times to enlarge the document, press [option] (Mac) or [Alt] (Win), then click three times to reduce the document.
3. Click the Zoom Level list arrow on the menu bar, then click 1200%.
4. Double-click 1200% in the Zoom Level text box, type **350**, then press [return] (Mac) or [Enter] (Win).
5. Click the Hand tool on the toolbar, then click and drag the document window to scroll around the page.
6. Double-click the Zoom tool.
7. Click the Selection tool, point to the center of the document window, then press and hold [command] [space bar] (Mac) or [Ctrl] [space bar] (Win) to access the Zoom tool.
8. Click three times, then release [command] [space bar] (Mac) or [Ctrl] [space bar] (Win).
9. Press and hold [space bar] to access the Hand tool, then scroll around the image.

10. Press and hold [command] [option] [space bar] (Mac) or [Ctrl] [Alt] [space bar] (Win), then click the mouse button multiple times to reduce the view to 25%.
11. Click View on the menu bar, note the shortcut key for the Fit Page in Window command, then click Fit Page in Window.

Work with rulers, guides, and the document grid

1. Click View on the menu bar, then note the Rulers command and its shortcut key.
2. Click the pasteboard to escape the View menu, then press [command] [R] (Mac) or [Ctrl] [R] (Win) several times to hide and show rulers, finishing with rulers showing.
3. Note the units on the rulers.
4. Click InDesign (Mac) or Edit (Win) on the menu bar, point to Preferences, then click Units & Increments.
5. In the Ruler Units section, click the Horizontal list arrow to see the available measurement options.
6. Set the Horizontal and Vertical fields to Picas.
7. Reopen the Units & Increments Preferences dialog box, change the Horizontal and Vertical fields to Inches, then click OK.
8. Click View on the menu bar, point to Extras, then note the Frame Edges command and its shortcut key.
9. Click the pasteboard to escape the View menu, then enter [Ctrl] [H] (Mac) or [Ctrl] [H] (Win) several times to hide and show frame edges, finishing with frame edges showing.
10. Click View on the menu bar, point to Grids & Guides, then note the Guides command and its shortcut key.

11. Click the pasteboard to escape the View menu, then enter [command] [;] (Mac) or [Ctrl] [;] (Win) several times to hide and show guides, finishing with guides showing.
12. Click View on the menu bar, point to Grids & Guides, then note the Document Grid command and its shortcut key.
13. Click the pasteboard to escape the View menu, then enter [command] ['] (Mac) or [Ctrl] ['] (Win) repeatedly to hide and show the document grid.
14. Click View on the menu bar, point to Grids & Guides, then note the Snap to Guides and Snap to Document Grid commands.
15. Click the pasteboard to escape the View menu.

Toggle screen modes

1. Click the View menu, point to Screen Mode, then click Preview.
2. Press [W] on your keypad to toggle between Preview and Normal modes, finishing in Normal mode.
3. Click View on the menu bar, point to Screen Mode, then click Presentation.
4. Press the ↓ on your keypad to scroll through the document to the last page.
5. Press the ↑ on your keypad to scroll up to the first page.
6. Press [esc] to leave Presentation mode.
7. Press and hold [shift], then press [W] to switch to Presentation mode.
8. Still holding [shift], press [W] again to return to Normal mode.

Work with multiple documents

1. Click InDesign (Mac) or Edit (Win) on the menu bar, point to Preferences, click Interface, verify that Open Documents as Tabs is checked, then click OK.

2. Open ID 1-2.indd, then click the tabs to toggle between viewing both documents, finishing with Hana.indd as the active document.
3. Position your mouse pointer over the bottom-right corner, then click and drag toward the center of the monitor window to reduce the window to approximately half its size.
4. Drag the Hana document out of the group to make it a floating window on its own.
5. Float the mouse pointer over the title bar of Hana, then click and drag it to group it as a tabbed document beside ID 1-2.indd.
6. Close ID 1-2.indd without saving changes.

Navigate through a document

1. Click the Page menu list arrow at the bottom-left of the document window, then click 3.
2. Click View on the menu bar, then click Fit Spread in Window.
3. Click the Next Page button.
4. Click the Previous Page button twice.
5. Show the Pages panel.
6. Double-click the page 6 icon on the Pages panel.
7. Double-click the page 3 icon on the Pages panel.
8. Double-click the numbers 2–3 beneath the page 2 and page 3 icons on the Pages panel.
9. Click Layout on the menu bar, then click First Page.
10. Enter [command] [J] (Mac) or [Ctrl] [J] (Win) to open the Go to Page dialog box, enter 5, then press [return] (Mac) or [Enter] (Win).
11. Save your work.

Apply color labels to thumbnails on the Pages panel

1. Click the page 5 thumbnail on the Pages panel.
2. Click the Pages panel menu button, point to Page Attributes, point to Color Label, then click Blue.
3. Click the page numbers 2–3 on the Pages panel to select both thumbnails.
4. Click the Pages panel menu button, point to Page Attributes, point to Color Label, then click Orange.
5. Save your work, then close the Hana document.

Work with objects

1. Open ID 1-4.indd, then save it as **Skills Objects**.
2. Click the Selection tool, then click to select the object.
3. Click and drag various handles, and note how the object is resized.
4. Undo all the moves you made.
5. Press and hold [shift], then drag the top-left corner handle toward the left edge of the document.
6. Undo the move.
7. Press and hold [option] (Mac) or [Alt] (Win), then click and drag any corner handle.
8. Undo the move.
9. Press and hold [command] (Mac) or [Ctrl] (Win), then click and drag any corner handle.
10. Undo the move.
11. Press and hold [shift] [command] [option] (Mac) or [Shift] [Ctrl] [Alt] (Win), then drag any corner handle.
12. Click File on the menu bar, click Revert, then click Revert (Mac) or Yes (Win) if you are prompted to confirm.
13. Select the text frame, then copy it.
14. Click Edit on the menu bar, then click Paste in Place.
15. Drag the copy to the right so it is beside the original object.

(continued)

16. Select the left object.
17. Press and hold [option] (Mac) or [Alt] (Win), then drag a copy of the object to the left so your screen resembles Figure 26.
18. Select all three objects.
19. Click and drag various handles to resize all three objects.
20. Click Edit on the menu bar, then click Cut.
21. Click Object on the menu bar, then click Show All on Spread.
22. Select all three objects, click Object on the menu bar, then click Group.
23. Click the Selection tool, click anywhere on the pasteboard to deselect all, then click the green diamond.
24. Click the pasteboard to deselect all, click the Direct Selection tool, then click the green diamond.
25. Select all, click Object on the menu bar, then click Ungroup.
26. Click the Selection tool, select the small circle, click Object on the menu bar, then click Lock.
27. Click Object on the menu bar, then click Unlock All on Spread.
28. Select all, click Object on the menu bar, then click Hide.
29. Click Object on the menu bar, then click Show All on Spread.
30. Hide the green diamond and the small blue circle.
31. Save your work.

Work with smart guides

1. Click (InDesign) (Mac) or Edit (Win) on the menu bar, point to Preferences, then click Guides & Pasteboard.
2. Verify that your Smart Guide Options section shows all four options checked, then click OK.
3. Click View on the menu bar, point to Grids & Guides, then click Smart Guides, if necessary, to activate it.
4. Click the yellow circle, then try to center it visually on the page.
5. Release the mouse button when both the horizontal and vertical smart guides appear, as shown in Figure 27.
6. Show the hidden objects, then hide the small circle.
7. Using the same method, align the center of the green diamond with the center of the yellow circle.
8. Show the hidden small circle.
9. Referring to Figure 28, align the vertical center of the small circle with the right point of the green diamond.
10. Save, then close the Skills Objects document.

Figure 26 Text frame copied and duplicated

Figure 27 Horizontal and vertical smart guides

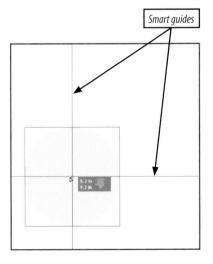

Figure 28 Completed Skills Review

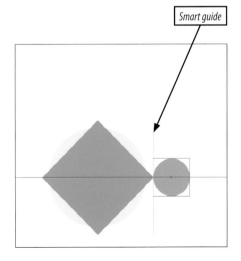

This set of steps will give you a refresher course for grouping and docking panels. You might want to consider how you would group and dock panels for your own customized workspace.

1. Open the file named Blank Page.indd.

2. Group the Paragraph and Character panels together, then click the Paragraph panel name tab so it is the active panel.

3. Dock the Pages panel to the bottom of the Paragraph panel group.

4. Group the Layers panel with the Pages panel, then click the Layers panel name tab so it is the active panel.

5. Dock the Swatches panel below the Layers panel group.

6. Group the Color, Stroke, and Gradient panels with the Swatches panel, then click the Gradient panel name tab so it is the active panel.

7. Dock the Align panel below the Gradient panel group.

TIP The Align panel is in the Object & Layout section of the Window menu.

8. Group the Transform and the Effects panels with the Align panel, then click the Transform panel name tab so it is the active panel.

TIP The Transform panel is in the Object & Layout section of the Window menu.

9. Compare your panels with Figure 29.

10. Close the Blank Page document without saving changes.

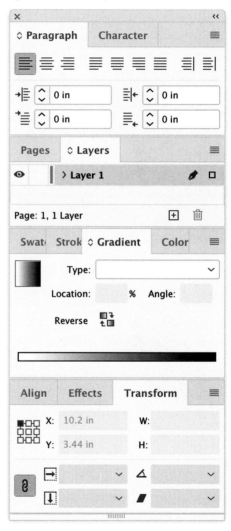

Figure 29 Completed Project Builder 1

Accessing the Zoom and the Hand tools with keyboard shortcuts is one of the most important skills you need to absorb in this chapter. This Project Builder will give you more practice at that.

1. Open ID 1-5.indd.

2. Click the Selection tool if it is not active, then press [command] [space bar] (Mac) or [Ctrl] [space bar] (Win) to access the Zoom tool.

3. Position the Zoom tool slightly above and to the left of the dog's left eye, click and drag the Zoom tool pointer to draw a dotted rectangle around the eye, then release the mouse button.

4. Press [space bar], then scroll with the Hand tool to the right eye.

5. Press [option] [command] [space bar] (Mac) or [Ctrl] [Alt] [space bar] (Win), then click the Zoom tool five times on the dog's right eye.

6. Move the image with the Hand tool so both the dog's eyes and his snout are visible in the window and your screen resembles Figure 30.

   Your magnification may differ from that shown in the figure.

7. Close ID 1-5.indd without saving any changes.

Figure 30 Completed Project Builder 2

Image courtesy of Chris Botello

DESIGN PROJECT

The page layout in this Design Project will strengthen your use of smart guides to position objects in relation to one another and in relation to the page.

1. Open ID 1-6.indd, then save it as **Squares and Targets**.

2. Use the techniques you learned in this chapter to recreate the layout in Figure 31.

TIP Try it on your own, then go through the following steps, and compare your results with those in the figure.

3. Verify that smart guides are activated.

4. Align the large yellow circle to the center of the page.

5. Center the large green circle in the large yellow circle.

6. Center the remaining three circles.

7. Copy the smallest yellow circle, then apply the Paste in Place command.

8. Center the pasted circle in the blue square.

9. Group the yellow circle and the blue square.

10. Click the Selection tool.

11. Drag and drop three copies of the group at the four corners of the document.

12. Save your work, then close the Squares and Targets document.

Figure 31 Completed Design Project

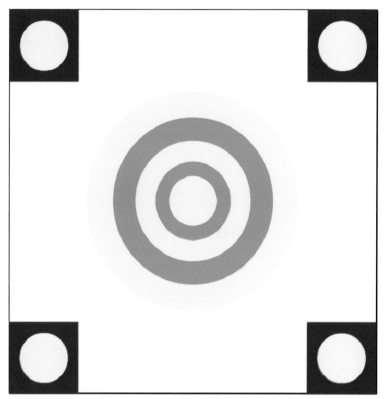

Jake's Diner

Early Bird Breakfast Menu

Eggs and Bacon

Two eggs any style, two strips of lean bacon, one biscuit with our homestyle gravy, and home fries.

$5.95

French Toast

Four triangles of thick peasant bread dipped in a cinnamon-egg batter. Served with French Fries.

$6.95

Egg Sandwich

One egg over easy, served with American or Jack cheese on a soft French croissant.

$5.25

Biscuits and Gravy

Light fluffy southern biscuits served with a hearty sausage gravy.

$3.95

Belgian Waffle

A golden brown buttery waffle served with fresh-picked strawberries, raspberries and blueberries. Whipped fresh cream on request.

$4.95

Eggs Hollandaise

Three eggs lightly poached served on a bed of romaine lettuce and topped with a rich Hollandaise sauce.

$6.95

Silver Dollar Pancakes

A stack of eight golden pancakes served with fresh creamery butter and warm maple syrup.

$4.95

Steak and Eggs

A 6 oz. strip of peppered breakfast steak cooked to your liking, served with two eggs, any style.

$7.95

13

WORK WITH TEXT

1. Format Text
2. Format Paragraphs
3. Create and Apply Styles
4. Edit Text
5. Create Bulleted and Numbered Lists

Adobe Certified Professional in Print & Digital Media Publication Using Adobe InDesign

1. Working in the Design Industry

This objective covers critical concepts related to working with colleagues and clients as well as crucial legal, technical, and design-related knowledge.

1.4 Demonstrate knowledge of key terminology related to publications.

C Understand and use key terms related to multipage layouts.

1.5 Demonstrate knowledge of basic design principles and best practices employed in the design industry.

C Identify and use common typographic adjustments to create contrast, hierarchy, and enhanced readability/legibility.

2. Project Setup and Interface

This objective covers the interface setup and program settings that assist in an efficient and effective workflow, as well as knowledge about ingesting digital assets for a project.

2.2 Navigate, organize, and customize the application workspace.

B Organize and customize the workspace.

C Configure application preferences.

2.6 Manage paragraph, character, and object styles.

A Load, create, apply, and modify styles.

4. Creating and Modifying Document Elements

This objective covers core tools and functionality of the application, as well as tools that affect the visual appearance of document elements.

4.2 Add and manipulate text using appropriate typographic settings.

A Use type tools to add text.

B Use appropriate character settings in a design.

C Use appropriate paragraph settings in a design.

E Manage text flow across multiple text areas.

F Use tools to add special characters or content.

4.3 Make, manage, and edit selections.

A Make selections using a variety of tools.

4.5 Use basic reconstructing and editing techniques to manipulate document content.

A Use various tools to revise and refine project content.

C Use the Story Editor to edit text within a project.

FORMAT TEXT

In this lesson, you will use the Character panel and various keyboard commands to modify text attributes.

Introducing the Min-Pin
by Christopher Smith

Creating Text

When you create text in InDesign, you do so by first creating a text frame. All InDesign text is in a text frame. Click and drag the Type tool anywhere on the page to create a text frame. You'll see a blinking cursor in the frame, prompting you to start typing.

You use the Character and Paragraph panels to format the text in the frame. You can also use the Text Frame Options command, located on the Object menu, to format the text frame itself.

Using the Character Panel

The Character panel, shown in Figure 1, is the command center for modifying text. The Character panel works hand in hand with the Paragraph panel, which is why it's wise to keep them grouped together. The Paragraph panel, as its name implies, focuses on manipulating paragraphs or blocks of text; the Character panel focuses on more specific modifications, such as font, font style, and font size.

Figure 1 Character panel

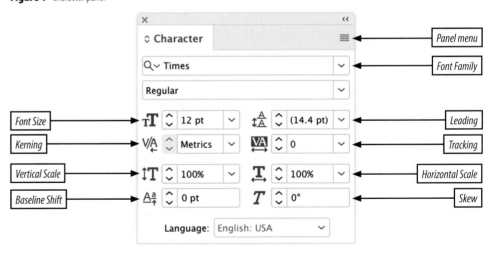

In addition to these basic modifications, the Character panel offers other controls for manipulating text. You can use the panel to modify leading, track and kern text, apply a horizontal or vertical scale to text, perform a baseline shift, or skew text. To select text quickly for editing, you can use the methods shown in Table 1: Keyboard Commands for Selecting Text.

TIP You can set the font list on the Character panel to show font names or font names and samples of each font. To enable or disable this feature, click Edit on the menu bar, point to Preferences, click Type, then click to add or remove a check mark in the Font Preview Size check box. Notice also that you can click the Font Preview Size list arrow and choose Small, Medium, or Large.

TABLE 1: KEYBOARD COMMANDS FOR SELECTING TEXT	
To select:	**Do the following:**
One word	Double-click word
One line	Triple-click any word in the line
One paragraph	Click any word in the paragraph four times
Entire story	Click any word in the story five times
Entire story	[command] [A] (Mac) or [Ctrl] [A] (Win)
One character to the right of insertion point	[shift] →
One character to the left of insertion point	[shift] ←
One line up from insertion point	[shift] ↑
One line down from insertion point	[shift] ↓
One word to the right of insertion point	[shift] [command] → (Mac) or [Shift] [Ctrl] → (Win)
One word to the left of insertion point	[shift] [command] ← (Mac) or [Shift] [Ctrl] ← (Win)
One paragraph above insertion point	[shift] [command] ↑ (Mac) or [Shift] [Ctrl] ↑ (Win)
One paragraph below insertion point	[shift] [command] ↓ (Mac) or [Shift] [Ctrl] ↓ (Win)

PASTING TEXT WITHOUT FORMATTING

When you copy text, then paste it, it is, by default, pasted with all of its formatting—its typeface, type style, type size, and any other formatting that has been applied. Sometimes, this can be undesirable. This is where the Paste Without Formatting command comes into play. It strips the copied text of all its original formatting, then formats it to match the formatting of the text frame where it is pasted.

Understanding Leading

Leading is the term used to describe the vertical space between lines of text. This space is measured from the baseline of one line of text to the baseline of the next line of text. As shown in Figure 2, the **baseline** is the invisible line on which text sits. Leading, like font size, is measured in points.

Scaling Text Horizontally and Vertically

When you format text, your most basic choices are which font you want to use and what size you want to use it. Once you've chosen a font and a font size, you can further manipulate the appearance of the text with a horizontal or vertical scale.

On the Character panel, horizontal and vertical scales are expressed as percentages. By default, text is generated at a 100% horizontal and 100% vertical scale, meaning that the text is not scaled at all. Decreasing the horizontal scale only, for example, maintains the height of the characters but decreases the width—on the horizontal axis. Conversely, increasing the horizontal scale again maintains the height but increases the width of the characters on the horizontal axis. Figure 3 shows four examples of horizontal and vertical scales.

TIP You can also control the vertical alignment of text inside a text box by selecting the text box, clicking Object on the menu bar, then clicking Text Frame Options. Click the Align list arrow, then click Top, Center, Bottom, or Justify.

Figure 2 Examples of leading

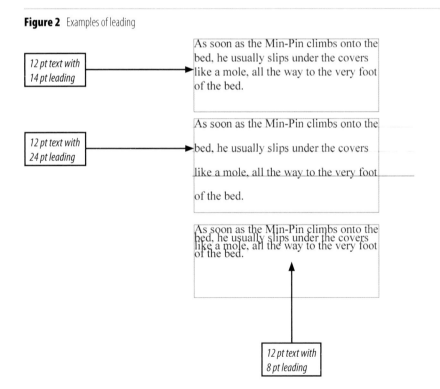

12 pt text with
14 pt leading

As soon as the Min-Pin climbs onto the bed, he usually slips under the covers like a mole, all the way to the very foot of the bed.

12 pt text with
24 pt leading

As soon as the Min-Pin climbs onto the bed, he usually slips under the covers like a mole, all the way to the very foot of the bed.

As soon as the Min-Pin climbs onto the bed, he usually slips under the covers like a mole, all the way to the very foot of the bed.

12 pt text with
8 pt leading

Figure 3 Scaling text horizontally and vertically

original text

50% horizontal scale

150% horizontal scale

50% vertical scale

150% vertical scale

Kerning and Tracking Text

Though your computer is a magnificent instrument for generating text in myriad fonts and font sizes, you will often want to manipulate the appearance of text after you have created it—especially if you have the meticulous eye of a designer. **Kerning** is a long-standing process of increasing or decreasing space between a pair of characters. Like kerning, **tracking** affects the spaces between letters, but it is applied globally to an entire word or paragraph.

Kerning and tracking are standard features in most word processing applications, but they are more about typography than word processing—that is, they are used for setting text in a way that is pleasing to the eye.

Spacing challenges with text are usually more prominent with large-size headlines than with smaller body copy—which is why many designers will spend great amounts of time tracking and kerning a headline. Figures 4 and 5 show examples of kerning and tracking applied to a headline.

The only mistake you can make regarding kerning and tracking is to ignore them. Especially when you're working with headlines, awareness of spacing is essential.

TIP Kerning and tracking are often used on body copy as a quick solution for fitting text within an allotted space. In other words, if a paragraph is taking up 12 lines and you want it to be 11 lines, tracking the text to have less space might do the trick.

InDesign measures both kerning and tracking in increments of 1/1000 em—a unit of measure that is determined by the current type size. In a 6-point font, 1 em equals 6 points; in a 12-point font, 1 em equals 12 points. It's good to know this, but you don't need to have this information in mind when kerning and tracking text. Just remember that the increments are small enough to provide you with the specificity that you desire for creating eye-pleasing text.

Creating Superscript Characters

You are already familiar with superscript characters, even if you don't know them by that term. When you see a footnote in a book or document, the superscripted character is the small number positioned to the upper-right of a word. Figure 6 shows a superscripted character.

Figure 4 Kerning text

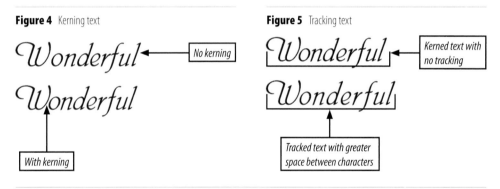

Figure 5 Tracking text

Figure 6 Identifying a superscripted character

The Superscript command, shown in Figure 7, is listed on the Character panel menu. There's a slightly tricky thing you need to remember about superscripts. If you select a 12-point character, for example, and then apply the Superscript command, the size of the character will decrease; however, its point size will still be identified on the Character panel as 12 points.

Creating Subscript Characters

The Character panel menu also offers a command for Subscript. You can think of Subscript as the opposite of Superscript.

Instead of raising the baseline of the selected text, the Subscript command positions the text below its original baseline. As with Superscript, the Subscript command makes the selected text appear smaller.

Of the two, Subscript is used less often. Though it is seldom used for footnotes, many designers use Subscript for trademarks and registration marks.

Underlining Text

InDesign offers different methods for underlining text and for creating **rules**, which

are horizontal, vertical, or diagonal lines. When you simply want to underline selected text, the most basic method is to use the Underline command on the Character panel menu. With this command, the weight of the underline is determined by the point size of the selected text. The greater the point size, the greater the weight of the line.

Searching for Fonts on the Character Panel

Font search enhancements in Creative Cloud make working with fonts and finding the font you want to use quick and easy. Creative Cloud lets you experiment with and search for fonts in powerful ways.

The top field on the Character panel contains a magnifying glass icon on the left side. Think of this field as both the font search and current font field because you can use this field to search through the available fonts on your system. Type any font name in the field—Garamond, for example—and a scrollable font menu will appear with all the Garamond typefaces on your system, grouped and listed together. You can also search for font styles such as bold, condensed, italic, and so on.

When you click the magnifying glass, you can choose between Search Entire Font Name or Search First Word only. Search First Word only is a helpful setting if you are unsure of the complete font name that you need.

Figure 7 The Superscript command on the Character panel menu

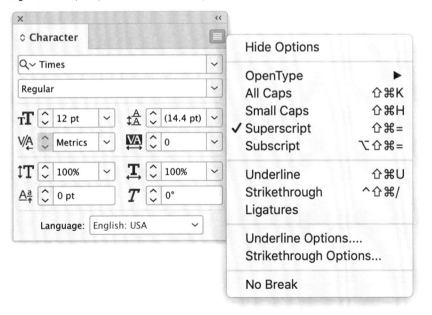

Modify text attributes

1. Open ID 2-1. indd, then save it as **Min-Pin Intro**.

2. Click **InDesign (Mac)** or **Edit (Win)** on the menu bar, point to **Preferences**, then click **Units & Increments**.

3. Verify that your settings are the same as shown in Figure 8, then click **OK**.

4. Click **Window** on the menu bar, point to **Workspace,** then click **[Typography]**.

5. Click **Window** on the menu bar, point to **Workspace,** then click **Reset Typography**.

6. Click the **Type tool** T, then double-click the word **Introducing** at the top of the page.

   Double-clicking a word selects the entire word.

7. Open the **Character panel**.

   The Character panel displays the formatting of the selected text.

8. Triple-click the word **Introducing**.

   Triple-clicking a word selects the entire line of text that the word is on.

9. On the Character panel, click the **Font Family list arrow**, click **Impact,** click the **Font Size list arrow,** click **48 pt.**, then verify that the **Leading text box** reads **57.6 pt.**, as shown in Figure 9.

   The parentheses surrounding the value in the Leading text box indicate that the leading is being auto-entered as a percentage of the point size. The default auto-leading percentage in InDesign is 120%.

   TIP Every function that you can perform on the Character panel can also be done on the Control panel.

Continued on next page

Figure 8 Units & Increments section of the Preferences dialog box

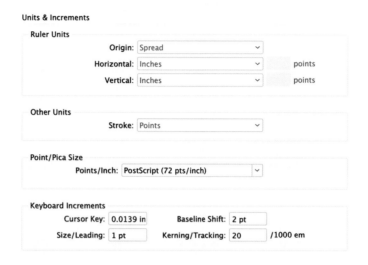

Figure 9 Character panel

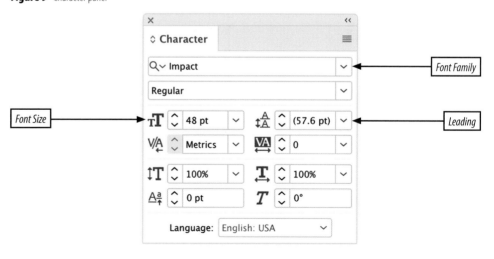

10. Press and hold **[shift] [command] (Mac)** or **[Shift] [Ctrl] (Win)**, then press **[<]** 10 times.

    The point size is reduced by one point size every time you press **[<]**.

11. Press and hold **[shift] [command] (Mac)** or **[Shift] [Ctrl] (Win)**, then press **[>]** two times.

    The point size is increased by two points.

12. Triple-click the word **by** on the second line to select the whole line, change the font to **Times New Roman** or a similar font, click the **Type Style list arrow**, click **Italic,** click the **Font Size list arrow**, then click **18 pt**.

13. Click the **Selection tool** ▶ , then note that the **text frame** is highlighted, and the **handles** are visible.

14. Click **Object** on the menu bar, click **Text Frame Options**, click the **Align list arrow** in the Vertical Justification section, click **Center**, then click **OK**.

    Your work should resemble Figure 10.

15. Save your work, then continue to the next set of steps.

You used keyboard commands and the Character panel to modify text. You then used the Text Frame Options dialog box to center the text vertically in the frame.

Track and kern text

1. Click the **Zoom tool** 🔍 , click and drag the **Zoom tool** 🔍 , around the **entire light green text frame**, then release the mouse button.

    When you drag the Zoom tool 🔍 , it creates a rectangle. When you release, the contents within the rectangle are magnified.

2. Click the **Type tool** T , then triple-click the word **Introducing**.

3. Click the **Tracking list arrow** on the Character panel, then click **200**.

    The horizontal width of each word increases, and a consistent amount of space is applied between each letter, as shown in Figure 11.

4. Reduce the **Tracking value** to **25**.

    Note that the space between the h and the e in the word "the" is inconsistent with the other spacing in the headline. The e is too far from the h.

5. Click **between the letters h and e in the word "the,"** click the **Kerning list arrow**, then click **−50**.

    The space between the two letters decreases.

6. Click the **Selection tool** ▶ to exit type editing mode.

7. Save your work, then continue to the next set of steps.

You used the Character panel to modify tracking and kerning values.

Figure 10   Selected text frame

Introducing the Min-Pin
by Christopher Smith

Figure 11   Increasing the tracking value of selected text

Introducing the Min-Pin
by Christopher Smith

Create superscript characters

1. Click **View** on the menu bar, click **Fit Page in Window**, click the **Zoom tool** 🔍, then drag a **selection box** that encompasses **all the body copy on the page**.

2. Click the **Type tool** T, then select the **number 1** after the words **Doberman Pinscher** at the end of the fourth paragraph.

3. Click the **Character panel menu button** ≡, then click **Superscript**.

   The character's size is reduced and positioned higher than the characters that precede it, as shown in an enlarged view in Figure 12.

4. Select the **number 2** after the word **cows** in the last paragraph, then apply the **Superscript command**.

   TIP When the Superscript command is applied to text, its designated font size on the Character panel remains the same.

5. Select the **number 1 beside the footnote at the bottom of the page**, apply the **Superscript command**, select the **number 2** below, apply the **Superscript command** again, then deselect the text.

   Your footnotes should resemble Figure 13.

6. Save your work, then continue to the next set of steps.

   You applied the Superscript command to format selected text as footnotes.

Figure 12 Applying the Superscript command

Figure 13 Using the Superscript command to format footnotes

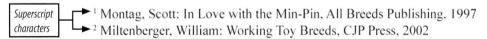

INSERTING FOOTNOTES AUTOMATICALLY

While you can insert footnotes using the techniques in this lesson, if you have many footnotes in a document, you can use the enhanced footnote feature to insert them quickly and easily. In InDesign, a footnote consists of a reference number that appears in document text and the footnote text that appears at the bottom of the page or column. To add a footnote, place the insertion point in the document location where you want the reference number to appear. Click Type on the menu bar, then click Insert Footnote. The insertion point moves to the footnote area at the bottom of the page or column. Type the footnote text; the footnote area expands as you type. If the text containing a footnote moves to another page, its footnote moves with it.

FORMATTING FOOTNOTES

If you use the Insert Footnote command to enter footnotes in a document, you can specify many formatting attributes. Click Type on the menu bar, then click Document Footnote Options. On the Numbering and Formatting tab, you can select the numbering style, starting number, prefix, position, character style, or separator. The Layout tab lets you set the spacing above and between footnotes, as well as the rule that appears above them. Formatting changes you make to footnotes affect all existing and new footnotes.

Underline text

1. Click **View** on the menu bar, click **Fit Page in Window,** click the **Zoom tool** 🔍 , then drag a **selection box** that encompasses **both footnotes at the bottom of the page**.

2. Click the **Type tool** T , then select **In Love with the Min-Pin** in the first footnote.

3. Click the **Character panel menu button** ☰ , then click **Underline**.

   Only the selected text is underlined.

TIP The weight of the line is automatically determined, based on the point size of the selected text.

4. Select **Working Toy Breeds** in the second footnote, then apply the **Underline command**.

5. Select the **entire first footnote** except the number 1 superscripted footnote, then reduce its size to **8 points**.

6. Select the **entire second footnote** except the number 2, then change its font size to **8 points**.

   Your footnotes should resemble Figure 14.

TIP To specify how far below the baseline the underline is positioned, click the Underline Options command on the Character panel menu, then increase or decrease the Offset value.

7. Save your work, then continue to the next lesson.

You selected text, then applied the Underline command from the Character panel menu.

Figure 14 Formatted footnotes

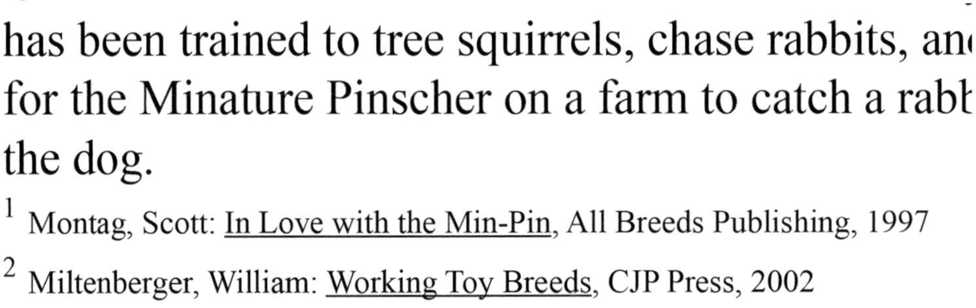

has been trained to tree squirrels, chase rabbits, and for the Minature Pinscher on a farm to catch a rabt the dog.

[1] Montag, Scott: In Love with the Min-Pin, All Breeds Publishing, 1997

[2] Miltenberger, William: Working Toy Breeds, CJP Press, 2002

FORMAT PARAGRAPHS

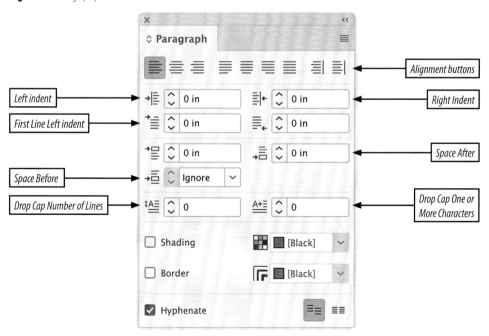

Using the Paragraph Panel

The Paragraph panel, shown in Figure 15, is the command center for modifying paragraphs or blocks of text, also known as body copy.

The Paragraph panel is divided into four main sections. The top section controls alignment. Of the nine icons offering options for aligning text, the first four—Align left, Align center,

Align right, and Justify with last line aligned left—are the most common. The remaining five options include subtle modifications of justified text and two options for aligning text toward or away from the spine of a book.

The next section offers controls for indents. With these controls, you can indent the left or right sides of a paragraph, or you can indent the first or last line.

Figure 15 Paragraph panel

Use the First Line Left Indent when you want the first line of each paragraph to start further to the right than the other lines of text, as shown in Figure 16.

At the bottom of the figure is what is commonly referred to as a pull quote. You have probably seen these in a magazine at some point. A **pull quote** is a typographical design solution in which text is used at a larger point size and positioned prominently on the page. Note the left and right indents applied to the pull quote. They were created using the Left Indent and Right Indent buttons on the Paragraph panel.

The third section of the Paragraph panel controls vertical spacing between paragraphs and drop caps. For large blocks of text, it is often pleasing to the eye to create either a subtle or a distinct space after every paragraph. In InDesign, you create these by entering values in the Space After or the Space Before text boxes on the Paragraph panel. Of the two, the Space After text box is more commonly used. The Space Before text box is often in conjunction with the Space After text box to offset special page elements, such as a pull quote.

Figure 16 First line indent and left and right indents

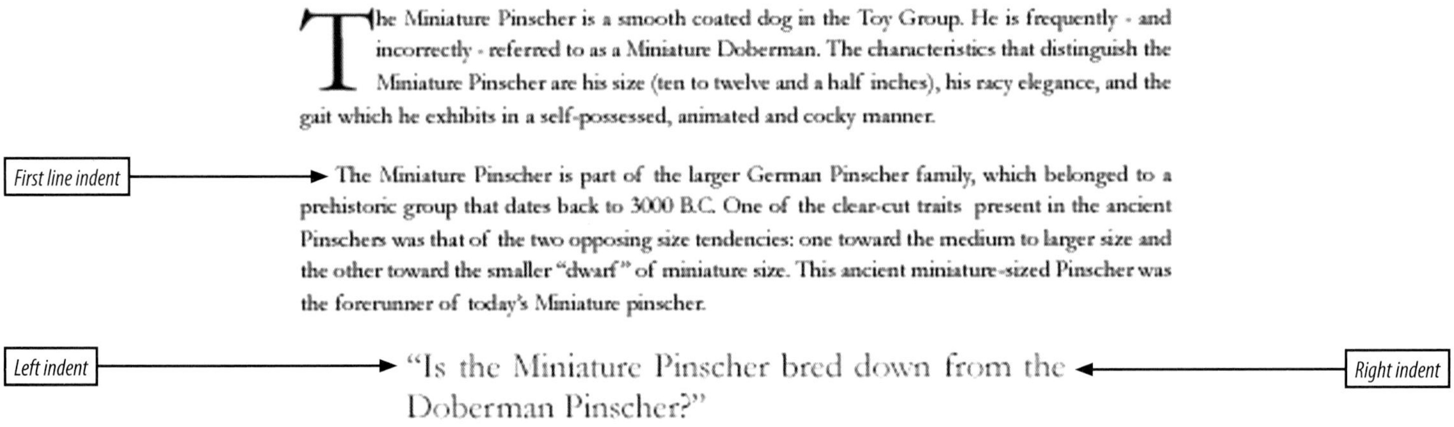

The Miniature Pinscher is a smooth coated dog in the Toy Group. He is frequently - and incorrectly - referred to as a Miniature Doberman. The characteristics that distinguish the Miniature Pinscher are his size (ten to twelve and a half inches), his racy elegance, and the gait which he exhibits in a self-possessed, animated and cocky manner.

First line indent ———————▶ The Miniature Pinscher is part of the larger German Pinscher family, which belonged to a prehistoric group that dates back to 3000 B.C. One of the clear-cut traits present in the ancient Pinschers was that of the two opposing size tendencies: one toward the medium to larger size and the other toward the smaller "dwarf" of miniature size. This ancient miniature-sized Pinscher was the forerunner of today's Miniature pinscher.

Left indent ———————▶ "Is the Miniature Pinscher bred down from the ◀——— Right indent
Doberman Pinscher?"

A **drop cap** is a design element in which the first letter or letters of a paragraph are increased in size to create a visual effect. In the figure, the drop cap is measured as being three text lines in height. If you click to place the cursor to the right of the drop cap and then increase the kerning value on the Character panel, the space between the drop cap and all three lines of text will be increased. Figure 17 shows a document with a drop cap and a 0.25-inch space after every paragraph.

The fourth section on the Paragraph panel allows you to highlight a paragraph and/or apply a border to a paragraph. When your cursor is positioned in any paragraph, activating the Shading or Border options will place a field of color behind the entire paragraph or a border around the paragraph. You can modify the color of each on the Paragraph panel.

At the very bottom of the Paragraph panel, the Hyphenate checkbox controls whether or not hyphens will be used to split words from line to line in a paragraph. If you uncheck Hyphenate, no words will be split with a hyphen.

Figure 17 A drop cap and paragraphs with vertical space applied after every paragraph

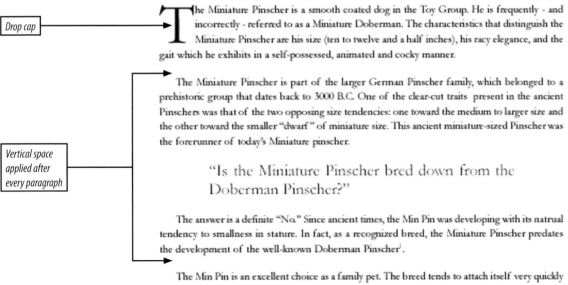

Drop cap

Vertical space applied after every paragraph

The Miniature Pinscher is a smooth coated dog in the Toy Group. He is frequently - and incorrectly - referred to as a Miniature Doberman. The characteristics that distinguish the Miniature Pinscher are his size (ten to twelve and a half inches), his racy elegance, and the gait which he exhibits in a self-possessed, animated and cocky manner.

The Miniature Pinscher is part of the larger German Pinscher family, which belonged to a prehistoric group that dates back to 3000 B.C. One of the clear-cut traits present in the ancient Pinschers was that of the two opposing size tendencies: one toward the medium to larger size and the other toward the smaller "dwarf" of miniature size. This ancient miniature-sized Pinscher was the forerunner of today's Miniature pinscher.

"Is the Miniature Pinscher bred down from the Doberman Pinscher?"

The answer is a definite "No." Since ancient times, the Min Pin was developing with its natrual tendency to smallness in stature. In fact, as a recognized breed, the Miniature Pinscher predates the development of the well-known Doberman Pinscher[1].

The Min Pin is an excellent choice as a family pet. The breed tends to attach itself very quickly to children and really delights in joining a youngster in bed. As soon as the Min-Pin climbs onto

Avoiding Typographic Problems

Widows and **orphans** are words or single lines of text that become separated from the other lines in a paragraph. Orphans are left alone at the bottom of a page and widows at the top of the next page or column. The Paragraph panel menu has many commands that allow you to control how text appears and flows, specifically at the end of a column or page, avoiding unsightly widows and orphans. The Keep Options command lets you highlight text that should always stay together instead of being split over two pages. The Keep Options dialog box lets you choose to keep the selected text together or choose how many lines to keep with the selected text. The Justification command opens the Justification dialog box in which you can define the percentages assigned to minimum, desired, and maximum word spacing, letter spacing, and glyph scaling. You can also change the Auto Leading value and tell InDesign how to justify a one-word line.

The Hyphenation Settings dialog box, which opens by clicking Hyphenation on the Paragraph panel menu, allows you to define how words should be hyphenated. You can turn hyphenation off completely by removing the check mark in the Hyphenation check box.

Understanding Returns

Most people think of a paragraph as a block of text, but in InDesign, a paragraph can be a block of text, a line of text, or even a single word, followed by a paragraph return. A **paragraph return**, also called a *hard return*, is inserted into the text formatting by pressing [return] (Mac) or [Enter] (Win). For example, if I type my first name and then enter a paragraph return, that one word—my first name—is a paragraph. When working with body copy, a paragraph is any block of text separated by a paragraph return.

When typing body copy, designers will often want a space after each paragraph because it is visually pleasing and helps to keep paragraphs distinct. The mistake many designers make is pressing [return] (Mac) or [Enter] (Win) twice to create that space after the paragraph. Wrong! What they've done is created two paragraphs. The correct way to insert space between paragraphs is to enter a value in the Space After text box on the Paragraph panel.

You can make a similar mistake when you want to force words from one line down to the next line. As you edit text, you may encounter a "bad line break" at the end of a line, such as an oddly hyphenated word or a phrase that is split from one line to the next. In many of these cases, you will want to move a word or phrase to the next line. Don't use a hard return to do this. Using a hard return means you are creating a new paragraph. Instead, do this by entering a soft return. A **soft return** moves words down to the next baseline but does not create a new paragraph. To enter a soft return, press and hold [shift] while pressing [return] (Mac) or [Enter] (Win).

You can avoid untold numbers of formatting problems by using correct typesetting behaviors, especially those regarding Space After and First Line Indent.

TIP When creating a first line paragraph indent, many users will press [spacebar] five or 10 times and then start typing. This is incorrect formatting. Paragraph indents are created using the First Line Left Indent setting on the Paragraph panel, not by inserting multiple spaces.

USING THE TYPE ON A PATH TOOL

Hidden behind the Type tool on the toolbar is the Type on a Path tool. The Type on a Path tool allows you to position text on any closed or open InDesign path. For example, you could draw a closed path, such as a circle, then position text on the circular path. Or you could draw a simple curved path across the page, then flow text along the path. Simply click the Type on a Path tool on the path. A blinking cursor will appear, and you can then begin typing on the path. The path itself remains visible and selectable; you can apply stroke colors and various widths to the path. You can format the size, typeface, and style of type on a path as well. Give it a try!

Use the Paragraph panel and Character panel to modify leading and alignment

1. Click **View** on the menu bar, then click **Fit Page in Window**.

2. Click the **Type tool** T , then double-click the **first word in the first paragraph**.

    Double-clicking a word selects the word.

3. Triple-click the **same word**.

    Triple-clicking a word selects the entire line of text.

4. Click the **first word in the first paragraph** four times.

Clicking a word four times selects the entire paragraph.

5. Click the **same word** five times.

    Clicking a word five times selects all the text in a text frame.

6. Click the **Leading list arrow** on the Character panel, then click **30 pt**.

    The vertical space between each line of text is increased, as shown in Figure 18. Because leading can be applied to a single selected word as well as to an entire paragraph, the Leading setting is on the Character panel (as opposed to the Paragraph panel).

7. Double-click **30** in the **Leading text box**, type **16,** then press **[return] (Mac)** or **[Enter] (Win)**.

8. Display the **Paragraph panel**, then click the **Justify with last line aligned left button** ≡ .

9. Click **Introducing** at the top of the document three times, then click the **Align center button** ≡ on the Paragraph panel.

10. Click **Edit** on the menu bar, then click **Deselect All**.

    Your document should resemble Figure 19.

    You modified the leading and alignment of a block of selected text.

Figure 18 Modifying leading

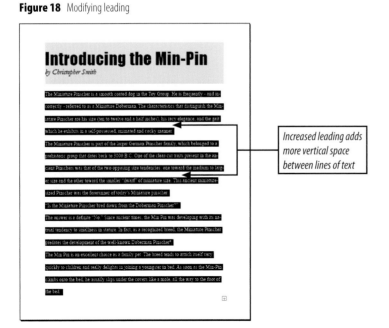

Increased leading adds more vertical space between lines of text

Figure 19 Modifying alignment

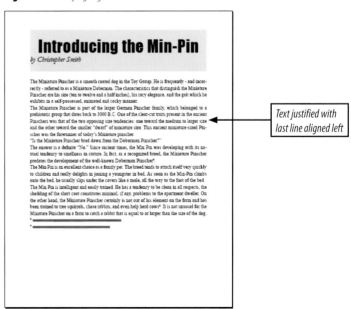

Text justified with last line aligned left

Apply vertical spacing between paragraphs

1. Click the **Type tool** T anywhere in the text frame, then enter **[command] [A] (Mac)** or **[Ctrl] [A] (Win)** to select **all the text in the text frame**.

2. Click the **Space After up arrow** ⬒ on the Paragraph panel three times so the value reads **.1875 in**, then deselect.

   As shown in Figure 20, 0.1875 inch of vertical space is applied after every paragraph.

3. Click and drag to select the **two footnotes at the bottom of the document**.

4. Double-click the **Space After text box** on the Paragraph panel, type **0**, then press **[return] (Mac)** or **[Enter] (Win)**.

5. Select only the **first footnote**, double-click the **0** in the **Space Before text box** on the Paragraph panel, type **.25**, then press **[return] (Mac)** or **[Enter] (Win)**.

   There is 0.25 inch of vertical space positioned above the first footnote.

6. **Deselect All**.

   Your document should resemble Figure 21.

7. Save your work, then continue to the next set of steps.

You used the Space After and Space Before text boxes on the Paragraph panel to apply vertical spacing between paragraphs.

Figure 20 Increasing the Space After value

Figure 21 Increasing Space Before value to move footnotes down

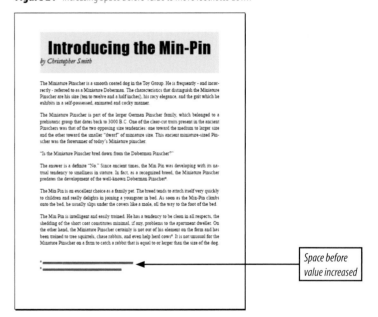

Space before value increased

Apply paragraph indents

1. Click **Type** on the menu bar, then click **Show Hidden Characters**.

   As shown in Figure 22, hidden characters appear in blue, showing blue dots for spaces, created by pressing [space bar], and paragraph marks for paragraph returns.

   TIP It's a good idea to memorize the keyboard command for hiding and showing hidden characters.

2. Select **all the body copy on the page** except the two footnotes, then click the **First Line Left Indent up arrow** ⬚ on the Paragraph panel four times to change the value to **.25 in**, as shown in Figure 23.

   The first line of each paragraph is indented 0.25 in.

Continued on next page

Figure 22 Showing hidden characters

The · characteristics · that · ← Space symbol

lf · inches), · his · racy · elegan

ocky · manner.¶ ← Paragraph return symbol

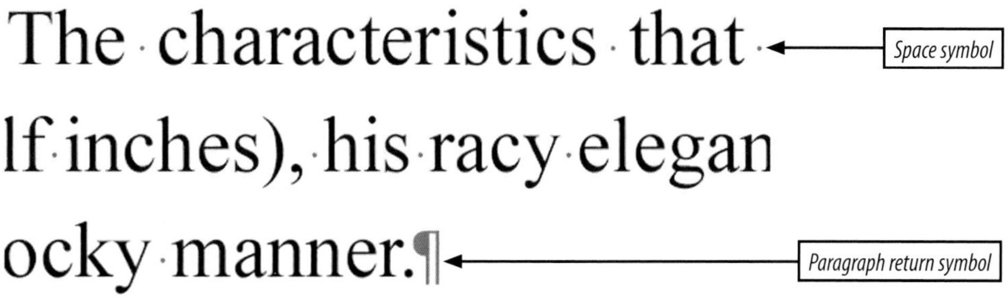

Figure 23 Applying a first line left indent

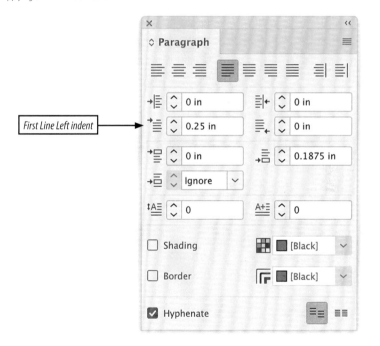

3. Select **by Christopher Smith**, then change the **Left Indent** ⁺⁼ ⌄ value to **.5**.

4. Click anywhere in the **third paragraph**, then change the **First Line Left Indent** ⁺⁼ ⌄ value to **0**.

5. Change the **Left Indent** ⁺⁼ ⌄ value to **.75 in**, then change the **Right Indent** ⁼⁺ value to **.75 in**.

6. Click **any word in the third paragraph** three times to select the entire line, change the **font size** to **18 pt.**, change the **leading** to **20 pt.**, then deselect the paragraph.

7. Save your work, then continue to the next set of steps.

   Your document should resemble Figure 24.

You showed hidden characters so that you could better identify each paragraph. You indented the first lines of every paragraph, and then you added substantial left and right indents to a paragraph and increased its point size to create a pull quote.

Apply drop caps and soft returns

1. Click the **Paragraph panel name tab**, click anywhere in the **first paragraph**, then change the **First Line Left Indent** ⁺⁼ ⌄ value to **0**.

2. Click the **Drop Cap Number of Lines up arrow** ¹ᴬ⁼ ⌄ three times so the text box displays a **3**, as shown in Figure 25.

   A drop cap with the height of three text lines is added to the first paragraph.

3. Select the **entire pull quote (the third paragraph)**, then click the **Align center button** ⁼ on the Paragraph panel.

   When centered, only the words Doberman Pinscher are on the second line of the pull quote. The goal now is to move more text from the first line to the second line so that the two lines are more balanced.

Figure 24 Using indents to format text as a pull quote

Pull quote formatted with increased left and right indents

Figure 25 Creating a drop cap

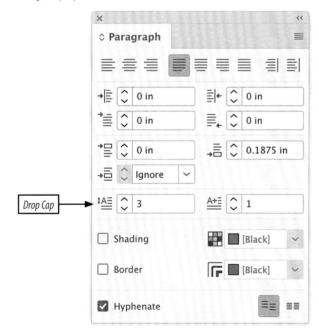

Drop Cap

4. Insert the **cursor** immediately **before the word** "**from**" in the first line of the pull quote, then press **[return] (Mac)** or **[Enter] (Win)** on your keypad.

As shown in Figure 26, a paragraph return formatting character appears at the end of the first line, and a space is added after the first line. Entering [return] (Mac) or [Enter] (Win) on your keypad creates what's called a hard return. With a hard return, all paragraph formatting is applied. Thus, the two lines in the pull quote are now two different paragraphs, and there's a space after amount applied to the first paragraph.

5. Undo Step 4, press and hold **[shift]**, then press **[return] (Mac)** or **[Enter] (Win)** on your keypad.

As shown in Figure 27, a soft paragraph return formatting character appears at the end of the first line. The words "from" and "the" are moved to the second line, but no space or other type of paragraph formatting is added because a soft return does not create a new paragraph; it just moves text from one line to another.

6. Use the keyboard command to hide hidden characters.

7. Press and hold **[shift]**, then press the **letter [W]** on your keypad.

The view changes to Presentation mode.

8. Compare your document to Figure 28.

9. Press **[esc]**, save your work, then close the Min-Pin Intro document.

You created a drop cap and a soft return, which moved text to the next line without creating a new paragraph.

Figure 26 Entering a hard return creates a new paragraph.

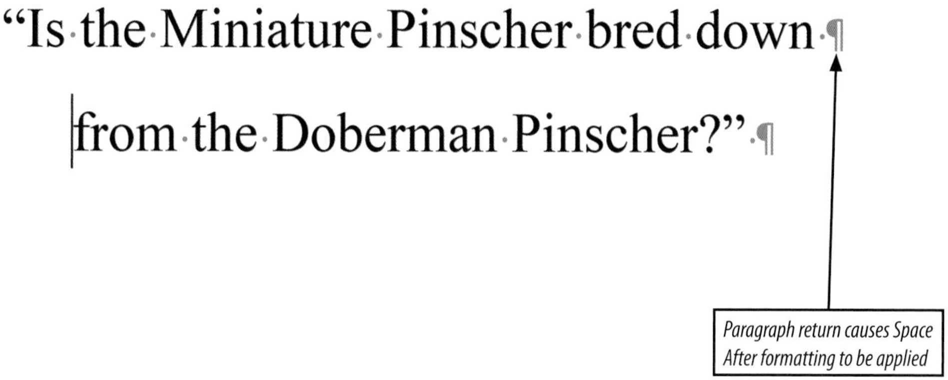

"Is·the·Miniature·Pinscher·bred·down·¶

|from·the·Doberman·Pinscher?"·¶

Paragraph return causes Space After formatting to be applied

Figure 27 Entering a soft return moves words to the next line but does not create a new paragraph.

"Is·the·Miniature·Pinscher·bred·down·⌐
from·the·Doberman·Pinscher?"·¶

Soft return only moves text to the next line

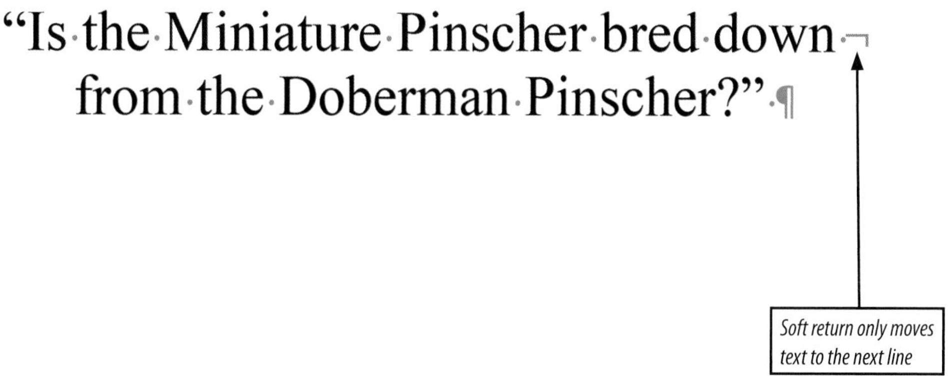

Figure 28 Final page layout with extensive formatting

Introducing the Min-Pin
by Christopher Smith

The Miniature Pinscher is a smooth coated dog in the Toy Group. He is frequently - and incorrectly - referred to as a Miniature Doberman. The characteristics that distinguish the Miniature Pinscher are his size (ten to twelve and a half inches), his racy elegance, and the gait which he exhittbits in a self-possessed, animated and cocky manner.

The Miniature Pinscher is part of the larger German Pinscher family, which belonged to a prehistoric group that dates back to 3000 B.C. One of the clear-cut traits present in the ancient Pinschers was that of the two opposing size tendencies: one toward the medium to larger size and the other toward the smaller "dwarf" of miniature size. This ancient miniature-sized Pinscher was the forerunner of today's Miniature pinscher.

"Is the Miniature Pinscher bred down from the Doberman Pinscher?"

The answer is a definite "No." Since ancient times, the Min Pin was developing with its natrual tendency to smallness in stature. In fact, as a recognized breed, the Miniature Pinscher predates the development of the well-known Doberman Pinscher[1].

The Min Pin is an excellent choice as a family pet. The breed tends to attach itself very quickly to children and really delights in joining a youngster in bed. As soon as the Min-Pin climbs onto the bed, he usually slips under the covers like a mole, all the way to the foot of the bed.

The Min Pin is intelligent and easily trained. He has a tendency to be clean in all respects, the shedding of the short coat constitutes minimal, if any, problems to the apartment dweller. On the other hand, the Miniature Pinscher certainly is not out of his element on the farm and has been trained to tree squirrels, chase rabbits, and even help herd cows[2]. It is not unusual for the Minature Pinscher on a farm to catch a rabbit that is equal to or larger than the size of the dog.

[1] Montag, Scott: In Love with the Min-Pin, All Breeds Publishing, 1997

[2] Miltenberger, William: Working Toy Breeds, CJP Press, 2002

CREATE AND APPLY STYLES

▶ *What You'll Do*

In this lesson, you will use the Character Styles and Paragraph Styles panels to create and apply styles to text.

Working with Character and Paragraph Styles

Imagine that you are writing a book. Let's say it's a user's manual for how to care for houseplants. This book will contain seven chapters. In each chapter, different sections will be preceded by a headline that is the same font as the chapter title, but a smaller font size. Within those sections, there will be subheads that, again, use the same font but in an even smaller size. Such a scenario is perfect for using styles.

A **style** is a group of formatting attributes—such as font, font size, color, and tracking—that is applied to text—whenever and wherever you want it to appear—throughout a document or multiple documents. Using styles saves you time and keeps your work consistent. Styles are given descriptive names for the type of text to which they are applied. Figure 29 shows three styles on the Character Styles panel. You use the Character Styles panel to create styles for individual words or characters, such as a footnote, which you would want in a smaller, superscript font. You use the Paragraph Styles panel to apply a style to an entire paragraph. Paragraph styles include formatting options such as indents and drop caps. The Paragraph Styles panel is shown in Figure 30.

Figure 29 Three styles on the Character Styles panel

Figure 30 Two styles on the Paragraph Styles panel

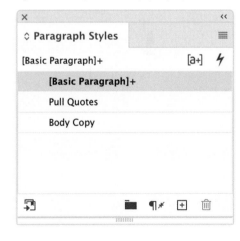

You can easily import character and paragraph styles from other InDesign documents. Click the Character Styles or Paragraph Styles panel list arrow, then click Load Character Styles or Load Paragraph Styles. You'll be prompted to navigate to the documents that have the styles you wish to import.

In the scenario of the houseplant book, if you weren't using styles, you would be required to format all seven chapter headlines one at a time. You would need to remember the font size, the font style, and any tracking, kerning, scaling, or other formatting. Then you would need to do the same for every section headline, and every subheadline. For any body copy, you'd risk inconsistent spacing, indents, and other formatting options. Using styles, you define those formats one time and one time only. A much better solution, don't you think?

Another important feature about styles is that they are useful when you change your mind and want to modify text. Simply modify the style, and all the text that is assigned to that style will be automatically updated throughout the entire document.

TIP Glyphs are type characters that you won't find on your keyboard. These include characters such as arrows, boxes, and trademark, registration mark, and cents signs. InDesign makes it easy to find and use glyphs. Click Type on the menu bar, then click Glyphs to display the Glyphs panel. Click the document window with the Type tool, then double click the glyph on the Glyphs panel that you wish to insert.

Choosing the Next Style

Once you have more than one paragraph style saved on the Paragraph Styles panel, you can program which style will come next when you are currently in one style and create a new paragraph. For example, imagine you are creating a catalog and you have two styles called Item and Description. Now let's say that each time you finish typing the name of an item, you want to type the description of that item using the Description paragraph style. Then, when you finish typing the description and start a new paragraph, you want to type the next item using the Item paragraph style. You can choose which style should follow which by double-clicking a style on the

Paragraph Styles panel, then clicking the Next Style list arrow in the Paragraph Style Options dialog box and choosing the name of the style that should come next.

Using Quick Apply

A quick way to apply a character or paragraph style is to use Quick Apply. The Quick Apply button is available on the Control panel, Character Styles panel, and Paragraph Styles panel. In the Quick Apply dialog box, there is a pull-down menu showing checked items, such as Character Styles. When Character Styles is checked, you can apply a character style quickly by typing its name in the Quick Apply text box. Your style will appear in a list below. Click the name in the list and your style is applied.

Quick Apply is not limited to applying styles. You can use Quick Apply to access menu commands and run scripts. Just be sure to click the Quick Apply list arrow in the Quick Apply dialog box and select Include Scripts and Include Menu Commands.

USING DATA MERGE

InDesign lets you create documents that are customized for each recipient, much like a mail merge in a word processing program, which you can use for items like letters, name labels, and postcards. In a **data merge**, you use a data source (usually a text file) that contains **fields** (labels like "First Name") and **records** (rows representing information for each recipient, such as "Bob Jones"). A **target document** is an InDesign file containing the text that will be seen by all recipients, such as a letter, as well as placeholders representing fields, such as <<First Name>>. In a data merge, InDesign places information from each record in the appropriate places in the target document, as many times as necessary. The result is a **merged document** containing the personalized letters.

To perform a data merge, click Window on the menu bar, point to Utilities, then click Data Merge. When the Data Merge panel opens, click the Data Merge panel menu button, click Select Data Source, locate the data source file, then click Open. This displays the merge fields on the Data Merge panel. Click in a text frame, and click field names to enter them in the frame. If you place placeholders on master pages, the merged document is connected to the data source, and you can automatically update the merged document with the most recent version of your data source.

To merge the document, click the Data Merge panel menu button, then click Create Merged Document. Select the records to include, then click OK.

Create character styles

1. Open ID 2-2.indd, then save it as **Jake's Diner**.

2. Display the **Character Styles panel**.

3. Click the **Character Styles panel menu button** ☰, then click **New Character Style**.

4. Type **Dishes** in the **Style Name text box** of the New Character Style dialog box, then click **Basic Character Formats** in the left column, as shown in Figure 31.

5. Click the **Font Family list arrow**, click **Impact**, click the **Size list arrow**, click **14 pt.**, click the **Leading text box**, type **16 pt.**, then click **Advanced Character Formats** in the left column.

6. Type **85** in the **Horizontal Scale text box**, then click **OK**.

   The style "Dishes" now appears on the Character Styles panel.

7. Click the **Character Styles panel menu button** ☰, click **New Character Style**, type **Descriptions** in the Style Name text box, then click **Basic Character Formats** in the left column.

8. Click the **Font Family list arrow**, click **Times New Roman** or a similar font, click the **Font Style list arrow**, click **Italic**, change the font size to **10 pt.**, change the leading to **12 pt.**, then click **OK**.

   The style "Descriptions" now appears on the Character Styles panel.

9. Click the **Character Styles panel menu button** ☰, click **New Character Style**, type **Prices** in the Style Name text box, then click **Basic Character Formats** in the left column.

10. Change the font to **Times New Roman** or a similar font, change the font style to **Bold,** change the font size to **12 pt.**, change the leading to **14 pt.**, then click **OK**.

    Your Character Styles panel should resemble Figure 32.

11. Save your work, then continue to the next set of steps.

You created three new character styles.

Figure 31 New Character Style dialog box

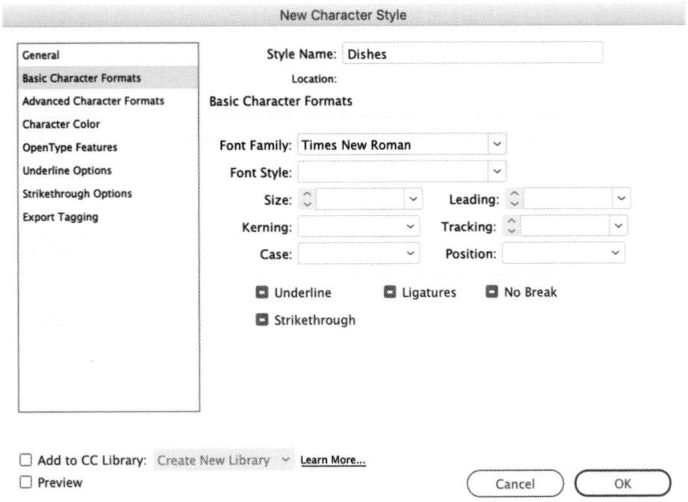

Figure 32 Character Styles panel

Apply character styles

1. Click the **Type tool** **T** , triple-click the word **Eggs** in the first title to select the entire title "Eggs and Bacon," then click **Dishes** on the Character Styles panel.

   The Dishes character style is applied to the title.

2. Select the **entire next paragraph** (beginning with the word Two), then click **Descriptions** on the Character Styles panel.

3. Select the **first price ($5.95)**, click **Prices** on the Character Styles panel, click **Edit** on the menu bar, then click **Deselect All**.

   Your first menu item should resemble Figure 33. If you used a different font, your text lines may break differently.

4. Select all the **remaining text** in the text frame, then apply the **Descriptions style**.

5. Apply the **Dishes style** to the **remaining seven dish titles**.

6. Apply the **Prices style** to the **remaining seven prices**, then deselect so that your document resembles Figure 34.

You applied character styles to format specific areas of a document.

Figure 33 Applying three different character styles

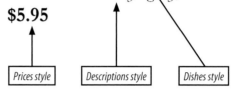

Eggs and Bacon
Two eggs any style, two strips of lean bacon, one biscuit with our homestyle gravy, and home fries.
$5.95

| Prices style | Descriptions style | Dishes style |

Figure 34 Viewing the document with all character styles applied

Jake's Diner
Early Bird Breakfast Menu

Eggs and Bacon
Two eggs any style, two strips of lean bacon, one biscuit with our homestyle gravy, and home fries.
$5.95

Egg Sandwich
One egg over easy, served with American or Jack cheese on a soft French croissant.
$5.25

Belgian Waffle
A golden brown buttery waffle served with fresh-picked strawberries, raspberries and blueberries. Whipped fresh cream on request.
$4.95

Silver Dollar Pancakes
A stack of eight golden pancakes served with fresh creamery butter and warm maple syrup.
$4.95

French Toast
Four triangles of thick peasant bread dipped in a cinnamon-egg batter. Served with French Fries.
$6.95

Biscuits and Gravy
Light fluffy southern biscuits served with a hearty sausage gravy.
$3.95

Eggs Hollandaise
Three eggs lightly poached served on a bed of romaine lettuce and topped with a rich Hollandaise sauce.
$6.95

Steak and Eggs
A 6 oz. strip of peppered breakfast steak cooked to your liking, served with two eggs, any style.
$7.95

Create paragraph styles

1. Close the **Character Styles panel**, then open the **Paragraph Styles panel**.

2. Click the **Paragraph Styles panel menu button** ≡, then click **New Paragraph Style**.

3. Type **Prices** in the **Style Name text box**, then click **Indents and Spacing** in the left column.

   TIP Note that the New Paragraph Style dialog box contains Basic Character Formats and Advanced Character

Formats categories—the same that you find when working in the New Character Style dialog box.

4. Click the **Alignment list arrow**, then click **Center**.

5. Type **.25** in the **Space After text box**, then click **Paragraph Rules** in the left column, as shown in Figure 35.

6. Click the **list arrow** directly beneath Paragraph Rules, click **Rule Below**, then click the **Rule On check box** to add a check mark.

7. Type **.125** in the **Offset text box**, type **.25** in the **Left Indent text box**, type **.25** in the **Right Indent text box**, then click **OK**.

   The paragraph style "Prices" now appears on the Paragraph Styles panel as shown on Figure 36.

8. Save your work, then continue to the next set of steps.

You created a paragraph style, which included a center alignment, a space after value, and a paragraph rule.

Figure 35 Paragraph Rules window in the New Paragraph Style dialog box

Figure 36 Paragraph Styles panel

Apply paragraph styles

1. Click the **Type tool** T, then select **all the text in the document** except for the two headlines at the top of the page.

2. Click the **Align center button** ≡ on the Paragraph panel.

    For this layout, all the menu items will be aligned center. It's not necessary to create a paragraph style for all items to align center because you can simply use the Align center button ≡ on the Paragraph panel.

3. Click the **first price ($5.95)** once, click **Prices** on the Paragraph Styles panel, click the **second price ($5.25)**, then click **Prices** on the Paragraph Styles panel again.

    Your first two menu items should resemble Figure 37.

    TIP When applying paragraph styles, just place the cursor in the paragraph you want to modify.

4. Apply the **Prices paragraph style** to the remaining prices in the document except the Silver Dollar Pancakes and Steak and Eggs prices.

    You don't need to apply the paragraph style to the last two items because you don't need rules at the bottom of the menu.

5. In the **"French Toast" item**, note that the last sentence of the description is split between two lines.

6. Click **before the word "Served"** in the description text for **"French Toast,"** press and hold **[shift]**, then press **[return] (Mac)** or **[Enter] (Win)**.

    "Served" is moved to the next line. Using the same method, add soft returns to break any other lines that you think could look better, then compare your work to Figure 38.

7. Save your work, then close the Jake's Diner document.

You applied a paragraph style to specific areas of the menu.

Figure 37 Applying a paragraph style to two prices

Eggs and Bacon

Two eggs any style, two strips of lean bacon, one biscuit with our homestyle gravy, and home fries.

$5.95

Egg Sandwich

One egg over easy, served with American or Jack cheese on a soft French croissant.

$5.25

USING THE TRACK CHANGES FEATURE

Whenever you're producing a document that involves a copy editor or more than one person making edits to copy, it becomes important that any edits made are recorded. For example, let's say you're the author of a story in a magazine. The copy editor goes through your text and makes various changes. You, as the author, will want to see what changes were made. You'll also want the option of approving or rejecting those changes, or at least the opportunity to debate whether or not the changes should be implemented.

The Track Changes feature allows for this important function within the editing process. The feature will identify each participant separately. Some of the changes that will be recorded include deleting, moving, and inserting new text. To view the changes, you use the Story Editor, accessed through the Edit menu. To accept or reject changes, use the Track Changes panel, located in the Window menu on the Editorial submenu.

Figure 38 Viewing the final document

Jake's Diner
Early Bird Breakfast Menu

Eggs and Bacon
Two eggs any style, two strips of lean bacon, one biscuit with our homestyle gravy, and home fries.
$5.95

French Toast
Four triangles of thick peasant bread dipped in a cinnamon-egg batter. Served with French Fries.
$6.95

Egg Sandwich
One egg over easy, served with American or Jack cheese on a soft French croissant.
$5.25

Biscuits and Gravy
Light fluffy southern biscuits served with a hearty sausage gravy.
$3.95

Belgian Waffle
A golden brown buttery waffle served with fresh-picked strawberries, raspberries and blueberries. Whipped fresh cream on request.
$4.95

Eggs Hollandaise
Three eggs lightly poached served on a bed of romaine lettuce and topped with a rich Hollandaise sauce.
$6.95

Silver Dollar Pancakes
A stack of eight golden pancakes served with fresh creamery butter and warm maple syrup.
$4.95

Steak and Eggs
A 6 oz. strip of peppered breakfast steak cooked to your liking, served with two eggs, any style.
$7.95

EDIT TEXT

▶ *What You'll Do*

In this lesson, you will use the Find/Change and Check Spelling commands to edit the text of a document.

Using the Find/Change Command

One of the great things about creating documents using a computer is the ability to edit text quickly and efficiently. Imagine the days before the personal computer. When you finished typing a document, you needed to read through it carefully, looking for any errors. If you found any, you had three options: cover it up, cross it out, or type the whole document again.

The Find/Change dialog box is a powerful tool for editing a document. With this command, you can search for any word in the document, then change that word to another word or delete it altogether with a click of the mouse button. For example, imagine that you have typed an entire document about Abraham Lincoln's early years growing up in Frankfurt, Kentucky. Then you find out that Lincoln actually grew up in Hardin County, Kentucky. You could use the Find/Change command to locate every instance of the word "Frankfurt" and change it to "Hardin County." One click would correct every instance of that error throughout the entire document.

TIP InDesign has many great features in the Find/Change dialog box. The Query menu lists predefined search options for finding (and changing) common formatting issues. For example, the Query menu has built-in searches for finding and changing dashes to en dashes and straight single or double quotes to typographer's quotes. There's a built-in search for trailing white space—useless extra spaces at the end of paragraphs or sentences—and there's even a search for telephone number formatting.

Checking Spelling

Since the earliest days of the personal computer, the ability to check and correct spelling errors automatically has been a much-promoted benefit of creating documents digitally. It has stood the test of time. The spell checker continues to be one of the most powerful features of word processing.

InDesign's Check Spelling dialog box is a comprehensive utility for locating and correcting typos and other misspellings in a document. If you've done word processing before, you will find yourself on familiar turf. The spell checker identifies words that it doesn't find in its dictionary, offers you a list of suggested corrections, and asks you what you want to do. If there is indeed a misspelling, type the correct spelling or choose the correct word from the suggested corrections list, then click Change to correct that instance or click Change All to correct all instances of the misspelling throughout the document.

Sometimes the spell checker identifies a word that is not actually a misspelling. For example, say you were typing a letter about your dog whose name is Gargantua. The spell checker is not going to find that word/name in its dictionary, and it is going to ask you what you want to do with it. You have two options. You could click Ignore, which tells the spell checker to make no changes and move on to the next questionable word. However, because in the future you will probably type the dog's name in other documents, you don't want the spell checker always asking you if this word/name is a misspelling. In this case, you'd be better off clicking the Add button. Doing so adds the name Gargantua to the spell checker's dictionary, and in the future, the spell checker will no longer identify Gargantua as a misspelling.

When you click the Add button, the word in question is added to the User Dictionary, which is InDesign's main dictionary. If you use the spell checker often, you will build up a list of words that you've chosen to ignore and a list of words that you've chosen to add to the dictionary. To see those lists and modify them, click the Dictionary button in the Check Spelling dialog box.

You can create your own user dictionary in the Dictionary section of the Preferences dialog box. Click the Language list arrow to choose the language with which you want to associate your dictionary, click the Add User Dictionary button, then select the user dictionary file. The user dictionary file is stored on the hard drive and includes a .udc or a .not extension. When you locate it, click Open. If you can't find the dictionary file, search your hard drive to locate the .udc files (try using *.udc or *.not in the search text box). The new user dictionary is added to the list under the Language menu. Then, when you are using the spell checker, click the Dictionary button, click the Target list arrow, then choose your new user dictionary from the list. You can add words to the new user dictionary using the Add button in the Check Spelling dialog box.

Using Dynamic Spell Checking

Another spell check feature is Dynamic Spelling. As you type, the program places a squiggly red line under words the spell checker thinks are misspelled. To prevent the program from flagging a proper name, you can add that name to your customized dictionary. To enable dynamic spelling, click Edit on the menu bar, point to Spelling, then click Dynamic Spelling.

Correcting Text Automatically

Autocorrect takes dynamic spell checking one step further. Instead of flagging a misspelled word, the Autocorrect feature corrects the misspelled word. For example, if you type the word "refered" and press [space bar], Autocorrect will change it to "referred."

Many commonly misspelled or easily mistyped words, such as "hte" for "the," are preprogrammed into the Autocorrect feature, and you can add words that might not already be listed. To turn on the Autocorrect feature, click Edit on the menu bar, point to Spelling, then click Autocorrect.

Use the Find/Change command

1. Open ID 2-3.indd, then save it as **Final Edit**.

2. Click **Edit** on the menu bar, then click **Find/Change**.

3. Type **Miniature Pincher** in the **Find what text box**, then type **Min-Pin** in the **Change to text box**, as shown in Figure 39.

4. Click **Find Next**.

   The first use of "Miniature Pincher" in the document is highlighted. As this is the first use of the term, you don't want to change it to a nickname.

   TIP Drag the dialog box out of the way if you cannot see your document.

5. Click **Find Next**, then click **Change**.

   The second use of "Miniature Pincher" is changed to "Min-Pin."

6. Click **Find Next** again, then click **Change**.

7. Click **Find Next** three times.

   You don't want to change all instances of Miniature Pincher to Min-Pin.

8. Click **Change**, then click **Done**.

9. Click **Edit** on the menu bar, then click **Find/Change**.

10. Type **Pincher** in the **Find what text box**, type **Pinscher** in the **Change to text box**, then click **Change All**.

    A dialog box appears stating that the search is completed, and 14 replacements were made.

11. Click **OK**, then click **Done**.

You used the Find/Change command to replace specific words in the document.

Figure 39 Find/Change dialog box

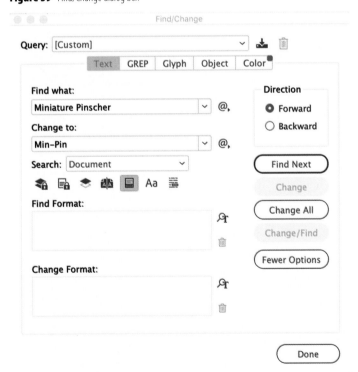

EDITING TEXT USING DRAG AND DROP

InDesign has a Drag and Drop text editing feature that allows you to move text to locations within a document without having to cut and paste. This means that you can select text and simply drag it from one text frame into another text frame. You can drag and drop text between text frames on different pages. You can even drag and drop text between documents. Dragging and dropping text is usually a lot faster and easier than cutting and pasting. You can also drag and drop a copy of selected text by pressing [option] (Mac) or [Alt] (Win) when dragging. You can turn Drag and Drop text on or off in the Type window of the Preferences dialog box. In the Drag and Drop Text Editing section, check both the Enable in Layout View and the Enable in Story Editor check boxes so the feature is activated for all your editing methods. Give it a try!

Check spelling

1. Click to the **right of the drop cap T** (between the T and the h) at the top of the page.

   Positioning your cursor at the top of a document forces the spell checker to begin checking for misspellings from the start of the document.

2. Click **Edit** on the menu bar, point to **Spelling**, then click **Check Spelling**.

   As shown in Figure 40, "refered" is listed as the first word the spell checker can't find in the dictionary. Suggested corrections are listed.

3. Click **referred** in the **Suggested Corrections list**, then click **Change**.

   The spell checker lists "racey" as the next word it can't find in the dictionary.

4. Click **racy** in the **Suggested Corrections list**, then click **Change**.

   The spell checker lists "Pinscher1" as not in the dictionary because of the number 1 footnote.

5. Click **Ignore All** for all remaining queries, click **OK**, then click **Done**.

6. Save your work, then close the Final Edit document.

TIP Never rely on the spell checker as the sole means for proofreading a document. It cannot determine if you have used the wrong word. For example, the spell checker did not flag the word "gate" in the first paragraph, which should be spelled "gait."

You used the Check Spelling dialog box to proof a document for spelling errors.

Figure 40 Check Spelling dialog box

Check Spelling

Not in Dictionary:

refered

Change To:

referred

Suggested Corrections:

refereed
referred
referee
revered
refer ed
refer–ed
referenced
referrer
deferred

Add To: User Dictionary

☐ Case Sensitive

Language: English: USA

Search: Story

Done

Direction
◉ Forward
○ Backward

Skip

Change

Ignore All

Change All

Add

Dictionary...

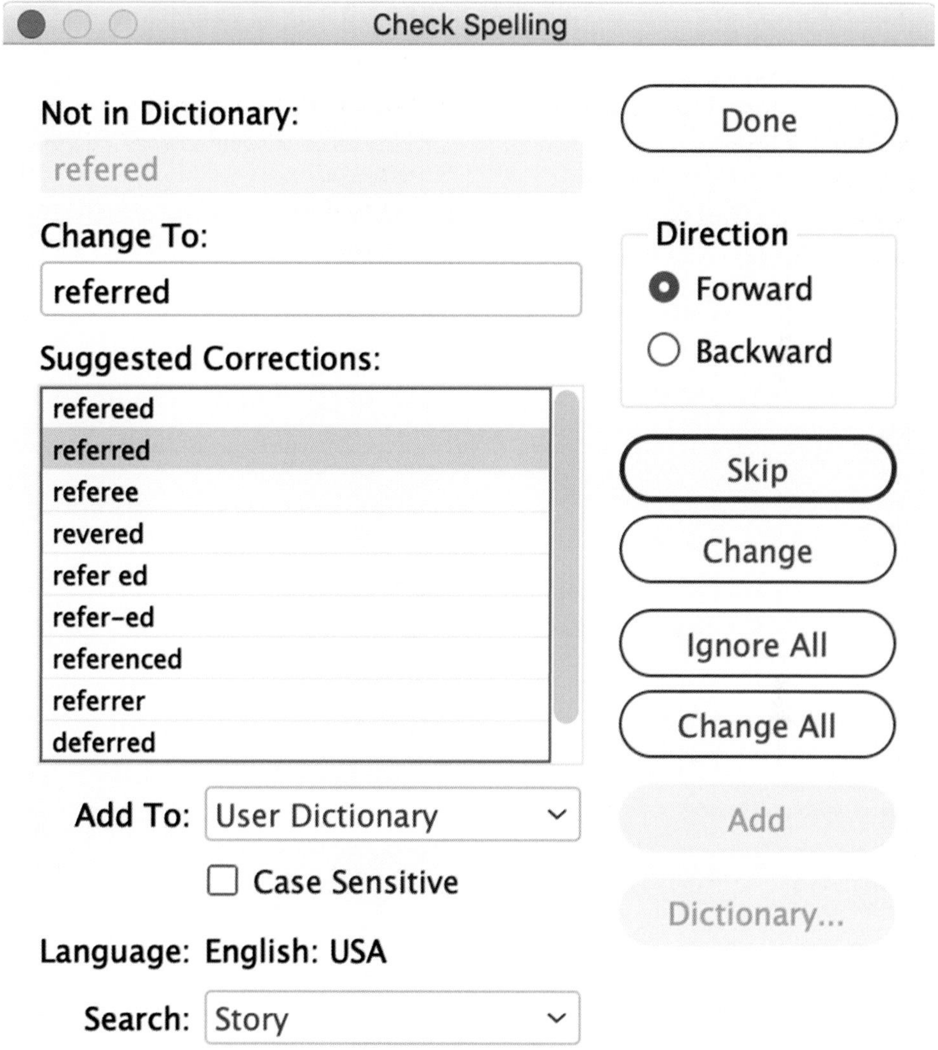

CREATE BULLETED AND NUMBERED LISTS

▶ *What You'll Do*

In this lesson, you will create bulleted and numbered lists, then change the typeface of the numbers.

Photoshop
Table of Contents

Chapter 1: Getting Started

Creating Bulleted and Numbered Lists

Creating numbered or bulleted lists is a common need in many types of layouts, and InDesign allows you to do so easily. The best way to start is to type the list first, without formatting. Select the list, point to the Bulleted & Numbered Lists command in the Type menu, and then choose whether you want to apply bullets or numbers to the selected text.

Bullets and numbers are like any other type of paragraph formatting. InDesign applies them to each paragraph of the selected text. At any time, you can select the text and change the marks from bullets to numbers or vice versa. You also use the same Bulleted & Numbered Lists command to remove bullets or numbers from selected text.

TIP By default, InDesign applies bullets and numbers with the same typeface, type size, and color of the selected text in the paragraph.

Modifying Bulleted and Numbered Lists

You can think of bullets and numbers as being applied "virtually" to a paragraph. Let's use numbers as an example. When you apply numbers, you can see the numbers, but you can't select them. If you select the entire paragraph of text, the numbers won't appear to be selected. This is because the numbers are applied as a format to the paragraph. For example, let's say you had a list of nine numbered entries, and then you inserted a 10th entry between numbers 5 and 6. The new entry would automatically be numbered with a "6," and the numbers on all the following entries would be automatically updated.

Once you've finished a list, you might find that you want to modify the numbers by changing the typeface, color, or size of the numbers.

To do so, you must first convert the list to text so that the numbers can be selected and modified. Click the Bulleted & Numbered Lists command, then click the Convert Bullets and Numbering to Text command, shown in Figure 41. When you do this, the numbers (or bullets) will be converted to regular text. The list will still appear to be numbered, but it will have lost the functionality of the list formatting. If you insert or remove any component of the list, the numbers won't be updated. InDesign will see it only as a block of text.

Figure 41 Convert Bullets to Text command

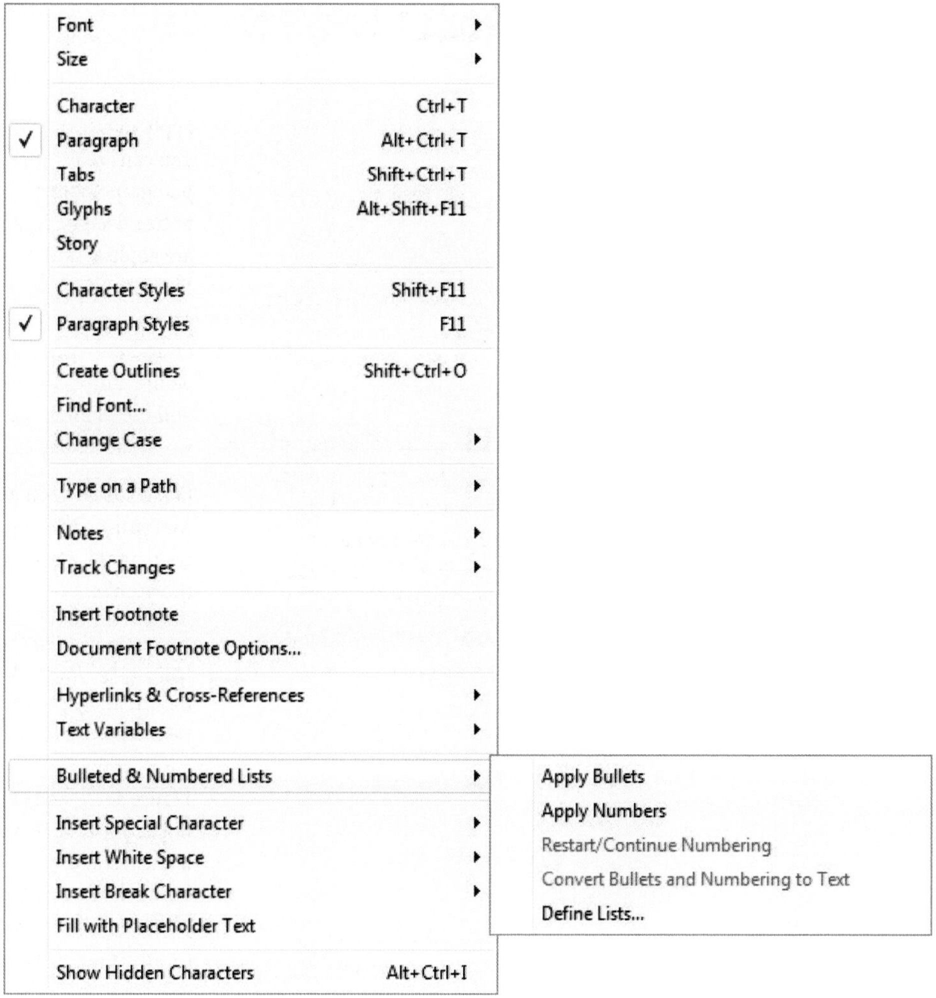

Font	▶	
Size	▶	
Character	Ctrl+T	
✓ Paragraph	Alt+Ctrl+T	
Tabs	Shift+Ctrl+T	
Glyphs	Alt+Shift+F11	
Story		
Character Styles	Shift+F11	
✓ Paragraph Styles	F11	
Create Outlines	Shift+Ctrl+O	
Find Font...		
Change Case	▶	
Type on a Path	▶	
Notes	▶	
Track Changes	▶	
Insert Footnote		
Document Footnote Options...		
Hyperlinks & Cross-References	▶	
Text Variables	▶	
Bulleted & Numbered Lists	▶	Apply Bullets
		Apply Numbers
Insert Special Character	▶	Restart/Continue Numbering
Insert White Space	▶	Convert Bullets and Numbering to Text
Insert Break Character	▶	Define Lists...
Fill with Placeholder Text		
Show Hidden Characters	Alt+Ctrl+I	

Create a bulleted and a numbered list

1. Open ID 2-4.indd, then save it as **TOC**.

2. Click the **Type tool** T ., then select **all the text below Chapter 12: Getting Started**.

3. On the Paragraph panel, set the **Space After value** .ᵃ◦ to **.125 in**.

4. Click **Type** on the menu bar, point to **Bulleted & Numbered Lists**, then click **Apply Bullets**.

   As shown in Figure 42, bullets are applied at each paragraph in the selected text. The text remains selected, though the bullets themselves do not appear selected.

5. Click **Type** on the menu bar, point to **Bulleted & Numbered Lists**, then click **Apply Numbers**.

   The bullets change to numbers that are the same typeface, size, and color of the selected text.

6. Save your work and then continue to the next set of steps.

You applied bullets to selected text, then changed the bullets to numbers.

Figure 42 Bullets applied to text

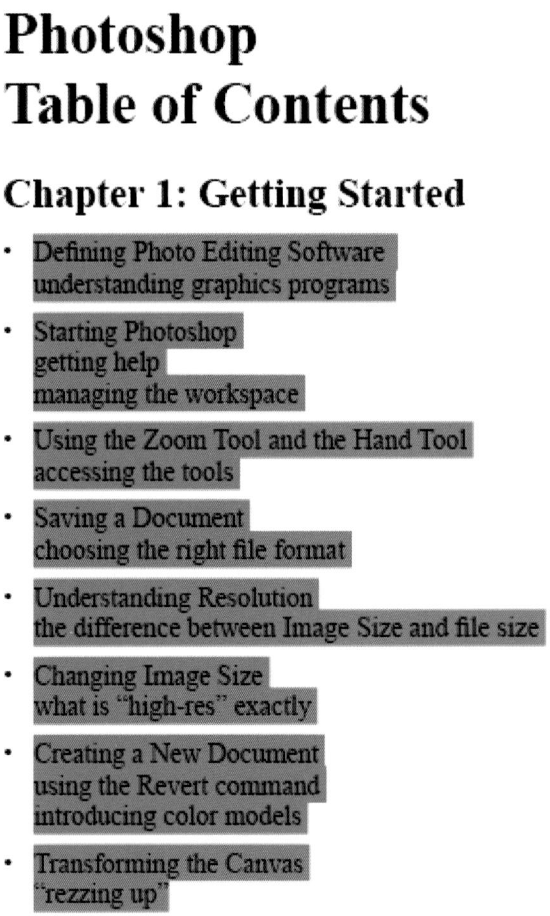

Photoshop
Table of Contents

Chapter 1: Getting Started

- Defining Photo Editing Software
  understanding graphics programs
- Starting Photoshop
  getting help
  managing the workspace
- Using the Zoom Tool and the Hand Tool
  accessing the tools
- Saving a Document
  choosing the right file format
- Understanding Resolution
  the difference between Image Size and file size
- Changing Image Size
  what is "high-res" exactly
- Creating a New Document
  using the Revert command
  introducing color models
- Transforming the Canvas
  "rezzing up"

Convert numbers to text

1. Verify that **all the numbered text** is still selected.

2. Click **Type** on the menu bar, point to **Bulleted & Numbered Lists**, then click **Convert Numbering to Text**.

3. Select the **number 8** and the **period** that follows it.

4. On the Character panel, change the **Type Style** from Regular to **Bold**.

5. Change **all the numbers** and the **periods** that follow them to bold so your list resembles Figure 43.

6. Save your work, then close the TOC document.

You converted numbering to text so you could format the numbers differently from the text in the list.

Figure 43 Reformatting the numbers in the list

Photoshop
Table of Contents

Chapter 1: Getting Started

1. Defining Photo Editing Software
   understanding graphics programs

2. Starting Photoshop
   getting help
   managing the workspace

3. Using the Zoom Tool and the Hand Tool
   accessing the tools

4. Saving a Document
   choosing the right file format

5. Understanding Resolution
   the difference between Image Size and file size

6. Changing Image Size
   what is "high-res" exactly

7. Creating a New Document
   using the Revert command
   introducing color models

8. Transforming the Canvas
   "rezzing up"

Format text

1. Open ID 2-5.indd, then save it as **Independence**.
2. Click Window on the menu bar, point to Workspace, then click Reset Typography.
3. Click the Type tool, then triple-click the word Declaration at the top of the page.
4. On the Character panel, type **80** in the Horizontal Scale text box, then press [return] (Mac) or [Enter] (Win).
5. Click the Font Family list arrow, click Impact, click the Font Size list arrow, then click 36 pt.
6. Press and hold [shift] [command] (Mac) or [Shift] [Ctrl] (Win), then press [<] two times.
7. Triple-click the word July on the next line; change the typeface to Garamond, if necessary; change the Style to Italic; then click the Font Size up arrow until the font size is 18 pt.
8. Click Object on the menu bar, click Text Frame Options, change the Align setting to Center, then click OK.
9. Triple-click the word July, if necessary.

10. Type **100** in the Tracking text box, then press [return] (Mac) or [Enter] (Win).
11. Click between the letters r and a in the word Declaration, click the Kerning list arrow, then click 10.
12. Click View on the menu bar, click Fit Page in Window, if necessary, click the Zoom tool, and then drag a selection box that encompasses all the body copy on the page.
13. Click the Type tool, then select the number 1 at the end of the first paragraph.
14. Click the Character panel menu button, then click Superscript.
15. Select the number 1 at the beginning of the last paragraph, then apply the Superscript command.

Format paragraphs

1. Click View on the menu bar, click Fit Page in Window, then click the first word When in the body copy five times to select all the body copy.
2. Select (12 pt.) in the Leading text box on the Character panel, type **13.25**, then press [return] (Mac) or [Enter] (Win).
3. Display the Paragraph panel, then click the Justify with last line aligned left button.

4. Click in the word Independence at the top of the document, then click the Align center button on the Paragraph panel.
5. Click the Type tool, if necessary; click anywhere in the body copy; click Edit on the menu bar; then click Select All.
6. On the Paragraph panel, click the Space After up arrow three times so the value reads .1875 in, click Edit on the menu bar, then click Deselect All.
7. Select the footnote (last paragraph of the document), double-click the Space Before text box on the Paragraph panel, type **.5,** then press [return] (Mac) or [Enter] (Win).
8. Apply the Deselect All command.
9. Click Type on the menu bar, then click Show Hidden Characters.
10. Select all the body copy on the page except for the last paragraph (the footnote), double-click the First Line Left Indent text box on the Paragraph panel, type **.25**, then press [return] (Mac) or [Enter] (Win).
11. Select July 4, 1776, beneath the headline, then click the Align right button on the Paragraph panel.

12. Double-click the Right Indent text box on the Paragraph panel, type **.6**, then press [return] (Mac) or [Enter] (Win).
13. Click anywhere in the first paragraph, then change the First Line Left Indent value to 0.
14. Click the Drop Cap Number of Lines up arrow three times so the text box displays a 3.
15. Click the Zoom tool, then drag a selection box that encompasses the entire second to last paragraph in the body copy.
16. Click the Type tool, position the pointer before the word "these"—the second-to-last word in the paragraph.
17. Press and hold [shift], then press [return] (Mac) or [Enter] (Win).
18. Click Type on the menu bar, click Hide Hidden Characters, if necessary, click View on the menu bar, point to Grids & Guides, and then click Hide Guides.
19. Click View on the menu bar, then click Fit Page in Window.
20. Compare your document to Figure 44, click File on the menu bar, click Save, then close the Independence document.

Figure 44 Completed Skills Review, Part 1

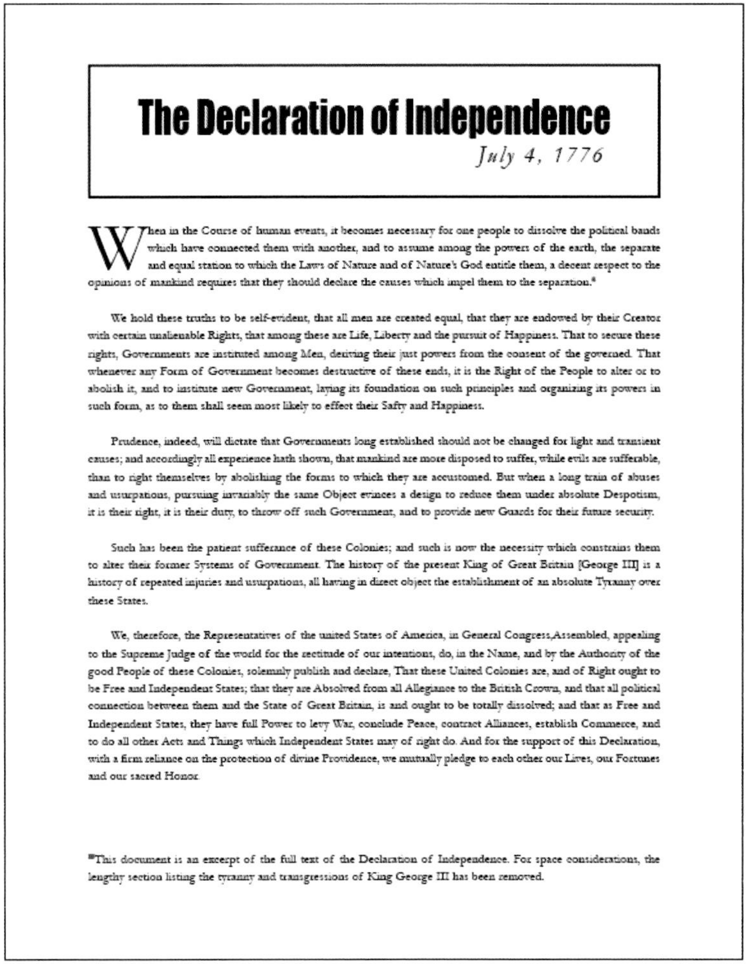

Create and apply styles

1. Open ID 2-6.indd, then save it as **Toy Breeds**.
2. Open the Character Styles panel.
3. Click the Character Styles panel menu button, then click New Character Style.
4. Type **Breeds** in the Style Name text box, then click Basic Character Formats in the left column.
5. Change the Font to Tahoma, change the Size to 14 pt., change the Leading to 16 pt., then click OK.
6. Click the Character Styles panel menu button, click New Character Style, type **Info** in the Style Name text box, then click Basic Character Formats in the left column.
7. Change the Font to Garamond, change the Style to Italic, change the Size to 10 pt., change the Leading to 12 pt., then click OK.
8. Select all the text except for the top two lines, then click Info on the Character Styles panel.

9. Double-click the Affenpinscher headline, then click Breeds on the Character Styles panel.
10. Apply the Breeds character style to the remaining seven breed headlines, then deselect all.
11. Open the Paragraph Styles panel.
12. Click the Paragraph Styles panel menu button, then click New Paragraph Style.
13. Type **Info** in the Style Name text box, then click Indents and Spacing in the left column.
14. Click the Alignment list arrow, then click Center.
15. Type **.25** in the Space After text box, then click Paragraph Rules in the left column.
16. Click the list arrow directly below Paragraph Rules, click Rule Below, then click the Rule On check box.
17. Type **.1625** in the Offset text box, type **1** in the Left Indent text box, type **1** in the Right Indent text box, then click OK.
18. Select all the text except for the top two lines, then click the Align center button on the Paragraph panel.

19. Click in the Affenpinscher description text, then click Info on the Paragraph Styles panel.
20. Apply the Info paragraph style to all the remaining descriptions except for the Pomeranian and the Pug.
21. Click View on the menu bar, point to Grids & Guides, then click Hide Guides.
22. Click before the word "bred" in the Manchester Terrier description, press and hold [shift], then press [return] (Mac) or [Enter] (Win).
23. Click before the phrase even-tempered in the Pug description, press and hold [shift], press [return] (Mac) or [Enter] (Win), click before the word and in the "Pug" description, press and hold [shift], then press [return] (Mac) or [Enter] (Win).
    Your text may break differently. Correct any other bad breaks you see.
24. Save your work, compare your screen to Figure 45, then close the Toy Breeds document.

Edit text

1. Open ID 2-7.indd, then save it as **Declaration Edit**.
2. Select the Type tool, then click at the beginning of the first paragraph.
3. Click Edit on the menu bar, then click Find/Change.
4. Type **IV** in the Find what text box, then type **III** in the Change to text box.
5. Click Find Next.

   You want to change the IV to III in George IV, as in George III; however, the spell checker finds all instances of "IV," such as in the word "deriving."
6. Click the Case Sensitive button Aa in the middle of the Find/Change dialog box.
7. Click Find Next.
8. Click Change All, click OK in the dialog box that tells you that two replacements were made, then click Done in the Find/Change dialog box. By specifying the search to be Case Sensitive, only uppercase IV instances were found and changed.
9. Click before the drop cap in the first paragraph, click Edit on the menu bar, point to Spelling, then click Check Spelling.
10. For the query on the word "Safty," click Safety at the top of the Suggested Corrections list, then click Change.

Figure 45 Completed Skills Review, Part 2

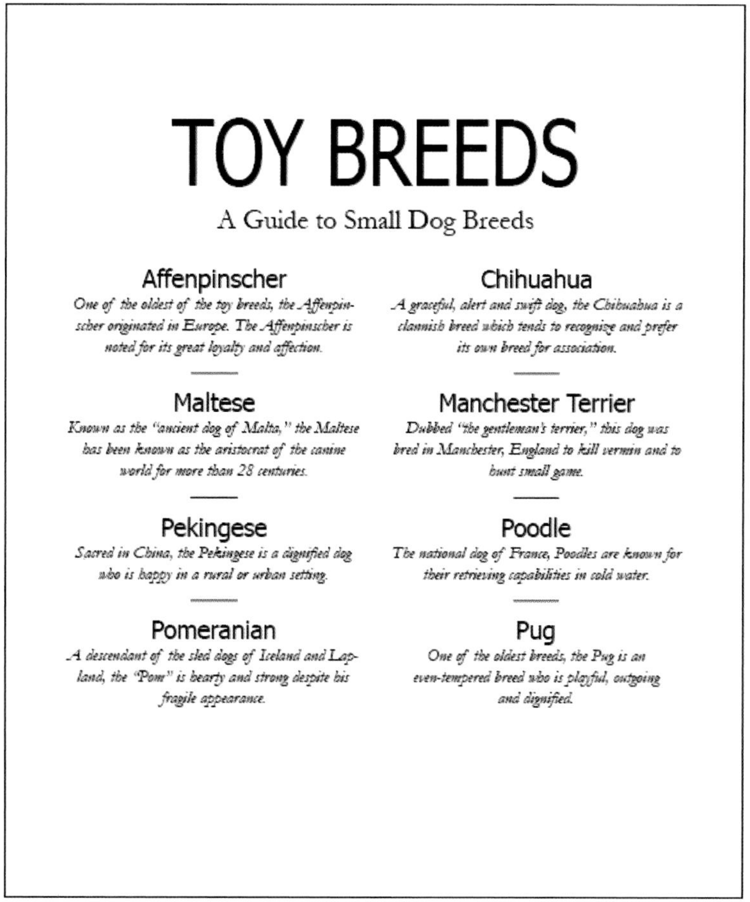

TOY BREEDS
A Guide to Small Dog Breeds

Affenpinscher
One of the oldest of the toy breeds, the Affenpinscher originated in Europe. The Affenpinscher is noted for its great loyalty and affection.

Chihuahua
A graceful, alert and swift dog, the Chihuahua is a clannish breed which tends to recognize and prefer its own breed for association.

Maltese
Known as the "ancient dog of Malta," the Maltese has been known as the aristocrat of the canine world for more than 28 centuries.

Manchester Terrier
Dubbed "the gentleman's terrier," this dog was bred in Manchester, England to kill vermin and to hunt small game.

Pekingese
Sacred in China, the Pekingese is a dignified dog who is happy in a rural or urban setting.

Poodle
The national dog of France, Poodles are known for their retrieving capabilities in cold water.

Pomeranian
A descendant of the sled dogs of Iceland and Lapland, the "Pom" is hearty and strong despite his fragile appearance.

Pug
One of the oldest breeds, the Pug is an even-tempered breed who is playful, outgoing and dignified.

11. Click Ignore All to ignore the query on hath.
12. Click Ignore All to ignore all instances of III.
13. Click before the capital "S" in "States" in the Change To text box in the Check Spelling dialog box, press [space bar] once, then click Change.
14. Click Done.
15. Save your work, deselect, compare your screen to Figure 46, then close the Declaration Edit document.

Create bulleted and numbered lists

1. Open ID 2-8.indd, then save it as **Chapter 13**.
2. Click the Type tool, then select all the text beneath Chapter 13: Selecting Pixels.
3. On the Paragraph panel, set the Space After value to .125 in.
4. Click Type on the menu bar, point to Bulleted & Numbered Lists, then click Apply Bullets.
5. Click Type on the menu bar, point to Bulleted & Numbered Lists, then click Apply Numbers.
6. Click Type on the menu bar, point to Bulleted & Numbered Lists, then click Convert Numbering to Text.
7. Select the number 1 and the period that follows it.
8. On the Character panel, change the Type Style from Regular to Italic.
9. Change all the numbers and the periods that follow them to italic.
10. Save your work, then close the Chapter 13 document.

Figure 46 Completed Skills Review, Part 3

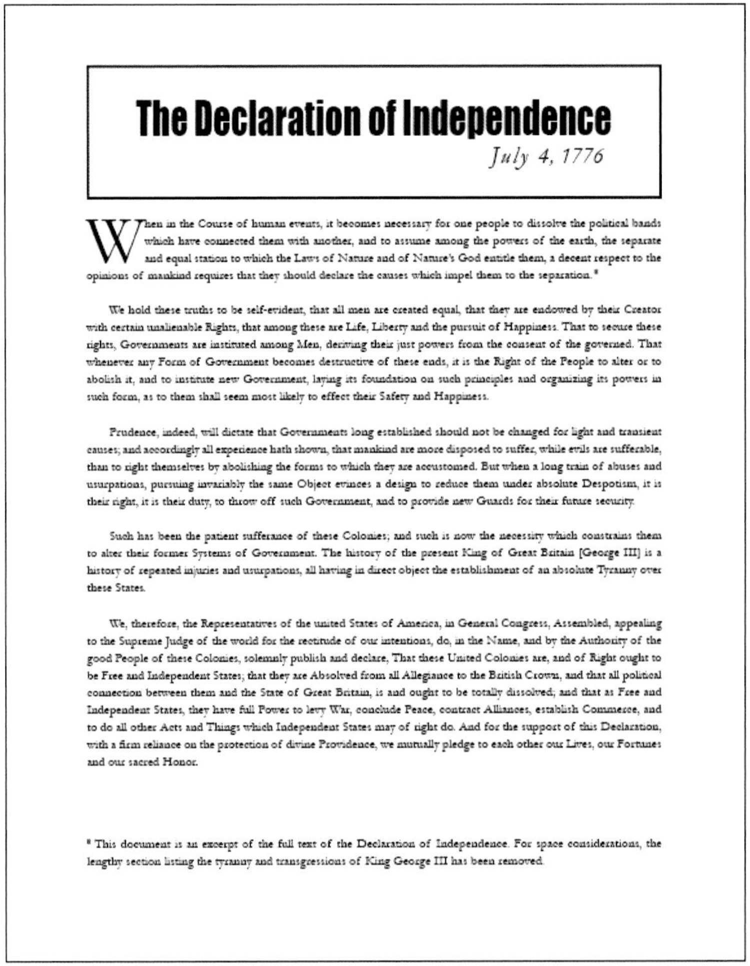

The Declaration of Independence

July 4, 1776

When in the Course of human events, it becomes necessary for one people to dissolve the political bands which have connected them with another, and to assume among the powers of the earth, the separate and equal station to which the Laws of Nature and of Nature's God entitle them, a decent respect to the opinions of mankind requires that they should declare the causes which impel them to the separation.*

We hold these truths to be self-evident, that all men are created equal, that they are endowed by their Creator with certain unalienable Rights, that among these are Life, Liberty and the pursuit of Happiness. That to secure these rights, Governments are instituted among Men, deriving their just powers from the consent of the governed. That whenever any Form of Government becomes destructive of these ends, it is the Right of the People to alter or to abolish it, and to institute new Government, laying its foundation on such principles and organizing its powers in such form, as to them shall seem most likely to effect their Safety and Happiness.

Prudence, indeed, will dictate that Governments long established should not be changed for light and transient causes; and accordingly all experience hath shown, that mankind are more disposed to suffer, while evils are sufferable, than to right themselves by abolishing the forms to which they are accustomed. But when a long train of abuses and usurpations, pursuing invariably the same Object evinces a design to reduce them under absolute Despotism, it is their right, it is their duty, to throw off such Government, and to provide new Guards for their future security.

Such has been the patient sufferance of these Colonies; and such is now the necessity which constrains them to alter their former Systems of Government. The history of the present King of Great Britain [George III] is a history of repeated injuries and usurpations, all having in direct object the establishment of an absolute Tyranny over these States.

We, therefore, the Representatives of the united States of America, in General Congress, Assembled, appealing to the Supreme Judge of the world for the rectitude of our intentions, do, in the Name, and by the Authority of the good People of these Colonies, solemnly publish and declare, That these United Colonies are, and of Right ought to be Free and Independent States; that they are Absolved from all Allegiance to the British Crown, and that all political connection between them and the State of Great Britain, is and ought to be totally dissolved; and that as Free and Independent States, they have full Power to levy War, conclude Peace, contract Alliances, establish Commerce, and to do all other Acts and Things which Independent States may of right do. And for the support of this Declaration, with a firm reliance on the protection of divine Providence, we mutually pledge to each other our Lives, our Fortunes and our sacred Honor.

* This document is an excerpt of the full text of the Declaration of Independence. For space considerations, the lengthy section listing the tyranny and transgressions of King George III has been removed.

You are a freelance designer. Your client returns a document to you, telling you that she wants you to make a change to a drop cap. She wants you to format not just the first letter but the entire first word as a drop cap so it is more prominent on the page.

1. Open ID 2-9.indd, then save it as **Drop Cap Modifications**.
2. Click the Zoom tool, then drag a selection box around the first paragraph.
3. Click the Type tool, click after the W drop cap, double-click the 1 in the Drop Cap One or More Characters text box on the Paragraph panel, type **4**, and then press [return] (Mac) or [Enter] (Win).
4. Click before the word in, in the top line, then type **100** in the Kerning text box on the Character panel.
5. Select the letters HEN, click the Character panel menu button, click All Caps, click the Character panel menu button again, then click Superscript.
6. With the letters still selected, type **–10** in the Baseline Shift text box on the Character panel.
7. Click between the W and H in the word WHEN, then type **–60** in the Kerning text box.
8. Save your work, compare your screen to Figure 47, then close the Drop Cap Modifications document.

Figure 47 Completed Project Builder 1

The Declaration of Independence
July 4, 1776

WHEN in the Course of human events, it becomes necessary for one people to dissolve the political bands which have connected them with another, and to assume among the powers of the earth, the separate and equal station to which the Laws of Nature and of Nature's God entitle them, a decent respect to the opinions of mankind requires that they should declare the causes which impel them to the separation.[1]

You have designed a document about Miniature Pinschers. Your client calls you with changes. He wants to show small pictures of Miniature Pinschers in the document, one beside each paragraph. He asks you to reformat the document to create space where the small pictures can be inserted.

1. Open ID 2-10.indd, then save it as **Hanging Indents**.
2. Select the four paragraphs of body copy, then change the first line left indent to 0.
3. Change the left indent to 2 in., then change the right indent to .5 in.
4. Create a half-inch space after each paragraph.
5. Type **−1.5** in the First Line Left Indent text box, then deselect all.
6. Save your work, compare your screen to Figure 48, then close the Hanging Indents document.

Figure 48 Completed Project Builder 2

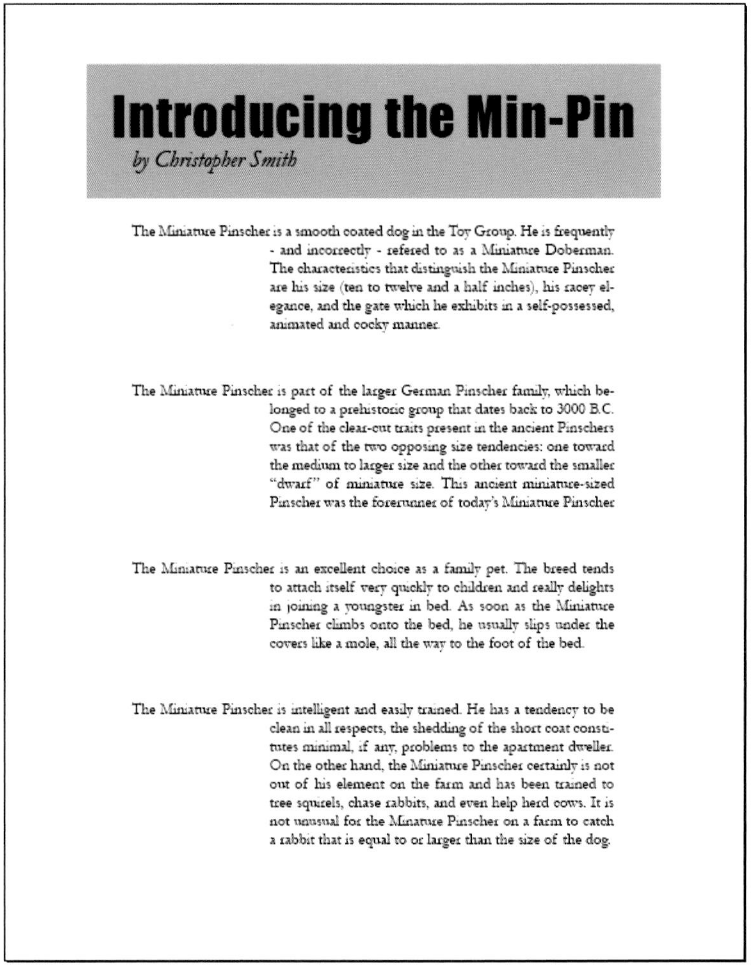

Introducing the Min-Pin
by Christopher Smith

The Miniature Pinscher is a smooth coated dog in the Toy Group. He is frequently - and incorrectly - refered to as a Miniature Doberman. The characteristics that distinguish the Miniature Pinscher are his size (ten to twelve and a half inches), his racey elegance, and the gate which he exhibits in a self-possessed, animated and cocky manner.

The Miniature Pinscher is part of the larger German Pinscher family, which belonged to a prehistoric group that dates back to 3000 B.C. One of the clear-cut traits present in the ancient Pinschers was that of the two opposing size tendencies: one toward the medium to larger size and the other toward the smaller "dwarf" of miniature size. This ancient miniature-sized Pinscher was the forerunner of today's Miniature Pinscher.

The Miniature Pinscher is an excellent choice as a family pet. The breed tends to attach itself very quickly to children and really delights in joining a youngster in bed. As soon as the Miniature Pinscher climbs onto the bed, he usually slips under the covers like a mole, all the way to the foot of the bed.

The Miniature Pinscher is intelligent and easily trained. He has a tendency to be clean in all respects, the shedding of the short coat constitutes minimal, if any, problems to the apartment dweller. On the other hand, the Miniature Pinscher certainly is not out of his element on the farm and has been trained to tree squirels, chase rabbits, and even help herd cows. It is not unusual for the Miniature Pinscher on a farm to catch a rabbit that is equal to or larger than the size of the dog.

You have been assigned the task of designing a headline for a billboard for the movie "Crushing Impact." The client has asked for a finished design in black letters on a white background. Before you design the title, you consider the following questions.

Discussion

1. Open ID 2-12.indd, then save it as **Crushing Impact**.
2. Look at the title for a full minute.
3. What font family might be best for the title?
4. Does the title demand a big, bold font, or could it work in a fine, delicate font?
5. Should the two words be positioned side by side or one on top of the other?
6. Does the title itself suggest that, visually, one word should be positioned on top of the other?

Exercise

1. Position the word IMPACT on a second line, select all the text, change the font to Impact, then change the Font Size to 64 pt.
2. Select the word IMPACT, change the Horizontal Scale to 200, then change the Vertical Scale to 80.
3. Select the word CRUSHING, change the Horizontal Scale to 50, change the Font Size to 190, then change the Leading to 190.
4. Select the word IMPACT, then change the Leading to 44.
5. Save your work, compare your screen to Figure 49, then close the Crushing Impact document.

Figure 49 Completed Design Project

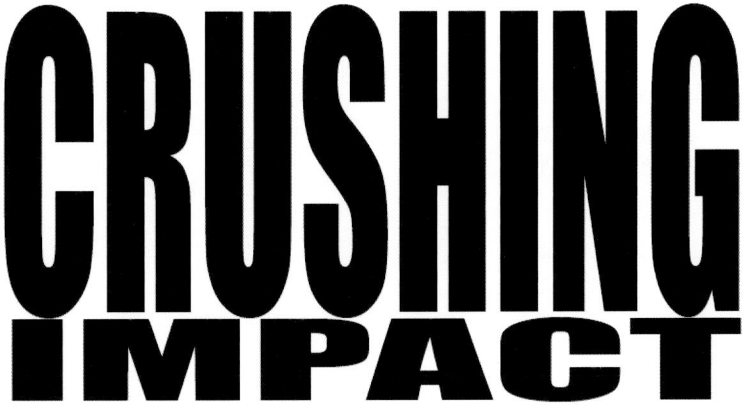

LOCATION
day/date

LOCATION
day/date

CHAPTER **14**

SET UP A
DOCUMENT

1. Create a New Document and Set Up a
   Master Page
2. Create Text on Master Pages
3. Apply Master Pages to Document Pages
4. Modify Master Pages and Document Pages
5. Place and Thread Text
6. Create New Sections and Wrap Text

**CERTIFIED
PROFESSIONAL**

**Adobe Certified Professional in Print & Digital
Media Publication Using Adobe InDesign**

2. Project Setup and Interface

*This objective covers the interface setup and program settings that assist in an
efficient and effective workflow, as well as knowledge about ingesting digital
assets for a project.*

**2.1 Create a document with the appropriate settings for web, print,
and mobile.**
  A Set appropriate document settings for printed and on-screen images.
  B Create a new document preset to reuse for specific project needs.

2.2 Navigate, organize, and customize the application workspace.
  A Identify and manipulate elements of the InDesign interface.
  B Organize and customize the workspace.
  C Configure application preferences.

**2.3 Use nonprinting design tools in the interface to aid in design
or workflow.**
  A Navigate a document.
  B Use rulers.
  C Use guides and grids.
  D Use views and modes to work efficiently.

2.5 Manage colors, swatches, and gradients.
  A Set the active fill and stroke color.

3. Organizing Documents

*This objective covers document structure such as layers, tracks, and managing
document structure for efficient workflows.*

3.2 Manage and modify pages.
  A Create, edit, and arrange pages in a document.
  B Edit and apply master pages.

4. Creating and Modifying Document Elements

*This objective covers core tools and functionality of the application, as well as
tools that affect the visual appearance of document elements.*

**4.2 Add and manipulate text using appropriate
typographic settings.**
  A Use type tools to add text.
  C Use appropriate paragraph settings in a design.
  E Manage text flow across multiple text areas.
  F Use tools to add special characters or content.

4.4 Transform digital graphics and media within a publication.
  B Rotate, flip, and transform individual frames or content.

**4.5 Use basic reconstructing and editing techniques to manipulate
document content.**
  B Evaluate or adjust the appearance of objects, frames, or layers using
    various tools.

CREATE A NEW DOCUMENT AND SET UP A MASTER PAGE

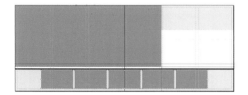

Creating a New Document

When you are ready to create a new document in InDesign, you begin in the New Document dialog box, shown in Figure 1. First you choose the type of document you need to create. Listed across the top of the dialog box are types of output categories, including Print, Web, and Mobile. When you click a category, blank document presets become available.

Figure 1 New Document dialog box

Saved presets are in the Saved category

Document categories

Enter number of pages you want here

Save Document Preset button

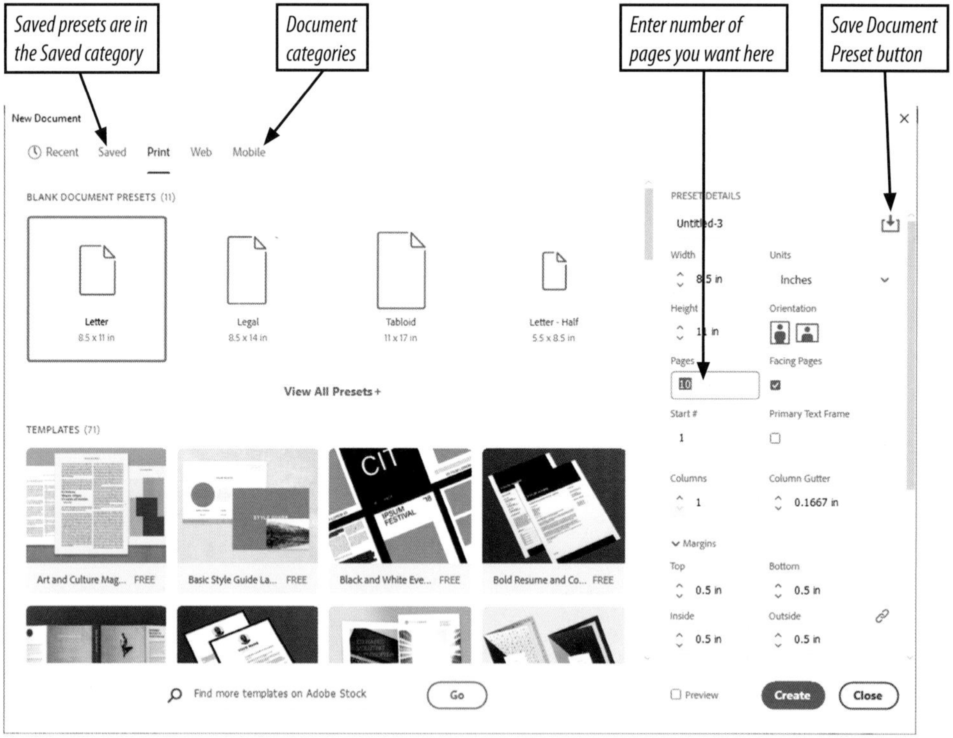

For example, if you are creating a layout for a phone, you would click the Mobile category. Blank presets including iPhone X and iPad Pro, among others, are available to choose from. After choosing a preset, you are ready to further define your document. The right side of the New Document dialog box is where you name the document and specify the number of pages the document will contain. You also specify the **page size**, or **trim size**—the width and height of the finished document. In addition, you specify whether or not the document will have **facing pages**. When you choose this option, the document is created with left and right pages that *face* each other in a spread, such as you would find in a magazine. If this option is not selected, each page stands alone, like a *stack* of pages.

The New Document dialog box also allows you to specify the width of margins on the outer edges of the page and the number of columns that will be positioned on the page. Margins and columns are useful as layout guides, and they play an important role in flowing text. When working with columns, the term **gutter** refers to the space between the columns. Figure 2 shows margins and columns on a typical page.

When creating a document with specific settings that you plan on using again and again, you can save the settings as a preset by clicking the Save Document Preset button next to the document name. Your named preset will then become available in the Saved category in the New Document dialog box.

Figure 2 Identifying margins and columns

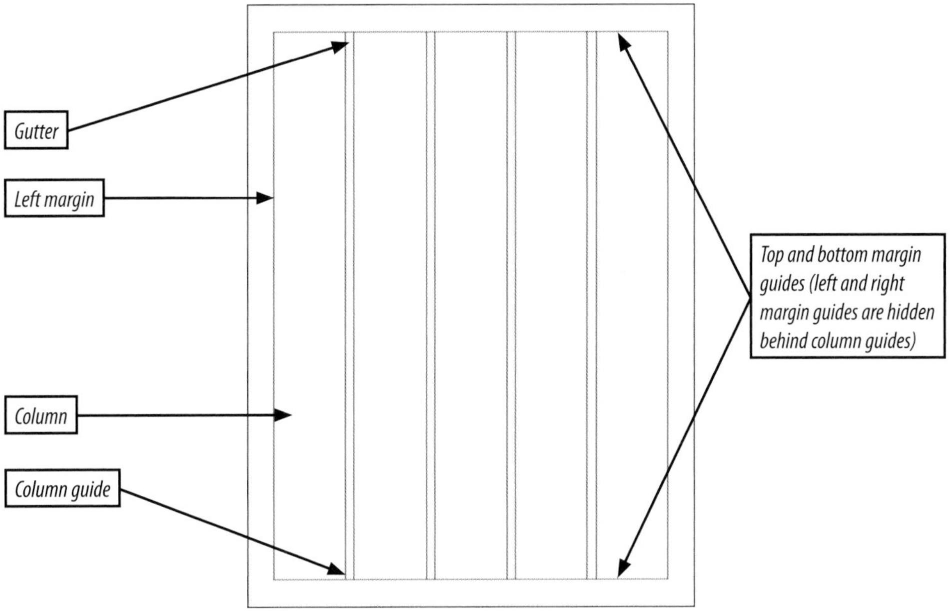

Gutter

Left margin

Column

Column guide

Top and bottom margin guides (left and right margin guides are hidden behind column guides)

Setting the Starting Page Number

Imagine that you are holding a closed book in your hands—perhaps this book—and you open the front cover. The first page of the book is a single right-hand page. If you turn the page, the next two pages are pages 2 and 3, which face each other in a spread. Now imagine closing the book and flipping it over so you are looking at the back cover. If you open it, the last page is a single left-hand page.

With this in mind, consider that whenever you create a multiple-page document with facing pages, InDesign always creates the first page on a single right-hand page and the last page on a single left-hand page. Figure 3 shows how InDesign, by default, would create a four-page document with a single right-hand page as the first page and a single left-hand page as the last page.

But what if you wanted to design those four pages as two spreads—what if you wanted the first page to be a left page?

You accomplish this in the Start # text box in the New Document dialog box. The number that you enter in this text box determines the page number of the first page and whether it is a left-hand or a right-hand page. If you enter a 2 (or any other even number), the first page will be a left-hand page. Figure 4 shows the same four-page document set up as two spreads. Note that the first page is page 2. It is a left-hand page. There is no page 1 in the document.

Modifying Margins and Columns

The New Document dialog box offers you options for specifying measurements for margins and the number of columns in the document. However, once you click OK, you cannot return to the New Document dialog box to modify those settings. The Document Setup dialog box allows you to change the page size and the number of pages, among other choices, but it does not offer the option to modify the number of columns. But don't worry; once you've created a document, you can modify the number of columns with the Margins and Columns command on the Layout menu. Margins can be changed in the Document Setup dialog box *and* the Margins and Columns dialog boxes.

Figure 3 Four-page document set up as facing pages

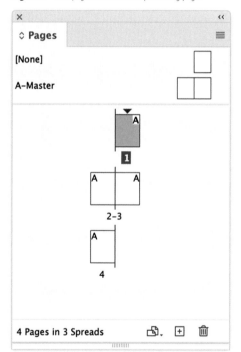

Figure 4 Four-page document set up as two spreads

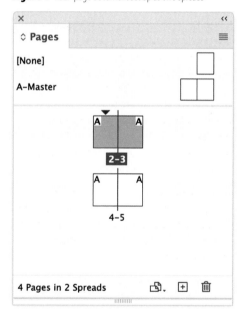

Understanding Master Pages

Imagine that you are creating a layout for a book and every chapter title page will have the same layout format. If that book had 20 chapters, you would need to create that chapter title page 20 times. And you'd need to be careful to make the layout consistent every time you created the page. Now imagine that you've finished your layout, but your editor wants you to change the location of the title on the page. That would mean making the same change—20 times!

Not so with master pages. **Master pages** are templates created for a page layout. Once created, you simply apply the master page to any document pages you want based on that layout. With master pages, you create a layout one time and then use it as many times as you like. Working with master pages spares you time-consuming repetition, and it offers consistency between document pages that are meant to have the same layout.

So what happens when your editor asks for that change in location of the title? Simply make the change to the master page, and the change will be reflected on all the document pages based on that master.

When you create a new document, one default master page is created and listed on the Pages panel, as shown in Figure 5. The Pages panel is command central for all things relating to pages and master pages. You use the Pages panel to add, delete, and apply master pages to document pages.

Figure 5 Default master page on the Pages panel

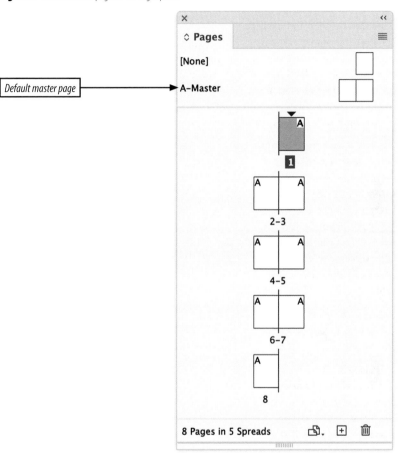

Creating Master Items on Master Pages

In InDesign, text is positioned in text frames. **Text frames** are boxes created with the Type tool in which you type or place text. Graphics are positioned in graphics frames. **Graphics frames** are frames in which you place imported artwork. You use the Rectangle, Ellipse, or Polygon tools to create graphics frames.

When you create a frame for text or graphics on a master page, it is referred to as a **master item**. All objects on a master page are called master items and function as "placeholders" where objects on the document pages are to be positioned. For example, if you had a book broken down into chapters and you created a master page for the chapter title pages, you would create a text frame placeholder for the chapter title text. This text frame would appear on every document page that uses the chapter title master page. Working this way—with the text frame placeholder on the master page— you can feel certain that the location of the chapter title will be consistent on every chapter title page in the book.

Creating Guides

Guides, as shown in Figure 6, are horizontal or vertical lines that you position on a page. As their name suggests, guides are used to help guide you in aligning objects on the page. You have many options for creating guides. You can create them manually by "pulling" them out from the horizontal and vertical rulers. You can also use the Create Guides command on the Layout menu. Once created, guides can be selected, moved, and deleted, if necessary. You can also change the color of guides, which sometimes makes it easier to see them, depending on the colors used in your document.

TIP Press and hold [command] (Mac) or [Ctrl] (Win), then drag a guide from the horizontal ruler to create a guide that covers a spread instead of an individual page in a spread.

Figure 6 Identifying guides

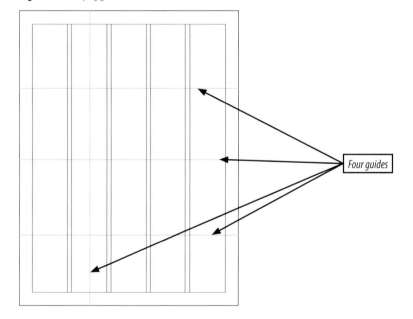

Four guides

Changing the Color of Guides, Margins, and Columns

By default, guides are cyan, column guides are violet, and margin guides are magenta. Depending on your preferences and the color of objects in the layout you are creating, you may want to change their colors.

In InDesign, you modify individual guide colors by selecting them, then clicking the Ruler Guides command on the Layout menu. Choosing a new color in the Ruler Guides dialog box affects only the selected guides. When you create more guides, they will be created in the default color.

You modify the default color of margins and columns in the Guides & Pasteboard section of the Preferences dialog box. Once you've modified the color of margins and columns, each new page you create in an existing document will appear with those colors. However, when you create a new document, the margins and columns will appear in their default colors.

Locking Column Guides

InDesign lets you lock column guides independently from any ruler guides you create. Click View on the menu bar, point to Grids & Guides, and then click Lock Column Guides to add or remove the check mark, which toggles the lock on or off. By default, column guides are locked.

Choosing Default Colors for Guides, Margins, and Columns

When you choose colors for guides, margins, and columns, you may want those choices to affect every document you create. You do so by making the color changes in the appropriate dialog boxes without any documents open. The new colors will be applied in all new documents created thereafter. Remember, if you change default colors when a document is open, the changes are only applied to that document.

Using the Transform Panel

The Transform panel identifies a selected object's width and height and its horizontal and vertical locations on the page. As shown in Figure 7, the width and height of the selected object appears in the Width and Height text boxes of the Transform panel.

When you position an object on a page, you need some way to describe that object's position on the page. InDesign defines the position of an object using X and Y Location values on the Transform panel. To work with X and Y locations, you first need to understand that the **zero point** of the page is, by default, at the top-left corner of the page. X and Y locations are made in reference to the zero point.

There are nine reference points on the Transform panel that correspond to the nine points available on a selected item's bounding box. Clicking a reference point tells InDesign that you wish to see the horizontal and vertical locations of that point of the selected object.

Figure 7 Transform panel shows location coordinates and size of selected frame

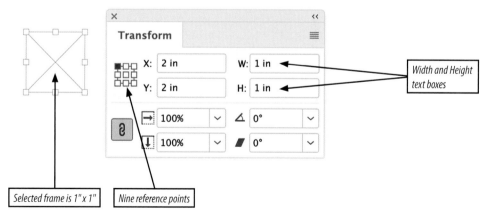

Width and Height text boxes

Selected frame is 1" x 1"

Nine reference points

When an object is selected, the X Location value is the horizontal location—how far it is across the page—and the Y Location value is the vertical location—how far it is down the page. The selected object in Figure 8 has an X Location of 1 inch and a Y Location of 1 inch. This means that its top-left point is 1 inch across the page and 1 inch down.

Why the top-left point? Because that is the reference point chosen on the Transform panel, also identified in Figure 8.

TIP X and Y Location values for circles are determined by the reference points of the bounding box that is placed around circles when they are selected.

Be sure to note that the text boxes on the Transform panel are interactive. For example, if you select an object and find that its X Location value is 2, you can enter 3 in the X Location text box, press [return] (Mac) or [Enter] (Win), and the object will be relocated to the new location on the page. You can also change the width or height of a selected object by changing the value in the Width or Height text boxes.

Figure 8 Identifying an object's X and Y locations

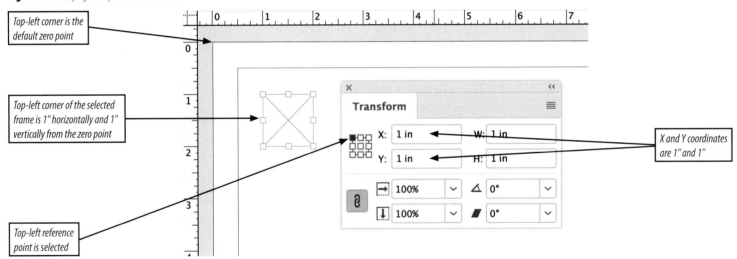

Using the Control Panel

You can think of the Control panel, docked at the top of the document window by default, as InDesign's "super panel." The Control panel mimics all the other panels, housing a wide variety of options for working with text and objects. Rather than always moving from one panel to another, you can usually find the option you are looking for on the Control panel.

The options on the Control panel change based on the type of object selected. For example, if a block of text is selected, the Control panel changes to show all the type-related options for modifying text, such as changing the font or font size. When any object is selected, the Control panel display is like the Transform panel. It offers X/Y coordinate reference points and text boxes and the same options for modifying a selected object. For example, you can change the width and height of a frame using the Control panel, just as you can with the Transform panel.

Unlike the Transform panel, the Control panel offers a multitude of additional options for working with frames, making the Control panel perhaps the most-used panel in InDesign. In Figure 9, the Control panel shows options for a selected graphics frame.

TIP You can perform calculations in the text boxes on the Transform panel. For example, you could select an object whose width is three inches. By typing 3 − .625 in the W text box, you can reduce the object's width to 2.375 inches. What a powerful feature!

TIP The Info panel displays information about the current document and selected objects, such as text and graphics frames. For example, if you click inside a text frame with the Type tool, the Info panel displays the number of characters, words, lines, and paragraphs in the frame. If you click the same text frame with the Selection tool, you can find out the size and location of the text frame. The Info panel is available only for viewing information. You cannot make changes to a selected object using this panel.

Using the Line Tool

The Line tool makes lines—no surprise there. Use the Line tool to make horizontal, vertical, and diagonal lines in your layouts. You can apply a fill color to a line, but generally speaking, you only want to stroke a line with color. You specify the weight of a line with the Stroke panel, and you can use the Line Length text box on the Control and Transform panels to specify the length. You can use all nine reference points on the Control and Transform panels to position a line in your layout.

Figure 9 Control panel

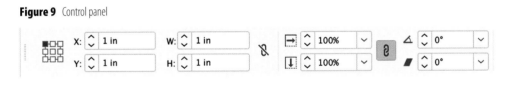

Transforming Objects

"Transform" is a term used to describe the act of moving, scaling, skewing, or rotating an object. You can do all of these actions on the Transform or Control panels. Figure 10 shows a rectangular frame that is 3" wide and 1.5" tall. Its center point is identified on the Transform panel because the center reference point is selected on the Transform panel. In Figure 11, the same frame has

been rotated 90°—note the 90° value in the Rotation Angle text box on the Transform panel. Note also that the object was rotated at its center point. This is because the center reference point was selected when the transformation was executed. The center point of the rectangle was the point of origin for the transformation. The **point of origin** is the location on the object from which the transformation is executed. Whichever reference point is selected determines the

point of origin for the transformation of the selected object.

Don't trouble yourself by trying to guess ahead of time how the choice of a point of origin and a transformation will affect an object. Sometimes it will be easy to foresee how the object will be transformed; sometimes you'll need to use trial and error. The important thing for you to remember is that the point of origin determines the point from which the transformation takes place.

Figure 10 A rectangle with its center point identified

Figure 11 Rectangle rotated 90 degrees at its center point

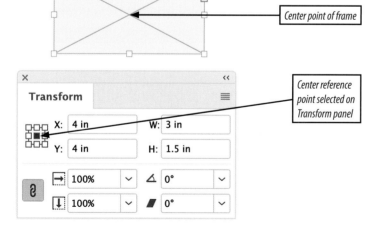

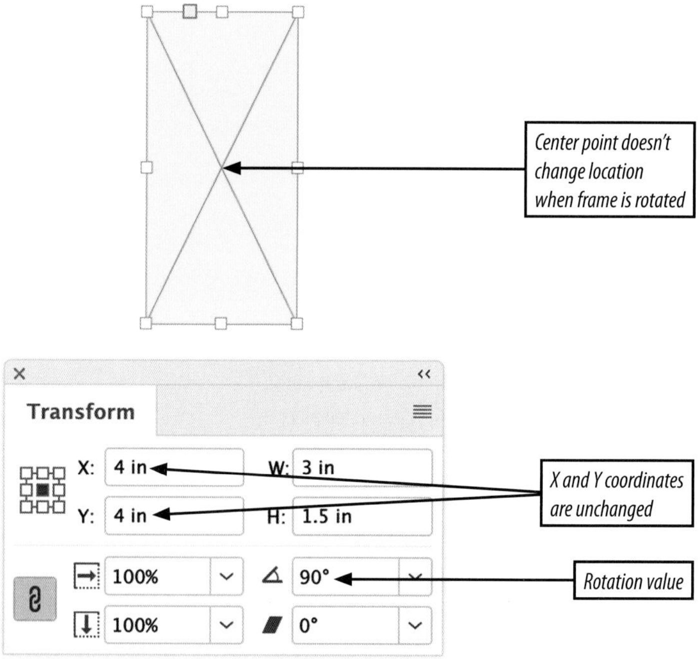

Center point of frame

Center reference point selected on Transform panel

Center point doesn't change location when frame is rotated

X and Y coordinates are unchanged

Rotation value

Transform

X: 4 in   W: 3 in
Y: 4 in   H: 1.5 in
100%   0°
100%   0°

Transform

X: 4 in   W: 3 in
Y: 4 in   H: 1.5 in
100%   90°
100%   0°

Using the Transform Again Command

The Transform Again command is a powerful command that repeats the last transformation executed. For example, let's say you rotate a text frame. If you select another text frame and apply the Transform Again command, the same rotation will be applied to the second object. The Transform Again command is useful for creating multiple objects at specified distances.

View a multipage document

1. Open ID 3-1.indd.

TIP When you open the document, a warning stating some images are missing or need to be updated will show. Click Don't Update Links, and the file will open.

2. Press **[shift] [W]** to enter Presentation mode.

3. Use the **right** and **left arrow keys** on your computer keypad to view all the pages in the document.

   The document is composed of five two-page spreads for a total of 10 pages. The document has been designed as a pamphlet for a travel company advertising destinations for a tour of Italy. Page numbers are visible at the bottom of every spread. The five spreads are based on three layout versions. The layout will be used for both a printed piece and for an interactive PDF that can be emailed.

4. Press **[esc]** to leave Presentation mode.

5. Press **[tab]** to show the panels, if necessary, then show the Pages panel.

   The first page of the document is page 2, and it is a left-hand page.

6. View **spread 4–5**.

Spread 4–5, shown in Figure 12 along with other spreads, is the basis for the document you will build using master pages in this chapter.

7. Close the file without saving changes.

You viewed a finished document that will be the basis for the document you will build in this chapter.

Figure 12 Layouts used as the basis for this chapter

Set preferences and create a new document

1. Verify that no documents are open.

2. Click **InDesign (Mac)** or **Edit (Win)** on the menu bar, point to **Preferences**, then click **Units & Increments**.

3. Click the **Horizontal list arrow**, click **Inches**, click the **Vertical list arrow**, click **Inches**, then click **OK**.

4. Click **File** on the menu bar, point to **New**, then click **Document**.

5. Click the **Print category** at the top of the dialog box, then click **Letter** in the **Blank Document Presets section**.

6. On the right side of the New Document dialog box, highlight the "Untitled" text at the top, then type **Setup** for the filename.

7. Type **10** in the **Pages text box**, verify that the **Facing Pages check box** is checked, then verify that the **Start #** is set to **1**.

8. Type **6.25** in the **Width text box**, press **[tab]**, type **4.75** in the **Height text box**, then click the **Landscape Orientation button** 📇.

TIP Press [tab] to move your cursor forward from text box to text box in the New Document dialog box. Press [shift] [tab] to move backward from text box to text box.

9. In the **Columns section**, type **2**, then verify that the **Gutter text box** is set to **.1667 in**.

10. Type **.5** in the Top Margins text box, then verify that the **Make all settings the same button** 🔗 is activated.

11. Compare your dialog box to Figure 13, click **Create**, then look at the Pages panel.

    Page 1 is a single right-hand page, and page 10 is a single left-hand page.

Figure 13 Settings in the New Document dialog box

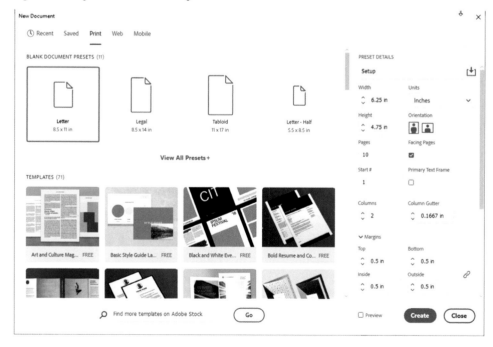

12. Click **File** on the menu bar, then click **Document Setup**.

Note that the Columns sections is not available in the Document Setup dialog box.

13. Change the **Start Page #** to **2**, click **OK**, then compare your Pages panel to Figure 14.

The document is now composed of five 2-page spreads, numbered 2–11. A reasonable question at this point would be "why create five spreads of ten 6.25" × 3.75" pages instead of as five 12.5" × 3.75" single pages?" By creating spreads, you have the option to print this as a document that folds into a 6.25" × 3.75" book or pamphlet. However, if you wanted to print it as a 12.5" × 3.75" printed book or pamphlet, the very same layout would service that choice as well. A document built as spreads can be output as single pages, folded pages, or as spreads.

14. Save your work, then continue to the next set of steps.

You set the Units & Increments preferences to specify that you will be working with inches for horizontal and vertical measurements. You then created a new document using the New Document dialog box. You specified the filename, number of pages in the document, page size for each page, and number of columns on each page. You then modified the start page number in the Document Setup dialog box to start the document on a left-hand page.

Modify margins and the number of columns on a master page

1. Set the **workspace** to **Essentials Classic**.

2. On the **Pages panel**, double-click the word **A-Master**, and note that *both* master pages in the Pages menu become blue and are targeted.

3. Note that the page menu at the lower-left corner of the document window lists A-Master.

A-Master is now the active page. You will modify the margins and the number of columns on a master page so your changes will be applied to all 10 document pages.

4. Click **Layout** on the menu bar, then click **Margins and Columns**.

The Margins and Columns dialog box opens.

5. Set the **number of columns** to **3**.

6. Reduce the **width of all four margins** to **.125 in**, then click **OK**.

Note that the width and height of the columns change to fill the area within the margins.

7. Save your work, then continue to the next set of steps.

You changed the number of columns and the width of margins on a master page.

USING THE MOVE PAGES COMMAND

If you have a multiple-page document, you can change the sequence of pages simply by moving them around on the Pages panel. Easy enough. But for documents with more pages—let's say 100 pages— dragging and dropping page icons on the Pages panel isn't so simple. Imagine, for example, trying to drag page 84 so it follows page 14. Whew! With InDesign's powerful Move Pages command, you can specify which pages you want to move and where you want to move them. Click the Pages panel menu button, click Move Pages, then specify options in the Move Pages dialog box. Be sure to check it out.

Figure 14 Pages panel showing a document starting on a left-hand page.

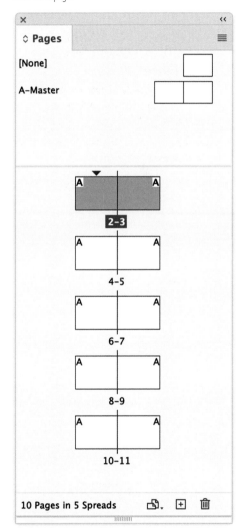

Add guides to a master page

1. If rulers are not visible at the top and left of the document window, click **View** on the menu bar, then click **Show Rulers**.

2. Click the **Selection tool** ▶, position the **pointer over the horizontal ruler**, then click and slowly drag down a guide, releasing it anywhere on the page.

    A guide is positioned only on the left page of the spread.

    TIP As you drag the new guide onto the page, the value in the Y Location text box on the Control panel continually changes to show the guide's current location. See Figure 15.

3. Click **Edit** on the menu bar, then click **Undo Add New Guide**.

4. Press and hold **[command] (Mac)** or **[Ctrl] (Win)**, then drag down a **guide** from the horizontal ruler, releasing it anywhere on the page.

    The guide extends across the entire spread.

5. On the **Control panel**, type **2.5** in the **Y Location text box**, then press **[return] (Mac)** or **[Enter] (Win)**.

    The guide jumps to the specific vertical location you entered: 2.5" from the top of the page.

    TIP For this entire chapter, you can use the Transform panel interchangeably with the Control panel.

6. While pressing **[command] (Mac)** or **[Ctrl] (Win)**, drag a **second spread guide** from the horizontal ruler, drop the guide anywhere on the spread, then set its **Y Location** to **3.5 in**.

7. Click **InDesign (Mac)** or **Edit (Win)**, point to **Preferences**, then click **Units & Increments**.

8. In the **Ruler Units section**, verify that **Origin** is set to **Spread**, then click **OK**.

    With the Origin value set to Spread, the ruler and all X values are continuous across the entire spread. In other words, there's one ruler across both pages, as opposed to one ruler for the left page and another for the right page.

Figure 15 Using the Control panel to position a guide

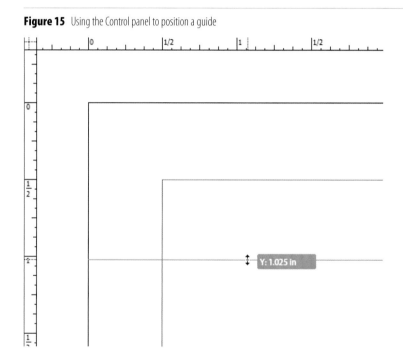

9. Drag a **guide from the vertical ruler** on the left side of the document window, then use the **Control panel** to position its **X value** at **8.35 in**.

10. Using the **Selection tool** ▶, click the **first horizontal guide** you positioned at **2.5 inches** to select it, double-click the **Y Location text box** on the Transform panel, type **3.4,** then press **[return] (Mac)** or **[Enter] (Win)**.

    The guide is moved to the new location.

TIP Selected guides appear darker blue.

11. Position a **third horizontal spread guide** at **3.25"** from the top of the page.

12. Compare your spread and guides to Figure 16, then save your work.

13. Continue to the next set of steps.

You positioned guides on the master page by dragging them from the horizontal and vertical rulers. You used the Control panel to position them at precise locations.

Figure 16 Master spread with guides in position

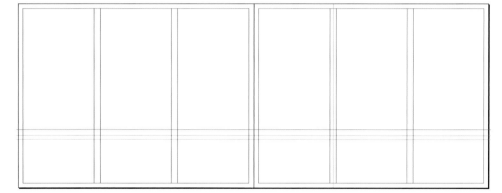

WORKING WITH CONDITIONAL TEXT

Using conditional text is a great way to create different versions of the same InDesign document. You create conditional text by first creating conditions and then applying them to text. Later, you hide or show the text that has the condition applied to it by hiding or showing conditions using the Conditional Text panel. Showing and hiding conditions works just like showing and hiding layers on the Layers panel. You assign a new condition to text, and then hide it by clicking the "Eye" (visibility) icon on the Conditional Text panel. When you have many conditions, you can create a **condition set**, which is a snapshot of the current visibility of the applied conditions. Click the Conditional Text panel menu button, then click Show Options. On the Conditional Text panel, click the Set list arrow, then click Create New Set. Name the set, then click OK. Instead of turning individual conditions on or off on the panel, you can choose a condition set to do the same job in one step.

Create placeholder text frames

1. Verify that the **fill and stroke buttons** on the toolbar are both set to **[None]**.

2. Click the **Type tool** T , then drag to create a **small text frame** anywhere in the rightmost column above the horizontal guides.

3. Click the **Selection tool** ▶ drag the **left and right handles** of the text frame so it is the full width of the column.

4. Drag the **bottom handle** down until it snaps to the topmost horizontal guide.

5. On the Control panel, click the **bottom-center reference point**, type **1.375** in the **Height text box**, then press **[return] (Mac)** or **[Enter] (Win)**.

   Your right page should resemble Figure 17.

6. Press and hold **[shift] [option] (Mac)** or **[Shift] [Alt] (Win)**, then drag and drop a **copy of the text frame** into the column to the left so your page resembles Figure 18.

   Note that the new text frames are difficult to distinguish from the ruler guides.

7. Save your work, then continue to the next set of steps.

You created two text frames, which will be used as placeholders for body copy in the document.

Figure 17 Positioning the text frame

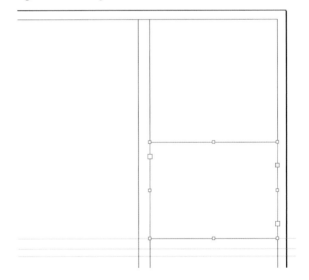

Figure 18 Duplicated text frame

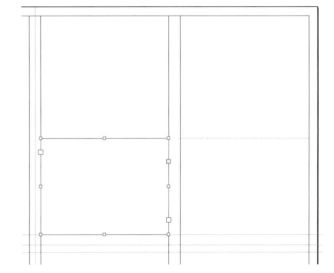

Change the color of guides, margins, and columns

1. Click **InDesign (Mac)** or **Edit (Win)** on the menu bar, point to **Preferences**, then click **Guides & Pasteboard**.

2. Verify that the **Guides in Back check box** is unchecked.

   When this option is deactivated, guides appear in front of all items on the document rather than hidden behind them.

3. In the **Color section**, click the **Margins list arrow**, then click **Light Gray**.

4. Click the **Columns list arrow**, then click **Light Gray**.

5. Click **OK**.

6. Click the **Selection tool** 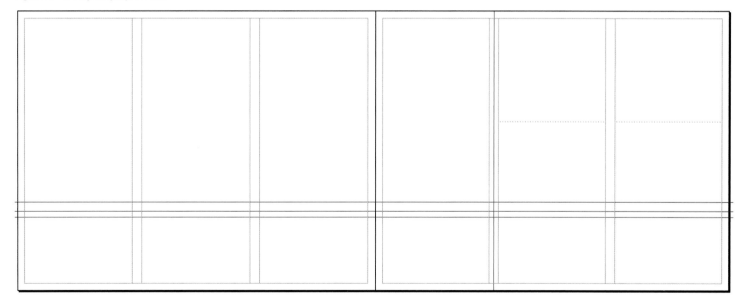, click the **vertical guide** to select it, press and hold **[shift]**, then click the **three horizontal guides** so all the guides you created are selected.

   All four guides appear dark blue.

7. Click **Layout** on the menu bar, then click **Ruler Guides**.

8. Click the **Color list arrow**, click **Red**, then click **OK**.

9. Click the **pasteboard** to deselect the guides, then compare your page to Figure 19.

You changed the color of margins, columns, and guides to improve your ability to distinguish text frames from page guides.

Figure 19 Viewing changed guide colors

Create color tint frames

1. Verify that the **fill and stroke buttons** on the toolbar are both set to **[None]**.

TIP You will learn much more about fills and strokes in Chapters 15 and 16.

2. Click the **Rectangle tool** ▢, then drag a **small rectangle** anywhere **above the two text frames** in the two rightmost columns.

3. Click the **Selection tool** ▶, click **Window** on the menu bar, point to **Object & Layout**, then click **Transform**.

The Transform panel appears.

4. Drag the **left handle** of the frame so it snaps to the red vertical guide.

TIP To verify that Snap to Guides is activated, click View on the menu bar, then point to Grids & Guides.

5. Drag the **right handle** of the frame so it snaps to the right edge of the document.

The Width text box on the Transform panel should read 4.15 in.

6. Drag the **top handle** of the frame so it snaps to the top edge of the document.

7. On the Transform panel, click the **top-center reference point**, then verify that the **Y text box** on the Transform panel reads **0**.

If the top edge of the frame is aligned to the top edge of the page, its Y coordinate must be zero.

8. On the Transform panel, change the **Height value** to **1.35 in**.

Because the Units & Increments preferences are set to Inches, you do not need to—nor should you—type the abbreviation for inches in the text box. Just type the number.

TIP Don't deselect the frame.

9. Fill the **frame** with **yellow**.

TIP Choose any shade of yellow.

10. Drag and drop a **copy of the yellow frame** straight down to the bottom of the page.

11. Drag the **top edge of the frame** down so it aligns with the bottommost of the three guides.

12. Drag the **left edge** to align with the left edge of the document.

Your spread should resemble Figure 20. The Width & Height text boxes on the Transform panel should read 12.5 in and 1.25 in, respectively.

13. Deselect all, then on the Swatches panel, click a **light blue swatch**.

14. Create a **small rectangle** anywhere in the **upper-left section** of the document.

The new rectangle is created with the light blue fill.

15. Click the **top-left reference point** on the Transform panel, enter **0** in the **X text box**, press **[tab]**, enter **0** in the **Y text box**, press **[tab]**, type **8.35** in the **Width text box**, press **[tab]**, then enter **3.4** in the **Height text box**.

16. Save your work, then continue to the next set of steps.

You created three color-filled frames on the page and used the Transform panel to position them and modify their sizes.

Figure 20 Two yellow rectangle frames positioned on the spread

Use the Line tool

1. Close the Transform panel, click **anywhere in the pasteboard** to deselect all, then click the **Line tool** ✏.

2. Position the **cursor** at the left edge of the document, press and hold **[shift]**, then click and drag to create a **line of any length**.

   Pressing and holding [shift] constrains the line so it is straight. Regardless of which colors are on the toolbar, once you create a line, both the fill and stroke colors change to [None]. A bounding box appears around the line.

3. Click the **stroke button** on the toolbar, then click **[Black]** on the Swatches panel.

4. Expand the **Stroke panel**, then increase the **Weight** to **4 pt**.

5. On the Control panel, click the **middle-left reference point**, type **0** in the **X text box**, press **[tab]**, type **3.5** in the **Y text box**, press **[tab]**, then type **12.5** in the **L (length) text box** so your spread resembles Figure 21.

6. Save your work, then continue to the next set of steps.

You created a line with the Line tool, specified its color and weight, then positioned it on the spread and specified its length with the Control panel.

Figure 21 Viewing the line

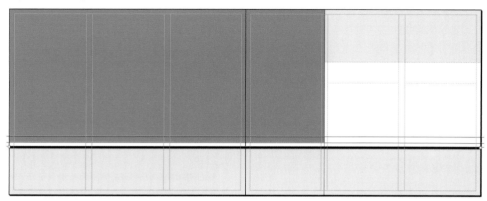

Use the Transform Again command

1. Click the **Rectangle tool** ▢, then draw a **small rectangle** in the first column anywhere at the bottom of the page.

2. On the Control panel, click the **top-left reference point**, type **0** in the **X text box**, type **3.6** in the **Y text box**, type **1.8** in the **Width text box**, then type **1** in the **Height text box**.

3. Press the **letter [I]** on your keypad to access the **Eyedropper tool** ✐, then click the **large blue frame** at the top of the page.

   The Eyedropper tool samples the fill and stroke colors from the large frame; the small rectangle takes on the same fill and stroke color.

4. Press the **letter [V]** to access the **Selection tool** ▶ press and hold **[shift] [option] (Mac)** or **[Shift] [Alt] (Win)**, then drag a **copy** that is positioned approximately **1/8" to the right of the original**, as shown in Figure 22.

5. Click **Object** on the menu bar, point to **Transform Again**, then click **Transform Again**.

   Step 4 is repeated, and a third frame is added.

6. Apply the **Transform Again command** two more times.

7. Select the **five small blue frames**.

8. On the Control panel, click the **center reference point**.

   With the center reference point selected, the X/Y coordinates on the Control panel now identify the center point of all five frames as a unit.

9. On the Control panel, change the **X value** to **6.25**.

As 6.25 is half of the full horizontal width of 12.5," the five frames, as a unit, are centered horizontally on the page.

10. Compare your layout to Figure 23, then save your work.

    Note that the 10 document pages on the Pages panel display an A because they are based on the A-Master by default. Their thumbnail icons reflect all the objects currently on the A-Master.

11. Continue to the next lesson.

You created a single rectangle, then changed its fill and stroke colors with the Eyedropper tool. You duplicated the rectangle with the drag-and-drop method and used the Transform Again command three times. You used the Control panel to center all five frames as a unit.

Figure 22 Duplicating the frame

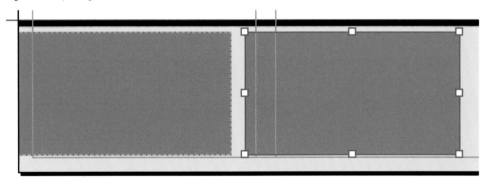

Figure 23 Viewing five frames centered horizontally on the spread

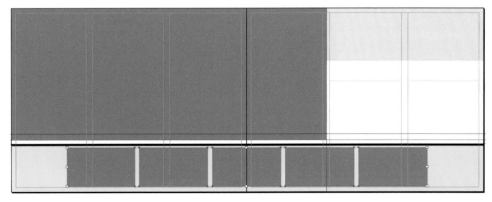

CREATE TEXT ON MASTER PAGES

▶ **What You'll Do**

In this lesson, you will position two headlines on a master page, create automatic page numbering, and create two new master pages.

Creating a New Master Page

You create new master pages by clicking the New Master command on the Pages panel menu. When you create a new master page, you have the option of giving the master page a new name. This is useful for distinguishing one master page from another. For example, you might want to use the name "Body Copy" for master pages that will be used for body copy and then use the name "Chapter Start" for master pages that will be used as a layout for a chapter title page.

When you create a new master page, you have the option of changing the values for the margins and for the number of columns on the new master page.

Loading Master Pages

You can load master pages from one InDesign document to another by clicking the Pages panel menu button, pointing to Master Pages, then clicking Load Master Pages. You will be prompted to navigate to the file that has the master pages you wish to load. Select the InDesign document, then click Open. The master pages are added to the Pages panel. You will be prompted to rename master pages that have the same name or replace the existing master pages.

Creating Automatic Page Numbering

When you create a document with multiple pages, chances are you'll want to have page numbers on each page. You could create a text frame on every page and then manually type the page number on every page, but think of what a nightmare that could turn out to be! You would have to create a text frame of the same size and in the same location on every page. Imagine what would happen if you were to remove or add a page to the middle of the document—you'd need to go back and renumber your pages!

Fortunately, InDesign offers a solution for this. You can create placeholder text frames for page numbers on your master pages. Click inside the text frame, click Type on the menu bar, point to Insert Special Character, point to Markers, then click Current Page Number. A letter will appear in the text frame, as shown in Figure 24.

That letter represents the page number. You can format it using any font, size, and alignment that you desire. On document pages based on that master, the letter in the text frame will appear as the number of the page. Page numbering is automatic. This means that the page number is automatically updated when pages are added or removed from the document.

When you work with multiple master pages, make sure that each page number placeholder is the same size, in the same location, and in the same format on each master page. This will make the appearance of page numbers consistent throughout the document, regardless of the master upon which a particular document page is based.

Inserting Space Between Characters

In Chapter 13, you learned that you should not press the space bar more than once to create extra spacing between characters. However, sometimes a single space does not provide enough space between words or characters. You may want to insert additional space to achieve a certain look. You could tab the text, or as you'll learn in this lesson, you can insert white space.

Figure 24 A text frame on a master page containing an auto page number character

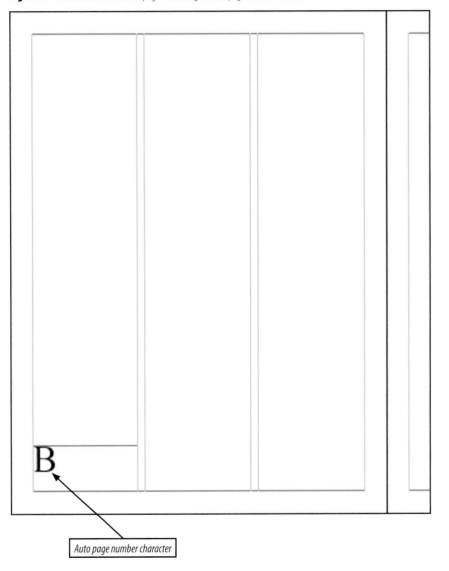

Auto page number character

The Type menu contains commands for inserting white space between words or characters. The two most-used white spaces are em space and en space. The width of an **em space** is equivalent to that of the lowercase letter m in the current typeface at that type size. The width of an **en space** is narrower—that of the lowercase letter n in that typeface at that type size. Use these commands—not the space bar—to insert white space. To insert an em space or an en space, click Type on the menu bar, point

to Insert White Space, then click either Em Space or En Space. Figure 25 shows an em space between a page number placeholder and a word.

Inserting Em Dashes and En Dashes

Sometimes you'll want to put a dash between words or characters, and you'll find that the dash created by pressing the hyphen key is not wide enough. That's because hyphens are shorter than dashes.

InDesign offers two types of dashes to insert between words or characters—the em dash and the en dash. The width of an em dash is equivalent to that of the lowercase letter m in the current typeface at that type size. The width of an en dash is narrower—that of the lowercase letter n in that typeface at that type size. To insert an em dash or an en dash, click Type on the menu bar, point to Insert Special Character, point to Hyphens and Dashes, then click either Em Dash or En Dash. Figure 26 shows an example of an en dash.

Figure 25 Identifying an em space

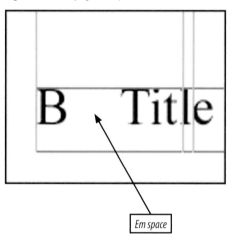

Em space

Figure 26 Identifying an en dash

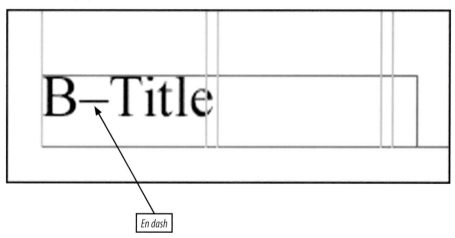

En dash

Creating a New Master Page Based on Another Master Page

Imagine that you've created a master page for a magazine layout. The master contains master items for the headline, the body copy, and the page number. It also contains master items for pictures that will appear on the page. Now imagine that you need to create another master page that will be identical to this master page, with the one exception that this new master will not contain frames for graphics. You wouldn't want to duplicate all the work you did to create the first master, would you?

To avoid repeating efforts and to create consistency between masters, you can create a new master page based on another master page. The new master would appear identical to the first. You would then modify only the elements that you want to change on the new master, keeping all the elements that you don't want to change perfectly consistent with the previous one.

Basing a new master on another master is not the same thing as duplicating a master. Duplicating a master creates a copy, but the original and the copy have no relationship.

When you base a new master on another, any changes you make to the first master will be updated on masters based on it. Think of how powerful this is. Let's say that your editor tells you to change the type size of the page numbers. Making a change in only one place offers you a substantial savings in time and effort and provides you with the certainty that the page numbers will be consistent from master to master.

Remember that all master items on new master pages will also be locked by default. To unlock a master item, you must press and hold or [shift] [command] (Mac) or [Shift] [Ctrl] (Win) to select those objects on the new master. InDesign does this so you don't accidentally move or delete objects from the new master or the original master.

Add placeholders for headlines

1. Verify that the **fill and stroke** on the toolbar are both set to **[None]**.

2. Click the **Type tool** T, then drag a **small rectangle** anywhere in the two rightmost columns above the two text frames already there.

3. Click the **Selection tool** ▶, then drag the **left handle** of the frame so it snaps to the red vertical guide.

4. Drag the **right handle** of the frame so it snaps to the right edge of the document.

   The Width text box on the Control panel should read 4.15 in.

5. Click the **bottom-center reference point** on the Control panel, then enter **1.35** in the **Y text box**.

   The text frame moves to align its bottom edge to the Y coordinate.

6. On the Control panel, change the **Height value** to **1.2**.

7. Click the **Type tool** T, click **inside the new frame**, then type **LOCATION** in all caps.

8. On the Control panel, click the **Align center button** ≡ to center the text.

9. Select the **text**, set the **typeface** to **Hobo Std Medium**, set the **Font Size** to **60 pt.**, then set the **Horizontal Scale** to **75%**.

10. Enter **[command] [B] (Mac)** or **[Ctrl] [B] (Win)** to open the **Text Frame Options dialog box**, click the **Align list arrow**, click **Bottom**, then click **OK**.

11. Deselect, then compare your text to Figure 27.

12. Click the **Selection tool** ▶, press and hold **[shift] [option] (Mac)**, or **[Shift] [Alt] (Win)**, then drag and drop a **copy of the text frame** anywhere straight down below the original.

13. Click the **Type tool** T, select the **duplicated text**, reduce the **Font Size** to **24 pt.**, then type **day/date** in all lowercase letters.

14. Click the **Selection tool** ▶, then verify that the **bottom-center reference point** on the Control panel is selected.

15. Type **1.75** in the **Y text box**, type **.35** in the **Height text box**, then compare your layout to Figure 28.

16. Save your work, then continue to the next set of steps.

You created and positioned two text frames on the master page, then formatted text in each.

Figure 27 Formatted headline on a master page

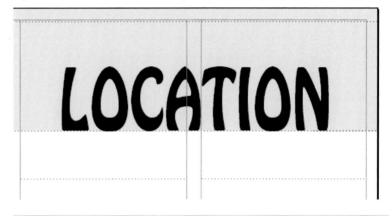

Figure 28 Formatted sub-headline on a master page

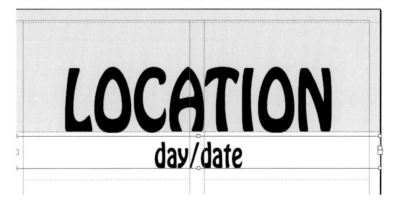

Create automatic page numbering and insert white space between characters

1. Click the **Type tool** T, draw a **text frame** anywhere in the **lower-right corner** of the spread, set its **Width** to **1.25**", then set its **Height** to **.25**".

2. Position the **text frame** in the **lower-right corner** inside the margin guide.

3. Type **City** in the text frame with no space after the word, choose any typeface and size you like, then verify that the text cursor is blinking to the right of the word.

4. Click **Type** on the menu bar, point to **Insert Special Character**, point to **Markers**, then click **Current Page Number**.

   The letter A appears in the text frame because this is the A-Master Page. This letter A will change on document pages to reflect the current document page. For example, on page 4, the A will appear as the number 4.

5. Click the **cursor between the y and the A**, click **Type** on the menu bar, point to **Insert White Space**, then click **Em Space**.

6. On the Control panel, set the **text** to **Align Right,** click **Object** on the menu bar, click **Text Frame Options**, then set the **Vertical Justification** to **Bottom.**

   Your text box should resemble Figure 29.

7. Copy the **selected text frame,** paste it in place, click the **bottom-left reference**

point on the Control panel, then change the **X value** to **.125**.

The text frame moves to the left page, inside the margin guide.

8. Reformat the text so the copied text frame resembles Figure 30.

TIP You copy and paste the em space just like any other character.

9. Save your work, then continue to the next set of steps.

You created automatic page numbering on the right and left pages of the master page and inserted em spaces.

Figure 29 Formatted text on the right-hand page

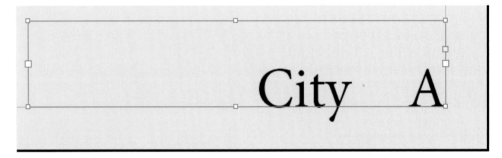

Figure 30 Reformatted text on the left-hand page

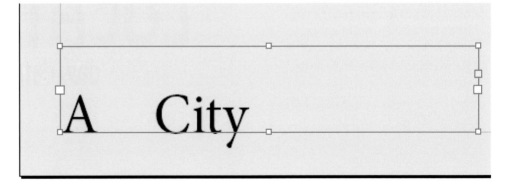

Create a new master page spread based on another master page spread

1. Expand the Pages panel, if necessary, click the **Pages panel menu button** ≡ , then click **New Master**.

2. Enter the settings shown in Figure 31, then click **OK**.

   The B-Master page icons are added to the Pages panel. Note that the B-Master icons on the Pages panel show an A because the B-Master is based on A-Master.

3. Double-click **B-Master** on the Pages panel to view the B-Master master page.

   B-Master is identical to A-Master, except that the automatic page number reads B rather than A.

4. Hide the guides.

5. Click the **Selection tool** ▶ , then try to select objects on the page.

   Objects on a master page based on another master cannot be selected in the standard way.

6. Press and hold **[shift] [command] (Mac)** or **[Shift] [Ctrl] (Win)**, then drag a **marquee** to select the elements shown in Figure 32.

TIP Make sure you start dragging on the pasteboard and not on the document or else you might accidentally select and move an object on the master.

Continued on next page

Figure 31 Settings for a new master page based on the A-Master

Figure 32 Selecting specific page elements

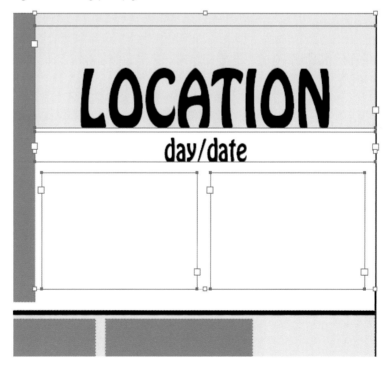

7. On the Control panel, click the **middle-left reference point**, then set the **X value** to **0**.

8. Select the **large blue frame**, click the **middle-right reference point** on the Control panel, then set the **X value** to **12.5**.

   Your B-Master spread should resemble Figure 33.

9. Save your work, then continue to the next set of steps.

You created a new master spread based on the A-Master spread. You modified the location of elements on the new master to differentiate it from the original.

Create a new blank master page spread

1. Click the **Pages panel menu button** ☰ , then click **New Master**.

2. Click the **Based on Master list arrow**, then verify that **None** is selected so your New Master dialog box resembles Figure 34.

3. Click **OK**.

   C-Master appears as two blank page thumbnails on the Pages panel.

4. Double-click the words **A-Master** in the top part of the Pages panel to view the A-Master spread, select all, then copy.

Figure 33 Five frames centered horizontally on the spread

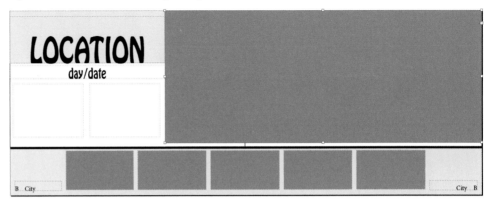

Figure 34 Creating a new master page not based on any other master

5. Double-click **C-Master** to view the C-Master spread, click **Edit** on the menu bar, click **Paste in Place,** then deselect all.

The A-Master layout is pasted into the C-Master spread. The only change is that the automatic page numbering reads C.

6. Click the **Selection tool** ▶, if necessary, then select the **five blue frames** at the bottom of the page as well as the **yellow frame** behind them.

Because C-Master is not based on A-Master, the items are not locked.

TIP Be sure you don't select either of the two automatic page number text boxes.

7. On the Control panel, click the **top-center reference point**, then set the **Y value** to **0**.

8. Click **Object** on the menu bar, then click **Hide**.

9. Select **all the objects above the horizontal black line**, click the **bottom-center reference point** on the Control panel, then set the **Y value** to **4.75**.

10. Delete the **automatic numbering text frame** at the bottom of the right-hand page.

Pages based on the C-Master will have page numbers only on the left page of the spread.

11. Show the **hidden frames**, then deselect all.

TIP To show the hidden frames, click Object on the menu bar, then click Show All on Spread.

12. Select the **large yellow frame** at the top of the page, click the **bottom-center reference point** on the Control panel, then note the **Y value**.

13. Select the **horizontal black line,** then set the **Y value** to be the same Y value you just noted.

Your C-Master spread should resemble Figure 35.

14. Save your work, then continue to the next lesson.

You created a new blank master spread not based on any other master. You modified the location of elements on the new master to differentiate it from the original.

Figure 35 Modified layout in C-Master

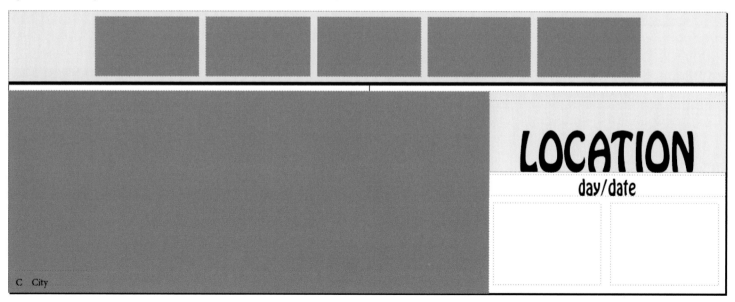

APPLY MASTER PAGES TO DOCUMENT PAGES

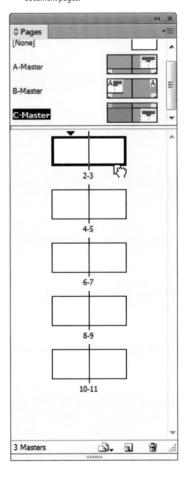

Applying Master Pages to Document Pages

Once you have created master pages, you then use the Pages panel to apply them to the document pages. One method for applying master pages is the drag-and-drop method. Using this method, you drag the master page icon or the master page name, in the top section of the Pages panel, down to the page icons in the lower section of the Pages panel. To apply the master to a single page, you drag the master onto the page icon. To apply the master to a spread, you drag the master onto one of the four corners until you see a dark border around both pages in the spread.

When you apply a master page to a document page, the document page

inherits all the layout characteristics of the master.

TIP You can apply the default None master page to a document page when you do not want the document page to be based on a master.

A second method for applying master pages to document pages is to use the Apply Master to Pages command on the Pages panel menu. The Apply Master dialog box allows you to specify which master you want to apply to which pages. What's great about this method is that you can apply a master to any page in the document—even inconsecutive pages—in one move. If you want to apply a master to multiple pages, use the Apply Master dialog box; it's faster than dragging and dropping.

Apply master pages to document pages

1. Click the **Pages panel menu button** ≡ , then click **Panel Options.**

2. In the **Pages section** at top, change the **Size** to **Extra Large**, then click **OK**.

   The page icons on the Pages panel are enlarged. Because the three master pages are similar in color, having larger page thumbnails will make it easier to see which masters have been applied to which spreads.

3. Scroll through the document and note that the A-Master has been automatically applied to all the pages in the document.

4. On the Pages panel, drag **B-Master by its name** to the **upper-left corner of spread 4–5** until a frame appears around the spread, as shown in Figure 36, then release the mouse button.

5. Using the same method, apply the **C-Master** to **spread 6–7**.

6. Click the **Pages panel menu button** ≡ , then click **Apply Master to Pages**.

Continued on next page

Figure 36 Applying the B-Master to the 4–5 spread

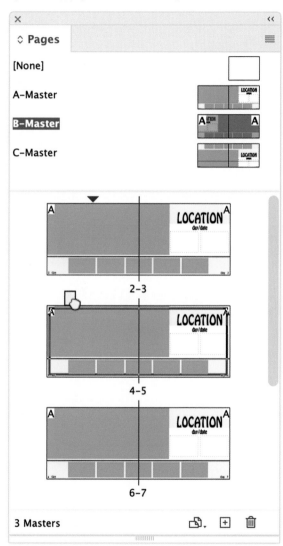

7. Click the **Apply Master list arrow**, then click **B-Master**.

8. Type **10–11** in the **To Pages text box**, then click **OK**.

   The master is applied to the spread. Your Pages panel should resemble Figure 37.

9. Navigate to **page 2**, then switch to **Presentation mode**.

10. Navigate through the spreads to see the masters applied and the automatic page numbering.

11. Exit **Presentation mode**, then save your work.

12. Continue to the next lesson.

You applied master spreads to document spreads using the drag-and-drop method and the Apply Master to Pages command.

Figure 37 Pages panel reflecting applied masters

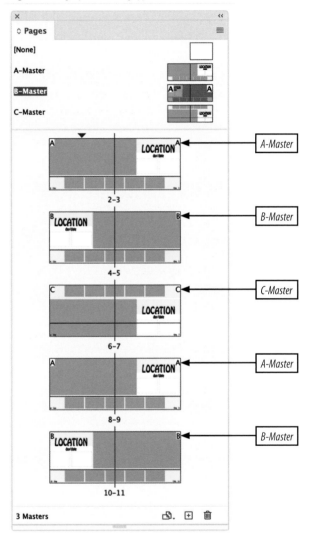

MODIFY MASTER PAGES AND DOCUMENT PAGES

Modifying Master Pages

When you modify a master item on a master page, that modification will be reflected on all document pages based on that master page. This is a powerful option. Let's say that you have created a layout for a 36-page book, and you decide that you want to change the typeface of all the headlines. If they were created on master pages, you could simply reformat the headline in the text frame placeholder on the master pages, and every document page in the book based on it would be updated.

Overriding Master Items on Document Pages

Master pages are designed to allow you to lay out the basic elements for a page that will be used repeatedly throughout a document. In most cases, however, you will want to make modifications to the document page once it is created—you might even want to delete some objects on the document page that were created on the master page.

Master page items on document pages are fixed objects and cannot be selected with normal methods.

You can modify a master page item on a document page, however, by overriding. You override a master item by pressing and holding [shift] [command] (Mac) or [Shift] [Ctrl] (Win), then clicking a master item. This makes the item selectable.

You might find that fixed master items on document pages are annoying! Long after the master page has served its purpose, you will find—especially with long documents—that the inability to just simply select master items with the Selection tool impedes your progress. You can quickly override all master items on a targeted document page by clicking Override All Master Page Items on the Pages panel menu.

Making changes to a document page is often referred to as making a local change. When you override a master item, that item nevertheless maintains its status as a master item and will still be updated with changes to the master page. For example, if you resize a master item on a document page, but you do not change its color, it will retain its new size, but if the color of the master item is changed on the master page, the master item's color will be updated on the document page.

Once a master item has been released from its fixed position, it remains selectable. You can return a master item on a document page back to its original state by selecting the item, clicking the Pages panel menu button, then clicking Remove Selected Local Overrides.

Detaching Master Items

When you are sure you no longer want a master item to be affected by updates made to the associated master page, you can detach a master item. To detach a master item, you must first override it by pressing and holding [shift] [command] (Mac) or [Shift] [Ctrl] (Win) while selecting it. Next, click the Pages panel menu button, point to Master Pages, then click Detach Selection from Master.

That's the official move. Note, though, that when you modify text in a text frame on a document page, the relationship between the text on the document page and the text on the master page tends to detach automatically. Therefore, when it comes to text, it's a smart idea to use master pages for the placement of text frames on the page but use character and paragraph styles for global formatting of the text itself.

Override master items on a document page

1. Verify that the document has been saved.

2. Double-click the **page 3 icon** on the Pages panel, click the **Selection tool** ▶, then try to select any of the objects on the page.

    Because all objects on page 3 are master items, they're fixed and cannot be selected with standard methods.

3. Press and hold **[shift] [command] (Mac)** or **[Shift] [Ctrl] (Win)**, then click the word **LOCATION**.

4. Click the **Type tool** T , select the **text**, type **MANAROLA**, then click the **pasteboard** to deselect.

5. Save your work, then continue to the next set of steps.

You overrode a master item on a document page.

Modify master items on a master page

1. Double-click the **right-hand page in the A-Master**, select the word **city**, the **em space**, and the **automatic page icon**, then set the **Font Size** to **12 pt.** and the **typeface** to **Times New Roman Regular**.

    This typeface is commonly available, but if you don't have it, use a similar serif face like Times, Garamond, or Baskerville.

2. Select only the word **City**, then change its **typeface** to **Times New Roman Italic**.

3. Make the same changes to the text on the bottom of the left-hand page of the spread.

    All the changes you are making to the A-Master are automatically updated on the B-Master but not on the C-Master.

4. Double-click the word **LOCATION** to select it, click the **Swatches panel**, then click **[Paper]**.

    The fill color of the text changes to white.

5. Click the **Selection tool** ▶, select the **two yellow frames** on the page, then change their **fill color** to **green**.

6. Select the **black horizontal line**, then change its **stroke color** to **red**.

   Your A-Master should resemble Figure 38.

7. Double-click **B-Master**.

   All the changes you made to A-Master, except one, are reflected on B-Master because B-Master was created based on A-Master. Note, however, the headline on B-Master is still black. Type tends to behave unpredictably on master pages. The fact that this frame has been relocated from its original position might explain why it didn't update.

8. Double-click **C-Master** to view the spread.

   None of the changes from A-Master affect C-Master.

9. View **spread 8–9**.

   All the changes you made on the master page, including the white headline, are reflected on the spread.

10. View **spread 2–3**.

    All the changes you made on the master page, except the white headline, are reflected on the spread. This is because you formatted the headline locally on the page itself. The change on the master page after the fact did not override the formatting you applied on the page.

11. Save your work, then continue to the next set of steps.

You modified elements on the A-Master and noted how those modifications affected B-Master, C-Master, and the pages in the document.

Figure 38 A-Master modifications

Remove local overrides and detach master items

1. View **spread 10–11**, then select the **large blue frame**.

2. Click the **Pages panel menu button**, point to **Master Pages**, then click **Detach Selection from Master**.

3. Double-click **B-Master**, then change the **fill color** on the **large blue frame** to **red**.

4. Scroll through the document to note the changes.

   The change is reflected on spread 4–5, but not on spread 10–11.

5. Navigate to **page 3** in the document, click the **Selection tool**, then select the **text frame of MANAROLA**.

6. Click the **Pages panel menu button**, point to **Master Pages**, then click **Remove Selected Local Overrides**.

7. Save your work, then close the Setup document.

You detached a frame from its master. You then modified the master, noting that the change did not affect the detached frame. You selected a modified master item on a document page, then used the Remove Selected Local Overrides command to restore the item's relationship to its master.

PLACE AND THREAD TEXT

In this lesson, you will place text, thread text from frame to frame, then view text threads.

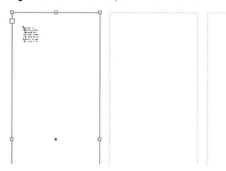

Placing Text

Once you have created a text frame—either on a master page or on a document page—you can type directly into the frame, or you can place text from another document into it. When creating headlines, you usually type them directly into the text frame. When creating body copy, however, you will often find yourself placing text from another document, usually a word processing document.

Placing text in InDesign is simple and straightforward. Click the Place command on the File menu, which opens the Place dialog box. Find the text document that you want to place, then click Open.

The pointer changes to the loaded text icon. With a loaded text icon, you can drag to create a text frame or click inside an existing text frame. When you position the loaded text icon over an existing text frame, the icon appears in parentheses, as shown in Figure 39. The parentheses indicate that you can click to place the text into the text frame. Do so, and the text flows into the text frame, as shown in Figure 40.

TIP The loaded text icon displays a thumbnail image of the first few lines of text that is being placed. This helps to make sure you are placing the correct file.

Figure 39 Loaded text icon positioned over a text frame

Figure 40 Text placed into a text frame

Text placed in text frame

Threading Text

InDesign provides many options for **threading** text—linking text from one text frame to another. Text frames have an in port and an out port. The **in port** is a small box in the upper left corner of a text frame that you can click to flow text from another text frame. The **out port** is a small box in the lower right corner of a text frame that flows text out to another text frame when clicked.

When threading text, you use the text frame ports to establish connections between the text frames.

In Figure 41, the center text frame is selected, and the in port and out port are identified.

The in port represents where text would flow into the text frame, and the out port represents from where text would flow out.

In the same figure, note that the out port on the first text frame is red and has a plus sign in its center. This indicates the presence of **overset text**—more than can fit in the frame.

To thread text manually from the first text frame to the second, first click the Selection tool, then click the frame with the overset text so the frame is highlighted. Next, click the out port of the text frame. When you position your cursor over the next text frame, the cursor changes to the link icon, as shown in Figure 42. Click the link icon, and the text flows into the frame, as shown in Figure 43. When the Show Text Threads command on the View menu is activated, a blue arrow appears between any two text frames that have been threaded, as shown in Figure 44.

Figure 41 Identifying in ports and out ports

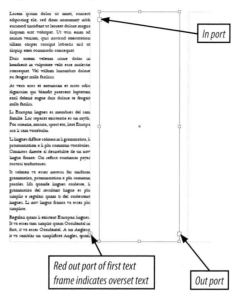

In port

Red out port of first text frame indicates overset text

Out port

Figure 42 Link icon

Link icon positioned over text frame

Figure 43 Threading text between frames

Figure 44 Showing text threads

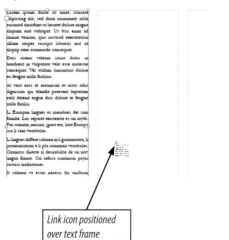

Text thread between frames

Place text on document pages

1. Open ID 3-2.indd, then save it as **Wraps and Sections**.

   This data file has the same parameters as the document you created at the start of this chapter. The only changes are that the local document pages have been colorized and the headlines and dates have been filled in. Also, small blue circle or square frames are positioned on each spread.

2. Click the **workspace switcher**, then click **Typography**.

3. Double-click the **page 3 icon** on the Pages panel.

4. Click **File** on the menu bar, click **Place**, navigate to the drive and folder where your Chapter 14 Data Files are stored, then double-click **Greek text**.

5. Position the **cursor** over the **interior of the left text frame**.

As shown in Figure 45, the loaded text icon appears in parentheses, signaling that you can insert the loaded text into the text frame.

6. Click the **loaded text icon** in the **left text frame**.

   Text flows into the frame. The red out port with the plus sign indicates there is overset text—more text than can fit in the text frame.

7. Click the **Type tool** $\boxed{T}$, click **any word** five times to select all the text in the frame, set the **typeface** to **Times New Roman Regular**, set the **Font Size** to **8 pt.**, set the **Leading** to **9 pt.**, then set the **alignment** to **Justify with last line aligned left**.

   TIP Clicking five times selects even the text that is not currently visible in the frame. If you just click and drag to select the text that is visible, only that text will be affected by your format change.

8. Click the **Selection tool** ▶, click the **red out port**, then position the **loaded text icon** over the **right text frame**.

   As shown in Figure 46, a link icon appears in the loaded text icon, indicating you are about to flow text from one frame to another. The red out port turns blue when you click it.

   TIP To unlink text frames, double-click the blue out port.

9. Click inside the **right text frame**.

   The text flows into the right text frame, and a new red out port appears at the bottom right of the right frame.

10. Save your work, then continue to the next set of steps.

You used the Place command to load text into a text frame, then threaded text from that frame into another.

Figure 45 Loaded text icon

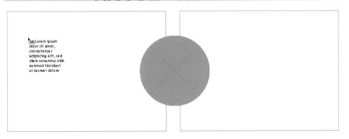

Figure 46 Loaded text icon with a link icon

Thread text through multiple text frames

1. Click **View** on the menu bar, point to **Extras**, then click **Show Text Threads**.

   With the Show Text Threads command activated, blue arrows appear between threaded text frames when they are selected.

2. Reduce the view of the document so you can see more than one spread on your monitor.

3. Click the **Selection tool** ▶, then click the **out port** of the right text frame.

   The loaded text icon appears.

4. Scroll so you can see both **pages 3 and 4** in the monitor window.

5. Press and hold **[option] (Mac)** or **[Alt] (Win)**, and position the **loaded text icon** over the **left text frame on page 4**.

6. Click, but do not release, **[option] (Mac)** or **[Alt] (Win)**.

   With the [option] (Mac) or [Alt] (Win) key pressed, the loaded text icon remains active. This means you won't have to click the out port of the left text frame to thread to the right text frame.

Continued on next page

7. Position the **pointer over the right text frame**, then click.

   As shown in Figure 47, the text is threaded through both frames on page 4.

8. Using the same process, thread text through the remaining pages of the document.

Note that when you're done threading, you will still have loaded text.

9. Save your work, then continue to the next lesson.

You threaded text between multiple text frames on multiple pages.

MAPPING STYLE NAMES WHEN IMPORTING WORD OR RTF FILES

When you place a Word document or RTF text in InDesign, you have many options to choose from regarding how text is imported. After you click Place on the File menu and find the Word or RTF document that you want to place, click the Show Import Options check box, then click Open. The Import Options dialog box opens. In this dialog box, you can choose to include or not include footnotes, endnotes, table of contents text, and index text. You can also choose to remove any previous styles applied to text and any table formatting. Conversely, you can opt to retain styles and table formatting applied to incoming text. You can import styles automatically by clicking the Import Styles Automatically option button and then tell InDesign how to deal with conflicts when incoming styles have the same names as existing styles in InDesign. Finally, you can map style names from the placed text file to specific styles in InDesign by clicking the Customize Style Import option button and then clicking the Style Mapping button. The Style Mapping dialog box allows you to choose which InDesign style to map to each incoming text style. For example, you can specify that the Normal style in Word is mapped to the [Basic Paragraph] style in InDesign.

Figure 47 Text threads showing text flowing from one spread to another

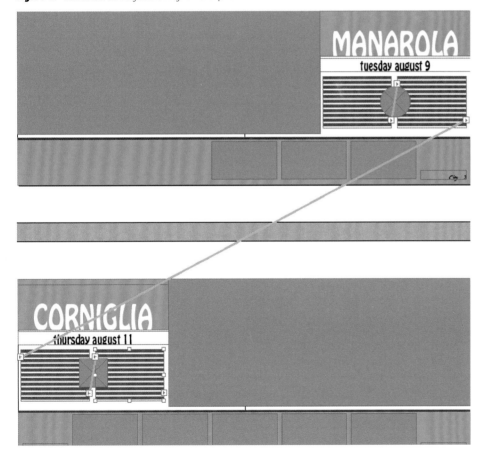

CREATE NEW SECTIONS AND WRAP TEXT

▶ *What You'll Do*

In this lesson, you will create two different numbering sections and create two text wraps around graphics frames.

Creating Sections in a Document

A **section** is a group of pages in a document with distinct page numbering from other groups of pages. For example, sometimes in the front pages of a book, such as in the introduction or the preface, the pages will be numbered with lowercase Roman numerals, then normal page numbering will begin with the first chapter. Or in a cookbook with different courses, the "Soup" section might run from pages 1–35 and be followed by the "Salad" section, which also begins on a page 1.

You can create as many sections in a document as you wish. You determine the page on which the new section will start by clicking that page icon on the Pages panel. Choose the Numbering & Section Options command on the Pages panel menu, which opens the New Section dialog box, shown in Figure 48.

> **TIP** The first time you choose a type of page numbering for a document, the Numbering & Section Options dialog box opens instead of the New Section dialog box.

Figure 48 New Section dialog box

New Section

☑ Start Section
○ Automatic Page Numbering
⦿ Start Page Numbering at: 1

Page Numbering
Section Prefix:
Style: 1, 2, 3, 4...
Section Marker:
☐ Include Prefix when Numbering Pages

OK
Cancel

Document Chapter Numbering
Style: 1, 2, 3, 4...
⦿ Automatic Chapter Numbering
○ Start Chapter Numbering at: 1
○ Same as Previous Document in the Book
Book Name: N/A

Wrapping Text Around a Frame

When you position a text frame or a graphics frame over another frame that contains text, you can apply a text wrap to the overlapping frame to force the underlying text to wrap around it. The Text Wrap panel offers many options for wrapping text around a frame.

Figure 49 shows a blue rectangular frame using the No text wrap option on the Text Wrap panel. Because there is no text wrap, the blue frame blocks the text behind it.

Figure 50 shows the same frame using the Wrap around bounding box option on the Text Wrap panel.

TIP To turn off text wrap in a text frame, select the text frame, click Object on the menu bar, click Text Frame Options, click the Ignore Text Wrap check box, and then click OK.

When you choose the Wrap around bounding box option, you can control the **offset**—the distance that text is repelled from the frame—by entering values in the Top, Bottom, Left, and Right Offset text boxes on the panel. The frame in Figure 50 has a 1.875" offset.

Figure 49 The blue frame has no text wrap and hides the text beneath it

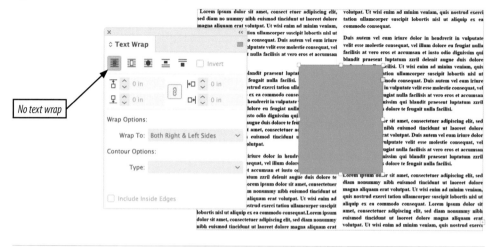

Figure 50 The frame has a 1.875" text wrap

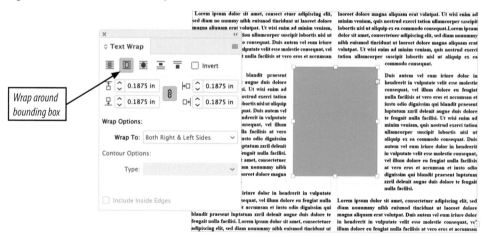

Formatting a Text Frame to Ignore a Text Wrap

There will be times when you will want text in a frame to be immune to a text wrap in another frame. For example, let's say you have an image in a square frame and you have added a text wrap so the body copy on the page wraps around the frame. Now let's say that you want to position a caption in another text frame under the image. You'll run into a problem because the text wrap on the image will repel the caption text in the separate text frame.

At any time, you can select a text frame, open the Text Frame Options dialog box on the Object menu, then click Ignore Text Wrap. With this activated, the selected text frame will be immune to any text wrap applied to any other frames.

Create sections in a document

1. Double-click the **page 8 icon** on the Pages panel.

   The document has been designed so page 8 represents a new section in the document. The color theme changes to red and blue, and the city is Firenze.

2. Click the **Pages panel menu button** ≡ , then click **Numbering and Section Options**.

   The New Section dialog box opens.

3. Verify that the **Start Section check box** is **checked**.

4. Click the **Start Page Numbering at option button**, then type **2**.

   Your dialog box should resemble Figure 51. With these choices, you are starting a new section at page 8, renumbered as page 2.

5. Click **OK**.

   The pages are renumbered. On the Pages panel, spread 8–9 is now spread 2–3.

   TIP If a warning appears, alerting you a page number in this section already exists in another section, click OK.

6. Save your work, then continue to the next set of steps.

You used the New Section dialog box to change the sequence of the automatic page numbering in the document.

Figure 51 Renumbering the document

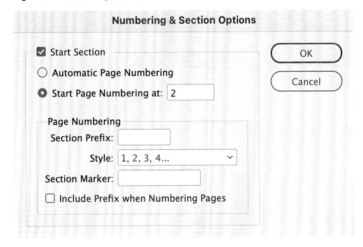

Wrap text around a frame

1. Double-click the **first page 3 icon** on the Pages panel, click the **Selection tool** ▶, then select the **small blue circle frame**.

2. Show the **Text Wrap panel**.

3. On the Text Wrap panel, click the **Wrap around bounding box button** ⊞ .

   The text wraps around the rectangular bounding box, not the circle shape.

4. On the Text Wrap panel, click the **Wrap around object shape button** ▦, then type **.125** in the **Top Offset text box**.

   The text wraps around the ellipse, as shown in Figure 52.

5. Navigate to **page 4**, select the **small blue rectangular frame**, then click the **Wrap around bounding box button** ▦ on the Text Wrap panel.

6. Click the **Make all settings the same button** 🔗 to deactivate it if necessary.

7. Enter the settings in Figure 53 on the Text Wrap panel.

   The text is offset at different amounts top and bottom versus right and left. You will use the space created below the rectangle to position caption text in the next set of steps.

8. Save your work, then continue to the next set of steps.

You used the Text Wrap panel to flow text around an object's shape and around a bounding box.

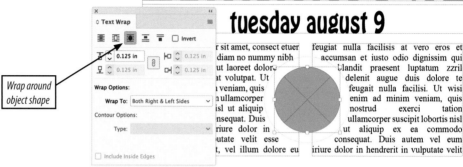

Figure 52 Text wraps around object shape

Wrap around object shape

Figure 53 Formatting different offsets for the text wrap

Offset textboxes are not linked

Format a text frame to ignore a text wrap

1. Find the **text frame** on the pasteboard **to the left of page 4** in the document.

    The text frame has 8 pt. bold text that reads, "Caption goes here in this box."

2. Move the **text frame** onto **page 4** and position it **below the blue rectangle**.

    Some or all the caption text disappears because it is being repelled by the text wrap on the blue rectangle.

3. With the **small text frame** still selected, click **Object** on the menu bar, then click **Text Frame Options**.

4. Click the **Ignore Text Wrap check box**, then click **OK**.

    As shown in Figure 54, the caption text is positioned under the blue rectangle and is not affected by the text wrap.

5. Save your work, then close the Wraps and Sections document.

You applied the Ignore Text Wrap feature to a text box, so it was not affected by the text wrap.

Figure 54 The caption text box set to ignore the text wrap

CORNIGLIA
thursday august 11

esse molestie consequat, vel illum dolore eu feugiat nulla facilisis at vero eros et accumsan et iusto odio dignissim qui blandit praesent luptatum zzril delenit augue duis dolore te feugait nulla facilisi. Lorem ipsum dolor sit amet, consectetuer adipiscing elit, sed diam nonummy nibh euismod tincidunt ut laoreet dolore magna aliquam erat volutpat. Duis autem vel

Caption goes here in this text box.

eum iriure dolor in hendrerit in vulputate velit esse molestie consequat, vel illum dolore eu feugiat nulla facilisis at vero eros et accumsan et iusto odio dignissim qui blandit praesent luptatum zzril delenit augue duis dolore te feugait nulla facilisi. Lorem ipsum dolor sit amet, consectetuer adipiscing elit, sed diam nonummy nibh euismod

Text frame ignores text wrap

Create a new document and set up a master page

1. Start Adobe InDesign.
2. Without creating a new document, click InDesign (Mac) or Edit (Win) on the menu bar, point to Preferences, then click Guides & Pasteboard.
3. In the Guide Options section, click the Guides in Back check box to select, if necessary. Then click Units & Increments in the Preferences list on the left side of the dialog box, verify that the Horizontal and Vertical ruler units are set to Inches, then click OK.
4. Click File on the menu bar, point to New, then click Document.
5. In the New Document dialog box, name the document **Skills Review**.
6. Type **8** in the Number of Pages text box, press [tab], then verify that the Facing Pages check box is checked.
7. Type **5** in the Width text box, press [tab], then type **5** in the Height text box.
8. Using [tab] to move from one text box to another, type **1** in the Columns text box.
9. Type **.25** in the Top, Bottom, Inside, and Outside Margins text boxes.
10. Click Create.
11. Click the workspace switcher on the menu bar, then click Advanced, if necessary.
12. Double-click the words A-Master on the Pages panel to center both pages of the master in your window.
13. Click Window on the menu bar, point to Object & Layout, then click Transform.
14. Click the Selection tool, press and hold [command] (Mac) or [Ctrl] (Win), create a guide across the spread using the horizontal ruler, releasing the mouse pointer when the Y Location on the Transform panel reads 2.5 in.
15. Create a guide on the left page using the vertical ruler, releasing the mouse pointer when the X Location on the Transform panel reads 2.5 in.
16. Click InDesign (Mac) or Edit (Win) on the menu bar, point to Preferences, click Units & Increments, click the Origin list arrow, click Page, then click OK.
17. Create a vertical guide on the right page, releasing the mouse pointer when the X Location on the Transform panel reads 2.5 in.
18. Verify that the fill and stroke buttons on the toolbar are set to [None], click the Rectangle Frame tool, then draw a rectangle anywhere on the left page.
19. Click the top-left reference point on the Transform panel.
20. With the rectangle frame selected, type **0** in the X Location text box on the Transform panel, type **0** in the Y Location text box, type **5** in the Width text box, type **5** in the Height text box, then press [return] (Mac) or [Enter] (Win).
21. Using the same method, create an identical rectangle on the right page.
22. If necessary, type **0** in the X Location text box on the Transform panel, type **0** in the Y Location text box, then press [return] (Mac) or [Enter] (Win).

23. Click the Pages panel menu button, then click New Master.
24. Type **Body** in the Name text box, click the Based on Master list arrow, click A-Master, then click OK.
25. Click the Selection tool, press and hold or [shift] [command] (Mac) or [Shift] [Ctrl] (Win), select both rectangle frames, then delete them.
26. Double-click B-Body on the Pages panel to center both pages of the master in your window.
27. Click Layout on the menu bar, then click Margins and Columns.
28. Type **2** in the Number text box in the Columns section, then click OK.

Create text on master pages

1. Click the Type tool, create a text frame of any size anywhere in the right column on the left page, then click the Selection tool.
2. Verify that the top-left reference point is selected on the Transform panel, type **2.6** in the X Location text box, type **.25** in the Y Location text box, type **2.15** in the Width text box, type **4.5** in the Height text box, then press [return] (Mac) or [Enter] (Win).
3. Click Edit on the menu bar, click Copy, click Edit on the menu bar again, then click Paste in Place.
4. Press and hold [shift], then drag the copy of the text frame onto the right page, releasing the mouse button when it snaps into the left column on the right page.
5. Click the Type tool, then draw a small text box anywhere on the left page of the B-Body master.
6. Select the text frame and verify that the top-left reference point is selected on the Transform panel, type **.25** in the X Location text box, type **4.5** in the Y Location text box, type **1.65** in the Width text box, type **.25** in the Height text box, then press [return] (Mac) or [Enter] (Win).
7. Select the Type tool, click in the text frame, click Type on the menu bar, point to Insert Special Character, point to Markers, then click Current Page Number.
8. Click Type on the menu bar, point to Insert Special Character, point to Hyphens and Dashes, then click En Dash.
9. Type the word **Title**.
10. Click the Selection tool, select the text frame, if necessary; click Edit on the menu bar, click Copy, click Edit on the menu bar again, then click Paste in Place.
11. Press and hold [shift], then drag the copy of the text frame so it is positioned in the lower-right corner of the right page of the master page.
12. Open the Paragraph panel, click the Align right button, then delete the B and the dash after the B.

TIP Switch your workspace to Typography to access the Paragraph panel if necessary.

13. Click after the word Title, click Type on the menu bar, point to Insert Special Character, point to Hyphens and Dashes, then click En Dash.
14. Click Type on the menu bar, point to Insert Special Character, point to Markers, then click Current Page Number.

Apply master pages to document pages

1. Double-click the page 2 icon on the Pages panel.
2. Drag the B-Body master page title to the bottom-left corner of the page 2 icon until you see a black rectangle around the page 2 and 3 icons, then release the mouse button.
3. Drag the word B-Body from the top of the Pages panel to the bottom-left corner of the page 4 icon until you see a black rectangle around the page 4 icon, then release the mouse button.
4. Click the Pages panel menu button, then click Apply Master to Pages.
5. Click the Apply Master list arrow; click B-Body, if necessary, type **6–8** in the To Pages text box, then click OK.
6. Double-click the page 2 icon on the Pages panel.
7. Hide guides.

Place and thread text

1. Click File on the menu bar, click Place, navigate to the drive and folder where your Chapter 14 Data Files are stored, then double-click Skills Review Text.
2. Click anywhere in the text frame in the right column on page 2.

3. Click View on the menu bar, point to Extras, then click Show Text Threads.
4. Click the Selection tool, then click the out port of the text frame on page 2.
5. Click the loaded text icon anywhere in the text frame on page 3.

Modify master pages and document pages

1. Double-click the page 6 icon on the Pages panel.
2. Click the bottom-middle reference point on the Transform panel.
3. Click the Selection tool, press and hold or [shift] [command] (Mac) or [Shift] [Ctrl] (Win), then click the large text frame.
4. Type **.3** in the Height text box on the Transform panel, then press [return] (Mac) or [Enter] (Win).
5. Double-click A-Master in the top section of the Pages panel, then select the graphics placeholder frame on the left page.
6. Click the center reference point on the Transform panel.
7. On the Transform panel, type **3** in the Width text box, type **3** in the Height text box, then press [return] (Mac) or [Enter] (Win).

8. Double-click the right page icon of the A-Master on the Pages panel, then select the graphics placeholder frame on the right page.
9. On the Transform panel, type **2** in the Width text box, type **4** in the Height text box, then press [return] (Mac) or [Enter] (Win).
10. View the two right-hand pages on the Pages panel that are based on the A-Master right-hand page to verify that the modifications were updated.
11. Double-click B-Body on the Pages panel, click the Rectangle Frame tool, then create a frame anywhere on the left page of the B-Body master page.
12. Click the center reference point on the Transform panel, then type **2** in the X Location text box, type **2.6** in the Y Location text box, type **2.25** in the Width text box, type **1.5** in the Height text box, then press [return] (Mac) or [Enter] (Win).

Create new sections and wrap text

1. Double-click the page 1 icon on the Pages panel, click the Pages panel menu button, then click Numbering & Section Options.
2. In the Page Numbering section, click the Style list arrow, click the lowercase style letters (a, b, c, d), click OK, then note the changes to the pages on the Pages panel and in the document.

3. Double-click the page e icon on the Pages panel, click the Pages panel menu button, then click Numbering & Section Options.
4. In the Page Numbering section, click the Start Page Numbering at option button, type **5** in the text box, then verify that the Style text box in the Page Numbering section shows ordinary numerals (1, 2, 3, 4). (If it does not, click the Style list arrow, and select that style.)
5. Click OK, then view the pages in the document, noting the new style of the page numbering on the pages and on the Pages panel.
6. Double-click the page b icon on the Pages panel, click the Selection tool, press and hold [shift] [command] (Mac) or [Shift] [Ctrl] (Win), then select the rectangular graphics frame.
7. Click Window on the menu bar, then click Text Wrap.
8. Click the Wrap around bounding box button on the Text Wrap panel.
9. Type **.125** in the Right Offset text box on the Text Wrap panel, then press [return] (Mac) or [Enter] (Win).
10. Click View on the menu bar, click Fit Spread in Window, then click anywhere to deselect any selected items.
11. Compare your screen to Figure 55, save your work, then close the Skills Review document.

Figure 55 Completed Skills Review

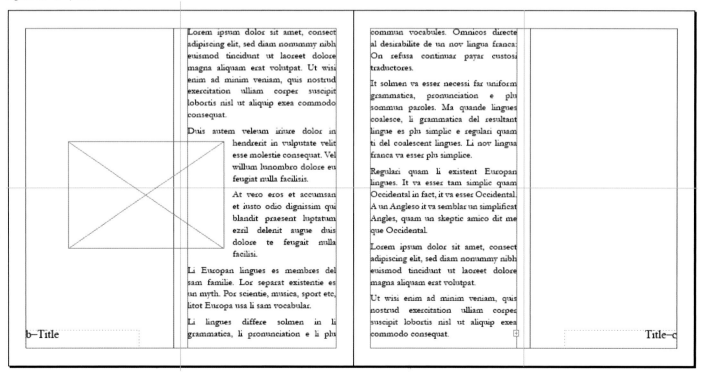

You are a graphic designer working out of your home office. A local investment company has contracted you to design its monthly 16-page newsletter. You've sketched out a design and created a new document at the correct size, and now you need to add automatic page numbering to the document.

1. Open ID 3-3.indd, then save it as **Newsletter**.
2. Double-click A-Master on the Pages panel.
3. Click the Type tool, then draw a text frame about one inch tall and one column wide.
4. Position the text frame at the bottom of the center column, being sure that the bottom edge of the text frame snaps to the bottom margin of the page.
5. Set the Preference settings so the guides are sent to the back of the layout—so all four sides of the text frame are visible.
6. Click the Type tool, then click inside the text box.
7. Click Type on the menu bar, point to Insert Special Character, point to Hyphens and Dashes, then click Em Dash.
8. Click Type on the menu bar, point to Insert Special Character, point to Markers, then click Current Page Number.
9. Click Type on the menu bar, point to Insert Special Character, point to Hyphens and Dashes, then click Em Dash.
10. Select all three text elements, and change their font size to 20 pt.
11. Click the Align center button on the Paragraph panel.
12. Click the dark blue swatch on the Swatches panel.
13. Click the Selection tool, click the bottom-center reference point on the Transform panel, double-click the Height text box on the Transform panel, type **.25**, then press [return] (Mac) or [Enter] (Win).
14. Double-click the page 5 icon on the Pages panel, compare your page 5 to Figure 56, save your work, then close the Newsletter document.

Figure 56 Completed Project Builder 1

You work in the design department for a bank, and you are responsible for creating a new weekly bulletin, which covers various events within the bank's network of branches. You have just finished creating three master pages for the bulletin, and now you are ready to apply the masters to the document pages.

1. Open ID 3-4.indd, then save it as **Bulletin Layout**.
2. Apply the B-Master to pages 2 and 3.
3. Click the Pages panel menu button, then click Apply Master to Pages.
4. Apply the C-Master to pages 4 through 6, then click OK.
5. Place Bulletin text.doc in the text frame on page 1.
6. Select the text frame, click the out port on the text frame, double-click page 2 on the Pages panel, then click anywhere in the text frame on page 2.
7. Thread the remaining text through each page up to and including page 6 in the document.
8. Click the Preview button, deselect any selected items, then compare your page 6 to Figure 57.
9. Save your work, then close the Bulletin Layout document.

Figure 57 Completed Project Builder 2

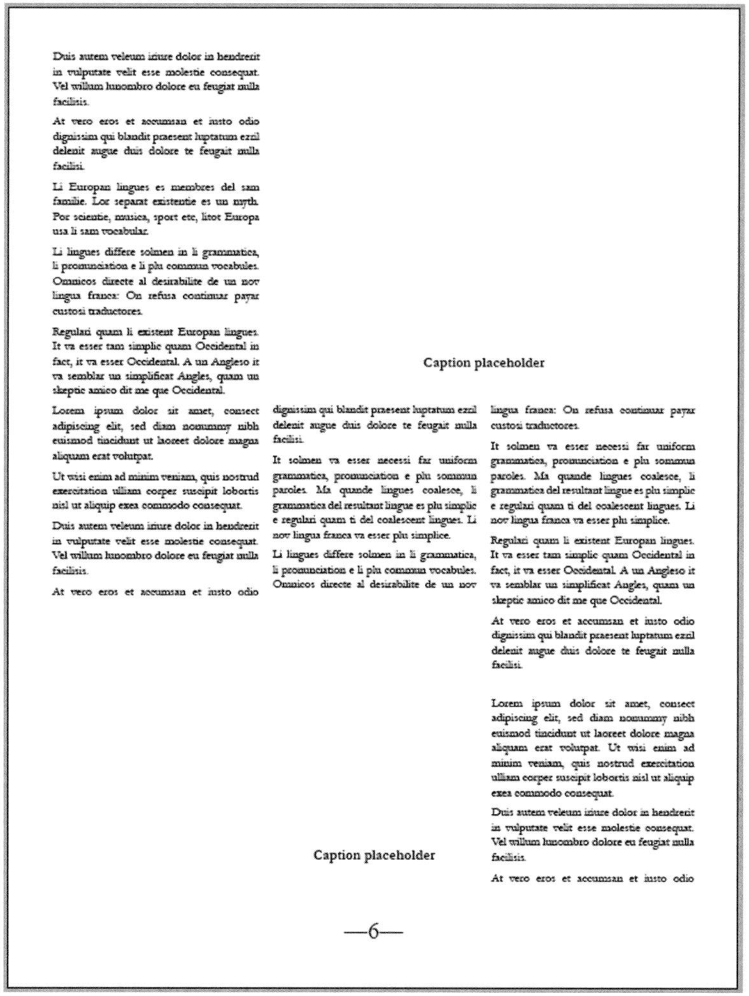

In this project, you're going to work on a fun puzzle that will test your problem-solving skills when using X and Y locations. You will open an InDesign document with two pages. On the first page are four 1-inch squares at each corner of the page. On the second page, the four 1-inch squares appear again—this time forming a large red square that is positioned at the exact center of the 7.75-inch × 7.75-inch document page. Looking at the second page, your challenge will be to write down the X and Y coordinates of each of the four boxes at the center of the page. Then, you will test out your answers with the boxes on the first page.

Setup

1. Open ID 3-5.indd, then save it as **Center Squares**.
2. On page 1, verify that each red square is 1" × 1", then deselect all.
3. Go to page 2, then press [tab] to hide all panels.
4. Do not select any of the squares at the center.
5. Write down what you think is the X/Y coordinate of the top-left point of the top-left square.
6. Write down what you think is the X/Y coordinate of the top-right point of the top-right square.
7. Write down what you think is the X/Y coordinate of the bottom-right point of the bottom-right square.
8. Write down what you think is the X/Y coordinate of the center point of the bottom-left square.
9. Press [tab] to show all hidden panels.

10. Go to page 1, select the top-left square, then click the top-left reference point on the Transform panel.
11. Enter the X/Y coordinates that you wrote down for this point, then press [return] (Mac) or [Enter] (Win).

12. Using the same method, test out the X/Y coordinates you wrote down for the other three squares.

TIP Be sure to click the appropriate reference point on the Transform panel for each of the three remaining squares.

13. When you are done, does your page 1 match page 2 exactly as shown in Figure 58?

Figure 58 Completed Project Builder 3

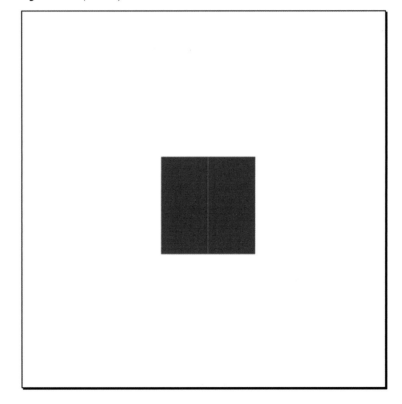

DESIGN PROJECT

This Design Project is based on the layouts you worked with in this chapter. This is your opportunity to create your own five-page layout of a five-city tour, similar to the one you created in this chapter.

1. Use Figure 12 in this chapter as a reference for the document you will create.
2. Choose five cities from anywhere in the world to profile in your document.
3. Go online and search for images that you can work with. For each city, find one photo that you can use as the large, dominant image for its page, then find at least three images you can use as smaller, secondary or support images.
4. Decide what your five-page document is. Is it a brochure, a magazine, a series of postcards, a five-page website?
5. Decide the shape and trim size of your document. Is it wider than it is tall or taller than it is wide? Or is it square? Decide the exact size for the finished document.
6. Create a new five-page document, then name it **Five Cities**.
   Note that for this project you will work with five single pages as opposed to five two-page spreads.
7. Using the skills you learned in the chapter, build a master page for your first layout.
8. Choose typefaces you want to use for your headlines, body copy, and captions.
9. Layout frames for your dominant image and for your supporting images.
10. Layout text frames for your headlines, body copy, and captions.
11. Create blocks of color for the page.
12. Use automatic page numbering for each page design.
13. Create at least two new master page versions of the layout based on the first master you designed.
14. Apply different masters to the five-page document.
15. When you are done, you should have your own original design based on the file named "Setup" that you created in the chapter.
16. Save your work, then close the Five Cities document.

Flowers
of the Desert

Lorem ipsum dolor sit amet, consect adipiscing elit, sed diam nonummy nibh euismod tincidunt ut laoreet dolore magna aliquam erat volutpat. Ut wisi enim ad minim veniam, quis nostrud exercitation ulliam corper suscipit lobortis nisl ut aliquip exea commodo consequat.

Duis autem veleum iriure dolor in hendrerit in vulputate velit esse molestie consequat. Vel willum lunombro dolore eu feugiat nulla facilisis. At vero eros et accumsan et iusto odio dignissim qui blandit praesent luptatum ezril delenit augue duis dolore te feugait nulla facilisi.

Li Europan lingues es membres del sam familie. Lor separat existentie es un myth. Por scientie, musica, sport etc, litot Europa usa li sam vocabular. Li lingues differe solmen in li grammatica, li pronunciation e li plu commun vocabules. Omnicos directe al desirabilite de un nov lingua franca: On refusa continuar payar custosi traductores.

At solmen va esser necessi far uniform grammatica, pronunciation e plu sommun paroles. Ma quande lingues coalesce, li grammatica del resultant lingue es plu simplic e regulari quam ti del coalescent lingues. Li nov lingua franca va esser plu simplice.

Regulari quam li existent Europan lingues. It va esser tam simplic quam Occidental in fact, it va esser Occidental. A un Angleso it va semblar un simplificat Angles, quam un skeptic

amico dit me que Occidental.

Lorem ipsum dolor sit amet, consect adipiscing elit, sed diam nonummy nibh euismod tincidunt ut laoreet dolore magna aliquam erat volutpat. Ut wisi enim ad minim veniam, quis nostrud exercitation ulliam corper suscipit lobortis nisl ut aliquip exea commodo consequat. Duis autem veleum iriure dolor in hendrerit in vulputate velit esse molestie consequat. Vel willum lunombro dolore eu feugiat nulla facilisis.

A windmill garden is a kite flyer's dream come true.

At vero eros et accumsan et iusto odio dignissim qui blandit praesent luptatum ezril delenit augue duis dolore te feugait nulla facilisi. Li lingues differe solmen in li grammatica, li pronunciation e li plu commun vocabules. Omnicos directe al desirabilite de un nov lingua franca: On refusa continuar payar custosi traductores.

Et solmen va esser necessi far uniform grammatica, pronunciation e plu sommun paroles. Ma quande lingues coalesce, li grammatica del resultant lingue es plu simplic e regulari quam ti del coalescent lingues. Li nov lingua franca va esser plu simplice. Regulari quam li existent Europan lingues. It va esser tam simplic quam Occidental in fact, it va esser Occidental. A un Angleso it va semblar un simplificat Angles, quam un skeptic amico dit me que Occidental.

Lorem ipsum dolor sit amet, consect adipiscing elit, sed diam nonummy nibh euismod tincidunt ut laoreet dolore magna aliquam erat volutpat. Ut wisi enim ad minim veniam, quis nostrud exercitation ulliam corper suscipit lobortis nisl ut aliquip exea commodo consequat.

WORK WITH FRAMES

1. Align and Distribute Objects on a Page
2. Stack and Layer Objects
3. Work with Graphics Frames
4. Work with Text Frames

CERTIFIED PROFESSIONAL

Adobe Certified Professional in Print & Digital Media Publication Using Adobe InDesign

1. Working in the Design Industry

This objective covers critical concepts related to working with colleagues and clients as well as crucial legal, technical, and design-related knowledge.

1.4 Demonstrate knowledge of key terminology related to publications.
    C Understand and use key terms related to multipage layouts.

2. Project Setup and Interface

This objective covers the interface setup and program settings that assist in an efficient and effective workflow, as well as knowledge about ingesting digital assets for a project.

2.4 Import assets into a project.
    B Place assets in an InDesign document.

2.5 Manage colors, swatches, and gradients.
    A Set the active fill and stroke color.

3. Organizing Documents

This objective covers document structure such as layers, tracks, and managing document structure for efficient workflows.

3.1 Use layers to manage design elements.
    A Use the Layers panel to modify layers.
    B Manage and work with multiple layers in a complex project.

4. Creating and Modifying Document Elements

This objective covers core tools and functionality of the application, as well as tools that affect the visual appearance of document elements.

4.1 Use core tools and features to lay out visual elements.
    A Create frames using a variety of tools.
    B Manipulate graphics in frames.

4.2 Add and manipulate text using appropriate typographic settings.
    E Manage text flow across multiple text areas.
    F Use tools to add special characters or content.

4.3 Make, manage, and edit selections.
    A Make selections using a variety of tools.
    B Modify and refine selections using various methods.

4.4 Transform digital graphics and media within a publication.
    A Modify frames and frame content.
    B Rotate, flip, and transform individual frames or content.

4.5 Use basic reconstructing and editing techniques to manipulate document content.
    C Use the Story Editor to edit text within a project.

ALIGN AND DISTRIBUTE OBJECTS ON A PAGE

▶ *What You'll Do*

In this lesson, you will explore various techniques for positioning objects in specific relationships to one another.

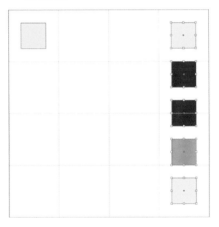

Applying Fills and Strokes

A **fill** is a color you apply to the inside of an object. A **stroke** is a color that you apply to the outline of an object. Figure 1 shows an object with a blue fill and a yellow stroke.

InDesign offers you many options for filling and stroking objects. The simplest and most direct method for doing so is to select an object and then pick a color from the Swatches panel. The color that you choose on the Swatches panel will be applied to the selected object as a fill or as a stroke, depending on whether the fill or the stroke button is activated on the toolbar.

Figure 1 An object with a fill and a stroke

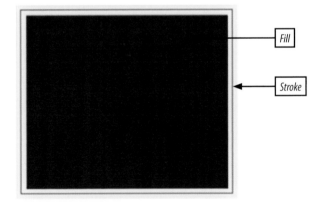

Fill

Stroke

To activate either the fill or the stroke button, click it once on the toolbar. The fill button is activated when it is in front of the stroke button, as shown in Figure 2. When the fill button is activated, clicking a swatch on the Swatches panel applies that swatch color as a fill to the selected object(s). When the stroke button is activated, as shown in Figure 3, the swatch color is applied as a stroke.

Once a stroke is applied, you can modify the **stroke weight**—how heavy the outline appears—using the Stroke panel. The Stroke panel is command central for all the modifications you can apply to a stroke, including making dotted and dashed strokes and varying stroke styles.

The Align Stroke section of the Stroke panel is critical for determining *where* on the object the stroke is applied. By default, a stroke is aligned to the center of the object's perimeter. This means that it's centered on the edge, halfway inside and halfway outside the object. For example, if you apply a 10 pt. stroke to a rectangle, five points of the stroke will be inside the object, and five points will be outside.

Figure 2 Fill is activated

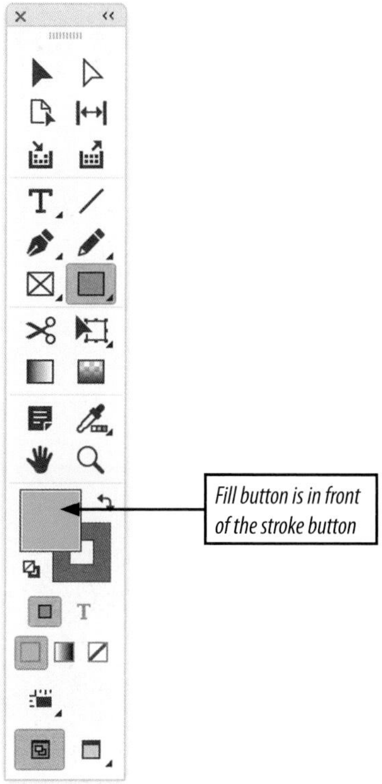

Fill button is in front of the stroke button

Figure 3 Stroke is activated

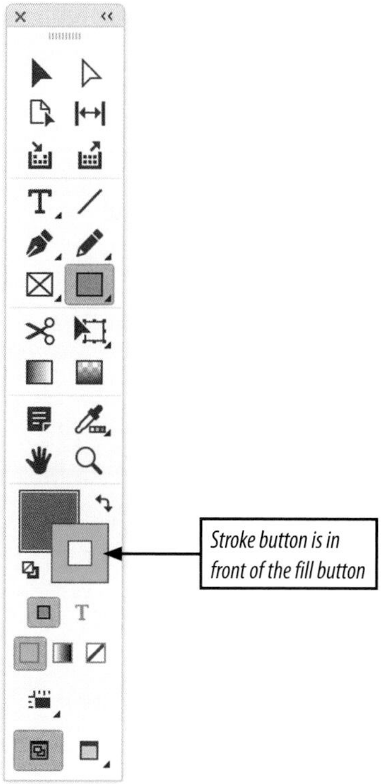

Stroke button is in front of the fill button

The Stroke panel offers three Align Stroke options: Align Stroke to Center, Align Stroke to Inside, and Align Stroke to Outside. Figure 4 shows three 2" × 2" frames with three different 10 pt. stroke alignments. Note that the object is different sizes in all three. In the first, the 2" × 2" frame is increased by 0.5 pt. on all sides because the stroke is centered. In the second, the frame with the 10 pt. stroke is 2" × 2" because the stroke is aligned to the inside. The third is the largest object, a 2" × 2" frame increased by 10 points on all sides, because the stroke is aligned to the outside.

Using the Step and Repeat Command

Many times, when laying out a page, you will want to create multiple objects that are evenly spaced in lines or in grids. InDesign offers many great utilities for accomplishing this, one of which is the Step and Repeat dialog box, as shown in Figure 5.

Figure 4 A 10 pt. stroke with three different alignments

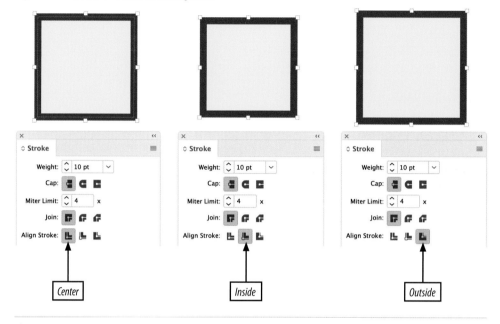

Figure 5 Step and Repeat dialog box

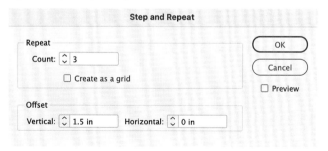

Before you choose the Step and Repeat command, you need to decide which objects you want to copy and how many copies of it you want to create. After selecting the object, choose Step and Repeat on the Edit menu. In the Step and Repeat dialog box, you choose the number of copies. You also specify the offset value for each successive copy. The **offset** is the horizontal and vertical distance the copy will be from the original.

TIP Click the Preview check box to see transformations before you execute them.

Figure 6 shows an original 1-inch square frame and three copies created using the Step and Repeat command. The horizontal offset is two inches, and the vertical offset is two inches. Thus, each copy is two inches to the right and two inches down from the previous copy.

Note that positive and negative offset values create copies in specific directions. On the horizontal axis, a positive value creates copies to the right of the original; a negative value creates copies to the left of the original. On the vertical axis, a positive value creates copies *below* the original; a negative value creates copies above the original. Figure 7 is a handy guide for remembering the result of positive and negative offset values.

Figure 6 Copying a frame with the Step and Repeat dialog box

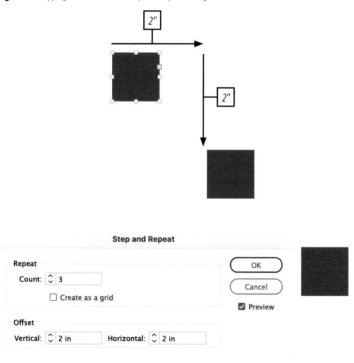

Figure 7 Understanding positive and negative offset values

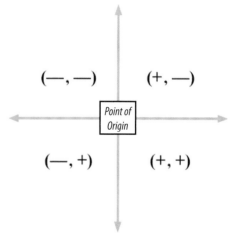

Use the vertical ruler on the left side of the document page to remember positive and negative values on the vertical axis. You are used to thinking of positive as up and negative as down, but remember that in InDesign, the default (0, 0) coordinate is in the top-left corner of the page. On the ruler, positive numbers *increase* as you move *down* the ruler.

Aligning Objects

The Align panel offers quick and simple solutions for aligning and distributing multiple objects on a page. To **align** objects is to position them by their tops, bottoms, left sides, right sides, or centers. To **distribute** objects is to space them equally on a page horizontally, vertically, or both. Using the top section of the Align panel, you can choose from six alignment buttons, shown in Figure 8.

Each option includes an icon that represents the resulting layout of the selected objects, after the button has been clicked. Figure 9 shows three objects placed randomly on the page. Figure 10 shows the same three objects after clicking the Align left edges button. Note that only the red and green boxes moved to align with the blue object. This is because the blue object was originally the leftmost object. Clicking the Align left edges button aligns all selected objects with the leftmost object.

Figure 11 shows the original three objects after clicking the Align top edges button. The red and yellow boxes move up so their tops are aligned with the top of the blue box.

TIP The Align panel has four choices for aligning objects. In addition to aligning objects using the boundaries of the selection, you can also align one or more objects to the page, margins, or spread.

Figure 8 Align Objects section of the Align panel

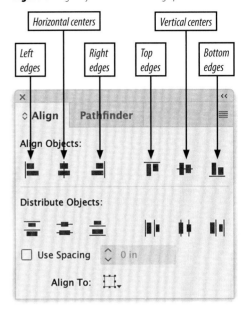

Figure 9 Three objects not aligned

Figure 10 Objects aligned with the Align left edges button

Figure 11 Objects aligned at their top edges

Distributing Objects

You use the Distribute Objects section of the Align panel to distribute objects. To distribute objects is to space them equally in relation to one another.

Figure 12 shows three objects that are not distributed evenly on either the horizontal or vertical axis. Figure 13 shows the same three objects after clicking the Distribute horizontal centers button. Clicking this button means that—on the horizontal axis— the distance between the center point of the first object and the center point of the second object is the same as the distance between the center point of the second object and the center point of the third object.

Figure 14 shows the same three objects after clicking the Distribute vertical centers button. Clicking this button means that—on the vertical axis—the distance between the center points of the first two objects is the same as the distance between the center points of the second and third objects.

Figure 12 Three objects randomly positioned

Figure 13 Horizontal centers distributed evenly

Figure 14 Horizontal and vertical centers distributed evenly

Using the Live Distribute Technique

When you select multiple objects, a bounding box appears around the objects. As you already know, you can drag the handles of that bounding box to transform all the selected objects. The Live Distribute option offers a different behavior. Instead of resizing the objects, you can use the Live Distribute option to proportionally resize the *space between* the objects.

To access the Live Distribute option, select multiple objects, start dragging a bounding box handle and then hold [space bar] as you drag. The spaces between the objects will be resized, and the alignment of the objects will change depending on where and in what direction you drag.

Figure 15 shows 20 frames aligned in a grid. Figure 16 shows the same 20 frames modified with the Live Distribute option. Note that the frames haven't changed size—only the space between them has changed.

Figure 15 Twenty frames

Images courtesy of Chris Botello

Figure 16 Space between frames increased proportionately with the Live Distribute option

Using the Gap Tool

When you're working with multiple objects, the Gap tool offers a quick way to adjust the size of the gaps between them. It also allows you to resize several items that have commonly aligned edges at once while maintaining the size of the gaps between them. Think of it this way: the Gap tool moves the gap.

Figure 17 shows a grid of 12 frames with the Gap tool positioned over the center gap. The shaded area indicates the length of the gap that will be modified by the tool. Figure 18 shows the result of dragging the Gap tool to the left. Note that only the gap moved; the size of the gap didn't change. The width of the associated frames changed.

You can use the Gap tool while pressing and holding various keys to perform other tasks as well, as shown in Table 1.

Figure 17 Gap tool positioned over a grid of frames

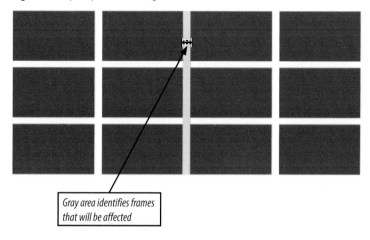

Gray area identifies frames that will be affected

Figure 18 Result of dragging the Gap tool to the left

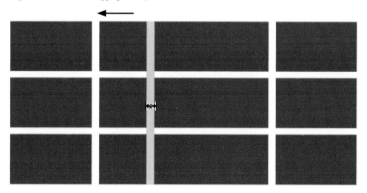

TABLE 1: GAP TOOL BEHAVIORS AND KEYBOARD COMBINATIONS		
Mac	**Win**	**Behavior**
[shift]	[Shift]	Affects the gap only between the two items nearest to the cursor
[command]	[Ctrl]	Increases the width and height of the gap
[option]	[Alt]	Moves the items with the gap instead of resizing the items

Align a stroke on an object

1. Open ID 4-1.indd, then save it as **Orientation**.

2. Verify that **guides** are showing.

3. Click the **workspace switcher list arrow** on the menu bar, then click **[Advanced]**.

4. Click the **Rectangle tool** ▢ , then click anywhere on the page.

TIP When a shape tool is selected on the toolbar, clicking the document window opens the tool's dialog box, where you can enter values that determine the size of the resulting object.

5. Type **2** in the **Width text box**, type **2** in the **Height text box**, then click **OK**.

   A 2" square appears on the page.

6. Switch to the **Selection tool** ▶ .

7. Fill the **square** with **Green**.

8. Stroke the **square** with **Brick Red**.

9. On the Stroke panel, type **6** in the **Weight text box**, then press **[return] (Mac) or [Enter] (Win)**.

10. Click the **Align Stroke to Outside button** ▣ .

    Note on the Control panel that adding the stroke has changed the width and height measurements of the 2" square. It is now 2.1667" because of the 6 pt. stroke positioned outside of the original frame.

11. Click the **Align Stroke to Inside button** ▣ .

    The dimension of the square is once again 2" because the stroke is completely inside the frame.

12. Click the **Align Stroke to Center button** ▣ .

The dimension of the square changes to 2.0833.

13. Click the **top-left reference point** on the Control panel, type **0** in the **X** and **Y text boxes**, then press **[return] (Mac)** or **[Enter] (Win)**.

    The top-left corner of the square with the red stroke is positioned at the top-left corner of the artboard.

14. Save your work, then continue to the next set of steps.

You created a square using the Rectangle dialog box. You then used the Swatches panel to choose a fill color and a stroke color for the square frame. You chose a weight for the stroke and tested three options for aligning the stroke, noting that the positioning of the stroke changed the dimensions of the square. Finally, you used the Control panel to position the square at the top-left corner of the page.

Use the Step and Repeat command

1. Make sure the **green square** is still selected, then change the **stroke color** to **[None]**.

   With the stroke removed, the green square is no longer exactly at the 0X/0Y coordinate at the top-left corner of the artboard.

2. Use the Control panel to position the **top-left corner of the frame** at the **0X/0Y coordinate**.

3. Click **Edit** on the menu bar, then click **Step and Repeat**.

4. Verify that the **Horizontal** and **Vertical text boxes** are set to **0** on the Control panel, type **3** in the **Repeat Count text box**, type **2** in the **Vertical Offset text box**, type **2** in the **Horizontal Offset text box**, then click **OK**.

   Three new squares are created, each one 2" to the right 2" down from the previous one, as shown in Figure 19.

5. Click the **Selection tool** ▶ , then click anywhere on the pasteboard to deselect.

6. Select the **top two squares,** click **Edit** on the menu bar, then click **Step and Repeat**.

7. Type **1** in the **Repeat Count text box**, type **0** in the **Vertical Offset text box**, type **4** in the **Horizontal Offset text box**, then click **OK**.

8. Select the **bottom two squares** on the page, click **Edit** on the menu bar, then click **Step and Repeat**.

9. Type **1** in the **Repeat Count text box**, type **0** in the **Vertical Offset text box**, type **−4** in the **Horizontal Offset text box**, then click **OK**.

10. Click anywhere to deselect the new squares, then compare your page to Figure 20.

11. Save your work, then continue to the next set of steps.

You used the Step and Repeat command to create a checkerboard pattern, duplicating a single square seven times.

Figure 19 Viewing results of the Step and Repeat command

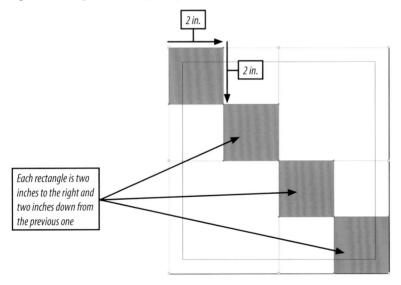

2 in.

2 in.

Each rectangle is two inches to the right and two inches down from the previous one

Figure 20 Checkerboard created using the Step and Repeat command

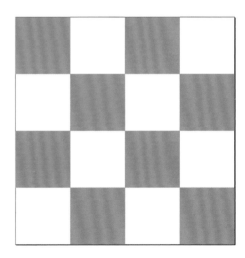

Use the Live Distribute technique

1. Select all, copy, then paste in place.

2. Click the **center reference point** on the Control panel, type **90** in the **Rotation Angle text box** on the Control panel, then press **[return] (Mac)** or **[Enter] (Win)**.

3. Verify that the **fill button is in front** on the toolbar, click **Dark Blue** on the Swatches panel, then compare your screen to Figure 21.

4. Select all, press and hold **[shift] [option] (Mac)** or **[Shift] [Alt] (Win)**, then click and drag the **upper-right handle of the bounding box** toward the center of the page, releasing the mouse button when your checkerboard resembles Figure 22.

   The objects are scaled from their center point.

5. Click and drag the **upper-right corner of the bounding box** toward the **upper-right corner of the document**; then, while you are still dragging, press and hold **[space bar]**.

   When you press [space bar] while dragging, the Live Distribute option is enabled. The space between the objects is modified—larger or smaller—depending on the direction in which you drag.

6. With the **[space bar]** still pressed, drag the **handle** in different directions on the document.

   Regardless of the direction you drag, the frames do not change size or shape—only the space between the frames changes.

7. With the **[space bar]** still pressed, press and hold **[shift] [option] (Mac)** or **[Shift] [Alt] (Win)**, then drag the **handle** to the **upper-right corner of the document** and release the mouse button.

   Pressing and holding [space bar] [shift] [option] (Mac) or [space bar] [Shift] [Alt] (Win) when dragging enlarges the space between the frames in proportion from the center. Your page should resemble Figure 23.

Figure 21 Viewing the complete checkerboard

Figure 22 Scaling the checkerboard in a standard manner

Figure 23 Expanding the space between frames with Live Distribute

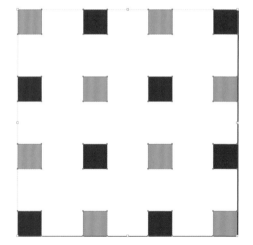

8. Begin dragging the **upper-right handle** of the bounding box slowly toward the **center of the document**.

9. As you're dragging, press **[space bar]** to activate Live Distribute, then press **[shift] [option] (Mac)** or **[Shift] [Alt] (Win)** and continue dragging toward the **center** until your artwork resembles Figure 24.

10. Deselect all, then save your work.

11. Continue to the next set of steps.

You pasted and rotated a copy of the squares to create a complete checkerboard. You selected all the frames, then dragged a bounding box handle to reduce all the objects in a standard manner. You then used the Live Distribute technique to modify the space between the objects.

Use the Gap tool

1. Click the **Gap tool** ⊷ on the toolbar.

2. Position the **Gap tool** ⊷ over the **middle-vertical gap**, then click and drag left so your grid resembles Figure 25.

3. Position the **Gap tool** ⊷ over the **bottom-horizontal gap**, then click and drag up so your grid resembles Figure 26.

4. Position the **Gap tool** ⊷ over the **gap between the top two frames in the upper-right corner**, press and hold **[shift]**, then click and drag to the left so your grid resembles Figure 27.

Continued on next page

Figure 24 Reducing the space between frames with Live Distribute

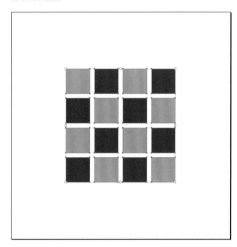

Figure 25 Moving the vertical gap

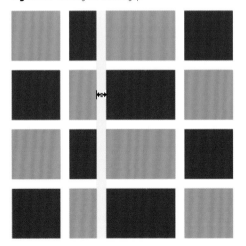

Figure 26 Moving the horizontal gap

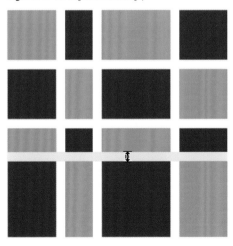

Figure 27 Moving the gap only between two rectangles

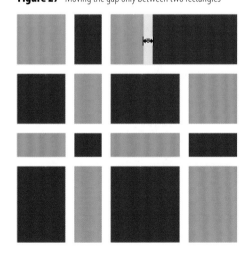

5. Press and hold **[command] (Mac)** or **[Ctrl] (Win)** then click and drag the **left edge** of the grid to the left.

The width of the four frames on the left is increased.

6. Press and hold **[option] (Mac)** or **[Alt] (Win)** to position the **Gap tool**  over the **bottom-horizontal gap**, then click and drag down.

As shown in Figure 28, the frames on both sides of the gap move. Neither the frames nor the gap are resized—only relocated.

7. Save your work, then close the Orientation document.

You used the Gap tool with various key combinations to affect the gaps in a grid of frames.

Align objects

1. Open ID 4-2.indd, then save it as **Alignment**.

2. Click **Window** on the menu bar, point to **Object & Layout,** then click **Align**.

The Align panel opens.

3. Press **[command] [A] (Mac)** or **[Ctrl] [A] (Win)** to select all **three objects** on the page, then click the **Align left edges button** in the Align Objects section of the Align panel.

The frames are aligned to the leftmost of the three.

4. Click **Edit** on the menu bar, then click **Undo Align**.

5. Click the **Align top edges button** on the Align panel.

As shown in Figure 29, the top edges of the three frames are aligned to the topmost of the three.

6. Undo the previous step, then click the **Align horizontal centers button**.

7. Click the **Align vertical centers button**.

The three frames are stacked, one on top of the other, their center points are aligned both horizontally and vertically.

8. Save your work, then close the Alignment document.

You used the buttons in the Align Objects section of the Align panel to reposition frames with various alignments.

Figure 28 Moving frames with the Gap tool

Figure 29 Aligning three objects by their top edges

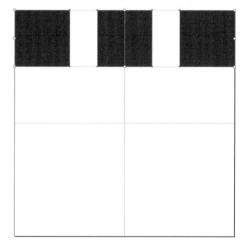

Distribute objects

1. Open ID 4-3.indd, then save it as **Distribution**.
2. Verify that **guides** are showing.
3. Select the **top two yellow squares** and the **two red squares,** then click the **Align top edges button** in the Align Objects section of the Align panel.

   The four objects are aligned by their top edges.

4. Click the **Distribute horizontal centers button** in the Distribute Objects section of the Align panel.

The center points of the two red squares are distributed evenly on the horizontal axis between the center points of the two yellow squares, as shown in Figure 30.

5. Click **Edit** on the menu bar, click **Deselect All**, select the **top-left yellow square**, select the **two red squares**, then select the **bottom-right yellow square**.
6. Click the **Distribute vertical centers button**, then compare your screen to Figure 31.
7. Select the **green square**, the **two red squares**, and the **bottom yellow square**, then click the **Align right edges button** .
8. Press and hold **[shift]**, then click the **top-right yellow square** to add it to the selection.
9. Click the **Distribute vertical centers button** .

   The center points of the five squares are distributed evenly on the vertical axis, as shown in Figure 32.

10. Save your work, then close the Distribution document.

You spaced objects evenly on the horizontal and vertical axes.

Figure 30 Distributing objects evenly on the horizontal axis

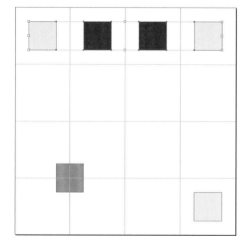

Figure 31 Distributing 4 objects evenly on the vertical axis

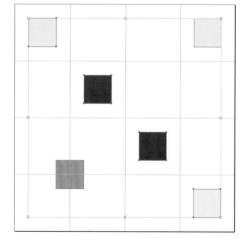

Figure 32 Distributing 5 objects evenly on the vertical axis

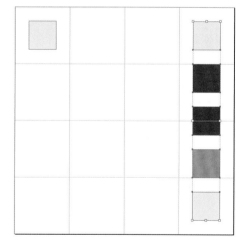

STACK AND LAYER OBJECTS

▶ *What You'll Do*

In this lesson, you will manipulate the stacking order of objects on the page, and you'll use the Layers panel to control how objects are layered.

Understanding the Stacking Order

The **stacking order** refers to how objects are arranged in hierarchical order. When you create multiple objects, it is important for you to remember that every object is on its own level. For example, if you draw a square frame, and then draw a circle frame, the circle frame is automatically created one level in front of the square, whether or not they overlap. If they did overlap, the circle would appear in front of the square.

TIP Use the word "level" when discussing the hierarchy of the stacking order, not the word "layer," which has its own specific meaning in InDesign.

You control the stacking order with the four commands on the Arrange menu. The Bring to Front command moves a selected object to the front of the stacking order. The Send to Back command moves a selected object to the back of the stacking order. The Bring Forward command moves a selected object one level forward in the stacking order, and the Send

Backward command moves a selected object one level backward in the stacking order.

Using these four commands, you can control and arrange how every object on the page overlaps other objects.

Understanding Layers

The Layers panel is a smart solution for organizing and managing elements of a layout. The Layers panel in InDesign is very similar to the Layers panel in Adobe Illustrator. It includes options for locking and hiding individual objects on a layer.

By default, every document you create in InDesign has one layer. You can create new layers and give them descriptive names to help you identify a layer's content. For example, if you were working on a layout that contained both text and graphics, you might want to create a layer for all the text frames called Text and create another layer for all the graphics called Graphics.

Why would you do this? Well, for one reason, you can lock layers on the Layers panel. Locking a layer makes its contents non-editable until you unlock it. In the example, you could lock the Text layer while you work on the graphic elements of the layout. By doing so, you can be certain that you won't make any inadvertent changes to the text elements. Another reason is that you can hide layers. You could temporarily hide the Text layer, thus providing yourself a working view of the graphics that is unobstructed by the text elements.

You can also duplicate layers. You do so by clicking the Duplicate Layer command on the Layers panel menu or by dragging a layer on top of the Create new layer icon on the Layers panel. When you duplicate a layer, all the objects on the original layer are duplicated and will appear in their same locations on the new layer.

Layers are a smart, important solution for organizing your work and improving your workflow, especially for complex layouts. Invest some time in learning layers—it will pay off with lots of saved time and fewer headaches.

Working with Layers

You can create as many layers on the Layers panel as you need to organize your work. Figure 33 shows the Layers panel with three layers. Notice the lock icon on Layer 2. The lock icon indicates that this layer cannot be edited. All objects on Layer 2 are locked. Clicking the lock icon will unlock the layer, and the lock icon will disappear.

Think of layers on the Layers panel as being three-dimensional. The topmost layer is the front layer; the bottommost layer is the back layer. Therefore, it follows logically that objects on the topmost layer are *in front* of objects on any other layer. Layers themselves are transparent. If you have a layer with no objects on it, you can see through the layer to the objects on the layers behind it.

Note that each layer contains its own stacking order. Let's say that you have three layers, each with five objects on it. Regardless of the stacking order of the top layer, all the objects on that layer are in front of any objects on the other layers. In other words, an object at the back of the stacking order of the top layer is still in front of any object on any layer beneath it.

Figure 33 Layers panel with three layers

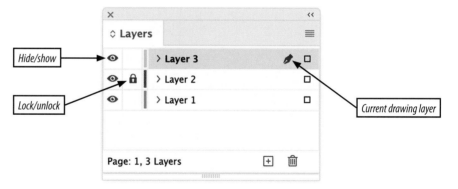

Hide/show

Lock/unlock

Current drawing layer

> Layer 3
> Layer 2
> Layer 1

Page: 1, 3 Layers

One great organizational aspect of layers is that you can assign a selection color to a layer. When you select an object, its bounding box and selection marks appear in the selection color of the layer on which it is placed, as shown in Figure 34.

You determine a layer's selection color by selecting the layer, clicking the Layers panel menu button, clicking Layer Options for the name of the selected layer, then choosing a new color from the Color menu. When you are working with a layout that contains numerous objects, this feature is a great visual aid for keeping track of objects and their relationships to other objects.

Manipulating Layers and Objects on Layers

Once you have created layers in a document, you have many options for manipulating objects on the layers and the layers themselves. You can move objects between layers, and you can reorder the layers on the Layers panel.

Clicking a layer on the Layers panel to select it is called **targeting** a layer. The layer you click is called the **target layer**. When you create a new object, the object will be added to whichever layer is targeted on the Layers panel. The pen tool icon next to the layer name is called the Current drawing layer icon. This icon will help remind you that anything placed or drawn will become part of that layer.

Figure 34 The selection color for objects on the layer

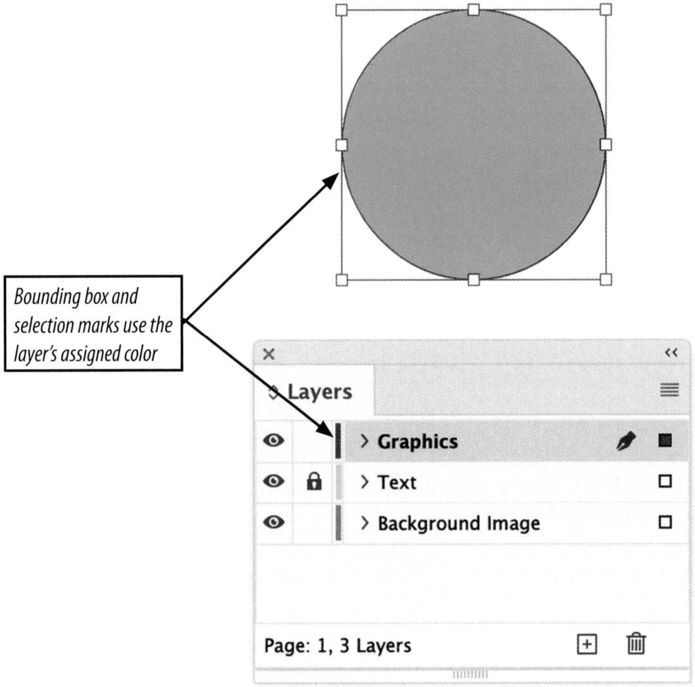

Bounding box and selection marks use the layer's assigned color

You can select any object on the page, regardless of which layer is targeted. When you select the object, the layer that the object is on is automatically targeted on the Layers panel.

When one or more objects are selected, a small, square icon on the far right of a layer on the Layers panel fills with color to show that items on the layer are selected as shown in Figure 35. The selected items button represents the selected objects. When you click and drag the selected items button and move it to another layer, the selected objects move to that layer. Therefore, you should never feel constrained by the layers you have chosen for objects; it's easy to move them from one layer to another.

You can also change the order of layers on the Layers panel by dragging a layer up or down on the panel. As you drag, a heavy black line indicates the new position for the layer when you release the mouse button.

Selecting Artwork on Layers

Let's say you have three layers in your document, each with six objects. That means your document has a total of 18 objects. If you apply the Select All command on the Edit menu, all 18 objects will be selected, regardless of which layer is targeted on the Layers panel.

In many situations, you'll want to select all the objects on one layer only. The easiest way to do this is with the selected items button. Even when nothing is selected, the button is available

Figure 35 The selected items button

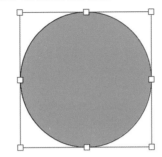

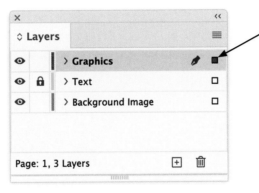

Indicates that items on this layer are selected

on every layer—as a hollow square. Click that button, and all objects on that layer will be selected. This is a powerful and useful option—make note of it.

Selecting Objects Behind Other Objects

When you have multiple overlapping objects on a page, objects behind other objects can sometimes be difficult to select. Pressing and

holding [command] (Mac) or [Ctrl] (Win) allows you to "click through the stacking order" to select objects behind other objects. Simply click the top object, press and hold [command] (Mac) or [Ctrl] (Win), then click the top object again; this will select the object immediately behind it. Click the top object again, and the next object down in the stacking order will be selected.

Use the Arrange commands to change the stacking order of objects

1. Open ID 4-4.indd, then save it as **Stack and Layer**.

2. Press **[V]** to access the **Selection tool** 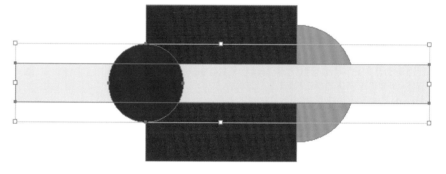, then click the **yellow rectangle**.

3. Click **Object** on the menu bar, point to **Arrange**, then click **Bring Forward**.

   The yellow rectangle moves forward one level in the stacking order.

4. Click the **red square**, click **Object** on the menu bar, point to **Arrange**, then click **Bring to Front**.

5. Select both the **yellow rectangle** and the **blue circle**, click **Object** on the menu bar, point to **Arrange**, then click **Bring to Front**.

   Both objects move in front of the red square, as shown in Figure 36.

6. Click the **green circle**, click **Object** on the menu bar, point to **Arrange**, then click **Bring to Front**.

7. Select all, then click the **Align horizontal centers button** on the Align panel.

   The blue circle is completely behind the green circle.

8. Deselect all, then click the **center of the green circle**.

9. Press and hold **[command] (Mac)** or **[Ctrl] (Win)**, then click the **center of the green circle** again.

   The blue circle behind the green circle is selected.

10. Click **Object** on the menu bar, point to **Arrange**, then click **Bring Forward**.

As shown in Figure 37, the blue circle moves forward one level in the stacking order, in front of the green circle.

11. Deselect all, select the **blue circle,** press and hold **[command] (Mac)** or **[Ctrl] (Win)**, then click the **blue circle center** again to select the green circle behind it.

12. Still pressing and holding **[command] (Mac)** or **[Ctrl] (Win)**, click the **blue circle center** again to select the yellow rectangle, then click the **blue circle center** once more to select the red square.

TIP Commit this selection technique to memory, as it is useful for selecting overlapping objects.

13. Save your work, then close the Stack and Layer document.

You used the Arrange commands to manipulate the stacking order of four objects.

Figure 36 Using the Bring to Front command with two objects selected

Figure 37 Sending the green circle backward one level in the stacking order

Create new layers on the Layers panel

1. Open ID 4-5.indd, save it as **Layers Intro,** then click **Layers** in the stack of collapsed panels to open the Layers panel.

   The Layers panel has one default layer named Layer 1. All the objects on the spread are on Layer 1.

2. Double-click **Layer 1** on the Layers panel.

   The Layer Options dialog box opens. In this box, you can change settings for Layer 1, such as its name and selection color.

3. Type **Tints** in the Name text box, then click **OK**.

4. Click the **Create new layer button** ⊞ on the Layers panel, then double-click **Layer 2**.

5. Type **Images** in the Name text box, click the **Color list arrow**, click **Orange**, then click **OK**.

6. Click the **Layers panel menu button** ≡ , then click **New Layer**.

7. Type **Text** in the Name text box, click the **Color list arrow**, click **Purple**, then click **OK**.

   Your Layers panel should resemble Figure 38.

8. Save your work, then continue to the next set of steps.

You renamed Layer 1, then created two new layers on the Layers panel.

Figure 38 Layers panel with three layers

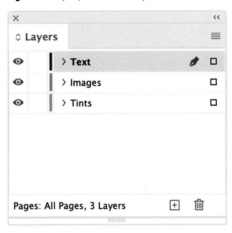

Position objects on layers

1. Press **[V]** to access the **Selection tool** ▶, then select all **seven images** on the spread.

   The Tints layer on the Layers panel is highlighted, and the selected items button ☐ appears next to the layer name.

2. Click and drag the **selected items button** ☐ from the **Tints layer** up to the **Images layer**.

   The seven images are moved to the Images layer. As shown in Figure 39, the selection edges around the frames are now orange, the color assigned to the Images layer.

3. Click the **eye icon** 👁 on the **Images layer** to hide that layer.

4. Select the **four text frames** on the left page, then drag the **selected items button** ☐ up to the Text layer.

   The text frames are moved to the Text layer and the selection marks are now purple. Be sure to note that the text wrap is still affecting the text, even though the image frame is on the Images layer and the Images layer is hidden.

5. Show the **Images layer**.

Figure 39 Seven images moved to the Images layer

6. Click the word **Text** on the **Text layer**, click the **Rectangle tool**, then draw a **small rectangle** anywhere on the page.

    Because the Text layer was selected on the Layers panel, the new rectangle is positioned on the Text layer.

7. Fill the **rectangles** with the **Tan swatch** on the Swatches panel.

8. Click the **top-left reference point** on the Control panel, enter **0** in the **X text box**, enter **0** in the **Y text box**, enter **12.5** in the **W text box**, then enter **4.75** in the **H text box**.

The rectangle covers the entire spread. Because the rectangle is the newest object created, it is at the top of the stacking order on the Text layer.

9. Click **Object** on the menu bar, point to **Arrange**, click **Send to Back**, then compare your spread to Figure 40.

Continued on next page

Figure 40 Rectangle moved to the bottom of the stacking order on the Text layer

The rectangle is at the back of the stacking order of the Text layer. Because the Text layer is at the top of the Layers panel, the rectangle is in front of all images and all tints on the layers below.

10. Drag the **selected items button** ☐ down to the **Tints layer**.

The rectangle is moved to the Tints layer. It is at the top of the stacking order on the Tints layer, so the green tints are not visible.

11. Click **Object** on the menu bar, point to **Arrange**, then click **Send to Back**.

As shown in Figure 41, the tan rectangle is at the bottom of the stacking order on the Tints layer.

12. Save your work, then continue to the next set of steps.

You used the Layers panel to move selected objects from one layer to another. You targeted a layer, then created a new object, which was added to that layer. You then pasted objects into a targeted layer.

Figure 41 Rectangle moved to the bottom of the stacking order on the Tints layer

Change the order of layers on the Layers panel

1. Switch to the **Selection tool** ▶, deselect all, then click and drag the **Tints layer** to the top of the Layers panel.

   A thick line appears, indicating where the layer will be positioned when dragged.

2. Drag the **Text layer** to the top of the Layers panel.

3. Drag the **Images layer** to the top of the Layers panel.

4. Click the **empty square** next to the **Text layer name** to lock the layer, then compare your Layers panel to Figure 42.

   The lock icon 🔒 appears when it is clicked, indicating the layer is now locked.

5. Save your work, then continue to the next set of steps.

You changed the order of layers and locked the Text layer.

Figure 42 Text layer locked

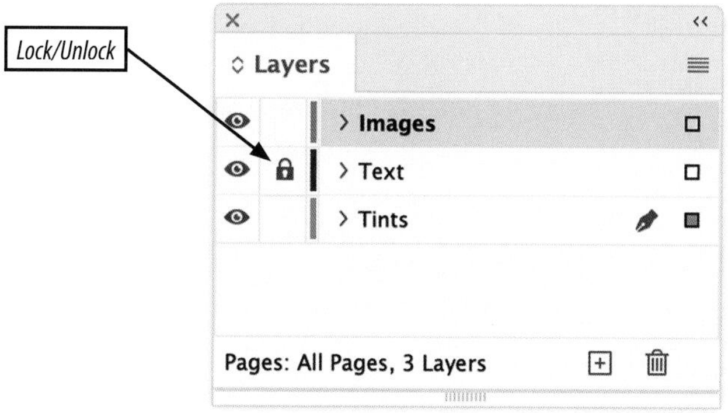

Lock/Unlock

Group items on layers

1. Click the **expand button** ❯ next to **Images** on the Layers panel.

   Expanding the layer shows the objects on the layer. The seven frames are listed on the layer with the name of the images pasted into them.

2. Select the **first four small frames** at the bottom of the layout on the page, starting with the leftmost frame.

   The selected items button ☐ becomes activated for each individual object that is selected.

3. Click **Object** on the menu bar, then click **Group**.

The four selected objects are moved into a folder named <group>.

4. Click the **expand button** ❯ to expand the <group> folder.

5. Select the **fifth thumbnail frame** on the layout, which is named Three Houses.tif.

   The selected items button ☐ is activated beside the fifth thumbnail layer on the Layers panel. Because this image is not part of the group, it is not within the <group> folder.

6. Click and drag the **fifth thumbnail layer** into the middle of the <group> folder.

   As shown in Figure 43, Three Houses.tif is now with the other four images in

the <group> folder and is grouped with them.

7. Deselect all.

8. Lock the <group> folder so your Layers panel resembles Figure 44.

   When you expand a layer, you can lock and hide individual objects on a layer. In this example, the Images layer has seven images on it, but only five of them are locked.

9. Save your work, then close the Layers Intro document.

You modified a group using layers. You grouped four of five frames. You then added the fifth frame to the group by dragging the fifth frame into the <group> folder on the Layers panel.

Figure 43 Moving the image into the <group> folder

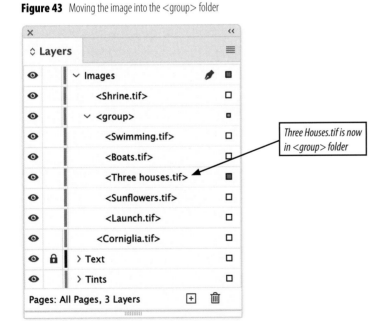

Three Houses.tif is now in <group> folder

Figure 44 Locking the <group> folder locks only the images in the folder

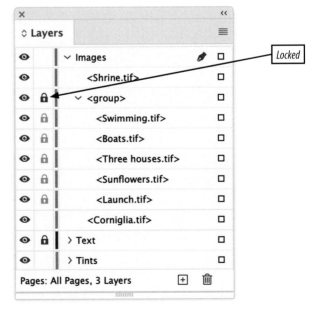

Locked

WORK WITH GRAPHICS FRAMES

Placing Graphics in a Document

The term graphic is quite broad. In its most basic definition, a **graphic** is an element on the page that is not text. A simple square with a fill color could be called a graphic. However, when you are talking about placing graphics in an InDesign document, the term "graphic" usually refers to bitmap images or vector graphics. **Bitmap graphics** are images that consist of pixels. They are created in a program like Adobe Photoshop, scanned in, or downloaded from the Internet or a digital camera. **Vector graphics** are artwork composed of geometrically defined paths and curves, usually illustrations created and imported from drawing programs such as Adobe Illustrator.

There are two essential methods for placing a graphic in a document. The first is to create a graphics placeholder frame using any of the InDesign's shape tools—Rectangle, Ellipse, or Polygon. Once you have created the frame and it is selected on the page, you use the Place command on the File menu to locate the graphic you want to import into the document. The graphic will appear in the graphics frame.

The second method is to place a graphic without first creating a graphics frame. If you click the Place command and then locate the graphic you want to import, your cursor will change to the loaded graphics icon, which is a thumbnail-size image of the image you chose.

Click the loaded graphics icon on the page to place the graphic. The graphic will be placed on the page in a graphics frame whose top-left corner will be positioned at the location where you clicked the loaded graphics icon.

Which is the better method? It depends on what you want to do with the graphic. If the size and location of the graphics frame is important, it's probably better to create and position the frame first, then import the graphic and make it fit into the frame. If the size and location of the frame are negotiable, you might want to place the graphic anywhere in the layout and then modify its size and location.

The Graphic vs. the Graphics Frame

One of the essential concepts in InDesign is the distinction between the graphics frame and the graphic itself. Think of the graphics frame as a window through which you see the placed graphic. Sometimes, the graphic will fit entirely within the frame. At other times, the graphic will be larger than the frame that contains it. In that case, you see only the part of the graphic that fits in the frame. The other areas of the graphic are still there; you just can't see them because they are outside of the frame.

Selecting Graphics and Frames

The difference between the graphics frame and the graphic itself is reflected on the toolbar. Anything you want to do to a graphics frame, you do with the Selection tool. Anything you want to do to the contents—to a graphic itself—you do with the Direct Selection tool. This concept is the key to manipulating graphics within a graphics frame.

Figure 45 shows a graphics frame selected with the Selection tool. The Transform panel shows the X and Y locations of the frame and the width and height of the frame. In this figure, the Transform panel shows no information about the actual placed image inside the frame.

Figure 45 Transform panel shows position info of the selected frame

tsuneomp/Shutterstock, Songquan Deng/Shutterstock

Transform panel showing info about the frame

Figure 46 shows the same object, but this time it has been selected with the Direct Selection tool. The image itself is selected. The selection frame is brown, which is the default color for a selected graphic. This frame is called the bounding box. The **bounding box**—always rectangular—is the frame that defines the horizontal and vertical dimensions of the graphic itself—not the graphics frame. Finally, note that there are parts of the graphic that you can't see. That's because the graphic is being cropped by the graphics frame.

It's important to note that the information on the Transform panel is rendered differently. The + signs beside the X and Y text boxes are a visual indication that the Transform panel is now referring to the graphic, not the frame. The X and Y values are *in relation to the top-left corner of the frame.* Let's explore this: The upper-left reference point on the Transform panel is selected. The X/Y coordinates on the Transform panel refer to the location of the upper-left corner of the graphic. The upper-left corner of the graphic is –0.0076" left and –0.0908" above the top-left corner *of the frame.*

You will seldom be concerned with the actual X/Y coordinates of a placed graphic. In most cases, you will instead place the image in the frame at a size and position that you like and not even note what the X/Y coordinates are.

Figure 46 Transform panel shows position info of the placed image

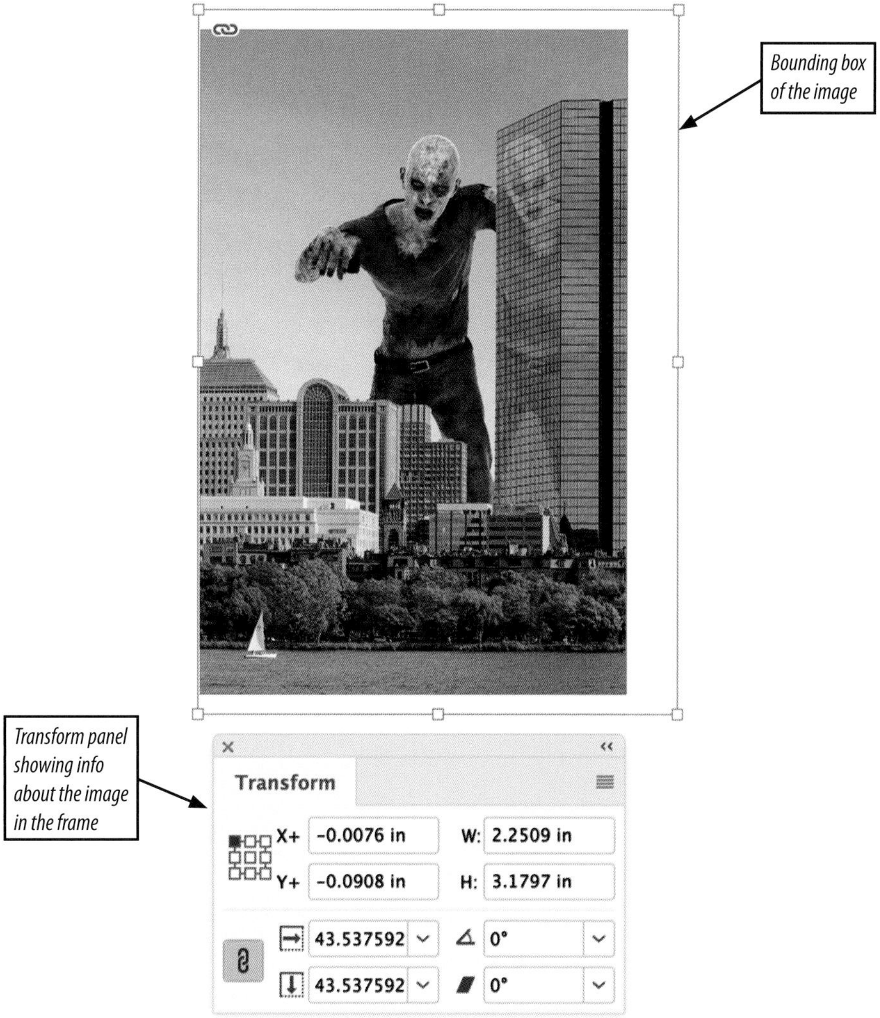

Bounding box of the image

Transform panel showing info about the image in the frame

Using the Content Indicator

When you're working with lots of graphics in lots of frames, you'll want a quicker solution for selecting graphics and frames. The quickest and easiest solution is to double-click the image. Double-clicking the image toggles between the frame and the graphic being selected.

The content indicator is a donut-shaped circle that's available whenever you float over a graphic placed in a frame. If you click the content indicator with the Selection tool, the graphic will be selected. Thus, the content indicator allows you to select the graphic with the Selection tool without having to switch to the Direct Selection tool.

You'll just need to make sure that when you intend to select a frame, you don't accidentally select the content indicator and, thus, the graphic.

Moving a Graphic Within a Frame

When you want to move a graphic within a frame, select the graphic by any method you prefer, then click and drag it. You can also move the selected graphic using the arrow keys on the keypad. When you click and drag the graphic to move it, you see a ghosted image of the areas that are outside the graphics frame. The ghosted image is referred to as a **dynamic preview**.

Once you release the mouse button, the graphic will be repositioned within the frame.

Using the Paste Into Command to Copy and Paste a Graphic

When designing layouts, you'll often find that you want to copy and paste a graphic from one frame to another. This is easy to do. First, select the graphic (not the frame), then copy it. Select the frame in which you want to paste the copy, then choose the Paste Into command on the Edit menu.

Resizing a Graphic

When you select a graphic with the Direct Selection tool, you can then resize the graphic within the frame. Changes that you make to the size of the graphic do not affect the size of the graphics frame.

CREATING A CAPTION BASED ON METADATA

Metadata is text-based information about a graphics file. For example, you can save a Photoshop file with metadata that lists information such as the image's filename, file format, and resolution. When the file is placed in an InDesign layout, you can specify that InDesign automatically generates a caption listing the metadata. These types of captions would be useful if you were creating a contact sheet of photography, for example, that listed important information about a bunch of photos on a DVD or server.

InDesign offers several methods for generating captions of placed images. The most exciting one is Live Caption. Simply click to select a frame containing an image, click the Object menu, point to Captions, then click Generate Live Caption. InDesign creates a text box immediately below the selected frame listing the metadata saved with the image—which is, at minimum, the filename. Here's the "Live" part: if you move that text frame to touch another frame containing a placed image, the text in the frame will update automatically to list the metadata information of the new image. To customize the data or formatting of the caption, click the Object menu, point to Captions, then click Caption Setup.

You can scale a selected graphic by dragging its handles or changing values in the Scale X Percentage and the Scale Y Percentage text boxes on the Transform or Control panels, as shown in Figure 47. You can also use the Transform/Scale command on the Object menu to scale the graphic. Remember, when the graphic is selected with the Direct Selection tool, only the graphic will be scaled when you use the Transform/Scale command.

Using the Fitting Commands

While it's not difficult to select a graphic with the Direct Selection tool and then scale it using the Transform panel, there are a lot of steps in the process.

For a quick solution, you can use the Fitting commands, located on the Object menu.

Figure 47 Scale X and Scale Y Percentages on the Control panel

Plus signs indicate that the Control panel is now referring to the image

X+ 0 in   W: 2.2748 in   44%

Y+ 0 in   H: 3.2135 in   44%

The Fitting commands offer different options for positioning the graphic in the frame. These commands are smart and useful, but beware—they're easy to confuse with one another. It's important that you keep each command straight in your head, because one of the commands distorts the image to fit the frame. See Table 2.

Of all the fitting commands, the Fill Frame Proportionally command is the one you're likely to use most often, because it resizes the placed graphic to a size that is guaranteed to fit the frame, with no negative space in the frame. This means that some of the graphic may not be visible if it exceeds the size of the frame, but you can be confident that it will not be distorted to fit the frame.

Wrapping Text Around Graphics with Clipping Paths

In Chapter 14, you learned how to use the Text Wrap panel to wrap text around a bounding box using the Wrap around bounding box button. You can also wrap text around a graphic inside the frame, as shown in Figure 48.

The Text Wrap panel offers many methods for doing so. In this chapter, you will focus on wrapping text around an image that was saved with a named clipping path in Photoshop. Figure 49 shows a Photoshop image with a clipping path drawn around a man. A **clipping path** is a graphic drawn in Photoshop that outlines the areas of the image you want to show when the file is placed in a layout program such as InDesign.

TABLE 2: FITTING COMMANDS		
Command	**Result**	**Proportion Issues**
Fill Frame Proportionally	The graphic is scaled proportionally to the minimum size required to fill the entire frame.	No proportion issues. The graphic is scaled in proportion.
Fit Content Proportionally	The graphic is scaled proportionally to the largest size it can be without exceeding the frame. Some areas of the frame may be empty.	No proportion issues. The graphic is scaled in proportion.
Fit Frame to Content	The frame is resized to the exact size of the graphic.	No proportion issues. The graphic is not scaled.
Fit Content to Frame	The content is resized to the exact size and shape of the frame.	The content will almost always be distorted with this fitting command.
Center Content	The center point of the graphic will be aligned with the center point of the frame.	No proportion issues. The graphic is not scaled.

Figure 48 Wrapping text around a graphic

Figure 49 A Photoshop image with a clipping path

Image courtesy of Chris Botello

Clipping path created in Photoshop

The text is able to enter the graphics frame to wrap around the picture

When you save the Photoshop file, you name the clipping path and save it with the file. When you place a graphic that has a named clipping path saved with it into your layout, InDesign recognizes the clipping path. With the graphic selected, click the Wrap around object shape button on the Text Wrap panel, click the Type list arrow in the Contour Options section of the panel, and then choose Photoshop Path, as shown in Figure 50. When you do so, the Path menu will list all the paths that were saved with the graphic file. (Usually, you will save only one path with a file.) Choose the path that you want to use for the text wrap.

TIP To define the way text wraps around a graphic, click the Wrap To list arrow in the Wrap Options section, then choose one of the available presets. Remember, in every case, you can manually adjust the resulting text wrap boundary. Though the clipping path is created in Photoshop, the text wrap itself is created in InDesign—and it is editable. As shown in Figure 51, you can relocate the path's anchor points using the Direct Selection tool. You can also use the Add Anchor Point and Delete Anchor Point tools to add or delete points to the path as you find necessary. Click the Add Anchor Point tool anywhere on the path to add a new point and increase your ability to manipulate the path. Click any anchor point with the Delete Anchor Point tool to remove it. Changing the shape of the path changes how text wraps around the path.

Figure 50 Choosing a path from Photoshop for a text wrap

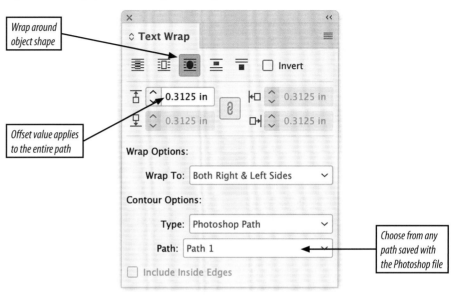

Wrap around object shape

Offset value applies to the entire path

Choose from any path saved with the Photoshop file

Figure 51 Manipulating the text wrap path

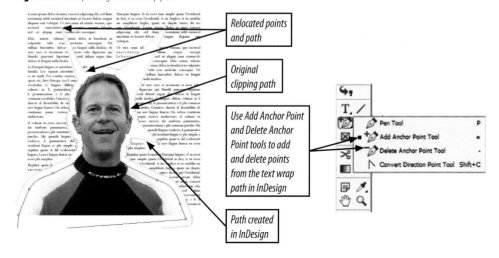

Relocated points and path

Original clipping path

Use Add Anchor Point and Delete Anchor Point tools to add and delete points from the text wrap path in InDesign

Path created in InDesign

Place graphics in a document

1. Open ID 4-6.indd, then save it as **Flowers**.

2. On the Layers panel, lock the **Text layer**.

TIP When a layer is locked, the contents of the layer cannot be selected or modified; this is a smart way to protect the contents of any layer from unwanted changes.

3. Click the **Background layer** to target it, click the **Rectangle tool** ▢, then draw a **graphics frame** in the center of the page that is approximately 3" × 3".

   The frame should have no fill or stroke. The bounding box of the frame is orange because orange is the selection color applied to the Background layer.

4. Click **File** on the menu bar, click **Place**, navigate to the drive and folder where your Chapter 15 Data Files are stored, then double-click **Windmills Ghost.psd**.

   Because the frame was selected, the graphic is placed automatically into the frame, as shown in Figure 52.

5. Click the **Selection tool** ▶, click anywhere to deselect the frame, click the **eye icon** 👁 on the **Background layer** to hide it, then click the **Images layer** to target it on the Layers panel.

Figure 52 Viewing the placed graphic

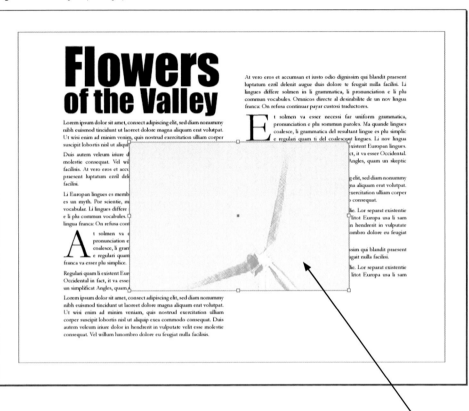

Placed graphic

6. Click **File** on the menu bar, click **Place,** navigate to the drive and folder where your Chapter 15 Data Files are stored, click **Girl at Windmills.psd**, then click **Open**.

TIP You can also access the Place command by pressing [command] [D] (Mac) or [Ctrl] [D] (Win).

7. Position the **pointer** over the **document**.

The pointer changes to the loaded graphics icon and shows a thumbnail of the graphic.

8. Click the **loaded graphics icon** on the **F** in the word **Flowers**.

As shown in Figure 53, the graphic is placed in a new graphics frame whose top-left corner is located where the loaded graphics icon was clicked.

9. Save your work, then continue to the next set of steps.

You imported two graphics using two subtly different methods. You created a graphics frame and then used the Place command to place a graphic in that frame. You used the Place command to load a graphic file and then clicked the loaded graphics icon to create a new frame for the new graphic.

Figure 53 Clicking to place a loaded graphic

sirtravelalot/Shutterstock.com

USING THE STORY EDITOR

InDesign has a feature called the Story Editor that makes it easier to edit text in complex documents. Imagine that you are doing a layout for a single magazine article. The text for the article is flowed through numerous text frames across 12 pages. Now imagine that you want to edit the text. Maybe you want to proofread it or spell-check it. Editing the text within the layout might be difficult—you'd have to scroll from page to page. Instead, you could use the Edit in Story Editor command on the Edit menu. This opens a new window, which contains all the text in a single file, just like a word processing document. Any changes that you make in the Story Editor window will be immediately updated to the text in the layout. It's a great feature!

Move a graphic in a graphics frame

1. Hide the **Images layer**.

2. Show and target the **Background layer**, click the **Selection tool** 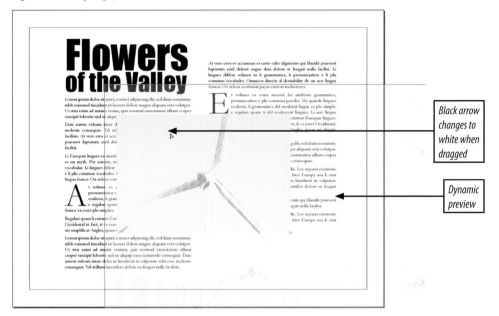, then click the **Windmills Ghost image** in the layout.

3. Click the **top-left reference point** on the Transform panel.

4. Click the **Direct Selection tool**, then click the **image**.

   As soon as you position the Direct Selection tool over the graphic, the pointer becomes a hand pointer. The X and Y text boxes on the Transform panel change to X+ and Y+, indicating that the graphic—not the frame—is selected.

5. Note the width and height of the graphic, as listed on the Transform panel.

   The graphic is substantially larger than the frame that contains it; thus, there are many areas of the graphic outside the frame that are not visible through the frame.

6. Press and hold the **hand icon** on the graphic until the hand icon changes to a black arrow; then drag **inside the graphics frame**, releasing the mouse button when the **windmill is centered** in the frame, as shown in Figure 54.

   The graphic moves within the frame, but the frame itself does not move. Note that the blue bounding box, now visible, is the bounding box for the graphic within the frame.

Figure 54 Viewing the graphic as it is moved in the frame

Black arrow changes to white when dragged

Dynamic preview

7. Click the **Selection tool** , then click the **image**.

   The orange graphics frame appears, and the blue bounding box of the graphic disappears. Note that the values on the Transform panel are again specific to the frame only.

8. Click and drag the **top-left selection handle of the graphics frame** so it is aligned with the **top-left corner of the document page**.

   The graphic within the frame does not change size or location when you drag a handle on the frame.

9. Drag the **bottom-right corner of the graphics frame** so it is aligned with the **bottom-right corner of the document page**.

   As the frame is enlarged, more of the graphic within the frame is visible.

10. Click the **Direct Selection tool** , click the **graphic**, type **0** in the X+ text box on the Transform panel, type **0** in the Y+ text box, then press **[return] (Mac)** or **[Enter] (Win)**.

    As shown in Figure 55, the top-left corner of the graphic is aligned with the top-left corner of the frame.

11. Save your work, then continue to the next set of steps.

You used the Direct Selection tool and X+ and Y+ values on the Transform panel to move a graphic within a graphics frame.

Figure 55 Viewing the entire graphic in the enlarged frame

Resize graphics frames and graphics

1. Drag the **Background layer** below the **Text layer** on the Layers panel.

2. Show and target the **Images layer**.

3. Press the **letter [A]** to access the **Direct Selection tool** ▷ , then click the **Girl at Windmills image** in the layout.

4. Verify that the **Constrain proportions for scaling button** 🔒 is activated on the Transform panel.

   The Constrain proportions for scaling button 🔒 is activated by default. If you click it, you will deactivate this feature and see a broken link icon 🔓 .

5. Type **50** in the **Scale X Percentage text box** on the Transform panel, as shown in Figure 56, then press **[return] (Mac)** or **[Enter] (Win)**.

   Because the Constrain proportions for scaling button 🔒 is activated, the graphic is scaled 50% horizontally and 50% vertically.

   The size of the graphics frame was not affected by scaling the graphic inside.

6. Deselect.

7. Press the **letter [V]** to access the **Selection tool** ▶ , then click the **image**.

8. Click **Object** on the menu bar, point to **Fitting**, then click **Fit Frame to Content**.

9. Click the **top-left reference point** on the Transform panel if it is not already selected.

Figure 56 Using the Transform panel to scale the image

Scale X and Y percentages both at 50%

10. With the **frame** still selected, type **4.5** in the **X Location text box**, type **3** in the **Y Location text box**, type **3.32** in the **Width text box**, type **2.125** in the **Height text box**, then press **[return] (Mac)** or **[Enter] (Win)**.

TIP When you resize a graphics frame using the Width and Height text boxes on the Transform panel, the graphic is not resized with the frame. In other words, this graphic is still at 50%.

11. Click **Object** on the menu bar, point to **Fitting**, then click **Fit Content Proportionally**.

The graphic is scaled proportionately to fit the resized frame. Note that on the right side of the image, the frame extends the actual image. This is not a problem, but some designers like to be very precise in their work and have all frames aligned with the graphic inside them.

12. Click **Object** on the menu bar, point to **Fitting**, then click **Fit Frame to Content**.

The right edge of the frame moves left to fit to the right edge of the graphic. Your image and Transform panel should match Figure 57.

13. Deselect all, save your work, then continue to the next set of steps.

You scaled a graphic using the Transform panel, noting that the graphics frame did not change with the scale. You then scaled the graphics frame with the Transform panel, noting the graphic itself was not scaled. Lastly, you used the Fit Frame to Content command to fit the graphic proportionally to the new frame size.

Figure 57 The frame is fit to the content

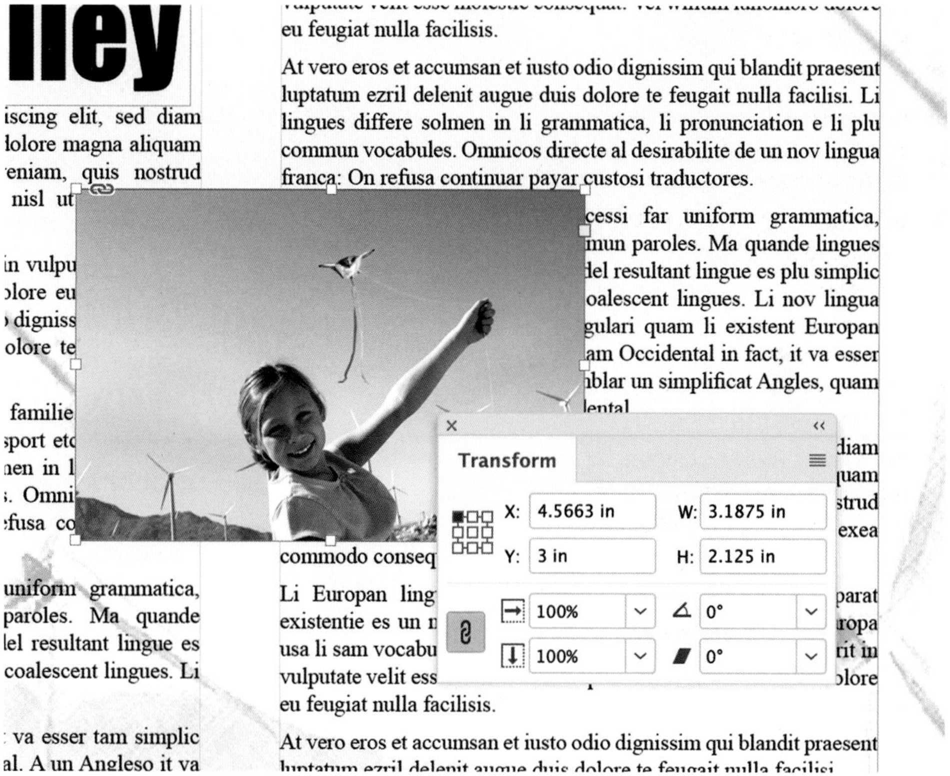

Wrap text around a graphic

1. Verify that the **center image of the girl** is selected.

2. Click the **Wrap around bounding box button** ⬚ on the Text Wrap panel.

3. Verify that the **Make all settings the same button** 🔲 is active, type **.125** in the **Top Offset text box**, then press **[return] (Mac)** or **[Enter] (Win)**.

   Your page and Text Wrap panel should resemble Figure 58.

4. Deselect all.

5. Press **[command] [D] (Mac)**, or **[Ctrl] [D] (Win)**, navigate to the drive and folder where your Chapter 15 Data Files are stored, then double-click **Windmills Silhouette.psd**.

6. Click the **loaded graphics icon** on the **F** in the word **Flowers**.

   Windmills Silhouette.psd was saved with a clipping path named "Path 1" in Photoshop. It has the same sketchy texture as the windmills in the background image.

7. Click the **Wrap around object shape button** ⬛ on the Text Wrap panel, click the **Type list arrow**, click **Photoshop Path**, then note that **Path 1** is automatically listed in the Path text box.

8. Type **.14** in the **Top Offset text box**, then press **[return] (Mac)** or **[Enter] (Win)**.

   The text wraps around the windmill's shape, as defined by the path created in Photoshop plus the 0.14" offset you specified.

9. Deselect all.

Figure 58 Text wraps on all four sides

10. Click the **Selection tool** ▶, then click the **windmill image** to select the frame.

11. Type **–1.25** in the **X Location text box** on the Transform panel, type **3.8** in the **Y Location text box**, then press **[return] (Mac)** or **[Enter] (Win)**.

    As shown in Figure 59, because of the shape of the path around the graphic, a couple of words appear in an odd position near the graphic.

12. In the Wrap Options section on the Text Wrap panel, click the **Wrap To list arrow**, click **Right Side**, then deselect the graphic.

    The words are moved to the right because the wrap option forces all items to wrap against the right edge of the graphic.

TIP Whenever you have a stray word or a stubborn area after applying a text wrap, you can fine-tune the text wrap using the Delete Anchor Point tool ✒, to remove unwanted anchor points along the path. You can also move anchor points along the path using the Direct Selection tool ▷.

13. Show the **Caption layer**.

    The text on the caption layer is meant to be positioned under the center image. However, you know the text wrap on the center image will "bump" the caption, so you must set the caption frame to ignore the text wrap.

14. Select the **frame** that contains the **caption text**, press **[command] [B] (Mac)** or **[Ctrl] [B] (Win)**, click **Ignore Text Wrap**, then click **OK**.

15. Center the **text under the center image**.

16. Click the **pasteboard** to deselect the frame.

17. Press **[W]** to change to **Preview**, then compare your work to Figure 60.

18. Save your work, then close the Flowers document.

You wrapped text around a graphic, specified an offset value, then specified wrap options.

Figure 59 Noting a minor problem with the wrap

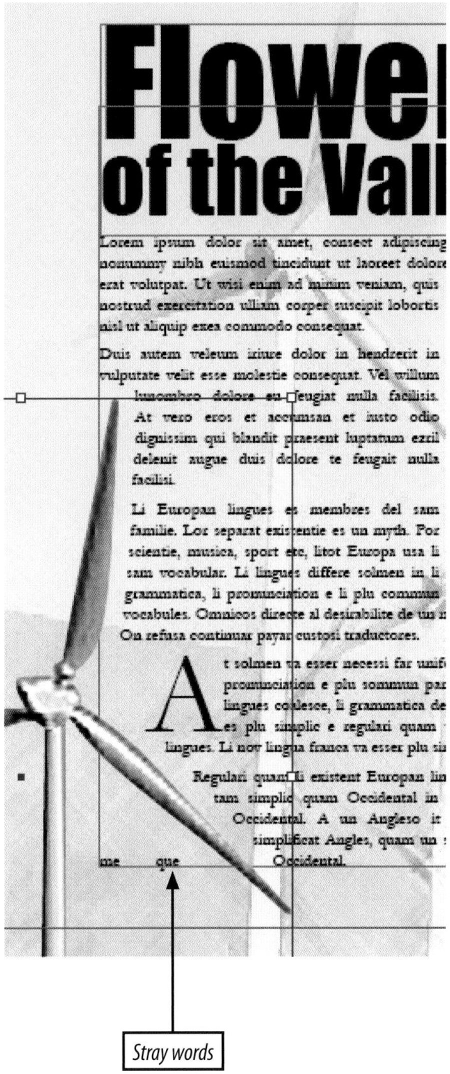

Stray words

Figure 60 The completed layout

Flowers of the Desert

Lorem ipsum dolor sit amet, consect adipiscing elit, sed diam nonummy nibh euismod tincidunt ut laoreet dolore magna aliquam erat volutpat. Ut wisi enim ad minim veniam, quis nostrud exercitation ulliam corper suscipit lobortis nisl ut aliquip exea commodo consequat.

Duis autem veleum iriure dolor in hendrerit in vulputate velit esse molestie consequat. Vel willum lunombro dolore eu feugiat nulla facilisis. At vero eros et accumsan et iusto odio dignissim qui blandit praesent luptatum ezril delenit augue duis dolore te feugait nulla facilisi.

Li Europan lingues es membres del sam familie. Lor separat existentie es un myth. Por scientie, musica, sport etc, litot Europa usa li sam vocabular. Li lingues differe solmen in li grammatica, li pronunciation e li plu commun vocabules. Omnicos directe al desirabilite de un nov lingua franca: On refusa continuar payar custosi traductores.

A t solmen va esser necessi far uniform grammatica, pronunciation e plu sommun paroles. Ma quande lingues coalesce, li grammatica del resultant lingue es plu simplice e reguliri quam ti del coalescent lingues. Li nov lingua franca va esser plu simplice.

Reguliri quam li existent Europan lingues. It va esser tam simplic quam Occidental in fact, it va esser Occidental. A un Angleso it va semblar un simplificat Angles, quam un skeptic

amico dit me que Occidental.

Lorem ipsum dolor sit amet, consect adipiscing elit, sed diam nonummy nibh euismod tincidunt ut laoreet dolore magna aliquam erat volutpat. Ut wisi enim ad minim veniam, quis nostrud exercitation ulliam corper suscipit lobortis nisl ut aliquip exea commodo consequat. Duis autem veleum iriure dolor in hendrerit in vulputate velit esse molestie consequat. Vel willum lunombro dolore eu feugiat nulla facilisis.

At vero eros et accumsan et iusto odio dignissim qui blandit praesent luptatum ezril delenit augue duis dolore te feugait nulla facilisi. Li lingues differe solmen in li grammatica, li pronunciation e li plu commun vocabules. Omnicos directe al desirabilite de un nov lingua franca: On refusa continuar payar custosi traductores.

A windmill garden is a kite flyer's dream come true.

E t solmen va esser necessi far uniform grammatica, pronunciation e plu sommun paroles. Ma quande lingues coalesce, li grammatica del resultant lingue es plu simplic e reguliri quam ti del coalescent lingues. Li nov lingua franca va esser plu simplice. Reguliri quam li existent Europan lingues. It va esser tam simplic quam Occidental in fact, it va esser Occidental. A un Angleso it va semblar un simplificat Angles, quam un skeptic amico dit me que Occidental.

Lorem ipsum dolor sit amet, consect adipiscing elit, sed diam nonummy nibh euismod tincidunt ut laoreet dolore magna aliquam erat volutpat. Ut wisi enim ad minim veniam, quis nostrud exercitation ulliam corper suscipit lobortis nisl ut aliquip exea commodo consequat.

WORK WITH TEXT FRAMES

▶ *What You'll Do*

In this lesson, you will explore options for autoflowing text through a document. You will also learn how to add column breaks to text.

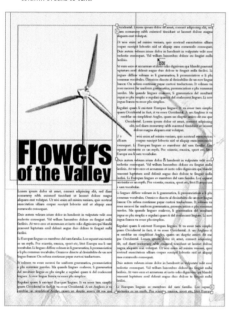

Semi-Autoflowing Text

In Chapter 14, you learned how to thread text manually—to make it flow from text frame to text frame. When you click the out port of one text frame with the Selection tool, the pointer changes to the loaded text icon. When you click the loaded text icon in another text frame, text flows from the first frame to the second frame—and the pointer automatically changes back to the Selection tool. That's great, but what if you wanted to keep threading text? Would you need to repeat the process over and over again?

This is where semi-autoflowing text comes in handy. **Semi-autoflowing** text is a method for manually threading text through multiple frames. When you are ready to click the loaded text icon in a text frame where you want text to flow, press and hold [option] (Mac) or [Alt] (Win), then click the text frame. Text will flow into the text frame, but the loaded text icon will remain active; it will not automatically revert to the Selection tool. You can then thread text into another text frame.

Autoflowing Text

You can also **autoflow** text, or automatically thread text through multiple text frames. This is a powerful option for quickly adding text to your document. Let's say you create a six-page document and you specify that each page has three columns. When you create the document, the pages have no text frames on them—they're just blank, with columns and margin guides. To autoflow text into the document, you click the Place command and choose the text document that you want to import. Once you choose the document, the pointer changes to the loaded text icon. Press and hold [shift], and the loaded text icon becomes the autoflow loaded text icon. When you click the autoflow loaded text icon in a column, InDesign creates text frames within column guides on that page and all subsequent pages and flows the text into those frames. Because you specified that each page has three columns when you created the document, InDesign will create three text frames in the columns on every page into which the text will flow.

If you autoflow more text than the document size can handle, InDesign will add as many pages as necessary to autoflow all the text. If your document pages contain objects such as graphics, the text frames added by the autoflow will be positioned in front of the graphics already on the page.

As you may imagine, autoflowing text is a powerful option, but don't be intimidated by it. The text frames that are generated are all editable. You can resize them or delete them. Nevertheless, you should take some time to practice autoflowing text to get the hang of it. Like learning how to ride a bicycle, you can read about it all you want, but actually doing it is where the learning happens.

Inserting a Column Break

When you are working with text in columns, you will often want to move text from the bottom of one column to the top of the next. You do this by inserting a column break. A **column break** is a typographic command that forces text to the next column. The Column Break command is located within the Insert Break Character command on the Type menu.

In Figure 61, the headline near the bottom of the first column would be better positioned at the top of the next column. By inserting a column break, you do exactly that, as shown in Figure 62.

Figure 61 Viewing text that needs a column break

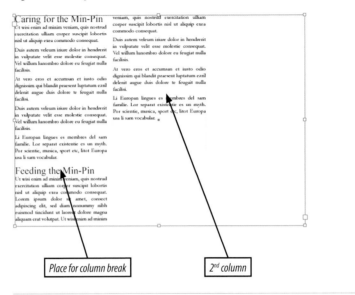

Place for column break   2nd column

Figure 62 Viewing text after inserting a column break

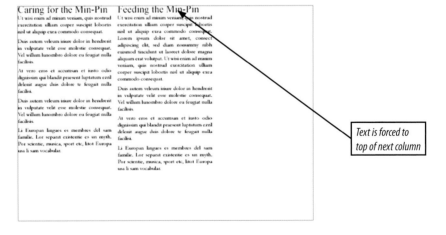

Text is forced to top of next column

Inserting a "Continued on page …" Notation

When threading text manually or autoflowing text, you will get to a point where text has filled all the text frames on the page and continues to another page. Usually, the text continues onto the very next page—but not always. In many cases, the next page will be reserved for pictures or other publication elements, such as tables or graphs. When readers get to the bottom of the page of text, they need to know on which page the text is continued. You can insert a "Continued on page …" notation to let the reader know where to go to continue reading.

If you've ever read a magazine or newspaper article, you are familiar with "Continued on page …" notations. In InDesign, a page continuation is formatted as a special character. Simply create a text frame, then type the words "Continued on page X." Select the X, then apply the Next Page Number command. The X changes to the page number of the page that contains the text frame into which the text flows. If, for any reason, you move pages within the Pages panel and page numbers change, the Next Page Number character will automatically update to show the page number where the text continues.

The Next Page Number command is located within the Insert Special Character command under Markers on the Type menu.

There's one important point you need to note when creating a "Continued on page …" notation. Below the text frame on the page of the text you are flowing, you will need to create another text frame to contain the "Continued on page …" notation. In order for the notation to work—for it to list the page where the text continues—the top edge of the text frame that contains the notation must be touching the frame that contains the body copy that is to be continued.

PARAGRAPHS THAT SPAN OR SPLIT COLUMNS

Imagine having one text box that contains five paragraphs, with the fourth needing to be split into two columns within the text box. Or imagine that you have a single text frame with three columns, and you want to run a headline across all three columns. With InDesign, you can format text to span multiple columns or split into columns within a single text frame. Not only is this feature unprecedented; it's remarkably easy to use. Simply click your cursor in the paragraph you want to modify. Choose the Span Columns command from the Paragraph panel menu, then select to split the paragraph or span the paragraph.

Autoflow text

1. Open ID 4-7.indd, save it as **Autoflow**, then look at each page in the document.

   Other than the text frame that holds the headline on page 1, there are no text frames in the document.

2. Click the **Selection tool** ▶ double-click the **page 1 icon** on the Pages panel, click **File** on the menu bar, click **Place,** navigate to the drive and folder where your Chapter 15 Data Files are stored, then double-click **Windmill text.doc**.

   The pointer changes to the loaded text icon.

3. Drag a **text frame** in the position shown in Figure 63.

   Note that once you have drawn the frame, the loaded text icon automatically changes back to the Selection tool ▶ .

4. Click the **out port** of the text frame, then position the **loaded text icon** over the **right column on the page**.

5. Press and hold **[option] (Mac)** or **[Alt] (Win)** so the pointer changes to the semi-autoflow loaded text icon.

Figure 63 Creating a text frame using the loaded text icon

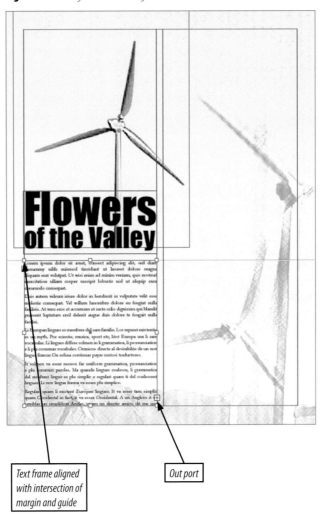

Text frame aligned with intersection of margin and guide

Out port

6. Still pressing and holding **[option] (Mac)** or **[Alt] (Win)**, click the **top-left corner of the right column** so a **new text frame** is created, then release **[option] (Mac)** or **[Alt] (Win)**.

Because you used the semi-autoflow loaded text icon, the pointer remains as a loaded text icon and does not revert back to the Selection tool ▶, as shown in Figure 64.

7. Double-click the **page 2 icon,** then click the **top-left corner of the left column** on the page.

A new frame is created, and text flows into the left column.

8. Click the **out port** of the **new text frame on page 2**, then position the **pointer** over the **right column on page 2**.

9. Press and hold **[shift]**, note the change to the loaded text icon, then click the **top-left corner of the second column**.

Because you were pressing [shift], InDesign created text frames within column guides on all subsequent pages. InDesign has added new pages to the document to accommodate the autoflow.

10. Save your work, then continue to the next set of steps.

You placed text by clicking and dragging the loaded text icon to create a new text frame. You flowed text using the semi-autoflow loaded text icon and the autoflow loaded text icon.

Figure 64 Flowing text with the semi-autoflow loaded text icon

Pointer remains as loaded text icon after text has been flowed

Reflow text

1. Double-click the **page 4 icon** on the Pages panel, then create a **horizontal guide** at **5.875 in**.

2. Click the **left text frame** to select it, drag the **bottom-middle handle** of the text frame's bounding box up until it snaps to the guide, then do the same to the right text frame, so your page resembles Figure 65.

   The text is reflowed in the document.

3. Double-click the **numbers 2-3** on the Pages panel to center the spread in the document window, click **View** on the menu bar, point to **Extras**, click **Show Text Threads**, then click the **right text frame on page 2**.

Figure 65 Resizing text frames

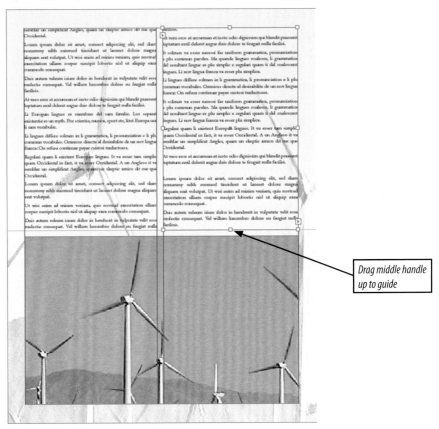

Drag middle handle up to guide

4. With the **right frame on page 2** still selected, press **[delete]**, then click the **text frame** remaining on **page 2**.

   As shown in Figure 66, the text is reflowed from the first text frame on page 2 to the first text frame on page 3.

5. Press **[command] [D] (Mac)** or **[Ctrl] [D] (Win)**, navigate to the drive and folder where your Chapter 15 Data Files are stored, then double-click **2 Windmills.psd**.

6. Click the **top-left corner of the right column on page 2**.

7. Create a **horizontal guide** at **5.375 in**.

8. Click the **text frame on page 2**, then click the **out port**.

9. Click the **intersection** between the guide you created and the **left edge of the right column**, beneath the graphic.

   As shown in Figure 67, text is now threaded through the new text frame.

10. Save your work, then continue to the next set of steps.

You resized two text frames, noting text was reflowed through the document. You deleted a text frame, then created a text frame, noting text continued to flow through the document.

Figure 66 Flowing text after deleting a text frame

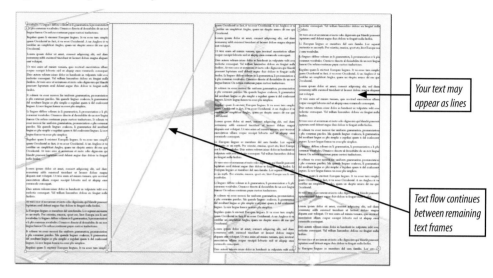

Your text may appear as lines

Text flow continues between remaining text frames

Figure 67 Threading text to a new text frame

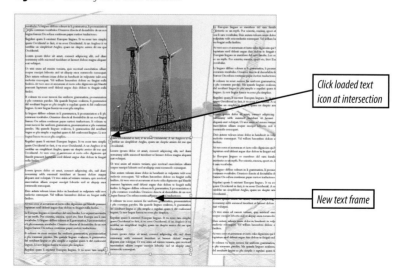

Click loaded text icon at intersection

New text frame

Add a column break

1. Double-click the **page 5 icon** on the Pages panel, then delete the **two text frames on page 5**.

2. Click **Layout** on the menu bar, click **Margins and Columns**, change the **number of columns** to **3**, then click **OK**.

3. Press **[command] [D] (Mac)** or **[Ctrl] [D] (Win)**, navigate to the drive and folder where your Chapter 15 Data Files are stored, then double-click **Sidebar copy.doc**.

4. Drag the **loaded text icon** to create a text frame, as shown in Figure 68.

5. Click **Object** on the menu bar, click **Text Frame Options**, change the **number of columns** to **3**, then click **OK**.

6. Click the **Type tool** **T**, then click to place the **pointer before the Windmill Speeds headline**.

Figure 68 Creating a text frame with the loaded text icon

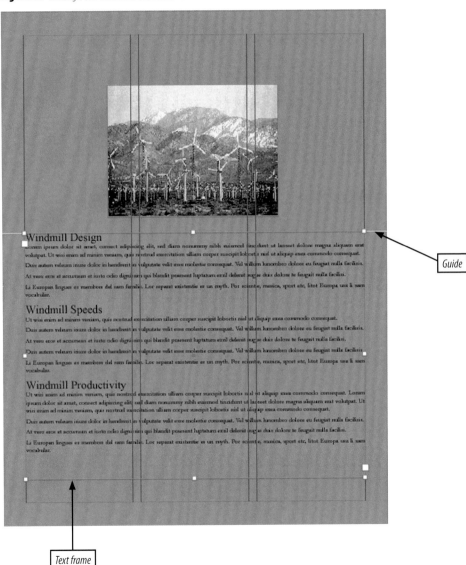

Guide

Text frame

7. Click **Type** on the menu bar, point to **Insert Break Character**, then click **Column Break**.

The Windmill Speeds text is forced into the second column.

8. Click before the **W** in the **Windmill Productivity headline**, click **Type** on the menu bar, point to **Insert Break Character**, then click **Column Break**.

Your page should resemble Figure 69.

9. Save your work, then continue to the next set of steps.

You deleted two text frames on a page and then changed the number of columns on that page. You then placed text, formatted the text frame to have three columns, and, finally, used the Column Break command to create two new column breaks.

Figure 69 Viewing the text frame with column breaks

Insert a page continuation notation

1. Double-click the **page 4 icon** on the Pages panel, then create a **horizontal guide** at **5 in**.

2. Click the **Selection tool** ▶, click the **text frame in the right column**, then drag the **bottom-middle bounding box handle** up until it snaps to the guide at **5 in**.

3. Click the **Type tool** T, then create a **text frame** between the two guides, as shown in Figure 70. The edges of the two text frames should overlap slightly at the guide, which is critical for page continuation notation to work.

4. Click **Object** on the menu bar, click **Text Frame Options**, change the **Vertical Justification** to **Center**, then click **OK**.

Figure 70 Creating a text frame for the page continuation notation

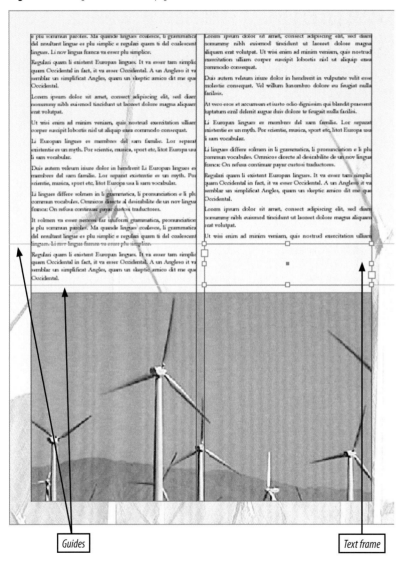

Guides

Text frame

5. Click the **Type tool** T inside the new text box, type **(Continued on page X)**, click **anywhere within the (Continued on page X) text**, show the **Paragraph Styles panel**, then click the style named **Continued**.

6. Select the **letter X**, click **Type** on the menu bar, point to **Insert Special Character**, point to **Markers**, then click **Next Page Number**.

   The text now reads (Continued on page 6), as shown in Figure 71.

   TIP You can use the Previous Page Number command along with "Continued from page . . ." text to indicate that a story is continued from a previous page.

7. Click the **Selection tool** ▶, click the **text frame** above the "Continued" text frame, then follow the text thread to verify that the text does indeed continue on page 6.

8. Save your work, then close the Autoflow document.

   You inserted a page continuation notation in the document.

Figure 71 Viewing the page continuation notation

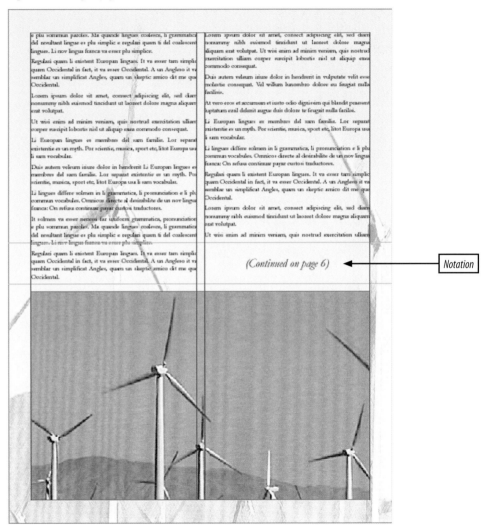

(Continued on page 6) ← Notation

Align and distribute objects on a page

1. Open ID 4-8.indd, then save it as **Dog Days**.
2. Click the workspace switcher list arrow on the menu bar, then click Advanced or Reset Advanced if Advanced is already checked.
3. Click the Type tool, then drag a text frame that fills the left column on the page.
4. Click the Selection tool, press and hold [shift] [option] (Mac) or [Shift] [Alt] (Win), then drag a copy of the text frame and position it in line with the right column.
5. Click the Rectangle Frame tool, click anywhere on the page, type **1.5** in both the Width and Height text boxes, then click OK.
6. Click the top-left reference point on the Transform panel, type **0** in the X Location text box, type **0** in the Y Location text box, then press [return] (Mac) or [Enter] (Win).
7. Verify that the frame has no fill and no stroke.
8. Click Edit on the menu bar, click Step and Repeat, type **1** in the Repeat Count text box, type **9.5** in the Horizontal Offset text box, type **0** in the Vertical Offset text box, then click OK.
9. Select both graphics frames, click Edit on the menu bar, click Step and Repeat, type **1** in the Repeat Count text box, type **0** in the Horizontal Offset text box, type **7** in the Vertical Offset text box, then click OK.
10. Click the Rectangle Frame tool, click anywhere in the left column, type **3** in both the Width and Height text boxes, click OK, then verify that the frame has no fill or stroke.
11. Click the Selection tool, press and hold [shift], click the top-left graphics frame, then click the top-right graphics frame so three frames are selected.
12. Click Window on the menu bar, point to Object & Layout, click Align, then click the Distribute horizontal centers button on the Align panel.
13. Deselect all, select the top-left and bottom-left graphics frames and the 3" × 3" frame, click the Distribute vertical centers button on the Align panel, then compare your page to Figure 72.

Figure 72 Completed Skills Review, Part 1

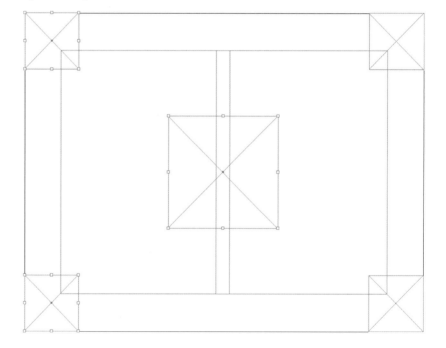

Stack and layer objects

1. Display the Layers panel.
2. Double-click Layer 1, type **Background Graphic** in the Name text box, then click OK.
3. Click the Create new layer button on the Layers panel, double-click the new layer, type **Dog Pics** in the Name text box, then click OK.
4. Click the Layers panel menu button, click New Layer, type **Body** in the Name text box, then click OK.
5. Click the Selection tool, select the five graphics frames, then drag the selected items button from the Background Graphic layer up to the Dog Pics layer.
6. Select the two text frames, then drag the selected items button from the Background Graphic layer up to the Body layer.
7. Verify the Body layer is selected, select only the left text frame, click File on the menu bar, click Place, navigate to the drive and folder where your Chapter 15 Data Files are stored, then double-click Skills Text.doc.
8. Click any word five times to select all the text, then format the text as Garamond 12-point font size with 14-point leading.

9. Click the Selection tool, click the out port of the left text frame, then click the loaded text icon anywhere in the right text frame.
10. On the Layers panel, drag the Body layer down below the Dog Pics layer.
11. Save your work.

Work with graphics frames

1. Click the Selection tool, select the top-left graphics frame, press [command] [D] (Mac) or [Ctrl] [D] (Win), navigate to the drive and folder where your Chapter 15 Data Files are stored, then double-click Red 1.psd.
2. Select the top-right graphics frame, press [command] [D] (Mac) or [Ctrl] [D] (Win), navigate to the drive and folder where your Chapter 15 Data Files are stored, then double-click Black 1.psd.
3. Select the bottom-left graphics frame, press [command] [D] (Mac) or [Ctrl] [D] (Win), navigate to the drive and folder where your Chapter 15 Data Files are stored, then double-click Red 2.psd.
4. Select the bottom-right graphics frame, press [command] [D] (Mac) or [Ctrl] [D] (Win), navigate to

the drive and folder where your Chapter 15 Data Files are stored, then double-click Black 2.psd.
5. Select the top two graphics frames, click Object on the menu bar, point to Fitting, then click Fit Content to Frame.
6. Deselect all, click the Direct Selection tool, press and hold the mouse pointer on the bottom-left graphic, then drag until the dog's nose is at the center of the frame.
7. Click the center reference point on the Transform panel, type **40** in both the Scale X Percentage and Scale Y Percentage text boxes, then click and drag to center the dog's head in the frame.
8. Deselect all, click the Selection tool, select the four corner graphics frames, click the Wrap around bounding box button on the Text Wrap panel, then type **.125** in all four of the Offset text boxes.
9. Select the center graphics frame, press [command] [D] (Mac) or [Ctrl] [D] (Win), navigate to the drive and folder where your Chapter 15 Data Files are stored, then double click Dog Silo.psd.
10. Click the Direct Selection tool, click the new graphic, then click the Wrap around object shape button on the Text Wrap panel.

11. Click the Type list arrow in the Contour Options section, choose Same as Clipping, type **.15** in the Top Offset text box, then press [return] (Mac) or [Enter] (Win).

12. Press [W] to switch to Preview, deselect all, compare your page to Figure 73, save your work, then close the Dog Days document.

Work with text frames

1. Open ID 4-9.indd, click Update Links, then save it as **Dog Days Part 2**.

2. Click the Selection tool, click the right text frame on page 1, then click the out port of the text frame.

3. Double-click page 2 on the Pages panel, position the loaded text icon over the left column, press and hold [shift], then click the top-left corner of the left column.

4. Click View on the menu bar, point to Extras, click Show Text Threads, double-click page 3 on the Pages panel, then click the eye icon in the Dog Pics layer on the Layers panel to hide it temporarily.

TIP Autoflowing the text created two text frames on page 3, but they weren't visible because the Body Copy layer is behind the Dog Pics layer.

Figure 73 Completed Skills Review, Part 2

Lorem ipsum dolor sit amet, consect adipiscing elit, sed diam nonummy nibh euismod tincidunt ut laoreet dolore magna aliquam erat volutpat. Ut wisi enim ad minim venim, quis nostrud exercitation ulliam corper suscipit lobortis nisl ut aliquip exea commodo consequat.

Duis autem veleum iriure dolor in hendrerit in vulputate velit esse molestie consequat. Vel willum lunombro dolore eu feugait nulla facilisis. At vero eros et accumsan et iusto odio dignissim qui blandit praesent luptatum eznil delenit augue duis dolore te feugait nulla facilisi.

Li Europan lingues es membres del sam familie. Lor separat existentie es un myth. Por scientie, musica, sport etc, litot Europa usa li sam vocabular. Li lingues differe solmen in li grammatica, li pronunciation e li plu commun vocabules. Omnicos directe al desirabile de un nov lingua franca: On refusa continuar payar custosi traductores.

At solmen va esser necessi far uniform grammatica, pronunciation e plu sommun paroles. Ma quande lingues coalesce, li grammatica del resultant lingue es plu simplic e regulari quam ti del coalescent lingues. Li nov lingua franca va esser plu simplice.

Regulari quam li existent Europan lingues. It va esser tam simplic quam Occidental in fact, it va esser Occidental. A un Angleso it va semblar un simplificat Angles, quam un skeptic amico dit me que Occidental.

Lorem ipsum dolor sit amet, consect adipiscing elit, sed diam nonummy nibh euismod tincidunt ut laoreet dolore magna aliquam erat volutpat. Ut wisi enim ad minim veniam, quis nostrud exercitation ulliam corper suscipit lobortis nisl ut aliquip exea commodo consequat. Duis autem veleum iriure dolor in hendrerit in vulputate velit esse molestie consequat. Vel willum lunombro dolore eu feugait nulla facilisis.

At vero eros et accumsan et iusto odio dignissim qui blandit praesent luptatum eznil delenit augue duis dolore te feugait nulla facilisi. Li lingues differe solmen in li grammatica, li pronunciation e li plu commun vocabules. Omnicos directe al desirabile de un nov lingua franca: On refusa continuar payar custosi traductores.

Solmen va esser necessi far uniform grammatica,

Images courtesy of Chris Botello

5. Verify that the Body Copy layer is selected, delete both text frames on page 3, then click the eye icon on the Dog Pics layer so the layer is visible again. The text now ends on page 2.

6. Go to page 2, click the Selection tool, click the right text frame on the page, then click the out port of the text frame.

7. Go to page 4, then click and drag the loaded text icon to create a text box across both columns on the page. The text now flows from page 2 to page 4.

8. Double-click page 2 on the Pages panel, select the right text frame, then drag the bottom-middle handle of the right text frame up so it slightly overlaps the top edge of the small text frame at the bottom of the column.

9. Click the Type tool, click the small text frame at the bottom of the right column, then type **Continued on X**.

10. Click the Continued style on the Paragraph Styles panel, then select the letter X.

11. Click Type on the menu bar, point to Insert Special Character, point to Markers, then click Next Page Number.

12. Deselect all, compare your page 2 to Figure 74, save your work, then close the Dog Days Part 2 document.

Figure 74 Completed Skills Review, Part 3

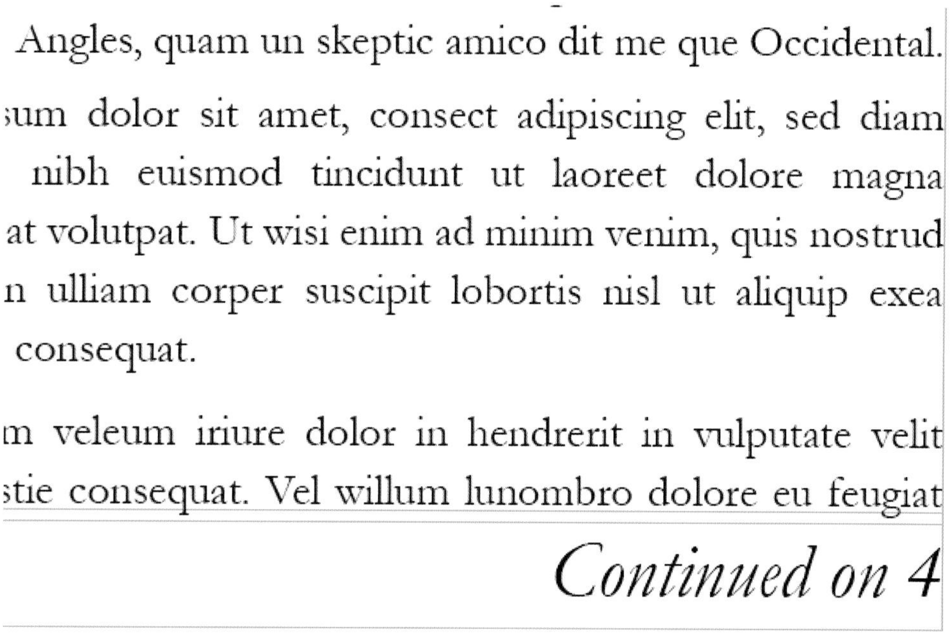

Angles, quam un skeptic amico dit me que Occidental.

sum dolor sit amet, consect adipiscing elit, sed diam nibh euismod tincidunt ut laoreet dolore magna at volutpat. Ut wisi enim ad minim venim, quis nostrud n ulliam corper suscipit lobortis nisl ut aliquip exea consequat.

m veleum iriure dolor in hendrerit in vulputate velit stie consequat. Vel willum lunombro dolore eu feugiat

Continued on 4

You work for a design firm, and you are creating a logo for a local shop that sells vintage board games. You decide to create an 8" × 8" checkerboard, which you will later incorporate into your logo.

1. Open ID 4-10.indd, then save it as **Checkerboard**.
2. Click the Rectangle Frame tool, create a 1" square frame anywhere on the board, fill it with black and no stroke, then position it so its top-left corner has a (0, 0) coordinate.
3. Use the Step and Repeat command to make one copy, one inch to the right of the original square.
4. Select the new square, if necessary, change its fill color to Brick Red, then select both squares.
5. Use the Step and Repeat command again, type **3** in the Repeat Count text box, type **0** in the Vertical Offset text box, type **2** in the Horizontal Offset text box, then click OK.
6. Verify that all squares are still selected, use the Step and Repeat command again, type **1** in the Repeat Count text box, type **1** in the Vertical Offset text box, type **0** in the Horizontal Offset text box, then click OK.
7. Deselect all, select the eight squares in the second row, click the center reference point on the Transform panel, then change the Rotation Angle text box to 180°.
8. Select all, use the Step and Repeat command again, type **3** in the Repeat Count text box, type **2** in the Vertical Offset text box, type **0** in the Horizontal Offset text box, then click OK.
9. Press [W] to switch to Preview, deselect all, then compare your work to Figure 75.
10. Save your work, then close the Checkerboard document.

Figure 75 Completed Project Builder 1

You are a designer at a design firm that specializes in travel. A client sends you a layout she created in InDesign. She wants you to use it as a template for future layouts. You open the file and decide it's best to move the basic elements onto layers.

1. Open ID 4-11.indd, then save it as **Brochure Layers**.
2. On the Layers panel, rename Layer 1 as **Background Colors**.
3. Create a new layer, then name it **Pictures**.
4. Create a new layer, then name it **Text**.
5. Select the four graphics frames, then move them onto the Pictures layer.
6. Select the two text frames, then move them onto the Text layer.
7. Use the Layers panel to select all the frames on the Pictures layer, then compare your work to Figure 76.
8. Save your work, then close the Brochure Layers document.

Figure 76 Completed Project Builder 2

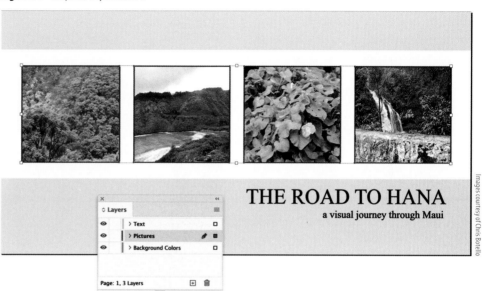

Images courtesy of Chris Botello

Figure 77 Positioning the graphics frame

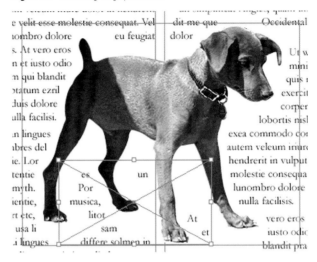

You lead the layout team for a design firm. Your client has delivered you a Photoshop file with a clipping path. He wants you to use it in the layout he has supplied. He tells you he wants the graphic placed in the middle of the page with text wrapping around it on all four sides. You import the graphic and realize you will need to modify the path that controls the wrap in InDesign.

1. Open ID 4-12.indd, then save it as **Four Leg Wrap**.
2. Click File on the menu bar, click Place, navigate to the drive and folder where your Chapter 15 Data Files are stored, then double-click Red Silo.psd.
3. Click the loaded graphics icon anywhere on the page, click the Selection tool, then center the graphic on the page.
4. Verify that you can see the Transform panel, press and hold or [command] [shift] (Mac) or [Ctrl] [Shift] (Win), then drag the top-left corner of the frame toward the center of the frame, reducing the frame until the Width text box on the Transform panel reads approximately 5 inches.
5. Click the center reference point on the Transform panel, type **4.25** in the X Location text box, type **4.2** in the Y Location text box, then press [return] (Mac) or [Enter] (Win).
6. Click the Direct Selection tool, click the graphic, click the Wrap around object shape button on the Text Wrap panel, then adjust the offset so it is visually pleasing.
7. Draw a graphics frame in the position shown in Figure 77, being sure the bottom edges of the two graphics frames are aligned.

8. With only the lower graphics frame selected, click the Wrap around bounding box button on the Text Wrap panel. Adjust the new frame as necessary to move any stray text.

9. Deselect all, press [W] to switch to Preview, then compare your work to Figure 78.

10. Save your work, then close the Four Leg Wrap document.

Figure 78 *Completed Design Project*

Lorem ipsum dolor sit amet, consect adipiscing elit, sed diam nonummy nibh euismod tincidunt ut laoreet dolore magna aliquam erat volutpat. Ut wisi enim ad minim veniam, quis nostrud exercitation ulliam corper suscipit lobortis nisl ut aliquip exea commodo consequat.

Duis autem veleum iriure dolor in hendrerit in vulputate velit esse molestie consequat. Vel willum lunombro dolore eu feugiat nulla facilisis. At vero eros et accumsan et iusto odio dignissim qui blandit praesent luptatum ezril delenit augue duis dolore te feugait nulla facilisi.

Li Europan lingues es membres del sam familie. Lor separat existentie es un myth. Por scientie, musica, sport etc, litot Europa usa li sam vocabular. Li lingues differe solmen in li grammatica, li pronunciation e li plu commun vocabules. Omnicos directe al desirabilite de un nov lingua franca: On refusa continuar payar custosi traductores.

It solmen va esser necessi far uniform grammatica, pronunciation e plu sommun paroles. Ma quande lingues coalesce, li grammatica del resultant lingue es plu simplic e regulari quam ti del coalescent lingues. Li nov lingua franca va esser plu simplice.

Regulari quam li existent Europan lingues. It va esser tam simplic quam Occidental in fact, it va esser Occidental. A un Angleso it va semblar un simplificat Angles, quam un skeptic amico dit me que Occidental. Lorem ipsum dolor sit amet.

Ut wisi enim ad minim veniam, quis nostrud exercitation ulliam corper suscipit lobortis nisl ut aliquip exea commodo consequat. Duis autem veleum iriure dolor in hendrerit in vulputate velit esse molestie consequat. Vel willum lunombro dolore eu feugiat nulla facilisis.

At vero eros et accumsan et iusto odio dignissim qui blandit praesent luptatum ezril delenit augue duis dolore te feugait nulla facilisi. Li lingues differe solmen in li grammatica, li pronunciation e li plu commun vocabules. Omnicos directe al desirabilite de un nov lingua franca:

On refusa continuar payar custosi traductores. It solmen va esser necessi far uniform grammatica,

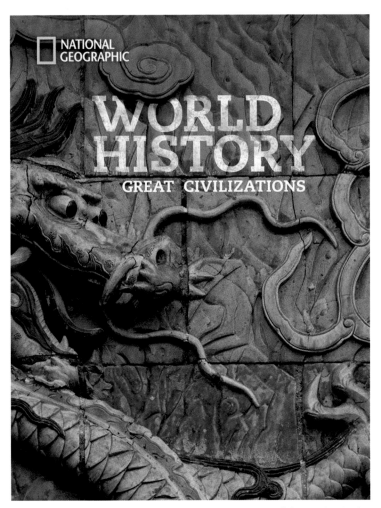

© Cengage Learning, Inc.

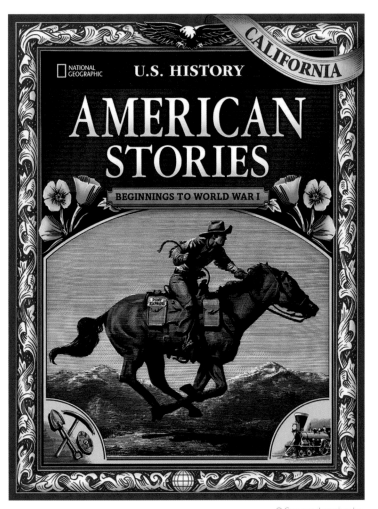

© Cengage Learning, Inc.

NATIONAL GEOGRAPHIC LEARNING	SCOTT BAKER **MANAGING ART DIRECTOR**

As a child, Scott Baker enjoyed creating comic books with his brother. Seeing their passion for art, their mother enrolled them in art classes. From an early age, Scott learned the importance of finding a creative mentor—and he has had many throughout his life. When it came time for college, Scott worked toward his BFA and Associate Degree in Illustration. After graduation, however, he wasn't sure of his career direction, so he traveled to London and worked as a freelancer for several music and fashion magazines. Those experiences opened many doors in the publishing industry upon his return to the states.

As Managing Art Director at National Geographic Learning, Scott manages a team of designers, and works to keep projects on time and within budget. In doing so, he places importance on the planning process. Scott suggests asking questions before starting work in order to establish the goal of the project and to understand the client's needs. He also values communication, both with colleagues and clients. He shares, "A big part of my job is not just creating effective designs but selling ideas, so having a good design vocabulary is extremely important."

This design vocabulary often helps Scott interpret criticism creatively. For example, if marketing requests a larger logo, Scott looks for a more elegant way to draw attention to the logo instead of simply enlarging it.

Although he has a variety of projects in his portfolio, Scott has always enjoyed designing book covers. He shares, "A cover creates a reader's first impression and sets the tone for the entire book." Creativity isn't just something Scott values while at work; it spills over into his free time as well. He enjoys drawing, writing, and painting, as well as growing fruits and vegetables in his backyard garden. Scott shares, "It's important for me to unplug whenever possible and just find time to do something more hands-on."

PROJECT DESCRIPTION

In this project, you will redesign the cover of your favorite book. You have complete creative freedom over the direction of the design. Think about the characters and events in the book. What stands out to you most? Explore all of your ideas and design a cover that will convey the feel of the book. The goal of this project is to give future readers visual insight into what the book is about.

QUESTIONS TO CONSIDER

What are the important events in the book?

What colors and images capture the tone of the book?

What is important to convey on the book cover?

GETTING STARTED

A book cover should allude to the plot or overarching theme of the book. From a design perspective, it should also stand out on a bookshelf and capture the reader's attention, making them want to open the cover and read more. Book covers take on a different tone, depending on the genre. If your chosen book is nonfiction—biography, how-to, historical, or commentary—it will carry a different feel than if it is a young adult novel or other fictional book.

Conduct an Internet search on book covers in your chosen book's genre. Compare the images. Pay close attention to the composition. Does the cover have a full illustration, photo, or graphic with the title and author's name centered, or does the text play a greater role, with a small abstract design in the corner? Look also at font choices and color choices. Then recall the events in your chosen book. Which elements from your Internet search would best convey the author's tone? Experiment with ideas and layouts until you create a cover that best represents the plot or theme of the book.

OAHU
living

FALL 2015 • $4.95

A•MAZE•ING
get lost in a
pineapple maze

TWIST & SHOUT
boogie-boarding
daredevils stare down
the north coast waves

MAVERICK
a sizzling interview
with Chef Mavro

16

WORK WITH COLOR

1. Work with Process Colors
2. Apply Color
3. Work with Spot Colors
4. Work with Gradients

Adobe Certified Professional in Print & Digital Media Publication Using Adobe InDesign

1. Working in the Design Industry

This objective covers critical concepts related to working with colleagues and clients as well as crucial legal, technical, and design-related knowledge.

1.4 Demonstrate knowledge of key terminology related to publications.

    B Demonstrate knowledge of how color is created in publications.

2. Project Setup and Interface

This objective covers the interface setup and program settings that assist in an efficient and effective workflow, as well as knowledge about ingesting digital assets for a project.

2.5 Manage colors, swatches, and gradients.

    A Set the active fill and stroke color.
    B Create and customize gradients.
    C Create, manage, and edit swatches and swatch libraries.

3. Organizing Documents

This objective covers document structure such as layers, tracks, and managing document structure for efficient workflows.

3.1 Use layers to manage design elements.

    A Use the Layers panel to modify layers.

4. Creating and Modifying Document Elements

This objective covers core tools and functionality of the application, as well as tools that affect the visual appearance of document elements.

4.6 Modify the appearance of design elements by using effects and styles.

    A Use effects to modify images or frames.

WORK WITH PROCESS COLORS

▶ *What You'll Do*

In this lesson, you will create new process colors and a tint swatch.

Understanding Process Colors

Process colors are colors that are created (and eventually printed) by mixing varying percentages of cyan, magenta, yellow, and black (CMYK) inks. CMYK inks are called **process inks**. Lighter colors are produced with smaller percentages of ink, and darker colors with higher percentages. By mixing CMYK inks, you can produce a large variety of colors, and you can even reproduce color photographs. Think about that for a second—when you look at any

magazine, most if not all the color photographs you see are created using only four colors!

In Adobe InDesign, you create process colors by creating a new swatch on the Swatches panel or in the New Color Swatch dialog box. You then mix percentages of CMYK to create the color. Figure 1 shows the New Color Swatch dialog box, where you name and define a color. You can choose Process or Spot as your type of color using the Color Type list arrow in the New Color Swatch dialog box.

Figure 1 New Color Swatch dialog box

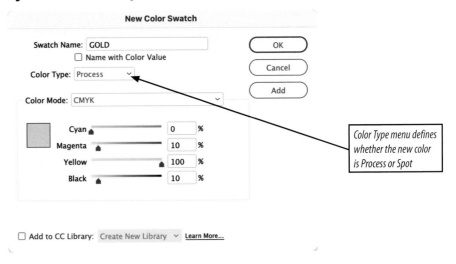

Color Type menu defines whether the new color is Process or Spot

Choosing Process defines the swatch as a process swatch, meaning that it is created with percentages of CMYK ink. Any color you create in this manner is called a **named color** and is added to the Swatches panel, as shown in Figure 2. You can choose to have the color's name defined by CMYK percentages, as shown in the figure, or you can give it another name, if you prefer.

One major benefit of working with named colors is that you can update them. For example, let's say you create a color that is 50% cyan and 50% yellow and you name it warm green. Let's say you fill 10 objects on 10 different pages with warm green, but your client tells you she prefers the objects to be filled with a darker green. You could simply modify the warm green color—change the cyan value to 70% for example—and every object filled with warm green would automatically update to show the darker green.

Figure 2 Swatch added to the Swatches panel

Panel menu button

Paper swatch

New swatch added

Understanding Tints

In the print world, the term "tint" is used to refer to many things. For example, some print professionals refer to all process colors as tints. In Adobe InDesign, however, the term **tint** refers specifically to a lighter version of a color.

Figure 3 shows four squares at the top. The first is filled with 100% cyan, the second is filled with a 50% tint of cyan, the third a 25% tint, and the fourth a 10% tint. Note the variations in color.

Here's the key to understanding tints—the four squares are all filled with the same cyan ink. The only difference is, in the lighter squares, the cyan ink is not solid; it does not cover the square entirely. Instead, some of the white paper is not covered, thus creating the appearance that the square is a lighter tint of cyan.

This is a key concept in printing, and the best way to keep it clear in your mind is to think of a checkerboard. In the figure, the 50% tint is enlarged. You can see it's a checkerboard pattern. 50% of the square is covered with cyan ink, and 50% is the white paper. Thus, the 50% square at the top appears significantly lighter than the 100% square. In the enlargement of the 25% tint, note that the cyan squares are all reduced in size. The square is 25% cyan ink and 75% paper.

Figure 3 Understanding the concept of tints

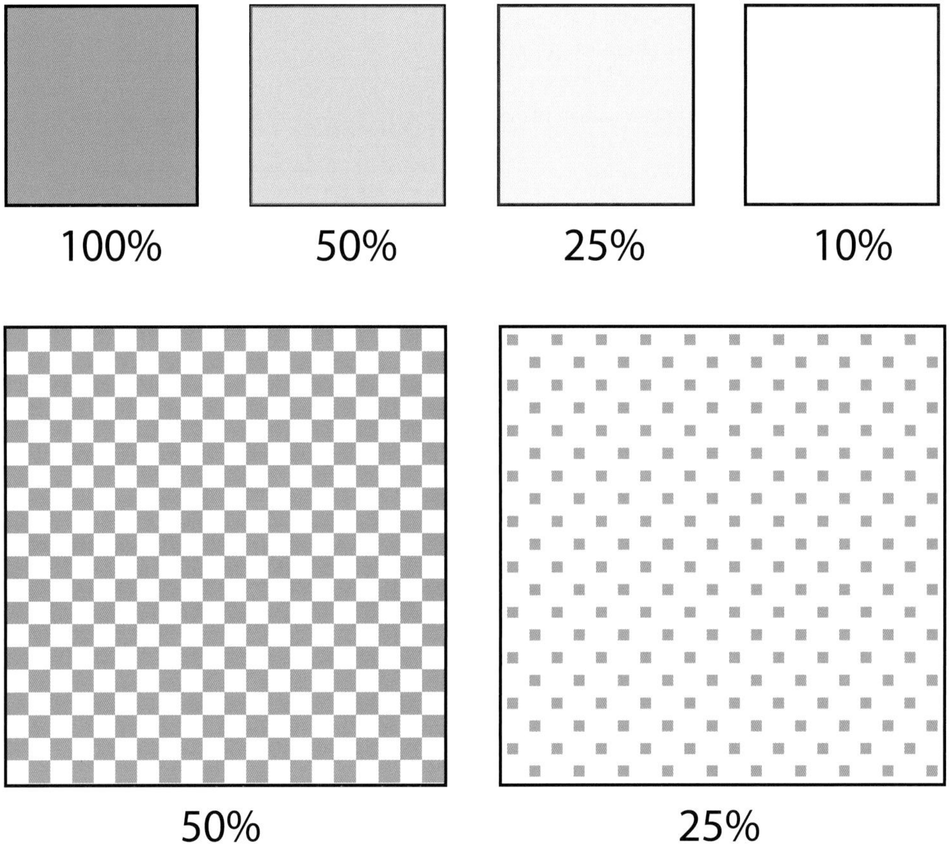

100%   50%   25%   10%

50%   25%

Tints can also be created from more complex process colors. Figure 4 shows a process color that is C16 M100 Y100. It follows logically that the 50% tint of the color is C8 M50 Y50. A tint of any process color is created by multiplying each of the original colors' CMYK values by the desired tint percentage.

Creating Tint Swatches

Like process colors, you use the Swatches panel to create tint swatches. You can select a swatch on the Swatches panel, and then create a tint based on that original swatch by clicking the Swatches panel menu button, clicking New Tint Swatch, and then dragging

the Tint slider to the desired percentage. The resulting tint swatch is given the same name of the color on which it was based, along with the tint percentage next to it, as shown in Figure 5.

If you modify the original swatch, any tint swatch that is based on the original will automatically update to reflect that modification.

For example, if your client says she wants that warm green color to be darker, then any modifications you make to warm green will affect all objects filled with tints of warm green.

Figure 4 A red process color and a 50% tint of that color

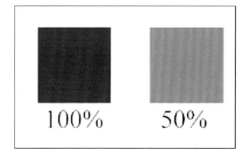

Figure 5 Tint swatch

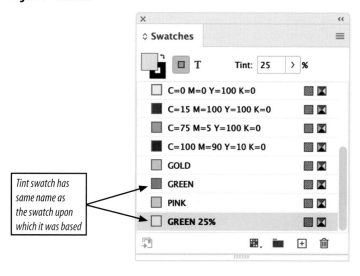

Tint swatch has same name as the swatch upon which it was based

Working with Unnamed Colors

It is not a requirement that you create named swatches for every color you want to use in your layout. Many designers prefer to use the Color panel, shown in Figure 6, to mix colors and apply them to objects. Using the Color panel, you can apply a color to an object by selecting it, then dragging the sliders on the Color panel until you are happy with the new color. As you drag the sliders, the color is continually updated in the selected object. In this way, you can experiment with different colors and allow the document's color scheme to evolve.

When you create colors using the Color panel, those colors are not saved anywhere. Any colors you create that aren't saved to the Swatches panel are called **unnamed colors**.

There's nothing wrong, per se, with working with unnamed colors. You can mix a color on the Color panel, then apply it to an object. No problem. But it's important to understand that the color is not saved anywhere. This can result in problems later on. For example, let's say you mix a royal blue color and apply it to a document, then you show the document to

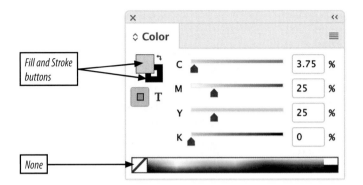

Figure 6 Color panel

your client who says he'd prefer it to be green. So you mix a new green color. Then the client says he prefers the royal blue after all. If you didn't write down the CMYK values of that royal blue, you are out of luck because InDesign does not retain a record of it for you.

Other problems can develop too. Let's say you used that royal blue to fill multiple objects throughout the document. If you wanted to modify the color, you would need to modify each individual usage of the color. This could get very time consuming.

Does this mean you'd be smart not to use the Color panel to mix colors? Not at all. Once you've decided on a color, simply save it on the Swatches panel. It couldn't be easier. Just drag the fill (or stroke) button from the toolbar or the Color panel into the Swatches panel. You can even drag the fill (or stroke) button from the top of the Swatches panel down into the Swatches panel. The swatch will instantly be added to the Swatches panel as a process color, and its CMYK values will be used as its name.

Create process color swatches

1. Open ID 5-1.indd, then save it as **Oahu Magazine Cover**.

2. Display the Swatches panel.

3. Click the **Swatches panel menu button** ▤, then click **New Color Swatch**.

4. Verify that the **Color Type text box** displays **Process** and that the **Color Mode text box** displays **CMYK**.

5. Remove the check mark in the **Name with Color Value check box**, then type **Gold** in the **Swatch Name text box**.

6. Type **0**, **10**, **90**, and **0** in the **Cyan**, **Magenta**, **Yellow**, and **Black text boxes**, as shown in Figure 7.

7. Click **OK**, click the **Swatches panel menu button** ▤, then click **New Color Swatch**.

8. Remove the check mark in the **Name with Color Value check box**, then type **Blue** in the **Swatch Name text box**.

9. Type **85**, **10**, **10**, and **0** in the **Cyan**, **Magenta**, **Yellow**, and **Black text boxes**, then click **OK**.

10. Create a **new process color** named **Pink**, type **20** in the **Magenta text box**, type **0** in the **Cyan**, **Yellow**, and **Black text boxes**, then click **OK**.

    Your Swatches panel should resemble Figure 8.

11. Save your work, then continue to the next set of steps.

You created three new process color swatches.

Figure 7 Creating a process color swatch

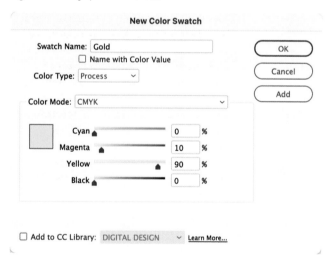

Figure 8 Three new process swatches

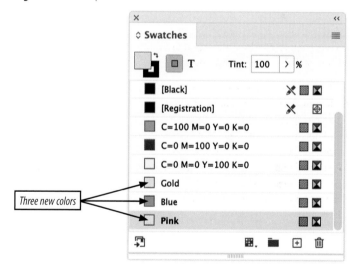

Create a tint swatch and modify the original color swatch

1. Click **Blue** on the Swatches panel, click the **Swatches panel menu button** ☰ , then click **New Tint Swatch**.

2. Drag the **Tint slider** to **25%**, then click **OK**.

   A new 25% tint swatch named Blue 25% appears on the Swatches panel.

3. Double-click the **original Blue swatch** that you created on the Swatches panel.

4. Rename it by typing **Green** in the **Swatch Name text box**, drag the **Yellow slider** to **100%**, then click **OK**.

   As shown in Figure 9, the blue swatch is renamed Green and the 25% tint swatch is renamed Green 25%.

5. Click **File** on the menu bar, then click **Save**.

   Be sure to save your work at this step, as you will later revert to this point in the project.

6. Continue to the next set of steps.

You created a new tint swatch. You then modified the original swatch on which the tint swatch was based, noting that the tint swatch was automatically updated.

Figure 9 Two swatches updated and renamed

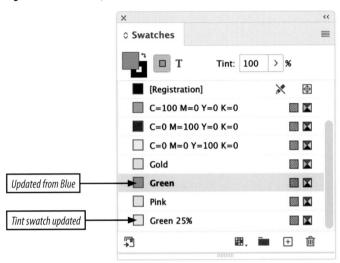

Updated from Blue

Tint swatch updated

Use the Color panel

1. Verify that the **fill button** on the toolbar is activated.

2. Click the **Selection tool** ▶, click the **Cyan-filled frame** that surrounds the image on the page, then display the **Color panel**.

3. Click the **Color panel menu button** ☰, then click **CMYK**.

4. Drag the **Magenta slider** on the Color panel to **50%**, then drag the **Cyan slider** to **50%**, as shown in Figure 10.

   The fill color of the selected frame changes to purple.

   TIP When you create a new color on the Color panel, it becomes the active fill or stroke color on the toolbar, depending on which button is active.

5. Drag the **Yellow slider** to **100%**, then drag the **Cyan slider** to **0%**.

   The purple color that previously filled the frame is gone because you never

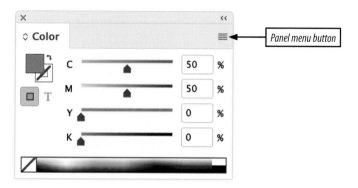

Figure 10 Color panel

actually saved the purple color on the Swatches panel.

TIP Colors that you mix on the Colors panel are not automatically saved on the Swatches panel.

6. Click the **green area** of the **CMYK spectrum** on the Color panel.

7. Drag the **Cyan slider** to **70%**, drag the **Magenta slider** to **20%**, then drag the **Yellow** and **Black sliders** to **0%**.

8. Save your work, then continue to the next set of steps.

You selected an object, then used the Color panel to change its fill to a variety of process colors, none of which were saved on the Swatches panel.

Save an unnamed color on the Swatches panel

1. Drag the **fill color** from the **Color panel** into the Swatches panel.

   A new color is created on the Swatches panel, named with the CMYK percentages.

2. Drag the **Tint slider** on the Color panel to **45%**.

3. Save the new color as a swatch by dragging the **fill button** from the **top of the Swatches panel** to the **bottom of the list of swatches on the Swatches panel**.

   Your Swatches panel should resemble Figure 11.

4. Double-click the **darker blue swatch** on the Swatches panel, remove the check mark in the **Name with Color Value check box**, type **Purple** in the Name text box, drag the **Magenta slider** to **100%**, then click **OK**.

   As shown in Figure 12, the darker blue swatch becomes purple, and the tint swatch based on the darker blue swatch is also updated.

5. Click **File** on the menu bar, click **Revert**, then click **Revert (Mac)** or **Yes (Win)** in the dialog box that follows.

6. Continue to the next lesson.

   The document is reverted to its status when you last saved. The new color swatches you created are no longer on the Swatches panel.

You saved an unnamed color on the Swatches panel, created a tint swatch based on that swatch, then reverted the document.

Figure 11   Adding a tint swatch to the Swatches panel

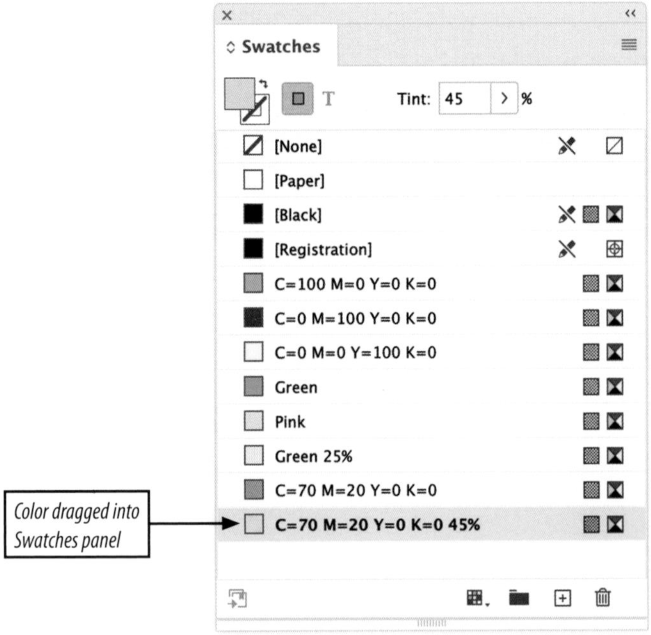

Color dragged into Swatches panel

Figure 12   Two swatches updated with a modification

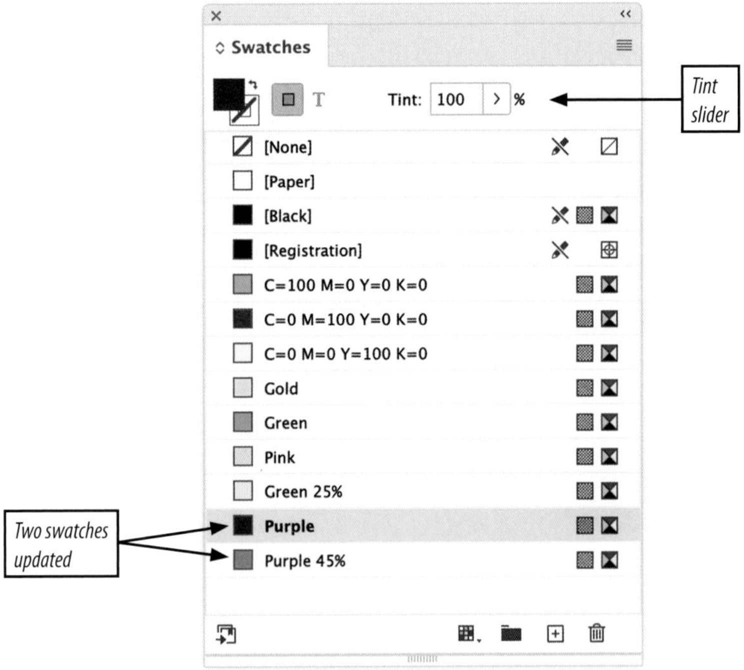

Tint slider

Two swatches updated

APPLY COLOR

In this lesson, you will explore various techniques for applying and modifying color swatches.

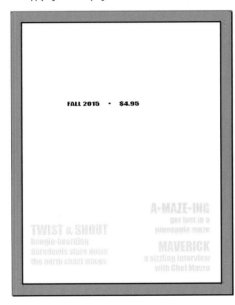

Applying Color to Objects

InDesign offers many options for applying fills and strokes to objects. The most basic method is to select an object, activate either the fill or the stroke button on the toolbar, then click a color on the Swatches panel or mix a color on the Color panel.

Both the Color panel and the Swatches panel have fill and stroke buttons that you can click to activate rather than having to always go back to the toolbar. When you activate the fill or stroke button on any panel, it will be activated in all the panels that have fill and stroke buttons.

Keyboard shortcuts also offer useful options. Pressing the letter [X] toggles between fill and stroke. In other words, if the stroke button is

activated and you press the letter [X], the fill button will be activated. Make a note of this. It's useful and practical and allows you to avoid always having to move the mouse pointer to a panel to activate the fill or the stroke.

Dragging and dropping is also useful. You can drag a swatch from the Swatches panel onto an object and apply the swatch as a fill or a stroke. Drag a swatch over the interior of an object and the swatch will be applied as a fill. If you position the pointer precisely over the object's edge, it will be applied as a stroke. What's interesting about the drag-and-drop method is that the object does not need to be selected for you to apply the fill or the stroke. You can use the drag-and-drop method with any panel that has fill and stroke buttons.

The toolbar offers useful buttons for working with color, as shown in Figure 13. The Default Fill and Stroke button reverts the fill and stroke buttons to their default colors—no fill and a black stroke. Clicking this button will apply a black stroke and no fill to a selected object. The Swap Fill and Stroke button swaps the fill color with the stroke color.

Finally, the three "Apply" buttons on the toolbar are useful for speeding up your work. The Apply Color and Apply Gradient buttons

display the last color and gradient that you've used. This makes for quick and easy access when you are using the same color or gradient repeatedly. The Apply None button is available for removing the fill or stroke from a selected object, depending on which button (fill or stroke) is active on the toolbar.

TIP If you are viewing the toolbar as a single column, you will not see all three of these buttons. Press and hold the current button on the toolbar, then click the desired button.

Understanding the Paper Swatch

If you were given a white piece of paper and a box of crayons and asked to draw a white star against a blue background, you would really have no other option than to color all of the page blue except for the star shape, which you would leave blank. The star would appear as white because the paper is white. The Paper swatch, shown in Figure 14, is based on this very concept. Use the Paper swatch whenever you want an object to have a white fill or stroke.

Figure 13 Useful color buttons on the toolbar

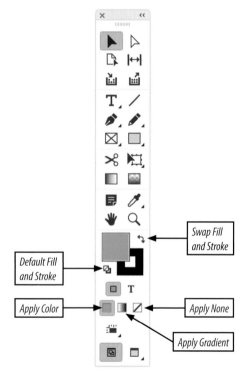

Figure 14 Paper swatch

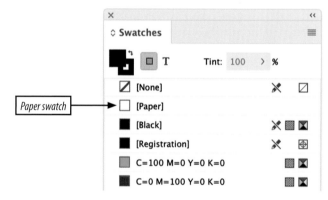

Don't confuse a Paper fill with a None fill. When you fill a frame with Paper, it is filled with white. When you fill it with None, it has no fill—its fill is transparent. Figure 15 illustrates this distinction. In the figure, two text frames are positioned in front of a frame with a yellow fill. The text frame on the left has None as its fill; therefore, the yellow frame behind the text frame is visible. The text frame on the right has Paper as its fill. If you were to print Figure 15, no ink would be used in the area with the Paper fill. The area would be white because the white paper would be visible.

Figure 15 Understanding a Paper fill

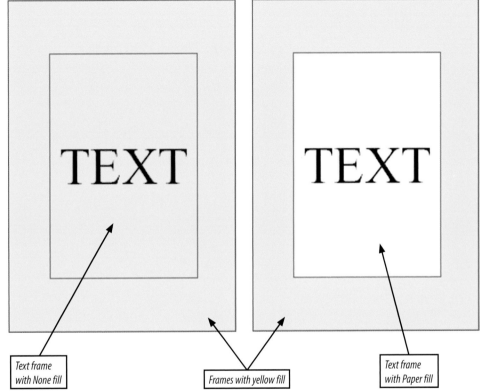

Text frame with None fill

Frames with yellow fill

Text frame with Paper fill

Applying Color to Text

Applying color to text is easy. There are two different methods for applying color to text, depending on whether you are using the Type tool or the Selection tool to select the text.

When you select text with the Type tool, the fill and stroke buttons on the toolbar display the letter T, as shown in Figure 16. This is a visual indication that you are filling or stroking text. Click a swatch on the Swatches panel or mix a color on the Color panel, and the text will be filled or stroked with that color.

> **TIP** The color of the T on the Fill and Stroke buttons is always the same color as the selected text.

When you select a text frame with the Selection tool, you need to tell InDesign what you want to do—apply a fill or stroke to the frame itself or apply a fill or stroke to the text inside the frame. If you want to apply color to the text, click the Formatting affects text button on the Swatches panel, identified in Figure 17. If you want to apply color to the frame, click the Formatting affects container button. It's that simple. Note that the two buttons can also be found on the toolbar and Color panel.

Figure 16 When text is selected, fill and stroke buttons display the letter T

Figure 17 Color formatting buttons

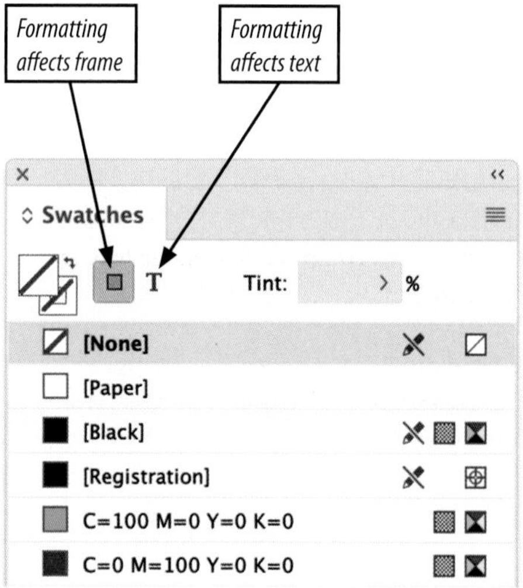

Formatting affects frame

Formatting affects text

Swatches

T   Tint: %

[None]

[Paper]

[Black]

[Registration]

C=100 M=0 Y=0 K=0

C=0 M=100 Y=0 K=0

Creating Black Shadow Text

When you position text against a background color or against a photographic image, sometimes it's not easy to see the text, as shown in Figure 18. To remedy this, many designers use the classic technique of placing a black copy of the text behind the original text, as shown in Figure 19. This trick adds much-needed contrast between the text and the image behind it.

TIP Placing a black copy of text behind original text produces a different effect than using InDesign's Drop Shadow command.

Figure 18 Text positioned against an image

Figure 19 Text with a black copy behind it

Black text placed behind purple text

Modifying and Deleting Swatches

Once you've created a swatch or added a swatch to the Swatches panel, it is a named color and will be saved with the document. Any swatch can be modified simply by double-clicking it, which opens the Swatch Options dialog box. Any modifications you make to the swatch will be updated automatically in any frame that uses the color as a fill or a stroke.

You can also delete a swatch from the Swatches panel by selecting the swatch, then clicking the Delete selected swatch/groups button on the Swatches panel or clicking the Delete Swatch command on the Swatches panel menu. If you are deleting a swatch that is used in your document, the Delete Swatch dialog box opens, shown in Figure 20.

You use the Delete Swatch dialog box to choose a color to replace the deleted swatch. For example, if you've filled (or stroked) many objects with the color warm green and then you delete the warm green swatch, the Delete Swatch dialog box wants to know what color those objects should be. You choose another named color that is already on the Swatches panel by clicking the Defined Swatch list arrow, clicking a color, and then clicking OK. When you do so, all the objects with a warm green fill or stroke will change to the named color you chose. Note that this can be a very quick and effective method for changing the fill (or stroke) color of multiple objects simultaneously.

If you click the Unnamed Swatch option button in the Delete Swatch dialog box, all the objects filled or stroked with the deleted color will retain their color. However, since that color is no longer on the Swatches panel, those objects are now filled with an unnamed color.

Figure 20 Delete Swatch dialog box

Drag and drop colors onto objects

1. Click **View** on the menu bar, point to **Extras,** then click **Hide Frame Edges**.

2. Drag and drop the **Green swatch** on top of the **blue frame**, then release the mouse button.

3. Click the **eye icon** 👁 on the **Photo layer** on the Layers panel to hide the background image.

   Your artboard should resemble Figure 21. The frame with the black stroke does not have a fill, so the larger frame with the green fill shows behind it.

4. Click to select the **frame with the black stroke**.

5. Click **Paper** on the Swatches panel to fill the selected frame.

   The frame is filled with white, as shown in Figure 22.

6. Save your work, then continue to the next set of steps.

You dragged and dropped a color from the Swatches panel to change the fill color of an object on the artboard. You applied the Paper swatch to fill a frame.

Figure 21 Selected frame has a black stroke and no fill

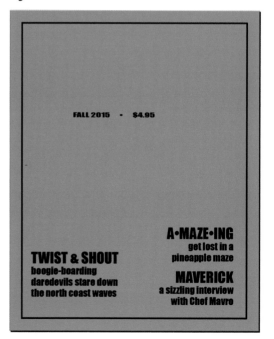

Figure 22 Viewing an object with a Paper fill color

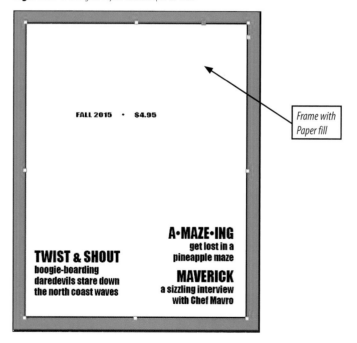

Frame with Paper fill

Apply color to text

1. Click the **Selection tool** , click the **TWIST & SHOUT text frame**, then click the **Formatting affects text button** T on the toolbar.

   As shown in Figure 23, the fill and stroke buttons display the letter T, indicating that any color you click on the Swatches panel will affect the text in the selected frame, not the frame itself.

2. Click **Gold** on the Swatches panel.

3. Click the **A·MAZE·ING text frame**, then note that the **Formatting affects container button** ☐ is active on the toolbar because you have selected a frame.

4. Click the **Type tool** T, then select **all the text in the A·MAZE·ING text frame**.

TIP When you select text with the Type tool T, the Formatting affects text button T on the toolbar is automatically activated.

5. Click **Pink** on the Swatches panel.

6. Click the **Selection tool** ▶, click the **MAVERICK text frame**, then click the **Formatting affects text button** T on the Swatches panel.

7. Click the **Green 25% swatch** on the Swatches panel so that your document resembles Figure 24.

You explored two methods for applying color to text. In the first, you selected text with the Selection tool, clicked the Formatting affects text button, then chose a new color. In the second, you selected text with the Type tool, then chose a new color.

Figure 23 Fill and stroke buttons with selected text

Figure 24 Viewing the colors applied to text

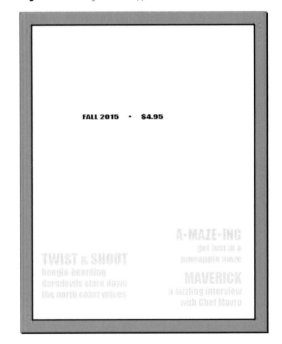

FALL 2015 • $4.95

A·MAZE·ING
get lost in a
pineapple maze

TWIST & SHOUT
boogie-boarding
daredevils stare down
the north coast waves

MAVERICK
a sizzling interview
with Chef Mavro

Create black shadow text

1. Show the **Photo layer** on the Layers panel, and then assess the legibility of the text in the three text frames against the background graphic.

   The text on the right is perfectly legible, but the text on the left is difficult to distinguish from the bright and busy background. You will add black shadow text to try to improve legibility.

2. Click the **Original Black Text layer** on the Layers panel, click the **Layers panel menu button** ☰, then click **Duplicate Layer "Original Black Text."**

3. Double-click the **Original Black Text copy layer** on the Layers panel to open the Layer Options dialog box.

4. Type **Color Headlines** in the Name text box, click the **Color list arrow**, then click **Orange** so your Layer Options dialog box resembles Figure 25.

5. Click **OK**, then hide the **Original Black Text layer**.

6. With the **Color Headlines layer** still selected, delete the **Fall 2015 text frame** on the Color Headlines layer since you will not need a duplicate of this text.

7. Hide the **Color Headlines layer**, then show the **Original Black Text layer**.

8. Click the **selected items button** ☐ on the **Original Black Text layer** to select all the objects on the layer.

9. Click the **Formatting affects text button** T on the Swatches panel, then apply a **100% Black fill** to all the text.

   You will need to use the Tint slider on the Swatches panel to make all the text 100% black.

10. Deselect all.

11. Show the **Color Headlines layer**, then click the **selected items button** ☐ to select all objects on the layer.

12. Press the **up arrow** on your keypad two times, then press the **right arrow** two times.

   Your work should resemble Figure 26. The black shadow goes far toward improving legibility. The gold text on the left is easier to read against the background, but it's not nearly as legible as the text on the right. You will take a different approach to improving its legibility later in this chapter.

13. Save your work, then continue to the next set of steps.

You duplicated a layer containing text. You changed the fill color of the text on the lower layer to black, then repositioned the colored text on the upper layer so that the black text acts as a shadow. By doing so, you added contrast to the colored text, making it more legible against the picture on the Photo layer.

Figure 25 Layer Options dialog box

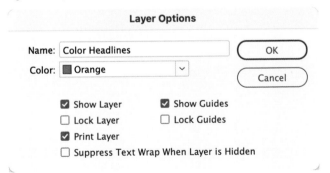

Figure 26 Using black shadow text to improve legibility

Modify and delete swatches

1. Deselect all, then drag the **Gold swatch** onto the **green frame** to change the green frame to gold.

2. Double-click the **Gold swatch** on the Swatches panel.

3. Activate the Preview option, if necessary; drag the **Black slider** to **5%**; then drag the **Magenta slider** to **100%**.

4. Click **OK**.

All usages of the Gold swatch—the frame and the "Twist & Shout" text—are updated with the modification to red.

5. Drag the **Gold swatch** to the **Delete selected swatch/groups button**  on the Swatches panel.

6. Click the **Defined Swatch list arrow** in the Delete Swatch dialog box, click **Pink**, as shown in Figure 27, then click **OK**.

As shown in Figure 28, all usages of the Gold swatch in the document are replaced by the Pink swatch.

7. Save your work, then continue to the next lesson.

You modified a swatch and noted that it updated throughout the document. You then deleted the swatch, replacing all its usages with a different swatch.

Figure 27 Delete Swatch dialog box

Figure 28 Gold colors replaced by pink colors

emperorcosar/Shutterstock

WORK WITH SPOT COLORS

In this lesson, you will create and apply spot colors, and import graphics that contain spot colors.

Understanding Spot Colors

Spot colors are non-process inks that are manufactured by companies. They are special pre-mixed inks that are printed separately from process inks. Though printing is based on the four process colors, CMYK, it is not limited to them. It is important to understand that although combinations of CMYK inks can produce a wide variety of colors—enough to reproduce any color photograph quite well—they can't produce every color. For this reason and others, designers often turn to spot colors.

Imagine you are an art director designing the masthead for the cover of a new magazine. You have decided that the masthead will be electric blue—vivid and eye-catching. If you were working with process tints only, you would have a problem. First, you would find that the almost-neon blue you want to achieve is not within the CMYK range; it can't be printed. Even if it could, you would have a bigger problem with consistency issues. You would want that blue to be the same blue on every issue of the magazine, month after month. But offset printing is never perfect; variations in dot size are factored in. As the cover is printed, the blue color in the masthead will certainly vary, sometimes drastically.

Designers and printers use spot colors to solve this problem. The color range of spot colors far exceeds that of CMYK. Spot colors also offer consistent color throughout a print run.

The design and print worlds refer to spot colors by a number of names:

- Non-process inks: Refers to the fact that spot colors are not created using the process inks—CMYK.
- Fifth color: Refers to the fact that the spot color is often printed in addition to the four process inks. Note, however, that a spot color is not necessarily the "fifth" color. For example, many "two-color" projects call for black plus one spot color.
- PANTONE color: PANTONE is a manufacturer of non-process inks. PANTONE is simply a brand name.
- PMS color: An acronym for PANTONE Matching System.

A good way to think of spot colors is as ink in a bucket. With process inks, if you want red, you must mix some amount of magenta ink with some amount of yellow ink. With spot colors, if you want red, you pick a number from a chart, open the bucket, and there's the red ink—pre-mixed and ready to print.

Creating Spot Color Swatches

You create spot color swatches in Adobe InDesign using the New Color Swatch dialog box. Instead of choosing CMYK values, as you would when you create a process color, you choose Spot from the Color Type list, then choose a spot color system from one of 30 systems in the Color Mode list. After you choose a system, the related library of spot colors loads into the New Swatch dialog box, allowing you to choose the spot color you want. Figure 29 shows the PANTONE+ Solid Coated color system.

Importing Graphics with Spot Colors

When you create graphics in Adobe Illustrator or Adobe Photoshop, you can create and apply spot colors in those applications as well. For example, you can create a logo in Adobe Illustrator and fill it with a spot color.

Because InDesign, Illustrator, and Photoshop are all made by Adobe, InDesign recognizes the spot colors applied to graphics created in those applications. In the previous example, when you place the graphic from Illustrator, InDesign identifies the spot color that was used and adds it to the InDesign Swatches panel. If you double-click the swatch on the Swatches panel, you will see that the swatch is automatically formatted as a spot color.

Figure 29 Creating a spot color swatch

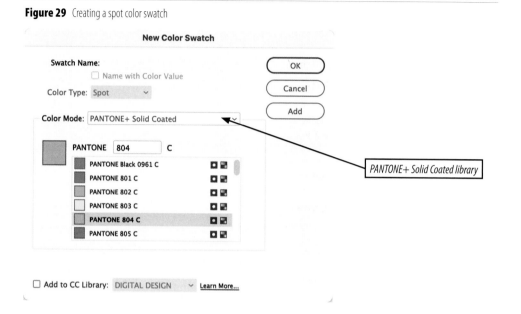

PANTONE+ Solid Coated library

Create a spot color swatch

1. Click the **Swatches panel menu button** ☰, then click **New Color Swatch**.

2. Click the **Color Type list arrow**, then click **Spot**.

3. Click the **Color Mode list arrow**, then click **PANTONE+ Solid Coated**.

4. Type **663** in the PANTONE text box so your New Color Swatch dialog box resembles Figure 30.

5. Click **OK**.

   The PANTONE swatch appears on the Swatches panel. As shown in Figure 31, the icons on the right are different from the process tints shown on the other colors.

6. Change the **fill of the pink frame** to **PANTONE 663**.

7. Change the **fill of the TWIST & SHOUT text** to **PANTONE 663**.

8. Save your work, then continue to the next set of steps.

You created a spot color swatch and then applied it to elements in the layout.

Figure 30 Creating a spot color

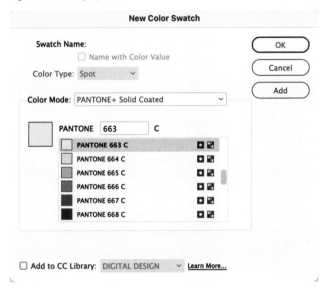

Figure 31 PANTONE swatch on the Swatches panel

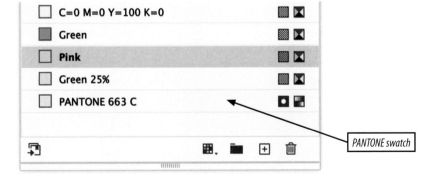

Import graphics with spot colors

1. Click the **Imported Graphics layer** on the Layers panel to target it, click the **Selection tool** ▶, then select the **frame** shown in Figure 32.

TIP Clicking in the general area of the selected frame shown in Figure 32 will select the frame.

2. Click **File** on the menu bar, click **Place**, navigate to the drive and folder where your Chapter 16 Data Files are stored, click **Living Graphic.ai**, then click **Open**.

3. Click **Object** on the menu bar, point to **Fitting**, then click **Center Content**.

    The graphic that is placed in the frame was created in Adobe Illustrator and was filled in Illustrator with PANTONE 159 C. Note that PANTONE 159 C has been automatically added as a spot color to the Swatches menu in InDesign.

TIP When you place graphics that are filled with spot colors, InDesign automatically adds those spot colors to the Swatches panel.

4. Select the **frame** shown in Figure 33.

5. Click **File** on the menu bar, click **Place**, navigate to the drive and folder where your Chapter 16 Data Files are stored, then double-click **OAHU graphic.ai**.

    OAHU graphic.ai is an Adobe Illustrator file. The fill color of O, A, H, and U is PANTONE 663—the same PANTONE 663 color that you created in InDesign. For this reason, PANTONE 663 does not need to be added to the Swatches panel.

6. Click **Object** on the menu bar, point to **Fitting,** then click **Center Content**.

7. Deselect all, then compare your document with Figure 34.

8. Save your work, then close the OAHU Magazine Cover document.

You imported a graphic that was created with a spot color in another application, then noted that the spot color was automatically added to the Swatches panel. Next, you imported a graphic that was filled with the same spot color that you had already created in InDesign.

Figure 32 Selecting a frame for a graphic

Figure 33 Selected frame

Figure 34 Magazine cover with all elements in place

WORK WITH GRADIENTS

In this lesson, you will create gradients and explore options for applying them to frames.

Creating Gradients

A **gradient** is a graduated blend of two or more colors. Every gradient must have at least two colors, which are commonly referred to as the **starting** and **ending colors** of the gradient. You can add more colors to a gradient—colors that come between the starting and ending colors. The colors that you add between the starting and ending colors are called **color stops**.

In InDesign, you create gradients by clicking New Gradient Swatch on the Swatches panel menu. This opens the New Gradient Swatch dialog box, shown in Figure 35. In this dialog box, you define all the elements of the gradient. You use the Gradient Ramp to define the starting and ending colors, as well as any intermediary colors for your gradient. You can choose your colors from a list of existing swatches, or you can mix colors using sliders.

Figure 35 New Gradient Swatch dialog box

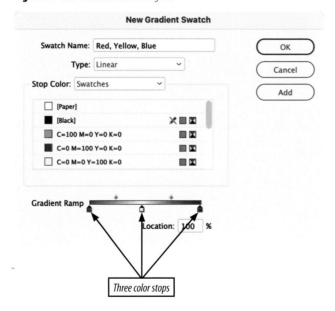

In this dialog box, you also choose whether your gradient will be radial or linear using the Type list arrow. You can think of a **radial gradient** as a series of concentric circles. With a radial gradient, the starting color appears at the center of the gradient, then radiates out to the ending color. You can think of a **linear gradient** as a series of straight lines that gradate from one color to another (or through multiple colors). Figure 36 shows a linear and a radial gradient, each composed of three colors.

Figure 37 shows the dialog box used to create the linear gradient in Figure 36. The Gradient Ramp shows the three colors in the gradient, and the yellow color stop is selected. The sliders show the CMYK values that make the yellow tint.

When you close the New Gradient Swatch dialog box, the new gradient swatch appears on the Swatches panel.

TIP On the Swatches panel, you can choose to view only swatches, only gradients, or only color groups by clicking the Swatch Views button ▦. on the Swatches panel and choosing Show Color Swatches, Show Gradient Swatches, or Show Color Groups. To view all swatches, choose Show All Swatches.

Figure 36 A linear and a radial gradient

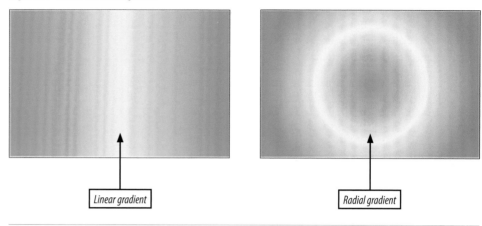

Linear gradient

Radial gradient

Figure 37 Cyan, Yellow, Green gradient settings

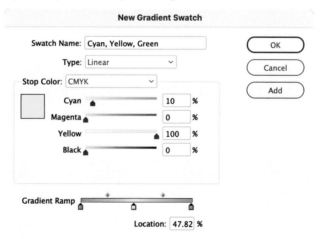

Applying Gradients

You apply a gradient to an object the same way you apply a color to an object. Simply select the object, then click the gradient on the Swatches panel. A gradient swatch can be applied as a fill or as a stroke.

If you use a gradient to fill an object, you can further control how the gradient fills the object using the Gradient Swatch tool. The Gradient Swatch tool allows you to change the length and/or direction of a linear or radial gradient.

To use the Gradient Swatch tool, first select an object with a gradient fill, then drag the Gradient Swatch tool over the object. For both linear and radial gradients, where you begin dragging and where you stop dragging determine the length of the gradient, from starting color to ending color. For linear gradients, the direction in which you drag the Gradient Swatch tool determines the angle that the gradient fills the object.

Figure 38 shows a rainbow gradient applied to objects in different ways. In the top row, the rainbow gradients fill each of the six boxes separately. In the second row, the Gradient Swatch tool is dragged across all six boxes, so the gradient itself extends across all six boxes. The black lines in the remaining four examples show how the Gradient Swatch tool was dragged across each row.

Figure 38 Using the Gradient Swatch tool

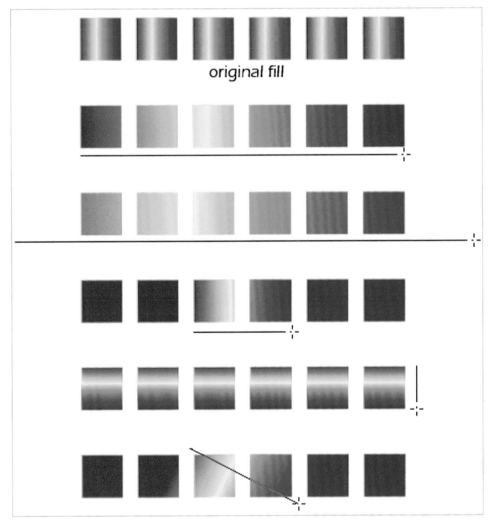

original fill

Modifying a Gradient Fill Using the Gradient Panel

Like color swatches, gradients can be modified. When you modify a gradient, all instances of the gradient used in the document will be automatically updated. Let's say you create a gradient and use it to fill 10 objects. Then you decide that in only one of those 10 objects, you want to modify the gradient by removing one color. What do you do? If you modify the gradient swatch by removing a color stop, it's going to affect all usages of the gradient. You could duplicate the gradient swatch, remove the unwanted color stop, then apply the new gradient to the single object. But there's a better way. You can use the Gradient panel, shown in Figure 39.

When you select an object with a gradient fill, the Gradient panel shows the Gradient Ramp you used to create the gradient in the New Gradient Swatch dialog box. You can manipulate the Gradient Ramp on the Gradient panel. You can add, move, and delete color stops. You can also select color stops and modify their color using the Color panel. Here's the great part—the modifications you make on the Gradient panel only affect the gradient fill of the selected object(s).

Figure 39 Gradient panel

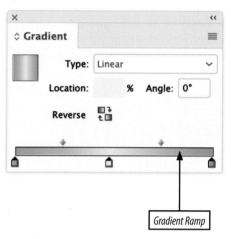

Gradient Ramp

Using the Gradient Feather Tool

The **Gradient Feather tool** causes a fill color to fade gradually to transparent. For example, if you have a frame filled with cyan and you drag the Gradient Feather tool from left to right over the width of the frame, the cyan color will fade from 100% cyan to 0% cyan.

From left to right, the cyan color will become increasingly transparent.

Figure 40 shows an image in a frame and an identically sized frame filled with black. Note that the text is difficult to read over the busy stripes in the image. In Figure 41, the Gradient Feather tool has been used to fade the black so it appears only at the bottom of the frame. When the black frame is positioned over the image, as shown in Figure 42, the effect is that of shadow that fades up from the bottom. It's a great effect, and it can be very useful for hiding problem areas of an image or, as in this case, for making text stand out better against a busy background.

Figure 40 Text over the image is difficult to read

Krakenimages/Shutterstock

Figure 41 Black fill fades with the Gradient Feather tool

Fades upward to None

Figure 42 Black fade makes text more legible and adds a visually interesting effect

CALL ME

Create a linear gradient swatch

1. Open ID 5-2.indd, then save it as **Making the Gradient**.

2. Click the **Swatches panel menu button** , then click **New Gradient Swatch**.

3. In the Swatch Name text box, type **Blue/Gold/Red Linear**.

4. Click the **left color stop** on the Gradient Ramp, click the **Stop Color list arrow**, then click **Swatches** so your dialog box resembles Figure 43.

When you choose Swatches, all the colors on the Swatches panel become available for the gradient.

5. Click the **swatch** named **Blue**.

The left color stop on the Gradient Ramp changes to blue.

6. Click the **right color stop** on the Gradient Ramp, click the **Stop Color list arrow**, click **Swatches**, then click the swatch named **Red**.

7. Click directly **below the Gradient Ramp** to add a new color stop.

TIP Click anywhere to add the new color stop. You can adjust the location using the Location text box.

8. Type **50** in the Location text box, then press **[tab]**.

The new color stop is located at the exact middle of the Gradient Ramp.

9. Click the **Stop Color list arrow**, click **Swatches**, then click the **swatch** named **Gold** so your New Gradient Swatch dialog box resembles Figure 44.

The new gradient swatch is added to the Swatches panel.

10. Click **OK**, save your work, then continue to the next set of steps.

You created a three-color linear gradient swatch using three named colors.

Figure 43 New Gradient Swatch dialog box

Figure 44 Adding a color stop

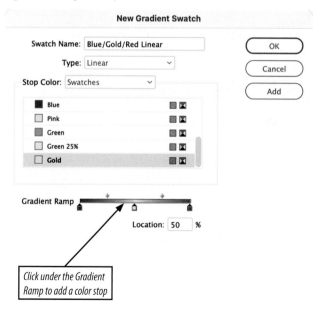

Create a radial gradient swatch

1. Click the **Swatches panel menu button** ≡ , then click **New Gradient Swatch**.

   The New Gradient Swatch dialog box opens with the settings from the last created gradient.

2. In the Swatch Name text box, type **Cyan Radial**.

3. Click the **Type list arrow**, then click **Radial**.

4. Click the **center color stop**, then drag it straight down to remove it from the Gradient Ramp.

5. Click the **left color stop** on the Gradient Ramp, click the **Stop Color list arrow**, then click **CMYK**.

6. Drag **each slider** to **0%**.

7. Click the **right color stop** on the Gradient Ramp, click the **Stop Color list arrow**, then click **CMYK**.

8. Drag the **Cyan slider** to **100%**, then drag the **Magenta**, **Yellow**, and **Black sliders** to **0%** so your dialog box resembles Figure 45.

9. Click **OK**, save your work, then continue to the next set of steps.

   The new gradient swatch is added to the Swatches panel.

You created a two-color radial gradient swatch using CMYK values.

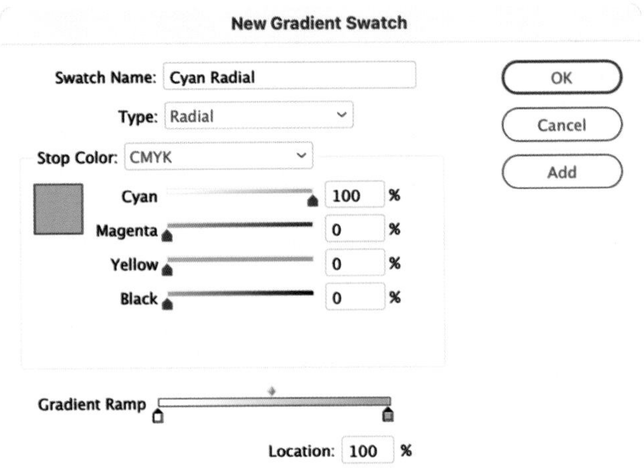

Figure 45 Settings for a radial gradient

Apply gradient swatches and use the Gradient Swatch tool

1. Click the **Selection tool** ▶, select the **top frame**, then fill it with the **Blue/Gold/Red Linear gradient** from the Swatches panel.

TIP Make sure you are in Normal view and that you are viewing frame edges.

2. Click the **Gradient Swatch tool** 🔲 on the toolbar. Then, using Figure 46 as a guide, place the mouse pointer anywhere on the **top edge of the rectangular frame**, click and drag down, and release the mouse button at the bottom edge of the frame.

Your result should resemble Figure 47.

TIP Pressing and holding [shift] while dragging the Gradient Swatch tool 🔲 constrains the movement on a horizontal or vertical axis.

3. Drag the **Gradient Swatch tool** 🔲 from the **bottom-middle handle** of the frame to the **top-right handle**.

4. Drag the **Gradient Swatch tool** 🔲 from the **left edge of the document window** to the **right edge of the document window**.

5. Drag the **Gradient Swatch tool** 🔲 a **short distance from left to right in the center of the frame**, as shown in Figure 48.

6. Click the **Selection tool** ▶, click the **edge of the circular frame**, then click **Cyan Radial** on the Swatches panel.

7. Click the **Gradient Swatch tool** 🔲, press and hold **[shift]**, then drag the **Gradient Swatch tool** 🔲 from the **center point of the circle** up to the **bottom edge of the center rectangle above the circle** so your document resembles Figure 49.

8. Save your work, then continue to the next set of steps.

You filled two objects with two different gradients, and you used the Gradient Swatch tool to manipulate how the gradients filled the objects.

Figure 46 Dragging the Gradient Swatch tool straight down

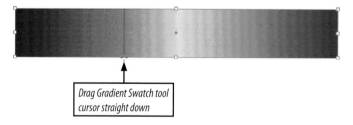

Drag Gradient Swatch tool cursor straight down

Figure 47 Linear gradient applied vertically to the frame

Figure 48 Dragging the Gradient Swatch tool from left to right

Figure 49 Gradients applied to two objects

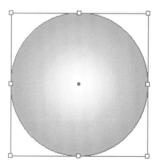

Use the Gradient Swatch tool to extend a gradient across multiple objects

1. Click **Window** on the menu bar, point to **Color**, then click **Gradient** to open the Gradient panel.

2. Deselect all, click the **Selection tool** ▶, then select the **three rectangular frames above the circle**.

3. Click **Blue/Gold/Red Linear** on the Swatches panel.

   As shown in Figure 50, the gradient fills each frame individually.

4. With the **three objects** still selected, click the **Gradient Swatch tool** ▣, then drag it from the **left edge of the leftmost frame** to the **right edge of the rightmost frame**.

   As shown in Figure 51, the gradient gradates across all three selected objects.

5. Click the **Selection tool** ▶, then click the **rectangular frame at the top of the document window**.

6. Drag the **Gold color stop** on the Gradient Ramp straight down to remove it.

   The gold color is only removed from the gradient fill in the *selected* frame. The original gradient on the Swatches panel (Blue/Gold/Red Linear) is not affected.

7. Save your work, then close the Making the Gradient document.

You selected three objects, applied a gradient to each of them, then used the Gradient Swatch tool to extend the gradient across all three selected objects. You then modified the gradient fill of a selected object by removing a color stop from the Gradient Ramp.

Figure 50 A gradient fill applied individually to three objects

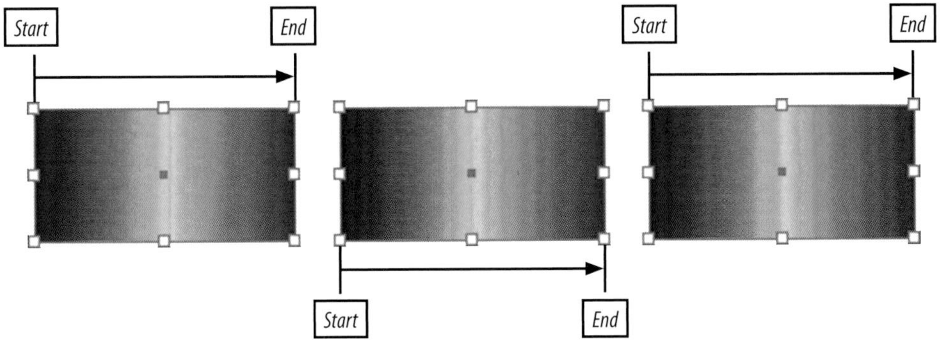

Figure 51 A gradient fill gradating across three objects

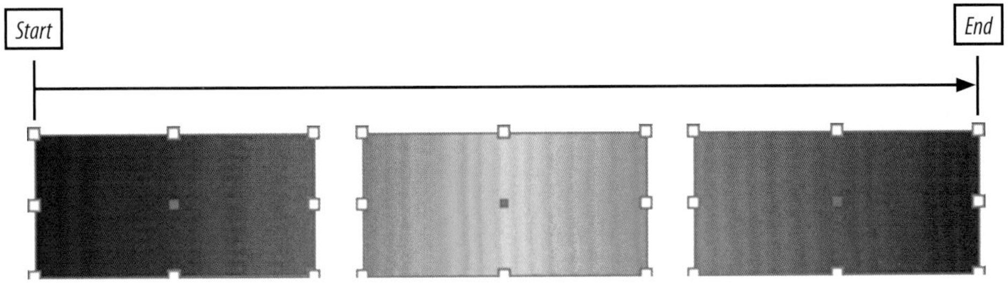

Fade color with the Gradient Feather tool

1. Open ID 5-3.indd, then save it as **Oahu Magazine Cover Final**.

    This file is at the same stage as it was when you completed Lesson 3 in this chapter.

2. Click the **Selection tool** ▶ , then click the **image** to select it.

3. Click **Edit** on the menu bar, click **Copy**, click **Edit** again, then click **Paste in Place**.

    A copy of the frame with the image is placed in the exact same location, above the original.

4. Click **Object** on the menu bar, point to **Transform**, then click **Move**.

5. Enter the settings shown in Figure 52, then click **OK**.

6. Deselect.

7. Click the **Direct Selection tool** ▷ , click the **center of the image** once to select it, then press **[delete]** on your keypad.

    The image is deleted and all that's left is the frame.

Continued on next page

Figure 52 Moving the copy 8" to the right

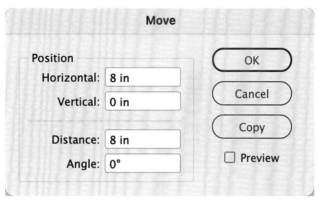

8. Fill the **frame** with the **100% Cyan** and **85% Magenta**, as shown in Figure 53.

9. Click the **Gradient Feather tool** .

10. Drag the **Gradient Feather tool** from the **bottom edge of the frame straight up**, and release it approximately one-third of the height of the frame.

Use Figure 54 as a guide.

11. Use the **Move dialog box** to move the frame **8" to the left**.

Your artwork should resemble Figure 55. The beach image behind the text on the left is now behind the blue fade. The beach image is still visible, but it's substantially more muted. As a result, the text on the left is now completely legible.

12. Save your work, then close the Oahu Magazine Cover Final document.

You duplicated the frame that contained the image, moved it exactly 8" to the right, then deleted the image. You filled the frame with blue, then faded it using the Gradient Feather tool. You then moved the frame to the left the exact same distance, using the blue fade to mute the background image and help the text on the left to be more legible.

Figure 53 Filling the frame with blue

Figure 54 Fading the blue fill with the Gradient Feather tool

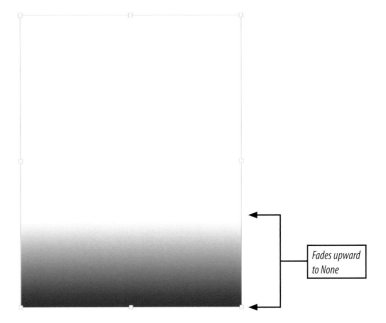

Fades upward to None

Work with process colors

1. Open ID 5-4.indd, then save it as **LAB cover**.
2. Verify that the Swatches panel is open, click the Swatches panel menu button, then click New Color Swatch.
3. Verify that Process is chosen in the Color Type text box and that CMYK is chosen in the Color Mode text box.
4. Remove the check mark in the Name with Color Value check box, then type **Pink** in the Swatch Name text box.
5. Type **15** in the Cyan text box, press [tab], type **70** in the Magenta text box, press [tab], type **10** in the Yellow text box, press [tab], type **0** in the Black text box, press [tab], then click OK.
6. Display the Color panel if necessary.
7. Click the Color panel menu button, click CMYK, then verify that the fill button is activated.
8. Drag the Cyan slider on the Color panel to 50%, drag the Magenta slider to 10%, then drag the Yellow and Black sliders to 0%.
9. Drag the color from the fill button on the Color panel to the Swatches panel.

10. Verify that the C = 50 M = 10 Y = 0 K = 0 swatch is still selected on the Swatches panel, click the Swatches panel menu button, then click New Tint Swatch.
11. Drag the Tint slider to 35%, then click OK.

Apply color

1. Duplicate the Text layer, then rename it **Colored Text**.
2. Click View on the menu bar, point to Extras, then click Hide Frame Edges.
3. Drag and drop C = 50 M = 10 Y = 0 K = 0 from the Swatches panel to the outermost, black-filled frame.
4. Click the Selection tool, click the BRUSH UP text frame, then click the Formatting affects text button on the toolbar.
5. Click the C = 5 0 M = 10 Y = 0 K = 0 swatch on the Swatches panel.
6. Click the Holiday Issue text frame in the lower-left corner of the cover, click the Formatting affects text button on the Swatches panel, then click the Paper swatch on the Swatches panel.
7. Click the Type tool, select all the text in the PUPPY LOVE text frame, then click Pink on the Swatches panel.

8. Select all the text in the FETCH text frame, then click the C = 50 M = 10 Y = 0 K = 0 35% tint swatch on the Swatches panel.
9. Click the selected items button on the Colored Text layer to select all the items on the layer.
10. Click Object on the menu bar, point to Transform, then click Move.
11. Verify that there is a check mark in the Preview check box, type **–.03** in the Horizontal text box, type **–.03** in the Vertical text box, click OK, then deselect all.

Work with spot colors

1. Click the Swatches panel menu button, then click New Color Swatch.
2. Click the Color Type list arrow, then click Spot.
3. Click the Color Mode list arrow, then click PANTONE+ Solid Coated.
4. Type **117** in the PANTONE text box, then click OK.
5. Change the fill on the C = 50 M = 10 border to PANTONE 117 C.
6. Click the Imported Graphics layer on the Layers panel to target it, click the Selection tool, then click between the dog's eyes to select the frame for placing a new image.

7. Click File on the menu bar, click Place, navigate to the drive and folder where your Chapter 16 Data Files are stored, click LAB.ai, then click Open.

TIP LAB.ai is an Adobe Illustrator graphic filled with PANTONE 117 C.

8. Click the Photo layer on the Layers panel, click the dog graphic in the document window, click Edit on the menu bar, click Copy, click Edit on the menu bar, then click Paste in Place.

9. On the Layers panel, drag the selected items button from the Photo layer up to the Imported Graphics layer.

10. Click File on the menu bar, click Place, navigate to the drive and folder where your Chapter 16 Data Files are stored, then double-click Wally Head Silo.psd.

TIP Wally Head Silo.psd is identical to the dog photo, with the exception that it was saved with a clipping path around the dog's head to remove the red background.

11. Deselect all, then compare your work to Figure 56.

12. Save your work, then close the LAB cover document.

Figure 56 Completed Skills Review, Part 1

Work with gradients

1. Open ID 5-5.indd, then save it as **Gradient Skills Review**.
2. Click the Swatches panel menu button, then click New Gradient Swatch.
3. In the Swatch Name text box, type **Red/Golden/ Green Linear**.
4. Click the left color stop on the Gradient Ramp, click the Stop Color list arrow, then click Swatches.
5. Click the Red swatch.
6. Click the right color stop on the Gradient Ramp, click the Stop Color list arrow, click Swatches, then click the Green swatch.
7. Click immediately below the Gradient Ramp to add a third color stop.
8. Type **50** in the Location text box, then press [tab].
9. Click the Stop Color list arrow, choose Swatches, click the Gold swatch, then click OK.
10. Click the Selection tool, select the border of the top rectangular frame, verify that the fill button is activated on the toolbar, then click Red/Golden/ Green Linear on the Swatches panel.
11. Click the Gradient Swatch tool, then drag from the top-middle handle of the rectangular frame down to the bottom-right handle.
12. Display the Gradient panel if necessary.
13. Click the Selection tool, deselect the top rectangular frame, then select the three lower rectangular frames.
14. Click Red/Golden/Green Linear on the Swatches panel.
15. Click the Gradient Swatch tool, and with all three objects still selected, drag the Gradient Swatch tool from the left edge of the leftmost frame to the right edge of the rightmost frame.
16. Deselect all, then compare your work to Figure 57.
17. Save your work, then close the Gradient Skills Review document.

Figure 57 Completed Skills Review, Part 2

You are a freelance graphic designer. You have recently been contracted to design a postcard that will be sent out in a mass mailing for the launch of a new fragrance. This is part of a larger worldwide campaign, and you are asked to work with only the colors from the bottle. The postcard will be printed with only four colors, so any tints you create must be process tints. You are told that no type can be white, because that is the color of the name on the bottle, and it should be the brightest type on the postcard.

1. Open ID 5-6.indd, then save it as **Swerve Postcard**.
2. Click the Eyedropper tool, then click the center of the perfume bottle to sample the color.
   The foreground color changes to the sampled color.
3. Open the Color panel, then set its sliders to CMYK so you can see the breakdown of the color, as shown in Figure 58.
4. Create a new Swatch named **Swerve Tan**, based on the values in Figure 58.
5. Create at least two tint swatches based on Swerve Tan.

Figure 58 Process tint breakdown on the Color panel

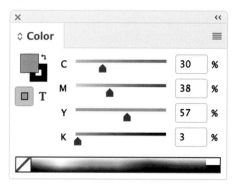

PROJECT BUILDER 1

(continued)

6. Colorize the magenta text and the promo label as you like with the new colors you've created. Figure 59 shows one result.

7. Save your work, then close the Swerve Postcard document.

Figure 59 One version of the postcard

You are a freelance graphic designer. You have recently been contracted to create a cover for LAB magazine. The magazine is usually published with only one color—in black and white—but the publishers have some extra money for this issue. They want you to create a design for this cover so it will print as a two-color job. It will be printed with black and one spot color. They provide you with the black and white version of the cover. You are free to choose the spot color and apply it in whatever way you think is best.

1. Open ID 5-7.indd, then save it as **2 Color Cover**.
2. Click the Swatches panel menu button, then click New Color Swatch.
3. Click the Color Type list arrow, then choose Spot.
4. Click the Color Mode list arrow, then choose PANTONE + Solid Coated.
5. Choose PANTONE 195 C, then click OK.
6. Click the Swatches panel menu button, then click New Tint Swatch.
7. Drag the Tint slider to 25%, then click OK.
8. Change the fill of the outermost frame that is filled with black to PANTONE 195 C.
9. Click the inner white border that is filled with Paper and stroked with Black, then change its fill color to PANTONE 195 C 25%.
10. Change the fill color on the three white headlines to PANTONE 195 C 25%.
11. Compare your cover to Figure 60, save your work, then close the 2 Color Cover document.

Figure 60 Completed Project Builder 2

DESIGN PROJECT 1

You have recently been contracted to create a logo for the Illusionists Foundation. A representative from the organization tells you that he wants the logo to be a circle filled with a radial gradient. Starting from the inside of the circle, the colors should go from white to black to white to black to white to black. He tells you that he wants each color to be very distinct. In other words, he doesn't want the white and black colors to blend into each other and create gray areas in the logo.

1. Open ID 5-8.indd, then save it as **Concentric Circle Gradient**.
2. Click the Swatches panel menu button, then click New Gradient Swatch.
3. Create a radial gradient named **Six Ring Radial**.
4. Add four new color stops to the Gradient Ramp, then position them so that they are equally spaced across the ramp.
5. Format the first, third, and fifth color stops as 0% CMYK (white).
6. Format the second, fourth and sixth color stops as 100% black.
7. Close the New Gradient Swatch dialog box, then apply the new gradient to the circle.
8. Hide the frame edges, then compare your work to Figure 61.
9. Save your work, then close the Concentric Circle Gradient document.

Figure 61 Completed Design Project 1

This project will strengthen your familiarity with process colors. You will open an InDesign document that shows 12 process colors. Each process color is numbered from 1 to 12. All 12 are very basic mixes. None of the twelve is composed of more than two process inks. Some are just one. The inks used to create the twelve colors are used at either 100% or 50%. Your challenge is to guess the CMYK components of each color.

1. Open ID 5-9.indd, then save it as **Guess the Tints**. The color squares are shown in Figure 62.
2. Write your answers on a sheet of paper numbered 1–12. For example, you could write **#3 = 100% Magenta**.
3. When you're finished, double-click each color on the Swatches panel to reveal the actual CMYK mix.
4. Tally your total number of correct answers, save your work, then close the Guess the Tints document.

Figure 62 Completed Design Project 2

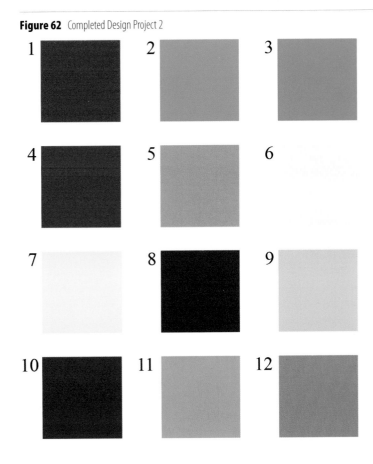

MANAROLA

tuesday august 9

Lorem ipsum dolor sit amet, consectetuer adipiscing elit, sed diam nonummy nibh euismod tincidunt ut laoreet dolore magna aliquam erat volutpat. Ut wisi enim ad minim veniam, quis nostrud exerci tation ullamcorper suscipit lobortis nisl ut aliquip ex ea commodo consequat. Duis autem vel eum iriure dolor in hendrerit in vulputate velit esse molestie consequat, vel illum do-

lore eu feugiat nulla facilisis at vero eros et accumsan et iusto odio dignissim qui blandit praesent luptatum zzril delenit augue duis dolore te feugait nulla facilisi. Ut wisi enim ad minim veniam, quis nostrud exerci tation ullamcorper suscipit lobortis nisl ut aliquip ex ea commodo consequat. Duis autem vel eum iriure dolor in hendrerit in vulputate velit esse molestie consequat,

precedente ◀

▶ seguente

④

FIRENZE

tuesday august 16

Lorem ipsum dolor sit amet, consectetuer adipiscing elit, sed diam nonummy nibh euismod tincidunt ut laoreet dolore magna aliquam erat volutpat. Ut wisi enim ad minim veniam, quis nostrud exerci tation ullamcorper suscipit lobortis nisl ut aliquip ex ea commodo consequat. Duis autem vel eum iriure dolor in hendrerit in vulputate velit esse molestie consequat, vel illum do-

lore eu feugiat nulla facilisis at vero eros et accumsan et iusto odio dignissim qui blandit praesent luptatum zzril delenit augue duis dolore te feugait nulla facilisi. Ut wisi enim ad minim veniam, quis nostrud exerci tation ullamcorper suscipit lobortis nisl ut aliquip ex ea commodo consequat. Duis autem vel eum iriure dolor in hendrerit in vulputate velit esse molestie consequat.

precedente ◀

▶ seguente

⑧

CHAPTER

17

WORK WITH
PLACED IMAGES

1. Place Multiple Graphics
2. Use the Links Panel
3. Explore Image Resolution Issues
4. Place Vector Graphics
5. Interface InDesign with Photoshop
6. Use CC Libraries

 CERTIFIED PROFESSIONAL

Adobe Certified Professional in Print & Digital Media Publication Using Adobe InDesign

1. Working in the Design Industry

This objective covers critical concepts related to working with colleagues and clients as well as crucial legal, technical, and design-related knowledge.

1.4 Demonstrate knowledge of key terminology related to publications.

    C Understand and use key terms related to multi-page layouts.

2. Project Setup and Interface

This objective covers the interface setup and program settings that assist in an efficient and effective workflow, as well as knowledge about ingesting digital assets for a project.

2.1 Create a document with the appropriate settings for web, print, and mobile.

    A Set appropriate document settings for printed and onscreen images.

    B Create a new document preset to reuse for specific project needs.

2.3 Use nonprinting design tools in the interface to aid in design or workflow.

    D Use views and modes to work efficiently.

2.4 Import assets into a project.

    B Place assets in an InDesign document.

4. Creating and Modifying Document Elements

This objective covers core tools and functionality of the application, as well as tools that affect the visual appearance of document elements.

4.1 Use core tools and features to lay out visual elements.

    B Manipulate graphics in frames.

4.2 Add and manipulate text using appropriate typographic settings.

    E Manage text flow across multiple text areas.

4.3 Make, manage, and edit selections.

    A Make selections using a variety of tools.

4.4 Transform digital graphics and media within a publication.

    A Modify frames and frame content.

4.5 Use basic reconstructing and editing techniques to manipulate document content.

    B Evaluate or adjust the appearance of objects, frames, or layers using various tools.

5. Publishing Digital Media

This objective covers saving and exporting documents or assets within individual layers or selections.

5.1 Prepare documents for publishing to web, print, and other digital devices.

    A Check document for errors and project specifications.

PLACE MULTIPLE GRAPHICS

Placing Multiple Images with the Place Command

The Place command on the File menu is the basic command used for placing graphics into an InDesign layout. In Chapter 15, you used the Place command to navigate to a single file, select it, then place it in a layout. You can also use the Place command to import multiple image files simultaneously. This is a great feature that offers substantial time savings when working with multiple images.

To place multiple images, click the Place command and navigate to the location where the graphics are stored. Select as many graphic files as you want to place, then click Place. The Place command will then display the **place thumbnail**, shown in Figure 1. The place thumbnail features a small, low-resolution thumbnail of a loaded image. When you've loaded multiple images, the thumbnail showing is the current loaded image, and the small number in the upper-left corner indicates how many total images are loaded. Use the right arrow and left arrow keys to scroll through all the loaded images. Click the place thumbnail on the page or in a frame and the current loaded image will be placed.

Figure 1 Place thumbnail icon

Number indicates the number of images loaded in the place thumbnail

Image courtesy of Chris Botello

When you place an image, you always have three options for how it's placed:

- Click the place thumbnail in an already existing frame, and the image will be placed into the frame.
- Click the place thumbnail on the page, InDesign will create a frame for the placed image. By default, the frame will be sized to display the entire image at 100%. In other words, the frame will be the same size as the image itself.
- Click and drag the place thumbnail to create a frame at the size that you want, and the image will be placed into that frame.

When placing graphics into frames, be aware the size at which the graphic is being placed. When you create a new frame and then place a graphic into that frame, the graphic will be placed at 100% by default—even if the graphic is larger than the frame itself. However, if you place a graphic into a "used" frame, the rules can change. For example, let's say you have a frame that contains an image, and that image has been resized to 74%. If you click the Place command and place a different image into the frame, the new image will be placed at 74%. In other words, when placing a graphic into a used frame, the new graphic is placed at the same size as the previous graphic.

Setting Frame Fitting Options

The Fitting command on the Object menu contains a submenu with many commands that affect how graphics fit into frames.

See Figure 2. Generally speaking, you'll find that the Fill Frame Proportionally and Fit Content Proportionally commands are the ones you'll use most often. The Fill Frame Proportionally command does just that: it scales the graphic so it fills the entire frame—without distorting the graphic. The Fit Content Proportionally command scales a placed graphic so the entire graphic is visible in the frame.

When you're placing many graphics into a layout, you will find it tiring to have to select the same fitting command over and over for each graphic. To alleviate this, you can set up options in the Frame Fitting Options dialog box. This dialog box allows you to define a specific fitting option for all graphics you place. If you apply settings in the Frame Fitting Options dialog box with a document open and no frames selected, the options will apply to all frames you create in that document only. If you apply frame fitting options to a selected frame, the options affect only that frame.

If you want the options applied to all frames you create in all future documents, set the frame fitting options with no documents open. By doing so, the frame fitting options you choose will be applied to all frames you create when you open a document.

TIP You can also use the Frame Fitting Options dialog box to specify the reference point for the alignment of the image in the frame.

Figure 2 Fitting commands

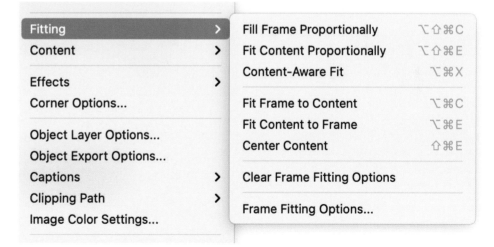

Working with Adobe Bridge

Adobe Bridge is a freestanding **content management application**.

What is content management? Imagine that you are designing a 200-page catalog, such as the quarterly catalog for L.L.Bean or IKEA. Think about the hundreds of images that you'll need to import to complete your layout. Now consider that those images—the ones that are actually used in the catalog—are only a subset of the thousands of product shots the photographers deliver after the photo shoot.

Adobe Bridge, shown in Figure 3, is designed to help you manage this content.

Let's say you have a folder with 500 image files. If you view that folder using Adobe Bridge as the interface, Bridge will show you a thumbnail of each file. You can choose the size of the thumbnail, enabling you to sample and preview each image quickly.

Adobe Bridge also allows you to apply color labels and text data to images to help you categorize them. Using the previous example of an L.L.Bean catalog, the photography team could apply the tag "shoes" to all shoe products they shoot, and "sweaters" to every sweater. Then you, the designer, could use Bridge to sort through the images to show only the shoe or sweater photographs.

You can access Adobe Bridge quickly and easily in InDesign. Just click Browse in Bridge under the File menu, and Bridge will launch.

Figure 3 Adobe Bridge interface

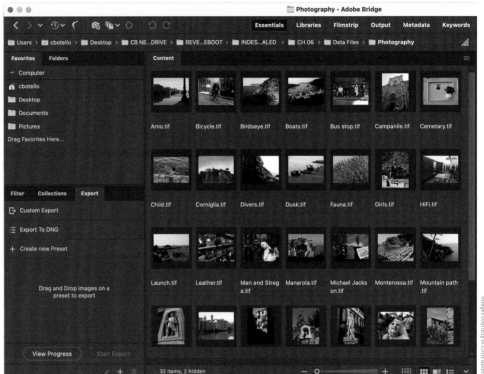

Images courtesy of Chris Botello

Using the Link Badge

When you place an image, the link badge appears at the upper-left corner of the image, as shown in Figure 4. If you hover over the link badge, the name of the placed file appears. Because it remains visible even when the frame is not selected, the link badge is useful, especially when you have a document that contains many placed images. You can simply mouse over the link badge and know immediately the name of the placed file.

If you press and hold [option] (Mac) or [Alt] (Win) and click the link badge, the Links panel will open with that image highlighted in the panel. This, too, is especially useful when you're working with many placed images.

To hide or show the link badge, click View on the menu bar, point to Extras, then click the Hide/Show Link Badge command.

Figure 4 Link badge

Link badge

Place multiple images with the Place command

1. Click **View** on the menu bar, point to **Extras**, then click **Hide Content Grabber**.

    For this chapter, you will double-click the image to toggle between selecting the frame and the image in the frame.

2. Click **View** on the menu bar, point to **Extras**, then verify that the **Link Badge** is not showing.

    For this chapter, you will access the Links panel directly.

3. Open ID 6-1.indd, then save it as **Multiple Placements**.

4. Click the **Selection tool** ▶, then select the **large blue frame** on pages 2-3.

5. Click **File** on the menu bar, click **Place**, navigate to the folder where your Chapter 17 Data Files are stored, open the **Photography folder**, then click the file **Corniglia** once to select it.

6. Press and hold **[command] (Mac)** or **[Ctrl] (Win)**, then click the following files in this order: **Townsfolk**, **Divers**, **Sheets**, **Fauna**, and **Dusk**.

7. Click **Open**.

    As shown in Figure 5, the place thumbnail is loaded, showing the Corniglia graphic and the number 6, indicating that six files are loaded.

Figure 5 Place thumbnail icon

Six images loaded

Image courtesy of Chris Botello

8. Press the **right arrow key** [→] on your keypad repeatedly to see all the files loaded in the place thumbnail.

   Despite the order in which you selected them when you chose them, the files are loaded alphabetically: Corniglia, Divers, Dusk, Fauna, Sheets, and Townsfolk.

9. Press the **right arrow key** [→] repeatedly until the **Corniglia image** is the visible loaded file.

10. Click the **place thumbnail** on the **large blue frame**.

    As shown in Figure 6, the Corniglia image fills the frame, and the place thumbnail now shows the next file in line.

11. Place the **remaining five loaded images** into the **five frames** at the bottom of the page in any order that you wish.

12. Select all **six frames**, click **Object** on the menu bar, point to **Fitting**, then click **Fill Frame Proportionally**.

13. Position the **images** in the frames (scale them if you like) so your page resembles Figure 7.

14. Save your work, then continue to the next set of steps.

You used the Place command to select six files to be placed, then used the arrow key to view those six files in the place thumbnail. You then placed the files and applied a fitting command to all the frames to verify that they were consistent.

Figure 6 Placing the Corniglia image

Place thumbnail and five loaded images

Figure 7 Six images loaded and fitted

Place multiple images with Adobe Bridge

1. Navigate to **spread 4-5**.

2. Click **File** on the menu bar, then click **Browse in Bridge**.

   Adobe Bridge launches and opens.

3. Navigate to the location where you store your Chapter 17 Data Files, then open the **Photography folder**.

4. Drag the **scale slider** at the bottom of the panel right to enlarge the thumbnails so only three thumbnails are visible left to right, as shown in Figure 8.

   The interface in the figure is set to charcoal; the thumbnail images tend to stand out better against a darker background.

5. Drag the **scale slider** left so nine thumbnails are visible in the panel.

6. Use the **scrollbar** on the right of the panel to scroll through all the thumbnails.

7. Click the file named **Manarola**, then note what the image looks like so you'll remember it.

8. Press and hold **[command] (Mac)** or **[Ctrl] (Win)**, then click the following five files: **Birdseye**, **Boats**, **Launch**, **Three Houses**, **Window**.

Figure 8 Bridge interface with enlarged thumbnails

Scale slider

Images courtesy of Chris Botello

9. Click **File** on the menu bar, point to **Place**, then click **In InDesign**.

The interface switches to InDesign, and the place thumbnail is loaded with the number 6, indicating that six files are loaded.

10. Press → to scroll through the loaded thumbnails, then scroll to the Manarola thumbnail.

11. Click in the **large blue frame** with the place thumbnail.

The Manarola image is placed into the frame.

12. Place the **remaining five loaded images** into the five frames at the top of the page in any order that you wish.

13. Select **all six frames**, click **Object** on the menu bar, point to **Fitting**, then click **Fill Frame Proportionally**.

14. Reposition any images in their frames as you like, then compare your result to Figure 9.

15. Save your work, then close the Multiple Placements document.

You previewed files on your computer using Adobe Bridge. You viewed and selected multiple files in Bridge and then placed them in an InDesign layout.

Figure 9 Placing and positioning six images

USE THE LINKS PANEL

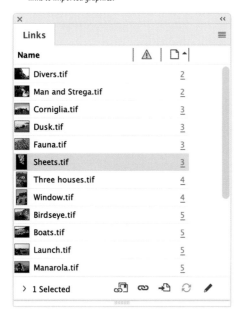

Understanding Preview Files

When you use the Place command to place a graphic file, the image you see in the graphics frame in InDesign is a **preview file**; it is *not* the graphic itself. Why does InDesign work this way? Because of file size considerations.

Remember that many graphics files—especially those of scanned photos or other digital images—have very large file sizes. Some of them are enormous. For example, if you had an 8" × 10" scanned photo that you wanted to use in a layout for a magazine, that graphic would be approximately 21 megabytes, at minimum. If you placed that graphic in your InDesign layout, your InDesign file size would increase dramatically. Now imagine placing 10 of those graphics!

The preview is a low-resolution version of the placed graphic file. As such, its file size is substantially smaller than the average graphics file. The role of the preview file in the layout is ingenious. As a proxy for the actual graphic, it allows you to see a representation of the graphic in your layout without having to carry the burden of the graphic's full file size.

Using the Links Panel

You can think of the Links panel, shown in Figure 10, as command central for managing the links to placed graphics. The Links panel lists all the graphics files that you place into an InDesign document. By default, text that you place in InDesign is not linked to the original text file and therefore not listed on the Links panel.

Also by default, graphics files are listed with a thumbnail of the graphic. Next to each listing is the page number on which the file is located. The Links panel menu offers options for sorting this list. For example, you can sort the list alphabetically or by page number.

You can use the Links panel to locate a placed file in your document quickly. If you select a file on the Links panel and then click the Go to Link button on the panel, InDesign will go to the page where the placed file is located and automatically select its frame. Conversely, when you select a placed file on the document, the file's listing is automatically highlighted on the Links panel.

Figure 10 Links panel

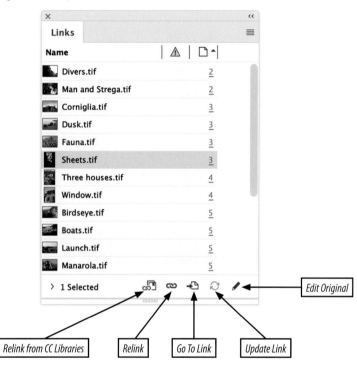

Viewing the Link Info Section of the Links Panel

Double-clicking a filename on the Links panel displays the Link Info section of the Links panel. Shown in Figure 11, the Link Info section displays important information about the placed file, including its file size, resolution, the date it was last modified, the application that created it, and its file format. The file format identifies what type of file it is, such as a Photoshop or an Illustrator file.

TIP You can also click the Show/Hide Link Information triangle to show this section of the panel.

It's always good to know the file format of a graphic and the application that created it in case you wish to edit the original. The Links panel is a big help in this regard. Click the Edit Original button on the panel, and the selected graphic will open in its original application (that is, if you have that application installed on your computer). For photographs, the original application will usually be Adobe Photoshop. For illustrations, it will usually be Adobe Illustrator.

Generally speaking, you will find the default information listed in the Link Info section of the panel to be more than satisfactory for your work. It might even be too much information. You can specify the categories of information you want to see listed in the Link Info section, by clicking the Links panel menu button, clicking Panel Options, then selecting only the check boxes of the categories you want to view.

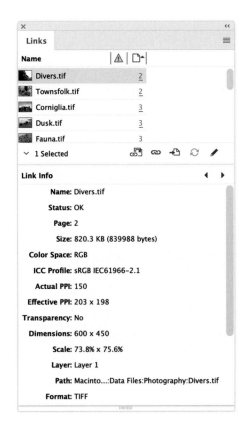

Figure 11 Link Info section of Links panel

Placing Text Files

When you place text in InDesign, the text is usually from a word processing program such as Microsoft Word. By default, when you place text in InDesign, the text is not linked to the original text file, and the placed text does not appear on the Links panel. The formatting changes you apply in InDesign don't affect the original text file, and more importantly, any changes that you may make to the original text file don't affect the formatting of the text in InDesign. You can override the default and link text you place in InDesign to the original text document. If you select the Create Links When Placing Text And Spreadsheet Files option in the File Handling preferences before you place a file, the name of the text file appears on the Links panel.

When text is linked to its original file in this manner, you can use the Links panel to update and manage the file. But beware—when you update a linked text file, any editing or formatting changes that you applied in InDesign are lost. That's why placed text in InDesign isn't linked by default: it's too risky. Even when you override the default and link text to its original file, text files in the InDesign document are not automatically updated when the original file is edited and saved. You must manually update the linked file using the Links panel.

Managing Links to Placed Graphics

When you place a graphic file, InDesign establishes a link between the graphics frame and the placed file. That link is based on the location of the file. When you first place the graphic, you must navigate through the folder structure on your computer to locate the file. You may navigate to a folder on your computer's hard drive, external drive, or network. In either case, InDesign remembers that navigation path as the method for establishing the location of the placed file.

The Links panel uses icons to alert you to the status of a placed file. The Missing icon appears beside the file's name when the established link no longer points to the file. In other words, if you move the file to a different folder (or delete it), *after* you place it in InDesign, the file will be listed as Missing on the Links panel. The Missing icon is a white question mark inside a red circle.

The Modified icon is a black exclamation point in a yellow triangle. A placed file's status is noted as Modified when the original file has been edited and saved *after* being placed in InDesign. For example, if you place a Photoshop graphic in InDesign and then open the graphic in Photoshop, edit it, and save changes, the graphic you placed in InDesign is no longer the most up-to-date version of the graphic. If you have the InDesign document open when you save the Photoshop file, InDesign automatically updates the graphic in the layout. Otherwise, the Links panel displays the Modified icon beside the file. Figure 12 shows files on the Links panel with the Missing and Modified icons.

The OK status does not have an icon. The OK status means that the established link still points to the location of the placed graphic, and the graphic itself has not been modified since being placed.

TIP If a linked or embedded file contains metadata, you can view the metadata using the Links panel. Select a file on the Links panel, click the Links panel menu button, click Utilities, then click XMP File Info.

Figure 12 Missing and Modified icons on the Links panel

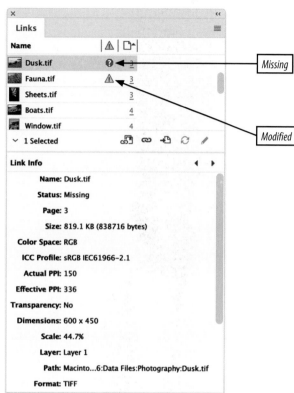

Updating Missing and Modified Files

When the Links panel displays Modified and Missing icons, those links need to be updated, meaning you need to reestablish the connection between the preview file and the graphic file that has been moved or edited.

It's easy to update modified files on the Links panel. To do so, you click the filename on the Links panel, then click the Update Link button on the panel. The link will update to the newest saved version of the file, and the status of the file will change to OK.

Files that have the Missing status need to be relinked to the graphic. To do so, you click the filename on the Links panel, click the Relink button, then navigate to the new location of the graphic file. Once the link is reestablished, the status of the file changes to OK.

When you reestablish a link, none of the formatting that you did to the graphic when you placed it the first time is lost. If, for example, you scaled a placed graphic to 35% and centered it proportionally in the graphics frame, those modifications will still be in place when you reestablish the link.

Embedding Files

InDesign allows you to embed a placed file into the InDesign document. When you embed a placed file, the file literally becomes part of the InDesign document; it no longer links to a source file.

You would embed images for one reason: to have a self-contained InDesign document without the need for supporting files. Rather than having to package an InDesign document with all its supporting files, an InDesign document with embedded graphics offers you the simplicity of having to work with only a single document.

To embed a placed graphic file, select it on the Links panel, click the Links panel menu button, then click Embed Link. The file will continue to be listed on the Links panel, but it will appear with the Embedded icon beside its name.

To relink an embedded file to its original file on your computer, click the file on the Links panel, click the Links panel menu button, then click Relink. You'll be prompted to navigate to the location of the source file to reestablish the link. The file will then be linked, not embedded.

Because an embedded file is part of the InDesign document, embedded files increase the file size of the InDesign document substantially, and this can lead to a slowdown in InDesign's performance. For this reason, you may want to avoid embedding files in InDesign and work with the standard methodology of linking to graphics.

CREATING AND USING SNIPPETS

In the same way that libraries let you store page elements for reuse, snippets let you export any elements from a document for reuse in other documents or in an object library. A **snippet** is an XML file with an .inds file extension that contains complete representation of document elements, including all formatting tags and document structure. To create a snippet, use the Selection tool to select the frames you want to reuse, click File on the menu bar, click Export, then choose InDesign Snippet from the Save as type list arrow. Remember that you can create a single snippet from multiple objects. For example, you can select all the objects on a page and create one snippet from everything on the page. (It's a good idea to group the elements before exporting the snippet.) An even easier method is to drag selected items onto the desktop, into Adobe Bridge, a Library panel, or an email message, each of which automatically creates a snippet file. To use a snippet in another file, you can use the Place command or just drag the snippet from the desktop into an InDesign document.

EXPORTING XML

XML is a versatile language that describes content—such as text, graphics, and design elements—in a format that allows that content to be output in a variety of ways. Like HTML, XML uses coded information, called "tags," to identify and organize content. Unlike HTML, XML does not describe how the information will appear or how it will be laid out on a page. Instead, XML creates an identity for the content.

XML can distinguish and identify such elements as chapter titles, headlines, body copy, an author's name, or numbered steps. Here's the hook: XML information is not specific to any one kind of output, so you can use that same information to create different types of documents, just as you can use the English alphabet to speak and write other languages.

For example, many designers work in XML to generate catalogs, books, magazines, or newspapers, all from the same XML content. The Tags panel and the Structure pane, which are two XML utilities in InDesign, interface smoothly with XML code and allow you to organize content and list it in a hierarchical order, which is essential to XML.

Before items can be exported to an XML file, they must be tagged, using the Tags panel. You can also apply an autotag to an item using the Autotag command on the Tags panel menu. When you do so, InDesign applies the default tag for that item type defined in the Tagging Preset Options dialog box. You can change the default tag settings in this dialog box by clicking the Tags panel menu button and then clicking Tagging Preset Options. All tagged items appear in the Structure pane. You can opt to show or hide tagged frames as well as tag markers using the Structure commands on the View menu. To export an XML file, click Export, then choose XML from the Format list menu.

Because XML tags are data descriptions and carry no formatting instructions, you will need to format XML content when you import it to a layout. A smart solution for doing that quickly and with consistency is to map XML tags to paragraph, character, table, or cell styles. As with all solutions involving styles, mapping tags to predefined styles makes formatting imported XML content easier and less time consuming.

To map XML tags to various styles, choose Map Tags to Styles from the Tags panel menu or the Structure pane menu. This opens the Map Tags to Styles dialog box, where you can choose an XML tag and apply a style to it.

Use the Links panel to update modified and missing graphics

1. Open ID 6-2.indd, then compare the warning dialog box you see to Figure 13.

   Your dialog box might differ from the figure.

2. Click **Don't Update Links**, then save the file as **Update Links**.

   Normally you would click Update Links and the modified links would be updated. The missing links wouldn't be updated because they are missing. For this lesson, you are instructed to not update links so you can do so manually on the Links panel.

3. Open the **Links panel**.

4. Scroll through the Links panel to view the list of the placed graphics.

   All the placed files in this document—except two—are located in the Photography folder in the Chapter 17 Data Files folder. Two files have been moved out of the Photography folder and into the Move Files folder to make them "missing" for this lesson.

   TIP Your Links panel might show all files as modified (an exclamation point in a yellow triangle). They are not really modified. This happens if you download the files to your computer.

5. Click the **Woman in Window.tif link** on the Links panel, then click the **Go to Link button** .

   As shown in Figure 14, the status of the Woman in Window.tif link is listed on the Links panel as Modified. This means that it has been modified in another program (in this case, Photoshop) after it was placed into this file.

Figure 13 Issues with Links dialog box

Issues with Links

This document contains links to sources that have been missing/modified. You can update the modified links now, or update these later using the Links panel.

2 – Missing Link(s)
1 – Modified Link(s)

Don't Update Links   Update Modified Links

Figure 14 Modified image on the Links panel

6. Click the **Update Link button** ⟳ .

   As shown in Figure 15, the link is updated, and the status of the graphic is OK.

7. If necessary, select any other **graphic files that show the Modified icon**, then click the **Update Link button** ⟳ .

8. Note that both the **Hat** and **Duomo graphics** are listed as Missing.

9. Click the **Hat graphic** on the Links panel, then click the **Go to Link button** .

   The image is selected.

10. Click the **Relink button** ∞ .

11. Navigate to the **Moved Files folder** where you store your Chapter 17 Data Files, click **Hat**, then click **Open**.

    An Information dialog box, shown in Figure 16, appears, indicating that one file has been found and relinked. This refers to the Duomo file. When you showed InDesign where the Hat file was located, InDesign also found Duomo and relinked it.

12. Click **OK**, then note on the Links panel that both missing files have been relinked.

13. Save your work, then continue to the next lesson.

You used the Links panel to update modified links, then you updated two missing links simultaneously.

Figure 15 Updated link on the Links panel

Figure 16 InDesign finds and relinks another missing graphic

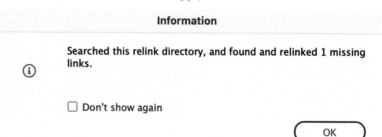

EXPLORE IMAGE RESOLUTION ISSUES

What You'll Do

In this lesson, you will learn about effective image resolution in an InDesign layout and how to modify image resolution in Adobe Photoshop.

Understanding Bitmap Graphics

Photographic images are created on computers using a rectangular grid of colored squares called **pixels**. Because pixels (a contraction of "picture elements") can render subtle gradations of tone, they are the most common medium for continuous tone images—what you perceive as a photograph on your computer. Graphics created from pixels are called **bitmap graphics**.

All scanned images and digital "photos" are composed of pixels. Figure 17 shows an example of a bitmap image. The enlarged section shows you the pixels that compose the image.

Understanding Image Resolution

The number of pixels in a given inch is referred to as the image's **resolution**. To be effective, pixels must be small enough to create an image with the illusion of continuous tone. The standard resolution for images for the web is 72 pixels per inch (ppi). For images that will be professionally printed, the standard resolution is 300 pixels per inch (ppi).

The term **effective resolution** refers to the resolution of a placed image based on its size in the layout. Effective resolution is a critical consideration whenever you're working with placed bitmap images.

Figure 17 Bitmap graphic

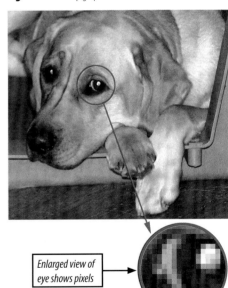

Enlarged view of
eye shows pixels

The important thing to remember about bitmap images in relation to InDesign is that the size of the image placed in the InDesign layout has a direct effect on the image's resolution. Think about it—if you enlarge a placed image in InDesign, the pixels that make up the image are spread out over a larger area. Thus, the effective resolution of the image goes down because there are now fewer pixels per inch. This decrease in resolution will have a negative impact on the quality of an image when it is printed.

Therefore, enlarging an image in InDesign usually creates a problem with effective resolution: the greater the enlargement, the lower the effective resolution of the image.

TIP The Link Info section in the Links panel, lists the effective resolution for all placed graphics.

Let's use a clear example to illustrate this. For a professionally printed bitmap image, the target resolution is 300 pixels per inch.

Let's say you have a Photoshop image that is 1" × 1" at 300 ppi. Since the image is at a resolution of 300 pixels per inch, it meets the target resolution and will print high-quality.

The image contains a total of 90,000 pixels (300 × 300 = 90,000).

Now, let's say you place the same image into a 2" × 2" frame and use the Fitting commands to enlarge the image 200% to fill the frame. Those same 90,000 pixels are now spread out to fill a 2" × 2" frame. Thus, the effective resolution is 150 ppi—too low for professional printing.

Figure 18 illustrates this example. Spend as much time considering this information as you need to thoroughly understand the concept of effective resolution. The main point is that the resolution of the original image is not the only consideration. Just as important is the size that it's used in InDesign. If it has been enlarged in InDesign, the effective resolution goes down.

Figure 18 Illustration of effective resolution

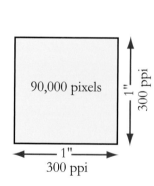

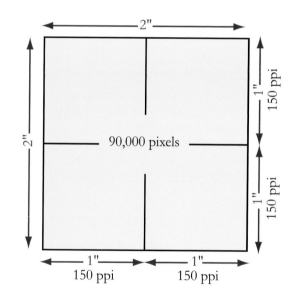

Enlarging a Graphic in Adobe Photoshop

Photoshop is the best-selling pixel-based image manipulation software application by Adobe Systems, the same company that produces InDesign. It's important to understand that scaling a graphic in Photoshop is different from scaling a graphic in InDesign. When you scale a graphic in InDesign, it either spreads the existing pixels over a larger area (enlargement) or squeezes them into a smaller area (reduction). Photoshop, because it specializes in image manipulation, allows you to actually change the number of pixels when you scale a graphic.

Let's continue with the same example from before. If you have a 1" × 1" graphic at 300 ppi, it has a total of 90,000 pixels. If you enlarge it in Photoshop to a 2" × 2" graphic, Photoshop offers you the ability to maintain the image resolution. Thus, after the scale, the image will still be 300 ppi, meaning the 2" square image will be 600 pixels wide and 600 pixels tall, for a total of 360,000 pixels. But from where do those extra 270,000 pixels come?

When enlarging a graphic in Photoshop, Photoshop creates the new pixels necessary to maintain an image's resolution by a process called **interpolation**. The color of the new pixels is based on the color information of the original pixels in the image. Thus, in the preceding example, the colors of the 270,000 new pixels are created based on the 90,000 original pixels.

TIP To be an effective designer in InDesign, you need to understand effective resolution issues and be able to work in Photoshop to modify an image's resolution.

Enlarging a bitmap graphic always results in a loss of quality—even if you do it in Photoshop. That's because interpolated data is only duplicated data—inferior to the original data that you get from a scan or a digital image that you download from your digital camera.

In a nutshell, you should try your best to create all bitmap graphics in Adobe Photoshop at both the size and resolution that they will be used at the final output stage. You then import the graphic into InDesign and leave its size alone.

If you find that you need to enlarge the graphic substantially (more than 10%), remember that all resizing of bitmap graphics should be done in Photoshop, not in InDesign. Use InDesign simply to place the graphics in a layout, create text wraps, and perform other layout-related tasks.

Is there any leeway here? Yes. If you need to reduce the size of a placed bitmap graphic in InDesign, you can do so without worrying about it too much. Reducing a bitmap graphic in InDesign is not a problem, because you *increase* the effective resolution of the bitmap graphic (the same number of pixels in a smaller area means more pixels per inch). If you need to enlarge a graphic slightly in InDesign, you can feel comfortable enlarging it up to 110%. For anything larger, enlarge it in Photoshop.

TIP Remember, nothing in this discussion applies to vector graphics. Vector graphics are resolution independent. You can feel free to enlarge and reduce placed vector graphics in InDesign to your heart's content.

Change the resolution of a placed graphic

1. Double-click **Dusk** on the Links panel, then click the **Go to Link button** 🔁 .

2. Compare your screen to Figure 19.

   The Link Info section shows that the Actual PPI of the image is 150, but the Effective PPI of the placed image is 336, making it high enough to print with quality. Because the image was placed at 44%, the effective resolution is more than double the actual resolution.

3. Double-click the **Corniglia link** on the Links panel, then click the **Go to Link button** 🔁 .

   The Actual PPI of the image is 150, and the Effective PPI is 144, which is too low for quality printing.

4. Click the **Edit Original button** ✏ on the Links panel.

   The image opens in Adobe Photoshop. You will need to have Adobe Photoshop installed on your computer to complete this lesson.

TIP Placed .PSD files will automatically open in Photoshop. Other formats, such as .TIF, must be specified in your computer's preferences to open by default in Photoshop.

Continued on next page

Figure 19 Viewing resolution info for Dusk

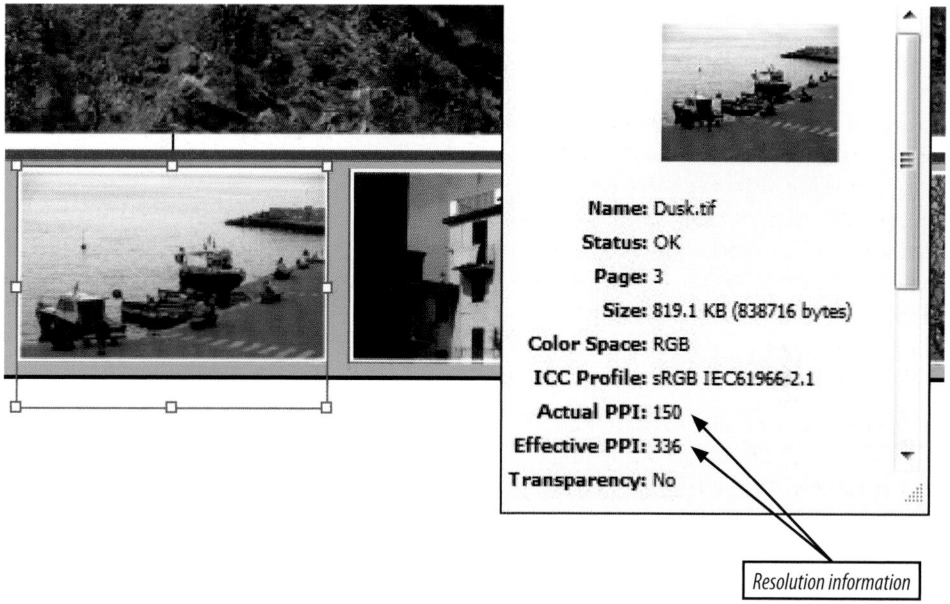

Name: Dusk.tif
Status: OK
Page: 3
Size: 819.1 KB (838716 bytes)
Color Space: RGB
ICC Profile: sRGB IEC61966-2.1
Actual PPI: 150
Effective PPI: 336
Transparency: No

Resolution information

5. In Photoshop, click **Image** on the menu bar, then click **Image Size**.

   The Image Size dialog box opens. As shown in Figure 20, the resolution of the image is 150.

6. Note that the **Resample Image check box** at the bottom of the dialog box is checked.

   The Resample Image option is a key option in the dialog box. When it is checked, Photoshop will add pixels to the image when enlarging, and it will remove pixels from the image when reducing. If you uncheck the option, changing the image size would be no different than doing so in InDesign— no pixels would be added or removed.

7. Verify that the **Resample Image check box** is checked.

8. Type **300** in the Resolution text box, then compare your Image Size dialog box to Figure 21.

   Note that the physical dimensions of the image do not change, but the number of pixels and the file size increase dramatically.

9. Click **OK**, click **File** on the menu bar, then click **Save**.

Figure 20   Image Size dialog box in Photoshop

Figure 21   Doubling resolution in Photoshop results in an increase of pixel data

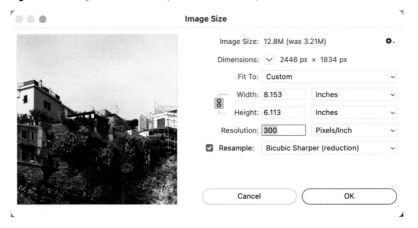

10. Return to the InDesign layout.

Because the InDesign document was open when you saved the change in Photoshop, the graphic in InDesign was automatically updated.

11. Click the **Corniglia image** on the artboard, then compare your screen to Figure 22.

The Actual PPI in the Link Info section now reads 300, and the Effective PPI is 293—close enough to 300 to be acceptable.

12. Save your work, then close the file.

You noted the Actual and Effective PPI for a placed graphic, opened the graphic in Photoshop, then increased its resolution.

Figure 22 Viewing updated resolution information

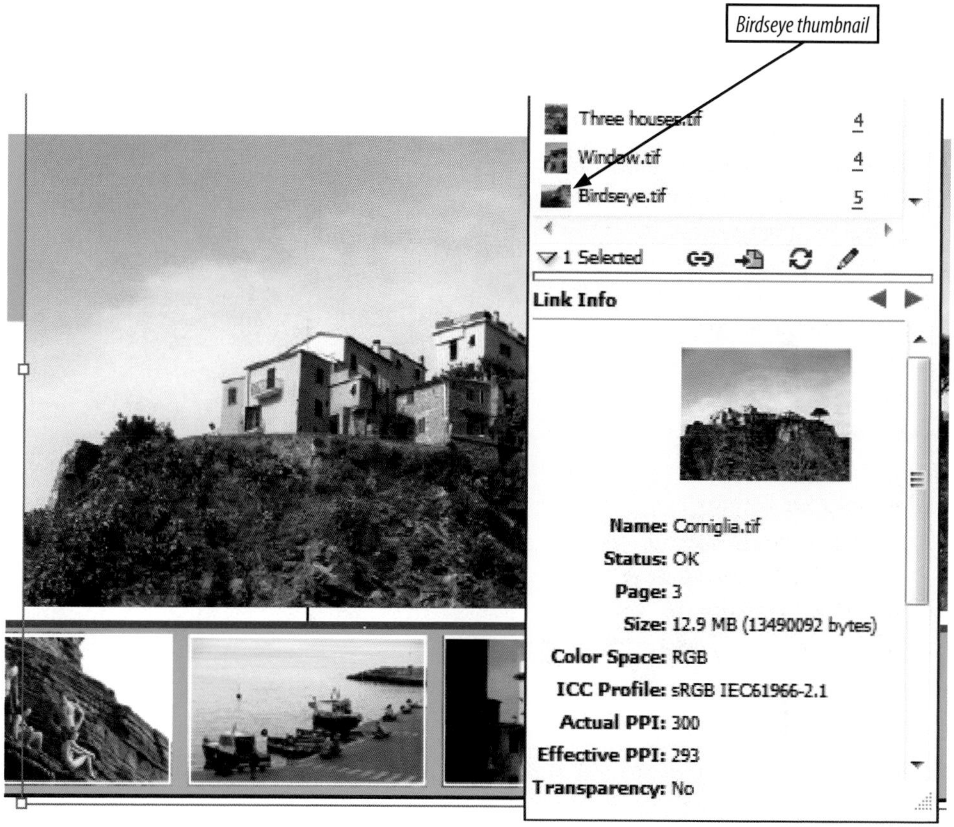

Birdseye thumbnail

Three houses.tif   4
Window.tif   4
Birdseye.tif   5

▽ 1 Selected

Link Info

Name: Corniglia.tif
Status: OK
Page: 3
Size: 12.9 MB (13490092 bytes)
Color Space: RGB
ICC Profile: sRGB IEC61966-2.1
Actual PPI: 300
Effective PPI: 293
Transparency: No

PLACE VECTOR GRAPHICS

What You'll Do

In this lesson, you will place vector graphics in InDesign, resize them, then choose display performance settings.

Understanding Vector Graphics

Graphics created in computer drawing programs, such as Adobe Illustrator, are called vector graphics. Vector graphics consist of anchor points and line segments, together referred to as **paths.** Paths can be curved or straight; they are defined by geometrical characteristics called **vectors**. Computer graphics rely on vectors to render bold graphics that must retain clean, crisp lines when scaled to various sizes.

Vectors are often used to create logos or "line art," and they are often the best choice for typographical illustrations.

Figure 23 shows an example of vector graphics used to draw a cartoon boy. The graphic on the left is filled with colors, and the graphic on the right shows the vector shapes used to create the graphic.

Because they are not based on pixels and therefore are **resolution independent**, vector graphics can be scaled to any size with no loss in quality. This means that the same graphic that you create in an application like Adobe Illustrator can be scaled to fit on a postage stamp … or on a billboard!

Figure 23 Example of vector graphics

Placing Vector Graphics in InDesign

When you place vector graphics in InDesign, you can enlarge or reduce them to any size because scaling a vector graphic does not have any impact on its visual quality.

When you place a vector graphic from Illustrator, only the objects that compose the graphic are placed. If you draw a 2" square on an 8" artboard in Illustrator, then place the file in InDesign, the 2" square will be placed, not the entire 8" artboard.

When you create a graphic in Illustrator, Illustrator draws an imaginary bounding box that defines the perimeter of the graphic. This will have an impact when the graphic is placed in InDesign. Let's say you create a 1" circle in Illustrator. When you place it in InDesign and apply a text wrap, the text will wrap around the imaginary 1" bounding box—not the circle. You must click Detect Edges in the Contour section of the Text Wrap panel to make the InDesign text wrap around the graphic. Remember this technique because, as shown in Figure 24, you can create interesting text wraps around a complex Illustrator graphic.

Choosing the Default Display Performance

When you place a graphic file in InDesign, a low-resolution preview file appears in the graphics frame. The appearance of the preview file—the quality at which it is displayed—is determined by default in the **Display Performance section** of the Preferences dialog box.

Figure 24 Placed Illustrator graphic with a text wrap

You can choose between Fast, Typical, or High Quality views of placed graphics.

- The Fast Display view shows no preview file. Instead, it shows a gray box within the graphics frame. Most up-to-date computers have enough memory that you won't need to resort to this option.
- The Typical Display view displays a low-resolution preview. This is an adequate display for identifying and positioning an image within the layout.
- The High Quality Display view displays the preview file at high resolution. This option provides the highest quality but requires the most memory. However, given the power and speed of today's computers, this is unlikely to be an issue. You may want to use High Quality Display to get a "final view" of a completed layout or to present the layout onscreen to a client.

The setting you choose in the Display Performance section of the Preferences dialog box will determine the default display for every graphic that you place in InDesign. In addition, there are two sets of Display Performance commands on the menu bar. There is one set on the Object menu and another set on the View menu. Use the View menu commands when you want to change the display performance of all the placed graphics in an open document. Use the Object menu commands when you want to change the display performance for graphics on an individual basis.

Placing Illustrator Graphics

There are two different ways you can put Illustrator graphics into an InDesign document. If you know you won't need to modify the graphic at all in InDesign, just place it using the Place command on the File menu. However, if you want to retain the option of editing the file from within InDesign, copy and paste the Illustrator graphic. When you copy and paste the Illustrator graphic into your InDesign document, it becomes an InDesign object—not a placed graphic—and will be fully editable in InDesign because InDesign is also an Adobe vector-based program. Figure 25 shows an Illustrator graphic placed in InDesign and selected with the Direct Selection tool.

Figure 25 Illustrator graphic placed in InDesign and selected with Direct Selection tool

Pasting an Illustrator graphic into InDesign is not a common practice, but it does have its uses. Once the graphic is pasted in InDesign, you can apply the layout's colors and gradients to the graphic rather than having to recreate those colors and gradients in Illustrator. You also have a bit more control for modifying the graphic to produce very specific text wraps. These are all minor considerations, however. In general, the best method for incorporating Illustrator graphics into your layouts is to place them.

Place vector graphics in InDesign

1. Open ID 6-3.indd, then save it as **Min-Pin Graphics**.

2. Go to **page 6**, then verify that **frame edges** are showing.

3. Click the **Selection tool** ▶, then click the **large graphics frame** at the center of the page.

4. Click **File** on the menu bar, click **Place**, navigate to the drive and folder where your Chapter 17 Data Files are stored, click **Montag.ai**, then click **Open**.

5. Click **Object** on the menu bar, point to **Fitting**, then click **Fit Content Proportionally**.

   Your screen should resemble Figure 26.

6. Go to **page 5**, fit the spread in the document window, then click **between the text frames** to select the **large graphics frame**.

   The graphics frame is behind the text frames in the stacking order.

7. Click **File** on the menu bar, click **Place,** navigate to the drive and folder where your Chapter 17

Figure 26 Montag.ai placed in the InDesign layout

Data Files are stored, click **Orange Dogs.ai**, then click **Open**.

8. Click **Object** on the menu bar, point to **Fitting**, then click **Fit Content Proportionally**.

   The graphic is enlarged to fit the frame. Note that the dramatic enlargement does not affect the quality of the lines and curves of the graphic.

   TIP If your dogs look bitmapped, go to Display Performance on the View menu and select High Quality Display.

9. Click the **No text wrap button** ▤ on the Text Wrap panel.

10. Deselect, switch to **Preview mode**, then compare your page to Figure 27.

11. Switch back to **Normal mode**, then save your work.

12. Continue to the next set of steps.

You placed two vector graphics in InDesign. You enlarged the second graphic dramatically, noting no effect on its quality.

Figure 27 Removing the text wrap from the graphic

the many faces of the Miniature Pinscher

Lorem ipsum dolor sit amet, consect adipiscing elit, sed diam nonummy nibh euismod tincidunt ut laoreet dolore magna aliquam erat volutpat.

Duis autem veleum iriure dolor in hendrerit in vulputate velit esse molestie consequat. Vel willum lunombro dolore eu feugiat nulla facilisis.

It solmen va esser necessi far uniform grammatica, pronunciation e plu sommun paroles. Ma quande lingues coalesce, li grammatica del resultant lingue es plu simplic e regulari quam ti del coalescent lingues. Li nov lingua franca va esser plu simplice.

Regulari quam li existent Europan lingues. It va esser tam

Li Europan lingues es membres del sam familie. Lor separat existentie es un myth. Por scientie, musica, sport etc, litot Europa usa li sam vocabular.

Duis autem veleum iriure dolor in hendrerit in vulputate velit esse molestie consequat. Vel willum lunombro dolore eu feugiat nulla facilisis.

At vero eros et accumsan et iusto odio dignissim qui blandit praesent luptatum ezril delenit augue duis dolore te feugait nulla facilisi.

Li Europan lingues es membres del sam familie. Lor separat existentie es un myth. Por scientie, musica, sport etc, litot Europa usa li sam vocabular.

Li lingues differe solmen in li grammatica, li pronunciation e li plu commun vocabules. Omnicos directe al desirabilite de un nov lingua franca: On refusa continuar payar custosi traductores.

It solmen va esser necessi far uniform grammatica, pronunciation e plu somplic

mun paroles. Ma quande lingues coalesce, li grammatica del resultant lingue es plu simplic e regulari quam ti del coalescent lingues. Li nov lingua franca va esser plu simplice.

Regulari quam li existent Europan lingues. It va esser tam simplic quam Occidental in fact, it va esser Occidental. A un Angleso it va semblar un simplificat Angles, quam un skeptic amico dit me que Occidental.

Lorem ipsum dolor sit amet, consect adipiscing elit, sed diam nonummy nibh euismod tincidunt ut laoreet dolore magna aliquam erat volutpat. Ut wisi enim ad minim veniam, quis nostrud exercitation ulliam corper suscipit lobortis nisl ut aliquip exea commodo consequat.

Duis autem veleum iriure dolor in hendrerit in vulputate velit esse molestie consequat. Vel willum lunombro dolore eu feugiat nulla facilisis.

At vero eros et accumsan et iusto odio dignissim qui blandit praesent luptatum ezril delenit augue duis dolore te feugait nulla facilisi.

Li Europan lingues es membres del sam familie. Lor separat existentie es un myth. Por scientie, musica,

sport etc, litot Europa usa li sam vocabular.

Li lingues differe solmen in li grammatica, li pronunciation e li plu commun vocabules. Omnicos directe al desirabilite de un nov lingua franca: On refusa continuar payar custosi traductores.

Regulari quam li existent Europan lingues. It va esser tam simplic quam Occidental in fact, it va esser Occidental. A un Angleso it va semblar un simplificat Angles, quam un skeptic amico dit me que Occidental.

Lorem ipsum dolor sit amet, consect adipiscing elit, sed diam nonummy nibh euismod tincidunt ut laoreet dolore magna aliquam erat volutpat.

Ut wisi enim ad minim veniam, quis nostrud exercitation ulliam corper suscipit lobortis nisl ut aliquip exea commodo consequat.

Duis autem veleum iriure dolor in hendrerit in vulputate velit esse molestie consequat. Vel willum lunombro dolore eu feugiat nulla facilisis.

At vero eros et accumsan et iusto odio dignissim qui blandit praesent luptatum ezril delenit augue duis dolore te feugait nulla facilisi.

It solmen va esser necessi far uniform grammatica,

Title   5

Wrap text around a placed vector graphic

1. Go to **page 6**, then select the **frame with the cartoon dog illustration**.

2. Click the **Wrap around object shape button** 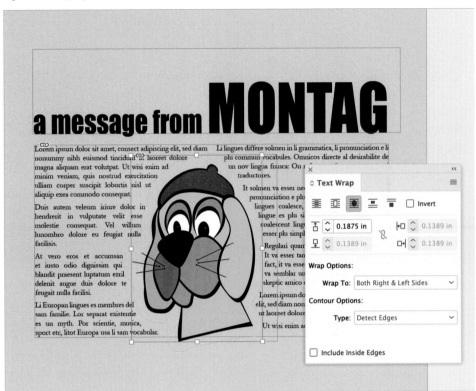 on the Text Wrap panel.

3. In the **Wrap Options section** of the Text Wrap panel, click the **Wrap To list arrow**, then click **Both Right & Left Sides**.

4. In the **Contour Options section**, click the **Type list arrow**, then click **Detect Edges**.

5. In the **upper section** of the Text Wrap panel, set the **Top Offset value** to **.1875**.

6. Compare your page to Figure 28.

   This figure highlights the terrific relationship between Illustrator and InDesign. You can draw an illustration in Illustrator, and InDesign will recognize its shape and run text around it—all with a couple of clicks on the Text Wrap panel. The result is a great effect that's so much more interesting and eye-catching than text running around a square (as in Figure 26).

7. Save your work, then continue to the next lesson.

You wrapped InDesign text around a placed Illustrator graphic.

Figure 28 Wrapping text around a vector graphic

INTERFACE INDESIGN WITH PHOTOSHOP

Understanding the Relationship of InDesign with Other Adobe Products

Adobe makes many software products. InDesign is a layout application. Illustrator is a drawing application. Photoshop is a photo manipulation application. Because they are all Adobe products, they have been engineered to work together, in most cases, seamlessly. This is a good thing. Also, because they are all Adobe products, many of their functions overlap. For example, you can draw complex graphics and manipulate bitmap images in InDesign. This overlapping of functions is also a good thing. It allows you to do things to placed graphics in InDesign, for example, without having to go back to either Illustrator or Photoshop. However, this overlapping can also blur the distinctions among the applications. So it's important that you keep clear in your head what those distinctions are—what you can and cannot and should and should not do to a placed graphic in InDesign. For example, though it is possible to enlarge a placed bitmap graphic 800% in InDesign, you must educate yourself to understand the ramifications of doing so and why it might not be something you *should* do even though it's something you *can* do.

Removing a White Background from a Placed Graphic

In many cases, bitmap graphics you place in InDesign will have a white background. One useful overlap between InDesign and Photoshop is that InDesign can identify the white background in a placed image and make it transparent using the Detect Edges function in the Clipping Path dialog box, shown in Figure 29.

InDesign can identify pixels in the graphic based on their values—from light to dark—and makes specific pixels transparent. The Threshold value determines the pixel values that will be made transparent. For example, if the Threshold value is set to 10, the 10 lightest pixel values (out of a total of 256 values from light to dark) would be made transparent.

Your best method for using this feature is to start with a Threshold value of 0—no pixels will be transparent. To make only the white pixels transparent, use a Threshold value of 1 and use the Preview function to see how that setting affects the image. If some unwanted almost-white pixels remain, increase the Threshold value until you are happy with the preview.

The Tolerance value determines how smooth the edge of the image will be once pixels are made transparent. A Tolerance value of 1 or 2 is usually acceptable.

Figure 30 shows a placed graphic, first with a white background, then with the white background removed using the Detect Edges section in the Clipping Path dialog box.

Figure 29 Detect Edges option in the Clipping Path dialog box

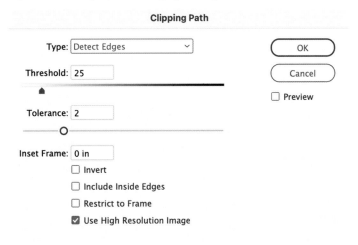

Figure 30 A placed graphic with a white background and with the white background made transparent

You can see that the utility works quite well. Not only does it make the white background transparent, InDesign can wrap text around the shape of the visible image. That's pretty amazing!

The Detect Edges feature works most effectively with darker foreground images against a white background. One drawback to using the Detect Edges feature is that it affects all white pixels, whether they are in the background or foreground. In other words, if you have an image of a man with a white beard against a white background, there's no way to make the white background transparent without making the white beard transparent as well. In that case, you'd need to explore other options working directly on the image in Photoshop.

Loading Alpha Channels in InDesign

Often, when working with bitmap graphics, you'll find you want to select only a specific area of the graphic. For example, you may want to isolate an image of a person from its background. Using selection tools in Photoshop, you can do just that. The selection, known as a **silhouette**, can be saved

with the Photoshop file for use in another Photoshop document or in another program, such as InDesign.

Alpha channels are selections created and saved in Photoshop. InDesign has the ability to load alpha channels that have been saved with a Photoshop file. This is another useful overlap between InDesign and Photoshop. Alpha channels are rendered in terms of black and white, with the white areas representing the selected pixels and the black areas representing the unselected areas.

Figure 31 shows a graphic in Photoshop and an alpha channel that was saved with the graphic. The white area of the alpha channel represents the area of the image that will be visible. The

black area of the alpha channel represents the area that will be transparent.

When you place the Photoshop graphic in InDesign, the alpha channel saved with it is not automatically loaded. The graphic will be placed by default as a **square-up**—the entire image, including the background, in the square format shown on the left side of the figure. You can then use the Clipping Path dialog box to load the alpha channel, thereby creating a silhouette in your layout. As with the Detect Edges option, InDesign offers you the ability to wrap text around the alpha channel.

Figure 31 A Photoshop file and an alpha channel

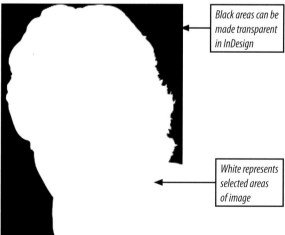

Black areas can be made transparent in InDesign

White represents selected areas of image

Loading Clipping Paths in InDesign

Like alpha channels, clipping paths are another type of selection you can create in Photoshop. Paths are created with the Pen tool, which is a sophisticated selection tool in Photoshop that allows you to make very specific selections. Once created, one or more paths can be saved or exported with a Photoshop file.

What's the difference between saving and exporting a path with a Photoshop file? It's a difference of intended usage. If a path is exported with the Photoshop file, the path will be loaded automatically when you place the graphic in InDesign. If you create a path for a Photoshop graphic and you know you want to use it to silhouette the graphic in your InDesign layout, you might as well export the path with the Photoshop file so you won't have to load it in InDesign.

If you save rather than export a path with a Photoshop file, it won't automatically load when you bring it into InDesign, but you can use the Clipping Path command in InDesign to load it. Sometimes you'll only want to save a path with a Photoshop document rather than export it, so you have the option to use the entire graphic or a silhouette in InDesign.

Of the three options we've explored for wrapping text around a bitmap image, creating alpha channels and clipping paths in Photoshop are the most accurate by far. Relying on Detect Edges in InDesign can work effectively, but your success will be mostly limited to images with white backgrounds and no other white areas.

Creating alpha channels in Photoshop is a more common skill than creating clipping paths. Creating alpha channels is generally easier because you do so with the Brush tool. That said, you can master both techniques with a bit of focus and commitment.

Placing a Graphic with a Transparent Background in InDesign

When placing a bitmap graphic with a feathered edge against a colored background in InDesign, the best solution is to save the graphic against a transparent background in Photoshop. You do this by making the selection with a feathered edge, then copying the selection to a new layer. You then make the original layer invisible. This solution is shown in Figure 32. Note that the graphic now appears against a transparent background (identified in Photoshop as a checkerboard). If you save the graphic in Photoshop with this configuration in the Photoshop Layers panel, when you place the graphic in InDesign, only the visible layer—the graphic with the feathered edge—appears.

Remember this solution. Someday, in some situation, you will encounter this scenario at work in a design department or production facility, and you can be the hero who has the answer!

Figure 32 Layers panel in Photoshop and a graphic against a transparent background

Remove a background from a placed graphic

1. Go to page 1, click the **Selection tool** , click the **center of the page** to select the **graphics frame**, then place the graphic named **Blake.psd**.

TIP Fit the page in the window if you cannot see it all.

2. Click **Object** on the menu bar, point to **Clipping Path**, then click **Options**.

3. Click the **Type list arrow**, then click **Detect Edges**.

4. Click the **Preview check box** to add a check mark if it is not checked.

   The Detect Edges option instructs InDesign to create a clipping path around the object. InDesign uses the Threshold and Tolerance sliders in conjunction with the given image to define where that path will be positioned in relation to the image. As shown in Figure 33, at the default Threshold and Tolerance settings, the white part of the background is made transparent, but the blue areas of the background are still visible.

5. Drag the **Threshold** and **Tolerance sliders** to **0**.

   The Threshold slider finds light areas of the image and makes them transparent—starting with white. At 0, no pixels are made invisible. The farther you move the slider to the right, the more the darker tones are included in the areas that are made invisible. That's why it's a smart idea to start with the Threshold set to 0. You want to use as small a Threshold value as possible.

Figure 33 Viewing transparency at default settings in the Clipping Path dialog box

6. Drag the **Threshold slider** slowly to the right until the entire background disappears.

   As shown in Figure 34, the Threshold slider needs to be set as high as 53 to make the entire background invisible. Note how many anchor points are on the brown clipping path.

7. Slowly drag the **Tolerance slider** all the way to the right, stopping along the way to view the effect on the path.

   The Tolerance slider defines how many points are used to draw the path and, therefore, how accurately the path is drawn. As you increase the Tolerance, the path is more inaccurate.

8. Keep the **Tolerance slider** at **0**, then click **OK**.

   Your result should resemble Figure 35.

9. Save your work, then continue to the next set of steps.

Using the Detect Edges feature in the Clipping Path dialog box, you were successful in making a white background from a placed graphic transparent.

Figure 34 An increased Threshold setting removes more of the background

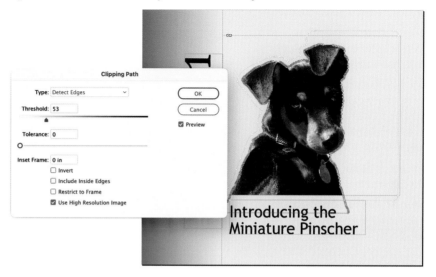

Figure 35 Background dropped out using Detect Edges

Load alpha channels in InDesign

1. Go to **page 7**, then select the **graphics frame**.

2. Looking at Figures 36 and 37, observe that Figure 36 shows a Photoshop file that has been saved with an alpha channel. Figures 37 shows the alpha channel in detail.

3. Click **File** on the menu bar, click **Place,** navigate to the drive and folder where your Chapter 17 Data Files are stored, then place **Red Silo with Alpha Channel.psd**.

4. Click **Object** on the menu bar, point to **Fitting**, then click **Fit Content Proportionally**.

5. Click **Object** on the menu bar, point to **Clipping Path**, click **Options**, then verify that the **Preview check box** is checked.

6. Click the **Type list arrow**, click **Alpha Channel**, click the **Alpha list arrow**, then click **Whole Body**.

Figure 36 Photoshop file saved with an alpha channel

Figure 37 Whole Body alpha channel

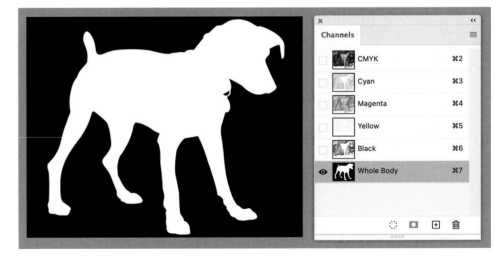

7. Click **OK,** deselect, then compare your page to Figure 38.

8. Save your work, then continue to the next set of steps.

You placed a file with an alpha channel. You loaded the alpha channel in the Clipping Path dialog box, which resulted in the background of the image becoming transparent.

Load clipping paths in InDesign

1. Go to **page 8**, then select the **frame at the center of the page**.

2. Place the file named **Puppies.psd**.

Puppies.psd is a Photoshop file saved with three paths.

3. Click **Object** on the menu bar, point to **Fitting**, then click **Fill Frame Proportionally**.

4. Click **Object** on the menu bar, point to **Clipping Path**, click **Options**, then verify that the **Preview check box** is checked.

TIP You may need to move the Clipping Path dialog box out of the way to see the results of your choices made in the dialog box.

5. Click the **Type list arrow**, click **Photoshop Path**, click the **Path list arrow**, then click **Blake Alone**.

Only the black dog is visible.

6. Click **Object** on the menu bar, point to **Clipping Path**, click **Options**, click the **Path list arrow**, then click **Rex Alone**.

Only the red dog is visible.

7. Click the **Path list arrow**, click **Blake and Rex**, then click **OK**.

8. Deselect all, then compare your page to Figure 39.

9. Save your work, then continue to the next set of steps.

You imported a file that was saved with three clipping paths. In the Clipping Path dialog box, you loaded each of the paths and previewed the results in the graphics frame.

Figure 38 Alpha channel used to remove background

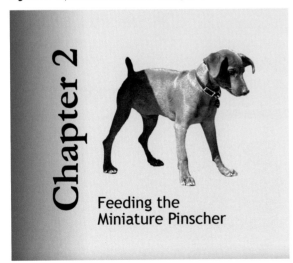

Figure 39 Background dropped out with a clipping path

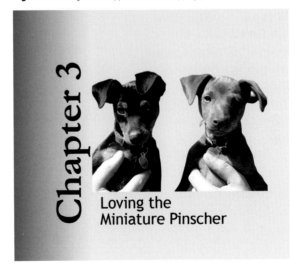

Place a graphic saved with a transparent background in InDesign

1. Go to **page 9**, click the **Selection tool** ▶ then select the **graphics frame** that is centered on the page.

2. Place **Dog Layer.psd** from the drive and folder where your Chapter 17 Data Files are stored.

    As shown in Figure 40, Dog Layer.psd is a Photoshop file containing two layers. Layer 1 contains an oval selection of the dog with a feathered edge against a transparent background. The Background layer contains the whole image, and it is hidden.

3. Click **Object** on the menu bar, point to **Fitting**, then click **Fill Frame Proportionally**.

4. Click **Object** on the menu bar, point to **Fitting**, then click **Center Content**.

5. On the Text Wrap panel, click the **Wrap around object shape button** ▣ , then set the Offset amount to **.3125**.

6. Deselect all, then compare your document to Figure 41.

    The bitmap graphic is placed in InDesign exactly the way it was saved in Photoshop, with a transparent background.

7. Save your work, then continue to the next lesson.

You placed a graphic in InDesign that was saved in Photoshop with a transparent background.

Figure 40 Photoshop file with artwork on a transparent layer

Figure 41   Photoshop artwork on a transparent layer placed in InDesign

Lorem ipsum dolor sit amet, consect adipiscing elit, sed diam nonummy nibh euismod tincidunt ut laoreet dolore magna aliquam erat volutpat. Ut wisi enim ad minim veniam, quis nostrud exercitation ulliam corper suscipit lobortis nisl ut aliquip exea commodo consequat.

Duis autem veleum iriure dolor in hendrerit in vulputate velit esse molestie consequat. Vel willum lunombro dolore eu feugiat nulla facilisis.

At vero eros et accumsan et iusto odio dignissim qui blandit praesent luptatum ezril delenit augue duis dolore te feugait nulla facilisi.

Li Europan lingues es membres del sam familie. Lor separat existentie es un myth. Por scientie, musica, sport etc, litot Europa usa li sam vocabular.

Li lingues differe solmen in li grammatica, li pronunciation e li plu commun vocabules. Omnicos directe al desirabilite de un nov lingua franca: On refusa continuar payar custosi traductores.

It solmen va esser necessi far uniform grammatica, pronunciation e plu sommun paroles. Ma quande lingues coalesce, li grammatica del resultant lingue es plu simplic e regulari quam ti del coalescent lingues. Li nov lingua franca va esser plu simplice.

Regulari quam li existent Europan lingues. It va esser tam simplic quam Occidental in fact, it va esser Occidental. A un Angleso it va semblar un simplificat Angles, quam un skeptic amico dit me que Occidental.

Lorem ipsum dolor sit amet, consect adipiscing elit, sed diam nonummy nibh euismod tincidunt ut laoreet dolore magna aliquam erat volutpat.

Ut wisi enim ad minim veniam, quis nostrud exercitation ulliam corper suscipit lobortis nisl ut aliquip exea commodo consequat.

Duis autem veleum iriure dolor in hendrerit in vulputate velit esse molestie consequat. Vel willum lunombro dolore eu feugiat nulla facilisis.

At vero eros et accumsan et iusto odio dignissim qui blandit praesent luptatum ezril delenit augue duis dolore te

Title   9

USE CREATIVE CLOUD LIBRARIES

What You'll Do

In this lesson, you will create a library to store the graphics you've placed in the document, then use them in another document.

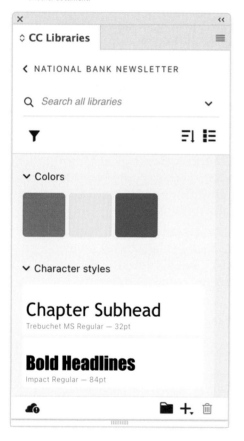

Working with Libraries

Libraries are collections of layout elements you save on a panel in your InDesign document. You can use this library panel to organize and store elements that you use often, such as text, images, character and paragraph styles, color swatches, ruler guides, and grids.

Library files exist as named files on your computer's hard drive, just like any other files. When you create a library file, you give it a name, and its status is saved as you work. You can open and close a library file just as you would any other file. Libraries exist independently of whatever InDesign document is open, and you can open multiple libraries, as needed.

For an example of the usefulness of libraries, imagine that you are an art director for an advertising agency. A major banking chain is your client. You design hundreds of ads for them throughout a given year. The bank has three divisions, each with a slightly different logo. Rather than having to place a logo every time you want to use it (and having to remember which filename refers to which version of the logo), you could simply create

a library and load all three of the bank's logos into that library. You could keep that library open whenever InDesign is launched. That way, you always have access to all three versions of the logo.

In a different scenario, imagine you are leading a team of three designers, all of whom are working from home. A big challenge is sharing assets among the team: logos, colors, character styles, paragraph styles, and so on. Libraries offer a great solution. You can share a library of assets via email.

When you use a file from a library in a document, you can edit the file however you like. The edits that you make to the file in the document do not affect the original file in the library in any way. For example, if you scale a graphic file that you used from the library in the document, the file in the library is not scaled. You can delete the graphic file from the document, but it won't be deleted from the library. Nothing you do to a graphic in the document affects any object in a library.

> **TIP** Snippets can be added to a library. Simply drag a snippet from the InDesign page into the Library panel to add it as a library element.

Create a new CC Library

1. Click **Window** on the menu bar, then click **CC Libraries** to open the panel.

2. On the panel, under Create New Library, type **Min-Pin Brochure**.

3. Click **Create**.

As shown in Figure 42, a new library opens on the CC Libraries panel.

You created a new library on the CC Libraries panel.

Add color swatches to a library

1. On the Swatches panel, click to select the **Background Orange**, **Sidebar Blue**, and **Background Tan swatches**.

2. At the bottom-left corner of the Swatches panel, click the **Add selected swatch to my current CC library button** 🔲 .

As shown in Figure 43, the three swatches appear in the Min-Pin Brochure library.

3. Continue to the next set of steps.

You added three colors to a library.

Figure 42 New library on the CC Libraries panel

Figure 43 Three color swatches added to the Min-Pin Brochure library

Add styles to a CC Library

1. Open the **Character Styles panel**.

2. Select the **three styles** listed on the panel.

3. At the bottom-left corner, click the **Add selected style to my current CC library button** 🔁 .

   As shown in Figure 44, the three styles appear in the Min-Pin Brochure library.

4. Open the **Paragraph Styles panel**.

5. Select the **Body Copy No Drop Cap style** on the panel.

6. Click the **Add selected style to my current CC library button** 🔁 .

   The paragraph style is listed by itself on the CC Libraries panel.

7. Save your work, then continue to the next set of steps.

You added two character styles and one paragraph style to a library.

Add a placed image to the CC Libraries panel

1. Go to **page 6** in the document, then click the **dog illustration** to select it.

2. On the CC Libraries panel, click the **plus sign** to show the menu, then click **Graphic**.

   The dog illustration is added to the CC Libraries panel.

3. Double-click the **name text field** below the graphic on the panel, then type **Dog Illo**.

   Your panel should resemble Figure 45.

4. Save your work, then continue to the next set of steps.

You added a placed graphic from the document to the library.

Figure 44 Three character styles on the CC Libraries panel

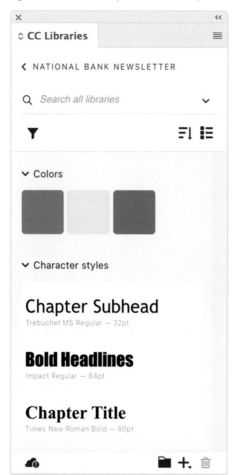

Figure 45 Graphic added to the library

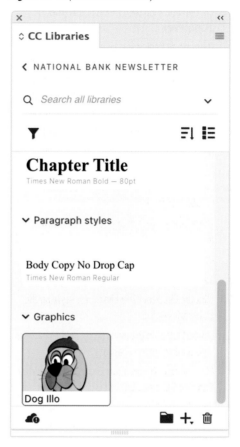

Apply library items to a document

1. Open ID 6-4.indd, then save it as **Chapter 16 Single Page**.

The concept behind this lesson is that you've already designed the brochure. Now it's months later, and you need to design a single-page flyer to promote the campaign. Rather than copy and paste elements, you will use the CC Libraries panel.

2. Select the **frame** that covers the entire page.

Note that the Swatches panel contains only default swatches.

3. Click the **Background Orange color** on the CC Libraries panel.

The frame fills with orange, and the Swatches panel now has a Background Orange swatch listed.

4. On the Swatches panel, set the **Tint** to **35%**.

5. Click to select the **Chapter 16 text frame**.

6. Click the **Chapter Title character style** on the CC Libraries panel.

The text takes on the formatting and the character style is added to the Character Style panel.

7. Click the **text frame** under Chapter 16, then click **Chapter Subhead** on the CC Libraries panel.

8. Press **[control] (Mac)** then click **Dog Illo** or **right-click (Win) Dog Illo** on the CC Libraries panel.

A context menu appears.

9. Click **Place Copy**.

The Dog Illo artwork is loaded as the place thumbnail.

10. Click **anywhere in the gutter** between the two columns of body copy text.

As shown in Figure 46, the graphic is placed along with the text wrap formatting that was applied when it was added to the CC Libraries panel.

11. Save your work, then close the Chapter 16 Single Page document.

12. Close the Min Pin Graphics document, saving changes if necessary.

You applied color, two character styles, and added a graphic, all from a library.

Figure 46 Library elements applied to a layout

Use the Links panel

1. Open ID 6-5.indd, click Don't Update Links, then save the document as **Program Cover**.
2. Click the Selection tool, click the spotlight graphic on page 1, then note that the graphic's name is highlighted on the Links panel.
3. Click Final Logo.ai on the Links panel, then click the Go to Link button.
4. Click susan.psd on the Links panel, then click the Go to Link button.
5. Click the Relink button, navigate to the EOU Moved folder, click susan.psd, then click Open.
6. Go to page 1, fit the page in the window, then click the center of the spotlight oval to select the empty graphics frame.

Place vector graphics

1. Click File on the menu bar, click Place, navigate to your Chapter 17 Data Files folder, click Logo with Shadow.ai, then click Open.
   Your page 1 should resemble Figure 47.
2. Go to page 2, click the Selection tool, then click the graphic named susan.psd.

Figure 47 Placed vector graphic

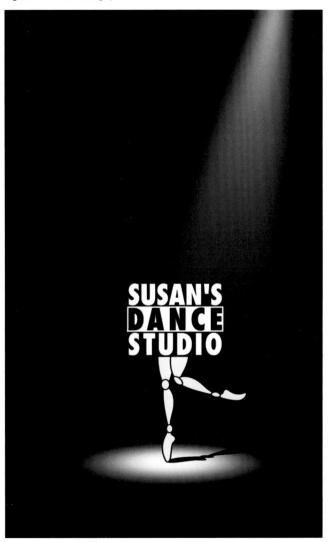

3. Click Object on the menu bar, point to Clipping Path, then click Options.
4. Click the Type list arrow, then click Detect Edges.
5. Verify that there is a check mark in the Preview check box.
6. Drag the Threshold slider to 40, then click OK.
7. With susan.psd still selected, click Object on the menu bar, point to Clipping Path, then click Options.
8. Click the Type list arrow, then click Alpha Channel.
9. Click the Alpha list arrow, then click Head Silhouette Only.
10. Drag the Threshold slider to 1, verify that the Tolerance slider is set to 2, then click OK.
11. With susan.psd still selected, click Object on the menu bar, point to Clipping Path, then click Options.
12. Click the Type list arrow, click Photoshop Path, then click OK.
13. Deselect all, then fit the page in the window.
14. Save your work, then close the Program Cover document.

Place multiple graphics

1. Open ID 6-6.indd, then save it as **Dog's Best Friend**.
2. Collapse all open panels.
3. Verify that the toolbar is showing.
4. Click File on the menu bar, then click Browse in Bridge.
5. Navigate to the location where you store your Chapter 17 Data Files.
6. Drag the scale slider at the bottom of the panel left and right to enlarge and reduce the thumbnails.
7. Use the scrollbar on the right of the panel to scroll through all the thumbnails.
8. Click the file named Black 1.psd.
9. Press and hold [command] (Mac) or [Ctrl] (Win), then click the following three files: Black 2, Red 1, Red 2.
10. Click File on the menu bar, point to Place, then click In InDesign.
11. Press the right arrow key to scroll through the loaded thumbnails, then scroll to the Black 1 thumbnail.
12. Click the place thumbnail in the top frame at the left of the page.
13. Place the remaining three loaded images into the remaining three frames in any order that you wish.
14. Select all four frames, click Object on the menu bar, point to Fitting, then click Fill Frame Proportionally.
15. Save your work.

Interface InDesign with Photoshop

1. Click the Selection tool, then click the graphic on the right-hand page.
2. Click the Wrap around object shape button on the Text Wrap panel.
3. Click Object on the menu bar, point to Clipping Path, then click Options.
4. Click the Type list arrow, then click Detect Edges.
5. Click the Preview check box to add a check mark, if necessary.
6. Drag the Threshold and Tolerance sliders to 0.
7. Drag the Threshold slider to 10, then click OK.
8. Save your work.
9. Verify that the large dog image on the right-hand page is selected.
10. Click Object on the menu bar, point to Clipping Path, click Options, then verify that the Preview check box is checked in the Clipping Path dialog box.
11. Click the Type list arrow, click Alpha Channel, click the Alpha list arrow, then click Petey.
12. Drag the Threshold slider to 1 and the Tolerance slider to 0.
13. Click OK.
14. Verify that the large dog image on the right-hand page is selected.

(continued)

15. Click Object on the menu bar, point to Clipping Path, click Options, then verify that the Preview check box is checked.
16. Click the Type list arrow, click Photoshop Path, click the Path list arrow, click Path 1, then click OK.
17. Deselect all, then switch to Preview mode.
18. Compare your page to Figure 48.

Explore image resolution issues

1. Verify that the large dog image is selected, double-click the thumbnail on the Links panel, then note the information in the Link Info section.
2. Click the Edit Original button on the Links panel. The image opens in Adobe Photoshop. You will need to have Adobe Photoshop installed on your computer to complete this lesson.
3. In Photoshop, click Image on the menu bar, then click Image Size.

4. Verify that the Resample Image option is checked.
5. Enter **600** in the Resolution text box, then click OK.
6. Click File on the menu bar, then click Save.
7. Return to the InDesign layout.
8. Verify that the dog graphic is selected, then note the change to the Effective PPI.
   The Actual PPI in the Link Info panel is now 600, and the Effective PPI is 319.
9. Save your work, then close the Dog's Best Friend document.

Figure 48 Completed Skills Review

You are a designer at a local studio. A client has delivered an Adobe Illustrator graphic for you to place in an InDesign document. The client wants you to place it with a text wrap and then display the results on your screen.

1. Open ID 6-7.indd, then save it as **Snowball**.
2. Switch to Normal mode if you are not already in it.
3. Select the graphics frame in the center of the page, then place the file Snowball.ai.
4. Fit the content proportionally in the graphics frame.
5. Click the Wrap around object shape button on the Text Wrap panel.
6. Click the Wrap To list arrow on the Text Wrap panel, then click Both Right & Left Sides.
7. Click the Type list arrow on the Text Wrap panel, then click Detect Edges.
8. Deselect all, then switch to Preview mode.
9. Save your work, compare your page to Figure 49, then close the Snowball document.

Figure 49 Completed Project Builder 1

You work for a print production service bureau. You have just been given a job to print 10 color copies of a supplied file. You open the file and realize that you need to update the links before printing the copies.

1. Open ID 6-8.indd, click Don't Update Links, then save the file as **Hawaii Links**.
2. Switch to Preview mode if you are not already in it.
3. Click the link for Tree coverage.psd that is on page 1, then click the Go to Link button.

TIP You will need to expand the Tree coverage.psd (2) link to see the two instances of the graphic, one on page 1 and one on page 2. See Figure 50.

4. Click the Relink button, navigate to the Hidden Tree folder in your Chapter 17 Data Files folder, click Tree coverage.psd, then click Open.
5. Relink Tree coverage.psd that is on page 2.
6. Update the remaining files on the Links panel if they are not updated.
7. Compare your Links panel to Figure 50.
8. Save your work, then close the Hawaii Links document.

Figure 50 Completed Project Builder 2

You are designing a cover for LAB magazine and run into a problem. The way the cover photograph has been shot, the dog's face is hidden behind the magazine's title. You open the photograph in Photoshop, then create a path around the dog's head. You are now ready to use the image in InDesign.

1. Open ID 6-9.indd, click Update Links, then save it as **Lab Cover**.
2. Switch to Normal view if necessary.
3. Verify that guides are showing.
4. Click the Selection tool, click the dog photograph, copy it, click Edit on the menu bar, then click Paste in Place.
5. Place the file Wally Head Silo.psd from your Chapter 17 Data Files.

TIP When the new graphic is placed, it will look exactly the same as the previous graphic.

6. Click Object on the menu bar, point to Clipping Path, then click Options.
7. Click the Type list arrow, click Photoshop Path, then click OK.

TIP The Direct Selection tool becomes automatically selected.

8. Click the Selection tool, then click the dog's face.
9. Click Object on the menu bar, point to Arrange, then click Send Backward.
10. Deselect all, click View on the menu bar, point to Display Performance, then click High Quality Display.
11. Hide guides, hide frame edges, then compare your page to Figure 51.
12. Save your work, then close the Lab Cover document.

Figure 51 Completed Design Project

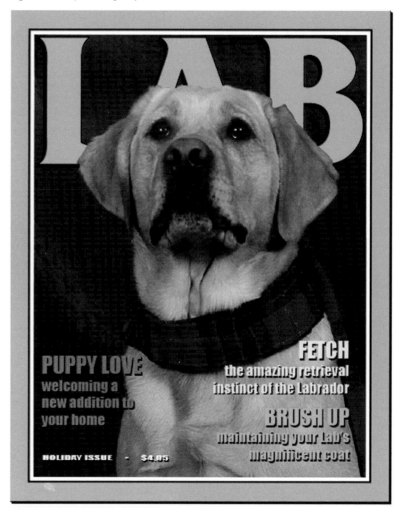

THE SUN IS STILL HIGH IN THE ALASKAN SUMMER SKY
WHEN THE CALL COMES IN AT 9:47 P.M.

SIRENS WAIL, AND EIGHT SMOKEJUMPERS race to the suit-up racks. Already in logger's boots, dark green pants, and bright yellow shirts, each man practically leaps into his Kevlar jumpsuit.

"First load to the box!" a voice blares over the intercom. Itchy, Bloemker, O'Brien, Dibert, Swisher, Koby, Swan, Karp, and Cramer are the men at the top of the jump list. All evening they've mostly been hanging around the operations desk at their base at Fort Wainwright, cracking jokes and razzing each other, anxiously and excitedly waiting for their turn to leap out of a plane to fight a backcountry forest fire.

Now they have exactly two minutes to suit up and be on the plane. It's a much practiced routine: Their hands fly nimbly around their bodies, strapping on kneepads and shin guards, zipping into jumpsuits, and buckling into heavy nylon harnesses. The jumpsuits are prepacked with gear—a cargo pocket on one pant leg is stuffed with a solar panel and raincoat. The pocket on the other leg holds energy bars and a 150-foot rope, plus a rappel device in case of a treetop landing. An oversize butt pouch contains a tent and a stuff sack for the parachute.

Other smokejumpers quickly surround them, helping the men put on their main parachutes and reserve chutes. Then each man grabs his jump helmet—fitted with a cage-like mask to protect his face during a descent through branches—and his personal gear bag, which holds a liter of water, leather gloves, hard hat, flares for lighting backfires, knife, compass, radio, and special aluminum sack that serves as a last-resort fire shelter.

Two minutes after the siren, they are waddling onto the tarmac, each laden with nearly a hundred pounds of equipment and supplies. Fully dressed, they appear awkwardly overstuffed, but every man carries a carefully curated, time-tested kit of the essential items a smokejumper needs to fight and survive a fire in some of the world's most remote and rugged forests.

Photographed by team member Mike McMillan, one of the crew, aims for a landing near the tail of the fire—where it started close to a group of cottages. The billowing smoke column signals a rapidly spreading "gobbler," a wildfire that's "off to the races," McMillan says.

Layout/design by Tim Parks. From "Into the Fire." *National Geographic Magazine*, Vol. 235, No. 5, May, 2019

850

PROJECT DESCRIPTION

In this project, you will explore the relationship between imagery and text using a model spread from *National Geographic*. You will then study the differences between various magazine spread layouts and work with a peer to create the layout for your own spread. Your group will choose an impactful photograph and write accompanying text to describe it. The goal of this project is to create a layout that is balanced in its imagery and text placement.

SKILLS TO EXPLORE

- Format Text
- Format Paragraphs
- Create and Apply Styles
- Edit Text
- Create Bulleted and Numbered Lists
- Create a New Document and Set Up a Master Page
- Create Text on Master Pages
- Apply Master Pages to Document Pages
- Modify Master Pages and Document Pages

SOFT SKILLS CHALLENGE

In print publishing, a "Wall Walk" is an opportunity to view all pages of a product before it goes to print. During this event, large format, full-color spreads are taped to the wall, so team members can view all pages in the book or magazine in one plane and discuss changes that need to be made to the design or layout.

In this challenge, you and your partner will engage in a Wall Walk. The goal of this project is to help refine your idea of what a balanced spread looks like. To prepare, look through old magazines or conduct an Internet search. Do not choose the first spreads you see. Instead, allow yourself to peruse different styles. Look for layouts, images, text placements, and font changes that capture your eye. Then select four or more full-color spreads that grab your attention. Lay the spreads on a table or tape them to the wall.

Then observe each element of the spreads carefully. Notice the details that differentiate the spreads from one another. During your Wall Walk, discuss the relationship between text and imagery, changes in font size or style, use of white space, and the balance on each of the spreads.

WALL WALK CHECKLIST

1. Partner
2. Four or more magazine spreads
3. Safe space to facilitate respectful conversation

◀ Alaskan smokejumpers parachute into remote forested areas to fight fires.

GETTING STARTED

As you prepare to create your own layout, compare the spreads you chose for your Wall Walk to the sample spread from *National Geographic*. Discuss ways these spreads are alike and different and point out your favorite elements in each of the spreads. Be sure to note the overall composition of the spread: How much real estate does the image take up? How is the spread divided? What plays a more prominent role: text or image?

1. Create a list of the various elements that call out to you and decide which of these you would like to use in your layout. For example, would it be more impactful to show a colorful photo, a black and white photo, or a design element? In terms of font, should all of the text be the same size, or would varied fonts and sizes make the layout more interesting? Are captions necessary?

The students created a list of design elements to use in their project.

- colorful photo
- varied font sizes
- all caps
- short caption

2. Create a sketch of your layout to get a feel for how the photo and text might work together to tell a story. Ensure that all elements from your list are considered. Don't worry about the actual fonts or sizes at the moment. This part of the project focuses on the composition itself. Place your image and text blocks. How does the page feel? If necessary, add other elements, or change up the text to make it more visually interesting.

After considering many elements, the student sketched a sample magazine layout.

These sample magazine layouts show multiple layout options for the spread.

zeber/Shutterstock

INTO

THE

FIRE

EACH SUMMER, ELITE TEAMS KNOWN AS SMOKEJUMPERS PARACHUTE
INTO ALASKA'S BACKCOUNTRY IN A DANGEROUS RACE TO FIGHT REMOTE FIRES.

BY MARK JENKINS
PHOTOGRAPHS BY
MARK THIESSEN

120

Layout/design by Tim Parks. From "Into the Fire." *National Geographic Magazine*, Vol. 235, No. 5, May, 2019

PROJECT DESCRIPTION

In this project, you will create a comprehensive spread based on the layout from your Design Project. Consider experimenting with font size and style, and using text elements such as bulleted lists, numbered lists, or captions. Play with graphic and text frames, and add color as you see fit. The goal of this project is to create a magazine-style spread that engages the reader using a balance of imagery and text.

SKILLS TO EXPLORE

- Place and Thread Text
- Create New Sections and Wrap Text
- Align and Distribute Objects on a Page
- Stack and layer Objects
- Work with Graphics Frames
- Work with Text Frames
- Working with Color
- Work with Process Colors

SOFT SKILLS CHALLENGE

Working with a partner in a creative project can present its challenges. Often, both people bring differing views and perspectives to the project. In order to create a project you are both proud of, you will need to work together. Be honest as you discuss your strengths and weaknesses with each other. Decide how to break up the work. Will you make every decision together, or will each partner have the opportunity to use their own creative skills? Look over your layout and the Skills to Explore. Work together to come up with a list of tasks for each person in your group. Practice your speech so you are confident while presenting. You want your audience to view you as an expert on the topic.

GETTING STARTED

It's often challenging to start with a blank screen. Allow your Design Project to guide you.

1. Look at the balance on your page. Should the image take up the whole spread with just a bit of text? Or would it make more sense to have a single-page image with text on either the right or the left? Should the text come before the image, or the image before the text? These small decisions greatly influence the visual feel of the spread.

2. Compare the two *National Geographic* spreads. Both use a feature image to capture the reader's attention, but one has much more text than the other. Which one are you more drawn to and why? Think about how you might have designed these spreads differently. For example, imagine the "Into the Fire" spread had more text. What would be lost? How might this impact the spread as a whole?

3. Challenge yourself to enhance the layout with text and graphic frames. Link text blocks together in interesting ways and experiment with placing text in different positions on the page. Think outside the box by arranging the text in a way that shows its importance. For example, you may be able to reduce a larger text block to three sentences and instead use small caps to convey the importance of the words.

4. Think about how best to include color in your spread, either through font, background, or a feature callout. Remember, the text and images should work together for the ultimate visual impact.

◀ Alaskan smokejumpers parachute into remote forested areas to fight fires.

SKILLS
INTEGRATION

CHAPTER 18
DESIGN A PROJECT THAT INCORPORATES
ILLUSTRATOR, PHOTOSHOP, AND INDESIGN

This graphic compilation blends pattern, texture, colo[r]
and line to create an abstract design atop a watercol[or]
background.

18

DESIGN A PROJECT THAT INCORPORATES ILLUSTRATOR, PHOTOSHOP, AND INDESIGN

1. Design Complex Typographic Artwork in Illustrator
2. Use Layer Styles in Photoshop to Add Dimension to Type
3. Use Images as Textures for Type in Photoshop
4. Create an Output Document for Print in InDesign

Illustrator

3. Organize Documents

This objective covers document structure such as layers and tracks, for efficient workflows.

3.1 Use layers to manage design elements.
    A Use the Layers panel to modify layers.
    B Manage and work with multiple layers in a complex project.

3.2 Modify layer visibility using opacity and masks.
    B Create, apply, and manipulate clipping masks.

4. Creating and Modifying Visual Elements

This objective covers core tools and functionality of the application, as well as tools that affect the visual appearance of document elements.

4.3 Make, manage, and manipulate selections.
    B Modify and refine selections using various methods.

5. Publishing Digital Media

This objective covers saving and exporting documents or assets within individual layers or selections.

5.2 Export or save digital images to various file formats.
    C Export project elements.

Photoshop

3. Organizing Documents

This objective covers document structure such as layers and managing document structure for efficient workflows.

3.1 Use layers to manage design elements.
    A Use the Layers panel to manage visual content.
    C Recognize the different types of layers in the Layers panel.

3.2 Modify layer visibility using opacity, blending modes, and masks.

4. Creating and Modifying Visual Elements

This objective covers core tools and functionality of the application, as well as tools that affect the visual outcome of the document.

4.4 Transform digital graphics and media.
    A Modify the canvas or artboards.

InDesign

2. Project Setup and Interface

This objective covers the interface setup and program settings that assist in an efficient and effective workflow, as well as knowledge about ingesting digital assets for a project.

2.1 Create a document with the appropriate settings for web, print, and mobile.
    A Set appropriate document settings for printed and on-screen images.

5. Publishing Digital Media

This objective covers saving and exporting documents or assets within individual layers or selections.

5.1 Prepare documents for print.

DESIGN COMPLEX TYPOGRAPHIC ARTWORK IN ILLUSTRATOR

▶ *What You'll Do*

In this lesson, you'll apply the Offset Path command to text outlines in Adobe Illustrator.

Offset paths in Illustrator

1. Start Adobe Illustrator.

2. Open AI 18-1.ai, then save it as **Jazz Offset Paths**.

3. Verify that your **Units Preferences** are set to **Inches** in the General category.

4. Select all.

   The 3" × 5" black rectangular object won't be selected because it is locked.

5. Click **Object** on the menu bar, point to **Path**, then click **Offset Path**.

6. Enter the settings shown in Figure 1, then click **OK**.

7. Open the Pathfinder panel, then click the **Unite button** ▪.

   Uniting the new path into a single object is an important step. Once it's united as a single object, it can be used to create the next offset path.

Figure 1 Settings for offsetting the path

Offset Path		
Offset:	0.06 in	
Joins:	Miter	⌄
Miter limit:	4	
☑ Preview	Cancel	OK

8. Click **Object** on the menu bar, point to **Arrange**, then click **Send to Back**.

9. On the Swatches panel, click a **light orange swatch**.

10. Click **Object** on the menu bar, point to **Path**, then click **Offset Path**.

11. Type **.06"** in the Offset text box, then click **OK**.

12. Click the **Unite button** ▪ on the Pathfinder panel.

13. Click **Object** on the menu bar, point to **Arrange**, then click **Send to Back**.

14. On the Swatches panel, click a **green swatch**.

    The Offset Path command resulted in an odd sliver of negative space inside the curve of the number 2. This happens often when offsetting paths, so it's good to know how to use the Delete Anchor Point tool to clean up these kinds of aberrations.

15. Click the **Delete Anchor Point tool** ✏️, then click the **three anchor points** indicated by white arrows in Figure 2.

TIP Zoom in for a better view of each anchor point.

16. Click the **Direct Selection tool** ▷, then click the **interior of the green object** so the entire object is selected.

17. Click **Object** on the menu bar, point to **Path**, then click **Offset Path**.

18. Enter **.06"** in the Offset text box, then click **OK**.

Figure 2 Identifying three anchor points to be deleted

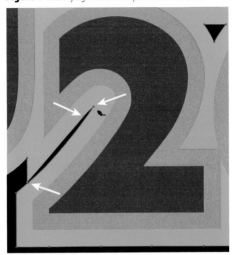

Figure 3 Completed offset path illustration

19. Click the **Unite button** on the Pathfinder panel.
20. Click **Object** on the menu bar, point to **Arrange**, then click **Send to Back**.
21. On the Swatches panel, click a **blue swatch**.

    Your artwork should resemble Figure 3. From a design perspective, there's much to appreciate about this artwork. Note the green object behind the number 2. Because you deleted the anchor points, the object is very clean. Now note the blue triangle between the *A* and the *Z* and the blue parallelogram between the two *Z*s. These blue objects are visible through the negative spaces in the green object. And finally, note the points and indents on the perimeter of the artwork. Interesting outcroppings are formed from the large letter *J*, the second *Z*, and the number 6.

Even though the top edge is straight, all other edges are unique and interesting.

22. Save your work, then continue to the next set of steps.

You used the Offset Path command three times to create a complex and visually interesting typographic illustration.

Create layered artwork in Illustrator

1. On the Layers panel, click the **Create New Layer button** four times to create four new layers.
2. From top to bottom, name the layers **RED**, **ORANGE**, **GREEN**, **BLUE**, and **BLACK**.
3. Click the **Direct Selection tool**, select the **eight red objects**, then move them to the **RED layer**.
4. Move the **orange object** to the **ORANGE layer**.

5. Move the **green object** to the **GREEN layer**, then move the **blue object** to the **BLUE layer**.
   Your Layers panel should resemble Figure 4.

Figure 4 Layers panel with layered artwork

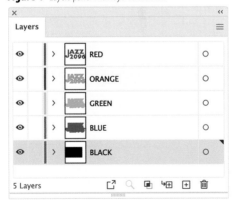

Continued on next page

6. Save your work, then continue to the next set of steps.

You created four new layers on the Layers panel, then moved artwork to different layers.

Export layered artwork from Illustrator to Photoshop

1. Click **File** on the menu bar, point to **Export**, then click **Export As** to open the Export dialog box.

2. Click the **Save as type list arrow**, then click **Photoshop (*.PSD)**.

Your Export dialog box should resemble Figure 5.

3. Click **Export**.

The Photoshop Export Options dialog box opens.

4. Enter the settings shown in Figure 6, then click **OK**.

The file is exported with the name Jazz Offset Paths.psd.

5. In Illustrator, save Jazz Offset Paths.ai, then close the file.

You exported a layered Illustrator file as a Photoshop (.PSD) document.*

Figure 5 Export dialog box

Figure 6 Settings for exporting Illustrator artwork to Photoshop

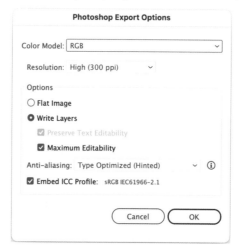

USE LAYER STYLES IN PHOTOSHOP TO ADD DIMENSION TO TYPE

What You'll Do

In this lesson, you'll use layer styles to apply complex effects to typographical artwork exported from Adobe Illustrator.

Combine Inner Shadow and Bevel & Emboss layer styles

1. Start Adobe Photoshop.

2. Open the Jazz Offset Paths.psd file that you exported from Illustrator, then save it as **Jazz 2096**.

   Note: If you did not complete the export from the previous lesson, or if you're not confident that you did it correctly, use the file 18-2.psd in the Chapter 18 Data Files folder.

3. Verify that your Units & Rulers preferences are set to **Inches** in the Rulers category.

4. On the Layers panel, hide all layers. Then show each layer, one at a time.

   The artwork and layer structure in Photoshop is identical to what you built in Illustrator.

5. Verify that all layers are showing.

6. Set the **foreground color** to **128R/128G/128B**.

   From this point on, we will refer to this color as "neutral gray."

7. Target the **RED**, **ORANGE**, **GREEN**, and **BLUE** layers one at a time, then activate the **Lock transparent pixels button** ▨ on the Layers panel for each layer.

   A lock icon will appear at the right side of each layer. When you're done, your Layers panel should resemble Figure 7.

8. Hide the **Red** and **Orange layers** so that only the Blue and Green artwork is visible.

9. Fill the **Blue layer** with **neutral gray**.

Figure 7 Transparent pixels locked on top four layers

10. Add a **Bevel & Emboss layer style** with the settings shown in Figure 8.

11. Click **OK**, then compare your results to Figure 9.

    With the 100-pixel size setting, the chiseled edge butts up against the edge of the green artwork.

12. Target the **Green layer**, then fill it with **neutral gray**.

13. Add an **Inner Shadow layer style**.

14. In the Layer Style dialog box, verify that the **Blend Mode** is set to **Multiply**, the **Opacity** is set to **75%**, the **Angle** is set to **45°**, and the **Use Global Light option** is checked.

The Use Global Light option allows you to set one "master" lighting angle that you can apply to layer styles that use shading. This is a great option for quickly applying a consistent light source to all your layer styles.

15. Drag the **Distance slider** to **11**, drag the **Choke slider** to **14**, drag the **Size slider** to **16**, then click **OK**.

    Compare your results to Figure 10. The illustration at this point is composed of two pieces of artwork on two different layers. The two layer styles are working in conjunction so the artwork appears as one object. The bevel and emboss effects create the outer edge of the object. The inner shadow creates indentations to the interior of the object. Take a moment to analyze the overall effect because it's a fine

example of an important concept: Don't get caught up in trying to make one layer style accomplish everything. More often than not, *many* layer styles work together to create a *single* effect.

16. Show and target the **Orange layer**, then fill it with **neutral gray**.

17. Add a **Bevel & Emboss layer style**.

18. Verify that the **Style** is set to **Inner Bevel**, click the **Technique list arrow**, then click **Chisel Hard**.

19. Drag the **Size slider** to **9**.

20. Click the **Gloss Contour list arrow**, click **Ring**, then click the **Anti-aliased check box** to activate it.

    Your dialog box should resemble Figure 11.

Figure 8 Bevel & Emboss settings

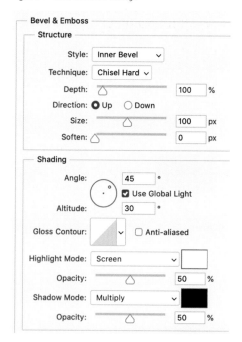

Figure 9 The Bevel & Emboss effect applied to the neutral gray artwork

Figure 10 Two layer styles producing one effect

Figure 11 Bevel & Emboss settings for Orange layer

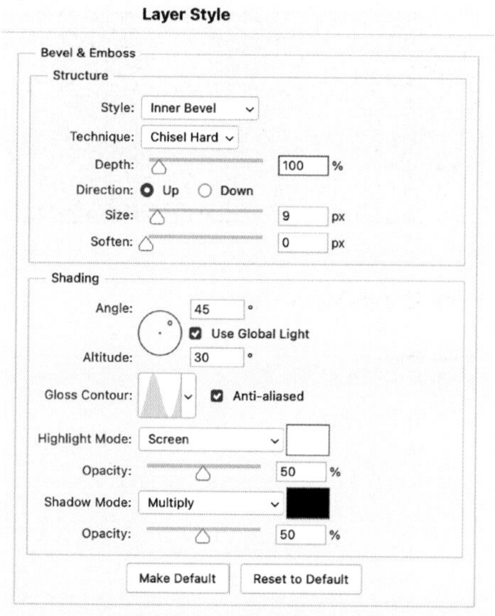

21. Click **OK**, then compare your results to Figure 12.

22. Show and target the **Red layer**, then fill it with **neutral gray**.

23. Add an **Inner Shadow layer style** with the settings shown in Figure 13, then click **OK**.

24. Compare your artwork to Figure 14.

25. Click the **Create new fill or adjustment layer button** ⬤ on the Layers panel, then click **Solid Color**.

26. Create a color that is **199R/75G/195B**, then click **OK**.

27. Clip the **new fill layer** into the **Red layer**.

Now that the illustration is almost finished, you'll make final adjustments to brighten highlights and add contrast.

Figure 12 The Orange layer, beveled and embossed

Figure 13 Inner Shadow settings

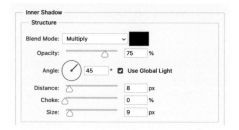

28. Double-click the **Bevel & Emboss layer style** on the **Orange layer** to open the Layer Style dialog box.

29. Increase the **Opacity** of the **Highlight Mode** to **80%**, then click **OK**.

This small change makes a big difference because the highlight on the emboss is now noticeably brighter. Sometimes the little adjustments you make at the end of a project make the biggest difference in the final image.

30. Compare your artwork to Figure 15.

31. Save your work, then continue to the next set of steps.

This exercise was an exploration of using multiple layers and layer styles all working together to produce one visually complex piece of artwork. The combination of the Bevel & Emboss effect on the Blue layer with the Inner Shadow effect on the Green layer was the best demonstration of how two layer styles on two different pieces of artwork can work together to produce one cohesive effect.

Figure 14 Four layer styles creating one piece of art

If you look back at the original artwork, it's pretty amazing that Photoshop can make an illustration this visually complex with just four layers and four layer styles. That said, the design itself works very well for this effect. Because the letter *J* is extra large, it integrates the two lines of text into one piece of artwork: the *J* is the bridge, so to speak. But even more importantly, the hook of the letter *J* delivers an interesting shape on the left side of the artwork that shows off the embossing and the inner shadow effects quite dramatically. This is mirrored on the right side of the artwork by the number *6*. Note how the point at the top extends farther to the right than the *Z* above it. That sharp point, along with the zig-zag of the letter *Z* above it, creates a unique and interesting sharp edge on the right that resolves itself with the friendly circle of the number *6* below it. These shapes all work so well with the layer styles and their effects.

Figure 15 The final artwork

USE IMAGE AS TEXTURES FOR TYPE IN PHOTOSHOP

In this lesson, you'll use a photograph as a texture clipped into type.

Clip images as textures

1. In the Jazz 2096.psd file, hide the **Red**, **Orange**, and **Green layers**, then target the **Blue layer**.

2. Open PS 18-3.psd, select all, copy, then close the file.

3. Paste the **copied image** into the Jazz 2096.psd file, then clip the **image** into the **Blue layer**. Your artwork should resemble Figure 16. Note that the layer style on the Blue layer affects the image clipped into it.

4. Show and target the **Green layer**, paste the **image**, then clip it into the **Green layer**.

5. Show and target the **Orange layer**, paste the **image**, then clip it into the **Orange layer**.

6. Change the **blending mode** on this clipped image to **Multiply**.

7. Show and target the **Red layer**, then drag the **Color Fill 1 layer** above it to the **Delete layer button** 🗑 to remove the purple fill color.

8. Paste the **image**, then clip it into the **Red layer**.

9. With **Layer 4** still targeted, add a **Hue/ Saturation adjustment layer** at the top of the Layers panel, then set its blending mode to **Overlay**.

10. On the Properties panel, drag the **Lightness slider** to **+16**.

    Your artwork should resemble Figure 17.

11. Save your work, then close the Jazz 2096.psd document.

You copied an image, then pasted it four times. Clipping each image into a different layer of the layered artwork allowed you to create contrasting effects as the image progressed through the layers. You then applied a Hue/Saturation layer with an Overlay blending mode to produce a high-contrast, glowing, and genuinely stunning piece of artwork.

Figure 16 Clipping the image into the Blue layer

Figure 17 The final image

CREATE AN OUTPUT DOCUMENT FOR PRINT IN INDESIGN

LESSON 4

▶ What You'll Do

In this lesson, you'll import the Jazz 2096 artwork into InDesign to be output as a printed postcard.

Document Setup

Intent: Print

Number of Pages: 1   ☐ Facing Pages

Start Page #: 1   ☑ Primary Text Frame

Page Size: [Custom]

Width: 6 in   Orientation: ▯ ▭

Height: 3 in

Margins

Top: 0.5 in   Left: 0.5 in

Bottom: 0.5 in   Right: 0.5 in

Bleed and Slug

	Top	Bottom	Left	Right
Bleed:	0.125 in	0.125 in	0.125 in	0.125 in
Slug:	0 in	0 in	0 in	0 in

ⓘ Adjust page elements to document changes   (Adjust Layout...)

☑ Preview   (Cancel)   (OK)

Understanding Bleeds

Before discussing bleeds, it's important to define trim size. **Trim size** is the size to which a printed document will be cut, or trimmed, when it clears the printing press. For example, an 8" × 10" magazine may be printed on a page that is 12" × 14", but it will be trimmed to 8" × 10".

Professionally printed documents are printed on paper or a "sheet" that is larger than the document's trim size. The extra space is used to accommodate bleeds, crops, and other printer's marks. **Bleeds** are areas of the layout that extend to the trim size. In Figure 18, the green background extends to the trim on all four sides; the yellow strip extends to the trim on the left and the right. Both are said to "bleed" off the edge.

Areas of the layout that extend to the trim—areas that are meant to bleed—must go beyond the trim size when the document is prepared for printing. Why? This helps accommodate for the margin of error in trimming.

Nothing is perfect, including the cutting device used to trim printed pieces when they clear the printing press. You can target the cutting device to slice the paper exactly at the trim size, but you can never expect it to be dead-on every time. There is a margin of error, usually 1/32" to 1/16".

Figure 18 Identifying areas that will bleed

Green extends to the trim size on all four sides

Yellow extends to the trim size on two sides

To accommodate for this margin of error, any item that bleeds must extend *beyond* the trim size in your final layout. The standard measurement that a bleed item must extend beyond the trim size is .125".

Creating Bleeds

You define a bleed area for a document in the Bleed and Slug section of the New Document dialog box when you're creating a document. If you want to define a bleed area after the document has been created, use the Document Setup dialog box, shown in Figure 19.

Figure 19 shows that the trim size for the document is 6" wide by 3" high and that a .125" bleed area is to be added outside the trim size. This bleed area is reflected in the document by a red guide, shown in Figure 20. You use this guide when you extend areas that bleed beyond the trim size.

As shown in Figure 21, the green background has been extended to the bleed guide on all four sides, and the yellow strip has been extended on the left and the right. If the trimmer trims slightly outside of the trim size (the black line), the extra bleed material provides room for that error.

Figure 19 Document Setup dialog box with .125" bleed

Figure 20 Identifying the bleed guide

Figure 21 Extending bleed items to the bleed guide

Create a document for print

1. Start Adobe InDesign, then verify that no documents are open in InDesign.

2. Click **InDesign (Mac)** or **Edit (Win)** on the menu bar, point to **Preferences**, then click **Units & Increments**.

3. Click the **Horizontal list arrow**, click **Inches**, click the **Vertical list arrow**, click **Inches**, then click **OK**.

4. Click **File** on the menu bar, point to New, then click **Document**.

5. Type **5** in the Width text box, press **[tab]**, type **3** in the Height text box, then click the **Landscape Orientation button** 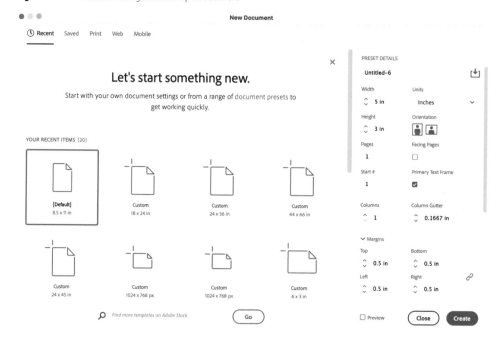.

6. Check the **Primary Text Frame check box**.

   Your New Document dialog box should resemble Figure 22.

7. Click **Create**.

   The margins on the page are ½ inch on all sides. This is generally the measurement for type safety. Any type positioned closer than ½ inch to the edge of the document is getting too close to the trim.

8. Save the file as **3 × 5 Postcard**.

   This document is intended to be a postcard that could be printed on card stock at a professional print house.

9. Click **Window** on the menu bar, point to **Workspace**, then click **[Essentials Classic]**.

10. Click **Window** on the menu bar, point to **Workspace**, then click **Reset Essentials Classic**.

11. Click the **Selection tool** , then select the **text frame** on the page.

    The text frame was created automatically at the size of the margins.

12. On the Control panel at the top of the window, click the **top-left reference point**.

13. In the **X, Y, W, and H text boxes**, type **0, 0, 5,** and **3**, respectively, then click **[Return] (Mac)** or **[Enter] (Win)**.

Figure 22 New Document dialog box set for a print document

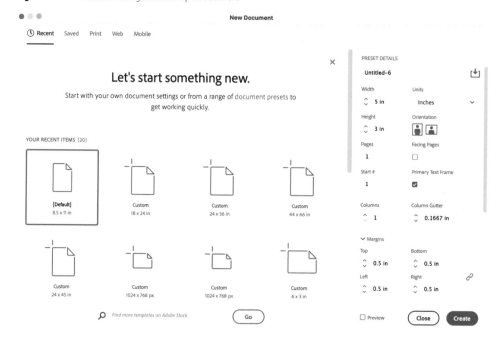

14. Click **File** on the menu bar, click **Place**, navigate to where your Chapter 18 Data Files are stored, then click the **Jazz 2096.psd** file you created in Photoshop.

The image fills the frame. Even though it was a default text frame, it is now functioning as a graphics frame. Your page should resemble Figure 23. Note that there are still two major steps to follow in order to print this postcard. Because this is a print document, the image must be converted to CMYK. CMYK (cyan, magenta, yellow, and black) is the color mode in Photoshop used for images that will be printed. Also, the perimeter of the image must be expanded by .125" on all four sides to create a bleed.

15. Save your work, then continue to the next set of steps.

You created a new document in InDesign, reset the workspace, resized an automatic text frame to the trim size of the document, then placed an image from Photoshop.

Convert an image from RGB to CMYK in Photoshop

1. Open the Links panel.

The Links panel lists all images placed in the document. Because the frame containing the Jazz 2096 image is selected, the image is highlighted on the Links panel.

2. Click the **Edit Original button** 🖉 on the Links panel.

The Jazz 2096.psd file opens in Photoshop.

3. Click **Layer** on the menu bar, then click **Flatten Image**.

Photoshop files with active adjustment layers cannot be converted between RGB and CMYK because doing so will create a dramatic shift in the appearance of the image. For that reason, it is better to flatten the RGB image and save a CMYK copy.

4. Click **Image** on the menu bar, point to **Mode**, then click **CMYK Color**.

TIP Click OK in any dialog boxes that pop up. Now that the image has been converted to CMYK, it's time to enlarge the canvas for the bleed.

5. Save your work, then continue to the next set of steps.

In Photoshop, you converted an RGB file to CMYK to be output as a print document in InDesign.

Figure 23 Placed 3" × 5" image

Expand the canvas size in Photoshop to create a bleed

1. Click **Image** on the menu bar, then click **Canvas Size**.

2. Enter the settings shown in Figure 24, then click **OK**.

   The canvas is increased .125" on all four sides, and the image is now surrounded by a white border.

3. Click the **Eyedropper tool** 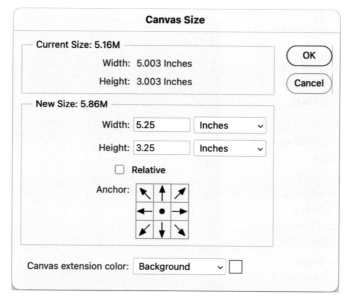, then sample the **black background of the image**.

4. Use any method you like to fill the white edge pixels with the black foreground color.

   It's important that you sampled the actual black color from the background for the fill. Even though all black pixels tend to look alike on your screen, they can print differently depending on their values. Always sample when you are extending a background. See the sidebar titled Sampling Color in the Canvas Size Dialog Box for an alternative method.

5. Click **File** on the menu bar, click **Save As**, then save the file as **Jazz 2096 CMYK**.

6. Return to the InDesign layout document.

7. Click **File** on the menu bar, then click **Document Setup**.

8. Expand the **Bleed and Slug section**, enter the values shown in Figure 25, then click **OK**.

Figure 24 Canvas Size dialog box

Figure 25 Entering values for a bleed

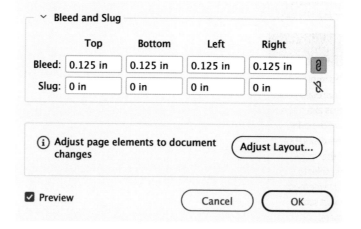

As shown in Figure 26, a red bleed guide appears surrounding the page. It's important to note that you have not changed the original page size of 5" × 3"; you have only added a guide around the page for a bleed.

9. Click and drag the **middle handles** on all four sides of the graphics frame to the bleed guide.

10. Click **File** on the menu bar, then click **Place**.

11. Place the Jazz 2096 CMYK.psd file.

12. Click **Object** on the menu bar, point to **Fitting**, then click **Fill Frame Proportionally**.

   The main components of the image—the type and the man playing the saxophone—have not changed size. All that has changed is the black background, which has been extended in Photoshop to meet the bleed guide on all four sides in InDesign.

13. Save your work, then close the 3 × 5 Postcard document.

You used the Canvas Size dialog box in Photoshop to expand the image to accommodate a bleed element. You then used the Document Setup dialog box in InDesign to create a guide for the bleed. You enlarged the frame in InDesign out to the bleed guide, then imported the CMYK version of the Jazz 2096 image.

SAMPLING COLOR IN THE CANVAS SIZE DIALOG BOX

Photoshop offers you the ability to sample color from the image while the Canvas Size dialog box is open. In Figure 24, note the Canvas extension color section at the bottom. Clicking the color picker square opens the Color Picker dialog box. With that open, you can float over the image with the Eyedropper tool to sample color to extend the canvas. This is an effective method for extending an image with the exact same color background that is already there.

Figure 26 Bleed guide surrounds the page

GLOSSARY

A

Additive primary colors Refers to the fact that red, green, and blue light cannot be broken down themselves but can be combined to produce other colors.

Adjustment layers Adjustments that are applied as layers and are always editable.

Adjustments Operations in Photoshop that affect the appearance of an image.

Algorithm An ordered set of instructions to process data in a certain way.

Aliased edge A hard edge.

Align To position objects in a specific relationship to each other on a given axis.

Alpha channel A grayscale image made in Photoshop that has been saved with a descriptive name and can be loaded into an InDesign document.

Anti-aliased edge A crisp but smooth edge.

Area text Text that is created inside an object.

Attributes Formatting that has been applied to an object that affects its appearance.

Autoflow The automatic threading of text through multiple text frames.

Average A command used to align two or more points on the horizontal axis, vertical axis, or both.

B

Base artwork Original artwork.

Base color The color of the pixel on the lower layer when a blending mode is applied.

Base layer The layer functioning as the clipping mask.

Baseline The invisible line on which text sits.

Bitmap graphics Images created by pixels in a program like Photoshop. Every digital image and scanned graphic is a bitmap graphic.

Bitmap image(s) Graphics created using a grid of colored squares called pixels.

Black point The very darkest pixel in an image.

Bleeds Areas of the layout that extend to the trim size.

Blend color The color on the layer in which the blending mode is applied. The blend color is above the base layer.

Blending modes Preset filters that control how colors blend when two objects overlap.

Bounding box A rectangle that surrounds an image and contains eight handles to click and drag in order to change the dimensions of the artwork.

Brightness A pixel's grayscale value. The higher the number, the brighter the pixel (the closer it is to white).

Brush Preset picker A menu that shows preset brushes and allows the user to create custom brushes.

Butt caps Squared ends of a stroked path.

C

Camera Raw A digital image that has not been compressed or otherwise processed.

Camera resolution The number of pixels per inch a camera can access to recreate an image.

Caps Define the appearance of end points when a stroke is added to a path. The Stroke panel offers three types of caps: butt, round, and projecting.

Captured data A digital image on a camera; the pixels in the image are data the camera captured.

Clipping Using artwork on one layer to mask the artwork on a layer (or multiple layers) above it.

Clipping path A graphic drawn in Photoshop that outlines the areas of the image to be shown when the file is placed in a layout program such as InDesign.

Color midpoint slider A diamond-shaped marker that determines where the gradient is a 50–50 mix between color stops.

Color model A mathematical model that describes how colors can be represented as numbers, usually as a way for computers to process color.

Color stops Small circles on the gradient slider that represent the colors used in the gradient.

Column break A typographic command that forces text to the next column.

Composite image An image that brings together many different images to create one new image.

Compound shape Two or more paths that are combined in such a way that "holes" appear wherever paths overlap.

Concentric Objects that share the same center point.

Cones Receptor cells in the human eye that perceive color.

Content Management Application A framework to organize and access electronic content, such as Adobe Bridge.

Contiguous check box An option to select only pixels that are contiguous to (touching) the pixel where you click the image.

Contrast The relationship between shadows and highlights of an image.

Corner point Anchor point joining two straight segments, one straight segment and one curved segment, or two curved segments.

Darken blending modes A commonly used blending mode in which white pixels become invisible and black pixels remain opaque.

Darker Color A blending mode in which the darker color will replace the lighter color when two colors overlap.

Data merge When a data source containing fields and records is merged with a target document to create personalized documents.

Destructive editing Working behavior in which changes are applied directly to the original image.

Digital image A picture in electronic form.

Direction lines Lines that emanate from an anchor point and determine the arc of a curved segment.

Direction points Handles at the end of a direction line used to reshape a curve.

D

Display Performance section A section of the Preferences dialog box that determines the quality at which the preview file is displayed.

Distribute To position objects on a page so they are spaced evenly in relation to one another.

Dock To connect the bottom edge of one panel to the top edge of another panel so both move together.

Document grid An alignment guide to which objects can be aligned and snapped.

Drag and drop a copy A command that allows the user to copy objects while dragging them.

Draw Behind drawing mode A drawing mode used to create an object behind a selected object or at the bottom of the stacking order.

Drop cap A design element in which the first letter or letters of a paragraph are increased in size to create a visual effect.

Dynamic preview An InDesign feature in which the entirety of a placed graphic, including areas outside a graphics frame, can be seen as the graphic is being moved.

E

Edge(s) The outline of a selection. The area of an image where highly contrasting pixels meet. Similar to strokes, edges are new shapes or areas created by the overlap of Illustrator objects when the Live Paint Bucket tool is applied.

Effective resolution Resolution of a placed image based on its size in the layout.

Electromagnetic spectrum The sum total of light radiation from the sun.

Em space A type of white space inserted into a text box. The width of an em space is equivalent to that of the lowercase letter m in the current typeface and type size.

Embed A command that copies and pastes a placed file into an Illustrator document.

En space A type of white space inserted into a text box. The width of an en space is equivalent to that of the lowercase letter n in the current typeface and type size.

Envelopes Objects that are used to distort other objects into the shape of the envelope object.

F

Facing pages Two pages in a layout that face each other, as in an open magazine, book, or newspaper.

Feathered edge A blended edge.

Fields Labels in a data source that categorize information in the records of a database, which are placed in a target document to specify how to do a data merge.

Fill A color applied to the inside of an object.

Flipping Creating a mirror image of artwork by turning it horizontally or vertically.

Frames Rectangular, oval, or polygonal shapes that you use for a variety of purposes, such as creating a colored area on the document or placing text and graphics.

G

GIF (Graphics Interchange Format) A standard file format for compressing images by lowering the number of colors available to the file.

Gloss contours A set of 12 preset adjustments that affect the brightness and contrast of a layer style to create dramatic lighting effects.

Gradient Graduated blend between two or more colors used to fill an object or multiple objects.

Gradient control bar A bar that appears in an object filled with a gradient; useful for changing the length, angle, and direction of a gradient.

Gradient Feather tool A tool that causes a fill color to fade gradually to transparent.

Gradient map adjustment Applies a gradient to the transition from shadows to highlights.

Gradient ramp A bar in the Gradient Editor dialog box that you use to add or remove color stops to create a customized gradient.

Graphic An element on a page that is not text. In an InDesign document, a graphic refers to a bitmap or vector image.

Graphics frames Frames in which you place imported artwork.

Grayscale image A single-color image, normally referred to as black and white.

Grayscale value A range of pixel values that span 0 to 255. Lower numbers represent darker shades while higher numbers represent lighter shades.

Group A type of layer in the Layers panel that resembles a folder and is used to organize layers.

Guides Horizontal or vertical lines positioned on a page. Guides are used to help align objects on the page.

Gutter The space between two columns.

H

Hardness A brush setting, measured in percentages. The higher the percentage, the more well defined the edge will be.

Highlights The lightest areas of an image represented by pixels in the top third of the grayscale range.

Histogram A graph of the image data and where that data is positioned on the grayscale range.

Hue Name of a color, or its identity on a standard color wheel.

Hue blending modes Commonly used blending modes that affect the color of pixels, specifically in terms of their hue, saturation, or brightness (luminosity).

I

Image-editing program A program that offers a wide variety of tools and settings to manipulate electronic images.

Image resolution The number of pixels per inch in an image file.

Image size The dimensions of a Photoshop file.

In port A small box in the upper-left corner of a text frame that you can click to flow text from another text frame.

Insertion mode Drawing mode in Illustrator that allows you to add a new object to a live paint group. A gray rectangle surrounding a live paint group indicates Insertion mode is active.

Interpolation The process by which Photoshop creates new pixels in a graphic to maintain an image's resolution.

Invert adjustment An effect made by flipping the grayscale image; black pixels change to 255 and white pixels change to 0.

Join A command used to unite two anchor points.

J

Joins Define the appearance of a corner point when a path has a stroke applied to it, such as miter, round, or bevel.

JPEG Joint Photographic Experts Group; standard file format for compressing continuous tone images, gradients, and blends.

K

Kerning Increasing or decreasing the horizontal space between any two text characters.

L

Lasso tool A tool that allows the user to make freehand selections of any shape or size.

Leading Vertical space between lines of text.

Libraries Collections of layout elements for organizing and storing graphics. Also called *Object Libraries*.

Lighten blending mode A commonly used blending mode in which black pixels become invisible and white pixels remain opaque.

Linear gradient A series of straight lines that gradate from one color to another (or through multiple colors).

Live paint group A group of objects that maintain a dynamic relationship with each other. When one object in the group is moved, the overlapping areas change shape and fill accordingly.

Location A text box below the gradient ramp that identifies a selected color stop's location, from left to right, on the gradient ramp.

Lock Transparent Pixels button An option to preserve the shapes of the type outlines when painting or filling rasterized type with colors.

M

Margin guides Page guides that define the interior borders of a document.

Marquee A dotted rectangle drawn around an object with the Zoom tool or the Selection tool to magnify or select an area of the document window.

Marquee tools Selection tools that select pixels. The Rectangular Marquee tool and the Elliptical Marquee tool create rectangular and square selections and elliptical and circular selections, respectively.

Master item An object on the master page that functions as a place where objects on the document pages are to be positioned.

Master pages Templates created for a page layout or for the layout of an entire publication.

Merged document A target document that has been merged with records from a data source.

Midpoint Point at which two colors meet in equal measure.

Midtones Sections of an image represented by pixels in the middle of the grayscale range.

Miter limit Determines when a miter join will be squared off to a beveled edge.

Modal control Allows you to save an action sequence once and use it in different ways for different projects.

Multiply A practical and useful blending mode in which the object becomes transparent but retains its color.

N

Named color Any color created in the New Color Swatch dialog box.

Noise Tiny, random, pixel-sized squares of color or gray applied to artwork to create texture over an image.

Nondestructive editing Working behavior in which original artwork is protected from permanent changes.

Nondestructive effect An applied effect such as a glow, shadow, bevel, and emboss that does not permanently change the graphic to which it is applied.

Nonproprietary format File formats that do not belong to a specific software company, such as JPEG, TIFF, GIF, and PNG.

Normal mode The default blending mode for the Brush tool.
Screen mode in which all page elements—including margin guides, ruler guides, frame edges, and the pasteboard—are visible.

O

Object An individual piece of artwork created in Illustrator.
Text or graphic element such as an image, a block of color, or a simple line that is placed in an InDesign document.

Offset The distance that text is repelled from a frame. Also, the specified horizontal and vertical distance a copy of an object will be from the original.

Opacity Determines the percentage of transparency; the lower the opacity, the higher the transparency.

Options panel A panel located under the menu bar that displays settings for the currently selected tool.

Orphans Words or single lines of text at the bottom of a column or page that become separated from the other lines in a paragraph.

Out port A small box in the lower-right corner of a text frame that flows text out to another text frame when clicked.

Outline A screen mode in which all objects are displayed as hollow shapes, with no fills or strokes.

Overlay blending modes Commonly used blending modes in which gray pixels become invisible and all pixels become transparent.

Overset text Text that does not fit in a text frame.

P

Page size The size a printed document will be cut when it clears the printing press.

Panel group A collection of panels.

Panel dock A gray vertical bar that contains a collection of panels, panel groups, or panel icons.

Panels Small control windows that house settings used to modify images.

Paragraph return Vertical space inserted into text formatting by pressing [return] (Mac) or [Enter] (Win). Also called a *hard return*.

Pass Through mode A blending mode that is applied to a group layer and functions only as an organizational tool to house layers.

Paste in Back A command that pastes a copy directly behind the original artwork.

Paste in Front A command that pastes a copy directly in front of the original artwork.

Pasteboard The area surrounding the document.

Paths Straight or curved lines created with vector graphics.

Pathfinders Preset operations that combine paths in a variety of ways; useful for creating complex or irregular shapes from basic shapes.

Pixels Picture elements; small, single-colored squares that compose a bitmap image.

Place thumbnail A small, low-resolution thumbnail of a loaded image or images.

PNG (Portable Network Graphics) A bitmap graphics file format that supports lossless data compression.

Point of origin Point from which an object is transformed; by default, the center point of an object, unless another point is specified.

Pull quote A typographical design solution in which text is used at a larger point size and positioned prominently on the page.

Preferences Specifications you can set for how certain features of an application behave.

Presentation mode A screen mode in which all nonprinting elements, panels, and menu bar are invisible and the page is centered and sized against a black background so the entire document fits in the monitor window.

Preview file A low-resolution version of a placed graphic file. As such, its file size is substantially smaller than the average graphic file.

Preview mode A screen mode in which all nonprinting page elements are invisible.

Process colors Colors that are created (and eventually printed) by mixing varying percentages of cyan, magenta, yellow, and black (CMYK) inks.

Process inks Cyan, magenta, yellow, and black ink; the fundamental inks used in printing.

Proprietary format A file format that is the property of a specific software company; PSD format is Adobe's format for Photoshop files.

R

Radial gradient A type of gradient in which the starting color appears at the center of the gradient and then radiates out to the ending color in a series of concentric circles.

Radius A value that determines how many pixels to change on each side of an edge.

Rasterize To convert type or vector artwork to pixels.

Records Rows of information organized by fields in a data source file.

Refraction A process in which white light can be broken down to make its component wavelengths visible.

Regions Similar to fills, regions are new shapes or areas created by the overlap of Illustrator objects; created when the Live Paint Bucket tool is applied.

Resolution The number of pixels per square inch in a digital image.

Resolution-dependent Graphics that should not be scaled when brought into other programs.

Resolution-independent Graphics that can be scaled with no impact on image quality. When an image has no pixels; usually refers to vector graphics.

Result color The color produced by blending the base and blend colors.

Rods Receptor cells in the human eye that process and perceive light as a range from highlight to shadow.

Rotating Moving an object clockwise or counterclockwise around a center point.

Round caps Rounded ends of a stroked path.

Ruler guides Horizontal and vertical rules you can position anywhere in a layout as a reference for positioning elements.

Rulers Measurement utilities positioned at the top and left sides of the pasteboard to help align objects.

Rules Horizontal, vertical, or diagonal lines on the page used as a design element or to underline text.

S

Sampling Taking information from a pixel or accessing its color.

Saturation Intensity of a hue. At 0% saturation, there is no color; full intensity or vibrance is at 100%.

Screen modes Options for viewing documents, such as Preview and Outline mode in Illustrator, or Preview, Normal, and Presentation mode in InDesign.

Section A group of pages in a document with distinct page numbering from other groups of pages.

Selection marquee Small lines that move in a clockwise direction around a selected object.

Semi-autoflowing A method for manually threading text through multiple frames.

Shadows The darkest areas of an image represented by pixels in the bottom third of the grayscale range.

Shape modes Preset operations that combine paths in a variety of ways; useful for creating complex or irregular shapes from basic shapes.

Silhouette A selection you make in Photoshop using selection tools, such as the Pen tool.

Smart Guides Nonprinting words that appear on the artboard and identify visible or invisible objects, page boundaries, intersections, anchor points, etc. Guides that appear automatically when objects are moved in a document and provide information to help position objects precisely in relation to the page or other objects.

Smooth points Anchor points that connect curved segments.

Snapshot A record of a project as it is at a given moment; stored on the History panel.

Snippet An XML file with an .inds file extension that contains a complete representation of document elements, including all formatting tags and document structure.

Soft return In typography, using the [Shift] key in addition to the [return] (Mac) or [Enter] (Win) key will move text onto the following line without creating a new paragraph.

Spot colors Non-process inks that are manufactured by companies; special premixed inks that are printed separately from process inks.

Spread Two pages that face each other—a left page and a right page—in a multipage document.

Square-up The default placement of a Photoshop file in InDesign that includes the entire image and its background.

Stacking order The order of how objects are arranged in front and behind other objects on the artboard.

Starting and ending colors The starting and ending colors of a gradient.

Stroke A color applied to the outline of an object.

Stroke weight The thickness of a stroke, usually measured in points.

Style A group of formatting attributes that can be applied to text or objects.

Subtractive primary colors Cyan, magenta, and yellow; colors created by subtracting one of the additive primary colors.

T

Target document An InDesign file containing text that will be seen by all recipients as well as placeholders representing fields in a data source with which it will be merged.

Target layer The layer selected on the Layers panel.

Targeting Clicking a layer on the Layers panel to select it.

Text frames Boxes drawn with the Type tool in which you type or place text.

Threading Linking text from one text frame to another.

Threshold adjustment A high-contrast effect made by manipulating the number of colors available per pixel.

TIFF (Tagged Image File Format) A standard file format that saves files with their layers intact.

Tint In InDesign, a lighter version of a given color.

Tolerance A setting on the Options panel that determines the number of pixels the Magic Wand tool either includes or doesn't include in the selection.

Tool tips Small windows of text that identify various elements of the workspace, such as tool names, buttons on panels, or names of colors on the Swatches panel.

Toolbar A collection of tools with icons to represent their functions.

Tracking Increasing or decreasing the space between letters of a word.

Transform Change the shape, size, perspective, or rotation of an object or image.

Trim size The size a printed document will be cut when it clears the printing press.

Units Standard quantities used in measurements, such as inches, picas, or points.

Unnamed colors Any colors you create that aren't saved to the Swatches panel.

Use Global Light An option to maintain a consistent light source for multiple layer styles.

Vector graphics Resolution-independent graphics created with the Pen tool. Artwork created entirely by geometrically defined paths and curves, usually created and imported from Adobe Illustrator.

Vectors Straight or curved paths defined by geometrical characteristics, usually created and imported from a drawing program.

Vignette A visual effect in which the edge of an image, usually an oval, gradually fades away.

Visible light Light waves that are visible to the human eye.

Visible spectrum Made of the colors red, orange, yellow, green, blue, indigo, and violet.

White light Concept that natural light on Earth appears to people as not having any dominant hue.

White point The very lightest pixel in an image.

Widows Words or single lines of text at the top of a column or page that become separated from the other lines in a paragraph.

Workspace Positioning of panels on an artboard or computer monitor; Illustrator includes preset workspaces targeted for specific types of work, such as Typography and Painting. Positioning of panels on an artboard or computer monitor.

Zero point By default, the upper-left corner of the document; the point from which the location of all objects on the page is measured.

INDEX

multiple objects, extending gradients across, 788

multiple open documents, working with, 567–568, 574

multiple-page document, 640

multiply blending mode, 46, 240–241, 267
  calculation, 242
  experiment, 242–243, 255
  groups, 244, 246
  inside groups, 249–250
  paint with transparent paint in, 53
  remove white background with, 248

multiply images, 250–251

N

named colors, 757, 770

National Geographic Creatives
  Baker, Scott, 752
  visual display of information, 850
  von Dallwitz, Alex, 431

National Geographic Storytellers
  Galimberti, Gabriele, 279
  Rao, Nirupa, 548
  Varma, Anand, 315–321
  Wright, Alison, 99

navigating documents, 575–578

negative offset values, 695

New Artboard button, 370, 372

New Character Style, 615

New Color Swatch dialog box, 756

New Document dialog box, 638–640, 648

New Gradient Swatch dialog box, 780, 781, 785

New Master command, 657

New Master dialog box, 664

New Mixed Ink Group command, 778

New Paragraph Style dialog box, 617

New Section dialog box, 677

Newspaper column formatted, 398

New Tint Swatch, 759

New View command, 434

Next Page Number command, 735

noise, 257

nondestructive editing, 184

None fill, 767

non-process inks, 775

nonproprietary formats, 18

normal blend mode, 244

Normal mode, 567

Numbering & Section Options command, 677

O

object(s), 579
  apply attributes, 454–456
  applying color to, 765–766, 771
  applying fill and stroke, 353
  behind other objects, selecting, 709
  copying, 342, 346–347, 580, 582
  duplicate, 346–347, 357, 582
  flowing text into, 395–399
  frames, 579
  grouping, 342–343, 348, 580, 583
  hiding, 342–343, 348, 580, 583
  hiding while working with text, 391
  locking, 342–343, 348, 580, 583
  moving, 355
  positioning, 356
  positioning on layers, 712–714
  resizing, 341–342, 346, 579, 581

unnamed colors, 760, 764, 770

updating, missing and modified files, 814, 816–817

use global light option, 153

User Interface preferences, 345

V

Varma, Anand, 315–321

vector graphics, 350–351, 717, 820, 824
  enlarging, 820

vectors, 351, 824

vertical type, 394

vertical type on a Path tool, 400

viewing
  commands, shortcut keys, 573
  metadata with Links panel, 813
  multi-page documents, 647

vignette, 72

visible light, 206

visible spectrum, 206

von Dallwitz, Alex, 431

W

warnings, links and fonts, 562

white light, 206

white points, 193

widows, 606

within stroke option, Gradient panel, 422

Word files, mapping style names when importing, 676

word processing program, 614, 812

workspace, 29, 326–332, 558
  areas, 558
  with Control panel, 559
  custom, 564
  customized, 327, 332
  switching between, 326–327
  toolbar, exploring, 560
  typography, 558
  working with panels, 561–562

wrapping text
  around a frame, 678, 680

around graphics, 722–723, 730–732
around placed vector graphics, 829

Wright, Alison, 99

X

XML, exporting, 815

Y

yellow, 208

yellow circle layer, 246

Z

zero point, 643

Zombie, 270

Zombie Reflection, 271

Zoom tool, 24–25, 333, 337, 560, 565, 569–570
  accessing, 565
  and Hand tool, 27